THE END OF CERTAINTY

CRITICAL ACCLAIM FOR PAUL KELLY

The Unmaking of Gough (1976) later republished as The Dismissal (1983)

'This is in many ways a model of lucid and instant history.'

Dr Neal Blewett

'Paul Kelly's is the reference we keep going back to.'

Peter Bowers, *Sydney Morning Herald*

'Of the books (about the dismissal) the one which to my mind puts the fairest construction on the course of events is Kelly's.'

Professor Geoffrey Sawer, *Canberra Times*

The Hawke Ascendancy (1984)

'The Kelly book is a superb account of dramatic political events . . . this is the real thing.'

Laurie Oakes

'Kelly at his best is a wordsmith and analyst without peer among those who make their living observing and reporting national politics.'

Alan Ramsey

'An outstanding job . . . indispensable reading for anyone who has any significant interest in Australian politics.'

Bob Hawke

THE END OF CERTAINTY

The story of the 1980s

Paul Kelly

ALLEN & UNWIN

First published in 1992
Allen & Unwin Pty Ltd
9 Atchison Street, St Leonards, NSW 2065 Australia

National Library of Australia
Cataloguing-in-Publication entry:

  Kelly, Paul
    The end of certainty.

    Includes index.
    ISBN 1 86373 388 4.
    ISBN 1 86373 227 6 (pbk).

    1. Political parties—Australia. 2. Australia—Politics and
    government—1976–1990. I. Title.

  324.294

Set in 10/12 pt Times by DOCUPRO, Sydney.
Printed by Southwood Press Pty Ltd, Marrickville NSW.

10 9 8 7 6 5 4 3 2 1

For my son, Joseph

Contents

Preface

This book is an account and an interpretation of Australia's political and economic experience during the 1980s and into the 1990s. It rests more in optimism than pessimism, reflecting the author's personal predilections. The argument is that the decade was a milestone in the redefinition of the ideas and institutions by which Australia is governed. It gives roughly equal weight to Labor and the coalition since the transforming impact of the 1980s was manifest on both sides of politics.

I would like to thank friends who helped me with ideas, information and advice. In particular I thank the many individuals whom I interviewed for this book over the past several years. My apologies are offered to those to whom I should have spoken but could not because of time constraints. I have kept a confidential set of footnotes in addition to the notes published here.

My thanks are extended to *The Australian* for permitting me a period of special leave for the book, my publisher Patrick Gallagher for his tolerance of my delays and his valuable cooperation, and staff on *The Australian* who helped me with typing, research and files.

Above all, I thank my family who lived with this book for too long—my wife, Margaret, for the hours she devoted to the ideas and the index and, in particular, for the editing she performed on the manuscript; to my son Joseph who finally gets back his printer and his dad for weekend football; and to Daniel whose birth was my original deadline and who celebrated his second birthday before publication.

Introduction

The story of the 1980s is the attempt to remake the Australian political tradition. This decade saw the collapse of the ideas which Australia had embraced nearly a century before and which had shaped the condition of its people. The 1980s was a time of both exhilaration and pessimism, but the central message shining through its convulsions was the obsolescence of the old order and the promotion of new political ideas as the basis for a new Australia.

The generation after Federation in 1901 turned an emerging national consensus into new laws and institutions. This was the Australian Settlement. Its principal architect was Alfred Deakin who became recognised as Australia's greatest prime minister. The feature of the Australian Settlement is that it was bipartisan and was accepted, sooner or later, by Liberal, Conservative and Labor politicians. Its universality provided the bonds for eight decades of national unity and progress despite its defects.

At its inception Australia had no Bill Of Rights or Declaration of Independence as a focus of national identity. The nation was founded not in war, revolution or national assertion, but by practical men striving for income, justice, employment, and security. The Australian Settlement was their creation. It is an achievement second only to the creation of Australian democracy, and its operation within that democracy has offered for most of this century the best definition of nationhood. But this Australia is in transition — in the 1980s, the Settlement ideas underwent a process of creative destruction from which there is no return.

The ideas which constitute the Australian Settlement, though devoid of formal definition, may be summarised under five headings—White Australia, Industry Protection, Wage Arbitration, State Paternalism, and Imperial Benevolence.

Australia was founded on: faith in government authority; belief in egalitarianism; a method of judicial determination in centralised wage fixation; protection of its industry and its jobs; dependence upon a great power, (first Britain, then America), for its security and its finance; and, above all, hostility to its geographical location, exhibited in fear of external domination and internal contamination from the peoples of the Asia/Pacific. Its bedrock ideology was protection; its solution, a Fortress Australia, guaranteed as part of an impregnable Empire spanning the globe. This framework—introspective, defensive, dependent—is undergoing an irresistible demolition.

The transformation in the 1980s of the Labor and non-Labor parties reflects this revolution and contributes to it. As the nation is remade so must the political parties be remade. By the year 2000 the Labor and coalition parties will be vastly different animals from those of 1980.

The fundamental divide in Australian politics in the late 1980s was no longer Labor versus Liberal. Party differences were real and bitter, but the underlying policy direction was the same. This was obscured because both sides deliberately exaggerated these differences. The 1980s saw the Labor–Liberal paradigm being eroded as the major battleground of ideas, though the tensions between the parties still dominated the political debate. The real division is between the internationalist rationalists and the sentimentalist traditionalists; it is between those who know the Australian Settlement is unsustainable and those who fight to retain it.

The first group believes in the power of markets, the internationalisation of Australian processes and the continuation of the direction established in the 1980s. The second group repudiates the 1980s economic orthodoxies, asserts that the power of the markets will succumb to a new triumph of government regulation, and denies the imperative for the internationalisation of the Australian economy. This division runs through the established parties, Labor and Liberal. It is a division between the visions of the new and old Australia; between the realistic and the sentimental.

This is the source of the identity crisis of the Labor and coalition parties, so manifest during the 1980s and certain to continue during the 1990s. The destruction of the old Fortress Australia Settlement cannot be denied though it can, at some cost, be delayed. The entire dynamics of 1980s politics originates within the collapse of the Australian Settlement, the struggle for a replacement credo, the demise of established interests, and the rise of new interests based upon the new rules. The starting point in grasping the 1980s story is an understanding of the old order and the forces destroying it.

The foundation idea of the Australian Settlement was White Australia. It was the unique basis for the nation and the indispensible condition for all other policies. It was established in the first substantive law passed by the federal Parliament—the mark of national individuality in an Empire of coloured races. White Australia was not just a policy, it was a creed which became the essence of Australian nationalism and, more importantly, the basis of national unity. It was endorsed by Labor and Conservatives, employers and unions, workers and housewives.

The first prime minister, Edmund Barton, predicted the demise of Western colonialism and the rise of new states in Africa and Asia. But Barton drew a false conclusion: he saw White Australia as a bulwark against this future age, not as its inevitable victim.

But the greatest exposition of the policy came from Deakin:

> The unity of Australia is nothing if that does not imply a united race. A
> united race means not only that its members can intermix, intermarry
> and associate . . . but implies one inspired by the same ideas . . . of a
> people possessing the same general cast of character, tone of thought,
> the same constitutional training and traditions . . . Unity of race is an
> absolute to the unity of Australia. It is more actually in the last resort,
> than any other unity. After all, when the period of confused local
> politics and temporary political divisions was swept aside it was this
> real unity which made the Commonwealth possible.'

Deakin's words betrayed, however, the insecurity lurking behind the assertion of White Australia. He said that Japanese should be excluded 'because of their high abilities' and that they 'would be our most formidable competitors.' With reference to Japan Deakin said, 'It is not the bad qualities but the good qualities of these alien races that makes them dangerous to us.'[1] This was the premonition of a challenge which would face Australia throughout the century. It surged with Japan's 1905 defeat of Imperial Russia, reached its zenith in World War II, and was reinvented in its contemporary form when Japan became an economic colossus.

White Australia, as Deakin also implied, transcended negativism and served as a dynamic basis for national action. It was notable for the eloquence of its defenders—Henry Lawson, the poet who created the mythology of the Australian identity; the liberal intellectual Frederic Eggleston; the socialist writer, Vance Palmer; and Australia's longest serving prime minister, R.G. Menzies. White Australia was the first and greatest ingredient in Australian nationalism; it was the chief motive driving Australian Imperialism. It was the first principle in the first platform devised by the Australian Labor Party caucus in 1901. Its last great racist champion was ALP leader, Arthur Calwell, who, as architect of the post-war immigration program, embodied in these contradictory impulses—immigration and racism—its final gasp.[2]

White Australia fell victim to decolonisation, the demise of Empire and the transformation of Australian national interests. At its 1965 National Conference, the ALP abandoned its commitment to White Australia. In

3

March 1966 the policy was abolished by the Holt coalition government. But its interment was accompanied by funeral obsequies which revealed that the principle of a homogeneous Australia remained alive. The nation had merely decided that racially based discrimination was officially unacceptable. There was no alternative vision to replace White Australia nor any intention to permit significant non-white immigration.[3]

In 1973 the Whitlam Government abolished the final vestiges of official racial discrimination. In the late 1970s the Fraser Government supported a major influx of refugees from Vietnam. This was the trigger which prompted an alternative national credo from Malcolm Fraser in the early 1980s—multiculturalism—which became the official definition of national direction. But for most people multiculturalism could never serve as an adequate or a sufficient re-definition of national identity.

It was the legacy of the post-war immigration program and the transformation of the Asia/Pacific from a region of military threat to one of economic progress which forced Australia to substitute multiculturalism and regional integration for the original idea of White Australia. Australia's future living standards are tied, in part, to the success of Australia's integration into the Asia/Pacific. It is the rise of a massive and prosperous middle class in the Asia/Pacific which will trade, travel and live in Australia that is the ultimate guarantor of a new identity. This involves changed immigration patterns and settlement policies, joint Australian/Asian ventures, a major tourist influx, greater foreign investment from Asia, educational exchanges, and the mutual search for new products and markets.

In short, it means a greater Asian presence in Australia and a greater Australian presence in Asia. It means, above all, more people-to-people intimacy and dialogue. In the 1980s Bob Hawke's declared objective was to 'enmesh' Australia in the Asia/Pacific, his term for the widest possible contact and intimacy. This transition in national identity has been uneven and stormy but the change is inevitable. The ultimate issue is the reconciliation between the growing Asianisation of Australia and maintenance of the dominant Anglo-Saxon Judaic-Christian value system.

The second pillar of the Australian Settlement was Protection. Its appeal transcended that of an economic policy. Protection was both a creed and a dogma. It was a philosophy that would make Australia powerful, secure its prosperity and assuage its insecurity. For its disciples, Protection was a policy for both war and peace. Protection and White Australia became fused into a self-reinforcing emotional bond. Protection was the core of Australia's consciousness.[4]

The first issue resolved within the new Federation was the contest between Protectionists and Free-Traders, symbolised in the struggle between Alfred Deakin and George Reid, the respective leaders of these groups. The victory for Protection was swift and decisive; Deakin was lionised and Reid was humiliated. The first moderate tariff was established in 1902, a more stringent tariff adopted in 1908 in the third Parliament, both delivered by Protectionist governments with support from a divided Labor Party.

Deakin was a Victorian and Reid was from NSW. These two colonies in the second half of the nineteenth century had chosen opposing solutions to the employment demands from the post-1850 trebling of Australia's population. Victoria had chosen Protection while NSW opted for free-trade. But the Victorian model prevailed in the new Commonwealth.

Deakin, politician, journalist and lawyer, had been converted to Protection by his patron, David Syme, the owner of *The Age*. It was a Damascus—'as we crossed the old Prince's bridge one evening', Deakin recalled. Deakin was 22 and his conversion owed more to political convenience than to economic understanding, never his forté. His conversion would be repeated by his successors for a century.[5]

George Reid had an economic brain and the common touch, a rare blend. He was, in fact, an economic libertarian and an old fox, a contemporary mixture of John Hyde and Reg Withers. Reid admired Adam Smith and Britain's nineteenth century free-trade champion, Richard Cobden. As early as 1875 Reid had attacked Protection using arguments which his intellectual inheritors would still be promulgating more than one hundred years later. Reid said the core of Protection lay in its neglect of principle, its resort to expediency and its refusal to address whether solutions were right or wrong.[6]

The Deakin–Reid battle was the first wet–dry contest in Australian national politics. It was a struggle not just over trade policy, but over competing visions of the new Commonwealth and whether its development would rest upon the principle of government intervention or that of individual enterprise. Deakin's victory was comprehensive and Reid slouched off as High Commissioner to London—a trail-blazer for the vanquished. It would be another eighty years before Reid's position would be vindicated.

The victory of Protection was sealed in three ways. First, Deakin's Liberals had been able to secure a coalition of support to put the Federation on the protectionist path. Second, the Labor Party, initially divided and uncommitted on the issue, finally settled for Protection. Third, when the non-Labor forces merged in 1909—the Deakin Protectionists and Reid's Free-traders—the newly created Liberal Party was pledged to Protection. Labor and non-Labor was Protectionist; the circle was all but closed.

The final step occurred in the early 1920s which saw the emergence of the Country Party. The non-Labor Nationalists under W.M. Hughes established the Tariff Board and then legislated for the highest and most comprehensive tariff schedules. This reflected the expansion of Australia's industrial base during World War I. But the decisive event of this period was the subjugation of the Country Party to Protection. It proclaimed a rebellion but settled for compensation. After threatening to attack the Protection edifice as a burden to primary producers, the Country Party was bought off.

During the 1920s the Country Party, under its first great leader, Earle Page, joined the Protection compact. The cost was a system of statutory marketing, growers' boards, public subsidies, price fixing and industry levies. The 'man on the land' who had promised to subvert tariff-raising and wage-fixing, was harnessed to the chariot wheels of Protection. Now a national stance of 'Protection All Round' was underwritten by the three major parties.[7]

From its inception Protection was seen as the basis for nation building. Deakin declared: 'No nation ever claimed national greatness which relied upon primary industry alone.' Protection was a policy which industries sought in their self-interest. It entrenched sectional interests and sectional politics and was justified by national leaders as a policy to build industrial strength.[8]

The flaws in the Protection edifice were known from the start and received periodic fanfare. In 1929 the Brigden Committee, reporting on the tariff, made an appeal for moderate protection but warned that 'the tariff has probably reached the economic limits and an increase . . . might threaten the standard of living.' It said that the burden of the tariff fell upon Australia's lifeblood—wool, wheat and mineral exports.[9] In fact, the average tariff level almost doubled in the decade to 1920 and doubled again by 1932 to become one of the world's highest.

The impact of Protection was known but unheeded—one industry's protection became another industry's cost through higher prices, thus forcing the second industry to demand, in turn, greater protection as compensation. Two works published in 1930 exposed the practice underpinning Protection, Edward Shann's *Economic History Of Australia* and W.K. Hancock's *Australia*. But ideas could not penetrate the political edifice of self-interest and perceived national interest. Indeed, during the post-World War II era, Protection experienced a resurgence under the leadership of a political giant, John 'Black Jack' McEwen, the toughest figure in post-war politics.

McEwen lived by the personal philosophy that 'a man who can't inspire fear in his opponents isn't worthy of the fight'. His vision was succinctly expressed: 'I have always wanted to make Australia a powerful industrialised country as well as a major agricultural and mining country. This meant that I was bound to favour broadly protectionist policies.' McEwen championed this vision throughout his twenty-nine years as Country Party deputy and leader—including 22 years as the minister responsible for secondary industry. He is the only post-war politician whose name was given to an economic philosophy—McEwenism. By 1970 Australia, apart from New Zealand, had the highest manufacturing tariffs within the industrialised world.[10]

When McEwen retired in 1971, his apparently immovable protectionist structure was under threat from an apparently irresistible anti-protectionist tide, furious at the longevity of its denial. It was during the 1970s and 1980s that the structure fell to successive assaults. The final timetable for Protection's virtual dismantling was announced by the Hawke government in March 1991. It offers a wonderful symmetry: that Australia will enter its second century as a nation in 2001 liberated from the protectionist shackles which stifled its first century.

Trade protection did not exist alone because its triumph involved the capture of the entire economy. The power of protectionism derived from its alliance with Arbitration, the third institution of the Settlement. This alliance, in fact, was called New Protection: its meaning was precise—the legal obligation upon employers who benefitted from protection to redistribute their profits to their employees in wages and working conditions provided upon a 'fair and reasonable' basis. New Protection left a legacy as powerful as any political idea in Australia. It was the device which tied both capital and labour to the post-Federation consensus. The Commonwealth Arbitration Court, later the Conciliation and Arbitration Commission, then the Industrial Relations Commission, became the forum for its entrenchment.

The depression of 1890s had been the dominant economic influence on the Australian Settlement. Its legacies were Protection and Arbitration and above all their fusion in the principle of New Protection. Arbitration was an Australian institution based upon the most distinctive of Australian ideas, the 'fair go' principle. It was Australian in its effort to restore order after the class conflict of the 1890s which neither unions nor employers wanted to repeat, in its egalitarian ethos, and in its solutions through bureaucratic legalisms.

The father of the Arbitration bill was the South Australian liberal, Charles Kingston, but it was introduced by Deakin in a *tour de force* of lyricism:

> This bill marks, in my opinion, the beginning of a new phase of civilisation. It begins the establishment of the People's Peace . . . which will comprehend necessarily as great a transformation in the features of industrial society as the creation of the King's Peace brought about in civil society . . . imperfect as our legal system may be, it is a distinct gain to transfer to the realm of reason and argument those industrial convulsions which have hitherto involved, not only loss of life, liberty, comfort and opportunities of well-being.[11]

The bill provided for conciliation between unions and employers and, if necessary, compulsory arbitration in the form of an award made by a new court which would determine the 'right' in industrial disputes. It was passed, finally, in 1904 after a series of political crises and re-drafting, becoming the major achievement of the second Parliament.

The philosophy of the Arbitration Act was that industrial relations required an umpire and could not be left to employers and employees. The aim was to remove the need for industrial action by paying workers a fair wage and guaranteeing equity across industries. The Australian system was unique because 'it provided regulation not only of the process for settling disputes but also direct regulation of the outcome . . . based on specific views about wage equity.'[12] This led to a system of national wage regulation and institutionalised comparative wage justice, an idea which defied the contrasting economic performance of different industries in varying regions. The Act enshrined trade union power and encouraged the growth of unions on a craft rather than an industry basis.

Arbitration was part of Labor's first federal platform in 1901. But the Labor Party, the beneficiary of its creation, did not establish the Arbitration system. It was an initiative of the Deakinite Liberals and it was secured, finally, by an alliance of Free-traders and Protectionists. It was supported by the Labor Party and the trade unions and resisted by the employers.[13]

The influential President of the Commonwealth Arbitration Court from 1907 to 1921 was Henry Bournes Higgins, a middle class radical and social reformer, appointed to this life's work by Deakin. Higgins as an outsider but a friend of the Labor Party, became Attorney-General in the first Federal ALP Government in 1904. For his biographer 'it was as though the working class was being officially received into the corridors of power with Higgins as its guide.'[14] Higgins was a rich lawyer and a man of fierce independence.

In his first case as President, Higgins put his stamp upon the Arbitration Court—the *Harvester* judgement of 1907 which enshrined New Protection. Excise duties were to be waived for manufacturers if the Court certified that they were paying 'fair and reasonable' wages. The parliament had left the Court to interpret this definition and Higgins chose Sunshine Harvester as the test case. He could not think of 'any other standard appropriate than the normal needs of the average employee.' He calculated them on the Melbourne household budget for about five people to which he made extra allowance for 'light, clothes, boots, furniture, utensils, rates, life insurance, savings, accident or benefit societies, loss of employment, union pay, books and newspapers, tram and train fares, sewing machine, mangle, school requisites, amusements and holidays, intoxicating liquors, tobacco, sickness and death, religion or charity.'[15]

The result was a wage of 42 shillings a week, a calculation influenced by Pope Leo XIII's *Rerum Novarum* encyclical, fairly primitive maths, and the worker's right to plan for a family of five. This established a wage fixation system based on human need, not on profits or productivity. It entrenched the idea that wages should be set by judicial decree. It enshrined the idea of a minimum wage which was sacrosanct and introduced the notion of family welfare into wage setting. It established the notion of cost-of-living as a basis for wage movements and underpinned the regulated wage structure. It was the rock upon which Higgins built his Court. This basic wage evolved as a wage for the unskilled with margins paid above it. Having taken his stand, Higgins was ruthless in its prosecution. This was revealed in the case involving BHP in 1909.[16]

Higgins told BHP that if it could not pay the minimum rate then it would be preferable to shut down the mine: 'If it is a calamity that this historic mine should close down, it would be a still greater calamity that men should be underfed or degraded.' Unemployment, by implication, was preferable to cheap labour.

Arbitration's dedication to wage justice and equity was an institutional bulwark against the growth of class warfare which a market system would have imposed, given the huge fluctuations in Australia's national income from commodity price movements. Yet the rejection of wage flexibility was also an institutional flaw for a nation whose export revenue depended upon fluctuating commodity prices. Higgins' interest was class power, not market forces. He said that Arbitration was needed to impose justice; to check the 'despotic power' and bourgeois spirit of employers.[17]

Higgins encouraged workers to trust Arbitration and strengthen their unions to utilise its advantages. The employers, after their initial resistance to the Court, were incorporated, finally, within the system. Arbitration grew in a turbulent but relentless manner as a joint federal-state structure of courts with union and employer organisations. The failure of the effort to abandon federal Arbitration by the coalition government of S.M. Bruce in 1929 which saw his Government defeated and the loss of his own seat, only reinforced the political weight of the system.

Arbitration was the greatest institutional monument to Australian egalitarianism and its quest for social order. It was an heroic endeavour founded in optimism that man could defy the anarchy of the marketplace and impose a system of just prices to secure his material dignity. Its longevity is a tribute to its ability to incorporate its opponents. But in the 1980s the conflict between the international economic pressures on Australia and centralised wage-fixation became irresistible. Higgins' effort to insulate wages from the international market finally began to collapse.

The Liberal–National coalition reversed a lifetime of virtual acquiescence in Arbitration when, in the 1980s, it declared its intention to dismantle the system. In the early 1990s the Labor Party and the trade union movement announced their own intention to move towards an enterprise bargaining system—evidence that the primacy of the central court and its system was crumbling.

The fourth element of the Australian Settlement was State Paternalism—individual happiness through government intervention. It originates not with Federation but from the white man's arrival in 1788 to establish a prison. Belief in state power was rooted in a society shaped by former convicts, military officers and a 'colonial secretary' mentality. From the start the state was involved in every form of commercial activity. The entrepreneur was divorced from the mechanism of the market. The individual looked first to the state as his protector, only secondly to himself.

This sentiment was reinforced by the growth of nineteenth century democracy. Australia's political consciousness was developed after the Industrial Revolution and the French Revolution. It fell into that period when the entire direction of politics was to demand political rights and secure economic benefits from the state. In Australia this process, culminating in the triumph of the Labor Party, was facilitiated by the absence of countervailing forces in the form of a property-owning aristocratic or entrenched ruling class.

The triumph of democracy in Australia was as comprehensive as anywhere in the world. But its nature involved a greater fusion between the interests of the individual and the state than in most other nations. During the 1890s and early 1900s Australia became a pioneer in progressive social laws which meant, in effect, the advancement of state power.

Deakin's liberalism was creative and dynamic. It was dedicated not just to the 'destruction of class privileges' but to the erection of laws and institutions to advance the individual through state power. Deakin declared: 'State socialism I fear only because of the weakness of the old social idea in us . . . run by selfishness nothing could exceed the corruption likely to be bred under a system of State Socialism but safeguarding this I have no desire other then to extend the sphere of State interference and control.'

The Labor Party supported Deakinite liberalism until it was strong enough to seize power from Deakin. Labor built upon the Deakin inheritance. It harnessed class power to the instrument of the state. Deakin sympathised with Labor but he could never join Labor. Deakin's liberalism was an appeal to the common interest but Labor campaigned on a class interest; a new appeal for a new century. Labor marched into the seats of the Deakinite liberals and stole the working class votes on which they had relied. Deakin saw the inevitable and opined that 'the rise of the Labor Party is more cosmic than the crusades.'[18]

The Australian Settlement had been achieved on the basis of Deakin's parliamentary alliance with the Labor Party; in effect, a Liberal-Labor alliance which is the key to the Settlement's longevity. It meant that faith in government power was shared by non-Labor and Labor as the century unfolded.

In 1930 when W.K. Hancock sought to capture Australia's political tradition he wrote: 'Australian democracy has come to look upon the State as a vast public utility whose duty it is to provide the greatest happiness for the greatest number . . . to the Australian, the State means collective power at the service of individualistic "rights". Therefore he sees no opposition between his individualism and his reliance upon Government.'[19]

The most penetrating account of state socialism came from Frederic Eggleston who held several Victorian state ministries on the non-Labor side

10

in the 1920s. Eggleston noted that Victoria's public services 'in proportion
to the size and the economic standing of the community, constitute possibly
the largest and most comprehensive use of state power outside Russia.' After
a detailed review of banking, railways, roads, water supply, electricity,
agriculture, forests, transport, ports and other services Eggleston concluded,
indeed he claimed to have proved, that state intervention was failing.[20]

Eggleston was a disillusioned interventionist convinced after his ministerial experience that the Victorian model required a retreat of state power,
a diagnosis that was never implemented. His central argument, documented
in detail, was that state socialism in practice undermined individual initiative
and responsibility.

It was this same belief, in fact, which drove the 1980s campaign to
secure smaller, less interventionist government and a more competitive
Australia. It was driven by the need to foster a more dynamic individual
citizenry. Its symptoms were a public sector surplus, an attack on government regulations, privatisation of public enterprise, needs-based welfare,
deregulation of the labour market, and micro-economic reform to achieve
better results in the economic lifelines that had been dominated by the
state—energy, communications and transport.

For example, in its 1988–89 report, the Industries Assistance Commission (IAC) estimated that an extra $12 billion annually would flow to GDP
from more efficient transport, aviation, communications and energy services.
The key to this lay in a reduction in government intervention. In its 1989–90
report the IAC complained that governments had distorted markets for much
of Australia's history and insisted that 'greater exposure to competition—
both at home and abroad—is the surest means of securing higher productivity.'

The final pillar of the Australian Settlement was Imperial Benevolence—the belief that Australian prosperity and security was underwritten
by the Empire. In 1901 the six states united in a Commonwealth under the
British crown. It was a union achieved by practical politicians who saw no
conflict between being both British and Australian. They sought to make
Australia strong by refurbishing the bond with Britain. A strong Empire
meant a strong Australia; nationalism and Empire loyalism were bedfellows.
The Royal Navy was the guarantor of White Australia. British finance and
trade preference underwrote Australian growth. Federation created a nation
but it could never create a sense of national identity or purpose.

Australia was a constitutional entity with a spiritual void at its core. It
longed for a test of national character. That came at Gallipoli which, in turn,
became a legend that was asked to do too much—to sustain a national
identity. The Australian psychology was trapped between the aspiration to
independence and the comfortable dependence upon Britain. It is extraordinary that it took Australia until the 1972 election of the Whitlam government
to begin to bury its inferiority complex. This glimpse of genuine national

confidence was fractured but the sentiment returned with firmer foundations in 1990. It was exhibited in the serious and growing movement to celebrate the centenary of the Commonwealth in 2001 by the declaration of a republic. In 1992 Paul Keating became the first prime minister to campaign for a shift in Australia's identity from a constitutional monarchy to a republic.

The party system evolved within the framework of the Australian Settlement. Labor and non-Labor had erected the structure and they worked within it. Labor was a party of moderate, sometimes doctrinaire reform, never revolutionary, socialist in its rituals rather than in its actions. No federal ALP leader ever talked about implementing a serious socialist agenda. One fashionable myth from the 1980s was that Labor was betraying a past of glorious socialism.

The landmark 1921 ALP Conference which carried the party objective— 'the socialisation of industry, production, distribution and exchange'—was immediately qualified by the passage of the 'Blackburn declaration' which said that private ownership would not be abolished where the owner employed it in a 'socially useful manner.' In short, give me socialism but not just yet! Labor's mission was usually an attempt to 'civilise capitalism.' In office it was usually practical, exaggerating the moderate advances it sought for its own constituents, and disguising its support for employers and capital. Whenever Labor succumbed to doctrine, for instance the attempt at bank nationalisation in the late 1940s, it was thrown from office by horrified voters.[21]

Australia has been governed mostly by non-Labor politicians for whom the decisive event was the 1909 'fusion' of the non-Labor forces against Labor. This is when the parties which Deakin and Reid had dominated decided that the threat from Labor transcended their hostility towards each other. It was a union of Conservative and Liberal, Protectionist and Free-Trader, thus establishing the Labor versus non-Labor party structure. Deakin, as a Liberal, took this decision with reluctance bemoaning that 'behind me (now) sit the whole of my opponents since Federation.' Deakin, finally, accepted Reid's outlook that the dominant political issue was 'socialism versus anti-socialism'. He buried his sympathy with Labor by joining with the Conservatives.[22]

From the formation of the modern party structure (from the 1910 election) until Hawke's 1983 victory, the non-Labor side governed for 52 of these 73 years. The Liberal–National Parties administered the Australian Settlement. They governed with caution, dedication, lack of inspiration, a pacification of sectional interests, and an appreciation of Australia's national insecurity complex. They sought not to make Australia great but, typically, to develop its resources for economic benefit and to exploit its national inferiority complex for political success. The two non-Labor traditions married in the 1909 fusion, liberal and conservative, were a source of strength for the Liberal Party for several decades. But in the 1980s they emerged as a source of internal tension, offering competing views of non-Labor identity.

Unions and employers, Protestant and Catholic, Liberal and Labor, buttressed the Fortress Australia system from the start. Fortress Australia fostered a weak domestically orientated business culture and a union mythology of a workers' paradise. The Australian political contest this century has not been about ideology—the system and its institutions—but rather about the terms and conditions on which they operate. It has been about the division of national income more than the generation of national income. Fortress Australia was bipartisan—an alliance between the conservative establishment and working class power—and this is the key to its endurance.

History imposed its own adjustments—the fall of Singapore in 1942; British entry into Europe in 1973; the US defeat in Vietnam in 1975; the transformation of America from a creditor to debtor power in the Reagan era; and, above all, the prolonged economic expansion in the Asia/Pacific built upon Japan as nucleus and spreading outwards.

Two trends coalesced during the 1980s—the internationalisation of the world economy in which success became the survival of the fittest; and the gradual but inexorable weakening of Australia's 'imperial' links with its two patrons, Britain and America. The message was manifest—Australia must stand on its own ability. Australians, in fact, had waited longer than most nations to address the true definition of nationhood—the acceptance of responsibility for their own fate.

The upshot is that the 1980s was Australia's decade of creative destruction. It witnessed business shake-out, financial excess, economic restructuring, individual greed, the making and breaking of fortunes and, for many, a struggle to maintain financial and family security. Despite the hopes it engendered, the decade closed in pessimism. But the significance of the 1980s transcends this pessimism; the decade saw the collapse of the Australian Settlement, the old protected Fortress Australia. In the 1960s it was shaken; in the 1970s the edifice was falling; in the 1980s the builders were on site fighting about the framework for the new Australia.

The obsolescence of the old order is documented. Since Federation Australia has failed to sustain its high standard of living compared with other nations. Australia's economic problems are not new; they are certainly not the result of the 1980s, the 1970s, or the 1960s. The malaise stretches back much further to the post-Federation Settlement. Australia's economic problem is a ninety-year-old problem. The legacy of the Settlement has been relative economic decline throughout the century. Australia is a paradox—a young nation with geriatic arteries.[23]

The evidence against the Settlement is overwhelming. In 1870 Australia's average income was about 40 per cent higher than any other nation. Over the next century Australia's GDP growth per head was worse than any industrial country. World Bank statistics show that from the late nineteenth century to 1980, Australia fell from first place to fourteenth in terms of GDP per head. During the nineteenth century the Australian economy was relatively open; in the twentieth century it was relatively closed.[24] The transition from success to failure ran parallel to a rise in protection.

In a separate analysis *The Economist* said: 'In 1870 . . . income per head was then 75 per cent higher in Australia than in America. By the end of the 1920's Australia had dropped to fourth place; by 1980, to 11th . . . On recent performance Singapore will overtake Australia within 10 years followed by Malaysia, Taiwan and South Korea within a generation.'[25]

Australia's share of world exports fell from 1.7 per cent in 1960 to 1.1 per cent in 1987, a measure of its closed economy and declining competitiveness. Australia was the only industrialised nation that failed to increase its proportion of exports to GDP over the thirty years from 1960. Australia's ratio stayed at 13.5 per cent when the expected growth should have taken this ratio to about 19 per cent. A feature of Australia's post-World War II progress has been the failure to diversify its export base and the lack of commitment to international standards.[26] This period saw the greatest expansion of wealth in human history, driven by the explosion in world trade, but Australia participated as a half-member, not a full member.

The 1980s campaign to re-invent the Australian political tradition was driven by economic crisis. The epitaph of the decade is writ large—Paul Keating's spontaneous warning in 1986 of the banana republic. The solutions adopted during the 1980s reflected both the free market orthodoxy in the English speaking world and a deep-rooted domestic reappraisal of the origins of the Australian malaise. The 1980s economic crisis has left the recognition that the solution lies not in addressing the symptoms but in basic institutional change.

This appraisal will not alter during the 1990s. The final decade of the twentieth century will witness a fresh political cycle, yet it is most likely that the direction of the 1980s will still be maintained. Australia is not going to find the solution to its problems in any reversion to the old and failed methods. But Australia's transition to sustained economic progress is sure to be a lengthy and turbulent process.

The superficial judgement of the 1980s is that it was a decade of greed, blunders, and excess. This is obvious and it is a scandal but it misses the real point—national transformation means inevitable and severe adjustment problems. For instance, one challenge for the 1990s is to manage the transformation of the labour market without the cost which eventually accompanied the transformation of the financial markets in the 1980s.

The demoralising impact of the early 1990s recession has imposed hardship, social division, a search for scapegoats and a national reassessment. Beneath the pessimism and its reverberations, new foundations were being laid. The decade of the 1980s saw the advance towards a multiracial

Introduction

Australia, the demise of Protection, the start of the long-waited assault on
Arbitration, a loss of confidence in state power and a turning away from
government paternalism, a shift towards market power and deregulation to
varying degrees, efforts to secure better enterprise productivity and workplace reform, a deeper sense of national self-reliance, a reappraisal of
welfare as a need not a right, and an emphasis on individual responsibility
as well as individual entitlement. Australia's economic orientation was more
outward-looking and its aspiration was to become an efficient and confident
nation in the Asia/Pacific.

The remaking of post-Federation consensus has meant, by definition, a
rethink by the major political parties of their own identity. The political
story of the 1980s is how Labor and Liberal, once joint upholders of the
old system, became joint architects of the new system.

The 1980s broke the power pattern of national politics which had
prevailed since Federation. It saw the triumph of Labor as a governing party
and its victory in four successive elections. It saw the conservative coalition
beaten and then falter under sustained new pressures.

It was the political era of Bob Hawke and Paul Keating and a regen-
erated Labor Party in its achievements and in its flaws. This was a Labor
Party which aspired to govern, reform and re-shape the traditional basis of
Australian politics. The irony for the Labor Party was that in addressing the
issue of international competitiveness it was destroying the ethos and
institutional pillars on which Labor's support had always been based. This
was the cruel historical paradox for Labor in the 1980s. The more successful
it was the more it destroyed the basis of Laborism.

Labor became the party of economic management—since this was the
path to election victories. This saw the creation in the 1980s of a new Labor
Party, the Hawke–Keating party. It was new because it sought to redefine
Labor's role in a society where the foundation of support for the old Labor
Party had collapsed or were falling—White Australia, Protection, Arbitra-
tion, trade union power, faith in government and class consciousness. The
Hawke–Keating Government had the courage to begin charting the new
direction. Yet those new directions would inevitably confront Labor with a
deeper political crisis because, if successful, they would make the old Labor
Party obsolete.

From the start of its third term in 1987 the Hawke Government was
under siege from both the right and left; the right attacking its timidity in
implementing the free market agenda and the left insisting that its
implementation of this ideology was a betrayal of Labor's history. The
traditionalists in the Labor and Liberal parties seek a return to the Settlement
or, at least, a retreat from the free market ideology. In fact, a return to the
old model is not a viable option. The issues for the 1990s are the speed
with which the Settlement is dismantled and the nature of the system which
replaces it.

15

The Liberal Party, the upholder of the status quo, underwent a regeneration in the 1980s and, having concluded that the status quo had failed Australia, adopted a series of radical free market reformist policies to destroy that status quo. This was the transforming event in the history of the Liberal Party—the transition from upholding the status quo to pledging to replace it. This was the turning point not just in Liberal history but in the history of the non-Labor parties. It meant that the next Liberal-National government would be judged by different standards because it had completely different goals; it aspired to be a government of radical reform.

Labor assumed a double role—as reformers and governors. The Liberals fought about reform, embraced a radical agenda but were unable to govern. Yet both sides moved to reject the original Settlement and agreed, broadly, on the future direction. The conservative critique of Labor in the 1980s was that it hastened too slowly. As Labor fades towards defeat in the 1990s the challenge for the Liberal and National parties is to continue the remaking of the Australian political tradition which Labor has launched.

The 1990s will answer the fundamental question raised by the 1980s—whether this decade laid the foundations for a new settlement or was merely a misguided aberration. It will resolve the battle between the reformers and the traditionalists; between those looking towards a new order and those merely tinkering with the old. It will determine whether Australia has the courage and insight to remake its political tradition or whether it buckles before the challenge and succumbs to an economic and social mediocrity.

PART I

THE REVOLUTION BEGINS

1
The new Labor Party

The new path of Australia after the fifth of March, 1983, will be national reconciliation, national recovery, national reconstruction.

Bob Hawke's pledge in his 1983 election policy speech

Bob Hawke and Paul Keating aspired to create a new Labor Party, first by instinct, then by conviction. The hallmark of their Labor Party was its ruling mentality. Their approach was dominated not by Labor history but by contemporary intellectual trends. Their motive was not hostility towards the mixed capitalist economy but a determination to improve its performance. Hawke and Keating realised, belatedly, that Australia faced a national economic challenge in the 1980s, and the preoccupation of their government was its response to this challenge. In the process they changed Australia, the Labor Party and the framework of politics. But finding a solution to the structural problems of the economy was a problem that outlived the Hawke–Keating 1980s era.

Hawke and Keating created in effect a new Labor model of governance. As is usual it arose from improvisation: from politicians making the best of the tools available at the time within the scope of their realisable political imaginations. Hawke and Keating knew from the start that the demands of the 1980s required a response which transcended Labor's penchant for economic intervention, income redistribution and class antagonism.

Their model evolved from a synthesis of contemporary Labor trends— Gough Whitlam's moderation, Bill Hayden's economic rationality, Neville Wran's pragmatism. Its foundations were the two great tactics which the Labor Party devised in the 1980s to secure electoral success. The first was a new basis of cooperation between the party and the trade union movement, and the second was the creation of new links and alliances with the business and financial community. Above all, the new Labor Party bore the stamp of its leaders. It inherited popularism and caution from Hawke, audacity and willpower from Keating.

Hawke and Keating were 'born to rule' Labor figures. They understood both the vulnerability of the old Liberal establishment and the obsolescence of the ALP policy tradition. The Hawke–Keating model was designed to usurp the conservative legitimacy by establishing Labor as the party of superior economic management. In office this was translated as the imperative to address Australia's economic malaise.

When Whitlam won in 1972, he assumed that ongoing economic growth was a given. When Hawke and Keating won in 1983 they assumed that their major task was to devise policies to produce sustained economic growth. They knew that this was the absolute precondition to the realisation of Labor's enduring objectives of income and social justice.

The Hawke–Keating path was marked by upheaval, success and setback as they discovered the depth of Australia's economic problems. Hawke and Keating sought a shift from sectional to national policies and from national to international consciousness. The new values they imposed upon the ALP were a belief in economic competition, a faith in market forces, a commitment to the internationalisation of the Australian economy, reform sanctioned by a consensus process, and government in collaboration with the ACTU leadership.

If Labor's performance in this period was often contradictory it was because these ideas conflicted with each other. Hawke and Keating sought simultaneously to resurrect the best of Labor's past and to destroy the worst of that past. Judgements of this nature are rarely precise. They clashed with Labor orthodoxy and their reforms undermined Labor ideology and ethos. Hawke and Keating were attacked as traitors to Labor's cause. They represented, in fact, the latest wave of that practical Labor tradition which gave preference to adapting the party ideology to community expectations rather than vice-versa.

Hawke and Keating were the heirs to Whitlam's mantle—a Labor Party that was middle class as well as working class, moderate and pragmatic. Gough Whitlam is the founder of the modern Labor Party just as surely as R.G. Menzies is the founder of the modern Liberal Party. Hawke and Keating built upon Whitlam's foundations.

Whitlam, an apocalyptic visionary with a schoolmaster's vocation, modernised the Labor Party in the three domains—ideology, structure and social composition. Under Whitlam the idea of nationalisation of industry was buried, the supremacy of the parliamentary wing over the machine was achieved in practice, and Labor became a respectable party for the expanding middle classes. Indeed, under Whitlam, Labor staked a claim to become the preferred party of the politically aware tertiary educated elite—the most influential force in Australian society in the post-1960s.

Whitlam's philosophy was formed in the 1940s, dominated by government-inspired post-war reconstruction. During the 1950s and 1960s Whitlam redefined both the means and ends of Labor's socialism. He saw Labor as a party of the future, not of the past; the party which must make itself relevant to aspiring middle class people in Australia's suburbs. He saw that blue-collar workers alone could never secure the ALP's future. Whitlam was not alone in reaching this conclusion; but he was unique in building a strategy from it. Whitlam fused Labor into a party resting upon working class and middle class votes, a necessity for survival.

The Whitlam credo was belief in state power and central government, in racial and sexual equality, social progress, economic justice, ethnic pluralism, nationalism at home, internationalism abroad, and government intervention to secure better education, health and welfare. Whitlam's philosophy was enshrined in the idea of equality of opportunity for all Australians.

When Whitlam became ALP leader in 1967, Australia was in transition. He exploited the Menzian legacy—economic prosperity and educational advancement, the pillars of the new age. The institutions and values of the status quo were under assault—parental authority, censorship, the great Australian mum, the RSL, the churches, the Liberal Party. The new log of claims put a premium on individual freedom, self-realisation and faith in state power. The flying wedge of the new age was the Women's Liberation Movement which undermined pre-existing family values, promoted women's equality and transformed the workforce.

Australian conservatism never recovered from the departure of its mesmeric godfather, R.G. Menzies, in 1966. His successors, Harold Holt, John Gorton and Billy McMahon, heard the beat for change but never caught its rhythm. The conservatives lost an entire generation of politically active young Australians in the Vietnam quagmire. This was the generation which underwrote Labor's governance in the 1980s. Labor succeeded in the 1980s because it had better leaders, politicians, organisers and strategists. These resources grew not like mushrooms but like trees—from seedlings nourished for over twenty years.

The two formative influences on the politically aware 1960s generation were Whitlam and Vietnam. It was Vietnam which drove this generation from the Liberal Party and Whitlam, finally, who tied it to Labor.

Whitlam's appeal was both practical and idealistic: from a better sewerage system to pride in Australian culture. Where Menzies lowered expectations, Whitlam raised them. His 1972 victory marked not just Labor's survival after 23 years of opposition but the transformation of Labor's ethos. Whitlam became for a while a hero; a leader with panache, wit and brains. But Whitlam embodied the 1960s grandest delusion—that continuous prosperity was Australia's destiny and that politics was about the distribution of wealth, not its creation.

The Labor Party was strong enough to endure Whitlam's flaws as prime minister, his dismissal, and his humiliations in the 1975 and 1977 elections. Shrewd commentators predicted the ALP's extinction but the party had too

21

much spirit, legend and tenacity to die. When, after Whitlam's retirement, Bill Hayden put away his Hamlet outfit and led Labor during the 1978-83 period, its maturity as a political institution was revealed. Labor defied its history, rebuilding in adversity through political logic and common sense.

The origins of the Hawke Labor Party lie in Malcolm Fraser's triumph over Whitlam. The post-Whitlam generation within the ALP learnt two lessons—that Whitlam's economic management failure must be rectified and that Fraser's political ruthlessness must be matched. These were the axioms which drove Hayden, Hawke and Keating all the way to Labor's return.

The transition had begun in the twilight of the Whitlam government as one generation surrendered to another. Whitlam, Frank Crean, Jim Cairns, Rex Connor and Clyde Cameron were giving way to Hayden, Hawke, Keating, John Button, John Dawkins, Ralph Willis and Peter Walsh. The old generation was a victim of Labor history, riddled with internal factionalism, class struggle and epic dreams. It had grown complacent on post-war economic growth and its weakness was economic management. The parliamentary leadership, ironically, was divorced from the trade unions and ignorant of the great business and financial houses. It was a generation ruined by isolation from the centres of power in Australian life. It lacked the experience to manage the economy and had no relevant model to guide it.

Whitlam helped to promote a more tolerant, diverse, educated society and ran a more independent foreign policy. But his government took office just before the first oil shock in 1973 which terminated the age of unbroken post-war prosperity. This negated the assumption underpinning the Whitlam program. Whitlam's economic management failed to meet this new challenge and Australia succumbed to high deficits, a wages explosion, high inflation and unemployment.

However a lasting economic memorial to the Whitlam government was its assault upon Protection. This occurred in two ways—the dramatic and electorally suicidal 25 per cent tariff cut, and the establishment of the Industries Assistance Commission (IAC) as a successor to the Tariff Board which became a watchdog on protection for all industries. The tariff cut, the single sharpest cut in protection levels, revealed Labor's crazy-brave character and the Liberal's ruthless exploitation of every opportunity to win votes.

The leader who kept Labor from despair after the Whitlam debacle was Neville Wran. Wran's election as NSW Premier in May 1976, just six months after Whitlam's dismissal, was proof that Labor could surmount its crisis. Wran gave Labor the best tonic any political party can have—election success. It came at the precise time that Labor's self-doubt was all-consuming. Wran did far more than just win. He consolidated, took control, kept winning, demoralised his Liberal opponents, and taught the entire Labor

Party that style, moderation and political professionalism was the route to Labor's return.

It was Wran who denied the conservative hegemony of the 1970s and seized a major beachhead while the rest of the Labor Party tried to regather its strength. Wran was a beacon of reassurance when Labor felt desperate. For half a decade Wran was the only ALP incumbent who could fight the non-Labor side, a task which he performed with skill, vigour and judgement. Wran occupies a special place in the Labor Party of the 1980s—he founded the contemporary leadership model. Every senior ALP figure was influenced by the Wran model in the late 1970s; Whitlam had faded but Wran was succeeding. Wran was always an alternative ALP federal leader and he would have switched to federal politics if Hawke had not made his own run.

The bridge in the ALP between the Whitlam and Hawke eras was provided by Bill Hayden's leadership. Hayden failed in a personal sense because he did not become prime minister. But his leadership was a success for the Labor Party. Hayden inherited the ALP during a period of electoral crisis. He brought realism to Labor's policies and over five years took Labor to the brink of reelection.

Hayden delivered one great message: that Labor must achieve economic management superiority over the Liberals. This idea took hold within the ALP. It was under Hayden that Labor accepted that its chief task in office was economic management in a turbulent post-1973 oil shock world where the assumptions of sustained international growth based on Keynesian economics had been terminated. The Hayden–Hawke–Keating generation decided that its priority must become economic growth—jobs, profits, security, better living standards. This decision had three consequences.

It meant the revitalisation of Labor's links with the trade unions through the inauguration under Hayden before the 1980 election of the ALP–ACTU prices-incomes policy. This later became the Accord—the central economic instrument of the Hawke government. Whitlam had ignored the unions but Hayden, under guidance from his shadow treasurer, Ralph Willis, sought to turn the union connection into a plus. The aim was to harness union support in the effort to generate economic growth with low inflation.

The second consequence was Labor's recognition that a successful economic policy required confidence and support from what Labor called 'the big end of town'—the centres of corporate and financial power. Labor became serious about this dialogue with business and for some ALP leaders it became an obsession. Thirdly, Labor began to accept as the source of its economic ideas the international orthodoxy. This was represented by the treasury, the finance department and the prime minister's department in Canberra, the economics profession, and the prescriptions disseminated to industrial nations by the International Monetary Fund (IMF) and the Organisation for Economic Co-operation and Development (OECD).

This meant that when Labor took office it was receptive to professional economic advice. Labor was ready to abandon its own internal resources—the dwindling advocates of socialist theory—as the source for its economic policy direction. It wanted to follow the experts and the experts were a new generation of Canberra-based economists commanding the senior posts in the major policy departments who believed in the efficiency of markets and deregulation.

The new ALP model revealed the distinction between the Hawke and Whitlam governments. The Accord meant a political partnership in office between Labor and the trade unions; financial deregulation exposed Australia to the full discipline of overseas capital markets. While Hawke believed in partnership with the unions and the power of the market, Whitlam really believed in neither. Hawke aspired to govern with the cooperation of labour and capital; Whitlam had a distaste for both.

Bob Hawke was the irresistible force offering to realise the ambitions of the reformed Labor Party under Hayden. Hawke's arrival in Parliament in 1980 transformed politics since he came with a messianic belief, verified by the opinion polls, that he was a certain election winner. Hawke was an Australian phenomenon—a populist, a budding statesman and an ocker. His authority lay not within the party, the parliament or the unions. It resided with the people and was the ultimate authority in a democracy.

Hawke delivered more than his backers ever asked. They made him leader to win an election. But Hawke won four successive elections to became Labor's most electorally successful prime minister, a record not likely to be broken. Hawke was the greatest political product of the television age and the subjugation of political institutions to television as the national forum of debate. He was a presidential candidate in a parliamentary system, ready to exploit both the decline of class as a voting determinant and the rise of the leadership cult.

The new Hawke, after his rejection of alcohol, was disciplined, moderate and boring. Only his ego was unaffected. Hawke was convinced of his special relationship with the Australian people and sought to preserve it with doses of chronic economic optimism and hefty promises. Hawke's ascension to the ALP leadership was driven by Labor's desperation to win, as John Button admitted.[1] It revealed the rapid collapse of the ALP's ideology in the post-Whitlam age. Hayden had promoted economic efficiency and a better deal for families, sound enough policies, but he failed to project them as a vision for Australia. Labor, in fact, was confused about its identify in the early 1980s and decided it would be preferable to resolve this problem in office.

The election of Hawke, 53, as leader in February 1983 was a climax in Labor's transition. Hawke was almost unique as a federal ALP leader in having a trade union career. Normally this had been a disqualification. Hawke, as a former ACTU president with close links to Australia's business community, was the perfect leader to manage the ALP–ACTU Accord and establish a rapport between the ALP government and the forces of capital.

Hawke, unlike Whitlam, had benefitted from a long line of patrons of whom Sir Peter Abeles was merely the best known. Hawke mixed easily in the 'mates' syndrome typified by the tribalism of the NSW right-wing. But Hawke's mates were never limited by Labor's class bias. Hawke, initially seen as a radical, soon proved to be a moderate. He liked being with businessmen and was happy to accept many of their favours. Hawke's political outlook was realistic, cautious and rooted in hostility towards the Labor left. Hawke was passionate about the American alliance, the defence of Israel and in his repudiation of the anti-uranium movement. But this concealed the deeper Hawke paradox, so notable in his prime ministership: beyond these few well publicised passions Hawke was devoid of both passion and commitment to policy positions.

However Hawke's career and persona captured the broader social base to which Labor had been appealing since Whitlam. Hawke was a Rhodes scholar and a unionist, a crusader against White Australia and supporter of multiculturalism, a hero of the underdog and respected by business, a sports fanatic with appeal to women voters, a leader whose image fused strength with the common touch. Hawke was a political freak. Indeed, he almost met Bagehot's description of a statesman, 'a man of common opinions and uncommon ability'.

Hawke brought only one great idea to the party he inherited—national consensus. For most politicians it would have been a gimmick; for Hawke it was genuine. Like most politicians with an idea, consensus was both Hawke's strength and his flaw. It was based upon an insight into his ability to resolve conflict and his grasp that Fraser's economic failure had left his confrontationalist style a liability. Hawke made consensus into an election-winning message. He aspired to harness Australian unity against economic hardship just as his hero, John Curtin, had fashioned unity during World War II. It was a personal mission.

In his 1983 policy speech, standing alone on the Sydney Opera House stage, Hawke called for an end to 'the politics of division'. In 'a commitment which embraces every undertaking' Hawke pledged 'to reunite this great community of ours, to bring out the best that we are truly capable of, as a nation'. For Labor it was poetic justice. Fraser, the leader who had forced the great political and constitutional crisis in 1975 to destroy Whitlam, was repudiated in 1983 by Hawke as the agent of national consensus.

However consensus had an even deeper meaning for Hawke:

> During my period at the ACTU I witnessed the unproductive nature of confrontation which was the practice of this country. More and more I became convinced of the necessity for an alternative approach. I knew that workers and employers were minimising their chances of getting the best economic results for themselves and the nation. I thought a lot

about this. I talked a lot about this. It was reflected in my 1979
Resolution of Conflict lectures and then just before the 1983 election
when I set out the philosophy. It was obvious to me that consensus
would deliver better results.[2]

So Hawke adopted the consensus model in the belief that this method
of government would improve Australia's economic condition. It was, of
course, an industrial relations conclusion, adapted to general economic
policy. Consensus harmonised with the economic model Labor was building—a collaboration between unions and employers. Hawke exploited consensus with a genius—it dressed him as a statesman, it gave Labor a
campaign theme, it seduced the business community, and it sold the Accord.

Consensus also became Hawke's method of government—within the
party, the Cabinet and the community. This brought stability to the Hawke
era. But it also became the great criticism of Hawke—that consensus was
a substitute for leadership and a rationale for inaction.

Paul Keating, 39, was Hawke's principal ally and future rival. Keating
was a mixture of ALP tradition and modernism. Possessed of a sharp brain
and an artist's eye, Keating was a born political salesman. He was an
enthusiast, a talker, a schemer, a manipulator, but with an architect's mind
in its penchant for clear lines and pure constructs. In the topsy-turvey world
of politics Keating operated at one speed—fast, fast, fast. He began as a
boy politician in the Labor Youth Council and became a premature political
veteran. He liked making friends and was never afraid to make enemies.
Keating left school at fifteen, completed his Leaving Cerificate at night
and had no tertiary qualifications.

Keating was self-made, soaked in Labor history handed to him from
Jack Lang and Rex Connor. He used the past but never succumbed to it.
His impatient mind was locked into the future. Keating was a reflex
politician who relied upon instinct first and argument later. His identity was
rooted in the Catholic Church, trade unionism and the NSW right wing, the
most tribal cabal within the most successful Labor branch. Keating got his
killer instinct early and then embarked upon on-the-job education. He was
street smart, picking up bits and pieces of life's jigsaw, half hustler, half
idealist. He raced into parliament at 25, the Whitlam ministry at 31 and
nearly became deputy leader at 33. Keating was hurtling towards the prime
ministership.

In Canberra Keating was pushy but narrow, the breadth coming later.
He admired the big men—Whitlam, John McEwen, Rex Connor—but noted
their mistakes. Whitlam had been a political reformer with the predictability
of a tertiary trained mind; Keating brought to the task a clever brain but
untrained mind. He grew on the job as he sought to fathom 'what made the
place tick and how it could tick better'. Keating worked the media and liked
the journalists. He was sharp and original, deft at exploiting Labor tradition,

aggressive towards the coalition. Keating had a lot to learn but was a fast learner. After the 1975 debacle he had plenty of fight amid defeatism. Keating dressed in Jesuitical severity, polished his parliamentary performance, developed a policy sense and assaulted the Liberals with refined savagery.

Keating rarely discussed ambition. For him action defined intent. He set Hayden against Whitlam in May 1977 in an unsuccessful effort to shorten Labor's time in opposition. Keating broke into prominence in the late 1970s as shadow minerals and energy minister, working the miners, mastering the detail, visiting Japan. Keating saw the lost economic opportunities and he became a zealot for economic growth. It became the Keating gospel, the text with which he assailed the Labor left as 'Balmain basket weavers' and the coalition as ruling class failures. Then Keating met Hawke.

In 1980 Hawke sought an alliance with Keating to run the party. They were right-wingers, divided by fourteen years, spanning Victoria and NSW—a basis for mutual self-interest. Keating said he would help Hawke but there was a proviso: he would not pull down Hayden. Keating told Hawke: 'The first Labor leader I tear down will be the one I replace.'3

This defined the permanent limits of the Hawke–Keating partnership. They became friends as politicians, never as men. It was politics which always dictated their relationship.

In 1982 when Hawke launched his challenge against Hayden, it was Keating who argued that the right-wing should support Hayden. Keating felt that Hayden was entitled to stay. Keating's own plan was to succeed Hayden in the future and to cut Hawke out of the leadership. Keating joined the Hawke revolt because he had no choice—not because he wanted to make Hawke leader. The right wing faction was going with Hawke so Keating was a reluctant conscript to Hawke's leadership. Keating, who prided himself on caucus leadership of the right wing, had to tolerate Hawke's elevation before him. Keating's very reluctant recruitment to the Hawke cause came during the famous 14 July 1982 meeting of the right wing power brokers at Sydney's Boulevard Hotel.

The irony is that in Hayden's fight for survival against the Hawke putsch, he unconsciously determined the nature of the future Hawke government. This arose from Hayden's January 1983 reshuffle when he sacked Ralph Willis and made Keating shadow treasurer. In a night of drama on 13 January 1983, Hayden tried to detach Keating from Hawke and thereby save his own leadership. Giving Keating the job of shadow treasurer Hayden said, 'You're the only bastard tough enough to handle John Stone.' Hawke was alarmed that Hayden's ploy might succeed. Keating was fearful, worried that he lacked the technical skill for the shadow treasury. He called the job 'a poisoned chalice'. Willis was merely devastated.4

When Hawke became prime minister he reluctantly accepted Keating as his treasurer. The truth is that Keating was Hayden's appointment, not Hawke's. Hayden, in fact, created the Hawke–Keating team in 1983 by his

January reshuffle and his February resignation. Hawke had wanted Willis, his longtime friend, as treasurer and Willis would have become Hawke's treasurer if Hayden had not appointed Keating as shadow treasurer seven weeks before Hawke won the election.

Hawke and Keating became one of the most successful teams since Federation. They had a policy affinity, an efficient rapport and complementary political skills. Hawke, unlike Fraser, gave his ministers political room. Keating was dominant within the Cabinet, Hawke within the country. Where Hawke was popular, Keating was dangerous. Hawke preached consensus and Keating wielded the economic knife. For much of the second half of the decade Hawke was de facto president, Keating de facto prime minister.

The alliance was a success in containing its rivalry. The turning point came only in 1988 when the leadership contest was joined. After an intense dispute between Hawke and Keating over the leadership, their working relationship was restored in late 1988 by a deal done at Kirribilli on a leadership transition during the fourth term. This secured another two years of Hawke–Keating collaboration. But Hawke's refusal to honour the deal and Keating's growing impatience revealed in his late 1990 Press Gallery dinner speech on leadership saw the eventual collapse of their partnership. It degenerated into a bitter personal and political power struggle which convulsed the Labor government.

Hawke and Keating posed a greater electoral threat to the coalition than had Whitlam before them. This was proved over four election victories. Hawke would not abdicate power through early mistakes or any rush of reformist blood. Hawke was determined not to defeat himself. The message from the Hawke–Keating government over four victories was that the Liberals were required to win on their merits, an unusual challenge for the non-Labor side. During the 1980s Hawke and Keating were determined to avoid loss by default, the experience of the three previous ALP governments in defeat—Whitlam in 1975, Ben Chifley in 1949 and Jim Scullin in 1931. The irony for Hawke and Keating is that the early 1990s recession suggested that, finally, they would suffer the same fate as their predecessors.

From the start Hawke and Keating saw longevity in office as the means by which their reforms would be entrenched. They rejected Whitlam's reformist rush, recognising that such haste betrayed the mentality of a government doomed to a fleeting life. They wanted to reclaim for Labor at the federal level the legitimacy which it had been denied or had forfeited through sublime blundering. They knew that the three Labor splits—over conscription in World War I, the Depression in the 1930s, and communist influence in the unions in the 1950s—had consigned Labor to a total of thirty years in the wilderness. This had been a blank cheque to the non-Labor forces for more than a third of Australia's history. Hawke and Keating, above all, sought to give Labor legitimacy as a governing party.

After Whitlam's dismissal, ALP historian Graham Freudenberg argued that Labor's core problem had always been its crisis of legitimacy. That is, the conservative establishment (based on pastoral, business, media and financial elites) had never accepted Labor's legitimacy despite the decisions of the voters—an interpretation made almost irresistible by the sabotage to which the Whitlam government had been subjected by the Senate and its dismissal by the Crown's representative.

But it is the task of governments to earn their own legitimacy. Hawke and Keating assumed their legitimacy from the start but their assertion went further: they claimed that the coalition had lost its legitimacy in the early 1980s recession.

Keating in particular promulgated the view that Australia's economic difficulties were a legacy of the 30-year post-war coalition rule. His aim was to destroy the legitimacy and the confidence of the Liberal–National parties and he enjoyed some success.

The Hawke–Keating government was assisted by the shift in the balance of political talent decisively in Labor's favour by 1983. The first post-Whitlam government ALP leader had been Neville Wran, who became NSW Premier in 1976. He was followed by John Cain in Victoria and John Bannon in South Australia, both in 1982, Brian Burke in Western Australia and Hawke in Canberra in 1983. Despite their subsequent mistakes each of these ALP leaders was manifestly superior to his Liberal opponent as a political leader and election winner. During Bill Hayden's five years as ALP leader the party had always had two formidable alternatives to him—Wran and Hawke, a somewhat luxurious position. The quality of the ministries Hawke appointed during the 1980s was further proof that Labor was reaping the dividend of the previous twenty years of political contest.

In the ten years from 1981 to 1990 there were 22 state and federal elections with Labor winning 17 and the non-Labor side only five. Two of these five victories were by Joh Bjelke-Petersen's National Party in Queensland. The senior coalition partner, the Liberal Party, won only three elections in this decade. Two of these wins occurred in the smallest, least influential state, Tasmania. On the Australian mainland the Liberal Party won only one election in the decade, that of Nick Greiner in NSW in 1988. The ALP won four federal elections, the three elections in Victoria, three in Western Australia, three in South Australia, while Neville Wran won his final two elections in 1981 and 1984. Labor lost in NSW in 1988 but regained office in Queensland and Tasmania in 1989. The decade overall was Labor's best and the Liberal–National parties' worst since Federation.

The factors underpinning this Labor success were better leadership, Cabinet authority over the party, and internal unity which amounted overall to superior political skills.

The 1980s, in fact, offered an insight into both the stability and the superiority of Labor's leaders in comparison with the Liberal Party's leaders in the period since Menzies' retirement in 1966. In this twenty-six years until 1992 Labor had four leaders, Whitlam, Hayden, Hawke and Keating. The non-Labor side had changed leaders nine times—Harold Holt, John Gorton, William McMahon, Billy Snedden, Malcolm Fraser, Andrew Peacock, John Howard, Peacock again, and finally, John Hewson.

Labor's leadership longevity was reinforced by its leadership unity, in relative terms, compared with the non-Labor side. Hawke was elected leader in February 1983 unopposed and was never opposed in any ballot until 1991 after he had already been leader for eight years! This was the Labor pattern, state and federal, during the decade. Most of the ALP leaders went unchallenged and without obvious rivals. The Liberals, by contrast, fought close leadership ballots throughout the decade with leaders unable to entrench their authority.

In his first fortnight as prime minister Hawke secured two fundamental internal changes. First, while caucus elected the ministry it agreed to a 13-strong inner Cabinet selected by Hawke. Second, the Cabinet agreed that it would operate on the solidarity principle, which meant that ministers must support Cabinet decisions within the party. In practice this meant the triumph of Cabinet authority over caucus sovereignty—a more hierarchically structured party.

The unity of the party was advanced by election wins, factional power-sharing and the collapse of the left-wing's ideological position. The left had no domestic issue on which to hang its anti-Americanism. Its campaign against the uranium industry had reached its zenith in 1977 but was declining during the 1980s. Its economic solutions were largely discredited and when Hawke offered the left genuine powersharing within his Cabinet the invitation was accepted—along with the responsibility this involved.

A major innovation was the three-faction system developed during Hawke's first term—right, centre-left and left. This became a mechanism for settling differences over policy, power and ministry appointments. Under Hawke the caucus become less important as power moved upwards to the Cabinet and outwards to the factions. The faction alliance between the right under Hawke and Keating, and the centre-left under Hayden delivered an ongoing majority within the party for Cabinet positions.

The Hawke–Keating Labor government was, like most governments, a product of its times. Labor was being reshaped in office which meant that it was being driven, above all, by the Cabinet's obligation in a democracy to address national problems. During the 1980s Australia faced its most severe economic crisis since the 1930s. This occurred against a backdrop of the globalisation of the world economy and the loss of national sovereignty which inevitably accompanied this revolution.

The response of the Hawke government was to apply the orthodox solutions of the age but adapt them to Labor's institutional needs. In short, it was a mixture of the OECD orthodoxy married to the ALP–ACTU Accord—a combination of prevailing economic beliefs and domestic labour movement innovation. This meant that Labor adopted its own unique model, a fact which Keating openly conceded in 1991 after his resignation. The Hawke–Keating era attempted an heroic fusion between the revised neo-classical economic wisdom and Labor's Accord commitment to growth and employment.

Labor won applause from around the world for its commitment to financial deregulation, free market economics, the achievement of a federal budget surplus, restraint of union claims, lower taxation rates, private sector restructuring through lower protection, higher profits and the reform of public enterprises. These remedies were applied with greater or lesser success at different times with varying commitments. But the direction is unmistakable.

That direction was a challenge to the Australian policy tradition, almost to the Australian way of life. It defied the stance which had been adopted by coalition and Labor governments over many decades. The Hawke–Keating direction was not just anathema to the Labor tradition. The government, in trying to apply a solution to the economic challenge, was really involved in the remaking of the Australian political tradition.

However Hawke and Keating were not alone. The revolution they launched in Australia was replicated by other Labour and Social Democratic parties around the world—in New Zealand, France, Italy, Spain, even Sweden—nearly everywhere that the left governed in the 1980s. It was part of an international movement which saw Labour parties admit that the power of the state to deliver prosperity and justice to its citizens was failing. It was a recognition of the failure of traditional policies and the embrace of market-based solutions which these Labour parties had always repudiated.

The most dramatic volte-face came in France, where under President Francois Mitterand the socialist orthodoxy was initially attempted with disastrous consequences, forcing a retreat on every front. Mitterand subsequently appointed Michel Rocard as prime minister, a Francophile exponent of policies that were similiar to those also followed by Hawke and Keating. The same process occurred in Italy under the Socialist leader Bettino Craxi and in Spain under Socialist Premier Felipe Gonzalez. The German Social Democrats who governed under Helmut Schmidt in the 1970s had pioneered the way. The New Zealand party under David Lange and Roger Douglas offered a fascinating parallel to Hawke and Keating. The climax to this decade of retreat from socialist theory in the Western democracies was the sudden collapse of the communist command economies in 1989, a decisive year in history.

This phenomenon of the 1980s reflected the worldwide policy consensus expressed in treasuries around the globe, notably in Canberra, and articulated forcefully within the forums of the IMF and the OECD. The international brotherhood of economic advisers was a dominant intellectual force throughout the decade.

But the policies of the Hawke–Keating era were never completely dominated by overseas orthodoxy because the political anchor of the government became the Accord. This represented the most concerted effort, possibly in the party's history, to turn the alliance between Labor and the trade unions into a tool of economic management. The Accord was the great institutional creation of the 1980s. It was, in effect, a last massive effort of the combined labour movement to salvage its power, institutions and influence in the more competitive world of the late twentieth century. The Accord was basic to Labor's political and economic strategy. It had a single overriding consequence—it committed the Hawke–Keating government to pursue policies designed to promote economic growth and employment.

During the 1980s the Hawke government was subject to attack at home from both the left and right. The ALP traditionalists and the left accused Hawke and Keating of betraying the Labor Party, a claim which became as fashionable as it was inevitable. It provided in fact an insight into the social transformation of the ALP captured by Kim Beazley Snr in his famous remark: 'When I first went as a young man to ALP forums those present were the cream of the working class, while now in many cases they represent the dregs of the middle class.'[5] A feature of Labor's 'middle classing' was the creation of an educated, above average income ALP constituency spawned from the 1960s often labelled the 'new class.' This was the source of much of the internal criticism from the left of the Hawke–Keating team and the ALP Cabinet.

The 'new class' was a coalition of white-collar professionals—teachers, social workers, university lecturers, journalists, reformist lawyers, environmentalists, civil servants and union officials—products of liberal education, affluence and the women's movement. It was skilled at promotion of its own interests in the name of the common interest. The 'new class' was part of the Hawke–Keating Labor Party yet alienated from it. The myth it propagated was that Labor was a socialist party undergoing an act of betrayal. The sharpest reply came in 1986 from the NSW Labor leader, Bob Carr, who said, 'The term socialist has had its day . . . it has been appropriated by the communist bloc. I say let them have it, let's use some other term like equity or social justice.'[6] But the real answer was the most obvious—the old-fashioned policies had failed and it was the task of politicians to find new policies which worked.

The Hawke–Keating experiment was a natural stage in Labor's evolution. It sprang from elements deep within Labor's nature—its adaptability, its economic rationalism, its aspirations for electoral success. Since Whitlam and Hayden, Labor's deepest policy commitment had been to make the economy work better in the national interest as opposed to sectional interest. The Hawke–Keating government was pioneering the latest effort to realise this objective. But the experiment would change the ALP forever. It was an attempt to incorporate into traditional Labor Party ideology the belief in an open economy, the value of competition and the utility of the market.

The new Labor Party

One of the main themes of Labor history is the tension between ALP governments and the party rank and file. Scullin, Chifley and Whitlam were subjected to a sustained campaign of denigration for betraying true Laborism. It is because Labor governments have only come once each generation that people forget that the criticism made of such governments is a reoccurring theme. The criticism of Hawke and Keating was even more intense than usual, but the reason is not hard to discover. It is because during the Hawke–Keating era it became apparent that the very institutions which had sustained the Labor Party throughout its history were being destroyed—Protection, Arbitration, trade union power, and the idea that domestic living standards could be quarantined from international market forces. The underlying dilemma of the Hawke–Keating years is that the policies needed to make Australia competitive would strike deep into the wellsprings of Labor's institutional base.

It was inevitable that many ALP supporters would be hostile and disillusioned and that there would be an alienation of the party rank and file. This was coupled with the apparent loss of the symbols by which the party faithful had lived. Hawke only accentuated this problem by his periodic public flirtation with the 1980s entrepreneurs. Keating made it worse with his penchant for arrogance, elitism and exclusivity—a trio of values that are hostile to both community and party outlook.

The real risk for Labor was not that the Hawke–Keating model would succeed but that it would fail. Failure would discredit the Labor Party and provoke another of its periodic crises of identity and direction. This was the threat posed by the deep recession of the early 1990s. The recession saw a renewal of the charge of betrayal from the ALP traditionalists. But more serious was the accusation from the federal coalition and the community that the Hawke–Keating model had failed the nation in terms of design, courage and execution.

2
The revolt against the Liberal tradition

For Australia's sake, we need to mend our ways.
Liberal backbencher John Hyde, October 1980, calling
for a new philosophy within the Liberal Party

The Fraser era finished in electoral defeat, tears and the eclipse of the philosophy which had dominated the Liberal Party since its inception, and non-Labor politics since Federation. The 1983 election terminated the vision of Australian progress which had been held by the 'born to rule' men of the Australian establishment. This election saw more than just the defeat of Malcolm Fraser, the principal heir of the Menzian mantle. It was a turning point because it triggered over the next decade the collapse of the ideas which had guided the Liberal Party.

The key to Liberal and National Party politics during the 1980s lies in the revolution within their own ranks and those of their supporters before the 1983 defeat. When the Fraser government lost, it was under assault not just from Hawke's Labor but from an internal revolt which championed a new brand of radical liberalism. Fraser had encouraged this movement by his rhetoric but disappointed it by his inanition. After his defeat, these radical liberals, who were given various labels—classical liberals, economic libertarians, the free market lobby, or drys—marched into the political vacuum that Fraser left.

In 1983 they constituted, in fact, a Liberal counter-establishment. Adherents were scattered through the parliament, academia, business, and the economic community. Their ideas were a synthesis of overseas opinions and a domestic policy reassessment of the Australian malaise. Their core belief was that government intervention must surrender to market forces. They supported small government, lower taxation, lower protection, industry deregulation, needs-based welfare, low inflation, genuine competition, an attack on trade union privileges, and allowing markets to set prices.

34

The revolt against the Liberal tradition

These radical liberals offered an alternative view of the Liberal Party and the national economic challenge. Their weapons were almost foreign to the Liberal Party—a body of ideas. They converted the majority of the Liberal Party to their position during the 1980s and their philosophy almost became an accepted orthodoxy. But their triumph inside the party was bitter, bloody and protracted. The non-Labor parties finished the decade still in Opposition with the radical liberals still awaiting the chance to deliver their program.

John Howard was the first radical liberal to lead the party and John Hewson the second. But it was only after Hewson's election as leader after the 1990 election defeat that the Liberal Party appeared to stabilise after its philosophical regeneration. But there was still no certainty that the Liberal revolution would succeed—that will be decided in the 1990s. It will be determined by the ability of a new Liberal government to implement its new ideology—a daunting task—and then for that ideology to be vindicated as the right prescription for Australia.

The radical liberals, like all successful reformers, were zealots. Liberal politics in the 1980s is their revolt against the old order. It was a revolt, though not always fully grasped at the time, against the Deakin-inspired Australian Settlement of the early post-Federation period which, in the post-war context, was embodied in the Menzies–McEwen–Fraser heritage.

Its force lay in two events. The first was the failure of Keynesian economics based on state intervention to keep delivering sustained prosperity. The onset during the 1970s of high unemployment and inflation—stagflation—prompted practical men to seek better solutions; the system wasn't working so the system needed to change! The second was the impact on Australia of the intellectual and political ferment in the two great democracies, Britain and America, where radical liberal ideas were espoused, if not always implemented, in the political revolutions of Margaret Thatcher and Ronald Reagan. Economic libertarianism was an idea whose time had come. The significance of Thatcher and Reagan for the Australian Liberals was that they were political winners. They won elections after Fraser had lost. They were upheld as evidence that the new politics worked and that Fraser's mistake had been faint-heartedness.

The drys were indigenous in their analysis and international in their outlook. The high priests of their doctrine were the eighteenth century philosopher and economist Adam Smith; the Austrian theorist Friedrich Hayek, and the American economist Milton Friedman. Fraser had entertained Hayek and Friedman at The Lodge during their visits to Australia. The radical liberals espoused a marriage between economic and political freedom which brought a new intellectual force to non-Labor politics. The audacity of the drys was soon revealed—they claimed to be restoring true liberalism to the Liberal Party.

From Adam Smith the drys seized the idea that both parties who freely enter an economic exchange can benefit and that a high correlation exists between individual interest and the public interest. From Friedman they took the notion that the failure of contemporary economics derived from the excessive role of the state. From Hayek they began to realise that they were not conservatives who merely sought to resist the socialist expansion of state power, but that they were liberals who sought a different direction— who sought to liberate the individual from state controls, direction and solutions. This was a political tradition which throughout Australian history had been particularly weak. Of course, not all the drys embraced all three notions.

The free market lobby attacked the Liberal and National Party establishment for sins ranging from closet socialism to bankrupt conservatism. In 1975 Malcolm Fraser was talking like the first radical liberal but in 1983 he was the chief obstacle to radical liberalism.

Upon his defeat Fraser won a lonely tribute from La Trobe University sociologist Dr John Carroll:

> It was a Roman resignation, honourable, decisive and pitiless. It told a society and times in which such character was almost never to be seen that the chaos and humiliation of a routed army can be stopped by the assertion of moral authority . . . It was time for orations in praise of the achievements of that Government and the virtues of the leader who made it.[1]

However, the Liberal Party had no stomach for tributes to Malcolm Fraser; the then second longest serving Australian prime minister would be dismissed inside and outside the Liberal Party during the 1980s as a leader who squandered a unique opportunity. Much of the criticism was with the benefit of hindsight, and hypocritical. But the Liberals descended into self-recrimination, abused the Fraser record and, having succumbed to Fraser's authority in office, dismissed him as too weak in defeat. Fraserism became the anti-model.

It is now apparent that Fraser's forcing of the 1975 crisis culminating in Whitlam's dismissal was the last gasp of the old Liberal establishment: the final fling of the 'born to rule' brigade. The men who sought to reclaim their destiny as rulers actually believed, with a sincerity conceived in arrogance, that Labor was ruining Australia and that a return to Liberal government would restore post-war prosperity. It was that easy! The Fraser–Anthony team, returned after three years in Opposition, was an unreconstructed coalition with new drivers. When the coalition failed it was obvious that Australia's economic problems were more deep-seated; the old formulas were irrelevant. This gave a new twist to Whitlam's dismissal: it became the trigger which finally shattered Australia's economic delusions.

The people took Fraser at his word and gave him a great mandate: for five and a half years he had control of the House of Representatives and the Senate. In 1975 and 1977 he won the biggest election mandates in

Australian history. Fraser faced a weakened ALP and a majority of non-Labor premiers. He was perfectly placed to implement national reforms.

But Fraser saw no imperative for major reform. His instinct and his character was for restoration. As a prime minister he was a disciplined traditionalist. Fraser sought to restore the status quo ante—to restore and cleanse the Australian tradition after the Whitlamesque excesses. Whitlam was ruining the nation; Fraser would redeem it. His slogan 'Turn on the Lights', conveyed the ease with which prosperity would return. Fraser's 1975 policy speech was an establishment fantasy.

He promised growth of 6–7 per cent, full tax and wage indexation, tax breaks for companies, as much protection as industry needed, a farm income fund, abolition of the means test on pensions, retention of Medibank and spending cuts to attack the budget deficit.

Fraser's achievement was to restore discipline. He announced the need to wind back the claims of the individual upon the state—a task he pursued with vigour but inconsistency. The average real increase in federal spending during the Fraser years was 2.2 per cent compared with 3.2 per cent for the Menzies era and 5.3 per cent for the McMahon era. Fraser halted Whitlam's expansionism and sought to revive the private sector.

Fraser was not an exponent of free market ideas. He believed in smaller government but, faithful to the Australian tradition, he was an interventionist. The alliance which dominated the Fraser Cabinet was the Fraser–National Party network, symbolised in the personal links between Fraser and the Nationals trio, Doug Anthony, Peter Nixon and Ian Sinclair. The Cabinet believed in protection, tolerated arbitration, and championed a managed exchange rate and strong government intervention in markets.

Fraser was a follower of the Menzies tradition. He described this tradition superbly when asked why he saw Menzies as Australia's greatest prime minister. Fraser replied:

> Because of the achievements that were introduced in his time. A health scheme that worked, a high level of home ownership, a capacity for people to plan ahead, the longest period of full and continuous employment in Australia's history, a very great deal of social progress, a very large number of social welfare programs introduced. There was an aura of predictability and certainty. People could plan their futures knowing those futures would be secure.[2]

The contradiction within Fraser was that this ruthless political giant-killer was a timid prime minister. Fraser fooled himself into believing that he was a man of action and of history when his government was dominated by his clever, scheming, cautious appreciation of vote-winning. Fraser could be pragmatic or ideological, depending upon the requirement. The final judgement upon Fraser is that he misread the times in which he governed, notably towards the end. Fraser made some concessions but never grasped that far more radical solutions were required to address the national deterioration. Australia faced a worse crisis in 1983 when Fraser lost than in 1975 when he won, the ultimate test.

Fraser was partly doomed by the divisions from the 1975 crisis. He admitted later that his caution as prime minister was influenced by a desire to repair the damage. His official biographer, Philip Ayres, says: 'After 11 November 1975 Australian society was more polarised than it had been since the conscription debate during the First World War . . . There was no point in exacerbating division. In Fraser's view . . . "It was one of the factors in us saying: it's time for negotiation and consultation with the union movement." '[3] This is an irony but not an excuse. Fraser's legitimacy worries were self-generated and they were exaggerated.

There were three distinct phases in Fraser's eight years in power. The first, which covers 1976, was that of Fraser reformism; the second, from 1977 to 1981–82, saw Fraser's broad acceptance of the John Stone treasury, 'fight inflation first' philosophy; and the third, which covers the final year, saw Fraser break from the treasury and attempt a series of interventionist experiments, notably an expansionary budget and a wages freeze to counter the recession.

The essence of Fraser's early reformism was the introduction of tax indexation—the discounting of tax increases due to inflation—for both individuals and companies. It was reinforced by discretionary tax cuts in 1977 which were 'sold' in television advertisements as a 'fistfull of dollars'. But Fraser betrayed both initiatives, cancelling the tax cuts in the following year, and abolishing tax indexation over several years.

Fraser's federal director, Tony Eggleton, believed that the voter cynicism over the cancelled tax cuts—the most publicised in history—was permanent. Fraser's chief adviser, Professor David Kemp, believed the retreat on tax indexation was a repudiation of Fraser's 'lower taxation and smaller government' position—the essence of his political commitment.

If Fraser had lost the 1980 election, the judgement upon him would have been that of a cautious prime minister who had restored discipline and made progress after the Whitlam stagflation. By this time inflation had been cut to 10 per cent compared with more than 15 per cent under Whitlam, unemployment was under 6 per cent, and a resources based investment surge was underway which Fraser declared 'promises to be as important to Australia and individual Australians as anything in the last 35 years'.[4] In Fraser's 1980–81 budget, spending as a proportion of GDP fell to 26 per cent compared with levels near 30 per cent under Whitlam.

However the 1980 election was a turning point after which the seeds were planted for history's adverse judgement on the Fraser government. This is when his policies failed. It was after 1980 that the radical liberals launched their revolt and the demand grew for free market policies. It is wrong to attack Fraser for failing to implement these policies in 1976 and 1977 when, frankly, virtually nobody was calling for them.[5]

38

But the climate changed post-1980, with a groundswell among a group of politicians, economists, journalists, senior public servants and businessmen that a change of national direction towards free market policies was necessary to solve Australia's problems.

The influence of the free market lobby within the Liberal Party was given formal expression on 28 October 1980 when, at the declaration of his poll, the West Australian backbencher and wheat farmer John Hyde launched the revolt against the old order. Hyde's speech was the inauguration of 'dry' power. It represented a deliberate decision by a small group to mobilise within and outside parliament for economic policies based on the free market philosophy.

Hyde warned that the Fraser government had lost its way, that it had failed to deliver on smaller government, less welfare and low inflation. He said: 'For Australia's sake we need to mend our ways.' Hyde said the election swing against Fraser was not because the government had followed tough policies. It was, in fact, the reverse—a disenchantment because Fraser's achievements had not matched his promises. Hyde warned that in the future he might be compelled to speak against government policies. He said that 'the art of leadership is explaining those things that are necessary to the future well-being of the nation'. Fraser was put on notice.[6]

As the informal leader of the free market lobby, Hyde's strengths were intellectual clarity and political courage. Hyde saw through the regulation of Australia's economic life to the poor productivity at its centre. He was not afraid to challenge Fraser—a rare thing in those days—because he was driven by policy results, not political ambition. Hyde was too rational to become a good Liberal politician.

The vanguard of the free market lobby within the Liberal Party was four backbenchers: Hyde and Peter Shack, both from Western Australia, and Jim Carlton and Murray Sainsbury from NSW. Shack and Carlton were ambitious politicians while Hyde and Sainsbury were sceptical of their political futures. The drys were zealots with a touch of naivety. They were political descendants of that stoic champion of free market forces, South Australian Liberal backbencher, C.R. 'Bert' Kelly, who had waged a lonely campaign against protection for years. Hyde paid Kelly the ultimate tribute: 'We stood on his shoulders . . . I never spoke out in the party room and found nobody on my side. But Bert did this for years.'[7]

Hyde's stand was a turning point in Liberal Party history. It was based upon a calculation made by the drys to challenge Fraser after the 1980 election. The decision was taken at two meetings in Carlton's office before the election, attended by Carlton, Hyde, Shack and Brian Buckley, senior adviser to Liberal deputy Phillip Lynch.

The free market lobby was driven by three perceived Fraser government failures. They were the renewal of the two airline agreement in a form which maintained the protected, consumer costly, cross-subsidised domestic airline duopoly of TAA and Ansett; the 'soft' 1980 Cabinet decision to reduce protection only gradually for the footwear, clothing and textile sector, the most inefficient, labour intensive and highly protected parts of manufacturing industry; and Fraser's failure to meet his money supply targets necessary to a successful prosecution of inflation.

This revealed the priorities of the free market lobby—lower protection, deregulation of domestic industry, and a low inflation economy. From 1980 the drys had a hard core dozen coalition backbenchers and could draw upon up to 25 depending upon the issue. They now mobilised within and outside the coalition parties.

An organisation called Crossroads became the symbol of their efforts and, in effect, a counter-establishment to the prevailing Fraser establishment. The name derived from the first comprehensive statement of the free market position articulated in a 1980 book, *Australia at the Crossroads*, the blueprint for an alternative Australia based upon radical liberalism. It was jointly conceived by the professor of economics at the University of NSW, Wolfgang Kasper, and the management of Shell Australia Ltd, in particular its chief economist, Douglas Hocking.

The book described Australia's direction as 'the Mercantilist trend' and provided an exposition of a better course titled 'the Libertarian alternative'. Its starting point was that Australia should improve on the 'stagnation mentality of the late 1970s'. Shell financed the study, which had five authors—in addition to Kasper and Hocking, they were the professor of economics at Flinders University, Richard Blandy; professor of agricultural economics at La Trobe University, John Freebairn; and Professor Robert O'Neill from the ANU Strategic and Defence Studies Centre. The assumption was that Australia had reached a turning point: the old ideas had failed and a new philosophy was needed.[8]

Crossroads said that Australia was suffering from the 'post-Whitlam blues', a mood in which 'bold initiatives are shunned and defensive protectionist reactions are widespread'. It pointed to the 1977 White Paper on Manufacturing Industry and the 1979 Crawford Study Group on Structural Adjustment—the two major secondary industry studies of the Fraser era—as symptomatic of the malaise. Both reports admitted that major, even bold, change was needed, yet they cautioned delay, victims of a 'wait-and-see' lethargy.[9]

The book argued that the logic from the Keynesian model's demise was the need for 'a new long-run strategy'. It warned: 'The longer Australia postpones the necessary reforms, the greater is the prospect of yet another decade of depressed economic conditions.'[10]

The authors identified a series of differences between the Mercantilist model and its Libertarian alternative: protection versus trade liberalisation; resistance to versus acceptance of new technology; a regulated versus a liberalised attitude towards capital flows; belief in centralised wage fixation as opposed to a shift towards collective bargaining; an expansion versus a reduction of government's role in health, education and welfare services; regulation versus deregulation of product markets. Their theme was that with a bold shift in direction Australia would win new export markets in growth areas such as food processing, raw material processing, minerals, chemical and energy products.[11]

The Libertarian alternative was named in honour of the international movement under way in the English-speaking world. The authors observed that liberal 'has become one of the weasel-words of modern politics' but that there were prospects that its true meaning might be rekindled 'in the tradition of such social philosophers as Adam Smith, Friedrich Hayek and Milton Friedman'.

The authors concluded:

> If Australia follows the Mercantilist Trend, we will not only see a
> continuing inability to cope with some aspects of economic
> welfare—such as high unemployment, particularly of the young,
> continued inflation, slow growth in living standards, and a more
> unequal distribution of income—but also serious failures in meeting the
> non-economic objectives to which Western societies aspire . . . [The
> Libertarian alternative] would amount to a new phase in the growing
> up of the Australian nation, a move from adolescence protected by a
> 'Mother State' to full maturity . . . The greatest obstacles to realisation
> of an alternative to the Mercantilist Trend are the Old Establishment (of
> money, private schools and clubs) and the New Establishment (of
> unions, media and academics) who will want to conserve their
> established positions from challenges and new ideas . . .[12]

Hyde described this book as the 'inspiration of the dry movement in federal parliament after the 1980 election'. At the end of the 1980s Hyde said that the book was the first blueprint for the ideas which dominated the decade.[13]

On 22 December 1980, Hyde wrote to forty prominent Australians to attend the inaugural Crossroads Conference. The aim was 'to discuss ways and means of moving Australia away from mercantilist policies and structures towards a market economy'. This was intended to be a meeting of believers. It was geared to action, persuasion, tactics. Jim Carlton says: 'The issue was how to get a market economy. We essentially saw both Fraser and Labor as espousing collectivist solutions.' Fraser ministers were not invited but prominent 'believers' among the advisers were present. Carlton picked the invitees. The first meeting was on 14–15 February 1981 at the Union Club, Sydney—ironically, an establishment citadel.[14]

The Crossroads Conference participants and those who joined later became, with some exceptions, the nucleus of the 'free market' counter-establishment of the 1980s. Those who stuck gave their careers, minds or money to the cause. Within the decade, the Crossroads core group and its ideas had taken control of non-Labor politics in Australia.

They included: from federal politics the core drys, Hyde, Carlton, Shack and Sainsbury, whose ideas would prevail within the Liberal Party; from NSW politics Nick Greiner, Bruce Baird and an adviser Gary Sturgess, the nucleus of the late 1980s NSW Liberal revival; the force behind the National Farmers' Federation (NFF), David Trebeck; the honorary founder of the dry movement, 'Bert' Kelly; and three key ministerial advisers, Professor David Kemp, later a Liberal frontbencher, Professor Cliff Walsh from Fraser's office, and Brian Buckley from Lynch's office.

Other participants included the radical liberal Andrew Hay; the Liberals' Research Director, Martin Rawlinson; and former IAC Commissioner Richard Boyer. Four of the *Crossroads* authors were involved: Kasper, Blandy, Hocking and Freebairn; from academia Professor Michael Porter from Monash University and Professor Ray Ball from the University of NSW; Austin Holmes from the Reserve Bank; the future director of Victoria's Institute of Public Affairs and later Senator, Rod Kemp; and the Director of the Centre for Independent Studies (CIS), Greg Lindsay.

Those from the corporate sector included Western Mining Corporation's (WMC) Executive Director, Hugh Morgan who, along with John Elliott, became the most influential businessmen within non-Labor politics during the decade; Bain & Company chief Maurice Newman; Australian Bank Managing Director Mark Johnson; Brisbane industrialist Don Swan; from Amatil, Phil Scanlan, later chairman of the Sydney Institute run by former Howard adviser Gerard Henderson; Sydney businessmen Neville Kennard and Roscoe Graham-Taylor, both strong supporters of Lindsay's new CIS; Andrew Kaldor, a former McKinsey man and close friend of Nick Greiner and Jim Carlton; and Jim Short, former Liberal backbencher and future frontbench Senator. The company economists included John Brunner from BHP, Don Stammer from Bain & Company and John McLeod from CRA.

Later participants included John Stone, after he left the treasury in 1984, and also Andrew Robb, future NFF director and federal Liberal Party director. On the fringe were another two influential advisers, Professor John Hewson from Howard's office, an occasional participant and future federal Liberal leader, and Professor John Rose from Fraser's office.

'Crossroads' met twice a year for about six years, well into the Hawke era. It was a network, a political cell for market policies, a talkfest, a lobby group on the Fraser government (which is why secrecy was crucial) and later a pressure point against Hawke. It became the first in a series of such groups which sprang up during the decade. Hyde says: 'It gave us courage when we needed it because we were challenging the leadership of our own party.'[15]

Within the parliament the drys were responsible for the establishment in 1981 of the Society of Modest Members, named after 'Bert' Kelly's newspaper column 'The Modest Member' in *The Australian Financial*

Review. The society's policy credentials were flexible—both Fraser and Andrew Peacock joined. But it highlighted the growing popularity of free market ideas and exploited the 'bandwagon' effect, the politician's search for group security.

The radical liberals were influenced by the most important department in Canberra—the federal treasury. John Stone's appointment as secretary to the treasury in 1979 guaranteed greater publicity and projection for its views. Treasury was fundamental in the reform agenda of the 1980s through its influence over government, and Stone emerged, almost irresistibly, in the guise of economic conscience for the Fraser government. The drys had access to Stone through the backbench economics committee and they supported Stone's 'fight inflation first' strategy against Fraser.

However for both 'Bert' Kelly and John Hyde the fight against protection was the preeminent struggle. It was the victory which they saw as the key because it would trigger the collapse of the entire Mercantilist structure. Protection was the bulwark of the non-Labor establishment and the fight against protection was a landmark.

This fight would liberate the Liberal Party from its past and it would terminate the National Party's future. The story of the anti-protectionist victory is the story of the National Party's lurch towards its death throes. The political revolt under way when Fraser lost office had consequences for the National Party as great as for the Liberal Party. By 1983 the foundations of protectionism had rotted as the result of events during the previous fifteen years. The crumbling of protection would dominate the politics of the 1980s.

Twenty years before in the 1960s protectionism had reached its zenith as the policy of the National Party leader and minister for trade and industry, John McEwen. McEwen's approach to assisting the wealth-creating sectors, mining, manufacturing and agriculture, was all-around protection. McEwen had forged an alliance between the Country Party and the manufacturing sector which led the veteran journalist Alan Reid, to liken his performance to that of a 'rider in a Roman amphitheatre with a foot on each of two horses. But in his case the horses were not harnessed together. They were kept together solely by the force of his personality.'[16]

The revolt against protection came from the Country Party's own base—graziers and many growers who decided, finally, to confront the McEwenist legacy. The political influence of farmers had been fading for many years, the product of fewer numbers, the rise of mining power and the clout of provincial town industries. The National Farmers' Federation (NFF) was created in 1979 to resolve the issues which the Country Party had refused to address. Under the influence of its full-time deputy director, David Trebeck, the NFF reviewed the protection/free trade issue and decided to commit to free trade. The National Party was put on notice, but it failed to heed the warning.

In this battle against protection the turning point was the creation of the Industries Assistance Commission, previously the Tariff Board. The three greatest opponents of McEwenism had been Liberal treasurer Billy McMahon, the chairman of the Tariff Board, Alf Rattigan, and Gough Whitlam. The final defeat of McEwenism was a triumph for a properly functioning democracy. It sprang from an irony, McEwen's misjudgement of Rattigan whom he appointed to head the Tariff Board only to discover that 'his man' became a convert to free trade.

In 1966 Rattigan used the Tariff Board to embark upon a review of tariff assistance to every industry, the publication of the level of effective protection for each industry, and encouragement of a public debate upon the costs of protection. Rattigan realised that once the true cost was laid on the bar of public opinion then protection was doomed. Secrecy was the lifeblood of Australian protectionism and Rattigan stripped it away in an epic battle with McEwen.[17]

Rattigan had many allies. A generation of Australian economists led by the ANU's Professor Max Corden—an international pioneer in protection theory—showed conclusively that the costs of protection outweighed the gains. An informal three-way alliance, bureaucrats–academics–journalists, arose to push the campaign. The advent of Max Newton as editor of the *Australian Financial Review* was another milestone. Newton, a fervent anti-protectionist, appointed the economic journalist Alan Wood to Canberra with the brief to make protection a national issue. But Rattigan found his greatest ally in Gough Whitlam post-1972.

Whitlam replaced the Tariff Board with the Industries Assistance Commission (IAC) in 1973. The purpose was to strengthen the role of rational analysis and weaken vested interests in protection policy. The IAC Act contained a 'mandatory' provision which obliged the minister to seek an IAC report before changing long-term assistance to any industry—which eliminated the scope for the special deal. The debate upon the IAC provided an insight into rural politics. The National Party led by Doug Anthony fought the bill but the farm organisations were quiescent. Rattigan noted that 'the farmers were more far-sighted and statesmanlike than the leaders of the party purporting to represent them'.[18]

David Trebeck explains the essence of the transition:

> The IAC was the turning point in the protection debate. The IAC
> became responsible for analysing assistance whether to primary,
> secondary or tertiary industries. It showed that the effective rate of
> protection for the rural sector was 6 per cent and for manufacturing it
> was 28 per cent. This meant that the debate changed fundamentally
> because it was clear that the level of assistance the farm sector got
> from government was relatively small. Droughts and commodity prices
> would come and go. But the rural sector aided by the IAC came to
> realise that it was issues beyond the farm gate which were determining
> its future—inflation, exchange rate, wage and protection policies. The

catalytic role played by the IAC during the 1970s in lifting the economic debate and explaining the impact of protection cannot be overstated. We fired the 'bullets' made by the IAC.[19]

This situation had three consequences. First, it drove a wedge between the farm leaders and the National Party. The Fraser–National Party Cabinet axis from 1976 onwards was pro-protection and launched a trench warfare against the IAC. The result is that the National Party created a revolt within its own constituency led by the NFF.

Secondly, when rural leaders saw that it was national policies which determined their fate, they sought strength in unity. Since its inception the Country Party had played 'divide and rule' with farm organisations. The move towards greater unity among rural groups denied the Country Party the use of this technique. These were the forces driving the creation of the NFF which campaigned for national not sectional policies.

Finally, the agenda of the NFF outlined in October 1979 at its first conference was a pure version of radical liberalism. It called for tight anti-inflationary policies, reduced expenditure, smaller government and lower taxation, more flexible wage policies, deregulation of the financial system, lower protection, a focus on competitiveness, and a freer international trade regime. The NFF was the first industry lobby in Australia to embrace the free market philosophy.[20]

This program was a repudiation of Country/National Party ideology, tactics and history. It was a direct threat to the existence of the National Party; a comprehensive revolt from the grassroots against the farmers' party and a rejection of its legitimacy. The NFF's charge was lethal—that the farmers' party had betrayed farm interests, that the protectionist policies of the coalition and the National Party were hurting the farm sector, not helping it. The NFF knew that the National Party would not change. It had only one option—to pit itself against the National Party.

The NFF's structure was tied to a series of grower committees which meant it had grassroots support. Its intellectual leadership came from Trebeck, qualified in agriculture and economics, who had spent the previous ten years with the Australian Woolgrowers' and Graziers' Council. It relied upon several industry and economic specialists, notably Andrew Robb and Ian Wearing.

Doug Anthony was a fine politician and a decent man. But Hyde identified the flaw: 'Doug was very loyal to the Country Party and then the National Party. But he couldn't conceive of putting the national interest before the party interest. Fraser and Anthony would criticise protection overseas and do the opposite at home. You had to be cynical about it.'[21]

Doug Anthony followed the McEwenist tactic of seeking to broaden the National Party base—protection for the clothing industry in provincial towns, playing the growers against the graziers on protection, assistance for the miners. But in catering for the many he forgot the core.

The end of certainty

While the Liberal Party was experiencing a revolt from the radical liberals who eventually assumed control, the National Party was being bypassed. The revolt was occurring outside and around the National Party. The Nationals were a relic of agrarian socialism; even when sufficiently embarrassed by this philosophy they had no substitute. The Nationals misread the times, perceiving the threat too slowly and failing to devise an adequate response.

The NFF had its own strategists, Trebeck, then its new director, Andrew Robb and his successor Rick Farley. It developed a greater financial base than the Nationals. It produced a more popular leader in the 1980s, Ian McLachlan. Once the dry philosophy took command of the Liberals the NFF gravitated towards the Liberal Party, joining forces with the radical liberals. It is no accident that Robb eventually succeeded Tony Eggleton as federal Liberal Party director nor that McLachlan became a Liberal frontbencher. In the 1980s the Liberal and Labor parties made inroads into the National's parliamentary strength. When John Hyde and his fellow drys surveyed the landscape after the 1980 election their most powerful industry ally was the NFF.

The rise of the radical liberals and the NFF coincided with a grassroots intellectual movement in the 1980s which began to shape the public debate. It was symbolised by a new group of think-tanks which won support from business and academic figures, a trend reflecting disenchantment with established universities. Small, privately funded, staffed by dedicated people, the Australian think-tanks became influential among opinion makers in the media, academia and politics.

Their most important backer was WMC's Hugh Morgan who assisted with moral and financial help. Morgan's influence on non-Labor politics in the 1980s is immense but indirect. He was an Australian business leader in the US tradition. Morgan aspired not just to run a business but to promote the public policy debate. He was associated with the three main think-tanks of the early 1980s—the Centre for Independent Studies (CIS) in Sydney, the revival of the Institute for Public Affairs (IPA) in Melbourne, and the Australian Institute for Public Policy (AIPP) in Perth.

Morgan also delivered many speeches during the decade, almost a body of work, in which he sought to shape the political agenda on Aboriginal land rights, industrial relations, foreign debt and the environment. Morgan collaborated in this activity with his adviser at WMC, Ray Evans, who was a speechwriter, soundingboard and intellectual activist. Evans was important in the intellectual revival of the right-wing in Melbourne and was the architect of the H.R. Nicholls Society, formed in the mid-1980s to agitate for radical reforms in industrial relations.

The best example of intellectual combustion was the creation of the Centre for Independent Studies (CIS) under the energetic guidance of a Sydney maths teacher, Greg Lindsay. Lindsay had become a classical liberal influenced by the writings of J.S. Mill and Hayek. His aim was to further the causes of free enterprise, capitalism and free choice.

Lindsay founded the CIS in 1976, a shell without financial support, when he was 26 years old. Later his path crossed that of a Melbourne group which wanted to establish an Australian version of the Institute of Economic Affairs (IEA), a London based free market think-tank. Lindsay began meeting the businessmen who wanted an Australian IEA—Hugh Morgan, Maurice Newman, South Australia's John Bonython, CRA's chief economist John McLeod, BHP's economist John Brunner, and Shell's Douglas Hocking. They felt that Australian universities had failed to lead Australia's intellectual debate. Maurice Newman had sponsored an earlier visit to Australia by Milton Friedman who left a lasting impression that new institutions were needed to promote the cause of freedom.

Lindsay's first notable conference, in April 1978, was on government intervention, with papers from two ANU economists, Ross Parish and Ted Sieper, along with John Hyde and Alf Rattigan. The conference and the CIS was given publicity when the *Australian Financial Review*'s economics editor, P.P. McGuinness, wrote an article headed 'Where Friedman is a Pinko', giving the CIS address and phone number, and Lindsay was flooded with expressions of interest. Later McGuinness donated his entire library to the CIS at the discount price of a dollar a book.

Lindsay's first backer was Sydney businessman Neville Kennard, who kept him afloat. After operating the CIS from a backyard shed at his Sydney home, Lindsay won his financial base in 1979. Six companies each put up $5000 a year for five years—WMC, CRA, BHP, Shell, Santos and *The Advertiser*. By the late 1980s Lindsay's budget was $850 000 annually and the CIS was a think-tank of world class, making a sustained contribution to the policy debate. Lindsay admitted a special debt to Kennard, Morgan, Bonython and Newman whose support along with his own outstanding commitment had made the CIS possible.

When Hyde was defeated in the 1983 election he formed the Australian Institute for Public Policy (AIPP) in Perth which had a research committee that included Wolfgang Kasper, David Kemp, and Patrick O'Brien from the University of Western Australia. Hyde was bankrolled initially by the Clough family which had a Perth engineering business. But he also received backing through Morgan, and AIPP embarked upon ambitious publications in economics, agriculture, transport and other areas.

However the biggest think-tank was the Victorian based Institute of Public Affairs (IPA), which underwent a revival in the early 1980s. This began in 1982 when Rod Kemp, brother of David, became its director. Kemp's father, Charles Kemp, had been one of the IPA's founders, its long-term director from 1943 to 1975, a major influence at the inception of the Liberal Party and probably the principal intellectual architect of the original Menzies platform. Rod Kemp was approached for this task by Sir

James Balderstone, who served on the boards of BHP, Westpac and the AMP. The board of the relaunched IPA included Balderstone, Hugh Morgan, the head of Potter Partners, Sir Charles Goode, and Nobby Clark from the National Australia bank.

Kemp ran the IPA on an annual budget of $1.4 million, recruited more than 1000 corporate subscribers, championed free market economics and promoted traditional values, the family, the Constitution, Christian morality and the ANZUS alliance. The IPA recruited former federal treasury deputy Des Moore, former senior WA treasury officer Les McCarrey, and former treasury secretary John Stone to spearhead its economics and finance work. It employed one of Australia's leading diplomats, David Anderson, as a foreign policy analyst and also drew upon Professor Owen Harries, formerly Fraser's senior adviser on foreign affairs. It hired Dame Leone Kramer to head its education unit and on the recommendation of La Trobe University's John Carroll, Kemp hired Dr Ken Baker to edit the *IPA Review*. This published John Stone, Geoffrey Blainey, Peter Costello, Michael Porter and Leonie Kramer among others.[22]

These developments were mirrored in Sydney when in 1986 the departing senior adviser to John Howard, Dr Gerard Henderson, a biting critic of the Fraser years, took over and revitalised the Sydney IPA, an organisation separate from its Melbourne counterpart. Henderson was appointed by the IPA board whose president was stockbroker Jim Bain, and whose members included the chairmen of Amatil and Westpac, Sir Noel Foley and Phil Scanlan. Later Henderson, who proved to be a shrewd publicist, turned the organisation into the more independent Sydney Institute, with Scanlan as chairman.

Another focus for free market ideas was Professor Michael Porter's Centre for Policy Studies at Monash University. Porter pioneered work on tax reform and advocated a flat rate personal income tax. When John Stone resigned from the treasury in 1984 he was jointly employed at Porter's centre and at the Victorian IPA.

The most influential organ for free market ideas was the *Australian Financial Review* whose politics were shaped by its managing editor, Max Walsh, and whose intellectual thrust came from P.P. McGuinness during 1980–85 when he was editor and then editor-in-chief. Under McGuinness the paper led the campaign against the power of the Arbitration Commission, likening the system to a 'club' and attacking its legitimacy. The paper backed budgetary restraint and lower protection and called for micro-economic reform, known as 'structural adjustment'. It became the virtual conductor of the free market orchestra in 1980–83, the phase of Fraser failure.

After 1980 Australia's political debate began to swing decisively as the forces for free market reform mobilised across a newly emerging agenda which would dominate the entire decade. Fraser's reputation as prime minister, as distinct from politician, was ruined in the 1980–83 parliament by this tide. When the Australian economy plunged into recession Fraser also lost his support within the wider community.

In his last term Fraser turned against this new agenda of change which was embodied in a series of issues that would dominate the decade—a broadly based indirect tax, protection policy, deregulation of the financial system, and a wages policy to manage high expectations from the 'resources boom'. Fraser's problem was that too often he consulted, pondered, then retreated. Sometimes his political judgement was right and on other occasions it was wrong. But the overall impression is inescapable—Fraser failed to tackle these issues with purpose.

The first major decision Fraser took after the 1980 election was to reject Howard's plan to implement a broadly based indirect tax to secure a change in the mixture of taxes before the 1983 election. The switch to indirect taxation would be sold to voters by steep cuts in personal income tax rates which it would make possible. Fraser had control of the Senate until mid-1981, the election had highlighted taxation as an issue, there was significant corporate support and the *Financial Review* editorialised in favour of the treasury position.

But Fraser equivocated, worried about the inflationary consequences. The National Party was strongly opposed, then, much to Howard's horror, the Nationals advocated one of the cargo cult ideas of the decade—flat rate tax. It was the first sign of the influence which the Queensland National Party premier, Joh Bjelke-Petersen, would exert on the 1980s. The tax debate went off the rails as Howard branded flat rate tax 'unworkable or unfair or both'.

The Cabinet was in no mood for taxation audacity and Fraser's two senior aides, David Kemp and John Rose, opposed Howard's indirect tax on grounds of both politics and economics. Howard was defeated in Cabinet on 23 February 1981 with only three ministers, Peter Durack, Ian Viner and Fred Chaney, supporting him. The Fraser–National Party axis was dominant. The indirect tax was put into deep freeze by the treasury, awaiting the next opportunity (which would come in 1985 with Paul Keating). Howard said the abandonment of the indirect tax option in 1981 was 'the worst mistake made by the Fraser government in its last term'.[23] This is a highly dubious assessment but the legacy of Fraser's decision endured for a decade. It left the free market lobby determined to introduce the tax and suspicious of Fraser, a mood which turned to alienation over the issue of protection.

The high tide of dry power was the Carlton–Hyde mobilisation of thirty-three backbenchers in December 1981 for a shock assault upon the high protection levels in the Lynch car plan proceeding through Cabinet. Phillip Lynch, pushing a policy based on GMH's world car strategy, was offering export assistance and ongoing protection for car makers. This revolt was the tremor which signalled the earthquake about to engulf non-Labor politics. The 'Bert' Kelly anti-protectionist 'minority of one' position had been transformed to the point where the free market lobby had actually come close to humiliating the Cabinet. The issue was sacred political terrain for the Liberal establishment—the restructuring of Australia's major manufacturing concern.

While Lynch prevailed, the revolt against his policy was decisive. It terminated Lynch's career and made Howard's. It led the drys to withdraw their support from Lynch and embrace Howard as their best supporter within a hostile Cabinet. Howard had offered futile resistance to the Cabinet protectionists but earned marks with the drys. Hyde and Carlton insisted that Lynch was finished. Howard succeeded Lynch as deputy leader six months later—primarily on the basis of this transfer of support from the drys. From this time Howard's career strategy became obvious—he became champion of the free market lobby.

The car decision revealed for the first time that numbers existed within the Liberal Party to reward free market politicians. The proof was Andrew Peacock's decision to launch his 1982 leadership challenge against Fraser by depicting himself as an advocate of free market policies. Peacock needed numbers, so he cast himself as a dry—a cause for which he had previously shown little enthusiasm. The irony is that Hyde and most drys were unimpressed. Hyde, in fact, tried to exploit Peacock's challenge against Fraser to get Howard, not Peacock, installed as prime minister. But in April 1982 Fraser easily prevailed against Peacock and Howard became his deputy.[24]

The best symbol of Howard's conversion to the free market ideology was his campaign for financial deregulation. This was an undertaking in which his senior adviser, John Hewson, was involved as a financial specialist. Hewson, in fact, was associated closely with Howard's efforts in the 1980–83 period to secure a broadly based indirect tax, lower protection, a freer financial system and a firm fiscal stance despite the recession.

Fraser lost the 1983 election on the back of three failures—the worst international downturn since the 1930s, the drought in rural Australia, and the domestic wages explosion which fed a severe dose of stagflation. Fraser had no responsibility for the first two but cannot escape culpability for the third.

It was Fraser who created the climate for the early 1980s wages explosion, first by raising hopes, second by failing to devise a wages strategy. Fraser campaigned in 1980 on a nirvana—a massive resources boom. In his 1981 Australia Day message Fraser pledged that 'the prosperity flowing from these great ventures will lift the living standard of every Australian family . . .' The resources boom left an appetite for easy money. Fraser had oversold the boom, inviting a comparison with the goldrushes, and the trade unions acted on his licence.

The government's wages policy was a form of partial indexation through the Arbitration Commission. As wage pressures rose in 1981 and unions launched industrial campaigns, Fraser's solution was to negotiate a deal with ACTU chief Cliff Dolan, to secure a peace by asking the full Bench to interpret the indexation system with more flexibility and offer further 'safety valve' wage rises. Fraser flew from this crisis to London for the Royal wedding of Prince Charles and Lady Diana. While Fraser paid homage in Westminster Abbey the Commission President, Sir John Moore, threw out the Fraser–Dolan deal, abandoned the indexation system because of lack of support from the parties, and put the torch to the Fraser era.

The government had no wages strategy to handle the resources boom expectations which it had created. Its last industrial minister, Ian Macphee, says: 'I remember Phillip Lynch saying in a Cabinet meeting—I was amazed he said it—that he was being asked all the time by industry what is our wages policy? Do we have one? To which there was a chorus including myself saying "no". Then there were rueful smiles. The truth is we never had one.'[25]

Fraser's luck had expired. The world recession killed off prematurely the resources boom; but the trade unions won the wage rises which Fraser promised—on their terms, not Fraser's. Stone lamented that 'wage claims were formulated in anticipation of benefits which had not, in fact, yet begun to flow'. The government responded to the wages breakout with a mixture of inaction and experimentation.[26]

The economy-busting deal came in late 1981 in the metals industry, with a collective bargaining agreement ratified by the Full Bench. It meant an average rise in hourly wages of 24 per cent for 400 000 metalworkers or 9 per cent of the work force. In 1982 wages rose across the workforce by 16 per cent with a resulting squeeze on profits. One of Australia's best economists, Max Corden, concluded that 'the recession's causes were as much domestic as foreign'.[27] The wages explosion saw Australia descend into double digit inflation and unemployment which destroyed Fraser's political career.

The damage represented a classic failure of Liberal politics. Fraser had fallen at the same hurdle as Whitlam—his inability to manage Australia's system of centralised wage fixation, craft union structure and strong demand conditions. Whitlam had been ruined in the 1974 wages explosion. Fraser, who had exploited the political benefits of that event, was felled by the same process in 1982. The responses to these failures within the Labor and Liberal Parties would dominate much of the rest of the 1980s. But Fraser compounded the damage.

Fearing the worst downturn since the 1930s, Fraser sought a budgetary expansion to counter the recession. Fraser was being a good Keynesian; Howard and the treasury were horrified. Stone walked away from the government. Fraser–Howard relations reached their nadir during the preparation of the 1982–83 budget.

Fraser and Howard snarled at each other across the Cabinet table as Howard's authority was flouted. Both Howard and Stone, separately and without contact, came to the verge of resignation from their posts in July 1982 in protest. Howard discussed a possible resignation with his wife Janette and his aide John Hewson, and decided to 'tough it out'. He said later: 'After having been told repeatedly that governments could not solve economic problems by spending the taxpayer's money, the people saw the 1982 budget as an attempt to do just that.'[28]

Fraser left office having failed to devise a method of securing sustained low-inflationary growth. At times he ran the economy slowly to get inflation down; but when growth took off Fraser was unable to prevent a wage-price spiral. The assumption of the Liberal establishment in 1975 that their return to power would restore prosperity had proven, ultimately, to be false.

Fraser also left with a dubious record in terms of his promise to cut spending and reduce taxation. Federal spending as a proportion of GDP was 29.9 per cent when Fraser left—exactly the same as when he arrived. But total tax as a portion of GDP had risen from 25 to 27.2 per cent during the Fraser era.

John Hyde was unforgiving: 'I think Fraser ran a poor government as governments go. Economic problems started to be evident during his time. He saw the problems yet did nothing or too little about them.'[29] By 1982 Hyde had defined his position in the manifesto 'The Year 2000: A Radical Liberal Alternative', which identified liberalism as a separate political force from socialism or conservatism and called for a free market policy revolution sweeping in its conception.

The Liberals were fixated by Fraser's failure. They were driven, above all, by the new breed of radical liberals who, denied legitimacy by Fraser, gradually saw their ideas vindicated by his defeat. Over the 1980s the Liberal Party accepted as policy each plank on which Fraser had resisted the free market lobby—low protection, decentralisation of wage fixation, financial deregulation, the broadly based indirect tax, and the rejection of fiscal policy as a counter-cyclical instrument. Fraser began by promising a new era for private enterprise but confirmed instead that his own policies were too timid and conventional to deliver this pledge. The judgement on Fraser by the free market lobby appeared too harsh but, on balance, it was not inaccurate.

The power of the free market lobby was rooted in the assertion that Australia had to break from its past, as implemented by the Liberal and National parties. Fraser's 1983 defeat was unique because of the existence within the coalition parties and their supporters of a counter-establishment, loosely united by a new ideology, networks, a mutual support mechanism and a comprehensive economic view of the Australian disease. Under this banner were Howard, Greiner, Hewson, McLachlan, Carlton, Hyde, Shack, David and Rod Kemp, Robb, and others who would dominate non-Labor politics during most of the 1980s and into the 1990s. They drew support from a new generation of academics, businessmen, public servants and journalists dedicated to the same philosophy.

But the radical liberals had not fully grasped the consequences of their challenge. They were striking at the power structure of conservative Australia. Their success would come only with the overthrow of the old order—and that dictated a clash of arms.

3
The Hawke–Keating model: the Accord

We are going to change the face of decision making in this country and the way government co-operates with important sectors of the Australian community.

Bob Hawke, 11 March 1983

The Hawke government was successful in reviving economic confidence and lifting the nation from its worst downturn since the Great Depression. Hawke was lucky being elected near the trough of the recession and riding the economic cycle upwards. His first two years in office saw the breaking of the drought, bumper crops, the international recovery, a rise in domestic demand and strong falls in Australia's high levels of unemployment and inflation. Hawke's prestige soared and the results dazzled the Labor Party.

After the 1983 election, Hawke's position was far stronger than that of Whitlam in 1972. Hawke had a 25-seat majority, the Australian Democrats holding the balance of power in the Senate, a grip on middle Australia, a majority of Labor premiers, a sympathetic media, a corporate sector ready for seduction, and an alliance with the union movement. Above all, Hawke had a discredited Opposition.

Hawke appeared as a potentially great leader, a prime minister of substance, skill and longevity. His strength rested upon his popularity which haunted the Liberals, the favourable international situation, and the new economic model which Hawke, Keating and their respective advisers would construct. He also benefited from Fraser's wages pause and budgetary expansion, both of which helped to kindle the recovery.

Hawke adapted quickly as prime minister and his personal approval rating stabilised at above 70 per cent—an unprecedented level. In John Button's famous letter to Hayden asking him to resign in favour of Hawke, he wrote that 'even some of Bob's closest supporters have doubts about his capacity to lead the party successfully'.[1] Hawke had the satisfaction of disproving this suspicion. He was a superb Cabinet chairman and revealed an immense capacity for self-discipline and long hours.

As a communicator his forte was television, never the parliament. Hawke, who came to parliamentary politics late in life, looked to the extra-parliamentary centres of power—unions, business and media—to entrench his support. It was a sharp contrast with Whitlam on each point. Hawke was a cautious leader, easily swayed by emotion but devoid of deep policy commitment. His sustaining force was his belief in his own political persona and his rapport with the Australian people. Yet this belief, far from encouraging Hawke to be audacious on policy, seemed to make him wary lest such a personal prize be damaged. It was as though Hawke's popularity was a delicacy to be preserved, not an asset to be utilised.

Hawke's skill was his ability to listen, absorb and synthesise. He was not an original thinker and lacked a strategic view of his government's direction. He tailored his views to secure party acceptance and was adroit in internal dialogue. He shunned confrontation and policies which provoked confrontation. Hawke was exceptionally fit, hard-working, moved paper quickly and rapidly mastered his briefs—but his penchant was for personal promotion. He mixed equally with the Prince of Wales, with revellers at the Royal Perth Yacht Club celebrating Australia's America's Cup win, and with chief executives from the business community. From the start Hawke loved the domestic comfort of the Lodge—the staff, the travel, the cars. His wife Hazel, after a tough life raising three children with a frequently absent husband, began the most rewarding phase of her life. But while Hawke thrived, Keating struggled as treasurer.

After the election Hawke had told his advisers: 'I want Ralph (Willis) as treasurer, not Paul. See if we can fix it.' Hawke saw Keating as an economic novice while Willis had been shadow treasurer for years. Hawke knew Willis better than Keating. Finally, Keating had struggled during the 1983 campaign and Hawke doubted his capacity for the task. But the NSW right-wing would not tolerate Keating's removal—the message came back from Graham Richardson. Nor would Keating's ambition permit such a humiliation.

The irony is that by mid-1983, just four months later, Hawke and Keating had formed a trusted working collaboration. Hawke's doubts about Keating had been despatched and Keating became closer to Hawke than did any other minister, in effect his de facto deputy. The Hawke–Keating partnership was sealed by mid-1983. It was tied by common interest and its strengths rested upon two factors—complementary political skills and similar policy instincts. It was never just a two-man government; but it was a government dominated by two men.

In 1983 the two principal instruments of the Hawke–Keating model were initiated—the Accord with the trade union movement, and deregulation of the financial system. These two forces would shape Australia's economic development during the 1980s. They imposed the limits within which policy would operate and became instruments for economic change. The Labor model was a hybrid, a mixture of tradition and innovation.

The Accord was a statement of faith in collective political action to secure economic benefits; the float of the exchange rate was a declaration of belief in the irresistibility of market forces. The Accord represented a sustained effort by the ALP and the trade unions to turn their historical association into an institutional asset for Labor in office. It was an attempt to harness Labor's history for future national progress and its success during the early 1980s was remarkable by international standards.

Labor's embrace of financial deregulation revealed far more than just Hawke–Keating pragmatism. They were Labor leaders sympathetic to the ideology of the market but, unlike the Liberals, devoid of vested interests and associations within the old business or corporate establishment. Hawke and Keating had no political inhibitions about putting the blowtorch of the market to the organs of capitalism. They were aggressive in seeking alliances with the business and finance 'counter-establishment'—those leaders and companies who embodied the apolitical spirit of the 1980s where it was balance sheets, not class loyalties, that mattered.

This is where Hawke and Keating operated with a ruthlessness and freedom which the Liberals had never displayed in power. They supported a series of revolutions within capitalism—the float; the entry of foreign banks to challenge Australia's financial institutions; the new breed of entrepreneurs of whom Alan Bond was the most spectacular; the BHP takeover bid by Robert Holmes a'Court; media changes which saw the older companies, the Herald and Weekly Times and John Fairfax and Sons, either fall or falter; and the most sweeping reductions of industry protection in Australia's history. If this was the path to efficiency, then Hawke and Keating saw no obstacle to its pursuit. It had the added plus of destroying the old anti-Labor establishment.

The Accord and financial deregulation meant that Labor was pledged to regulate the wages market but to liberate the financial market. This reflected the fact that Labor had vested interests in the labour market but not in the financial sector. The government was seen abroad to be pioneering a unique model during the 1980s. The initial overseas appreciation was that Labor was oldfashioned in its pursuit of an incomes policy which had been discredited during the 1970s, notably in Britain, but innovative in the rapidity with which it implemented financial deregulation, the new orthodoxy.

The orientation of the Hawke government was determined decisively within the first week. Hawke and Keating met secretary of the treasury, John Stone on 6 March, the day after their victory, to be briefed on two crises. There was a huge capital outflow which suggested the need for a substantial $A depreciation. But the bombshell was Stone's advice that the projected budget deficit for the next financial year, 1983–84, was $9.6 billion; this compared with Fraser's planned deficit for 1982–83 of $1.7 billion which, Stone said, had now blown out to an estimated $4.3 billion. Stone said the budget outlook 'at best, can be regarded as alarming' and that 'the magnitude of the fiscal imbalance is unprecedented in Australia during peace time, as is the level of government spending'. The speed of the deterioration was 'remarkable'. Stone's memo, marked SECRET, was a clinical demolition of the Fraser regime, a condemnation before history and a savage introduction to office for the Hawke government.[2]

The upshot was a 10 per cent devaluation to settle the capital markets. Hawke and Keating exploited Stone's $9.6 billion 'shock' to abandon the program of Keynesian expansionism on which they were elected, much to the treasury's relief. The Stone memo was exploited by Keating for years to denigrate the Liberals; it became one of the most lethal documents in Australia's political history. At this point Keating decided to retain, not fire, Stone as treasury chief. The Victorian economic adviser who came to assist the transition, Peter Sheehan, was despatched back to Melbourne where he would dominate Victoria's economic policy for the rest of the decade.

In the space of four days Hawke and Keating had ditched Labor's economic program, rejected the Keynesian model, struck an alliance with their new official advisers, and found a weapon to use against their opponents for years. It was a dramatic case study in the impact of power.

Hawke, in fact, had had a pre-election tip about the deficit blowout. He had reserved his right before voting day to modify Labor promises if, upon winning, the accounts showed a fiscal horror. The $9.6 billion projected deficit meant that Fraser had already implemented the fiscal expansion which Hawke had promised during the campaign. It was an exquisite irony—Fraser, unbeknown to Labor, had secretly implemented ALP policy, at least in its fiscal magnitude!

The urgent economic advice to the Labor government was to cut back this figure, not boost it, advice put by the treasury and the prime minister's department where the senior advisers were Stone and Ed Visbord respectively. The instincts of both Hawke and Keating were to follow this advice and enshrine a 'sound money' reputation for their government.

The chief requirement for an incoming government is to establish a competent advisory structure in which it trusts. Hawke was fortunate to secure an impressive private office where the three senior figures were—a public servant with economic and diplomatic experience, Graham Evans as private secretary, the former political journalist and Wran adviser, Peter Barron, as political adviser, and an ANU academic, Dr Ross Garnaut, as economic adviser.

Hawke's reliance upon his own office was greater than that of most leaders. Hawke lacked any ministerial experience but his needs transcended this deficiency. He required emotional support from his staff and sought to find in them the policy conviction which he was unable to muster within himself. Hawke had little grasp of institutional power or inclination to use his own department. He preferred to rely upon those whose loyalty he had sanctioned by appointing them to his personal staff.

As a prime minister he made the mistake of having his primary relationship with his own office, not his Cabinet. Evans provided the self-effacing reliability, Barron the political ballast, and Garnaut obtained the magic fusion between economics and emotion. Ed Visbord said later: 'Hawke never took my advice on a single economic issue unless it coincided with that of Ross Garnaut.' Garnaut was a strategic thinker whose influence on Hawke was never remotely matched by any subsequent economic adviser. Evans, Garnaut and Visbord formed a sound policy advising troika for Hawke. Barron had a natural political touch and rare ability in human persuasion. Barron never left tracks by putting pen to paper. But the influence of Hawke's political advisers tended to be negative rather than positive, telling him not to take risks.

When Hawke interviewed Garnaut during his first week in office he asked whether Garnaut had any reservations. 'Yes. The expansionist economic program on which you were elected,' Garnaut replied. But Hawke shot back: 'After the briefing we've had from treasury you won't have to worry about that.' Hawke hired in Garnaut a dedicated anti-protectionist and pro-market economist.

Hawke was fortunate to inherit a talented Cabinet which fitted neatly his retiring style of prime ministership. The senior ministers included Lionel Bowen, John Button, Don Grimes, Keating, Hayden, Mick Young, Gareth Evans, Peter Walsh, John Dawkins, Ralph Willis, and Susan Ryan, with the junior ministry including Kim Beazley, John Kerin, Brian Howe, Neal Blewett and Michael Duffy, all later promoted to Cabinet. Hawke was never the interventionist leader in the Fraser mould. He left his ministers to their tasks and he stuck to being prime minister. Hawke saw his ministers in the Cabinet room and in parliament. When issues arose they were called to his office. But Hawke kept his ministers as a group away from the Lodge; home was for family, staff, recreation and the occasional ministry favourite.

Hawke says: 'I had, from the start, a Cabinet of considerable talent. I've always believed the best approach to people management is to recognise talent and allow that talent to exercise itself . . . Ministers didn't have me poking about and interfering in any continuous way.'[3]

Keating's decision to retain Stone was in the interests of himself, Stone and the government. Labor was unhappy since it had anticipated Stone's execution as a ritualistic symbol of the transition of power. His retention meant that Keating would court the treasury, renowned for its policies of restraint all round. Keating, alive to the Whitlam legacy, was sending a message: this Labor administration believed in harnessing the support of the economic institutions. On the Monday after the poll Keating had told a small group of senior treasury officers, 'I want a strong treasury. It's an important national institution.'

The situation was ripe for the development of the Keating–treasury relationship which became central to the government's character. The treasury's relations with the outgoing Fraser government had virtually collapsed. Stone's memo was a model of strict bureaucratic loathing. The treasury had reached the stage where any government would represent an improvement. It found in Keating a clever novice but fast learner who possessed both personal candour and Cabinet clout. The treasury was sick of being beaten in Cabinet during the Fraser years. Now it had a minister who would restore its authority. Stone did not accept the validity of the Accord; but he took a conscious decision to work with Keating and the new government.

Keating's personal adviser, Barbara Ward, said: 'Within the government there was the background that Keating was a bit insecure and not really on top of his portfolio—there's no denying that . . . His view was that he had to rely on treasury and he had to get them on side. It was a conscious decision not to get rid of Stone.'[4]

The adviser Keating had inherited from Willis, John Langmore, later an ALP backbencher and the architect of the 1982 ALP expansionary program, left Keating's office in disgust. Langmore depicted Keating as an innocent manipulated by the treasury. In the Labor lobbies Keating was the victim of a whisper that he was 'John Stone's puppet'.

But Keating, like Hawke, fashioned a formidable office. His private secretary was Tony Cole, a career treasury officer, later chairman of the Industry Commission and then treasury secretary, on whom Keating relied immensely. His adviser was the academic Dr Barry Hughes, and his political support came from long-time aide Barbara Ward, who later went to a senior post in TNT.

The instincts of Hawke and Keating coincided with their advice, both departmental and private. They moved towards a middle course in economic policy—a cut, not an increase, in the $9.6 billion deficit projection but overall a more expansionary program than contained in Fraser's last budget. This was too tough for the Labor Keynesians but too slack for the economic purists. Keating said: 'I think that the financing of a $10 billion deficit would put too much pressure upon interest rates.'[5] This line came direct from treasury. From the start Keating's instinct was to create jobs in a private sector recovery, not just a public sector expansion.

Within the first weeks Hawke and Keating had defied the Labor expansionists by shooting for an $8.5 billion deficit for 1983–84. This figure was settled upon in talks involving Hawke, Keating, Garnaut and David Morgan (treasury). Stone signed a minute written by Morgan recommending this figure. The decision was made less than a month after the election, before the National Economic Summit and far ahead of the start of budget

Cabinet talks. Why? Hawke and Keating went for the lowest deficit they felt was politically feasible and proceeded to lock-in the Cabinet and party as early as possible. Keating sold the $8.5 billion deficit as the highest figure consistent with containing inflation!

This battle over the degree of fiscal expansion determined the direction of the Hawke government and who would control it—a battle which Hawke and Keating won decisively. The advocates of a more expansionary policy were the former shadow treasurer Ralph Willis, the ALP premiers John Cain, John Bannon and Brian Burke, the Victorian treasurer Rob Jolly, economic guru Peter Sheehan, reinforced by the Labor left with cheering from the Melbourne Institute of Applied Economic and Social Research and sections of the influential Melbourne *Age*.

The victory of Hawke and Keating meant that they took firm control of the government. At this point they broke from the Keynesian philosophy to which Willis had pledged the ALP from opposition. The result was an alternative basis for the Hawke government's economic policy, an alliance between Hawke and Keating and an advisory structure which institutionalised this approach.

The message shining through every statement from Hawke and Keating was the need to deliver the central pledge of Hawke's 1983 election—to fight unemployment and inflation simultaneously. It was because Labor was serious about inflation that it refused to expand the deficit even further and, equally, it was because Labor was serious about addressing the extent of unemployment that it supported such an expansionary budget. It was a fine balance.

The origins of Hawke's pledge to fight inflation and unemployment simultaneously lie in the chief innovation of his government—the ALP–ACTU Accord; a compact dedicated to economic growth and job creation.

Hawke promised in his 1983 campaign to create 500 000 new jobs in his first three years, which required a rate of economic growth far superior to Australia's recent performance. In mid-1983 the ANU's Professor Fred Gruen said: 'The Labor Party's promise to create some 500 000 jobs in three years may not sound very ambitious, given the levels of open and disguised unemployment . . . [but] it exceeds by some 37 000 the greatest number of new jobs generated in the economy in any three year period since 1967.'[6]

The target was achieved by November 1985, five months before the deadline, defying most economic forecasters. The 10 per cent levels of unemployment and inflation under the Fraser legacy were beaten back when inflation fell and stabilised at 5 to 5.5 per cent in 1984–85, and unemployment fell to below 8 per cent in 1985. A strong increase in employment began in 1983–84 in construction, wholesale and retail trade, finance, property, community and business services, recreation and communications.

While demand drove this job creation it was reinforced by another factor—the wage restraint imposed by the Hawke government through the

Accord. Wage restraint became a feature of Labor's policy during the mid-1980s and its dividend was a healthy labour market, a triumph for theoretical economics and for Labor politics.

The experience of the 1980s proved that reductions in labour costs did lead to a strong growth in employment. This was a vindication of the belief of the Accord partners. It was a win for the ALP and ACTU leaders who had implemented the Accord with these exact hopes. It was a vindication for the treasury which had argued this case during the Fraser years, in particular for its future secretary, the late Dr Chris Higgins, who spearheaded this work in the department. Finally, it was a repudiation of much of the left-leaning economic doctrine within Labor and the unions during the 1970s which refused to concede the job generating impact of wage restraint.

The first point to make about the Accord in the 1980s is that it achieved its objectives—to help revive the economy, create jobs and generate conditions for strong economic growth. The second is that the Accord was devised to solve the economic growth problems of the 1970s and early 1980s—but Labor found that those problems were superseded by others by the late 1980s and early 1990s. As the decade advanced it became clear that Australia's real problem was poor productivity, of which the Accord may have been a cause rather than a solution.

The origins of the Accord lay in a rethink by the political and industrial wings of the labor movement after the Whitlam failure.[7] The Accord arose directly from the failures of Whitlamism. The Whitlam years were conspicuous for the policy and public antagonism between the political and industrial wings of the labour movement. The breakdown was symbolised in the personal rancour existing between Whitlam and Hawke, who was then ACTU president. The Accord sprang from the belief that the institutional bond between the ALP and the unions was useless if it remained as a political negative. If the link were to survive then it must be converted into a political plus. Whitlam had seen the unions as a negative and therefore kept them at a distance. Under Hawke the Accord harnessed the potential of the unions to help Labor's economic management.

The 1979 ALP National Conference first endorsed the Accord concept and Bill Hayden ran on a 'prices-income' policy in the 1980 election. The architects of the Accord were Ralph Willis and Bill Kelty with great assistance from the ACTU's Jan Marsh, and it arose from the belief of Willis and Kelty that a basis of common interest could be established.

The Accord's chief purpose for a Labor government was to prevent a wages explosion during periods of strong economic growth and thereby deliver sustained growth. The aim was to prevent a repetition of the wages explosions of 1974 and 1982 which had destroyed Whitlam and Fraser. Hayden and Hawke believed that if the next Labor government failed due to a wages explosion the consequence could be terminal for the ALP.

The principles of the Accord were further entrenched at the 1982 ALP

National Conference. The ACTU leaders supported Hawke against Hayden as leader in early 1983 in the expectation of working with him as prime minister. A Special Unions Conference on 21–22 February 1983, after Fraser had called the election, approved the Accord document on which the Hawke government relied in its early years.

The document was a compact for a partnership in office between the ALP and the trade unions. The Accord covered every area of domestic concern: the economy, industrial relations, tax, welfare, foreign investment, health, education, industry and immigration. Prior consultation with the unions was required for virtually all government decision making. An Economic Planning Advisory Council (EPAC) was to be set up with union and employer representatives to advise government. No previous Australian government had been elected with such a formal policy agreement with one sector of society. Of course, former Liberal governments had given the corporate sector such privileges in practice, but they had never formalised the partnership.

The critics depicted the Accord as a step towards a corporate state or the entrenchment of trade union power. Opinion among many economists was that Australia was recycling failed incomes policies from the British Labour Party. In fact, the Accord gave the unions access to government power but in return the government sought union responsibility. The document contained three central trade-offs which would shape the politics of the 1980s.

First, union acceptance of wage restraint to generate more jobs. Second, a shift in union emphasis from money wages to the social wage in recognition that living standards were set not just by income but by the full range of benefits government provided through tax, health insurance, education and welfare. Third, immunity for unions from punitive civil laws or common law penal sanctions in return for settlement of disputes by conciliation and arbitration.

The Accord was premised on wage indexation, that is, wage rises matching price rises, a concept which economists mistrusted. The wage adjustments would be handed down by the Full Bench, which meant a return to centralised wage fixation. The principle of a return to wage indexation after Fraser's wage pause was a victory for the unions—but they were forced to accept concessions in two vital provisions.

First, in exchange for indexation the unions guaranteed 'that there shall be no extra claims except where special and extraordinary circumstances exist'. This was designed to prevent a repeat of the wages explosions and ensure that the decisions by the Full Bench were not supplemented by overaward payments. Second, it said that real wage maintenance could be achieved 'over time'. This meant that if the economic situation was perilous the unions would accept real wage cuts for a temporary period. The Accord also specified that both the living standards of wage earners and non-wage earners should be 'through time increased with movements in national productivity'—a provision later used to reform Australian superannuation.

Above all, the Accord was an agreed basis for an economic philosophy to fight unemployment and inflation simultaneously.

The early 1980s recession—caused by the domestic wages explosion and the overseas recession—had finished Fraser and traumatised the unions. It was the first time since the Great Depression that unemployment broke the 10 per cent barrier. The unions had paid a crippling price for their high pay rises in the early 1980s—the loss of 100 000 jobs alone in the metal trades industry. Unemployment in seasonally adjusted terms increased by 266 100 over the year to the June quarter 1983 to a total of 719 300. The unemployment rate rose over that year from 6.6 to 10.3 per cent.

The union leaders had pursued a course resulting in disaster for their members—a fact which Kelty later admitted. The upshot was a greater impetus for the Accord concept. The conversion was best reflected in a leader of the 1981 wage push, the veteran unionist and communist, Laurie Carmichael, a senior official from the metalworkers' union. Carmichael became a champion of the Accord and later an apologist for the real wage cuts it delivered. His conversion reflected that of many union leaders, the lions of the left wing along with the moderates: Tom McDonald (building workers), Tas Bull (waterside workers), George Campbell (metalworkers), Ivan Hodgson (transport workers) and, of course, Simon Crean (storeman and packers), who would replace Hawke's successor Cliff Dolan as ACTU president.

The trade union commitment to the Accord predated the 1980s recession. But the depth of this commitment can only be grasped in terms of the employment holocaust the unions visited upon their own members by excessive wage claims during the early 1980s. This legacy was basic to the high level of compliance the ACTU leaders were able to extract from their constituent unions during the rest of the decade.

The collective decision taken by the unions on the Accord was historic. It was a choice which shaped the politics of the 1980s. The unions abandoned their traditional campaign for redistribution of the national income from profits to wages in favour of a collaborative economic strategy with the Hawke government to increase economic growth. Their aim was to reap the benefits from the subsequent expansion in employment. They would share greater national wealth rather than aspire to a greater share of lower national wealth. This strategic rethink was the essence of the Accord.

The Accord betrayed the weakness of the trade union movement, an obvious but poorly appreciated feature of the 1980s. Union power was in retreat. The recession hurt people, destroyed the market power of the unions, exposed the absurdity of their tactics, and raised questions about their legitimacy. The issue was clear: by whose authority and for whose interest had such disastrous wage claims been launched?

The Accord meant a search for solutions through economic policy rather than industrial action. Unions accepted the deal because their more astute leaders knew that democratic Australia was challenging their legitimacy and that their industrial 'success', which meant higher wages at the cost of productive investment, only resulted in uncompetitive industry and fewer jobs. The weakness of the unions was implicit in their acquiescence in Fraser's December 1982 wage pause.

The Accord was made possible only by union leaders prepared to display a type of restraint which Hawke as ACTU chief had never offered Whitlam. A decade later Hawke became prime minister with two convictions—that wage restraint was basic to sustained recovery and that his own persona would enable him to win the cooperation of the unions through the Accord. Hawke was a reformed arsonist selling a fire-prevention policy.

Hawke put the issue very simply in his early days as prime minister: the central defect in Australian post-war economic policy had been the lack of an effective wages policy. The Labor Party was now in a position to rectify this breach.

The Accord was a natural reconciliation between a Labor government and the system of conciliation and arbitration which Labor had upheld since its inception. It was, in effect, a double fusion. First, the shaping of a common purpose between Labor and the trade unions. Second, the manipulation of the arbitration system to achieve that common purpose. The question is not why the Accord arose, but why it took so long to arise. The answer is that for the previous thirty years the Labor Party and the trade union movement, despite their institutional links, endured an intellectually sterile and politically corrupting relationship. The unions funded Labor and Labor was beholden to the unions. But Labor distrusted the unions and the unions knew that Labor was impotent, at least federally.

The Accord was rooted in the principle of centralisation of power and discipline by constituent unions. It sought not just to restore to primacy the power of the Arbitration Commission but to enhance its power. The Accord sought a return to centralised wage fixation after the early 1980s disastrous experiment with collective bargaining. But it envisaged the Commission setting not just minimum rates but setting, in effect, the overall wage rates through indexation principles. The Full Bench would be more powerful than ever. The Accord aspired to give the old idea of arbitration a new prestige.

At the same time the Accord represented a centralisation of power within the union movement—it was a decision to increase the power of the ACTU. This coincided with a decade of outstanding ACTU leadership embodied in the Crean–Kelty partnership, Crean as presidential figurehead and Kelty as the powerbroking strategist. It was Kelty's cross-factional support within the unions, his tactical skills over wages policy and his influence with government and employers that made the structure viable.

Hawke was Labor's first federal parliamentary leader to have held high office within the trade unions. His grasp of the unions and the wage system was far superior to that of any of his predecessors. He harnessed the weight of arbitration to Labor's own needs. It was an institution which Hawke understood and through which he had carved his career.

Hawke's political appeal transcended the Accord because he projected the ideas of consensus and reconciliation to the people. Hawke reached out to the business sector, the so-called natural constituency of the Liberal Party. His most brilliant piece of political theatre was the National Economic Summit of April 1983.

Hawke had a mandate for the Summit—a unique gathering of Australia's political, business, financial and union leaders chaired by Hawke to address the national crisis. It was convened when Hawke's influence was at its peak. It was held in the House of Representatives chamber, a privilege Hawke extended to participants—and thereby gaining a psychological advantage over them. Dinners were at the Governor-General's residence and at the Lodge. For the business chiefs the event was heavy with the smell of power and the weight of responsibility.

At the Summit Hawke secured the two objectives he needed. He won the support of the employers for a return to centralised wage fixation on the terms specified in the Accord. He also won their agreement to Labor's economic approach of fighting inflation and unemployment simultaneously. Both aims were essential to his model. Both were sanctioned by the Summit. These were tangible victories, but Hawke achieved more.

Hawke secured the respect of the cream of Australia's capital class at the Summit—business, finance and employers. There was a distinct sense that they were given guest status at the policy-making banquet and left intoxicated. Hawke had harnessed reconciliation as a device to win business goodwill on his own terms.

The participants included senior economic ministers, state premiers and an ACTU delegation including the president, Cliff Dolan, Charlie Fitzgibbon and Bill Kelty; representatives from all employer groups and business organisations—miners, manufacturers, farmers, bankers, retailers—and individual businessmen including Sir Peter Abeles (TNT), Sir Keith Campbell (Hooker), Sir Roderick Carnegie (CRA), Brian Loton (BHP), Brian Kelman (CSR), Sir Arvi Parbo (WMC), Bill Dix (Ford), John Utz (Wormald) and Alan Coates (AMP).

Hawke's opening speech called for a common purpose, invoked the spectre of the next generation, declared his belief in the Australian people who had just elected him, and, inevitably, contained his John Curtin analogy:

> The first problem is how to arrest the explosion in unemployment and then move towards its steady reduction with the ultimate goal of genuine full employment—the bipartisan goal adopted for the first three decades of the post-war era . . . total unemployment in 1932—the worst year of the Great Depression reached 29 per cent. Unemployment today in the 15 to 19 age group is already at least as high as that.[8]

However Keating's speech, written over a weekend with a hand-picked treasury official, David Morgan, a Stone protégé, was a treasury-inspired effort to keep Labor serious about an anti-inflation stance. The Accord, Keating said, would enable Australia to return to higher economic growth without the penalty of higher inflation. But Keating, in fact, had serious doubts about the utility of the Accord to achieve this objective. He enunciated the original treasury position on the Accord—a stance it would abandon during the decade—by insisting that the Accord must reinforce traditional fiscal and monetary policy, not substitute for such policy, in the fight against inflation. Keating warned of the costs of high inflation—that it would threaten recovery through higher interest rates and balance of payments deficits.

Keating said the economic growth required to turn around the unemployment tide could be as much as 4 per cent annually, a daunting challenge. The Summit was given three scenarios which had been prepared in the prime minister's department—high wage, medium wage (the Accord option) and low wage. The projections over a three year period showed that it was the low wage option which delivered the most employment and the lowest inflation.

There was support for the low wage scenario, notably from the late Keith Campbell, precisely because it was best for jobs and inflation. But at this point an insight into the entire nature of 1980s Labor politics was revealed. Hawke's old friend and employers' representative, George Polites, killed the 'first-best' low wage option by saying it was 'beyond the limits of consensus available at this conference'.

This was a startling admission of political truth. It revealed the corporatist character of the Accord which meant, by definition, 'best' results had to be surrendered to 'consensus' results. The three scenarios were merely a political trick to maximise Summit endorsement for the middle or Accord option—the medium wage outcome. It was the first of many Labor exercises in political manipulation during the 1980s to build community support for its middle-ground economics.

The most arresting speech at the Summit came from ACTU secretary Bill Kelty, who underwrote its success. It was the speech of a new leader—a baby-faced, prematurely grey-haired midget who riveted his audience, offering economic analysis in a whining nasal tone, supremely confident of his authority within the unions and aware of his intellectual dominance of the employers. Kelty left the impression that he knew the future, it was the Accord, and Kelty had its key. Kelty spoke as few union leaders have ever spoken before. He made the union cause sound clear, just and strong, but above all, Kelty never spoke in sectional terms. He spoke only about national advancement.

Kelty said the Accord only had meaning within a return to centralised wage fixation: 'An acceptance by the trade union movement in this country of the belief that the market, left unfettered, should determine wage rates would represent an abandonment of our fundamental beliefs and an acceptance that the value of the trade union movement, as we know it, will be destroyed.'[9]

Having flashed his steel, Kelty played his violin. The Accord was a vehicle of long-term planning for companies, the chance for an anti-inflationary policy, better understanding between unions, employers and government which meant fewer industrial disputes and a mechanism to win sustained economic growth. Kelty spoke for the entire union movement, the symbol of the power transfer from individual unions to the ACTU.

The next speaker, Roderick Carnegie, called the speeches of Keating and Kelty 'incredible' in terms of 'the commitments they made to the good of Australia'. For most employers and chief executives it was their first exposure to Kelty, economics graduate and industrial strategist. Their response was a mixture of astonishment, admiration and alarm. But Kelty was still a support player to Hawke. The business chiefs, many of whom had known Hawke for years, felt they had no choice. They were backing Hawke's model and they accepted Hawke's terms.

The Summit communiqué, primarily drafted by Abeles and Kelty, was a comprehensive victory for Hawke. The participants—with Joh Bjelke-Petersen the sole dissenter—approved the return to centralised wage fixation, noting the union commitment to wage restraint. They endorsed Labor's expansionary fiscal policy to the extent it was consistent with inflation reduction. Hawke got business to endorse the Accord, a compact which it had not drafted and to which it was not a party. Business was outsmarted by Hawke, Keating and Kelty. But what choice did it have?

Peter Abeles, part of the Hawke apparatus, said that business felt 'as though we had been invited to play singles tennis against a champion doubles combination'. Hawke showed the power inherent in prime ministerial authority when employed at the right time. Few participants would have believed then that Hawke would fail so singularly to marshal such authority again.

The Summit was a warning to the Liberals. It revealed Hawke's ability to secure corporate support, even enthusiasm, for his economic model. The Summit, in its atmospherics, repudiated the class bias of ALP politics. Hawke never aspired to a labour versus capital model, arguing instead the mutual interests of labour and capital. At the Summit Hawke dealt as easily with Carnegie and Abeles as he did with Kelty and Carmichael.

Business was responsive to Hawke for three reasons. First, it believed Hawke was genuine in pioneering a better government-business relationship and its leaders were susceptible to flattery: sitting in the chamber, dining at the Lodge and Yarralumla, chatting in the lobbies with Hawke and Keating. Second, the corporate sector was disillusioned with the Liberals following the Fraser debacle, a fact which Hawke exploited. Third, Hawke followed the Summit with results, partly because he was lucky—in 1983–84 the drought broke, domestic demand lifted, the overseas economy picked up, and corporate profits surged.

For Hawke the Summit was a double plus. He secured support for the Accord and he introduced another idea—the ALP as a business government.

The early months of power were the steepest challenge of Keating's career. At one stage his confidence nearly cracked and Keating confessed to Hawke personal doubts over whether he could master the technicalities. Hawke saw that Keating was experiencing a crisis of confidence and he offered patronising but genuine support. Keating's 1983 transition had been dramatic—from shadow resources minister to treasurer.

The irony is that Keating, later the orchestrator of the Accord, began as a sceptic. Keating had not enjoyed any previous rapport with the ACTU, hardly knew its officials and had the benefit of treasury's fears. Barbara Ward recalls: 'At the start Paul had severe doubts about the Accord.' Keating held out monetary policy as the anti-inflation insurance if the Accord crumbled. At one point Keating raised his doubts with Hawke but was dismissed. 'Paul, you've got to realise that Bill Kelty is solid gold,' was Hawke's cerebral reply. Keating told his staff about this exchange laughing at Hawke's naive belief in the Accord with his old mates. Keating was a non-believer—until he began to know Bill Kelty and Laurie Carmichael.

Kelty offers a graphic account:

> We weren't friends at the start. I'd met Paul Keating a couple of times during the 1970s. I was not an enthusiast and he struck me as an opportunist . . . We had developed the Accord with Ralph Willis. We had a very strong personal commitment to Ralph. He was the person you trusted; the person I trusted. He was the person on whom we had developed our whole relationship with the incoming government.
>
> Then Bill Hayden dumped Ralph for Paul. When we first met Paul to discuss the Accord he made it clear he didn't think much of the Accord. He told us that incomes policies never worked. He wasn't going to be lumbered with an Accord-type strategy. So I must admit that in that initial period I thought that if Paul was going to be the treasurer there wasn't going to be any long term future for the Accord. I thought we'll get through the election campaign and then treasury will dominate it and that will be it.
>
> But Paul I think realised that there were a lot of genuine people who wanted to transform the labour movement in terms of employment, the social wage, social gains, superannuation, that these people weren't crazy—the Carmichaels, the McDonalds, the Fitzgibbons. I think he came to trust us and when he trusted us we always delivered and, in return, he always delivered. That's what was the basis for our friendship.[10]

Keating was fortunate to have moved his family to Canberra where they rented a house, just a few minutes from Parliament House and the

Lodge. Keating spent his toughest winter in his basement office, fighting off fitful colds with an electric bar radiator for extra warmth. He was tentative in parliament and pressured at his desk. This was a deeply personal struggle—to master the material, to locate the arcane secret of the economic machine.

His office operated under a regime of relaxed intensity. The staff called him Paul, but Keating's obsessive nature compelled performance from his staffers. Keating had almost no secrets and no false airs with his advisers. As he learned, Keating delved deeper into Stone's treasury, dealing more with the senior officials, not just Stone, establishing personal relationships, evaluating people as he went.

For Keating the Stone treasury was magic. Here were experts, true experts, people who knew the economy like the NSW right knew politics and spoke with the same conviction. These advisers were technicians and believers, and Keating learned the jargon and he moved into their world. The treasury flattered Keating and Keating flattered the treasury. In the early months Keating turned his back on the political side of his life. He spent much of his time with senior treasury officers, even becoming friends with them. Keating had charm and speed, and unlike Howard was never aloof. He was building a great alliance.

Keating made a habit of leaving his office and walking the four hundred yards past the Lobby restaurant to the department. The day after his May Statement he had a take-away Chinese lunch with Stone. This was not the way that treasurers usually behaved, but this was Keating psychology in action. Keating was courting the treasury and the staid old treasury began to open its heart. It told Keating how terrible it was to work for Howard and Fraser, of how much better he was—and the treasury meant it.

The treasury saw that with Keating it could return to its former pre-eminence after fifteen years of strife spanning the pre-1972 coalition era, the Whitlam and Fraser regimes. Keating was a certain winner at the Cabinet table. The treasury had every reason to embrace Keating. Apart from Hayden, its ministers since 1969 had been an uninspired lot—Leslie Bury, Billy Snedden, Frank Crean, Jim Cairns, Phillip Lynch and finally Howard, who had been kneecapped by Fraser.

Keating approached the economy as an architect searching for the interconnections and the links which gave the structure meaning. Keating loved the treasury's mission—to impose an order for economic analysis that often never existed within the real economy. It aspired to bring exactitude to an inexact science.

Keating defended his links with treasury which his critics depicted as dependence: 'If it meant I had to engineer John Stone's sacking to prove that I am in charge of economic policy I can assure you that no such act of cowardice would be entertained by me . . . What my party wanted was to have the treasury brought back into the mainstream of economic policy thinking . . . that is the mission I was given and it has been achieved.'[11]

But Keating also demolished a persistent myth of the decade, most virulent at the start—that he was Stone's or treasury's puppet. He replied:

> It would be fair to the treasury to say that if it had its way, the budget deficit would be very much lower than what the government will accept . . . I don't think the treasury has ever supported centralised wage fixation . . . There's always this concern in the Labor Party that the treasury would not accept the position of the government. When the treasury does accept them, people argue the government is accepting the Treasury policies.[12]

The truth is that the treasury had no choice but to accept the Accord and its expansionary fiscal policy—despite its personal distaste for both.

The early mileposts for the Hawke government were the Summit, the May Statement and then the August 1983 budget—each of which helped Keating to build his confidence. The May 1983 Statement was the first of fourteen major economic statements delivered by Keating in his eight years as Labor's longest-serving treasurer. This represented, in total, a body of economic decision-making far more extensive than that of any previous treasurer.

The preparation for the May Statement saw the first operation of the Cabinet Expenditure Review Committee (ERC) which initially comprised Hawke as chairman, Keating, Willis, Walsh and Dawkins. It cut the prospective 1983–84 deficit by $1 billion, 'quality' cuts which would grow to $2.2 billion two years later, and re-ordered spending priorities. Labor's social and employment priorities were reflected in the new programs—Medicare, the Community Employment Program (CEP) and the First Home Owners' Assistance Scheme.

The May Statement established the ERC as the engine-room of the Hawke government. It promoted the ERC's self-concept as the Cabinet's elite. It created the initial ERC working relationship between Keating and Dawkins, previously antagonists. It was, in effect, the first step in the evolution of Keating's alliance with the yet-to-be-formed centre-left faction, an alliance in which shared policy beliefs overcame personal distrust. Keating struggled in this first ERC but Dawkins and Walsh were prominent; evidence that they were destined to play fundamental roles within the government. Finally, it helped to bring Keating closer to Kelty when they disagreed over the ERC's proposal to tax lump sum superannuation. Keating said: 'Bill, why don't you just concede on this? We can't agree.' In politics adversity often breeds respect and friendship.

By mid-year the Hawke–Keating bond was sealed and their relationship reached its zenith. Often, late at night Keating would walk up the stairs to Hawke's office, just above his own, and they would chat into the early hours. Barron would get Hawke to ring Keating after the treasurer's press conferences to congratulate him. Some Sundays Keating would join Hawke at the Lodge to review their progress. Often Keating's wife Annita would come to see Hazel Hawke.

Hawke took the unusual step of inviting Keating to join his mid-year US trip. Before his meeting with President Reagan Hawke said: 'I think I'll tell Reagan that we're friends and that friends have the right to disagree.' But Keating dissented and told Hawke not to say this. 'You're the first Labor Prime Minister to come here since Whitlam. There's lots of bad history. Tell Reagan that we're friends. Don't compromise the message by saying we can disagree.' Hawke took the advice.

By mid-1983 Keating was de facto deputy. Hawke's preference for Willis was long gone. Later in 1983 Hawke returned taxation responsibility to Keating.

Keating was the only minister who could walk into Hawke's office, the ultimate form of body language in handling a prime minister. But their alliance was based on politics, not personal friendship. Hawke's interests were horses, sport, tennis, all Keating's weak suit. Keating's non-political obsessions were clocks, antiques and classical music, which left Hawke cold.

In his August 1983 budget Keating brought down an $8.4 billion deficit, a middle ground compromise. Keating won both sides of the equation: he introduced a stimulatory budget but gained a reputation for responsibility by reducing Fraser's deficit legacy. By spending cuts and tax rises Keating had cut the prospective deficit by $1.8 billion. But the Keating deficit was still large—4.7 per cent of GDP compared with a deficit result of 2.8 per cent of GDP the previous year. Keating told Labor the deficit would turn the employment market, that it was 'a big enough bang'.

In an effort to persuade the cognoscenti Keating said the deficit was designed to provide 'the maximum fiscal stimulus' that was consistent with controlling inflation 'without placing undue burdens on interest rates or the balance of payments'. But within three years high interest rates and a balance of payments crisis would threaten to finish the government.

The budget papers contained a warning authored by Stone, who was alarmed that the structural deficit was increasing significantly. Stone identified the 'success or failure' question for Labor: 'Expansionary fiscal policy is predicated on the assumption that the Accord will be successful in combating inflation. If that assumption is not realised, the viability of that approach to fiscal policy will be immediately called into question.'[13]

Stone's official warning captured the essence of Labor's challenge. Its economic policy was driven by the Accord; it was the Accord which demanded an expansionary fiscal policy since the Accord existed to create employment growth and jobs for workers; but the expansionary fiscal policy was viable only if the Accord, in turn, by delivering wage restraint was able to keep inflation in check. The political and economic logic of Labor's structure was inescapable: the Accord must succeed as an anti-inflationary weapon if the Accord's employment objectives were to be realised. This was the central policy issue for the first Hawke government.

Stone was sceptical about Labor's ability to deliver but he was proved wrong. The Accord delivered—exactly as it had been intended, at least at the start.

The Accord underwrote three wage achievements for the Hawke government in its first term. It was a re-entry vehicle for the unions into the wage fixing system after Fraser's successful wages pause. The unions agreed to surrender any wages catch-up after the pause, which meant that Hawke retained the full anti-inflation benefits from Fraser's pause. This was a singular triumph. Naturally Hawke denied Fraser any credit.

Second, the Accord secured the smooth return to centralised wage fixation from October 1983 on the basis of six monthly adjustments with the unions adhering to their pledge not to seek extra claims.

Finally, the Accord secured a new twelve-month de facto wages pause from April 1984. This saw a fall in Australia's inflation rate to nearly 5 per cent in Labor's second year. It left the Hawke–Keating team with an aura of economic success.

This de facto wages pause was achieved by two Accord 'deals' negotiated by Keating and the ACTU. The first deal stemmed from the introduction of Medicare, which by cutting private health premiums resulted in a negligible Consumer Price Index (CPI) for six months. The effect was to reduce the measured CPI by about 2.5 percentage points, thereby securing a wage cut of the same magnitude in mid-1984. Medicare was an endorsed Accord policy and Keating and Kelty had known from the very start that its introduction would deliver this 'inflation bonus' in Labor's second year.

Keating followed this gain by announcing in his second Budget, in August 1984, the first of the wages/tax deals which characterised the Labor government. The tax cut, effective from 1 November 1984, was given as a substitute for another six monthly pay rise. The cuts, worth $2.1 billion in a full year, were heavily slanted towards low and middle income earners— the Kelty target groups.

In his 1984 budget speech Keating said that inflation was running at 5 per cent which meant it 'is finally falling to about the same level as our major trading partners'. There was a strong recovery in profits and falling interest rates setting the scene for an investment surge. Australia's growth rate over the previous year had been the highest in the OECD. Keating hailed Labor's model as a success and identified the Accord as the centrepiece.

By this stage, with his second budget, Keating was emboldened—confidence became his hallmark. He described the wage tax deal as 'a breakthrough in Australian economic history because it has provided unprecedented wage restraint in a period of economic recovery. It provides Australia with an opportunity to really break the back of inflation'.[14]

But the treasury sounded its own warning: so far, so good. But how long could deals be done? The task was to 'maintain income restraint over the medium-term as recovery strengthens'. The issue was whether the Accord could deliver throughout the decade or whether it would disintegrate. That was the question on which the corporate-investing community was fixated and it didn't know the answer. The business community was impressed by Labor's achievements but plagued by two chronic worries: how long would the Accord last and how long would it deliver low inflation? Keating appealed for business investment but business stayed wary.

From 1984 onwards Keating saw himself as a manipulator of economic policy, exploiting the Accord like an architect intent on locating the built-in benefits. Labor found itself in a luxurious condition—presiding over an expanding economy where unemployment and inflation were falling simultaneously—just as Hawke had pledged.

The result was that when Bob Hawke sought his reelection in December 1984 the inflation rate had been halved and was heading towards 5 per cent and 270 000 jobs had been created in the eighteen months since the Summit. Hawke had luck, an international recovery and astute political management on his side. The Accord after eighteen months was more successful than Hawke, Keating or Kelty had dared to hope.

But as Hawke promoted national consensus to build a store of electoral goodwill, his position was being usurped within the government in the process of Accord management. Keating had become the manager of the Accord and, in fact, was now an Accord zealot. Keating and Kelty were gaining great confidence in each other. If Stone made Keating apprehensive about the Accord, then Kelty had left him confident. Keating hardened Kelty's economic thinking and Kelty deepened Keating's commitment to income equity. Impressed by the Accord's apparent flexibility, Keating was engaged in the first of his three attempts during his eight years as treasurer to tie Australia into a low inflation pattern.

Hawke sold the Accord as a symbol of community consensus but Keating was more dynamic: he sold the Accord as a mechanism for sweeping institutional reform. Keating moved to exploit the Accord as a weapon of Labor's management superiority over the Liberals, the type of argument in which he had no peer. Keating declared that 'the Accord provides a mechanism by which agreements can be reached on the key determinants . . . wages, taxes and government programs'.

Then Keating focused on the principal reform—sustained growth. The Accord, he insisted, enabled Labor not just to beat inflation, but to beat it without Fraser's terrible crunch. Labor had found the missing link in Australian economic policy—the mechanism which allowed wages to be used as a policy tool; the device which would enable Australia to sustain an economic growth which resurgent inflation would not throttle. Labor, only Labor, possessed this weapon, Keating declared.

He diagnosed Labor's success: 'The Accord, centralised wage fixation and wage indexation are based on a recognition that pure market forces simply do not work satisfactorily in the Australian labour market. Half-baked attempts to impose market processes in the employment area are doomed to failure. The simple analogy with deregulation in other areas of the economy just cannot be made.' The wages market had to be politically managed and only Labor could manage it. Keating was explicit in his defence of the budget stimulus and wage restraint mixture of the first two years: 'The government does not consider that the best deficit is necessarily the lowest deficit.'

This was a testimony to Keating's compulsion to establish a Labor model, to sell a framework for governance, to twist the political knife into the coalition, and to his incurable electoral oversell. It is the best admission of the corporatist nature of the Accord and Labor's management model. Finally, it reveals the Hawke–Keating commitment to economic growth, jobs and investment as the ultimate goal of Labor reformism in the 1980s.[15]

It was inevitable that such early success would diminish Labor's insights into the difficulty of making its strategy a long-term success. Fighting inflation and unemployment simultaneously was not wrong in principle. But it is a truly formidable task. It could only work—as treasury explained—if fiscal and monetary policy were used to support the incomes policy and provided Labor never believed that the Accord was a substitute for firm fiscal and monetary policy.

Labor's unique model of fiscal expansion and wage restraint through consensus attracted much overseas attention. In its 1984–85 report upon Australia, the OECD pointed to its doubts about the viability of Australia's course and the fact that Australia had chosen a growth path which differed from the rest of the world. The report said:

> The current policy approach in Australia differs from that followed in the late 1970s and early 1980s both in Australia and in most other OECD countries. The orthodox approach had stressed the need to reduce fiscal deficits, re-establish external equilibrium and to fight wage and price inflation through tight fiscal and monetary policies. Incomes policy has been regarded as self-defeating over the longer run and there has been general concern that expansionary demand-management policies would lead to an acceleration of wage increases at higher level of unemployment than in the past.[16]

The Hawke–Keating model was audacious because it tried to defy the rest of the world. Most, though not all, OECD nations, had embraced pain and discipline, a crunch against inflation and the tolerance of high unemployment—the international practice of the early 1980s. But Australian confidence, internal politics and Labor's Accord drove Australia to seek more: to secure growth and low inflation together. It would have been a singular achievement, but then Hawke and Keating were ambitious and arrogant men and their government assumed their character. Of course, when trade-off time came in the mid-1980s, Labor would choose growth at the cost of higher inflation.

In the interim Labor overdosed during 1984, watching the economy boom and inflation fall. It was Labor's golden year. The party was agog with its dazzling double. It seized upon the Accord as the policy of the decade, perhaps the policy discovery of the generation. Then it unveiled a truly spectacular companion piece.

4

The Hawke–Keating model: the float

Markets by their essence are unled. They are always looking for leadership. When the government gives markets something real they will always give you more back in return.

Paul Keating on financial deregulation[1]

The most influential economic decisions of the 1980s were the floating of the Australian dollar and deregulation of the financial system. Although spread over several years spanning the Fraser and Hawke governments, the centrepiece was the historic announcement by Paul Keating on 9 December 1983 of the float of the dollar and abolition of exchange controls. The float transformed the economics and politics of Australia. It harnessed the Australian economy to the international marketplace—its rigours, excesses and ruthlessness. It signalled the demise of the old Australia—regulated, protected, introspective.

The revolution of financial deregulation embodied four main reforms—surrendering official control of the exchange rate, abolishing exchange control over movements of capital inside and outside Australia, deregulation of interest rates, and foreign bank entry. It meant a freer, faster, market-determined financial system which would affect nearly every business and family in the nation.

It was, in effect, four revolutions—the market would set domestic interest rates terminating the age of regulation; the market would set the price at which Australia's currency exchanged with the world; banks would be competing not just with one another but with overseas banks allowed to establish in Australia; and the exchange controls on capital flows which prevented Australian acquisition of significant overseas assets were lifted.

The move to financial deregulation was the decisive break made by the Hawke–Keating government with Labor dogma and Australian practice. It was the sharpest repudiation of regulation made by a federal government. The decision transformed the financial sector. It was based on the belief

76

that deregulation would mean a more efficient financial sector and that market forces, not official intervention, would better direct capital to achieve a more efficient economy—a proposition that would be severely challenged in the late 1980s.

But financial deregulation would never stand alone. This move was an irresistible catalyst to further deregulation of Australian society—its markets for goods, labour and services. That meant, in effect, an economic and political revolution.

When Hawke and Keating took this decision they sought to expose Australia to the anti-inflationary discipline of overseas forces, an opinion Keating offered in these exact terms to journalists the evening of the announcement. Keating also believed that financial deregulation would destroy the parochial and conservative mentality of Australia's financial establishment, a point he argued repeatedly inside the ALP. Keating tapped that deep reservoir of anti-bank Labor sentiment to win approval for the exposure of local banks to foreign competition.

Neither Hawke nor Keating foresaw the full impact of deregulation, notably the credit explosion, asset boom and corporate crashes which the new system spawned later in the 1980s. Nobody could have foreseen these events. The era after deregulation was akin to large-scale experimentation in a chemical laboratory where previously unmixed elements were combined.

But Hawke and Keating acted in the knowledge that they were severing the old controls, that the future was unpredictable and that it was best to stake national progress on the market rather than on the failing regulatory mechanisms of the Reserve Bank. They chose to elevate belief in market forces to an article of faith for their government and the ALP—an historic step. Reserve Bank governor Bob Johnston says: 'It's just as well they did not foresee all the consequences otherwise we might not have got the change.'[2]

The float had a psychological significance almost greater than its monetary effects. It sealed a de facto alliance between the government and the financial markets; it made Keating hero of the markets. For a while Labor became the fashion within the financial sector and even in sections of the corporate sector, notably the 'new money'. The float turned politics upside down because Labor displayed courage where the Liberals had squibbed the issue the previous year. Finally, it brought the former Fraser government into disrepute among its own kind because the socialists had shown more faith in market forces than Malcolm Fraser!

Financial deregulation in tandem with the ALP–ACTU Accord provided the twin pillars for Labor's unusual economic management model. It meant that financial markets operated on market forces but the labour market relied on political agreement. The Hawke government was sufficiently divorced from vested financial interests to deregulate the financial system but it was unable to deregulate the labour market because of its vested ties to the trade unions. The moral, perhaps, is that Labor was more ruthless in discarding old habits with business and finance while the Liberals could be more ruthless with the unions.

The embrace of financial deregulation was contrary to ALP policy and to the terms of the Accord. Rarely has such a reversal of an established philosophy been accomplished so swiftly, so comprehensively, with so little internal trauma. Financial deregulation is the quintessential example of a revolution imposed upon the ALP by its leaders. It is a classic case study of a new government using its authority and its mystique—never to be under-estimated in exchange rate policy—to overwhelm its own members.

Financial deregulation had a long history but eventually it came with a rush. It originated with Malcolm Fraser's decision to have an inquiry into the financial system based upon a recommendation from his two principal economic advisers, Ed Visbord and John Rose. Cabinet agreed to the inquiry in February 1978 but it took an inexperienced John Howard and his aide John Hewson a year to find an inquiry team which was led by the chief of Hookers, Sir Keith Campbell. The inquiry was set up only in January 1979. Its 1981 report was comprehensive and coherent in its recommendation of financial deregulation and its view that market-related mechanisms would maintain economic stability. But the challenge for the government was immense since the treasury opposed the report's core and the Reserve Bank was equivocal.[3]

Howard decided on a 'bit by bit' approach to Cabinet for fear of seeing the entire Campbell Report lost. Fraser had a farmer's suspicion of banks and in Visbord's view 'his opposition to deregulation was to moves that could have given the banks more influence, more freedom, more power'. The dominant Fraser–National Party Cabinet axis wanted to keep controls on bank lending rates, where Howard favoured the principle of deregulation. Howard was unable to overcome his two chief opponents, his own leader Fraser and his chief adviser, treasury secretary John Stone. Howard never asked Cabinet to float the exchange rate because he knew the Fraser–Anthony axis would kill any such submission.[4]

While Fraser had reservations about greater freedom for banks and a floating currency, his government did back some forms of deregulation—for instance, lifting controls on several key interest rates, notably Commonwealth government securities. Change was slow despite the reformist drive from John Rose and John Hewson, private advisers to Fraser and Howard respectively. Foreign bank entry was endorsed by Cabinet in early 1983. Rose said later that on many deregulatory initiatives, 'the action, the drive, the change came from Fraser, it did not come from Howard'. But Howard told a different story, insisting that Fraser had been the barrier to further progress.

The situation was manifest—Fraser would never become a pure deregulator; Howard lacked reforming drive and clout in Cabinet; and Stone was obstructionist. The Fraser government gave credence to financial deregulation but lacked speed and conviction in its execution. This appeared a minor issue at the time but was seen later within the Liberal Party as a major failure.

The Labor Party had attacked the Campbell Report and foreign bank entry. Yet by mid-1983, just a few months after their election, Hawke and Keating had been converted separately to financial deregulation. It was a function of three factors—an emerging crisis in the management of the currency; the growing conviction of their advisers that deregulation was the best option; and their own ability to free themselves from the dead hand of the past.

In 1983 the majority of the ALP rejected the Campbell Report as free market dogma which had no place in a Labor administration. But this was a decision made in Opposition by a party removed from exchange rate policy, which was always conducted within a government's inner sanctum. Exchange rate reform, in fact, was the ideal area for policy change from above. It is not by accident that the first step towards deregulation came with the floating of the dollar. This was the 'make or break' decision, taken without reference to the party. Once the currency was floating the bulwark against full financial deregulation had sustained an irreparable breach.

The milestones along the path were the float of the dollar and the abolition of exchange controls in December 1983; the removal of remaining interest rate ceilings in 1984 and 1985; and foreign bank entry in 1985. The decision to float was not taken in a vacuum. It was a response to a monetary crisis which had its origins in the growing integration of the Australian financial system and the international economy.

The momentum for financial deregulation came from the 1970s international phenomenon of the rapid integration of world financial markets. Capital markets were being transformed as huge sums were being traded by the day and, courtesy of new technology, by the minute. This assault by capital and computer was redefining the notion of national economic sovereignty. The world was becoming an integrated market in a financial sense. Pension fund managers sitting at their desks in London, Tokyo and New York directed their funds on a global basis to secure the best return.

The Bretton Woods system of fixed exchange rates had collapsed in 1971, ushering in a period of managed exchange rates. Australia had subsequently tied its exchange rate to sterling, then the $US, then to a basket of currencies. By 1980 nations were experimenting with varying systems of exchange rate management, including floats—allowing the market to set the rate with a minimum of official intervention. From the late 1970s Australia's rate was set by four senior officials from the Reserve Bank, the treasury, finance and the prime minister's department. But this 'managed' system became unsustainable during 1983 as the volumes of funds shifting in and out of Australia became much larger.

The proof of this was the reversal during 1983 of the 10 per cent $A depreciation, the first decision of the new Labor government taken in March 1983. During the year the $A returned almost to its pre-depreciation level, evidence that the authorities were finding great difficulty setting a rate in the teeth of market forces. The market would test and move the $A with speculative capital. The message for a relatively small nation such as Australia was that the market 'was bound to overwhelm any attempt to hold exchange rates against market forces for prolonged periods of time'. It was becoming obvious that the markets were able to impose a crisis and disrupt interest rates and the money supply.[5]

The changes in the international financial system were described by the Reserve Bank's John Phillips:

In the ten years between, say, 1973 and 1983, we saw a rapid and wide-ranging innovation in financial markets, perhaps to a greater extent than in any previous decade. Australia's financial markets became much more closely integrated with markets overseas, particularly in Asia . . . Corporate treasurers became more active and skilled in managing their foreign exchange exposures and in fund management more generally. They recognised and took advantage of opportunities for covered arbitrage between foreign and domestic financial markets and there was increasing scope for exchange rate speculation without the need for players to put all their cash up front . . . There we sat, fixing the exchange rate each morning and committing ourselves to take on board at that rate whatever net flows of foreign exchange developed during the day.[6]

The consequence of this system was that exchange rate management was starting to founder. The post-March 1983 revaluations—imposed by the market upon the authorities—were evidence of a protracted currency crisis. The exchange rate management committee was being outfoxed by speculators boosting capital inflow, forcing the dollar upwards and then taking their profits. It was a one-way bet for the speculators. There was too much capital inflow, a firm monetary policy was being threatened and the government had to try to soak up the excess liquidity. The system meant that Australia was taking overseas financial volatility more on its domestic money supply and interest rates rather than its exchange rate.

Within the government during mid-1983 there was a series of meetings to debate exchange rate policy and devise a better way. It was in this climate that most but not all of the government's economic advisers began to conclude that the best solution was a float. No formal decision was taken by the Reserve Bank but its governor, Bob Johnston, felt that the system was untenable and that the choice was either 'massive capital inflow controls or letting the rate float'.

The Hawke–Keating model: the float

Johnston says: 'The restoration of the March depreciation had convinced a lot of people that the existing system was unacceptable. We didn't make a formal decision to float until the deathknock. We said that if the existing system can work then we'll give it a try but it didn't look hopeful. It was a situation where a bold solution was required.'[7]

The outstanding feature of the subsequent decision is that Hawke and Keating both believed as early as mid-1983 that a floating currency was inevitable. The predilection within the Reserve Bank for a float was reinforced by advice from Hawke's and Keating's offices.

As early as May 1983 Keating moved to appoint a new inquiry into the financial system, headed by the chairman of the Mutual Life and Citizens Assurance Company, Vic Martin. The Martin Committee was a mechanism Keating needed to resurrect the financial deregulation agenda which Labor had rejected in the form of the Campbell Report. Martin's real purpose was suspected but not known at the time: the inquiry was established because Keating was planning to deregulate the financial system. His main adviser and later treasury secretary, Tony Cole, says: 'From the time Martin was set up Keating was heading for deregulation.'[8] Keating's longtime aide, Barbara Ward, says: 'Keating always believed the float was the best option but he faced very strong opposition from Stone which made him cautious.'[9] Keating's private office was unanimously for the float—Cole, Barry Hughes, Greg Smith and Barbara Ward—though this was not a treasury position. Stone was filled with grave reservations about full financial deregulation but Cole, a believer in the float and deregulation, was determined to combat Stone.

Around mid-1983 Keating complained about the exchange rate mechanism to Johnston: 'This system has had it.' Johnston was happy to see Keating's willingness to change. From this time the Reserve Bank began to prepare its 'war book'—a step-by-step blueprint for the transition to a float. Johnston says: 'I think Keating confronted the idea of floating the exchange rate pretty early in the piece. We had conversations about the consequences of the float for the economy and the speculators.'[10]

Meanwhile a similar process was taking place with Hawke, but with less pain. By mid-1983 Hawke's economic adviser, Ross Garnaut, had decided that a float and the removal of exchange controls was the best solution. Garnaut gave Hawke a consistent message—the key to Labor's growth strategy lay in a mixture of wage restraint through the Accord, backed not by a fiscal expansion but by a depreciation to increase the competitiveness of Australian industry. Garnaut had written to Hawke and Keating as early as the 1983 campaign identifying the balance of payments as Australia's main economic issue and advocating a solution which combined depreciation plus wage restraint. He believed that the existing system was unworkable and that a float would ultimately deliver the depreciation that Australia needed.

Garnaut's advice was almost identical with that from the prime minister's department, whose chief economic adviser, Ed Visbord, was a veteran of numerous currency crises, a student of exchange rate policies around the world, and a practitioner of $A management through the officials' committee. Visbord had decided from bitter experience that the system was unmanageable, that allowing a market-determined rate would be more efficient and that the government should be audacious—a view not universally shared among the economic advisers within the department, although Hawke's senior aide, Graham Evans, reflected the Garnaut–Visbord perspective. So Hawke's advisers were settled and Hawke was also settled. Hawke, who had served when ACTU president on the Reserve Bank board, saw the float as inevitable. He was even relaxed about the difficulties. It was just a matter of timing. Hawke was sailing, with almost cavalier serenity, towards the free market ocean.

The principal opponent of the float was not the Labor Party but the treasury. John Stone's weapons were the authority of his department, his intellectual conviction and his passion. Cole told Keating that Stone was never likely to agree to the float but it might be possible to isolate him within the treasury. Cole felt that a lot of senior officials would favour a float. The split within treasury was revealed during a meeting of senior officers with Keating around September or October 1983 which canvassed exchange rate policy. Stone opposed a float vigorously. According to the unwritten rules of treasury, the department speaks to its minister with only one voice, its secretary. But this time the rules were broken. A senior treasury officer, later to become Keating's favourite, Ted Evans, a Stone protégé, split with Stone: 'Treasurer, I don't agree with that. I think we should float.' Keating knew he was penetrating; powerful forces were stirring within the treasury.

In October 1983 there was a capital inflow crisis, the most severe to that time. Keating met his senior advisers one evening at the Reserve Bank quarters in Canberra—Johnston, John Phillips and Don Sanders from the Bank and the relevant treasury officers—Stone, Des Moore and Bob Whitelaw. The meeting was split, with all treasury officers opposed to the float thereby ending Cole's hopes of isolating Stone. Keating, his office and the Bank favoured a float. But Keating was not prepared to press the button. He wanted the treasury to come with him.

Stone was able to stop the float—this time. When the meeting finished Keating muttered: 'John, this is the last time you'd hold me on this.' His real message to Stone was—you've got a few weeks to come aboard or be humiliated. Keating had made his final concession to Stone.[11]

A subsequent meeting of the advisers with Hawke and Keating was held in Hawke's office on 27 October. The situation was reviewed and a compromise adopted on Garnaut's suggestion—a technical change, the floating of the forward rate. Stone was implacable in his hostility towards a float. Garnaut wanted to float then and there. This was the consensus of the meeting, except for Stone. From this point Hawke, Keating, their advisers and the Reserve Bank felt that the float was inevitable. Garnaut actually saw an advantage in floating the forward rate: it would take the element of surprise from the float because it would signal the final destination. Hawke, not Keating, announced the float of the forward rate on 28 October 1983.[12]

Keating was becoming frustrated with Stone. 'That's the last time he stands me up,' he told his staff. But Keating had a dilemma. Keating was an institutional person; he wanted the treasury with him. He knew the decision was historic; he knew the consequences were unpredictable. He didn't want the markets, domestic and abroad, thinking that the Australian treasury had opposed the move. Both for the record and his own reassurance Keating wanted the treasury on board. Stone, however, refused to concede.

The turning point came in December with a worse crisis than before. Funds poured into Australia to exploit another revaluation of $A. The authorities were unable to check the momentum and in the week to Friday 9 December there was a massive capital inflow. On the afternoon and evening of 8 December Johnston and John Phillips from the Bank spoke to Keating's office about a mounting crisis. Their message was that international financiers had targeted Australia with as much as $800 million. It was enough to increase the money supply by one per cent and smash the Bank's efforts to conduct a proper monetary policy to contain inflation. The managed exchange rate system was falling apart.[13]

The crisis was forcing a decision from Hawke and Keating. Phillips, the Reserve's financial markets manager, says: 'The Reserve Bank found itself buying almost $1.5 billion of foreign exchange in just a few days . . . The Bank and the government had to face up to how long they would let that continue given the damage it was doing to monetary management.'[14] Hawke and Keating spent several hours together that night in Hawke's office talking by phone to Stone and the Reserve Bank. Their advisers moved in and out of the office as more data was gathered and opinions sought.

The debate was not over the principle of the float—that was assumed. It was about timing. It was whether the decision to float should be taken now in this crisis or deferred for due process. And if Labor didn't float now then how did it handle the crisis? At the early stages the advisers assumed a float was inevitable—but they underestimated Stone.

Johnston and Stone gave the same tactical advice: if the government decided to close the foreign exchange market the next day then it had to float the dollar. They insisted that once this step was taken Labor had to follow through with the fundamental change. Here they split; Stone opposed the float and Johnston supported it.

Stone's opposition was the major internal problem and he argued with force on economic and national interest grounds. Hawke and Keating listened, pondered, then dallied. They would never admit it, but Stone shook them. Stone said the dollar would become a speculators' toy; it was inappropriate for a nation of Australia's size to float its currency; the exchange rate was a weapon of policy and should never be surrendered to the markets. The question went to the core of national sovereignty.

The advisers began to grow alarmed; Garnaut, Cole, Visbord and Evans were all involved at various stages. Keating's problem was insoluble: he wanted Stone to approve but Stone was the critic.

The advisers had waited six weeks to take this decision. Now was the hour. But Stone fought to deny this moment. He pleaded with Garnaut to stop the move. Stone was a figure of domestic influence and international standing. When Stone had broken from the Fraser government over economic policy he had inflicted immense damage upon it. Keating was apprehensive about the impact of Stone's opposition on the decision. Keating's problem, in fact, was Stone.

Before midnight Keating returned to his basement office without any decision. The talks continued in both Hawke's and Keating's offices. It was the last sitting night of 1983, the year of Labor's return, and the parties were just gaining momentum for the run until 5 am. The old building rocked with life. But Hawke faced his gravest decision.

By midnight the mood in Hawke's office was black and the advisers went into Hawke's personal office for further talks. Garnaut now warned of a disaster the next day; he pressed the need for a bold decision. Hawke systematically reviewed the options again and agreed with Garnaut—they had to float. Peter Barron was despatched to bring Keating back for a decision. But Keating had reached the same conclusion.

It was in Hawke's office around 1 am on 9 December that Hawke and Keating took the historic decision to cut the dollar loose and float, along with the abolition of exchange controls. Stone later called this the most important single economic decision made by an Australian government since World War II. It was still transmitting shock waves through the economy a decade later. The complex, chaotic and confused story of the 1980s was the result of thousands of responses and interactions to this transforming decision.

It was agreed to close the markets that day and bring senior Bank officials to Canberra to formalise the float. It was also agreed to abolish exchange controls, as the Reserve had advised. Keating rang Johnston at his Sydney home about 1.30 am to tell him. Johnston was ready. Johnston, Sanders and Phillips took the first plane to Canberra that morning. They carried the Bank's 'war book' on the float, the guide to action.

Late that night Keating sought out three ministers who would be critical in the formal decision-making process—Hayden, Dawkins and Willis. When Keating left the building he had their support. The party-goers were still revelling, oblivious to the making of history.

Keating met the Bank officials just after breakfast and gave them two messages: the aim was to secure a formal decision to float the dollar, and the Bank must counter Stone's opposition. At 10 am Hawke, Keating, the advisers, officials and Bank officers gathered in the Cabinet room. Hawke chaired the meeting, committed to the float but staying his hand. Stone knew it was over. But due process must be followed; now came the formal arguments. Stone spoke long and hard, employing economics, emotion and, towards the Bank, a dose of sarcasm.

Stone warned that the dollar, if floated, would rise to a significant level, perhaps an appreciation of 10 per cent. A torrent of cheap imports would undermine the competitive position of Australian industry. Stone pointed to the smallness of the Australian economy, the mammoth size of financial markets. He said a float was totally inappropriate for Australia; it was too small and would be swamped. In the longer term he predicted much volatility for the dollar. Conditions within the traded goods sector of the economy—Australia's lifeblood—would become very hazardous. Stone felt the economy would become hostage to the financial sector rather than the financial sector service the economy's needs. He urged the government not to be stampeded into a float but to accept, instead, in the short-term, capital controls.

Stone was an economic rationalist and Australian nationalist. He believed that the exchange rate and exchange controls were too important as economic levers to be surrendered. His culture was that of the treasury professional: running the economy with the weapons available, and that included the exchange weapons. Stone distrusted the markets' setting the $A price. But his position was not supported by the majority of senior officers beneath him. Stone was stunned by one aspect of the affair—the decision was being made, in effect, by just two ministers without Cabinet papers and proper documentary briefings.

Johnston, in reply, put the case for the float. He said the existing system had failed comprehensively. Speculators were making their money against the Australian government, the Bank was now unable to conduct a proper monetary policy, the speculation had thrown monetary growth—vital in controlling inflation—beyond the planned range. The government had to find a solution—the alternative to the float was a steep increase in regulation in an effort to stem the speculative inflow, such as a Variable Deposit Requirement (VDR)—in effect, a tax on capital inflow. The choice was a float or a massive re-regulation.

Johnston says: 'I told them those were the two possible courses. But if they went for the capital controls I doubted that they would work. If they were going to work they would have to be very stringent and cause a great deal of disruption. If they were totally opposed to floating that was the only alternative. I was saying that Australia is confronted with this situation and this is the choice.'[15]

Neither the Bank nor the government had any desire to open the Pandora's box of re-regulation. The growing size and sophistication of financial markets had made government intervention far less effective.

Johnston said the float and abolition of exchange controls was the best solution. Under a float the speculators would speculate against each other. He predicted, contrary to Stone, that the $A would gradually depreciate once floated—the same assessment that Garnaut had given Hawke. Under a float the market would determine the exchange rate and the Bank through the purchase and sale of dollars could smooth out fluctuations.

The meeting finished with Hawke and Keating announcing that they would float and abolish exchange controls. Stone had his final parting shot in a remark to Hawke, a lunge at Labor's psychological flaw: 'This decision will bring more damage to the Australian economy than the Whitlam government's tariff cut.'[16] It was the ultimate line to frighten Hawke and Keating. But they had crossed the Rubicon. The Bank was asked to make all the administrative arrangements. A meeting of Cabinet's economic committee was called—which included Hayden, Dawkins, Willis, Button and Kerin. Keating gave an exposition, Johnston took questions and there was no opposition. Stone had drifted back to the treasury, defeated. His senior officers helped Keating put the package together. At 5 pm on Friday 9 December 1983 Keating convened a media conference, with Bob Johnston by his side. After announcing the decision Keating said:

> This means that the Reserve Bank will no longer announce a
> trade-weighted index or indicative exchange rates for the $A and the
> $US. Nor will the banks be required to settle their foreign exchange
> positions at the end of each day. In future exchange rates will be
> determined by the market. These reforms of the exchange rate
> management system will also assist the conduct of the Government's
> monetary policy.

The abolition of exchange controls meant that Australians had the freedom to direct their funds—invest, lend or borrow abroad. The abolition of these controls was more significant than the float—it meant that unless Australia performed then capital would move offshore.

Keating pointed to Australia's persistent higher inflation rate compared with the other OECD nations. He said the float would force Australia into the necessary economic adjustments. Keating explained later:

> You can't defend an exchange rate against the market. There's too
> much money out there. Why, if we tried to defend an unsustainable
> exchange rate against the market, we'd have to sacrifice our foreign
> exchange reserves.
> What for? Trying to stop an exchange rate going where the market
> sends it. That would be just crazy.
> One of the things is that the born-to-rule brigade—the coalition—
> have never lived with the discipline of a floating exchange rate. They
> think their mere presence will affect how the world markets treat them.
> It won't matter a tinker's curse. The float is the decision where

86

Australia truly made its debut into the world and said, 'O.K., we're now an international citizen.'[17]

After the float Bob Johnston said:

It's a better economy for it. A floating exchange rate can deliver harsh judgements . . . There is always the possibility of mistaking the messenger for the message—blaming the exchange rate for what really are faults in the economy—but the exchange rate will certainly tell you if things are out of kilter . . . the market wins in the end.[18]

These decisions were most important in the internationalisation of the Australian economy during the 1980s. The float and financial deregulation were, arguably, the greatest blow struck against the protectionist, introverted, regulatory apparatus of the Deakinite Settlement in the eighty years since its inception.
Johnston called them 'the decisions of the decade'.

It was the overt breaking of our isolationism. Without it, there is the mentality of living behind the moat. The float linked the Australian economy, for better or worse, with the rest of the world. It would teach us some very severe lessons but we have to learn those lessons. The great advantage was that we had reserves running out of our ears.[19]

Hawke and Keating saw the move as probably inevitable, according to Johnston. He says: 'We had passed the point where a managed rate was defensible.'[20] But Stone was brooding. After a newspaper article claiming that Keating's office knew that a majority of senior treasury officials supported the float, Stone sent a memo to senior officers quizzing them in an effort to find the basis of this report. Its assessment was accurate.

The decision to float and abolish exchange controls was the product of a monetary crisis. But the crisis did not produce the solution. Hawke and Keating had been charting a path towards deregulation of Australia's financial system from mid-1983. Their direction was unmistakable and is confirmed by their respective advisers. It had to be disguised since deregulation was contrary to official Labor policy and ethos. But the signs were telling: Keating's creation of the Martin inquiry, the Reserve Bank's 'war book' on the float, the October floating of the forward rate, the nature of the debate over the float on 8–9 December. Events shaped the timing of deregulation, not its fact.

In February 1984, Keating received the Martin Report—its recommendations were similar to those of Campbell. Martin asserted that deregulation was preferable to controls to deliver 'an adequate supply of finance at a reasonable cost for the housing, rural and small business sectors'. Martin meant that Labor could now be its own master; it could claim authorship and legitimacy for its own deregulation. But the internal ALP debate was dominated by the float. The float had never gone to the ALP caucus for decision because it was a currency issue. By 1984 when the caucus debated deregulation, the horse had bolted.

Keating's approach in 1984 and 1985 was fast, exploiting the momentum of deregulatory fashion. Each step was another victory. A study of the period asserts:

> The sheer breadth of Keating's program should be acknowledged for it included the granting of sixteen foreign bank licences, the deregulation of interest rates, the dismantling of controls on foreign investment and international capital movements, the deregulation of the stock market, alterations to the asset reserve requirements of the banks and insurance industry and the dissolution of the distinctions between savings and trading banks.[21]

From April 1984 Keating began to force the pace through Cabinet— with prior caucus consultation. His success earned the admiration of many outsiders including the former Liberal adviser John Hewson, who called Keating's performance a 'masterstroke.'[22] The float, financial deregulation and foreign bank entry were endorsed by the 1984 ALP National Conference on right wing and centre-left votes. Conference bowed to its Cabinet and to pressure from Hawke, Hayden and Keating. It endorsed positions that would have been heresy two years earlier. The transforming impact of power weakened the resistance.

The pace of Australia's deregulation was swift by any standard. In 1985 Bob Johnston said: 'We have deregulated the financial system as far and as fast as any country; few have deregulated domestically and externally at the same time.'[23] Only in the late 1980s did the authorities begin to speculate that the pace of reform had been so fast that Australia's institutions, notably the banks, had panicked.

The party debate in 1984 was about foreign bank entry. Keating carried it with spectacular arguments: the domestic banks had done nothing for Labor, so here was a chance to apply the blowtorch of competition. He promised, in effect, to smash the old anti-ALP financial establishment with deregulation. This stunning rhetoric had an unintended consequence—the banks listened and went into a survival frenzy. Once the market opened, they chased market share with a crazy ruthlessness that defied their image.

The reform came so fast partly because there was so little opposition. It was a reversal of the Australian experience of industries resisting their own liberalisation. It was an idea whose time had come. An alliance for financial deregulation had grown over the previous several years, conditioned by the Campbell Report. It included the commercial banks, the Reserve Bank and the weight of official economic advice.

The driving force for 'internal' deregulation, allowing interest rates to be market determined, came from the banks, which were being outpaced. The banks went for deregulation because the existing controls prevented them from competing with the non-bank sector which had more freedom. By 1980 more than 50 per cent of Australia's financial assets had passed to non-bank control whose innovations included currency hedge markets and cash management trusts. The choice facing government was clear—either extend the arms of regulation to cover the non-banks or deregulate the entire system.

It was assumed that giving the banks more freedom would lead to economic efficiencies. Johnston says: 'I was as much moved as anybody by the belief that the banks were efficient fund gatherers and efficient lenders and it was a step towards a more efficient economy for the banks to be free in these areas.'[24]

In 1991 Tony Cole, an architect of deregulation, then treasury secretary said:

> It's true that financial deregulation was oversold at the time. But that's inevitable when you're trying to convince people about the need for change. The benefits were exaggerated and the negatives were under-estimated. The problem was that nobody predicted the Australian banks would take such risks for market share. They didn't know how to risk-assess and nobody knew how incompetent they were. The entry of foreign banks came too quickly on the heels of deregulation. The banks didn't have time to learn the new system. In the old days when credit was rationed you never went near a bank unless you were solid. Back in 1984 and 1985 we kept selling the transforming impact of overseas banks. We got the local banks terrified, convinced that they were going to get creamed. Keating was promising that foreign banks would unclog the arteries of the financial system and some of our banks began to think they'd lose their corporate clients. We all undervalued the traditional retail banking activities and the dominance the established majors had in that area.[25]

Deregulation was embraced with enthusiasm inside and outside the ALP. The Wran and Cain governments, far from criticising the breach of ALP policy, were chasing the benefits. Both governments began promoting their capitals, Sydney and Melbourne, as financial centres for the region. The ACTU was acquiescent but Kelty was openly supportive. Most business and industry groups, particularly exporters, farmers and miners, were firm supporters. The media was enthusiastic and praised Labor's courage. Financial deregulation was a popular reform and in this sense was easier for Labor to implement than many others.

The decision was the making of Keating as treasurer. At this point Keating broke free of Stone. Keating had outmanoeuvred Stone, backed his own judgement against Stone's, and no longer needed him. It gave Keating a new confidence. It was the issue on which the loyalty of the 'best and the brightest' treasury generation beneath Stone was transferred from Stone to Keating. The seeds of the remarkable Keating–treasury axis began to grow—without Stone.

The end of certainty

Stone never recovered from this defeat. He believed that Keating and Johnston had settled on the new policy behind his back. Stone felt that his position as treasury secretary as becoming untenable. Cole now advised Keating to sack Stone as secretary but Keating declined. 'Let's wait, he might just resign anyway,' Keating said — a shrewd calculation.

The outcome was a stunning triumph for the Reserve Bank and Johnston over Stone. It established the basis of the Keating–Johnston relationship for the next five years: mutual respect and deep accord. Keating emerged in a powerful position inside and outside the government. Inside he had the respect and support of a powerful functioning troika—his personal office, the treasury and the Reserve Bank. Outside he began to project an aura of successful and sweeping reform.

The pace of Australia's financial deregulation attracted international attention. In late 1984 Keating went to America where he received the *Euromoney* award as finance minister of the year. This was the origin of the famous label 'the world's greatest treasurer', which passed into the language first as a term of praise, later of sarcasm. The magazine's editor, Sir Patrick Sergeant, declared: 'In Australia we find the hour has brought forth the man', and he called Keating 'the most impressive Treasurer since the war . . . his moves have been bold, brilliant and above all, brave'.

The decision also gave Keating confidence against Hawke. This is a deep irony since Hawke believed that he had dragged a reluctant Keating to the float, a perception based upon Keating's apprehension before the decision. But Keating now made financial deregulation the testament of his career. In later years there would be an intense private rivalry between Hawke and Keating over who was entitled to assume the chief credit for this historic decision, with each of them convinced that he had been the driving force.

The early impact of financial deregulation launched Keating into the political stratosphere. Keating was realising the compulsive force within himself; he was, to use his own words, 'painting the big picture'. His political skills—persuasion, power and theatre—were applied with great effect to the financial markets over coming years. For a while market confidence in Australia was a function, partly, of Keating's own presence.

Deregulation, in fact, had consequences of varying predictability and some that defied prediction:

First, Australia's competitive weakness would be revealed in a series of sharp depreciations during the mid-1980s which would force Labor into economic restructuring, a plus from the float which was anticipated by many of its advocates.

Second, financial deregulation helped to feed into the 1980s sharemarket and investment boom—but this also had its adverse side: a rise in unsustainable private debt, a decline in corporate standards, the technique of the high-leveraged buy-out, and the substitution of paper profits for 'real' profits.

Third, the freeing of domestic controls helped to trigger a credit

90

The Hawke–Keating model: the float

explosion as banks and other financial institutions competed for market share—an explosion which involved many poor commercial decisions and led to corporate crashes and damage to Australia's overseas reputation. It revealed that neither borrowers nor lenders were mature enough to handle their new freedom.

Fourth, investment flows in and out of Australia were facilitated resulting in a sharp rise in Australia's national debt, which reached $150 billion by 1992. On the other hand Australian corporations exploited the abolition of exchange controls to invest heavily overseas and by the end of the 1980s had assets abroad worth an estimated $50 billion.

Fifth, the process facilitated the exit of Australia's old business elite and the rise of a new band of high-debt entrepreneurs. They inherited a unique opportunity—lower wages, higher profits, easy money and world growth—but many squandered that chance, to their individual cost and that of Australia.

Sixth, deregulation changed the rules of monetary policy management by the authorities. Controls were exercised through the price of money—interest rates—rather than by direct controls on the volume of money lent. Deregulation meant that monetary targets were abandoned as strict policy objectives. Throughout the world central banks were plunged into a crisis of monetary theory as they struggled to devise new guidelines in the unprecedented context of international financial market integration. Monetary policy operated in a sea of uncharted waters during the 1980s, as Labor discovered, a critical fact in the 1990 recession.

Seventh, during the late 1980s the markets set an $A rate too high, too often, which misjudged Australia's economic fundamentals and hurt exporters. The float had failed to set an exchange rate which kept demand and supply for foreign exchange in balance—the hope of some, but not all, of its advocates. The problem was that the exchange rate and the current account seemed to be 'uncoupled'. The advocates of the float in 1983 believed that it would help, not hinder, in setting an $A rate to address Australia's subsequent central economic problem—the deficit on the current account—but the experience by 1990 was not hopeful. Markets set the rate not on trading fundamentals but on capital flows.

The early 1990s recession prompted a rush of arguments against deregulation. A more valid assessment is that there were costs, sometimes high costs, in the adjustment of institutions to a new reality. The lesson was that extracting the benefits of deregulation required better judgement from people and institutions. Yet for Australians as a whole, deregulation delivered better services at lower economic cost, a cardinal point. Overall, it was a plus.

Financial deregulation was driven by the change in the world economy and the integration of international financial markets. This was a phenomenon from which Australia was unable to escape. Long before the float Australia's financial markets were being integrated with those overseas.

Merchant banks and foreign banks were represented here; Australia's capital inflow had ceased to be dominated by long-term equity investment; short-term capital flows began to drive the exchange rate; there was a dramatic change from equity to debt in capital inflow. The government was losing control of the exchange rate, which was being transformed from a tool of policy into a consequence of policy.

These trends were beyond Australia's control but demanded a response. They reflected the fact that goods, capital, information and ideas were being transmitted through international markets. The old world was being destroyed. Australia had no choice but to swim in the ocean. It is hard to refute Stone's view that the financial deregulation decisions were the most important in economic policy in the post-World War II era.

Claims that the Hawke government should have deregulated the labour market before the financial market are unrealistic for two reasons. First, the debate about financial deregulation was very advanced because of the Campbell Report, while debate about labour market deregulation scarcely existed in 1983. Second, the opportunity to deregulate the financial system was produced by the monetary crisis of 1983 and in politics, as in life, opportunities exist to be seized. By contrast, the opportunity for labour market deregulation did not exist, with a new ALP government pledged to the Accord and centralised wage fixation.

However, a related proposition is certainly true—that the government should have made a greater effort to deregulate the real economy in closer proximity to its deregulation of finance—and this became a theme of the late 1980s.

The move to financial deregulation was a step of historic magnitude for the Labor Party. From its inception Hawke and Keating saw financial deregulation as a fundamental element of their economic strategy. Keating described the financial system as the economy's main artery; improve its efficiency and the body functioned better. Hawke and Keating were never apologetic about the float; they were always aggressive. Financial deregulation was presented by Keating from 1984 onwards as basic to the achievement of economic growth, to the improvement of economic efficiency through restructuring, and to maintenance of an anti-inflationary discipline. Labor drew a new equation: deregulation would promote growth and help to beat inflation. Keating said:

> There has been a revolution in the national attitudes to our existing
> institutional arrangements. There has been a new acceptance of the
> need for change—to adapt to new world realities. Australians are
> dissatisfied with the mediocrity of our economic performance in the
> post-war years . . . I do not think it is particularly surprising that it has
> been a Labor Government which has sought most comprehensively to
> capture this new mood and to express it in policy reforms.[26]

The Hawke–Keating model: the float

In terms of philosophy and method, financial deregulation signalled a break with the ALP tradition. Throughout its existence the Labor Party had sought to improve or civilise the capitalist economy through the intervention of the state. Under Hawke and Keating it sought to improve the economy by unleashing the weapon of the market. This was a fundamental leap in Labor politics. It became in fact a theme of the Hawke government, because deregulation of finance could not be quarantined from other sectors. The ideas underpinning financial deregulation were a belief in markets, a faith in competition, a conviction that the economy must be internationalised.

The mixture of the float and the Accord provided the ingredients for Labor's 1980s growth strategy. The float was to secure a major depreciation; the Accord was to deliver the wage restraint to retain the competitive advantages of the depreciation. In this way Labor hoped to attack and eradicate the balance of payments weakness and the constraint it imposed on growth and employment. The aim was to create a framework which allowed Australia to grow faster than the rest of the world. This was necessary for two reasons—to reduce unemployment, and to absorb Australia's fast growing population, the result of immigration.

Financial deregulation would promote deregulation in other areas of the economy: labour, trade and product markets. The financial sector could never be quarantined. The consequences of financial deregulation for other sectors of the economy were only partly realised at the time by Hawke and Keating. During the 1980s Labor would try to promote deregulation in some sectors and resist it in others.

The Hawke–Keating model was a hybrid. Hawke and Keating were zealots for financial deregulation but equally zealous to keep a regulated labour market. When it came to the labour market the government was pledged to a political compact, not a market adjustment. The slow burning fuse for Labor was the prospect that financial deregulation would destroy the Accord; that a deregulated financial system would smash a regulated labour market.

Labor did, however, accept deregulation of industrial protection. In late 1983 Hawke announced in Bangkok an initiative to seek through the General Agreement on Tariffs and Trade (GATT) a cut in agricultural protection in a new trade negotiation round. This inaugurated Australia's most sustained international initiative of the decade, a decision taken by Hawke knowing that Australia's credibility would be upheld only by ongoing cuts in its own industrial protection. Hawke and Keating delivered these cuts in two principal decisions in 1988 and 1991. Hawke's commitment to financial deregulation and lower protection was driven by Ross Garnaut—the most influential economic adviser of his prime ministership.

Financial deregulation meant that the Hawke–Keating government would be contemporary, just as the Accord meant it would be traditional. Hawke and Keating, by the way they sought to improve the capitalist system and the Australian economy, had sown the seeds for an internal debate about

Labor's identity. The principle involved was clear and was enunciated by Hawke in his Curtin lecture in September 1983: 'Social Democrats have no reason to deny the capacity of markets to allocate resources efficiently . . . I see no virtue in regulation of economic activity for its own sake and I believe that where markets are working efficiently they should be left to do their job.'[27] This was an ideological leap for the ALP.

The floating rate and exchange control abolition meant that currency and capital markets would test every major economic policy decision made by Australia. The nation would be under permanent examination with savage consequences for failure. The values of the markets were far removed from those of the old ALP. During the 1980s the discipline imposed by the markets through the float and capital movements imposed severe policy changes upon Australia. It forced Labor towards small government, real wage cuts, lower taxation and industry deregulation. The left wing would be reduced to impotent rumbles in 1986 about what it saw as the economic Darwinism of the float.

Financial deregulation also led Hawke and Keating to another concept—the promotion of a new generation of Australian businessmen. The new system created a new business generation that played by new rules—rules Labor had encouraged. Keating said the old business and financial establishment had failed the nation. Financial deregulation was a revolution within the capitalist citadel. It was a perfect policy for Labor. It would demolish the old order and introduce a new generation of business leaders based on merit and, by definition, devoid of the old anti-Labor prejudice. Hawke and Keating looked towards the new business generation. It was assumed that they would be smarter, just as Hawke and Keating were smarter than the Liberals.

On the eve of the float Doug Anthony told Howard that he intended to make a statement saying that a float was against the national interest. Howard replied: 'If you say that, I'll have no option but to repudiate your position as shadow treasurer.' They argued, then Anthony relented. A short time later he left politics.

In electoral terms Labor had seized supposedly Liberal terrain—it was pushing non-Labor to the right. Keating applied his skills to torment the Liberals. In fact, he mocked them for a decade: the deregulators who had been scared to deregulate. It was Keating who had delivered for finance, business and the markets. Keating never let the Liberals or the markets forget. No Labor treasurer had ever attacked the Liberals from this direction.

As 1984 unfolded, Hawke seemed invulnerable; the Hawke–Keating duo had put in place a remarkable alliance of organised labour and capital markets through the Accord and financial deregulation. It was unique and its success was proved in rising activity, falling inflation and falling unemployment. But the Liberals were undergoing their own revolution.

5

The Liberal revolution

A host of reasons has been advanced for the recent decline in the party's support . . . one reason more than any other was put to the committee again and again—loss of credibility . . . we did not practice what we preached.

Report of the 1983 Liberal Party Committee of Review

The 1983 election loss drove the Liberal Party to a reassessment of its past and the impotence of Opposition assisted a transformation in its policies. In the brief 21 months before the 1984 poll there was scant joy for the coalition facing Hawke, but non-Labor politics underwent a quiet revolution. The free market lobby moved from the wings to take virtual control of the Party. The Liberal Party began to torch the edifices of its past.

The deepest frustration for Liberals after 1983 was the absence of a leader to market its new beliefs. This absence is the cause of nearly every 'crisis' the party endured in the 1980s. Modern parties are vulnerable to disunity when they attempt to recast their ideology. The absence of a strong leader to give coherence to reform accentuates its costs and obscures its benefits. This was the experience of the Liberals during their three terms in Opposition from 1983 to 1990.

On Sunday 6 March 1983, the day after the defeat, at Melbourne's Windsor Hotel a beaten Malcolm Fraser put his hand on Andrew Peacock's forearm in an anointing of his successor. Fraser's action was unusual since he and Peacock had been ferocious rivals over two decades. They were personality opposites and power rivals inclined to conspiratorial views of each other. Fraser's anointing of Peacock reflected the power of Victorian tradition in the Liberal Party and a rejection of his deputy, John Howard, the most senior adherent of the free market ideas which Fraser saw as too impractical and too puritanical.

Peacock defeated Howard 36–20 to become the new leader in a ballot dominated by electoral appeal, not policy. Howard was still unpopular from his period as treasurer and his retrospective 'bottom of the harbour' tax laws. It was an easy win for Peacock but it also entrenched Howard as alternative leader.

The Liberal Party's combined reversals in 1982 and 1983 were the worst since its formation by Menzies nearly forty years earlier. By the end of 1983 the Liberals governed only in Tasmania (the Nationals held power in Queensland). The Liberals held only 21 out of the 78 metropolitan House of Representatives seats, just one in four. The coalition had polled particularly badly among female and young voters in the election but it had lost support everywhere. Since 1977 the Liberal vote nationally had remained at about three million while the Labor vote had increased to 4.3 million.[1]

The social base, organisational structure and political ethos of the Liberal Party would be revealed as inadequate over the next decade. The advent of a strong ALP government reluctant to self-destruct would expose the bankruptcy of Australia's status quo party. The free market lobby might win control of the formal policy direction, but the internal culture of the Liberal Party was remarkably impervious to change.

This culture was rooted in respect for private property before a genuinely competitive economy, good manners before intellectual combat and states' rights before national imperatives. These ideas would cripple the Liberals during the 1980s and severely retard the push to reinvent Liberalism. Politicians can alter policy but political culture is more enduring. During the decade the Liberal instinct for property rights, individual and corporate, would inhibit its attack on economic privilege. Its dedication to federalism would prevent the party from making the transition from six state divisions to a robust national body. Finally, the intellectual weakness and lack of power within the Liberal organisation contributed to both a demoralised rank and file and to an inept organisational leadership, much inferior to the ALP's.

But the equilibrium of Australian politics still prevailed. Even after Labor's redistribution in this parliament, the Opposition required only a moderate 3.2 per cent uniform swing to regain office at the next poll. It revealed a theme of the decade: the coalition was always within striking distance of Hawke. Its position was never hopeless on the statistics, but it kept faltering at the politics.

Within a short time after Fraser's departure the party had embraced the ideas which he had resisted or accepted only in qualified terms—financial deregulation, lower protection, a move away from centralised wage fixation, large-scale privatisation, a shift from direct to indirect taxation, belief in markets, and a rejection of Keynesian pump-priming as a means to combat unemployment.

The transformation of the Liberals was driven by four factors: the retirement of an older generation of Liberal politicians; the loss of office which facilitated the reassessment of ideas in the safety of Opposition; the extent to which the Hawke government embraced free market policies, which shocked the Liberals and provoked them to become even more purist; and finally, the influence of the free market philosophy among opinion-makers at home and abroad.

A generation of conservatives retired from politics or the front bench before, at or just after the 1983 election—Fraser, Doug Anthony, Sir Phillip Lynch, Peter Nixon, Sir John Carrick, Robert Cotton, Jim Killen and Tony Street. They were the post-Menzies generation, believers in the middle course, tough, pragmatic, mostly shrewd politicians, and more practical than ideological. These men would have been reluctant to embrace the purist doctrines of the free market since they believed this would jeopardise the traditional lifelines of Liberal support.

Defeat gave licence to the new fashion. Radical ideas flourished since there was no immediate test of implementation. The success of Ronald Reagan and Margaret Thatcher sent an important message to the Liberals— that a more aggressive advocacy of free market capitalism could deliver better electoral success than the compromises which had typified the Fraser era. The perception took hold that Fraser lost because he lacked conviction. This became an orthodoxy within vital constituencies—party rank and file, business and finance, the Liberal blue rinse set and the economic advisers.

Fraser was denigrated as a wimp, often unfairly, frequently by Liberals who broke with him only in hindsight. The rejection of Fraser grew in intensity over the next few years. The inaugural attack from the right-wing intelligentsia came from Dr Gerard Henderson, a DLP refugee and frustrated Fraser government staffer. Henderson wrote an article two days after Fraser's defeat which offered a contemptuous dismissal of Fraser's record as either a tough or reforming leader. It was a contrast to the 'noble Roman' depiction of Fraser from John Carroll.[2] Henderson said:

> In spite of the continuing difficult economic situation, Malcolm Fraser was really a bit of a bleeding heart. In the last Whitlam Labor Budget, Commonwealth Government expenditure on social security and welfare was estimated at 21.8 per cent of total budget outlays . . . By 1982 the figure had grown to 28.2 per cent . . . Likewise, it is nonsense to suggest that a government which consistently overshot its money supply targets, and maintained high tariffs and quotas to protect local industries, was implementing Milton Friedman's advice.

> One of the paradoxes of his period in office was that Malcolm Fraser suffered sustained public criticism for his perceived hardness, but was not able to achieve the economic benefits that would have flowed from a real, as distinct from rhetorical, tough-mindedness. In other words, he lost both ways.[3]

Within nine months Henderson had become Howard's senior adviser and the critique made by the radical liberals had assumed gospel status. Its acceptance by the rank and file was reinforced by the 'victim' theory of politics. Liberal 'wet', former Senator Chris Puplick, explains:

> When Hawke first became a public figure as ACTU president he was regarded by almost everybody in the Liberal Party as a foul-mouthed drunken barbarian who had no class. Later when Malcolm lost the election the reaction was—'how bad do you have to be to lose to Hawke?' The Party was unforgiving and resentful. The reaction was intense and Fraser became a scapegoat. A mythology started to be built by his former close associates about what Fraser had failed to do in office at their urging.[4]

After the defeat the Liberal Party sought to repudiate its own ideas and policies—the platforms on which the party had relied not only since its inception in 1944 but on which the non-Labor side had relied since the Deakin Settlement. Figures such as Howard and John Hyde understood the magnitude of the revolution. In the lobbies Howard would tell the journalists that the Liberal Party was at a turning point: the Fraser–McEwen legacy would be buried forever.

The Liberal Party, for the first time in its history, was abandoning its guise as protector of the status quo or pragmatic reformer of the free enterprise system. The ultimate political significance of dry economics in the Australian context was that the Liberals, in effect, were recasting themselves as the free market radicals. Protection, arbitration, and state paternalism were the bulwarks of the status quo with which the bulk of business, employers and farmers were familiar and comfortable. The Liberals were now saying they should be dismantled.

The argument of the radical liberals was that the inherited Australian Settlement was the core of Australia's economic problem. The system which purported to be free enterprise was hostile to free enterprise. So the system of intervention, regulation and protection, supported by coalition governments for so long, had to be dismantled and replaced by competitive markets. By such logic the Liberals became pledged to dismantle, not defend, the old edifice, a political and economic position which cast them as radicals. Herein lay the problem—the new gulf between Liberal ideology and Liberal ethos.

Most Liberals had no conception of a radical political position. They were unable to think, act or mobilise as political reformers. Many never realised that the overall content of their new policies had cast them as radicals because they had no grip on the history of their own country and little feel for the historical role of their own party. Fashion, not conviction, drove more than a few. Many reforms were accepted with a casual disregard of their true economic import and political risk.

The Liberals didn't have the slightest idea of how to formulate a political strategy to mastermind the dismantling of the Australian Settlement—the biggest attack on vested interests ever envisaged. It was easy to say that vested interests created by tariffs, the industrial system and government regulation had to be attacked. But how? The party had no political tradition that was commensurate with its new economic beliefs; no tradition that would help them mobilise, persuade and propagandise to achieve far-reaching institutional and cultural reforms. The drys were strong on economic theory and weak on political techniques, strategy and tactics. This discrepancy, which lies at the core of their dilemma, would plague the Liberal and National forces throughout the rest of the 1980s.

The task of piloting the Liberals fell to Peacock and Howard, supported by Ian Macphee, who ran second to Howard in the deputy's ballot, and Fred Chaney, who became Senate leader. This quartet was all that remained of the senior echelon from the Fraser years. The Liberal story of the 1980s is the story of their failure to cooperate sufficiently to meet the challenge with the strength, skill and cohesion required.

The Peacock–Howard team, the best for the Opposition after the 1983 defeat, had the potential to blend image and ideology. But it was never realised. The coalition faced a popular prime minister in Hawke, a Cabinet superior to that of Fraser, and a recovering economy, a formidable trio.

The imperative for Liberal unity was cooperation between Peacock and Howard, since mutual trust had been absent from their relationship during the Fraser years. But it was Peacock–Howard rivalry, always intense but remarkably unresolved, which dominated and disrupted the Liberals during the decade. It had a triple impact: it denied the prospect of strong leadership; it divided the party; and it made a transition to free market policies far more difficult.

Peacock's election as leader realised his destiny, manifest to many since his 1966 entry into Parliament as a 27 year old in Menzies' seat. Appointed a federal minister at 30, Peacock was a bright hope in the pre-1972 period for a younger generation of Liberals, with his charismatic pretensions and interest in the social trends of the sixties generation.

As a 'boy' minister Peacock won admiration with his commitment to independence for Papua New Guinea, perhaps his main achievement in politics. But Peacock fell victim to an Australian version of the Kennedy tragedy, doomed as a career politician to try to realise the destiny which his friends, the media and the party always ordained for him. Peacock's tragedy was that he lacked the inner strength which leadership demanded yet was unable to purge himself of the leadership ambition to which his life was chained. What else was he to do?

Peacock's career reveals a pattern of miscalculation. In 1975 when Fraser was stalking Snedden it was Peacock, supposedly Snedden's loyal backer, who triggered the crisis, presumably to try to seize the leadership for himself rather than Fraser. The effect was to precipitate the precise situation Fraser had wanted by forcing a Fraser–Snedden showdown.

Fraser's victories in 1975 over Peacock, Billy Snedden and then Whitlam were comprehensive, guaranteeing the Liberals five years of strong leadership and relative unity.

In September 1980 Peacock plunged the Fraser Cabinet into turmoil when he threatened to resign on election eve and finally did resign six months later with a melodramatic attack on Fraser. Peacock strutted for a year on the backbench, willing to wound but afraid to strike. Finally in 1982 Fraser forced the challenge and demolished Peacock 54–27. Fraser simultaneously sponsored Howard to replace the fading Phillip Lynch as deputy leader. These events terminated the long Fraser–Peacock power struggle and inaugurated in its place the Howard–Peacock struggle. Henceforth Howard would be Peacock's rival in future Liberal leadership contests.[5]

Peacock had always been a popular politician and an electoral asset for the Liberals. But he lacked the drive to master the economic and industrial issues which dominated politics from the mid-1970s onwards; Peacock was not a believer. As conservative politics became more dominated by ideas, Peacock's lack of them was transparent.

Peacock had no killer instinct, a fact which a politician like Keating would exploit. Peacock was a good bloke and a decent man, but he had little inclination for the long hours and hard work which are the companions of power. Peacock's assets were his television presence, personal charm and campaigning ability. Yet his lazy affability concealed a political time-bomb: here was a politician unable to imagine any other road to power but that which Liberal history told him was the orthodoxy—the ritual of manoeuvre, strike and challenge. Peacock was cavalier about the havoc which his ambition caused but he lacked the ruthlessness of a Fraser to achieve a party coup of lasting success.

Peacock was a student of fashion, in life and in politics. As the times changed so did Peacock. He rose to prominence in the Liberal Party in the late 1960s, coming from the party's left progressive wing. But by 1982 Peacock presented himself as an economic dry although he had pushed such dry policies only rarely at the Cabinet table and most of the drys were sceptical of him. Doubting his sincerity, they looked to Howard. Peter Shack was almost alone among the original drys in his belief that Peacock was the best leader. Peacock was always presentable but rarely convincing.

Peacock won the leadership in 1983, drawing upon his electoral appeal and his long-established base of about a third of the parliamentary party. He was also the beneficiary of a deeper trend—a dearth of leadership figures on the non-Labor side after Menzies' retirement.

This was the period when a post-war generation of confident Australians was leaving its stamp on all Australia's institutions, including the Labor Party. The Liberals—the party which by 1983 had governed for thirty-one out of the previous thirty-four years—largely failed to attract the quality from this generation. In the twenty-four years from Menzies' retirement in

100

The Liberal revolution

1966 to Peacock's second resignation as leader in 1990, the Liberal Party produced only one genuinely successful leader—Malcolm Fraser. Fraser won three elections, ran a united party for five years and had moderate success before his failed third term. None of the other leaders—Harold Holt, John Gorton, William McMahon, Billy Snedden, Peacock, Howard and Peacock again—can claim real success, with the possible exception of Holt (but there is little doubt that the seeds of decay were advanced in Holt's term and were beyond his management). After the Liberals lost the 1972 election, their leadership choice lay between Billy Snedden and Nigel Bowen; after their 1983 loss it was between Peacock and Howard. They were relatively uninspiring options for a party of the ruling order. The conclusion is that the Liberals during most of the post-Menzies era were plagued by leadership inadequacy.

Peacock, 44, carried the hopes of the Victorian establishment from which he had come. His claim to the leadership lay in the unwritten law of Liberal political primitivism: he posed as the best election winner. Carrying the Menzian mantle but unable to wear it, Peacock, too weak to beat Fraser, stepped into the Liberal breach created by Hawke.

John Howard, 43, his deputy, was an aspirant to the leadership. Howard was a living embodiment of the force of Menzies' 'forgotten people' pledge from the 1940s—decent, hard-working, thrifty. Howard came from Sydney's western suburbs, a government school, a small business background and Methodist upbringing. Belief in hard work, respect for properly earned profits, and faith in authority—God, kin, country and family—were the values he absorbed. Political faith came early.

Howard was a recruit to the Liberals from the small capitalist class, a perfect fit into the 1950s Liberal hegemony based on anti-communism, the US alliance, free enterprise rhetoric and family values. Howard grew within the narrow confines of his background—university, law, Young Liberals. His performance was modest, his progress steady, his narrow path never allowed any personal revolt. He became a protégé of John Carrick; some Liberals said that 'Howard was the son Carrick never had'.

Howard was a party loyalist unlikely to question its faiths, either Vietnam or the anti-communist campaigns. As an instructing solicitor his briefs were authoritative and he was sympathetic to the underdog. Howard entered parliament at the 1974 election to witness the follies of the Whitlam government which confirmed his prejudice against the ALP. He backed Fraser against Snedden and became a minister in Fraser's government.[6]

Howard, true to his life, was a conventional Liberal politician. It was 'yes sir, no sir' to Fraser. As minister for business and consumer affairs he was a faithful protectionist; he implemented Fraser's muzzling of the Industries Assistance Commission (IAC). When outgoing IAC Chairman Alf Rattigan recommended as his successor the economic rationalist Austin Holmes, then head of the Priorities Review Staff, his advice was spurned.

The end of certainty

Howard appointed Bill McKinnon, Director and General Manager of the AIDC, often known as the 'McEwen-Westerman Bank'.[7] Howard was an orthodox Liberal and keen to support the Fraser regulatory philosophy.

The turning point in Howard's career was Lynch's resignation as treasurer before the 1977 poll and Fraser's audacity in giving Howard the job. During the campaign his strengths were manifest—the mastery of a brief, the determination, the good performer. Howard remained treasurer for five years which was his making as a politician of substance.

Exposure to the economic debate converted Howard to dry economics, promoted him into the deputy leadership and provoked his bitter breach with Fraser. The intellectual conversion was slow but decisive. By his last year, 1982, Howard was an advocate of financial deregulation, reduction of industry protection, and an opponent of a counter-cyclical fiscal policy to combat the recession. On each issue Howard fought with Fraser and lost. Howard could never break the Fraser–National Party Cabinet axis but he became a dedicated opponent of Fraser Liberalism.

He concluded that Fraser was too deceptive a politician—that the initial denial of his move against Snedden and then his blocking of Supply in 1975 meant that his electoral mandate was flawed from the start. Howard concluded that being 'straight' in politics was best, a view which harmonised with his upbringing.

Howard left office tarnished after the treasury misjudged the economic slowdown. The 1982–83 deficit blew out and Howard was unable to stem a torrent of post-budget election-eve decisions which made the deficit even higher. Keating taunted Howard for years with the famous memo from John Stone which projected a $9.6 billion deficit on the forward estimates for 1983–84. Keating hung three crosses on Howard—his failure to win at the Cabinet table, his fiscal legacy, and the double digit inflation and unemployment of the early 1980s recession.

But Howard's place in the Liberal Party in 1983 was secure—deputy leader, the senior NSW figure, the shadow treasurer, the most experienced economic spokesman. With the Fraser generation gone Howard saw his destiny manifest. When the Liberals went into Opposition nobody had a clearer concept of the role he would play than Howard—he would lead the Liberal Party to the truth of free market economics. After Fraser's exit, Howard would secure the victory which Fraser had denied him in office. He set out to chart a new direction for the Liberal Party.[7]

Howard was professional but contemptuous towards Peacock: he would work with the leader. But the psychology was the key. Howard, distrustful of pretension and 'show ponies', had no time for Peacock. When the pressure had mounted in the Fraser government, Peacock melted into resignation; Howard stayed to fight. Howard had long since decided he was harder, tougher and better than Peacock. Howard thought he was a good chance to become the next Liberal prime minister.

The Liberal revolution

After leader and deputy, the two most important Liberals at this stage were Ian Macphee and Fred Chaney. Macphee, 44, was a social progressive who became the de facto leader of the Liberal wets. Macphee had studied law, economics and history and when working in Papua New Guinea had become friendly with Hawke, who had helped to forge Macphee's own dream of becoming prime minister.[8] Macphee had considered joining the Labor Party, a significant point in view of his later alienation from the Liberals. Macphee knew the industrial system well and had worked with the Chamber of Manufacturers where he had been an associate of Hawke's close friend, George Polites, the employers' spokesman.

In parliament Macphee backed Fraser against Snedden and championed social justice and a social contract with the trade unions. He warned Fraser against blocking Supply in 1975 but later served in productivity, immigration and ethnic affairs and finally employment and industrial relations. The last two portfolios saw a Fraser–Macphee concord based on their belief in a non-discriminatory immigration program buttressed by a domestic philosophy of multiculturalism and a conciliatory approach towards the trade unions. Fraser and Macphee were united in industrial relations and multiculturalism, two areas of turbulence looming in the 1980s.

Thus was born the role to which Macphee appointed himself during the decade: upholder of the Fraser legacy. As the Liberals moved towards free market policies and attacked Fraser's performance, Macphee emerged as the chief point of resistance. He upheld what he called tolerant and compassionate liberalism. He abhorred the imitators of Thatcher and Reagan. He defended state power, social justice, feminism, media ownership diversity, multiculturalism and the Arbitration Commission.

The paradox of Macphee is that such a mild man could generate such animosity. As his fight with the drys and later the New Right intensified, Macphee fell victim to paranoia. Macphee, a whiskey in hand by 5 pm with a journalist in his office, was a model of conspiracy. He was fighting the radical liberals and that meant, above all, fighting Howard. Macphee saw Howard as the internal enemy of the party; the agent who would terminate the finest instincts of the old Deakin/Menzian/Fraser Liberal Party which Macphee had joined in the early 1970s in preference to Labor. So Macphee fought to justify his choice of party and secure his future.

The wet–dry rivalry was personalised in the Macphee–Howard conflict. They fought over the future direction of the party, a battle which began in Fraser's last year and continued in Opposition, where Macphee was the champion of Fraserism in its final form and Howard became its chief critic.

The new Senate leader, Fred Chaney, was an excellent communicator, but too precious. Chaney was a Perth lawyer who had served in the Aboriginal Legal Service and helped to establish the WA Legal Advice Bureau to assist the poor. It was to his misfortune that Fraser had called him 'the conscience of the Party' without a trace of sarcasm. Chaney had been minister for aboriginal affairs and later social security. He was close to Howard and they became a familiar double at party functions. They called each other 'flint face' and 'human face'; it sounded clever in the days when Liberals could laugh at each other.

But Chaney was riven by a confusion—he sought power but paraded purity. He failed to perceive that politicians who offer to uphold such standards invite retribution from their colleagues if they fail their own test. Chaney's career would founder in the late 1980s on those issues of loyalty and trust on which he had put such emphasis. Chaney was impressive but left doubts about his toughness. After 1983 he rated behind Peacock and Howard in the leadership stakes.

Liberal Party history bred the expectation of a return to power into the 1983 leadership generation of Peacock, Howard, Macphee and Chaney. After all, the Whitlam government had lasted just three years and Hawke was unproven. But this generation lacked talent in depth and its fate, obvious in retrospect, was to serve as a bridge between the Fraser government and a future Liberal government. It became a generation half-chained to Fraser, half-pioneers of a post-Fraser era. It would fail to return the Liberals to power, the ultimate test.

Peacock's shadow Cabinet was balanced between wets and drys—these were very loose groups, not factions in the ALP sense. The drys were united by a philosophy; the wets, a more disparate group, were united mainly by hostility to dry policies. The main drys were Howard, Chaney, Peter Durack and Jim Carlton; the wets were Macphee, Steele Hall, Michael Hodgman, Peter Baume and sometimes Reg Withers, perhaps more cynic than wet.

Peacock was interested in numbers not ideas. His power base lay with the wets but he recognised that the drys were the rising power and that this was his vulnerability. So Peacock's tactic was to appease the drys, the core of Howard's support. By denying the drys any reason to remove him Peacock thus hoped to prosper. The upshot was that Peacock encouraged the triumph of dry policies.

The risk for Peacock was that he would irritate the wets and never convince the drys. Peacock was a pragmatist and an opportunist, skilled at image cultivation, shallow in commitments, friendly but elusive. Peacock allowed the drys to take command of the Liberal Party.

This had an important consequence: it gave Howard the status of intellectual leader of the party. This was a mistake by Peacock. He forgot the leadership axioms put forward by David Kemp in his essay after the 1972 loss—that it is the leader's task to define and articulate the philosophy of the party. Given the ideological transformation under way, the power of ideas was greater than ever. Once Peacock surrendered this mantle to Howard, he invited appeals for Howard to replace him.

The reorientation of Liberal policy in this parliament was achieved through two vehicles. First, the Committee of Review chaired by NSW president John Valder, a Howard loyalist, which was set up by the Federal Executive in April 1983 to conduct a detailed reassessment of the party and its beliefs. This became known as the Valder Report. The second was a Parliamentary Policy Review chaired by Howard to reshape policy for the next election.

The Valder committee was pluralist containing Brisbane's Mayor Sallyanne Atkinson; prominent wet Chris Puplick; South Australian leader John Olsen; but its clout lay with the drys: Valder, Jim Carlton, Peter Shack and David Kemp. Its secretary was Nick Minchin, deputy federal director.

The report presented in September 1983 was dominated by three themes: the philosophy of economic libertarianism; the need to reinvigorate the ailing party organisation with more members, better staffers and significantly, to increase the central authority of the party at the expense of the states; and thirdly, the need to ensure that in office the Liberal Party laid down its own priorities for the Public Service rather than the reverse.

In this report the Liberal Party embraced officially the damning interpretation which the free market lobby had laid against the Fraser government: it had failed because it lacked the courage to implement economic libertarianism and thereby succumbed to expediency, inconsistency and the fatal gap between rhetoric and action. Analysing the reasons for Fraser's failure the report said: 'One reason more than any other was put to the Committee again and again—loss of credibility. Often our performance in government did not match our rhetoric. Opportunities were missed. We did not practice what we preached. Too often we were seen to be inconsistent, too pragmatic and finally too expedient.' Once the Liberals accepted this view of their own government it was inevitable that others would also accept it.

The report diagnosed Australia's sickness as the expansion in the size of government in the 1970s: this was the root cause of high inflation, high unemployment and low economic growth. It admitted that Australia was one of the first democratic nations to develop a substantive role for government. But the system had led to an overdependence of individuals on governments, a welfare mentality in both corporate and individual terms—a criticism of the Deakin inheritance:

> Australians have tended to see government authority as a solution to many problems. In the 1970s an historic turning point was reached. The cost of imposing excessive responsibilities on government became apparent in the disruptive effects of large and growing government on the rest of the social and economic fabric of the nation.

The Valder Committee found the solution required:

> . . . decentralised decision making, in government, the economy and in other areas of social life. In economic life, the system of private enterprise coordinated by an efficient pricing system and market disciplines is more essential than ever before to achieving the values of

105

Australians. The extension of market coordination in education, in health, in welfare and in relation to many services previously centralised in government should be an objective of any future Liberal government . . .

The big institutions of Australian society—the public sector, business and trade unions—must be effectively accountable to the Australian people. The accountability of business is best achieved by the promotion of effective competition in the marketplace, not by the imposition of increased government control . . . The committee believes that the development of a program to deal with union power is a major obligation of the Liberal Party to the Australian community.[9]

The report called upon the Liberals to 'plan a major democratisation and rationalisation of the government sector'—regulation should be cut and a 'substantial privatisation of government commercial activities' be undertaken. The report said that 'taxation must be as low as practicable'—but it confronted the tax issue honestly: 'If taxes are too high, then government spending is too high.' Spending restraint was the key to low tax and a balanced budget. One consequence was the need to 'concentrate welfare benefits on those in need'. Welfare must no longer be seen as a 'system from which almost everyone could obtain something'. The link between high wages and high unemployment had to be explained to people. A more flexible labour market with wage differentials for skills was needed. The economic rigidity of centralised wage fixation penalised enterprise and small business.

The committee upheld the integrity of Australia's national institutions and symbols. Regard for the Constitution, the monarchy and the parliamentary system should be strengthened, not weakened. But Australia should accept its diversity:

The Liberal Party has actively pursued the principle of the multicultural society based on diversity within one national community. This is a principle so vital to the future well-being of the Australian national community that active government programs to foster it at this stage of our development are highly desirable . . . The Liberal Party rejects utterly racism, and other forms of discrimination based on group characteristics . . .[10]

The Valder report captured the 'free market' mood of the party rank and file. It confirmed the free market lobby as the dominant intellectual force in the party. Summarising the report's significance, one of its authors, Jim Carlton, said:

It was essential to have an officially authorised document which spelt out the course that the Liberal Party should have been taking prior to the 1983 elections, but hadn't. It was a seal of approval for a basic change of direction; a document moving the Liberal Party towards an open economy.[11]

106

The Liberal revolution

The report identified the erosion of the Liberal Party's organisational base, which would be central to its subsequent election defeats in the 1980s. Party membership was only 103 000, just 3.5 per cent of the national Liberal vote, compared with 10 per cent and 25 per cent respectively for its counterparts in Britain and New Zealand. The implication was that the Liberal Party was not 'properly representative of either its own voting supporters or of the whole Australian electorate'. There was a need for fresh members, renewal of branches, revival of state divisions and for a 'dramatic increase' in financial support.

The critical recommendation for the party organisation was to reshape the Liberals as a more truly national party. It was contentious because it meant some surrender of state autonomy—one of the most sacred concepts of the party and one of its chief liabilities in the 1980s.

The report advocated a stronger Federal Secretariat, more independent of the leader's office, which would coordinate national activities and direct both the federal campaign and a marginal seats campaign across all states. It called for a stronger Federal Executive which, while not having the power to intervene in the affairs of the states (unlike Labor), would increase its role in watching and supporting political operations in each state.

Most of these sensible recommendations were not adopted. Many were too imprecise, others were deferred because they were too challenging—the political willpower did not exist to force them. So the Liberals remained during the decade with an organisational structure that paid homage to states rights and lacked national authority and professional depth. They were easy prey to Labor's superior campaign techniques. The Liberals, in fact, were paralysed by their 'states rights' dogma. Tony Eggleton actually reread the Valder Report after the 1990 election to see if the Liberal Party, after four successive defeats, might yet accept some of its organisational reforms!

The Liberals, however, suffered from three other legacies.

First, the Liberal tradition of parliamentary policy authority over the organisational wing had helped to demoralise the party rank and file. Second, the poverty of internal debate and organisational vigour meant that full-time party officers were grossly inferior to their ALP counterparts in political and campaign skills. Third, the Liberals had not adjusted to the media revolution of the 1970s which left working journalists and editors, not proprietors, with a new power in shaping the agenda and results of national politics. The Liberals had a distaste for and suspicion of the new 'media' generation in newspapers and television and the upshot was a failure to communicate effectively to the people.

The enduring value of the Valder Report was its policy direction. In Peacock's speech to the October 1983 Federal Council he embraced the report's policy approach and, in effect, accepted its direction as his own. Peacock called the report 'one of the most important documents' in the party's history. He praised its criticism of the Fraser years, agreeing that 'we were seen to be inconsistent, too pragmatic and finally, too expedient'. The master of expediency solemnly told the delegates: 'Those are very telling words. We must remember them. They will be deeply embedded in the minds of all members of the next Liberal Government.'

In his speech Peacock went beyond the normal Liberal pledges of higher profits, economic growth and lower taxes: 'Government intervention in the economy will be limited to the bare minimum needed to ensure the efficient operation of free market forces which determine the allocation of rewards in our society.'[12]

Australia was too dependent on government 'as the first rather than the last port of call'. Peacock enunciated the 'freedom to choose' principle in education and pledged the Liberals 'to a competitive market in medical insurance'—a policy they would fail to master over the decade. Peacock stressed the party's commitment to deregulation of financial markets and opposition to 'unnecessary regulation' of interest rates. He pledged gradual but clearly phased reductions in trade barriers. The wages system 'must be sensitive to market influences and stress the basic link between profitability and employment'. This meant recognition of the 'sharp variations' in the capacity to pay between different employers.

Peacock was a conscript of history—the tentative prophet of a new order. He was an unlikely candidate for this role. No previous Liberal leader had made such a comprehensive pledge to free market economics. In one sense Peacock's motives were unimportant. The drys were determined to hold him to these pledges.

The October 1983 Liberal Federal Council was a turning point for the Liberals. Peacock endorsed the drys' agenda—but he won no respect from them. The wets like Macphee were edgy, seeing that Peacock was sliding away. The wets knew Peacock was weak, but to exonerate him they made Howard and Carlton into the demons. Meanwhile Howard was thriving, daily more popular within the NSW division, seen as a man for the times—a convert to the ideas of Thatcher and Reagan, liberated by Fraser's departure.

Howard and Valder were natural allies though not close friends. Valder, a confidant of Eggleton, aspired to become the next federal president. There was a growing assertiveness within the NSW division, described by Chris Puplick:

> The line was—we'd lost, we needed drastic and dramatic change at all levels. Now Peacock had never been in the business of dramatic change. He tried to accommodate but he was sniped at from day one.[13]

Formal approval for the new economic direction was given by the shadow ministry and coalition parties in autumn 1984 when the policy review chaired by Howard came to fruition. Its general economic principles (but not details) were released by Peacock, Howard and National Party leader Ian Sinclair on 12 April 1984.

The central elements were: opposition to big government and big budget deficits (Howard pledged to cut the $7 billion deficit by $2 billion); full and fast deregulation of the financial system including the abolition of controls on bank interest rates; restraint in the total tax burden with cuts in income tax and a shift towards more indirect taxation; a priority for deficit reduction before tax cuts; the dismantling of the ALP–ACTU Accord; cuts in real wages; a winding back of regulation of the economy; privatisation of the AIDC, Medibank Private and the Housing Loans Insurance Corporation, with other enterprises to be considered for sale including Telecom, TAA, Aussat, OTC, ANL and the Commonwealth Bank; a gradual lowering in tariff protection; and a 'freeing up' of Medicare.

This program was a triumph for Howard but no help to Peacock in winning an election. It was not designed for this purpose. It was crafted as a set of medium to long-term principles which reflected a new vision for Liberalism and the coalition. Every sensible Liberal knew the coming federal election was lost. The aim was to entrench a new direction for the party and a new program on which it would win a later election. The eventual leadership plans of the drys did not include Peacock. Peacock knew the problem with the free market agenda was that it would lose votes rather than win them. Peacock's greatest problem remained—how could he win an election? The drys were scarcely interested. That was Peacock's problem.

The coalition's major policy package received a mixed response. Some pundits recognised its long-term significance; others said it would be an electoral failure; a third group merely said that Fraser had broken his promises and there was no reason to believe the Liberals now. *The Australian*'s Des Keegan called the policy 'rational and hard-headed' and a tilt towards Thatcherism.[14] The *Sydney Morning Herald*'s Ross Gittins said: 'The only word is amazing . . . there is nothing in it aimed at winning votes and quite a lot which could lose votes . . . dry policies are an indulgence which can only be afforded by a party which knows it has nothing to lose.'[15] The commentator Max Walsh said: 'The Liberals have saddled themselves with a policy approach which . . . is not going to be implemented so long as the Liberals have to rule with the Nationals and that looks like being forever.'[16]

During 1984 the growing rivalry between Peacock and Howard began to spill into the media. But Howard had no wish to become Opposition leader ahead of certain electoral defeat. The Liberal leadership was a poisoned chalice, as Hawke's reelection was certain. Howard concluded that if the party was doomed to lose then it must lose under Peacock.

The coalition had two difficulties in marketing its economic framework. First, Hawke's economic policy was a success and second, there was little appeal in the coalition policy—just the opposite with its pledge of small government, enterprise sell-offs, real wage cuts and higher indirect taxes.

The tragedy for the 1983 Peacock–Howard generation is that it failed to function as a team throughout the decade. There were three possible obstacles to a Liberal return—the entrenchment of internal divisions, the emergence of a formidable Hawke ALP government, and a deepening repudiation of the Fraser era throughout the community—each of which eventuated. The irony for the 1983 generation is that while repudiating Fraserism it was tainted by its association with the Fraser years.

The initial victory of the free market lobby within the Liberal Party was achieved with only meagre resistance. There were squabbles over policies but no comprehensive traditional or wet philosophy was offered as a counterpoint. The drys never defeated the wets; they just occupied a vacuum. The Liberals had rarely lived by ideas. When faced with a new phenomenon—a comprehensive fashionable free market theory—the Liberal Party just rolled over and acquiesced.

The victory of the radical liberals was the trigger for a new set of problems. The task was to make dry economics into successful politics. The Liberal Party had been established as a coalition of special interest groups— this was partly the reason for Menzies' success. The Liberal constituency included business, finance, farmers, returned soldiers, pensioners, home owners and housewives. Each group would be affected by free market liberalisation which would terminate their certitudes and the special sectional arrangements they enjoyed.

Embracing a new economic philosophy meant that the Liberals needed to invent a new political strategy. But in 1984 this point was not even comprehended. The political strategy had to serve two purposes. It had to persuade voters and convince the party's own ranks that free market policies were necessary. It also had to combat the Hawke–Keating party, which would pursue a dual tactic of 'theft and assault'—stealing some of the free market policies but attacking others.

6
The attack on Justice Higgins

The time has come when we have to turn Mr Justice Higgins on his head.

John Howard, August 1983

The most formidable target of the radical liberals was the Conciliation and Arbitration Commission—the issue which dominated the internal Liberal Party struggle. It was the oldest debate since Federation but this time it had a new twist. The issue was not just about wage rates and the division of national income between wages and profits. It was about the system itself; whether a comprehensive legal alternative should be established as the first step towards the dismantling of the Arbitration process.

The contest was between the centralised and decentralised industrial relations models. It was here that the Liberal traditionalists fought to halt the progress of the free market lobby. This was a battle between Ian Macphee, shadow industrial minister and John Howard who, as deputy, led the charge to free market reform. The contest was crucial in its own right and as a symbol of the dry/wet struggle for the Liberal Party's future.

Industrial relations was the field in which the wets were best equipped to fight. Macphee was knowledgeable, experienced and determined to resist Howard. He believed in the system of arbitration and was a reformer within that system. Howard's aim was to undermine the old system by having wages set by the market based on the different conditions in each enterprise. In its crudest form Howard wanted a humane Americanisation of the workplace.

The conciliation and arbitration framework had become the strongest pillar of the old Deakin Settlement. It had shaped the trade union and employer structures, the culture of employer–union dialogue and a network of complex legal processes. The dismantling of the industrial system was the greatest single challenge confronting the Liberal free market zealots.

111

The end of certainty

The Accord had a profound impact upon the Liberal Party. The Liberals believed the Accord would collapse in a public humiliation of the Hawke government—a misjudgement of Labor politics. But they were more accurate in grasping that Labor's financial deregulation would eventually destroy centralised wage fixation.

The Accord meant that the Liberals were confronted by an unprecedented alliance between Labor and the unions that was manipulating arbitration for its agreed ends. The Liberals realised as the 1983–87 period unfolded, more clearly each year, that the legacy of Deakin and Higgins had been claimed comprehensively by Labor.

Hawke made the efforts of former Liberal prime ministers to harness the centralised wage system for their own objectives seem vapid and inept. When this perception was reinforced by the necessity for an Opposition to find an alternative policy, it became timely for the non-Labor side to take an historic step and set itself against the Deakin legacy, against arbitration and the centralised wage system.

Industrial relations policy had bred economic failure under former Liberal and Labor governments. Fraser had paid the ultimate price when he lost power on the back of the 1981–82 wages explosion and subsequent recession. The magnitude of this failure is enormous, since Fraser had always identified the reduction in union power as an objective for the Liberal Party. But after seven years of office Fraser found that union power and employer acquiescence had destroyed his economic credibility.

Post-1983 Howard sought two industrial goals—a reduction in union power and a wages system which reflected market conditions. There were three groups which had agitated along these lines: the free market liberals, the treasury, now muzzled by the Hawke government, and the National Farmers' Federation (NFF).

The first strike against the industrial establishment had come from the NFF. After its formation in 1979 the NFF took a conscious decision to try to destroy the organised monopoly power of the trade union movement. The turning point for the farm leaders had been the 1978 live sheep export dispute when the farm organisations cooperated under the leadership of Ian McLachlan to defeat union bans on the export trade. This victory had assisted the formation of the NFF itself.

In this dispute the farmers had refused to compromise, to accept 'help' from the Commission or mediation from the Fraser government. They had relied instead upon the threat of action under s45D of the Trade Practices Act, which had the potential to impose stiff fines on the meatworkers' union which was halting sheep exports. This extension of the Trade Practices Act to union conduct had been made by the Fraser government in 1977 and was to become a landmark. It prohibited two or more people acting in concert to prevent a third person supplying goods to, or acquiring goods from, a fourth person. It was enforceable in the Federal Court. From the live sheep export dispute onwards this law became the basis for a new employer confidence.

In 1981 the industrial committee of the NFF adopted a hardline position in a strategy to change the balance in Australia's industrial system. The committee included future NFF president, Ian McLachlan, and a new organiser, Paul Houlihan, a former union official. The NFF sought a freer industrial system, a bolder stance from employers and reliance upon legal remedies against strikes. During the early to mid-1980s the NFF achieved two great industrial victories—the wide combs dispute and the confrontation at Mudginberri, both important in changing the industrial power balance. The NFF saw the post-1983 Liberal moves to redraft its industrial policy as welcome but belated.

Howard had concluded that the misjudgement of the Fraser era had been to accept the industrial relations status quo. The Fraser Cabinet had never addressed any alternative to the system during its 1975–83 tenure. After Hawke won he made the Liberals look fools by turning industrial relations into a devastating electoral plus for Labor. He preached consensus, responsibility between the partners and a greater role for the Commission. Hawke taught the coalition a great lesson—that Labor could master the centralised system better than the Liberals.

In September 1983 Gerard Henderson published his article 'The Industrial Relations Club'—a clever attack on the status quo. His aim was to debunk and de-authorise the system. The article drew upon Henderson's three years in the industrial relations bureaucracy. It brought Henderson to Howard's attention and inaugurated their brief but vital relationship.

Henderson described the rituals of the IR Club—wine and song, compliant journalists, client academics, the pervasive ethos of negotiate, compromise, concede, and the annual ILO trip to Geneva. He depicted a life of comfortable belonging, occasional drama and elaborate ritual:

> The IR Club exudes an ethos of complacency and self-congratulation. Here can be found men and women who are reasonable and moderate. They alone understand industrial realities; they alone know how the system works. And it is they who can do deals and fix agreements. Within the Club there is no time for confrontation . . . The task is to secure industrial harmony. Economic realities take what is very much second place, if that.

Then he proceeded to the charge:

> A key sector of the Australian economy is virtually controlled by Club members. The Commission determines overall wage levels which have a direct impact on Australia's ability to compete on world markets. The Department of Industrial Relations advises the Government on industrial relations issues—including wages policy and proposed legislative amendments to the C & A Act. Union and employer members of the

Club have considerable influence within the ALP and L–NP respectively. Club members have been so successful in promulgating their IR ethos that it has become one of the sacred cows of Australian politics.

Henderson concluded that breaking the Club and its culture would be a formidable task:

> The IR Club is almost eighty years old and its impact cannot be suddenly overturned. Ironically the Club's longevity is used as a rationalisation for its continued existence. The Liberal spokesman on employment, Ian Macphee, has disparaged the view that 'somehow 80 years of history' can be banished. Normally this would be regarded as a tradition-bound (almost reactionary) position. But to members of the Club it is simple realism—nothing more, nothing less. A reforming government which seeks to achieve changes in industrial relations will have to take on not only the union leadership and the IR bureaucracy—it will also have to confront the industrial 'heavies' in some employer peak councils.[1]

Henderson argued that the Fraser government had threatened draconian legislation against the unions, but the IR Club was left intact after the Fraser era, safeguarded at the end by Ian Macphee.

Columnist Des Keegan from *The Australian* praised the article.[2] This was the day of Howard's August 1983 address to the National Press Club and after reading Keegan's piece he felt inspired to add to his speech the declaration: 'The time has come when we have to turn Mr Justice Higgins on his head.'

This provided the historical perspective for the political war Howard had launched. The Liberals as well as Labor had accepted to this stage the Higgins framework in the Arbitration Court inheritance. Macphee nearly had apoplexy. He saw that Howard was invading his own terrain; that Howard in this speech revealed that he wanted to bring down the arbitration house and reverse eighty years of history.

Howard had rung a dubious Macphee the previous night to say that he would be urging a more market-based wage system. But he did not mention the Higgins reference. Macphee says:

> It was a red rag to a bull. There's no way of getting the labour movement more against you than attacking the sacred cow of Higgins and the Harvester judgement and the basis of wage fixation. You may please the finance world but you'll have shopfloor ructions. Even the employers won't be happy.[3]

Howard attached great significance to this Press Club appearance:

> I regarded that speech as, in a sense, beginning the long fight to free up the labour market. It's interesting to reflect now that it predated by several years pronouncements by some of the latter day "new rightists"

on labour market deregulation. I think when you look back now, years after the event, that the philosophic change at that time was really quite mammoth.[4]

A few weeks later Howard wrote to Henderson that his article was 'an excellent analysis of the situation . . . very similar to many views I have recently expressed about the rigidities present in our wage fixing system . . . As I see it, getting away from comparative wage justice is fundamental to any effective alternative system.'[5] Comparative wage justice was a pillar of the system—the linking of pay rates across and within industries on an 'equal work, equal pay basis', thereby denying individual enterprises the capacity to set their own rates.

Henderson seized his opportunity and became Howard's senior aide. His first advice was: 'You've got to be stronger.'[6] Howard sensed that Henderson would try to run him intellectually.

Henderson recognised that Howard could see through the symptoms to the core of Australia's malaise. The problems of protection, government intervention, poor productivity and welfare dependence could be traced to a deeper culture—arbitration and the IR Club. This was the sustaining institution. Break this and the rest of the system collapsed.

The achievement of the Howard–Henderson partnership came in their first six months. They secured the opening breach in the coalition's support for the system. Once the breach was made the tide was irresistible. Their targets were Macphee, the coalition industry policy, the IR Club and the Deakin Settlement.

Henderson says: 'Howard had been very much traumatised by the early 80s recession. That was true on the left and it was true on the right. I think from this stage Howard started looking seriously to find an alternative industrial relations system.'[7]

Henderson's arrival as Howard's senior adviser was another sign of the radicalisation of the Liberals. Henderson's history was strongly anti-Liberal Party. Like Santamaria, he had dismissed the 1960s Liberals for their inability to prosecute their Vietnam policy. This perception was reinforced when Fraser failed to deliver on his hard economic rhetoric during the next decade. Henderson joined Howard to test whether radical reform was possible through the Liberals.

Macphee wanted to strengthen the existing industrial system by reform yet give the Liberals a position from which to attack Hawke. Macphee was a champion of the Deakin–Higgins legacy and described himself in these terms. As a former practitioner Macphee was skilled in industrial relations argument and complained that his critics didn't understand the system. His argument fell within the traditional Liberal industrial position. Macphee's problem, ultimately, was that the Liberal Party mood was turning against him. Macphee sounded too much like a Labor politician—in his endorsement

115

of a system the Liberals had always endorsed—at a time when the Liberals wanted an alternative philosophy to Hawke's. It was Howard who offered the break from the past.

Macphee warned of an electoral disaster if the drys got control of the coalition's industrial policy: 'It's hardly smart to tell your constituents they'll get a cut in real wages plus a confrontation with the trade unions at the very time that Hawke is winning with consensus.'[8]

Macphee opposed the Accord; he had no political choice. He attacked it for being anti-profits and, like all Liberals, argued that it could never endure. But Macphee then called for 'maximum efforts' to obtain consensus with the unions. He sought to revitalise arbitration, preserve centralised wage fixation yet improve the system.[9]

In his February 1984 draft policy, Macphee's ambition was to reconstitute the Commission as a tribunal with two arms—one to make awards, the other to enforce them. His approach was reflected in two themes. First, the tribunal would be required to pay greater attention to the economic consequences of its decisions. It would be limited to setting minimum award rates based on national productivity, not cost-of-living adjustments as provided by the Accord. Collective bargaining between employers and employees would be encouraged in over-award agreements which would be registered by the tribunal.

Second, in recognition of the need for greater sanctions the tribunal would gain extra powers of enforcement for its own awards. Macphee wanted the tribunal, not the Federal Court, to exercise the sanctions power. He proposed that action against secondary boycotts and the abuse of power by unions, under sections 45D and 45E of the Trade Practices Act, would be withdrawn and such powers vested in the tribunal. In addition Macphee wanted to empower the Commission to help restructure unions on an industry basis.

Macphee's was a variation on the Hawke model. The differences were that Macphee wanted informal consensus with the unions, not a formal Accord; that wage adjustments by the tribunal be based on productivity not indexation; and that greater sanctions be provided by the tribunal itself rather than the court system.[10]

Henderson went for Macphee's jugular in a memo to Howard:

> The end result of this policy would be to ensure that the Commission has virtually untrammelled powers in the area of industrial relations . . .
>
> No adequate reasons are given for withdrawing the right of individuals to take action in the Federal Court re certain limited industrial relations matters . . .
>
> The paper makes no reference to any 'opting out' procedures. Accordingly no pressure is placed on the Commission to perform responsibly—for there is no possible alternative to it . . . Outside the Commission there is no industrial relations salvation.

No attempt is made to define national productivity or to suggest how it is consistent with a flexible approach to wages policy.[11]

Howard challenged Macphee in his own paper to the shadow Cabinet. The essence of the reform sought by Howard was to secure an 'opting out' provision which meant that those employers and employees who desired it would be able to bypass the Commission completely. This became, in fact, the fundamental principle on which reform of the industrial system was based—the right to settle wages on an agreed basis without any resort to the Commission. It would establish the precedent on which an alternative system could be built.

Howard also sought to retain the rights of employers and employees to take civil action in the courts rather than hand this jurisdiction to the Commission. The reformers would never tolerate Macphee's effort to negate the new powers in the Trade Practices Act—on which the NFF had put such weight—by surrendering this authority to the very institution that they were trying to subvert!

Throughout the mid-1980s the government and the Opposition were obsessed with the need for a system which delivered competitive wage results. The politicians lived in the shadow of the early 1980s recession which in turn had its domestic origins in the 1981–82 wages explosion. For them the imperative was to reform the wages system to deliver competitive results and prevent yet another wages break-out which would further undermine Australia's efficiency and wealth.

Macphee argued that the discipline of the centralised system would mean lower wage rises than a deregulated system where employers would be exposed to the force of union power. In the mid-1980s this seemed correct, when Labor used the Accord to persuade the unions to accept voluntary real wage cuts ratified by the Commission. Macphee said his policy was competitive and that Howard was driven by ideology, not results.

Macphee's argument had power because many corporate chiefs, particularly in manufacturing, supported him. Business was familiar with the system; it wanted the protection offered by the Commission. Howard would face immense difficulty in persuading employers to accept his model, because it placed a new responsibility on employers who had grown secure with arbitration.

Macphee used against Howard the legacy of the 1981 wages explosion which Macphee (and Hawke) claimed as a case study of the dangers flowing from abandonment of centralised wage fixation through the Commission. In his strongest attack upon Howard's 'opting-out' proposal Macphee wrote:

None of the experts who appeared before our Committees, nor those who have written on the subject (Blandy, Gregory, Gruen, Hughes, Isaac, Mitchell of the Brookings Institute, Niland) believe that the wage outcome in Australia would be better under a collective bargaining system.

> While a tribunal continues to exist, it seems to me unlikely that many employees would voluntarily opt out of the protection of the tribunal, in order to negotiate for themselves wages and conditions below those set by the tribunal.
> Companies or industries most likely to opt out would include those most able to pass on their costs in higher prices (eg, the oil industry) and those with unions strong enough to survive outside registration (eg, the BLF).
> The effect of comparative wage justice in a highly-unionised workforce (53 per cent of the workforce, compared to 20 per cent in the United States) organised across trade rather than industry lines, tends to encourage flow-on to other industries regardless of the capacity to pay. Opting-out therefore raises the prospect of a second stream of wage-fixation acting as a pace-setter for the tribunal, and therefore a worse wage outcome rather than a better one . . .
> An opting-out policy will inevitably be portrayed as confrontationist by Hawke, particularly while the Accord lasts . . . (it) would be opposed not only by the trade union movement and the States, it would be opposed by major employer bodies.[12]

These were strong arguments but Howard offered two rebuttals. First, he was seeking enterprise agreements in the small business low-unionised sector, not collective bargaining at an industry level. Second, he said the early 1980s wages explosion was not the result of a true deregulated wages system. It was rather the product of industry-based collective bargaining, pay rises being passed on to the workforce through the Commission itself.

When the issue went to shadow Cabinet, Macphee and Howard were deadlocked and others were lost in technicalities. A working paper was requested to identify the disputed points. The basic split centred on Howard's 'opting out' proposal—the essence of his attack on Macphee. This would create a 'second stream' industrial system which Macphee was fighting ferociously. The secondary battle was Howard's determination to stop Macphee from making the Commission even stronger at the expense of employer resort to sanctions through the Trade Practices Act.[13]

The Howard–Henderson tactic was to open the door towards an alternative industrial system and eventually to see the infant strangle the parent. It was a medium-term strategy, not an overnight revolution. Their 'opting out' was geared in Howard's famous phrase 'towards the soft end of union power'. Howard saw the small business sector as a constituency of political support and an agent for industrial change. Henderson wrote: 'The opting-out proposal is aimed at newly established industries where unions have yet to obtain significant power (eg, high technology) and those areas where unionism is weak (eg, some service industries, some areas of small business, some exporters).'[14]

Overall 40 per cent of employees were covered by federal awards, 50 per cent by state awards, while 10 per cent were award free. Opting-out was intended to boost the final category. The trouble was that implementation meant breaking through the reinforcing federal–state system. Macphee said that Howard's scheme for an alternative system could work only with joint federal–state legislation, a problem when two-thirds of the states were run by the ALP. Henderson wrote:

> The opting-out procedure could most readily come about if the Commonwealth and the States (or a particular State) enacted complementary legislation . . . The recently announced small-business policy of the NSW Opposition makes such legislation a real possibility—in the State in which about 40 per cent of Australian employees live.[15]

As the battle neared its climax Howard gave the shadow Cabinet a note on 28 March 1984, arguing that the ultimate gain from his 'opting out' reform was superior productivity. This was the seminal argument. In the coming years it would become the centrepiece of the Liberal campaign to deregulate the labour market. Howard said that the existing system had a

> harmful impact on employment and productivity. Employers and employees should have the freedom to enter into voluntary work contracts covering such areas as starting and finishing times, hours and weeks worked, lunch breaks, annual holidays, penalty rates and wage levels (above a specified minimum rate) . . . This would encourage the creation of new jobs . . . Voluntary contracts would have to comply with Minimum Standards of Employment legislation covering such areas as: minimum pay; maximum hours; and safety, health and welfare.[16]

Henderson said: 'I thought the real issue was productivity, not wages. You can pay higher wages if you get higher productivity.'[17]

Andrew Peacock had tried to avoid taking sides between Howard and Macphee, his dilemma being that opinion was evenly balanced. Henderson said: 'Peacock didn't like argument, he found it frustrating and distracting.'[18] When the shadow Cabinet met on 2 April Peacock finally backed Macphee. Peacock had acquiesced in the other policy wins by the drys and to retain credibility with the wets he had to back Macphee on industrial policy. It had become too much a direct confrontation. Howard's agenda was radical and politically hazardous. If Peacock supported Howard he would underwrite too great a win for his deputy at too great an alienation of the wets and his own power base. But Peacock's vacillation before showing his hand pleased nobody. Macphee, a Peacock ally, offers this critique:

> Peacock wasn't confident enough in the economic areas to discern what was the right policy and how to deal with the people who would be offended by its adoption. The result was that on wages and industrial relations he was chairing a meeting which was evenly divided and he

119

seemed to have great difficulty in coming down on one side or another.[19]

The shadow Cabinet split 6–6 between the Howard and Macphee options. Ralph Hunt was unable to make up his mind and abstained, a disappointment to Howard who had hoped to secure him. Peacock then appointed a troika, Howard, Macphee and Durack, to finalise an agreeable form of words to bridge their differences.[20] Durack drafted a compromise formula which Howard showed Henderson who snapped it up. Henderson recalls:

> We now abandoned all other claims except for voluntary agreements. This was the achievement we won. The rest of the policy was Macphee's. I was very surprised that Macphee accepted the voluntary agreement provision. It was on this basis that Howard was able to run through the next two years saying that Liberal policy allowed for an alternative industrial relations system. It was the 1984 document that was the victory. But the Press Gallery didn't understand this and many saw the result as a defeat for Howard.[21]

Macphee's mistake was to conclude that because he had contributed 90 per cent of the policy document he had defeated Howard. He was correct in claiming that Howard's voluntary agreements wouldn't work as proposed; that few employees would chose to opt out; that the system was unworkable without complementary laws; that the heavily unionised building and transport sectors might bust enterprise agreements wide open and finally, that Howard was not offering a more competitive wage outcome.

The Liberals were doomed to lose the next election and this policy was never seen as a practical document for action. Its significance lay in one basic achievement—the breach of the centralised system. Enterprise agreements were a small step in themselves but an historic principle. The door was now opened towards a new system based upon enterprise bargaining. Howard and the free market lobby could now propagandise for this with the sanction of official policy. The voluntary agreements proposal still provided for changes to pay rates embodied in contracts to be approved by the arbitration tribunal—a qualification dropped later in the decade. But the voluntary agreements principle which Howard had won would guarantee the eventual eclipse of Macphee's model.

The policy limited the wage-fixing powers of the new tribunal to minimum awards on a national productivity basis and the capacity of the economy to pay. It rejected Labor's wage indexation as a recipe for more unemployment and inflation, a judgement the Hawke government embraced during the subsequent economic crisis. It provided for over-award payments to reflect the different conditions prevailing in, say, Port Hedland and Bankstown. These were Macphee's own proposals which represented a change towards more flexibility within the centralised system.

The truth is that any transition towards deregulation would take years, during which a majority of workers would remain within the Commission's ambit. This was recognised in every Liberal industrial policy through to the 1990 election, and is why the shift in Macphee's policy towards Commission determined wage rises based on productivity was so critical.[22]

The industrial relations policy revealed the influence of Howard and the animosity his rise was breeding. Macphee says: 'Howard assumed the right as deputy to speak out across every portfolio. In government he would never have done that. But Peacock let him get away with it. I wasn't the only shadow minister that went to Peacock complaining about Howard pre-empting policy decisions.'[23]

The reaction to the coalition industrial policy focused on the risk of a wages blow-out, a testament to Labor's control of the terms of the debate. The argument was that encouraging wage settlements outside the centralised system in a period of strong economic growth would finish in pay explosion. the *Sydney Morning Herald* warned: 'What happens when we are in our next boom and wages are threatening to go through the roof? Does a Liberal PM simply shrug his shoulders? Will Mr Stone and the Treasury write . . . that wages are not a problem because they are only reflecting market forces? Of course, they won't . . . the Opposition's policy is a victory of the Right over commonsense.'[24]

The strongest attack came from *The Age*'s Geoffrey Barker: 'The Peacock Liberal Party is a qualitatively different party from the party of either Menzies or Fraser. For Menzies Liberalism did not imply any commitment to laissez-faire policies . . . Under Andrew Peacock the Liberals have become gung-ho Adam Smith Liberals committed to the destruction of concepts like comparative wage justice which reflect rules of equity and justice . . .'[25]

Macphee, Peacock and Howard saw the policy in different ways. For Macphee it was the final concession to a limited form of wages deregulation: 'Australians have always wanted consensus. Certain aspects of our society, notably egalitarianism, are deeply entrenched. So we had to modify the system. Get away from indexation but keep the spirit of Higgins. You had to build on what Hawke had done.'[26]

Peacock saw the result as a success in damage control. It had resolved the Howard–Macphee split. But it gave Peacock no electoral bullets to use against Hawke. The success of Hawke's consensus, the economic upturn and the fall in industrial disputes, meant that industrial policy would remain a plus for Labor at the polls.

For Howard the policy was about control of the long-term agenda of the Liberal Party and the nation. Howard knew the dam wall had been breached and the irresistible waters were rolling towards a new industrial system. This 1984 battle was the decisive contest within the coalition over industrial policy. It set the future direction, sealed by Peacock's post-election decision to move Macphee to another portfolio which delivered control of this area to the free market lobby.

However, the attack upon the arbitration system came not just from the federal Opposition. The coalition's policy reflected a growing tide of opinion which drew upon support from farmers, small business and exporters. But it possessed another quality, an aggressive intellectual leadership. This was a reaction against both the Accord and the Australian Settlement tradition.

While the shadow Cabinet fiddled over technicalities, prophets were stirring in the land, launching a furious, urgent, self-righteous campaign against the industrial establishment. Some said these men were crazy; others that they were prophets of genius. In late 1984 Western Mining Corporation's (WMC's) Hugh Morgan and the departing treasury secretary, John Stone, took to their pulpits.

Morgan embodied the interests of the miners and exporters trying to compete on overseas markets; Stone, as the retiring senior economic adviser, represented the advisory school that wanted wages set by the market. They knew where to begin their attack—at the foundations—so they sought to destroy the reputation of H.B. Higgins, Chief Judge of the Commonwealth Arbitration Court, 1907–21, as a prelude to the destruction of his institution. Stone and Morgan, like Howard and the NFF, put the proposition straight— unless the Higgins heritage was destroyed, it would destroy Australia.

In June 1984 Morgan delivered a speech, 'Our Higgins Problem', to the IR Society of Victoria which drew sweeping conclusions: that in Australia's economic decline from the late nineteenth century era of 'Marvellous Melbourne' to the 1980s, the arbitration culture was a dominant factor. The Court, said Morgan, 'is a profoundly anti-market institution . . . incompatible with a dynamic, successful, growing economy'. Morgan complained that Higgins had been a classical scholar who enshrined in his Court the values of the Roman Republic along with its distaste for the man of commerce, the hero of the modern age.

Morgan quoted Higgins—'the more wages, the less profit; the less wages, the more profit'—to expose the economic primitivism on which Higgins' order was built. This static model, which assumed a zero sum game, denied the income generating capacity of capitalism. Then he turned the knife by quoting Higgins in the 1909 *Broken Hill* case, namely, it is better for a capitalist to close his business than to cut his wage rates. Branding this 'high-minded heartlessness', Morgan said Higgins embodied the fusion between lofty benevolence and total economic confusion and had created the Court on this basis. (The pen of Morgan's adviser, Ray Evans, could be detected in this attack. The H.R. Nicholls Society was approaching.)

Meanwhile in his swansong John Stone brought his destructive logic down on Justice Higgins. Using the lecture in honour of E.O.G. Shann, one of Australia's greatest economists, Stone went for the jugular. Ray Evans later called this speech 'the most significant attack on the founder of our arbitration system since Billy Hughes sought to undermine Higgins in 1917'.[27]

Stone resurrected Shann's immortal description of Higgins' achievement, namely, that he had 'renovated as a novel extension of democratic jurisprudence the mediaeval idea of the just price'. Stone recalled Shann's 1930 classic *An Economic History of Australia* to show that the intellectual bankruptcy of the Higgins' system was known and documented at that time, though ignored. He quoted Shann's 1930 assessment that Australia's greatest economic evil was distortion of the labour market stemming from the interaction of trade union power with the regulation through arbitration of wages. Stone identified the three 'malignant influences' responsible for Australia's ongoing wage-setting process—union monopoly power, self-serving arbitral bureaucracies, and short-sighted governments.

It was one thing, Stone said, for the authorities to construct labour market policy ignoring the role of supply and demand. But it was nonsense to believe that supply, demand and price effects did not operate in labour markets. The results were measured in the levels of unemployment. Stone said the wage system had become a 'national self-delusion'. He quoted Shann saying, as the Great Depression began, that the system 'concentrates the burden through unemployment upon the minority least able to bear it'. Stone insisted that during times of hardship like the 1980s recession it was absurd to have a wages system which prevented burden-sharing and which tried to deny employees and employers the right to cut wages to save jobs.

There was an intellectual rage in Stone's demolition. He likened the corporate state mentality in Australia to 'the industrial philosophies of Fascism'. He described the growth of arbitration to a 'pitch of idiocy . . . which has laid so sharp an axe at the roots of our national productive capacity'. Australia faced a potential crisis and arbitration was the core of the national malaise. Stone attacked the Commission's Accord-sanctioned principle of full wage indexation, saying that it 'is clearly completely at odds with any meaningful effort, as distinct from hypocritical rhetoric, to reduce unemployment'. Stone demanded the abolition of legal minimum award rates payable to people under 21 years which priced youths out of the job market.

Stone finished with a charge, then hope. The system of wage determination constituted 'a crime against society'. Australia's political leaders were 'accomplices to that crime'. The solution, as before, lay in the realisation of Shann's belief that 'in Australia free enterprise to solve the secrets of a strange and inscrutable country is in our blood'.[28]

Peacock had little interest in the ideology of Stone, Morgan and Ian McLachlan. He could pretend to ignore these men but he could not ignore their ideas. The critics were on the march and Howard would keep the Liberal Party in the vanguard.

7
Beyond White Australia
—a new identity

*If necessary a ceiling can be placed on Asian immigration—placed
openly and honestly.*

Geoffrey Blainey, August 1984

In the early 1980s the nation faced the consequences of the abolition of
White Australia, an event which had taken place less than two decades
earlier. They were manifest in the mass arrival post-1975 of Asian refugees
and immigrants which began to transform the social and ethnic nature of
whole suburbs in Sydney and Melbourne. This process raised two questions—whether the rate of Asian immigration was appropriate, and whether
or not Australia's ultimate identity was that of a Eurasian nation.

These issues were highlighted by one of Australia's prominent histori-
ans, Professor Geoffrey Blainey, on 17 March 1984 in a speech at
Warrnambool. His argument was elaborated three days later in *The Age*.
Blainey ignited a fuse that would burn with spasmodic fury during the
1980s. He said:

> I do not accept the view, widely held in the Federal Cabinet, that some
> kind of slow Asian takeover of Australia is inevitable. I do not believe
> that we are powerless. I do believe that with goodwill and good sense
> we can control our destiny . . . In the past 30 years the Government
> has moved from the extreme of wanting a White Australia to the
> extreme of saying that we will have an Asian Australia and that the
> quicker we move towards it the better . . . It is public opinion which
> ultimately decides whether an immigration program will succeed. At
> present the Government is shunning a vital section of public opinion. It
> is in the interests of those Asian immigrants already here, and
> especially those who have contributed so much to this country, that the
> pace of Asian immigration should be slower.[1]

The previous year, Blainey had visited an old Victorian goldfield which the Chinese diggers had once occupied. He had stood on a yellow-grassed hill above the diggings at dawn, the place where a century before Australians had discovered that multiculturalism could be fatal. Blainey, who was Chairman of the Australia–China Council, was rethinking the equation. He felt that Australia's tolerance was under too great a strain. His conclusion as an analyst of the Australian psyche was that a slowdown in Asian immigration was essential.

Blainey said that Asian immigrants were 'very conspicuous' and vulnerable in high unemployment suburbs. He said that with 2 per cent of the population Asian, it was a mistake to have 40 per cent of the migrant intake from Asia. He complained that national guilt was driving policy—guilt from the Vietnam involvement, guilt from international criticism on racial issues.

In mounting a response to criticism, Blainey hardened his position. He called Labor's policy a 'surrender-Australia' stance, warned there could be 'a Birmingham in Australia in 10 to 15 years time', accused the Hawke government of being the most anti-British in Australia's history, claimed that Labor's immigration policy was a formula to maximise the number of Asians, and said that democracy would not necessarily survive if Labor's 'Asianisation' policy continued. He recalled that during the Lambing Flat anti-Chinese riots in the 1860s, Asians were only 3 per cent of the population. Blainey's tone was restrained but his content was emotive. He resented the many McCarthyist accusations that he was a racist, but he should not have been surprised.[2]

Blainey did not want a return to White Australia, but he was motivated by an alternative vision of Australia to that implied by official policy. Blainey was a passionate nationalist who loved the Australian tradition and who recalled the remark of the Federation Father, Sir Henry Parkes, 'The crimson thread of kinship runs through us all'. He warned that government promotion of multiculturalism was cutting that crimson thread of national unity, that it was wrong to suppose Australia's future identity was as 'a nation of all the nations'.

Blainey complained about the disowning of Australia's past and the caricaturing of its history as a land seizure from the native people, one of exploitation and violence. Australia's wealth was forged by generations of its people's sweat, grit and ingenuity, a truth that was almost overlooked. To Blainey Australia was not just a large tract of good fortune to be shared with the rest of the world. It was a sovereign nation with traditions to be maintained within an immigration program.[3]

The dismantling of White Australia had been facilitated by political bipartisanship. But during the 1980s the issue became whether the introduction of racial pluralism into Australia would see this bipartisanship retained or broken. It was about whether Labor and Liberal would broadly agree upon the new identity for Australia or whether the parties would fracture around this fundamental.

The Hawke government had no policy to 'Asianise' Australia. The only reference of this sort had come from Bill Hayden, who predicted in September 1983 that in another two-hundred years Australia would be a Eurasian nation. But a spokesman for immigration minister Stewart West had told Blainey that 'increasing Asianisation was inevitable'—a remark which influenced his perceptions of the government.[4]

On trends at that time, 4 per cent of the population would be Asian by the year 2000, which would be more than three decades after the abolition of White Australia. Many saw this rate as evidence of realism, not surrender. The bipartisanship underwriting this trend was substantial, manifested in the Fraser era in the bond between immigration minister Ian Macphee and shadow immigration minister Mick Young during the intake of 90 000 refugees from South-East Asia initiated by Malcolm Fraser. Their aim had been to assist acceptance of these people from Asia and they had succeeded. Hawke, far from changing Fraser's policy, merely continued it.

The proportion of Asians within the intake in 1983–84 had risen but the reasons for this, some temporary, were identifiable. The main factor was that the Vietnamese refugees were now sponsoring their kin under the family reunion program. As this cycle passed the hump in Asian immigration would smooth out. Of course, there were underlying factors driving a long-term trend in Asian entry—the decline in Australia's appeal to European immigrants, improved European living standards and the rise in interest from Asia. (With more than 2 per cent of the population from Arab nations a similar argument could have been mounted against Australia being 'Arabised'.)[5]

Blainey turned his warning into a campaign, almost a crusade, as he predicted that immigration would become the most important issue at the 1984 election. He wrote a book and considered running for the Senate. He attacked on several fronts—claiming that the policy of multiculturalism since 1978 threatened to destroy stability and social cohesion; he criticised the size of the program and advocated a cut in the program, perhaps halving it, until unemployment fell; he wanted fewer refugees and more genuine refugees; a scrapping of much of the family reunion scheme, which he called 'farcical and prodigal'; and finally, fewer Asian immigrants, achieved through 'if necessary, a ceiling . . . placed openly and honestly'.[6]

The defect in Blainey's position was that his policy would reintroduce a racial basis to the immigration program. Given the legacy of White Australia at home and abroad, the consequences of a shift to the reintroduction of race would be adverse and far-reaching. The only alternative to a non-discriminatory policy was a discriminatory policy. Hawke in his recent visit to North-East Asia had declared that Australia must 'enmesh' with the region. The word was chosen carefully and would be repeated throughout his prime ministership. The practical and symbolic consequences for Australia of discrimination against Asian immigrants would render this objective an absurdity.

Blainey's argument that social stability was at risk was hard to prove. How many tensions are too many? Some tensions are the inevitable cost of social pluralism; others, the inevitable cost of economic reform. During the 1980s the Liberal Party's free market lobby was prepared to accept the social tensions involved in economic reforms like labour market deregulation and less government benevolence because it asserted that such policies served the national interest.

The basis for a non-discriminatory immigration program which accepted workers, businessmen, family reunion entrants and refugees from the Asian region was national self-interest. If Australia wanted better integration with the Asia/Pacific then it could hardly discriminate against the Asia/Pacific in immigration.

Blainey's opponents also believed that his case rested on exaggeration of the difficulty which Asian immigrants faced in finding a mutually acceptable position within Australia. Resentment had always been present against the latest immigrant wave—from Italy, Greece, Yugoslavia—now it was the Asians. Despite their high levels of unemployment, many Asian immigrants were hard-working, Christian, natural recruits to capitalism; they were upwardly mobile and spanned a wider socio-economic range than their counterparts from Western and Eastern Europe thirty years earlier. This suggested that their ability to integrate might be higher than that of other immigrant groups.

Blainey's campaign raised the risk that it would encourage the community fears on which he put such weight. Many Labor ministers said that he was making racism respectable; others that he was making Asians an unjustified target for economic blame. The *Sydney Morning Herald* editorialised that Blainey's 'mistaken view that we have an "Asian Australia" policy comes very close to a racist canard'.[7] The reaction to Blainey was an insight into the attitudes of government and opposition.

The parliamentary Labor Party was virtually united against Blainey, a measure of the transformation of Labor's racial attitudes. It was less than fifteen years since Whitlam had struggled with his immigration spokesman, Fred Daly, in Labor's last internal fight over its abandonment of White Australia—an idea which had been fundamental to Labor radicalism since the early 1900s. Contemporary Labor historian Graham Freudenberg believed that in the past Labor's 'commitment to White Australia was probably the Party's greatest single source of electoral strength'. Yet by the 1980s this source of strength had disappeared, and been replaced within the party, virtually from top to bottom, by a new faith.

It had been the 1960s generation of Labor leaders, Whitlam, Don Dunstan, Lionel Murphy, Bob Hawke and Bill Hayden, who symbolised the breaking of the nexus. The tradition was not only purged. It was replaced by a new ideology, initially racial equality, which grew into multiculturalism. These were strong political concepts within the ALP of the 1980s, beliefs underwritten by electoral benefits, as the ALP was a net beneficiary over the coalition among ethnic voters. It was Whitlam who pioneered the drive for the immigrant vote and by the 1980s there was a network of personal and institutional links between the ALP and ethnic Australia.

The important exception to Whitlam's record was his opposition to Vietnamese refugees, based upon domestic political legacies. Whitlam believed that the Vietnamese would provide the right wing with another influx of rabid anti-communist recruits to torment another generation of Labor just as the post-war Eastern European immigrants had become a constituency for the right wing.

However, within the coalition Blainey exposed a crisis of faith. During the Menzian era the Liberals had backed immigration on the bipartisan 'populate or perish' ethos. Succeeding Liberal governments had modernised the program—Holt began the abolition of White Australia; Fraser inaugurated a new phase of Asian entry and multiculturalism in a period when the program had lost its national security rationale. It is sometimes forgotten that before he left office Fraser nominated the growth of a genuine multiculturalism as his greatest achievement. But with high unemployment and Asian faces in the suburbs, resentment had begun to mount. There was confusion over the central issue—the national interest purpose of the immigration program.

Blainey posed the coalition the question: What did it believe? Did it back an immigration program including an Asian component underpinned by a domestic multiculturalist philosophy? Or did the coalition want modifications to limit racial differences and social disruption in the cause of a more united nation and the primacy of the Anglo-Celtic culture and Crown, flag and English heritage? It was a bedrock issue for Australian Liberalism. Its social conservatives feared the pace of change and its cynics saw votes in slowing the march towards the new order.

Immigration had been the sleeping issue of Australian politics for some years, a fact revealed in private party research. The 1984 immigration debate revealed the strains involved in the abandonment of the first article of the Australian Settlement. This was an emotional time, which saw the coalition flirt with the Blainey position only to retreat when it saw the consequences. In this debate neither side was properly served by its spokesman. The immigration minister, Stewart West, a left-winger, was slow, sanctimonious and prone to branding his critics as racists. His shadow was the Tasmanian publicity addict, Michael Hodgman, a right-winger, defender of God, Queen and Commonwealth, renowned for talking before thinking and branded 'the mouth from the South'. Hodgman had launched a campaign against Labor's removal of the oath of allegiance to the Queen in citizenship ceremonies.[8]

On 8 May 1984, nearly two months after Blainey had begun his campaign, Andrew Peacock, during a major parliamentary debate, declared his concern about the racial 'mix' or 'balance' in the immigration intake.

Peacock, in fact, was supporting the line which Hodgman had been developing since Blainey began his campaign. Peacock's statement came during a day of drama which saw Labor backbencher Lewis Kent climbing over the benches towards the Opposition shouting, 'You're racist bastards.'

In the debate Hodgman accused Labor of bringing about 'a substantial reduction in British and European migration' and 'altering dramatically the traditional proportions of Australia's successful immigration policies'. Hodgman declared there was no longer bipartisanship over immigration policy and pledged that a Liberal government would restore balance to the program.[9] A few days earlier Hodgman had set the tone by accusing the government of wanting to 'stab the knife deep into the back of the Queen'.[10]

The divisions within the Liberal Party were apparent on the floor of parliament. Macphee as a former Liberal immigration minister denied that there was any dramatic increase in Asian immigration under the Hawke government. He said the trend 'has gone exactly as I foreshadowed it would' from the period of his own administration. In an obvious criticism of his own side Macphee said: 'This debate has fuelled some anti-Asian sentiment and that is tragic for this country.'[11]

In a careful speech Hawke explained the hump in Asian immigration; he identified Fraser's 1977–78 boost in the refugee intake after the Vietnam War and the influx of just under 90 000 refugees, many of them from Asia. When the Hawke government took office it cut the immigration intake from 93 000 to 70 000 because of high unemployment. But it kept the family reunion program and the right of the Asian refugees who had settled here to secure entry for their families. It was the operation of the family reunion program for the Vietnamese within a smaller overall intake which lifted the proportion of Asians in the mix during the early years of the Hawke government. This was readily understood by politicians on both sides.[12]

In an appeal to the parliament, Hawke seized upon the image of the brilliant heart surgeon, Dr Victor Chang, who was fighting in a Sydney hospital to save the life of the young Fiona Coote:

> I do not know the antecedents of Dr Chang but I am sure it was not Gundagai or Tallarook. It was somewhere in Asia. Dr Chang has already saved the lives of some Australians. He has saved the life of an Australian shearer . . . these are human beings we are talking about, people who share the same sorts of aspirations and hopes for themselves and their families as we do.

Hawke then turned to a hard-headed appraisal:

> We are a country of just over 15 million people in a world of seven and a half billion but in a region of billions of people. We have to understand as Australians that that is where our future lies. It is where our capacity to provide a better life for our children and their children lies . . .. anything that this country does which is, in fact, or which is

seen to be, in terms of prejudice against that region would be not only immoral but also manifestly against the present and future best interests of the people of this country.[13]

Then Peacock unveiled a formula which he could use to address the issue Blainey had raised. He said the 'right number' of Asians were arriving but the number of Europeans should be increased to rectify the overall balance. Through this formula Peacock was accepting the essential point in Blainey's argument. He praised Blainey for identifying 'a dangerous drift in the country's immigration policy'. Peacock said: 'The Caucasian component has dropped and the proportion of Asian intake has risen . . . the Minister has to explain why the imbalance has occurred and what he is prepared to do to correct it.'[14]

Peacock charged that the Hawke government had altered the racial balance of the intake, with the result that immigration minister West was 'providing fodder for the active minority of racists in this community'. Peacock concluded: 'We want to see that the European nature of this nation continues in the sense that there is a balance in the migration intake . . . When the Minister says that he is not pro-Asian he is saying it not because we have raised it but because, firstly, some of his own people have said that has to be his policy and, secondly, his current figures give weight to that being a trend.'[15]

That afternoon Peacock and Macphee openly clashed over this new policy direction. During a bitter evening exchange in the leader's office Peacock demanded that Macphee backtrack, but was met with defiance. Macphee told Peacock that Hodgman was a dangerous clown and that Peacock, not himself, was in error since until the party endorsed a new policy the old policy prevailed (Macphee's policy from his ministerial period). Macphee said the Liberals should attack Labor's administration of the non-discriminatory policy but defend the principle, a sentiment which had strong support within the parliamentary Liberal Party.

Reinforcing these internal divisions, Peacock was rocked further by the response of the quality press. The *Sydney Morning Herald* editorialised:

> The Opposition, desperate for an issue on which to attack the
> Government yesterday signalled that it is prepared to run hard on
> immigration. And running hard on immigration means running hard on
> race . . . It is the Opposition and not the Government that is seeking to
> depart from bipartisan policy . . . It seems that Mr Peacock does not
> want a constructive debate. The Opposition just wants to make a quick
> killing.[16]

The *Australian Financial Review* said: 'Mr Hodgman is riding the tiger of racial prejudice' but that Peacock's offence 'is in a sense worse' because as the alternative Prime Minister he had supported Hodgman 'in the hope of scoring political points'.[17]

Referring to the Peacock tactic of pledging to reduce the proportion of

Asians by taking more Europeans *The Age* political correspondent, Michelle Grattan, said: 'It is a neat but cheap ploy, a way of trying to keep yourself clean while you hope the political dirt will hit your opponents.'[18]

In a subsequent statement Hawke commented that the coalition when in office had never identified racial mixture as a policy aim. However, his speech revealed the central ambiguity in the administration of immigration. Hawke said that his government 'does not consider that a balance or mix in our immigration program determined on racial grounds can have any place in our society'. But he added that his government 'acknowledged the need to ensure that our migration program does not threaten the stability and fabric of Australian society'.[19]

The figures for 1983–84 showed 20 per cent of migrants from Britain and Ireland, 16 per cent from Europe, 36 per cent from Asia and 29 per cent from other sources. Labor's policy change, in fact, had come not in the racial balance but in the skills balance. Labor lifted family immigration at the expense of skilled immigration, its concession to the recession. This switch would trigger a late 1980s debate about the economics of immigration.[20]

The shadow Cabinet had examined the immigration issue during this period and there had been much informal talk among shadow ministers. The original decision to reinforce Blainey's concerns was taken after talks involving the senior figures, notably Peacock, Howard and Chaney. It was obvious that the minister, Stewart West, was a vulnerable and a tempting target. Hodgman had been breathing fire. For the Liberals it made sense to rough up Hawke and shatter his protracted honeymoon. They needed an issue to break the pro-Labor political cycle.

Peacock was a realist and pragmatist on immigration policy. He was able to expound with equal sincerity the imperatives for both non-discrimination and social cohesion. Peacock let Hodgman run with the issue, offered him public support, but when the climate turned nasty was sensible enough to call a halt. Peacock saw there was some mileage in the issue for the Opposition but he would not sanction any deliberate racial campaign which he knew would be counterproductive. But he was determined to insist upon the Opposition's right to attack Labor and offer a new policy rather than succumb to Hawke's clever talk of the need for bipartisanship.[21]

Howard was ambivalent on the issue. He respected Blainey and believed that he was making legitimate points. Howard felt that the Liberal Party's record on immigration was a proud one, which gave it a moral basis from which to speak frankly. Howard was worried about Labor's downgrading of national symbols and in May 1984 delivered an unprovoked warning to Labor against changing the Australian flag. Howard respected the bipartisan immigration policy and its value in containing community divisions. But Howard was a social conservative and a national traditionalist who put a high premium on social cohesion.

Chaney believed that Blainey's comments had struck a chord within the community which should be addressed by the Opposition. Chaney, an opponent of any reversion to White Australia, said there was a need for a racial balance in the intake and that the Opposition should find a form of words to give effect to this policy. Chaney criticised Hodgman for trying to exploit the race issue for political gain and he repudiated any such tactic. But Chaney felt that political prudence required the Liberals to devise a response to community fears and he put this view to the shadow Cabinet.

Meanwhile, Hodgman had excited deep antagonism within the party. At one stage Peacock told Gerard Henderson: 'Blainey's a good bloke and he's onto a big issue here.' Henderson bitterly complained about Hodgman: 'He's the only anti-communist I know who can single-handedly turn thousands of anti-communist Vietnamese into Labor voters.'[22]

On 20 June Blainey declared that Labor would lose 'many swinging seats' on the immigration issue and that it would be forced to modify its policy. He predicted that immigration could be the major issue at the election.[23] The next month Hodgman said that the Opposition could win twelve marginal seats on the immigration issue, a misjudgement prompted by exuberance. At this point Peacock rejected Hodgman's prediction. It was clear that rank and file Liberal opinion was against Hodgman and rejected any racial element in the policy.

Meanwhile Blainey proved to be his own worst enemy. He pushed his argument to the assertion that because Asian nations lacked Australia's values—democracy, civil liberties, press freedom, religious tolerance—the arrival of Asian immigrants might prejudice the maintenance of these values at home.[24]

Professor Henry Reynolds, the author of pioneering works on Aboriginal history, replied:

> Blainey has exaggerated the threat posed by current and projected levels of Asian immigration . . . He said that while Asians were worthy of respect 'we do not have to see them as the inevitable possessors of this land' . . . Racists will certainly use his ideas, claim legitimacy from his writing, turn his phrases into slogans of hate. He will become, unwittingly, the patron-professor of the rag-bag right . . . current policies will see the Asian component of the population increase from just 2 to 4 per cent by the end of the century. It grossly exaggerates both the capacity and desire of newcomers to change deeply entrenched institutions and customs.[25]

In July 1984 the shadow Cabinet decided that the basis of its immigration policy should be a set of nine principles similar to those which applied under the Fraser government. They involved an assertion of Australian sovereignty over the intake, entry on the basis of Australia's national interest, maintenance of social cohesion and a non-discriminatory policy.

There was a major debate within the shadow Cabinet over the potential conflict between two of the principles: non-discrimination versus social cohesion. The issue was: if we're going to have a socially managed program then shouldn't that be admitted. Carlton and Chaney, one way or another, wanted this question resolved. But the traditionalists, led by former immigration ministers Ian Macphee and Michael Mackellar, carried the day. They said it would be a mistake for the Liberal Party to divide the nation, to depart from its policy under Fraser and be seen to be helping the racists. It was decided to retain the words of the nine principles and that the Liberals would not make race or the racial balance of the immigration program an election issue. It was a position which Peacock and Howard happily accepted. So the Liberals after the initial flirtation with the Blainey 'doctrine' retreated to the orthodox.

However the immigration debate was revived in parliament on 23 August by the foreign minister, Bill Hayden, in a tactical error. Hayden was agitated after a recent ASEAN foreign ministers' conference where criticism had been made of Australia for its anti-Asian sentiments. Hayden, worried that Australia's reputation was being damaged, decided to assault the Opposition in the House. He attacked the Liberals for a weak policy towards South Africa, quoted Flo Bjelke-Petersen supporting the League of Rights, caricatured Hodgman as 'vaseline slicked oozing his way into the contemptible barrel of racist bigotry' and claimed that former Nazis were speaking for the National Party. The attack was calculated and it misfired.

Ian Sinclair moved a censure motion against Hayden but the debate was dominated by John Howard, whose speech had a deep impact on the House and the media and probably had some influence in his rise to the leadership. There were two themes in Howard's remarks.

First was the Liberal Party's rejection of any stand against Asian immigration and Howard's personal rejection of this position—the theme which attracted media attention. But Howard devoted most of his speech to his second theme—the assertion of the Liberal Party's right to take positions on immigration policy without being branded as racist. Howard recalled Whitlam's opposition to Vietnamese refugees in 1975 and Hawke's implied opposition in 1977. He pointed to the Liberal record of tolerance on immigration. He said that Labor had no moral authority to make racist accusations against the Liberals and the Liberals would never be intimidated by this tactic.

This speech helped to make Howard briefly fashionable in the press gallery. Howard's performance was damaging to Peacock although this was not intended. It was final confirmation of Howard as a superior parliamentary performer to Peacock. It left the impression of Howard as a more honest politician than Peacock since his repudiation of the Asian immigration electoral tactic was contrasted with Peacock's flirtation with this tactic in May. Howard won a tremendous media. He was expected to outshine

Peacock in economics; now it was immigration. Peacock's leadership was being threatened by a potent danger—a superior performer.

At the launch of the Opposition policy on 18 October, Hodgman was deliberately low-key. He retreated from earlier calls for more European immigration in order to achieve a better racial mix. Hodgman confessed that he had been wrong in saying the previous July that immigration could win twelve seats for the Liberals. The coalition did not favour an overall lift in the intake but put greater emphasis on skilled and business immigrants. Hodgman refused to comment on the racial mixture but he defended Geoffrey Blainey as a 'great Australian'. During the campaign, away from the national media, he reverted to type.

In his 1984 policy speech Peacock championed the line 'One Nation One Future' and declared that Australia's social cohesion was one of its greatest achievements. Peacock warned that its maintenance would require judgement, notably on immigration and Aboriginal land rights. He said the Liberals supported the retention of the flag and the monarchy—thereby rejecting republicanism—as traditions which 'are binding influences in our society'. The Liberals could hardly imagine that within a few years Labor would be campaigning on republicanism as well as multiculturalism.

Peacock reaffirmed the principle of non-discrimination and said that 'the size and composition of the immigrant intake should not jeopardise social cohesiveness and harmony'. Labor was blamed for departing from a bipartisan policy and the Liberals pledged to restore it. But there was no longer any pledge to restore the racial balance. Peacock, in effect, bowed to the reality of immigration bipartisanship.

The 1984 immigration debate focused on racial balance but Blainey's concerns were driven by two other factors—his critique of multiculturalism and alarm about the economic implications of the program. These two issues would become the centre of the immigration debate as the 1980s unfolded. In fact, Blainey had made a sensible review of these issues more difficult because he had based his case on Asian immigration.

The coalition, after its flirtation with Blainey's invitation, declined to adopt his position. This reflected the majority sentiment within the Liberal Party for bipartisanship on a non-discriminatory policy. There were two lessons from this episode. First, Blainey had touched a nerve-centre of discontent with many aspects of immigration and multiculturalism which struck a responsive chord within non-Labor politics. Second, the anchor of Australian politics still lay in the moderate centre with common ground shared by government and opposition. Its strength would be tested during the decade with attacks from extremists of the right and left. The 1984 debate revealed that the long march beyond White Australia was strife-torn but irresistible, with a majority of both sides likely to support a multicultural future.

8
Hawke—from messiah to mortal

Hawke went to campaign with a two per cent plus swing to Labor and he came back with a one per cent plus swing to the Liberals. Hawke blew three per cent of the vote.

Paul Keating's diagnosis of the 1984 election

The 1984 election campaign revealed a vulnerability within Bob Hawke which left doubts about his judgement and conviction. It was at this stage that the central criticism emerged which would plague Hawke's entire prime ministership—that he lacked the policy belief and personal strength to dominate his government. Bob Hawke won the 1984 election by a comfortable margin. But he suffered a loss of political and personal prestige within and outside the Labor Party.

This election terminated the image of Hawke as an electoral messiah. He was reduced to mortal status, just a man subject to tears, blunders and setbacks. Hawke's campaign featured all three. The magic had to expire some time and perhaps Hawke was lucky that his transition to mere mortal in political terms came when his government was able to sustain it. The 1984 election represented a conjunction for Hawke of political failing and personal tragedy.

The failing was the shattering of Labor's dreamy optimism as its majority was reduced from 25 to 16 seats in a 1.4 per cent two-party preferred swing to the Opposition. The result was actually worse than that, since Labor's notional majority on the new boundaries was 30 not 25 seats so its majority was virtually halved. The polling trend for a year had pointed the opposite way: a pro-ALP swing.

In this 1984 election Hawke secured one of the best wins of any ALP prime minister. But it was a win seen as a rebuff, because Hawke failed to meet expectations. Hawke, in fact, was judged by new criteria. First, the Hawke magic was assumed to provide certain victory so ALP hopes, raised by opinion polls, were for a smashing victory. Second, Hawke was expected to repeat the astonishing electoral command which Neville Wran had established in NSW.

The NSW right wing was Hawke's closest source of political advice—specifically Paul Keating, Graham Richardson and Peter Barron. They had the mentality of political killers. They saw conservative politics at its weakest in their lifetime and the 1984 election as time for the killing. Hawke was their instrument. Their gospel was that Hawke should accomplish in federal politics what Wran had achieved in NSW at his first reelection in 1978. That was the famous 'Wranslide'—turning the knife-edge 1976 win into a landslide which guaranteed Wran at least another two terms and demoralised the NSW Liberals for nearly a decade.

Barron and Richardson had been Wran's close advisers. Their aim was the entrenchment of Labor at the federal level; the seeding in national politics of the deepest instinct of the NSW right, the proprietorial concept, revealed by their slogan that NSW was 'the Labor state'. For Keating especially this was a reflex response. In 1984 the NSW right readied for the kill. The trouble was that its leader was unfit for battle, disabled on emotional grounds.

The Hawke tragedy began during the Caesarean operation to deliver a child for his daughter, Rosslyn, when the doctors discovered that she was a drug addict. Mother and baby required treatment. Hawke was told by Hazel on 9 August, just minutes before his official talks with Malaysian Prime Minister Dr Mahathir. A shocked Hawke reacted in a pattern repeated through his life—he externalised the emotion. Hawke told Mahathir what had happened, much to the shock of his advisers. For months Hawke was consumed with grief and guilt, pondering whether his daughter's habit was a function of his paternal defects. Hawke, in the kinder words of one adviser, 'took an emotional sabbatical'.

Before the official dinner for Mahathir, Hawke broke down again with Keating as he told the treasurer about Rosslyn. Hawke was in tears and Keating was nearly in tears as the terrible story tumbled out. Keating always remembered these events. Years later he dated this, perhaps unfairly, as the turning point in his relationship with Hawke—the night when, according to Keating, Hawke stopped being prime minister.

Hawke was unready to face the people or even to run an administration. It is a periodic event in the realms of power, a leader distracted by a personal crisis, but since on this occasion it was election time the dangers were greater than normal. Barron and Bob Hogg tried to pull Hawke together. Finally Barron just administered a drip, in the form of a campaign script, hoping that Hawke wouldn't try to improvise. Hawke's performance in the 1984 election was the worst of the four campaigns he fought as ALP leader—1983, 1984, 1987 and 1990—and he was blamed by the ALP for the poor result. Several months after the election Hawke attributed his dismal effort to the distress from his daughter's potentially fatal addiction.

Hawke—from messiah to mortal

Hawke's calling of a 1 December 1984 election just 21 months after his initial victory in March 1983 was natural and justifiable. Hawke didn't have to run a three year term, thanks to the efforts of Malcolm Fraser. Fraser's calling of the double dissolution on 3 February 1983 meant that the terms of the short-term Senators in the new parliament would expire on 30 June 1985, which necessitated an election for half the Senate before mid-1985. That meant a Senate election in either autumn 1985 or, according to more established practice, in late 1984, since pre-Christmas was the usual election period. In order to spare the voters two separate elections Hawke was expected to hold the House of Representatives election at the same time as the Senate election, again normal practice.

In summary, from the time Fraser called the double dissolution in February 1983 it was clear that if Hawke won, the natural length of his first term would be only 20 months. This meant a second election before the honeymoon phase of such a popular leader had expired.

The constitutional rules which underwrote this were arcane, but they had been defended for years by an alliance which involved the Senate, the states and, when in opposition, the federal coalition. Referendums to enshrine simultaneous elections and terminate the separate life of the Senate had been defeated by disgraceful and deceiving campaigns mounted by the non-Labor side. Hawke was now the beneficiary of this conservative mania.[1]

Hawke faced an electoral killing field. Through luck and good management he had presided over strong growth, falling unemployment and falling inflation. The Hawke–Keating relationship was at its high tide. Hawke saw Keating as his chief asset in retaining the prime ministership—Keating's guise as rival was yet to materialise. Hawke praised Keating and publicised him as 'the world's best treasurer'. The pillars of Labor's economic policy—the Accord and financial deregulation—were both hailed as successes.

The Hawke government was, like all governments in the Australian political system, a short-term reactive outfit, smarter and luckier than most. While its ministers were superior to their predecessors they had the fortune of good economic news to help smooth their path.

But the 1984 election exposed several doubts about Hawke's own judgement. Labor's best tactic was obvious—a short formal campaign along 'business as usual' lines to convert Labor's strong lead into votes. Hawke's first mistake, born of foolish optimism, was to experiment with a campaign of just under eight weeks, unusually long by Australian standards. Its consequence was to give the Opposition the time to erode Labor's lead. Hawke was warned but felt that he knew better.

In his post-election report ALP National Secretary Bob McMullan said: 'I believe it would be universally agreed that the election campaign period was too long . . . the Party did not examine the implications of the length of the campaign for its strategy, particularly for its impact on the Senate campaign and for the timing of the "Great Debate".'

137

Having embarked upon a campaign of absurd duration, Labor failed to devise an optimum strategy for the torture. McMullan concluded: 'It appears certain that support for the Labor Party . . . fell during the course of the election campaign—perhaps by as much as 1 to 1.5 per cent.' And this was a modest estimate. Labor conceded that the Opposition won the campaign, if not the election. In his damning post-election report McMullan said:

> Strategic planning in my view was almost non-existent. At most stages during the evolution of the 1984 election campaign the party had no or insufficient knowledge of: the Government's intentions with regard to major policy areas; statements of substance made during the election campaign; the content and tone of the policy speeches . . . Post-election research confirmed the view current during the course of the campaign that the setting of the agenda remained firmly in the hands of the Opposition for the duration of the campaign.[2]

The problem was not just the campaign's length. It was the lack of leadership, planning and purpose—it was Hawke. Certain of his superiority over his opponent, Hawke's folly was to underestimate Peacock severely.

Andrew Peacock confronted a series of problems in the 1984 election, his first as Opposition leader. Peacock had no hope of victory, a fact conceded on all sides. Peacock's first task was to prevent a Hawke landslide—the objective of the Labor hardheads. He knew a bad result would provoke a post-election leadership challenge from Howard and others. Howard was stalking Peacock, ready to nominate for the leadership after a worse Liberal defeat than 1983.

However, the dilemma facing the Liberals in late 1984 ran far deeper. The history of conservative politics revealed an inability to sustain the structure of the party in opposition. The non-Labor side had fought under four successive identities over the previous seventy years—Liberal, Nationalist, United Australia Party and then Liberal Party again. The Liberal 1972–75 phase was the first in which the non-Labor side of politics did not undergo disintegration and recreation when in opposition. The rumblings within non-Labor politics were soon recognised by those with a sense of history.

The focus of discontent was the Queensland National Party. It was successful, arrogant, populist, operating in an arena of chronic ALP weakness, and was profoundly anti-Liberal. The Nationals relied upon Sir Joh Bjelke-Petersen as vote-winner and Sir Robert Sparkes as strategist. The party had seen Malcolm Fraser as a menace and now viewed Peacock as an amiable feather duster. The Queensland Nationals were flirting with grand ideas. Sparkes believed that the eventual defeat of the Hawke government could see the Nationals replace the Liberals as the core force in a new Australian conservative party.

Sparkes was influenced by the Thatcher and Reagan models. He believed in radical tax policies and rejection of Aboriginal land rights and was appalled by moves to undermine family values and the Queen.

'We can't at this stage say what should be done by the anti-Socialist forces if we were badly trounced by the ALP,' Sparkes said before the 1984 poll. 'We would have to look at all sorts of measures . . . The National Party is in a position, philosophy and policy-wide, to capture a very significant proportion of the anti-Socialist vote . . . People are sick of the middle-of-the-road, wishy washy approach.' Sparkes smelt the weakness in the Liberals.[3]

The paranoia gripping the Liberals was revealed in the pressure Fraser applied to Howard to challenge Peacock. It came at a posh Liberal dinner in Melbourne in late 1984 to celebrate the party's fortieth anniversary. Fraser hammered Howard: 'This Party could be doomed. You've got to do something about it. For all I know Sparkes might put his plans into operation for a new conservative party. Andrew's not performing, he's not making any impact. You should challenge and take over the leadership now.' Howard was incredulous. He told Fraser: 'That's impossible. It's unthinkable now that Hawke has called the election.'

After dinner a group of six went to the flat of state Liberal Tom Austin—the Frasers, Austins and Howards. Fraser tried again with Howard: 'You've got to put your hand up, John.' The passion of his repeated urgings stunned Howard. After they left, Janette and John Howard came to a conspiratorial conclusion—that Fraser wanted to eliminate Howard and Peacock simultaneously. Janette Howard told her husband: 'Fraser wants to finish you both.'

The next morning Howard bumped into Fraser at the airport and got the same message. As the six and a half foot former prime minister headed off to his plane he turned back to Howard, put his hand in the air, and said: 'Do it John, put your hand up and be counted.' These were strange days for the Liberal Party. At the dinner tables of its supporters in Sydney, Peacock was dismissed as a lightweight, in Brisbane the National Party was all-powerful, and in Melbourne, the party's cradle, the ALP was dominant.

Peacock's 1984 campaign success was an assertion of Liberal strength against two rival forces—the drive for a Hawke-inspired Labor hegemony, and the incipient revolt of the rebel Nationals. Peacock's achievement was to liberate the Liberals from their forebodings of doom. Tony Eggleton's post-election report captured the Liberal's euphoric relief at escaping from a potential calamity. He wrote:

> Against all the odds, the outcome was a stunning rebuff for Labor . . .
> the Liberals, led by Andrew Peacock, outmanoeuvred and
> out-performed the Hawke Labor Government in the 1984 election . . .
> it's generally conceded that we won the campaign. The Party and the
> leader confounded the media, the pollsters and the political pundits . . .

Far from sustaining its aspiration as the 'natural' party of government, the result left Labor defending a relatively narrow majority.[4]

However, before the election Peacock had betrayed signs of desperation. Peacock in late 1984 looked like a loser, had few committed friends within the Liberal Party and knew the sharks were circling. Defeatism was rampant and was usually self-fulfilling. Peacock's assets were his wife Margaret St George, a loyal though often ineffective staff, some old mates—Peter Shack and Reg Withers—both of whom joined his team to help, and, above all, his own determination.

In his 1984 campaign Peacock had two agendas. The formal agenda was the coalition's endorsement of a radical free market economic program which was a sharp departure from previous non-Labor policy. This was outlined in Peacock's policy speech but received scant attention in the campaign because it offered little hope of attracting the voters. Peacock had spent most of 1984 casting about for issues on which to nail Hawke and shatter his confidence. The three areas on which Peacock focused his election efforts were crime, the assets test on the pension, and taxation, an agenda driven by Peacock's sheer desperation—but it worked, finally.

At the start, however, Peacock had launched a counter-productive attack upon Hawke for being soft on organised crime. He had seized upon Labor's decision to terminate early the work of the Costigan Royal Commission and transfer ongoing investigation to a new National Crime Authority (NCA) whose powers were less than Costigan believed were required. Under parliamentary privilege Peacock accused Hawke of undermining the fight against the drug trade, of protecting 'some of the most powerful criminals in Australia', of being himself 'a little crook' and 'a perverter of the law' who 'associates with criminals and takes his orders from criminals'.

Hawke, in reply, said that Peacock had suffered a moral deterioration and denied that he was either a crook or an associate of criminals. The backdrop to these events was a heavy focus on crime, accusations about several prominent public figures, and inquiries by Parliamentary Committees and Royal Commissions which helped to generate a strong media coverage. These issues included a long series of corruption allegations within NSW police and political circles, the allegations of impropriety against former ALP Senator and High Court judge Lionel Murphy, and the sensational leaking of material from within the Costigan Commission which concerned the powerful media proprietor, Kerry Packer, who subsequently and successfully sought damages against the Fairfax newspaper group.

The climax to some of these events came when Hawke broke down and cried at a Canberra press conference on 20 September 1984 in front of startled journalists. Hawke's tears were provoked by a question about a media report concerning a drug case involving his daughter Susan. But the real reason for Hawke's display of emotion was publicly revealed a few days later by Hazel Hawke—that their other daughter Rosslyn was in a serious condition from drug use.

Hawke's aide Peter Barron was surprised but not shocked at the tears. He knew that Hawke liked being the emotional focus of attention. Hawke was guilt-ridden about his daughter. Once he had told the public he could cope better with the guilt—he felt better when the whole world knew. It was melodrama as therapy. After the media conference Hawke dropped into Barron's office. 'Sorry, it won't happen again,' he said. 'It had bloody better not,' grumbled Barron. But a few days later Hawke was almost sobbing on the John Laws show.

Hawke's composure had been shaken by the sustained attack to which he had been subjected by Peacock. Yet Peacock's attack did more harm to the Opposition leader than to the prime minister. Peacock never raised the matter of the Hawke children or criticised them; it was the Hawkes who took the extraordinary step of revealing the drug problem of their own daughter. Peacock said that Hawke's tears betrayed an emotional instability inappropriate for a prime minister. But Hawke's tears only assisted him to obtain public sympathy; a reward, in fact, for his self pity.

The policy issues were lost—whether the Costigan Commission should be wound up when the NCA was established and whether the NCA's powers should be greater or circumscribed.

Within the inner sanctum the Hawke crisis had produced intense exchanges before and during the campaign. Barron was appalled at Hawke's self pity. During the campaign he told Hawke, 'Your performance is a fucking disgrace. You want the whole country to feel guilty because your daughter got a drug habit. You want people to feel sorry for you. Well, it won't work.'

Hawke's personal crisis was profound. He was in a state of shock, depression and low self-esteem, an unusual condition for him. This coincided with a series of political difficulties. The trauma of discovering Rosslyn's drug condition took Hawke to the brink of resignation as prime minister. 'I was within minutes of resigning from office at that time,' Hawke confided later. 'I was very emotionally distraught.' Hawke considered resignation very seriously although he did not discuss this option with Hazel; she had enough worry about her daughter. Hawke said later that he was 'very close to resignation'. But, as usual in a crisis, the survival instinct prevailed.

The toughest decisions of the first Hawke government were a natural target for Peacock. They were the introduction of an assets test on the pension; the imposition of a tax on lump sum superannuation to encourage retirees to fund their retirement through annuities rather than spend their benefit; and an incomes test on the over-70s pension which only affected those with a hefty private income. These decisions had inaugurated needs-based welfare as a central theme of the decade.

These retirement policy decisions struck deep into Australia's emotional expectations. The 30 per cent tax on lump sum super to encourage retirees to make proper lifetime provision for retirement challenged Australia's almost tax-free lump sum mentality—virtually unique within the OECD. Labor wanted to kill the rort of 'double dipping' whereby people took a lump sum, purchased assets and then took a retirement pension too.

The assets test decision in the 1983–84 budget tightened pension eligibility and helped to direct payments to the needy. About 330 000 people would be worse off under the assets test while 170 000 would actually benefit. The decision was undermined by very bad public relations and Labor's failure to foresee the backlash. It provided a launch point for a pensioner or Grey Power movement. The coalition, the Australian Democrats and sections of the ALP made public protests. The scheme was modified by the Cabinet and then stalled in the Senate.

The shadow Cabinet decided to abolish Labor's lump sum tax and asset test when it returned to office. It was an apparent vote-winner for the coalition; it was also evidence that the new economic rationalism of the Liberals was merely surface deep. If smaller government, a touchstone of this philosophy, had any meaning it meant a tighter welfare budget and that necessitated, in turn, a needs-based welfare policy. The coalition might accept this in theory but its decision to put votes before savings on the assets test suggested that it did not accept this in practice.

John Howard, absent from this meeting of the shadow Cabinet, was upset by the result. Howard told Peacock that he disagreed with the decision—yet it remained well into Howard's own leadership period. Peacock exploited the assets test with deft cynicism, won votes at the margin but, in the process, undermined his own economic stature.

Hawke's assets test actually removed benefits being paid to some people, an action which violated the safety principle by which the Fraser Cabinet had lived: never withdraw benefits from anyone. Labor had a deeper belief in welfare equity than Fraser and was prepared to terminate some middle class welfare. The Hawke government had more political courage than Fraser's.

Peacock campaigned relentlessly on the assets test abolition and was assisted by a newspaper campaign conducted by the now defunct Melbourne *Herald*. It is hard to identify from this decade any other newspaper campaign conducted with such vehemence for so long against such a worthwhile public policy. It was the origin of the anger Hawke and Keating held towards the Herald and Weekly Times group of newspapers.

The assets test was never a primary poll issue, affecting only a small portion of the population. Peacock needed a bigger weapon—as usual, he stuck by Liberal practice and picked taxation.

In late 1984 taxation was looming as the main political issue of the next few years. Hawke was vulnerable here because of Labor's historic objective of a more equitable tax system through a capital gains tax or other wealth taxes. The taxation issue was linked to economic policy and to the criticism of Labor's second budget, its 1984–85 budget, for being too soft on spending. After this budget Peacock attacked Labor for its record spending and record taxation. Labor's response was central not just to the election but to Australia's fate post-election.

Labor's 1984–85 budget was an election budget. It offered tax cuts worth $1.3 billion as a trade-off for wage restraint and a real growth in spending of 6.1 per cent, down from the 7.7 per cent of Labor's first budget. The deficit was trimmed from $8 to $6.7 billion and the economy was starting to boom. The key to the budget was clear: the revenue surge from higher growth would finance both the tax cuts and a modest cut in the record deficit.

But Labor was running too strong a public sector in tandem with the private sector recovery. The government was fighting yesterday's problems, not tomorrow's. It was still spending its way out of recession when the task was to discipline the public sector to create scope for private sector expansion. The budget was too soft because Hawke and Keating knew they were having an election before Christmas.

Concern over the soft budget was shared by Canberra's economic establishment, the senior advisers within the treasury and the prime minister's department. But the most savage critic of Labor's policy was its chief economic adviser, John Stone. The split between Labor and John Stone—inevitable from the start—came in August 1984. Having reached the early retirement option Stone smashed his public service chains and released his long pentup intellectual passions. Stone and Keating parted as friends with Stone organising farewell champagne in the treasurer's office. But the relationship was doomed to a rapid decline.

Stone's departure had no immediate political impact but it helped to establish the economic foundations for criticism of the Hawke–Keating model during the rest of the decade. In his August 1984 Shann memorial lecture, titled '1929 And All That', Stone offered a new view of the economy based upon a parallel between the economic conditions of the late 1920s and the mid-1980s. He asserted the problems now were the same—financial mismanagement, protectionism and ossified labour markets.

Stone's speech made him one of the first prophets of Australian decline in the eighties. The main target of his attack was the Deakin legacy. He warned of the rapid growth in debt imperiling Australia's credit rating; the vulnerability of Australia to the fragile international financial situation; the risk of commodity price shocks undermining Australia's export earnings and its capacity to service its external debt. Stone said that while Australia's standard of living was much higher than in the 1920s, the rigidities in its economy had grown worse. He attacked the sharp rise—a doubling—in public sector borrowing over the previous two years, debunked the notion of borrowing to solve unemployment, and said that fiscal policy 'reflected a failure on the part of successive governments to come to grips with the real problems confronting Australia for the past fifteen years'.

Stone praised Keating's float of the dollar as 'the most important single step in economic policy . . . in the post-War period' (a reversal of his 1983 stance). Now he wanted public spending and the labour market tackled. He offered a dramatic departure from the buoyant consensus about the economy—he predicted a crisis, seeing great parallels with the crisis of the 1930s. Stone was ignored for the moment; his time would come in 1986 when Keating also saw a crisis.

In late 1984 the adviser best placed to impose damage control on fiscal laxity was Ross Garnaut, on whose advice Hawke would act. Garnaut had written a memo to Hawke in July 1984 warning against a soft budget. He told Hawke that if spending rose in 1984–85 as a proportion of GDP it would be a sign of policy failure—which is precisely what the budget papers showed. Spending as a proportion of GDP was estimated to rise to 31.1 per cent in 1984–85, compared with 29.9 per cent two years earlier and 30.5 per cent the year before.[5]

Hawke, at Garnaut's urging, exploited the budget criticism and the election climate to make a far-reaching pledge about budgetary and taxation policy for the next three years which became known as the 'trilogy'. The trilogy—restraint in public spending, taxation levels and the budget deficit—was created in three steps. In Cabinet on 3 September 1984 Hawke delivered a report on the means Labor could adopt to counter the criticism of the budget's excessive spending. As a result the Cabinet decided upon a deficit reduction strategy of ensuring that future spending fell as a proportion of GDP. Garnaut's identified 'mistake' in the 1984–85 budget would not be repeated. This was the first leg of the trilogy and it was sealed a fortnight after the budget. It put spending on a downward trajectory to generate scope for the private sector investment the government wanted—the first step in a journey that would finish later in the 1980s in a fiscal revolution and a record budget surplus.

Reduction of the budget deficit was inseparable from taxation policy—the issue which Hawke admitted was his main post-election challenge. The 46 cents marginal income tax rate applied at 1.5 times average weekly earnings, an onerous burden for too many. Political necessity demanded a taxation rethink but Labor had not yet applied itself to tax reform. Hawke had no tax policy for the election so he promised instead an inquiry.

Hawke and Keating wanted to survive the election with their tax options open. It was a perfect situation for a Liberal tax scare campaign, a technique which the Liberals had used successfully in past elections, notably 1980. It was the sort of campaign at which Peacock excelled.

Labor's bogey was a capital gains tax, which Hawke had ruled out during his first term. What of his second term? Labor believed in capital gains taxes and wanted to be reelected with an open mandate on this issue. Hawke was not selling a tax policy; he was asking the voters to 'trust me' on taxation.

Peacock targeted taxation, declaring in a famous cliché that 'as certain as night follows day' Labor would introduce capital gains, death and gift taxes. The turning point came over 17–18 October when industry minister John Button said that capital gains taxes, wealth taxes and death duties would be examined in Labor's taxation review: 'We are not going to be blackmailed out of an intelligent review of the taxation system.'

Hawke was now forced into successive retreats. Everyone in politics remembered Hawke's 1982 ALP National Conference remark about a capital gains tax: 'If we can't sell this proposition . . . then we shouldn't be in the bloody business of politics.'

On 19 October, on Perth radio, Hawke took a snap decision and declared that a national taxation summit was 'a good idea', catching the entire Labor Party by surprise. Graham Richardson spent two days making desperate phone calls to Hawke and Button warning that the capital gains tax issue would have a damaging impact in Sydney, that Labor needed an urgent meeting to rethink its taxation tactics. It was called at the Lodge on Sunday 21 October, the day before Peacock released his own tax policy, and it was a seminal encounter, attended by Hawke, Keating, ALP officials and Hawke's advisers.

Hawke's staff liked the tax summit proposal because it could defuse the tax issue for the election. Hawke was pledging a summit and reform based upon consensus. Keating, more orientated to the mechanics of a 1985 tax package, was unhappy about any summit—but Keating had to accept it.

Hawke released his detailed proposal for a tax summit and the nine principles which would govern it on 30 October, placing the initiative within the consensus framework which he had pioneered as prime minister. The tax summit became in effect a clever political device used by Hawke to avoid enunciating a taxation policy at the 1984 election. It rekindled the image of the successful National Economic Summit, allowing Hawke to rely on his 'trust me' message on taxation.

One of Hawke's nine tax principles as drafted by Garnaut was that overall tax burden on the community would not rise as a result of Labor's reforms. This, in fact, became the second leg of the trilogy—that the revenue share of GDP would not rise over the next three years. The third leg arose because Hawke had to guarantee that lower levels of taxation would not be financed the easy way—through a blowout in the budget deficit. It was formalised as a pledge that there would be no rise in the budget deficit as a proportion of GDP over the next three years.

The trilogy committed the Hawke government to a smaller public sector, lower taxation and lower budget deficit in his second term by a series of exacting pledges. It meant a new economic policy during the second term based upon public sector restraint and private sector growth.

The end of certainty

In his 15 November 1984 policy speech, Peacock outlined an alternative model of government to that of both the Hawke and Fraser eras. This was not Peacock's personal vision but a reflection of the philosophical changes which had swept through the Liberal Party since the 1983 defeat. The Liberal election policy was a philosophical marriage of free market radicalism—thereby marking a break in the Liberal tradition—and social stability. The contradiction between these ideas never registered with the Liberals. Peacock said that Australia's lasting prosperity depended upon 'a series of fundamental changes which aim directly at improving our international competitiveness'—a phrase which symbolised the eventual demise of Liberal provincialism. He argued that Australia's recovery from recession had been achieved by forces beyond Labor's control—the wage pause, the international upturn and the breaking of the drought.

The Liberal model outlined by Peacock had four elements: First, a freer, decentralised, flexible industrial relations system—a reform seen even in 1984 as the Liberals' most far-reaching pledge. Second, a gradual reduction in the overall tax burden and, in another breakthrough commitment, a shift in the tax base from direct to indirect taxation. Third, a reduction in the size of government and the level of government spending in the first budget and a reduction in the deficit. Fourth, the embrace of deregulation as the paradigm for business and finance with a phased reduction in industrial protection and in the financial sector complete deregulation of markets and interest rates. This model was a triumph for the Liberals drys and, above all, for Howard.

This free market radicalism had more appeal to the Liberal branches than to the voters. In 1984 it was irrelevant whether a Peacock government would have possessed the guts and brains to implement its platform. Indeed, this question, which dominated future debate about the Liberals, was not even asked in 1984.

Peacock did not promote this model during the campaign since he was desperate to win votes, indeed, to hold votes. On the hustings Peacock hammered another set of vote-winning pledges. For families with children a special deal through income tax cuts and child care rebates. For pensioners he pledged the abolition of the assets test; for the retired the abolition of Labor's higher tax on superannuation; for small business special tax concessions. He promised there would be no capital gains or wealth tax. The National Party secured a raft of tax concessions for the farmers. In a drive to entrench the coalition 'family' image Peacock pledged a crackdown on drugs and organised crime and an inquiry into pornography.

But the Liberal policy was modest on overall tax cuts. Howard had little interest in securing Peacock's election with a razzle-dazzle tax offer that sent voters weak at the knees. His priority was a broadening of the indirect tax base, a euphemism for the new indirect tax which he had wanted since 1981. Howard made the assessment that Labor would not exploit this indirect tax pledge because Keating had similar intentions. Hawke admitted under pressure that Labor might extend the indirect tax system. The ACTU, which opposed greater indirect taxation, was aghast. The issue was summarised by *The Age*'s Michelle Grattan: 'Whichever way you vote on 1 December, you are almost certainly voting for higher consumption taxes.'[6]

The second arm of Liberal tax policy, the family emphasis, was the revival of a Liberal ritual perfected by Menzies. The Liberals sought to give parents a choice on whether one should remain at home caring for children by offering a system of splitting their total income for tax purposes up to a set limit. The benefit would flow to all one-income families, regardless of wealth. They also offered a bonus for the two-income family—a childcare tax rebate for families where both parents worked at least part-time. These two ideas—a bias in the tax system towards the family and a tax break for working parents—were advocated by the Liberal Party for much of the 1980s and would be central to Peacock's 1990 campaign package.

In 1984, for the first time in forty years, a Labor government went to the people perceived as a superior economic manager to the coalition. Labor's model—the Accord, financial deregulation, fighting inflation and unemployment together—was a successful novelty. The Australian electorate, notoriously disinterested in ideology, paid attention to results. Hawke had results—the creation of 270 000 jobs in 18 months since the National Economic Summit, a fall in the jobless from 10.4 to 8.6 per cent, a fall in inflation from 11.5 to nearly 5 per cent, a decline in the bank bill rate from 16 to 11 per cent, and a year in which Australia had experienced the strongest growth within the OECD. Hawke said the economic outlook was the best in ten years and was taken seriously.

In his policy speech on 13 November 1984, again at the Opera House, Hawke claimed a 'supreme vindication' of the trust the voters had bestowed at the 1983 election. He said the nation had emerged from the early 1980s recession—its deepest economic crisis in fifty years—as a result of 'a new national approach which had never been tried in Australia in peacetime, the course of national reconciliation, national recovery and national reconstruction'.

For Hawke and Keating these were heady days. Their first term had been too easy, but politicians make their own luck. Hawke and Keating were convinced that Labor had devised, finally, a model which delivered a superior economic management performance to the coalition's. They felt that Labor had reached an historic breakthrough point, a turning point in its history as a party. They believed they had unlocked the door to a long tenure in government through two keys. First, they had shown an ability to run the economy by burying the ALP's traditional hostility to market forces. Second, they had created the best working relationship any ALP government had enjoyed with the trade union movement, a great source of political strength and legitimacy. The Hawke–Keating optimism was fed by a favourable business cycle and a world growth surge.

Hawke identified 'a new spirit of confidence in Australia' reflected by business sentiment, consumer confidence, falling industrial disputes, the trends in jobs, inflation and growth, and it provoked him to ask the Opera House audience, 'Is it any wonder that Paul Keating has been nominated as the world's best Treasurer?'

Hawke identified the Accord as the 'absolute condition' for producing a sustained recovery without inflation. It was the cornerstone of the Labor model which the coalition was pledged to destroy. In 1983 Hawke had sold his own persona to the nation as the symbol of consensus; in 1984 he sold both himself and the idea of the Accord as an institutional success. Hawke could now credibly attack the coalition for opposing the Accord since it embodies 'the spirit of cooperation and the process of consultation between government, business and unions, which has enabled Australia, at last, to break out of the cycle of inflation and recession'.

That a Labor prime minister could make this assertion, confident of reelection, was a measure of Australia's political transformation. The Accord was an arrangement between two parties, government and unions. It did not include business. This mirrored the party's priorities—it liked to help business as its 'special guests' but the unions were still the 'family'. Of course, the family could also be conscripted for sacrifices which guests might not tolerate.

Normally such an ALP–ACTU instrument at the apex of a federal government would be a liability. In the 1960s the idea would have been inconceivable on electoral grounds. But Hawke had achieved it and turned the Accord into an apparent electoral plus. One reason was that he initially obscured the institution of the Accord with the ethos of consensus.

Hawke named three tasks for Labor's second term—strong economic growth without inflation, major tax reform, and a drive to eradicate poverty and win a fairer society. His growth strategy envisaged a more export-oriented industry supplying technology, services and manufactures as well as primary products to the Asia/Pacific.

Labor's direct promises were kept to a minimum. Hawke tried to neutralise the weak points—saying the Medicare levy would not rise and the assets test would not become more stringent. His toughest pledge was to keep inflation below 5 per cent. Pensioners were not given any timetable on lifting the pension to 25 per cent of average weekly earnings and Hawke retreated on Aboriginal land rights. Hawke, in fact, was chasing more swinging voters. At the end of the speech his voice broke and his eyes glistened.[7]

During the campaign Keating outlined his economic framework—inflation would be addressed through the Accord and budget policy, not interest rates. Monetary policy—the use of high interest rates—was not a 'viable mechanism' for beating inflation and would be conducted to allow growth in money supply to accommodate expected GDP growth. Hawke and Keating held out the prospect of a lasting change in Australia's fortunes. They paraded their self-image as figures of destiny. They were shooting for a permanent lift in Australia's performance.

But Peacock campaigned better than anybody expected, surprising the Liberals as well as Labor. He displayed icy nerves and a capacity to remain immune from the terrible polling results for the entire seven weeks. He was disciplined and determined and refused to become rattled. Peacock was assisted by two other factors—Hawke's complacency and the media's reluctance to assess Peacock as an alternative prime minister because they assumed he couldn't win. Peacock's wife, Margaret, was a source of strength and often Andrew and Margaret breakfasted with the travelling media. Hawke by contrast was aloof and devoid of news for the media. When the journalists caught up with him Hawke was shrunken, withdrawn yet fascinating. (One night he predicted the internal collapse of the Soviet Union and the decline of the Eastern bloc.)

The 1984 campaign was notable for the televised Hawke–Peacock debate, an innovation which should become a permanent feature of federal campaigns. Hawke was right to have the debate despite the platform such a forum gives an Opposition leader. Peacock would have exploited Hawke's fear of facing him if Hawke had reneged. Hawke, however, was emotionally unprepared. He performed creditably but was not outstanding—Peacock, who looked straight down the lens, won the post-debate polling. Labor's real mistake was to allow the debate at the start of the last week of the campaign, thereby giving Peacock renewed impetus.

The contrast between Hawke and Peacock on election night was dramatic. Barron walked into Hawke's luxury suite in Sydney's Regent Hotel at 9 pm on election night. The tension had been severe and Hawke had flicked channels compulsively, searching for good news. Early in the count a Peacock win had seemed possible. But Barron found Hawke alone, staring at a gymnastics program. He had given the election coverage away. 'It's OK mate, we're there,' Barron said. 'You can stop worrying. But it's not a pretty result and you'll have to live with it.'

Hawke had to live with more than the result. Just before the election Hawke had virtually conceded a three-term horizon on his prime ministership, a concession born in weakness which would be used against him for years, notably by Keating. Hawke had said of his future: 'I haven't made up my mind but . . . I hope to serve this next term after the election on December which will take us to about 1988. I think I would like to serve another term then. By that stage I would be in my early 60s and I think by about that time I would probably think about retiring from the leadership.'[8] In short, Hawke suggested that three terms would probably be enough.

The loser was hailed at Melbourne's Southern Cross Hotel like a winner.

Peacock began the election with a leadership rating of 19 per cent and finished with 54 per cent. The long campaign, the debate, Hawke's complacency and Peacock's determination had transformed Liberal fortunes. Peacock had walked past his political death to live again. He had confounded the ALP, the media and much of his own party.

The final results showed a 1.4 per cent two-party preferred swing from Labor towards the coalition. In two-party preferred terms Labor polled 51.8 per cent and the coalition 48.2 per cent of the total vote. Hawke's majority in the next parliament was a modest 16 seats. The result defied the entire course of politics over the previous 18 months, which had pointed towards a pro-ALP swing—some Labor strategists had hoped that swing would be as high as 2 per cent.

John Howard, shocked by the results, looked doomed to the role of loyal deputy. Howard watched the results with his family, party workers and friends at his Sydney home. He never betrayed the frustration of the hungry heart. He had expected and did not fear a bad Liberal defeat; he would have relished the chance it gave him.

Howard had convinced himself that a major defeat could be beneficial, that an anti-Peacock swing was merely a necessary stage in the reform of Australian Liberalism. Just as the 1983 election had finished Fraser, so the 1984 election would finish Peacock. Peacock's demise would leave only one man to complete the transformation of the Liberal Party and to recover the prime ministership from Labor—and that man was Howard.

Howard and Janette had to rethink his plans for his ascension to the leadership. Only one Liberal advised him to challenge Peacock despite this result—his former economic adviser, John Hewson, a political amateur with a ruthless streak. But Howard cheered Peacock, forced a smile and deferred the pursuit of his ambition.

The election result terminated for the moment the rumblings from the Queensland National Party. Bob Sparkes' pre-poll view was that Peacock was too weak and that an amalgamation between the National Party and the conservative wing of the Liberal Party was the best option. He had canvassed this idea in private and hinted in public. Sparkes believed the 1984 election could become a trigger: a bad non-Labor result, as appeared likely, would intensify the pressure. Sparkes saw a merger leading to a new conservative party more similar to the Nationals than to the Liberals.

The apprehension within the Liberals over this danger is manifest in Tony Eggleton's post-election report. After noting that the main election consequence had been to revitalise the coalition, he listed five other implications of the poll: a reinvigorated Liberal Party at all levels; a silencing of the critics predicting the early demise of the (Liberal) Party; a reminder to the Nationals of 'the limits of their constituency'; an elimination of 'speculation about new political parties'; and a vulnerable Hawke and shaken ALP.

The 1984 election, a triumph for Peacock as a campaigner, also created false hopes about his ability. Peacock had averted a Hawke landslide, but he was never seriously judged as an alternative prime minister in 1984—that only came at the 1990 poll. The result, in fact, created a false confidence within the Liberal Party. Convinced that they were heading back towards power, the Liberals lacked the drive to reform their party in the 1984–87 term. This election was their false dawn.

At the technical level there were two defects in Labor's campaign. There was a breakdown between the government and the party in Labor's first campaign from the treasury benches since 1974. There was also a failure within the ALP campaign apparatus, notably its ANOP research, to identify and respond to the deterioration in Labor's position during the campaign.

In a criticism of ANOP in his post-election report, ALP national secretary Bob McMullan said: 'The failure of almost all research including our own to detect the substantial late move away from the Labor Party and the potential for it which existed is a factor which must be incorporated in future planning . . . [Labor] must also assess its relationship with ANOP.'

However it was Hawke who bore all the Labor recriminations. The 1984 campaign was an opportunity for Hawke to outline his vision of Australia. But he failed singularly in this task, offering instead banalities for nearly six weeks, emotionally destabilised by his daughter and politically paralysed. Post-election there was no hint of shared responsibility. Hayden was the cruellest: 'The drover's dog will win again but it looks a bit clapped out this time.' Hawke was even humble at the right-wing faction meeting: 'Some people felt they were going to this poll to win two elections. We've only won one.'

Above all, the election killed the fantasy about Labor being the natural party of government. The Hawke honeymoon was over. The gods had spoken and Hawke's status was cut to mortal dimensions. Labor was put on notice: it had to earn its votes. The ALP had to improve its skills across the board—persuading the voters to accept reforms, eliminating factional disunity and boosting its campaign performance.

In policy terms the 1984 campaign had seen Hawke develop two important promises. The first was to hold a National Taxation Summit which became the vehicle for the major issue of 1985. The second promise was the trilogy, which meant that Hawke, Garnaut and Keating had boxed the Cabinet into a new budgetary structure of restraint for the 1984–87 term. This was long before any economic crisis made such restraint an imperative.

The second Hawke government lived with the peril of a moderate majority, not a landslide. For the six years from 1984 Labor fought in the political trenches because it never won the high ground. That eventually made the 1987 and 1990 election wins greater political achievements—based on the degree of difficulty principle—but the toll was greater too. It was measured in personal attrition and electoral concessions from optimum policy.

The 1984 result changed Labor's psychology. Keating had smelt Hawke's weakness, his personal crisis, his failure to finish the Liberals. The NSW right concluded that Hawke lacked Wran's killer streak. Keating was emboldened when he saw the messiah mantle drop from Hawke's shoulders. Hawke had won but he was vulnerable. Keating judged that Hawke had been a poor campaigner who lacked toughness and the will to dominate his government. Keating could not help himself—he stepped forward to occupy the vacuum. Hawke had a finite period for his prime ministership—three terms, Keating gave him. Then Keating would seize the mantle.

But Keating, like the Liberals, read too much into Hawke's bad performance. The 1984 election became Hawke's political cross; he made a personal pledge to prove it was an aberration.

PART II

THE ECONOMIC CRISIS

9
The Tax Summit

*I think it's a bit like Ben Hur. We have crossed the line with one
wheel off, but we have crossed the line.*

> Paul Keating, 4 July 1985, explaining his
> position after the taxation summit

The Hawke government was reelected with a mandate to reform the taxation
system and a nine month debate ensued whose climax was the mid-1985
National Taxation Summit. This was dominated by Paul Keating's proposal
for a broadly-based consumption tax, which he pursued with a passion that
demanded reevaluation of his character as a politician. Keating lost his
consumption tax but still secured the most detailed tax reform package of
the decade, which was implemented during Labor's second term. The
paradox is that Keating's tax defeat was a hidden victory—Labor would
probably have lost the next election if burdened by a consumption tax.

The Keating package included a capital gains tax, fringe benefits tax,
elimination of loopholes and shelters, abolition of 'double taxation' of
dividends, and a lower personal tax scale with a top rate of 49 per cent.
Labor subsequently defied the conventional wisdom by winning its third
election in 1987 in a campaign heavily based on taxation issues.

The taxation debate was conducted in the shadow of a deeper issue—the
growing realisation that Australia's current account deficit posed a national
crisis. Taxation was the last issue of the Hawke years finalised on the
assumption of a relatively benign economic outlook.

The taxation debate of 1985 was one of the most intense public policy
debates in Australian history. To an extent the entire nation was swept along
by its momentum. Keating would have preferred a government decision
without any Summit; that would have been much easier. Confronted with the
Summit, it was Keating who shaped its intensity, agenda and atmospherics.

Keating's campaign was one of the best examples during the 1980s of
the forces remoulding Australian politics and the ALP. His tax policy came

155

from the treasury, not the party; it was legitimated in terms of the internationalisation of the economy; it was sold as part of a series of political and corporate trade-offs which typified the 1980s ALP; it was an amalgamation between Labor's traditional equity goals and the economic efficiency ethic of the Labor modernists; but it provided the best insight into the gulf—in the case of the consumption tax an unbridgeable gulf—between Labor's self-image as a party still supporting the working man and the realisation of its role as 'first-best' economic reformer.

The treasury convinced Keating of the need for a consumption tax just as it had convinced John Howard. The timing and the situation were perfect. Keating was at the apex of his authority, inexperienced enough to feel invincible and sufficiently blooded to be formidable. Labor had a new three year term ahead. The voters wanted a better tax system and the ALP had an opportunity to impose a fairer tax system.

However, there were three problems. The ALP was divided, hopelessly, about the design of a tax reform package. Secondly, the Tax Summit was a serious obstacle to reform since it required consensus about income redistribution where there was a complicated pattern of winners and losers. Agreement was only possible if interest groups put the national interest before self-interest, hardly an Australian characteristic. Tax policy by its nature is an arena for resolute decision-making by Cabinets, not for opinion tasting. Finally, Hawke's late 1984 malaise, originating with his family problems, far from being cured, had advanced into a prime ministerial slough that affected Labor's ability to govern.

The tax struggle opened a spectacular window on the Hawke–Keating relationship—an effective working partnership and a mounting power struggle. It captured these competing elements, almost daily, just as a sheet of glass when tilted offers an example of both refraction and reflection. It implanted in the public consciousness for the first time the impression of Keating as the dominant force and Hawke as the cautious arbiter; Keating as crazy brave, Hawke as phoney tough. It revealed a panache and fatalism in Keating which mocked his stereotyping as a narrow NSW right-wing operative and invited another comparison: with Whitlam's 'crash through or crash' compulsion.

The tax debate provided an explosive political climate within the ALP during 1985. It asked the party, in effect, to identify its trade-off point between good policy and political survival. It forced every major community group, the ACTU, the business community, and welfare organisations, to address the need for a better tax system—a bonus from the Summit. But the greatest paradox is that the tax issue over which Labor agonised finally throttled the Opposition, an unexpected dividend.

The Opposition repudiated Labor's final tax package. Indeed, the coalition became mesmerised by taxation. Convinced that taxation was its election salvation, the Opposition sank into populism and a series of tax-induced convulsions which finished in its 1987 campaign ignominy. The coalition cannibalised itself over taxation, offering concessions to sectional interests and pandering to the community interests which Labor policy was attempting to subsume in the general interest.

A few days after the 1984 election, Hawke, Keating and their advisers met at the Lodge to discuss tax reform. They had the nine principles for reform as announced in the campaign: no overall tax increase; more cuts in personal income tax; a crackdown against tax avoidance and evasion; a simpler tax system; a more progressive system in which tax is paid according to capacity to pay; no disadvantage to welfare beneficiaries; no indirect taxation expansion that might prejudice wage restraint; a package which facilitated investment and employment; and finally, proposals which had wide community support—a list impossible to realise in full.

It was decided to conduct a feasibility study into the major options, in particular a broadly-based indirect tax, through the creation of a task force. This was later refined as a draft White Paper. The task force was chaired by a senior treasury officer, Ted Evans, serviced by the treasury, and included among others David Morgan (treasury), Greg Smith (Keating's office), Ross Garnaut (Hawke's office) and Ed Visbord (prime minister's department), as well as tax office experts.

It was an immediate battle. Keating and the treasury had made a blood pact: they would force through a mega-reform with a new indirect tax. The treasury saw that it had a 'once-in-a-generation' opportunity to secure these structural changes. The treasury was emboldened by Keating's political flair and clout, just as Keating was strengthened by treasury steel and expertise. The decision was akin to a chemical reaction. Evans and Morgan were zealots for a sweeping reform package; so was Keating's office, led by Tony Cole and Smith, both treasury officers. Treasury, long accustomed to political cowardice, grew excited now and began to burn the edifices of policy mediocrity.

The Keating–treasury tactic was to hijack the tax agenda. The treasury was not interested in an analysis of options; its mind was set. For the cognoscenti this was an old debate. The Asprey Review in the early 1970s, twelve years before, had provided a sustained argument for a broadly-based indirect tax. It was the norm in most OECD nations and overwhelmingly supported in the tax literature. The gameplan was conceived: the treasury wanted to broaden the tax base on the principle that the broader the base, the more scope to cut tax rates. The economics meant a more efficient tax system. The politics lay in using the lower rates to sell the broader base.

Keating believed that Labor could win the next election on a three year program of economic performance and tax reform. But the only method of making steep and lasting cuts to the income tax scale was by raising extra revenue from an indirect tax. The Opposition had campaigned at the 1984 election on a major extension of the indirect tax base. Politicians had to address the situation where the marginal tax rate on average weekly earnings was now 46 per cent, an unacceptable burden.

Keating's plan was to beat the Opposition to this reform—implement the massive switch from direct to indirect taxation; lock in the steep cuts in the personal rate scale as the selling point; and finally, unlike the Liberals, maintain the progressivity of the overall system by attacking the tax shelters of the better-off and introducing a capital gains tax. It was an audacious gameplan but Keating believed its economic and political symmetry would deliver success.

Hawke, unlike Keating, was surrounded by sceptics of two types: political and economic. His political advisers, Peter Barron from the right wing and Bob Hogg from the left wing, urged extreme caution. Their fear was that Labor would be sucked into electoral suicide. The NSW right held that tax increases were electoral poison but Labor was talking about an even greater risk—the introduction not just of a new tax, but a series of new taxes, each likely to alienate a section of the community. The capital gains tax would strike the rich and the middle class, the consumption tax the poor. Despite the offsetting income tax cuts it was a potential electoral nightmare. Labor would alienate the working class and the middle class.

Graham Richardson, speaking for the right wing, told Hawke in March 1985 that if Labor implemented a capital gains tax it would lose the next election. Meanwhile the left wing was horrified: here was a tax package which seemed to achieve a unique double: violate Labor principles on indirect taxation and lose an election.

Hawke's main economic advisers, Garnaut and Visbord, grew more hostile with each task force meeting. Garnaut advised Hawke at the start that a consumption tax was 'desirable' provided it didn't damage Labor's other policy priorities. But he finished a dedicated opponent. Visbord was a veteran of this issue from previous tax battles. He told Hawke that a sensible tax package was possible without a new indirect tax. He felt the treasury exaggerated the economic gains from such a tax, underestimated the difficulties in the transition, and misjudged the economic policy risks.

Garnaut insisted that treasury must demonstrate that an indirect tax would not disrupt Labor's central economic objective of wage restraint to secure a sustained recovery. What economic impact would such measures have? How would the ACTU react? What guarantee was there that the total package would be progressive? Garnaut feared the glint in treasury's eye.

Keating, in fact, had to persuade the Cabinet, caucus, parliament and the people, a daunting prospect. But Keating's actions were consistent with a challenge of this magnitude. Success depended upon conviction. The treasury sensed that in Keating it had a combination of persuasive politician and policy zealot. Who knew what was impossible? Autumn 1985 in the treasury was a time for the believers. Keating sought the reform monument which had earlier been denied to Howard.

Hawke's office began to protest that treasury was pushing a specific package, that it was not trying to assess feasibility. Garnaut and Visbord would probe and question—but answers never came. At one task force meeting Ted Evans announced the White Paper would be devoted to an exposition of the indirect tax. When Hawke's people protested, Evans replied, 'That's the instruction we're under.' When drafts of the White Paper were prepared, Garnaut and Visbord complained that it assumed the decision for an indirect tax had been taken. Treasury just ploughed ahead. Garnaut and Visbord complained to Hawke; but Hawke just fiddled.

Hawke's advisers now grew agitated. In March 1985, Hawke travelled to Canada and the advisers hammered him in the plane. Upon his return Hawke held a Lodge dinner for his staff—Graham Evans, Garnaut, Barron, Hogg and media aide Geoff Walsh. Each spoke separately; each was against Keating. Garnaut felt sure that Hawke would kill the package but, typically, Hawke wouldn't reveal his hand. And that was becoming a problem.

The debate was a contest for Hawke's favour. Barron found its elemental nature remarkable. He would persuade Hawke against the package by week's end. But on Sunday Keating would go to the Lodge and talk Hawke back to his side. Barron would find at the start of the next week he had to begin again. Keating saw its funny side; he talked about getting Hawke back 'in the tax cart'. The Keating tax cart became one of the extended metaphors of politics. But it was not the only one. Keating, complaining to the press about Hawke's staff, said, 'They're offering Hawkie caviar, I go up and tell him to bite a shit sandwich.'

As autumn swept over Canberra, Hawke's dilemma was that he would have to choose between his treasurer and his own advisers. Here was an insight into Hawke's leadership—he led from behind. Admirers said that Hawke invited parallels with Menzies: giving his ministers scope, reserving his authority, holding his judgement. In truth, Hawke was crippled from within.

Barron and Richardson sensed his malaise. They were used to Neville Wran's panache and aggression. Hawke, by contrast, was a small, hunched figure, cautious, often isolated, unwilling to exercise control over the workings of his government.

Whispers began to mount about Hawke's indecision. In February 1985 the first Morgan poll appeared showing an Opposition victory (52 to 48 per cent). Hawke was damaged by the MX missile crisis in early 1985 when he had to withdraw approval for US missile testing near Australia; this in turn helped to trigger a major $A depreciation. Hawke called the financial markets 'irrational' but he failed, along with Keating, to explain how his government would respond to the depreciation. The more indecisive Hawke appeared on tax the more questions about his leadership style were raised. Hawke had taken a decision by refusing to take a decision—he would give Keating his chance to carry the tax package. Hawke believed in Keating;

yes, he would give Keating his chance. Hawke was in awe of Keating's will.

Officials within the treasury supporting the task force worked mammoth hours, all week, then at weekends. As deadlines for drafts neared they worked harder. Some stayed at the office all night, bedding down in sleeping bags next to desks covered with estimates and calculations. Wives ran support services, take-away dinners to the office, often bringing small children with them who bedded down as well. This was a treasury with an ethic of public policy belief which its critics, the well-paid financiers and Sydney money men, would never understand, because it was rooted in an idealism foreign to their nature.

For treasury now was the hour; it bonded with Keating in a common purpose, disgusted with the tax rorts and fragmented tax base. One of Canberra's most experienced correspondents, Michelle Grattan, said as early as April: 'I can't recall any recent policy issue where the positions were held with such passion.'[1] It was a passion which originated with Keating.

Keating's tactic was to destroy Labor's options. He depicted the existing system as unsustainable, therefore it had to be changed radically. Keating's aim was to generate such a momentum for reform that the politics would be transformed—that retreat would be seen as political cowardice and that biting the tax bullet would become the lesser electoral risk. Keating's message was that 'failure to act now will pose even greater difficulties'. It was a classic hijack.

This decision by Keating frightened the party—what would be the consequences for the government of repudiating the treasurer? It was a serious problem, the origin of the alarm within Hawke's office over Keating's tactics. It was a triple fear: that the public impression was that Keating, not Hawke, was running the country; that Keating was putting his own future into jeopardy; finally, that Keating was destabilising the Hawke government itself.

In the end Barron and Richardson called Hawke's bluff and broke the cycle. Barron told Richardson, 'Hawke wants the tax but not the problems it will cause.' Barron had told Hawke to oppose Keating but Hawke had refused. Barron sensed that Hawke wanted him to solve the problem with Keating—but that was hopeless since nobody controlled Keating. The upshot was that Barron and Richardson decided the best method of terminating Labor's tax paralysis was to support Keating. Richardson was convinced that the debilitating sense of drift within the government had to be ended. Their decision had an inevitable consequence—it forced Hawke to commit to Keating. It was a victory for Keating's tactics.

On 2 May Richardson declared: 'I have come to the conclusion that if this government does not move forward on tax reform it will be branded weak and indecisive.' Richardson declared the Keating package was equitable and saleable.

The same day Hawke moved behind Keating: 'I and the Treasurer have been and remain as one on the most desirable course in regard to tax reform.' Hawke said it was 'self-evident arithmetic' that steep income tax cuts could only be achieved through greater indirect taxation. Then he addressed the issue on which the ALP and the community were most worried: he expressed his confidence that suitable compensation arrangements could be devised for three million low income and welfare recipients for the extra burden which a consumption tax would impose upon them. Hawke and Keating were tied together; but Hawke had declared for Keating from political necessity, not conviction.

The vital constituency Keating needed was the ACTU—but the unions had always fought indirect taxes as inequitable. The Tax Summit was a political nightmare for the ACTU which was forced to choose between its tax principles and its political loyalties. The first session Keating held with the ACTU was a shocker, a fact which he managed to conceal from the media. The ACTU shot down treasury's plan and tore its framework to pieces. Treasury retreated, pleading for more time. The upshot was the most sustained dialogue on any issue between the government and the ACTU in the Hawke era. Before the Summit about ten meetings were held between the Keating and ACTU tax teams—about fifty hours of talks. The main unionists involved were Bill Kelty, Jan Marsh, John MacBean and Bill Mansfield.

These meetings fell into a pattern: the ACTU complained about the redistributional and economic impact of a consumption tax. Keating sought more time to convince them and kept telling Hawke that the ACTU would join his 'tax cart'. But Garnaut and Ralph Willis, both of whom spoke to the ACTU, reported the opposite—they told Hawke the ACTU could not be persuaded. Indeed, at one stage Kelty had wanted to shut the issue down.

During the second half of May the Cabinet held three meetings and spent 23 hours discussing the draft White Paper before Keating emerged victorious with Cabinet endorsement of his option as the preferred government position for the Summit. It was an extraordinary event: only Hawke, Gareth Evans, Kim Beazley and Susan Ryan supported Keating's position; it was carried against the numbers. Keating talked, seduced and intimidated the Cabinet into submission, leaving a legacy of bad blood. It was a decision devoid of conviction. Most ministers were unenthusiastic and some were horrified; but they knew that Keating's package would face severe attack at the Summit.

Walsh was Keating's main opponent in Cabinet. Walsh's finance department, much to Keating's fury, had devised an alternative package—a reform of the wholesale/sales tax system and an extension of the sales tax to selected services. This avoided indirect taxes on the necessities of life—food, clothing, shelter. It had smaller income tax cuts and less impact on the CPI. Walsh opposed Keating's package on two grounds—firstly, that it was inequitable and that adequate compensation was unavailable for all the disadvantaged, and secondly, that an indirect tax would take inflation to a new plateau.'

Walsh says: 'There would have been an increase in the price level of around 6.5 per cent. Far from there being any guarantee that the unions would not try to recover that through wage increases, the ACTU had virtually served notice that it would try to recover this . . . that meant an ongoing plateau of higher inflation.'[2]

Walsh believed that the politics of Keating's package would fail. There was a 1 February 1987 consumption tax start date that Walsh felt would not allow the downside to be washed away before an election. He predicted that Labor would lose the election on the consumption tax and the Liberals would reinstitute the tax shelters that Labor was planning to abolish—a comprehensive failure for the ALP.

Keating would have been doomed without Hawke's backing. Hawke felt obliged to support Keating but he also felt the indirect tax was the best option if it were feasible. Hawke wasn't prepared to veto Keating himself. He was abdicating his leadership role to the unpredictability of the Summit. The centre-left ministers Dawkins and Walsh were very unhappy, Willis was a persistent critic and the left wing led by Brian Howe was hostile. Keating's treasury 'boys', Evans and Morgan, told the Cabinet that the economic implications of the tax package were 'manageable'.

Keating prevailed because he made the issue implicitly one of confidence. He had deliberately put his position as treasurer at stake. But the result was a dramatic omen—it signified the decline of Cabinet government during the Hawke era and the rise of the 'Führer' principle—the capacity of the man of power to impose unilateral decisions.

Keating was not prepared to lose in Cabinet. His technique was often to avoid Cabinet—notably on all monetary policy decisions—and where avoidance was impossible, such as on taxation, he demanded approval almost by right. (Later in the 1980s another variation of the 'Führer' principle was embodied in Hawke's so-called 'right' as leader to prevail on environmental issues, a principle enunciated by Beazley within the Cabinet room which was tantamount to subverting the true operation of Cabinet government.)

The draft White Paper was released on 4 June 1985. For the first time the debate was anchored in specific proposals, not media leaks. The afternoon of the release Hawke and Keating bumped into each other in the Press Gallery. A journalist asked whether Hawke was still in the tax cart and Keating shot back, 'He's right there in the chariot.' A beaming Hawke put his arm around Keating.

It was a snapshot for history, yet highly deceptive. The fractures were starting to show. It was known in the Press Gallery that Keating had tagged Hawke 'jellyback' for his lack of nerve—a description which Peacock even raised in Parliament. Keating was unable to conceal his patronising attitude towards Hawke, made manifest in repeated private references to having 'to get Hawke back in the tax cart'. Keating spoke about Hawke as a schoolmaster dealing with an unruly head prefect.

Hawke said his relationship with Keating was 'extraordinarily close' and added 'our families have a close personal relationship'. But Keating, not Hawke, had become the transfixing figure of the government. The contrast they offered was sharp: Keating raced towards his Armageddon or his triumph without hesitation; but for months Hawke had been indecisive and ambivalent, supporting Keating but covering his options.

The White Paper was a sophisticated polemic designed to lead to one conclusion—acceptance of the famous Option C, the Keating–treasury tax package. The 280-page document began with a devastating critique of the existing tax system and its untenable reliance upon personal income tax. It showed that personal income tax contributed 52 per cent of total federal revenue compared with 35 per cent in the mid-1950s.

The marginal tax rate on average income earners was 46 per cent compared with 19 per cent in 1955. The average tax rate was 25 per cent compared with 10 per cent in 1955. In 1955 only one per cent of employed persons paid a marginal tax rate of 46 per cent or more; in 1985, 40 per cent of employed people (2.1 million taxpayers) paid this marginal rate. In 1955 the top rate (67 per cent) began at an income level 18 times average weekly earnings, which was equivalent to $400 000 at current (1985) values, but the 1985 top rate (60 per cent) began at $35 000, only 1.6 times average weekly earnings.

The system had become far less progressive. The rich paid less in proportionate terms and the middle class far more. Many sources of income such as capital gains and fringe benefits were virtually untaxed. This meant that the tax base had narrowed and as the base narrowed the rates required to raise the same proportion of revenue had to be higher. The burden was carried by wage and salary earners since the potential for avoidance (legal tax minimisation) and evasion (illegal tax dodging) rested more with the relatively wealthy.

The White Paper revealed that Australia was a low-tax nation. In terms of total tax revenue as a proportion of GDP Australia ranked 17 out of 23 OECD nations, similar to America but below Canada, Britain and New Zealand. But Australia's system was lopsided, biased towards personal income tax as opposed to indirect tax.

The treasury, from this analysis, identified two directions for reform. First, the income tax base must be broadened. If income from all sources were taxed, the extra revenue would fund a cut in marginal income tax rates. This was the White Paper's Option A. Its main proposals were: a comprehensive tax on capital gains discounted for indexation with the home being exempt; a fringe benefits tax imposed upon the employer; abolition of tax deductibility for entertainment expenses; curtailment of negative gearing on rental properties; a national identification system for tax and social security purposes to improve compliance and reduce tax evasion; restrictions on the write-off for farm losses; a tax on gold mining income; reduction of the film industry concessions; and a foreign tax credit system for foreign source income of Australians. This tightening of the income tax system would raise an extra $700 million initially, rising to $1.8 billion by 1987–88.

Option A represented a rare fusion between treasury and ALP ideology. The treasury was offended at the size and scope of loopholes which compromised revenue gathering efficiency and mocked the nominal progressivity of the system. The ALP was anxious to ensure that the relatively rich beneficiaries of such concessions were made to meet their tax obligations. A wealth tax was considered but rejected. But the Option A list was a political hornet's nest and would guarantee myriad fights with business, employers, farmers, capital owners and film-makers. Yet it was merely the first step in reform for Keating and the treasury.

The White Paper explained that the extra revenue from Option A measures would finance only a modest cut in the marginal income tax rates. The rates for average wage earners would fall from 46 to 40 per cent—still 'discouragingly high and incentives to evade and avoid tax would remain strong'. A major enduring reduction in marginal tax rates could only be obtained from the second path towards reform—a broadly-based indirect tax, a consumption tax on all goods and services being the favoured type.

Two consumption taxes were proposed, Option B with a 5 per cent rate and Option C at 12.5 per cent. The lower rate was included to demonstrate the superiority of the higher rate. The argument was that only with a higher rate consumption tax would sufficient revenue be raised to make a substantial cut in the income tax rates.

The Keating position, Option C, therefore involved a 12.5 per cent consumption tax which would replace the existing wholesale sales tax which applied to selected goods and no services, a hotchpotch, inconsistent and confusing tax, levied at different rates.

The merit of a uniform 12.5 per cent tax on the broadest possible base was revenue efficiency and administrative simplicity. Goods for business use would be exempt. A tax at this rate would increase the CPI by 6.5 percentage points, assuming that the tax-induced component in the CPI did not flow through to wage rises under the indexation system. That is, the cooperation of the trade unions was assumed in accepting discounting from wages for the CPI effect of the tax, a cardinal point. It meant that ACTU collaboration was fundamental in its introduction. The tax could be operational during 1986–87 and Keating's intent was to have a minimum 15 months gap between its introduction and the next election, sufficient to see the bulk of the CPI effect washed away and inflation return to the underlying rate by voting day.

As a result of intense party pressure, the draft White Paper contained compensation provisions for low income earners, the needy and welfare recipients who would be disadvantaged by higher consumer prices. This was a real and emotive issue since the new indirect tax would apply to food, clothing and shelter—the necessities of life. The compensation came through the increase in the tax-free threshold, above-indexation increases in welfare payments and, where necessary, new welfare payments to catch the undercompensated. But the treasury was honest enough to admit that even comprehensive arrangements did not guarantee that 'every needy individual would be compensated fully'.

It is a fact, however, that Keating's plan devoted $1.9 billion to compensation, over and above the income tax cuts. This was a very substantial figure, largely dismissed by welfare groups, who may find a future government unwilling to be nearly as generous. It is true, however, that not everybody could be compensated and that some people would be worse off from the changes.

After compensation, the consumption tax and the Option A measures raised extra revenue of $8.6 billion. Devoting all these funds to a lower rate scale, the 46 per cent average income tax rate could be cut to 35 per cent. Low and middle income earners would win through an increase in the tax-free threshold and a substantial cut in the marginal rates. The top rate would be cut from 60 to 50 per cent as a trade-off for the extra taxes the wealthy would pay.

The White Paper estimated that under Option C all income groups would be better off, that is, their income tax cuts would exceed their extra indirect tax burden. It said the result would be a more efficient and fairer tax system. The White Paper endorsed Option C as the preferred position— the Keating stance. From the start of this debate Keating was an absolutist. He wanted the whole package; he insisted that its integrity lay in its totality.

The package contained a number of trade-offs. Keating was offering the ALP a closure of tax shelters in return for his consumption tax. He was offering business the consumption tax, which it supported, on the condition that it accept the crackdown on tax shelters. Finally, Keating was offering the ACTU a net tax cut for its members to abandon their hostility towards an extension of indirect taxation. This was Keating's bait for the unions—a net gain of $12.60 a week for the average wage-earner on $22 500 a year with two children. How can the ACTU say 'no', Keating snorted. In fact, the rate scale Keating proposed had been devised with the ACTU.

Despite its polemical defects the White Paper was distinguished by its realism. Its message, which the non-Labor side refused to acknowledge, was that genuine tax reform was a hard, not a soft, political option. The paper buried years of political bunkum: it showed that a fairer and efficient tax system meant a crackdown on concessions and loopholes. Serious tax reform required political courage. It was separate from electoral bribery, notably Fraser's fistful of dollars, which had given tax reform a bad name.

The White Paper posed the toughest question: did voters want a more efficient tax system which, by definition, closed loopholes and taxed capital as well as income? Or did people prefer a system that could be rorted and was filled with black holes for avoidance/evasion games?

After Cabinet approval, Keating began his 'chariot of fire' selling tour around the nation. Option C was rejected by state ALP conferences, the left and the centre-left factions. But Keating had become Paul the evangelist: 'This is the most comprehensive and ambitious document on tax ever produced in this country.' He bemoaned that 'the country has not been working to the peak of its achievable capacity'. People who were surprised about Labor's tax package had misunderstood the government's nature. Keating declared it was a quality government and the voters would recognise its quality.

In selling his package Keating betrayed an absolutism which stunned his colleagues. He signalled that he might resign from politics unless it was accepted. 'If this sort of proposal doesn't get up, one has to decide if there's much point in someone like me worrying about the Australian institutional processes and in Australian institutions much longer.'³ Keating conceded that he might fail but asked what such a failure meant. 'If finally there is a failure it may be a failure of the institutional process rather than my own failure.'⁴ The tactic was Whitlamesque, crash through or crash. The tax debate demanded a major reappraisal of Keating.

It revealed Keating as a believer—a believer in tax reform just as he was a believer in financial deregulation and the Accord. It was the depth of passion Keating injected—revealed in arrogance, abuse and commitment—which mocked the NSW right-wing cynic stereotype with which he had been branded for years, typified by Craig McGregor profile pieces.

The chemistry within Keating's treasurership was the fusion between his will to power and his passion for achievement. The clue had always been there—his self-proclaimed Labor heroes, Jack Lang and Rex Connor. No politician dedicated to the narrow road to power could have been so fascinated by this pair of gargantuan megalomaniacs who created such spectacular fireworks before blowing themselves to electoral extinction. This predilection was combined with Keating's capacity to grow as treasurer, just as he had grown in politics. He was linked to the old party—unions, machine and faction—yet he was intellectually free of them. The NSW right now whispered that Keating was questioning his own political culture.

Keating knew that if he carried the tax debate and it secured Labor's reelection, than he was claiming the leadership transition from Hawke.

Yet Keating's tax fatalism was also a tactic. Keating had to be uncompromising; the first sign of weakness and his package would have collapsed. Keating knew that the man who makes history is the man who cuts off his

166

options, a fundamental difference between Keating and Hawke. Keating ran free from the party but the party could not afford to lose Keating. So Keating dared it to follow. After the draft White Paper was released Keating said: 'My mind is made up, but it is not closed.'

The opposition to Keating's Option C was based upon four propositions. First, that the proposal was a political catastrophe for the ALP and would ensure its defeat. Second, that it was too regressive and would disadvantage too many people; this came from the ALP, the ACTU and the welfare lobby. They said the poor, low income earners and welfare recipients could not be adequately compensated; that no mechanism existed to ensure that nobody was worse off.

The third criticism came from business and industry. On 19 June the Australian Chamber of Commerce, the Australian Mining Industry Council, the Business Council of Australia, the National Farmers' Federation and the Confederation of Australian Industry issued a joint statement warning that the package would lift business costs by 30 per cent. They felt the Keating package overall would reduce private investment and economic growth and undermine incentive through the capital gains and fringe benefits taxes, and the crackdowns on shelters.

The fourth complaint was that Keating's package would jeopardise Labor's economic management. This one was advanced by Garnaut, who now emerged within Hawke's office as Keating's strongest opponent, indeed, his rival. Garnaut told Hawke that economic growth, not an indirect tax, was Labor's chief priority and that treasury's priorities were misplaced.

From the day of Hawke's election, Garnaut had believed that the key to Labor's growth policy lay in a depreciation combined with wage restraint. The depreciation which arrived in 1985 would give the economy a new competitiveness and wage restraint would retain this advantage. The key to wage restraint was to use the Accord to discount wage rises for the inflationary impact of the depreciation. Garnaut asserted that this model would underwrite Labor's governance in the 1980s.

Garnaut's fear with the indirect tax was that the Accord would become overloaded. He asked how many concessions could be requested of the ACTU. The success of any indirect tax depended on agreement with the ACTU to discount from wages the CPI boost caused by the new tax, which would be about 6.5 per cent. Without this, the tax would merely build a higher inflation rate into the economy. This is why ACTU support for the tax was strictly a 'make or break' question for Labor. Garnaut's fear was that Labor could never secure ACTU approval for two discounts, covering both the indirect tax and the depreciation. If only one discount were possible, then it had to cover the depreciation. But treasury, he believed, was jeopardising economic policy by going for both; it was risking the ALP model of employment growth and inflation control.

Keating, however, believed that he could accomplish both discounts.

He was confident that the ACTU would endorse most of his package. Keating in fact had made a misjudgement. He had courted the ACTU so persuasively for so long that he mistook its sympathy for its support. Keating grasped a fundamental aspect of Kelty's character—that Kelty would not allow the ACTU to veto sound government policy. But Keating forgot that if the policy was under community assault then Kelty could not offer ACTU immunity from rejection.

On Summit eve on 27 June, Hawke and Keating met Kelty, Crean and MacBean to find that the ACTU tax committee had finalised its own proposal. It was a compromise: the indirect tax extension would be limited to services only with smaller personal income taxes, the closing of loopholes and a capital gains tax. The ACTU was halfway, but still far short of Keating. But Keating saw this concession as the start, not the end, of ACTU tolerance.

The Tax Summit was far different from the National Economic Summit two years earlier. Hawke and Keating were seeking approval for a compli- cated tax package which affected every interest group and individual. It was a package which defied consensus-building.

Hawke opened the Summit of 160 delegates in the House of Represen- tatives chamber on 1 July 1985 with an appeal to delegates to restore 'equity, efficiency and integrity' to the tax system. Hawke had said the disadvantaged would be adequately compensated under Keating's package. Now he made a further pledge: '. . . all Australians require an assurance that the least privileged among us will not suffer as a result of the changes. I give that assurance unreservedly.'[5]

The first delegate to speak was president of the Business Council (BCA) Bob White, and his speech doomed Keating. White cast an uncompromising psychology over the Summit. Keating, busy for weeks lobbying the ACTU and the welfare groups, had made the mistake of taking business for granted. Keating and his officials should have spent more time before the Summit with the BCA. They didn't because they knew that business supported a consumption tax.

But White rejected the trade-off implicit in the package for business. He said that business:

> does not support approaches A, B or C. We are not on the
> Government's cart. We are on another cart. The Government's preferred
> option . . . imposes substantial additional imposts on business to an
> extent which will discourage investment and economic growth . . . This
> makes it impossible for us to support any of these (options) without
> major qualifications.[6]

This opening speech, in fact, was the turning point of the Summit. Once business—the main lobby backing a consumption tax—had revealed its hardline stance, then every other lobby was similarly encouraged. Sectional interest was put before national interest—a decision that would condemn

168

Keating. The irony is that White had tried for the week before the Summit to contact Keating—but the treasurer had not taken his calls. White reflected the resentment of business at the extra taxes being imposed upon it as part of the package. But his hardline speech was partly by design and partly by accident; it left a more uncompromising impression than intended.

The second blow was delivered by the welfare lobby, whose chief spokesman was the president of the Australian Council of Social Services (ACOSS), Bruce McKenzie. He attacked the White Paper: 'Is it progressive? No. Is it redistributive? No . . . The broad-based consumption tax, so-called Option C, is rejected totally, [it] can be likened to the logic of punishing all citizens for a crime instead of vigorously pursuing the guilty . . . The tax is a fundamentally unsound approach and would be a disaster, not only to poor people but also to the community as a whole.'[7]

Speaking for the ACTU Bill Kelty raised serious doubt about the consumption tax. He said that indirect tax was more regressive than income tax, that the scope of Option C was greater than in most countries, that doubts remained about its inflationary impact and its effect on unemployment, that its impact on women would be deleterious, and that its income redistribution was unacceptable with the lowest earning groups gaining only $2.40 to $3.30 a week. Kelty said the consumption tax proposal as outlined was unacceptable to the ACTU but he did not rule out some extension of indirect taxes, a concession to Keating. Kelty's speech was not a negotiating ploy but a warning to Hawke and Keating that the consumption tax must be modified to win union backing.

Keating's package never recovered from this sustained assault on the first day of the Summit. It was a self-reinforcing circle of opposition as speaker after speaker explicitly rejected Option C—unions, ALP premiers, farmers, big and small business. The fact that both business and welfare groups attacked the package made it impossible for the ACTU—which was divided—to adopt any course other than deep scepticism. One delegate, Sir Joh Bjelke Petersen, called for an alternative flat rate 25 per cent income tax, an omen of a future furore.

Hawke and his advisers, particularly Garnaut, believed that Option C was finished on the first day. In his concluding speech on day one Keating tried a salvage operation. He said that too many contributions were 'divided, sectional and too uncompromising' and rightly pointed out that the benefits of Option C were almost universally ignored. His sting was reserved for business. Keating said that business taxation had declined significantly over the last decade yet business only assessed the package in terms of the increase in business costs, ignoring the transforming impact of lower marginal rates on economic activity and wage fixation. Keating told all delegates there was no magic pudding in tax reform.

Hawke now realised that the politics of Option C were impossible. Hawke and Keating were split: Hawke searched for a compromise while

Keating tried to save his package. From the Summit's first evening events moved with speed and drama as Hawke began a series of private talks to locate a compromise.

Neville Wran had opened the door to compromise in his speech by backing a consumption tax with food exempted, thus easing the burden for low income earners. It was the type of emotional concession always effective within the ALP. Wran and Barron were negotiating a fallback. Before the Summit, asked about a food exemption Keating had replied, 'I'm killing it stone dead.' Keating knew that exemptions only created added complexity and cut the revenue from which to offer tax cuts.

But in his concluding remarks on the second day Hawke conceded that the government had begun work on an amended package to meet 'the main areas of concern' revealed at the Summit. That evening Hawke, Keating, Kelty and Barron met in Hawke's office to canvass a compromise. Barron told Keating: 'I can get Wran to back you with food excluded.' What would the ACTU wear? Kelty said that with food excluded and incentives for housing, he could carry the package 'possibly'. But petroleum was a problem, perhaps an exemption was needed. 'Can you wear it, then?' Barron asked. 'Yes, I think we can get it up,' Kelty replied. Barron thought it was the crack of light. As they left he joked to Keating, 'You're home, mate.' He was shocked when Keating shot back: 'Not me mate. I want the lot. We're not wearing any soft cop.' Barron was incredulous. Keating, in fact, was prepared to compromise, but not just yet.

But Keating misjudged the mood. His determination had anaesthetised his political antennae. Day three began with publication in the *Bulletin* of a disastrous Morgan poll showing the Opposition heading Labor 49 to 41 per cent and Peacock heading Hawke for the first time in approval ratings. It had an important psychological effect; the ALP was being torn apart. If debate about Keating's package had done such harm what fate for Labor after its implementation? The third day was really about the compromise point at which the government and the ACTU would meet.

Crean and Kelty wanted to help Keating but they were mere mortals with their own constituency. They needed exemptions to sell the tax. But Keating knew that major exemptions would render the tax futile. At the end of day three Keating lamented: 'It has to be understood that by cutting out the broad-based consumption tax, we cut out the heart of the package and with it the opportunity for significant increases in benefits and reductions in tax rates.'

At this point Hawke, who had played second fiddle to Keating for six months, moved to terminate the issue. Hawke acted from political necessity and with a sound conscience. He felt that he had given Keating every chance. He had supported him during the drafting of the White Paper, in Cabinet and at the Summit. He had watched Labor's position slide to the point where the party held serious doubts about its electoral recovery. The

The Tax Summit

Summit had rejected the consumption tax and Hawke felt that in this situation the ALP would not accept it. Opposition within the left and centre-left was mounting. Hayden was prepared to postpone an overseas trip to spearhead Cabinet opposition to the consumption tax. The Keating package fell victim to a strange alliance—business, the ACTU, the centre-left and left wing, the welfare lobby and the Joh Bjelke-Petersen and John Stone flat rate tax mania; opponents threw rocks from every vantage point.

The final deal between Hawke and the ACTU was sealed on Wednesday night when Hawke, unbeknownst to Keating, visited Crean and Kelty in their hotel on the opposite side of the lake. Hawke came to bury the consumption tax, to drop his demands on the ACTU, to liquidate the government position. Keating later accused Hawke of betrayal. Hawke said that he had obligations to the government, not just to Keating.

Hawke did not ask Crean and Kelty to back a modified consumption tax. He simply took the position with which the ACTU entered the Summit—a tax on services, a rationalisation of the wholesale sales tax system and a crackdown on tax shelters. The ACTU leaders agreed—Hawke sued for peace largely on their terms.

Keating, for once, had been outfoxed. The same night, just after Hawke had cut his deal with the ACTU, Keating and his advisers—deluded optimists to a man—were still hoping to reverse the tide. A gallery journalist, John Short, rang David Morgan late that night to check a story. Short told Morgan that Option C was finished but Morgan laughed at him—the Keating camp was the last to know. The joke was on Keating and his advisers. Keating only knew of Hawke's deal and the sellout when he read the Thursday morning papers. Keating's breakfast was ruined; Option C had past into legend, not law.

On the last day of the Summit Hawke left the chair to his deputy, Lionel Bowen, and convened a series of meetings involving ministers and advisers to clear his fallback package. An emotional Hawke then marched into the Summit to announce a defeat but disguise it as a victory. Barron quipped, 'If I see a tear in your eye, I'll crown you.' The parliament was awash with rumours; the $A was already falling on the back of Keating resignation rumours. But Hawke had the perfect excuse for a backdown: what else but consensus? He invoked principle nine of the tax reform guidelines—that any package must have widespread community support—to justify the abandonment of the consumption tax.

In this speech and in a subsequent Hawke–Keating press conference an effort was made to decorate the wreckage that remained after what Hawke called amid the sniggers 'an extraordinarily successful Summit'. Hawke now assembled a new tax cart from the broken pieces. It was the worst type of policy improvisation. The government was left with an odd group of ill-fitting taxation parts—like a stunned schoolboy whose prize invention has just exploded.

171

All speakers offered tributes to Keating at the Summit's end, none more so than Hawke. With his jaw trembling Hawke said: 'The contribution that Paul Keating has made to lifting the level of community debate, both before and at this Summit, has been without parallel and without equal . . . No Prime Minister could have asked for better, closer, more effective cooperation than I have enjoyed with Paul Keating. Thank you, Paul.'[8] Hawke's voice quivered badly. Keating reached out to pat his arm.

Despite the rumours, Keating wasn't resigning, indeed, he had never contemplated resignation. In Keating's final comments to the Summit he launched a tribute to the treasury—the men who made his bullets and drafted the White Paper. He took a savage swipe at John Stone, saying that 'no conceptual thinking had been done in the Treasury on taxation before Bernie Fraser became Secretary'.[9] Then, like a defeated but unbeaten general, Keating sealed his loyalty to his troops. He said: 'The Treasury is a very important institution in this country. It has not been prepared over the years to offer soft advice to governments. It stands its ground. Often in a sea of weakness it stands up. You have to have institutions which stand up and it stands up. I have been very proud to have executive responsibility for the Treasury.'[10]

Hawke, under pressure at the joint press conference, fell into his customary hectoring style. But Keating, in defeat, stole the show. Asked if his tax cart had been derailed he replied: 'I think it's a bit like Ben Hur. We have crossed the line with one wheel off, but we have crossed the line.' Asked if he had been dumped Keating replied: 'We tugged at the ends of power in this country to put it on the table . . . but we couldn't get that support.' Keating paid tribute to Hawke: 'Without his support there wouldn't have been a White Paper . . . I am pleased to say that in the time I have been Treasurer that support has been unqualified.'[11]

This was the public face of Hawke–Keating unity. But the private visage was quite different. The qualities of trust and respect by which men honour each other are tested only in adversity. At the drinks that night in Keating's office the believers—Keating, his staff and the treasury officials—were joined by the ACTU. Surely a paradox, Keating and the ACTU officials who beat him?

The moral is that no defeat is total; no victory is absolute. Human emotions and political power operate in unpredictable ways. The ACTU saw that Keating had fought for his position beyond the point of self-interest. That won Keating the respect of the ACTU. But Keating won their trust by the exhaustive dialogue in which he had engaged the ACTU for months. This forged the Keating–ACTU and, in particular, the Keating–Kelty relationship.

The ACTU felt guilty at denying Keating so they came bearing a gift. It was to commemorate Keating's message that there was no magic pudding in tax reform. The book which Kelty presented to Keating was Norman Lindsay's *The Magic Pudding*, and it was inscribed inside the cover to

Keating 'with our respect and thanks for your efforts in tax reform and the promotion of greater equity for Australians'. It was signed by the entire ACTU executive. Keating treasured the book, beyond most other gifts. As the wake continued in Keating's office Hawke suddenly arrived. An unwelcome guest. 'It was like a cold shower,' Keating said later.

Keating showed skill in transferring blame for his defeat to Hawke and business, not to the ACTU. He abused Barron and complained about Garnaut. His loathing for Hawke's office, which he called the 'Manchu Court', intensified. His senior adviser Cole had a screaming match with Barron. The treasury was filled with contempt for Hawke who was cast as the villain, the classic weak man, the 'jellyback'.

From this night onwards Keating, typically, manufactured his own history. He insisted that he could have won—but for Hawke's betrayal. Keating believed that Kelty would never have allowed the ACTU to veto the consumption tax. He was convinced that the consumption tax with exemptions was available for the taking. But Hawke decided not to take it; that Hawke, facing a disastrous opinion poll, lost his nerve and ran.

But the evidence does not sustain Keating's interpretation of the Tax Summit. The final judgement upon whether the ACTU could have delivered for Keating rests with Kelty, and his assessment leaves little doubt that Hawke's conclusion was accurate. Kelty says:

> I don't think it would have been possible for the ACTU to have gone further. We were prepared to support an indirect tax on services provided the income was redistributed in a fair way. That was largely the consensus that arose out of the Tax Summit. I think we'd gone as far as we could because in essence, that is a consumption tax minus a range of things. Now the government's argument was that you either have a consumption tax or you don't; that a consumption tax with exemptions defeats its purpose. On that basis, I don't think we could have got a consumption tax.[12]

The next day Keating lunched at The Lobby restaurant with journalists who were surprised to find him relaxed, dismissive about his defeat, relishing the task of turning the tax wreckage into a great package. But Keating nursed his anger at Hawke's 'betrayal'.

Hawke was furious at weekend newspaper reports suggesting that he had pulled the mat from under Keating. When he complained to Keating he found that Keating hit back. He wouldn't tolerate any humbug. 'If I'm coming after you Bob, you'll be the first to know about it,' he said. 'Right now I'm cruising. I'm not even trying. If I come after you, you'll know.'

It was an exposure of the ultimate issue between them—the leadership. Keating would seek Hawke's job—but not now. Hawke and Keating both knew this. In the interim their interests were similar so they would collaborate. But Keating never forgot this warning to Hawke, not even six years later when the challenge finally materialised. Keating had promised to tell Hawke first when he attempted the coup. It was a matter of honour between colleagues; when Keating came to assassinate Hawke he approached from the front—and in 1991 that helped Hawke to save himself.

The Tax Summit legacy, like so many hasty compromises, was unworkable. Five weeks after the Summit, on 13 August 1985, Keating announced the final retreat. The plan for a consumption tax on services and to extend the wholesale sales tax regime was 'unworkable, impractical and inconsistent with the basic objectives of tax reform'. The treasury costed the extra revenue at $2.5 billion but the compensation required for the needy at $2.8 billion; the government actually lost money. The exercise was a farce. Keating had closed the circle—having been denied his broadly-based consumption tax in July he buried the last remnants of the consumption tax in August. Keating had liberated himself from the Summit's legacy; now he had a chance to salvage the policy wreckage.

In September 1985 Keating unveiled Labor's final tax package—constructed from the Summit's residue. From July to September Hawke had fluctuated between distrust and disinterest as Keating reconstructed a tax package. After the Summit Hawke moved to contain Keating by having a Cabinet committee set up to filter the tax submissions. In September Hawke announced that the full ministry, not just the Cabinet, would debate and authorise the final tax package, a move that infuriated Keating. Keating knew that his reputation couldn't sustain another defeat on taxation. The ministry met over the weekend of 14–15 September and again on the Monday to approve the package.

On the second day Hawke left to attend Papua New Guinea's tenth anniversary celebrations. Keating, during his more melodramatic reflections, felt the symbolism was exquisite—Hawke had stabbed him at the Tax Summit and was now deserting him. Hawke, in fact, abdicated responsibility to Keating—again.[13]

Keating's final package was based upon two trade-offs. First, a closing of loopholes and the introduction of capital and fringe benefits taxes in return for a lower marginal tax scale. Second, the elimination of double taxation of company dividends (full dividend imputation) as a quid pro quo for the extra taxes being imposed upon the investment community through the capital gains and fringe benefits taxes. The dividend reform, which came from Keating, not treasury or the tax department, was an effort to pacify business, the main loser from the Summit.

Keating sought to repair a system which he said was debauched by avoidance, evasion and minimisation so that its progressivity was a fiction and the 60 per cent top rate was honoured more in the breach. Keating told the ministry and the people that every sectional rort or tax dodge imposed a greater burden on the general community.

In the ministry meeting Keating fought a long battle with Tom Uren and

174

Ralph Willis to win the abolition of 'double taxation' of company dividends. But he suffered one great loss in this meeting—he failed to secure a far tougher capital gains tax. The ministers forced a grandfathering provision which exempted existing assets so the capital gains tax applied only to realised assets which had been purchased after the start-up date. Keating had wanted a capital gains tax without a grandfathering exemption—a tax which would apply to all currently held assets when they were sold.

The Keating–treasury capital tax position was undermined by Chris Hurford who persuaded the ministry on the basis of accounting advice that Keating's plan was too dangerous and complex and meant that every asset would have to be valued when the policy was announced. The majority opinion was to weaken the capital gains tax—either by imposing a lower rate or by grandfathering. The treasury opposed both options but grandfathering was adopted, probably the right political choice. The electoral consequences of Keating's preferred position would have been extremely harsh for Labor.

When the ministry meeting broke Keating returned to his office euphoric. He had a package—not the best, not a consumption tax, not steep income tax cuts, but a series of genuine reforms. Keating could even call them 'historic' by the pedestrian standards of Australian tax change. In fact, Keating had talked the ministry into a package which terrified much of the caucus when they saw it.

On 19 September Keating unveiled the package in parliament before a jubilant Opposition that smelt an electoral killing. He announced a fringe benefits tax levied on the employer at the company rate directed towards cars, cheap loans, free housing and other benefits; the denial of deductions for entertainment expenses; a requirement for substantiation of employment related spending deductions; a prospective tax on realised capital gains discounted for inflation with the main exemption being the family home; a rationalisation of the wholesale sales tax system to three rates and its extension; a national identification system called the Australia Card; the quarantining of farm losses; a lift in company tax from 46 to 49 per cent to help to finance the abolition of 'double taxation' of company dividends, thereby offering more incentive to sharemarket investment.

He cut the top rate from 60 to 49 per cent, a new psychological ceiling, and for average earners from 46 to 40 per cent. But the new scale was not indexed, a great flaw. He rejected comparisons with Ronald Reagan's 'supply side' economics although only $1.5 billion of tax cuts totalling $4.5 billion was being financed by the tax shelter crackdown. The rest had to come from fiscal drag and spending cuts. Keating used the tax cuts to underwrite another wage-tax deal, the second for the Hawke government.

The package was a courageous attack on entrenched tax shelters which would strike at business and capital-conscious middle Australia. It alienated business, large and small, farmers and employers. The Opposition was able to taunt Keating for losing the heart of his reform, the indirect tax. It mocked Hawke for rejecting the indirect tax on consensus grounds by asking him what consensus existed for taxes on capital gains and fringe benefits. It said, correctly, that the failure to tax gold mining was a political sop to WA premier Brian Burke. Labor insisted that overall the September package was progressive.

Keating had only one reply—to argue on national interest grounds, not sectional grounds. Overall his package did contribute to a more efficient and fairer tax system, a recognition that took some years. Keating's package sought to achieve taxation progressivity by closing loopholes and taxing capital rather than through the rate scale, a victory for Keating over Peter Walsh. Yet the company tax innovation, by eliminating the 'double taxation' on dividends, encouraged greater investment in the sharemarket and was a practical sign of Labor's belief in a nation of citizen shareholders. The Australia Card, however, was an unforeseen provocation for a Democrat–Opposition alliance that would later trigger the 1987 election.

Keating's tax package faced further struggles in the Senate and modifications, yet it was gradually introduced during the second term, ready for the 1987 election battle. The package quickly helped to repair the direct tax base—the proof being the surge in federal revenue over the next few years which was basic to Labor's success in cutting public spending from 1986.

The Opposition, after watching Labor's nine months of taxation agony, had a dilemma. Should it reaffirm its own indirect tax policy for the next election? Peacock said 'no' and Howard 'yes'. This issue would plague the Liberals throughout Hawke's second term. In the interim the coalition was convinced that Keating's September taxation package would deliver it the next election, an inaccurate judgement.

The 1985 tax debate revealed the strength and the flaw within Keating. Once set he became an absolutist, brooking no retreat. He possessed the strength but lacked the balance. The debate reinforced the Hawke–Keating stereotype: Hawke as peacemaker and man of compromise; Keating as the pacesetter, the man of resolution. It revealed Keating as Labor's agent for change and Hawke as the arbiter who decided how far Keating would get. The tax debate left the indelible impression in the minds of the party, the press and the public of Keating's claim to lead the government. Above all, it revealed Keating as the fascinating politician within the ALP, more complex than was recognised, allied with Hawke yet ready to break from Hawke.

Keating was impressive in his fightback after the Tax Summit; he returned with a package of substance many of whose reforms endured in the tax system. Others like the Australia Card eventually collapsed. In the transition Keating switched the politics of the package: before the Summit he offered business its consumption tax in return for closing down the tax shelters, while post-Summit his deal to the investment community was the abolition of the double taxation of dividends (full imputation) in return for the tax shelter crackdown.

The debate revealed Keating as a policy elitist. He promoted treasury options within a Labor framework and with the arrogance of the NSW right. Yet Keating had made a gross misjudgement at the Tax Summit of his capacity to carry the consumption tax. Afterwards he displayed an ability to insist upon his infallibility even when he changed direction. The tax debate revealed Keating's consultative skills, notably with the ACTU, but it betrayed equally his elitism in handling the party and the public. It left the voters impressed with his will but with reservations about his judgement.

Hawke's ability to direct his government was left severely damaged, a fact Barron recognised. Hawke lacked the will to policy; his definition of leadership was often mere occupation of the throne. It was Keating who inspired to use the power. Hawke was exposed as a weak policy strategist as opposed to Keating who excelled in this domain. The tax debate revealed the extent to which Hawke would shun any personal confrontation with Keating and suggested that he was even intimidated by Keating. But it left another legacy within Hawke—the seeds of a suspicious reappraisal of Keating's loyalty, judgement and balance.

Yet the debate had identified the limits to Keating's political persuasion. Keating concluded in turn that his power base within the Cabinet was not broad enough, that the Hawke–Keating axis was no longer a guarantee of Cabinet victory since he could no longer trust Hawke. So Keating decided to build an alliance with the centre-left, a decision symbolised in his efforts to secure a personal rapprochement with John Dawkins, a senior centre-left minister and former Keating rival. Keating told Dawkins that they weren't real rivals, that he would beat Dawkins in any future leadership contest, that Dawkins would better secure his Cabinet victories working with Keating not against him. Dawkins in turn had changed his own view of Keating. He concluded that they were policy soul-brothers and that Keating had transcended the primitivism of his NSW right origins.

So Dawkins joined with Keating, a fateful personal and political relationship. It was an alliance founded on mutual suspicion of Hawke and mutual policy self-interest. But nobody could have predicted the future political fireworks created by this Keating–Dawkins bonding.

Keating emerged from 1985 stronger, not weaker, with a grip on the four central economic institutions—the treasury, the Reserve Bank, the taxation office and the ACTU. He had a bond with the four men who headed these institutions—Bernie Fraser, Bob Johnston, Trevor Boucher and Bill Kelty respectively. Within the party he called upon the support of the right and was building links to the centre-left. Keating held the reins of power in his hands as few treasurers ever had. Yet 1986 would unleash an economic tempest.

10
The Peacock surrender

Next stop, the Lodge!
Janette Howard, September 1985, after John Howard's
election as Liberal leader

John Howard had not accepted the December 1984 election result as a vindication of Peacock's leadership. A post-election challenge was impossible so Howard would bide his time but intensify the pressure. Howard had been happy to give Peacock one election—but two elections was a luxury. Howard did not envisage a coup, that was too bloody. He resolved to press his own claims and force the Liberals to recognise his superiority over Peacock.

Howard's feelings were made apparent the day after the election in a phone call that became famous within politics. A Canberra journalist, Peter Rees, rang Howard at home and was startled at the warm greeting he received when Howard mistook Rees for his Victorian backbench ally, Peter Reith. Howard said: 'Peacock has had his chance. We don't really know what he stands for,' and continued with several blunt remarks: 'I don't think Andrew is ever going to be prime minister. He has some fundamental weaknesses. We have been directionless for 18 months. I'm not certain that he won't fall over next year [1985].'

Their talk was interrupted and Howard suggested that Rees call back a little later. But when that happened Howard was confused: 'Sorry, who did you say it is?' Rees repeated his name and his newspaper, the *Melbourne Sun*. Howard was appalled. 'I thought you were Peter Reith,' he said. Howard asked Rees not to publish his remarks because they were given on the basis of mistaken identity. Rees agreed and published only after Howard became leader.[1] Those who said Howard did not covet the leadership were either politically naive or ignorant of Howard.

A decade of political success had fuelled in Howard a deep ambition. Howard was affronted by Peacock. He had long since been convinced of

178

his superiority to Peacock on every criterion: toughness, drive, policy and media skill. Howard was scornful of Peacock and his political style. But Howard had 'no plan or plot in my mind to depose Peacock'.[2]

Peacock won three cheers when he walked into the post-1984 election party meeting which confirmed both leader and deputy unopposed. Yet within hours Peacock's elation turned to anger. At their joint press conference after the meeting, Howard refused to rule out a leadership challenge before the next election.

Asked directly about a challenge, Howard, with Peacock next to him, refused to answer. When asked again Howard said: 'Given all of the circumstances, given the unanimous re-election of Mr Peacock as leader, given the track record of loyalty I have always displayed towards leaders that I have served, I don't believe that it is necessary for me to add to the answer that I have given and I don't propose to.'[3]

Peacock was furious at Howard's refusal to dismiss any challenge and was justified in wanting such a statement. Political parties expect the deputy to support the leader, not to undermine him. Howard, in fact, had changed his leadership formula. During Peacock's first term, he said unequivocally that Peacock would lead the party to the next election, but after the 1984 election he refused to give such an endorsement.

Peacock spoke to one of his backers, Ian Macphee, about forcing Howard to recant. From the very start, Peacock identified Howard's position as a fundamental problem and flirted with forcing the issue. A political wedge had been inserted between the two men and their relations were doomed to deteriorate.

Howard had studied the Fraser assault on Snedden. Fraser's tactics were brutal and brazen: brutal because he resolved to assassinate the leader and brazen because he always denied it. Howard found such tactics distasteful. He was not called 'Honest John' for nothing; Gerard Henderson referred to Howard's 'Sunday school honesty'.

Howard wanted to realise his ambition but keep his purity. He was determined to avoid the accusations of hypocrisy levelled against Fraser from which Fraser had never recovered. Howard was not going to be trapped by dismissing a challenge one day and launching it the next. The truth about Howard is that he had no plot to become leader. He lacked the stomach to organise the assassination of Peacock. Howard just assumed that somewhere, somehow, over the next three years, Peacock would stumble; the Liberal elders would rally; opinion would shift. By being an honest challenger Howard excited more rancour than would a devious pretender. The irony of Howard is that the frankness of his intent was not equalled by a ruthlessness of purpose.

Peacock was a bolder leader after his reelection. He told all and sundry that he would take a greater role in the policy process and he was ruthless in reshaping the shadow ministry. The test for a leader is to be daring but not foolhardy; unfortunately Peacock was both. He dropped among others three senior NSW shadow ministers—Jim Carlton, John Spender and Wal Fife—all close to Howard. Peacock sent a message to Howard and the NSW party that he would punish his rivals. The shadow ministry was cut from 30 to 27 and the number of NSW shadow ministers from nine to five.

The upshot was that Howard refused to endorse the reshuffle, saying only that Peacock as leader had the right to hire and fire. But NSW president John Valder complained that 'some of our [NSW] most highly regarded members have lost their positions'. The reshuffle reflected Peacock's 'phoney tough' stance and penchant for taking decisions based on allegiance, not merit. Hostility towards Peacock deepened throughout the NSW party.

Peacock's weakness as leader, both in 1985 and again in 1989, was his lack of intellectual authority. After the election Peacock continued his cultivation of the Liberal drys—he identified privatisation and labour market deregulation as the two policies on which he would run. So Ian Macphee, the focal point of resistance to a deregulated labour market, was dumped from the industrial job—proof that Peacock was settling this policy in favour of the free market lobby.

Two sentiments towards Peacock shaped Liberal thinking in 1985—that he was soft on policy issues but that he could win an election. The myth of Hawke, the supra-politician, had been exploded by the 1984 result. As 1985 unfolded, the Hawke government was plagued by two issues which turned the climate towards the Opposition. They were the MX missile crisis and the tax debate, both of which had revealed Hawke's weakness as a leader. Peacock was the beneficiary of these upheavals.

Peacock moved at every step to protect his flank from Howard. He promoted the idea of Peter Shack as a future leader—the man whom he expected to succeed himself. He tried to block the bid by the NSW president and Howard loyalist, John Valder, to become the next federal president of the party. He removed Howard from the party policy committee which Howard had previously chaired, thereby putting distance between the deputy and policy development.

However, it was the Valder issue which consumed Peacock and became a lightning rod for the Peacock–Howard tussle. Peacock's distrust of Valder was profound. He had never forgiven Valder for his remark on Sydney radio in 1984 that Peacock had to 'lift his game'. This had prompted a sharp retort from Peacock's wife, Margaret, who declared: 'Andrew could have chucked in the towel ages ago . . . That's why I think this thing is pretty outrageous. It's just so cruel when Andrew's trying so hard. I like John [Valder] very much and I don't want to be nasty to him, but I think loyalty is a pretty important thing. He's chucked a bucket just at a time when the Liberal Party has to be so together.' When wives go public it is a sign of earth tremors.

Peacock spoke to Valder in early April 1985, trying to divert him from seeking the federal presidency at the July Federal Council meeting. Peacock's problem was to find an alternative; he flirted with his mate, Reg Withers, and even tried to persuade a reluctant Dr Jim Forbes to remain in the job.

Peacock and Howard fell out during 1985 over Labor's taxation agenda. Peacock saw the consumption tas as a political catastrophe for Labor which he should exploit. But Howard saw a broadly-based indirect tax as basic to the Opposition's own economic policy. In early 1985, there was a de facto alliance between Keating and Howard to facilitate this reform. The shadow Cabinet on 19 February 1985 endorsed a submission from Howard supporting an indirect tax with as few exemptions as possible. Howard's aim was to encourage Keating and to ensure that the indirect tax was not lost because of Opposition hostility. In early May, Peacock complained to Howard that Keating was getting too easy a ride from the Opposition. But Howard rejected Peacock's complaint, along with its implied criticism of himself.[4] Howard was conscious that as treasurer he had espoused this tax reform before Keating. He called for a 'constructive though critical' approach from the Opposition.[5]

Howard said: 'If the government is doing something you agree with, for Heaven's sake let's say so and get on to the next issue. I think the public is tired of automatic opposition.'[6]

Before the winter recess Peacock told Tony Eggleton that Howard's ambition had outpaced his loyalty. Eggleton urged Peacock to use the recess to 'bridge the gap and improve relations'. Eggleton was convinced that terrible staff relations were an important issue—the two men's staffs were filled with mutual paranoia that infected their leaders.

The July Liberal Federal Council elected Valder as the new federal president and he promptly confirmed Peacock's fears with a series of inexcusable comments on the leadership. Asked whether, under any circumstances, he could foresee a challenge to Peacock, Valder equivocated: 'Well, I don't suppose you can ever rule out "under any circumstances" because you don't know what those circumstances might be. But certainly at this stage I think . . . there's no question of a leadership challenge around.' When the media suggested it was provocative to leave the possibility open, Valder began to ramble: 'I have a bad habit of being a provocative sort of fellow. We live in the real world, don't we? We don't live in a make-believe world. Any circumstances means any circumstances that might arise in the future. We might all be blown up here despite the security people that have been in this hotel the last few days.'[7]

These comments were a pure indulgence. A federal president has only one job in this situation—to support the leader. It is not his task to speculate about unpredictable events that may undermine the leader. Peacock was enraged because he knew that Valder was adopting the Howard formula—refusing to rule out a leadership challenge. Peacock had both his deputy and his president keeping open the option to depose him. But Peacock did to Valder what he could not do to Howard—demand a retraction. After a sharp private drubbing from Peacock, Valder declared categorically for his leader.

At the Council Saturday night dinner, football coach and media personality Alan Jones dumped on a shaken Valder, declaring he had broken the loyalty bond and his behaviour had been 'unworthy, unacceptable and unsatisfactory'. While the Howard group said Peacock had overreacted, the Peacock group accused Valder of treachery. Valder himself said his next stop was Heaven; Peacock said Valder would go through Hell first and Howard refused to criticise Valder. There was more farce than malice in the Liberal Party.

The Valder gaffe turned Peacock's mind to the possibility of confronting Howard and forcing either a change in his leadership formula or his removal as deputy. Peacock and his advisers realised that Valder was merely an extension of the Howard problem. Peacock knew he had the numbers against Howard on the leadership and began to ruminate on the prospect of using his strength against Howard. Peacock was influenced by the way Fraser had waited for the right moment and successfully ambushed Peacock himself in 1982 when he had been preparing to challenge Fraser.

Peacock was a mixture of insecurity and assertion. He was contemplating a strike against Howard when another Valder gaffe was revealed on 1 August 1985. The story broke about a video interview recorded by Valder for the Westpac Number One program, a monthly discussion of financial issues sent to top clients. Valder had argued that big cuts in government spending meant tackling the social welfare area. Referring to the Hawke government's assets tests abolition (which Peacock had made a campaign issue) Valder said: 'If I can be a little candid on your private program, [it] was a very small step in that direction.' Valder also supported Keating's effort to tax fringe benefits while saying the treasurer had been foolish to attempt so much so fast. Again, this undermined the Liberal attack on the fringe benefits tax. Valder's conclusion was superb irony:

> So, I have said many times, you know, let the Labor Party get on implementing the more necessary but perhaps less popular parts of our policy. And let's hope they get them into place and promptly lose office. And I think that would be a very good scenario, don't you?

Valder was elevating political hypocrisy to an art form. The reaction was typified by a *Financial Review* editorial:

> The underlying implication is that in opposing such initiatives in the assets test, the tax on fringe benefits and other proposals of the Government, the Liberals are engaged in a sham. Actually, they want the Government to succeed in imposing such measures, draw a full

measure of public wrath (whipped up by the Opposition piously proclaiming contrary policies) and then go down to defeat.[8]

A jetlagged Peacock arrived home from America the same morning this editorial appeared. He rang Valder immediately and instructed him to put out a statement saying that the Liberal parliamentary party, not outsiders, set policy. Hawke applauded Valder for being 'devastatingly honest'.[9]

Valder was not trying to ruin Peacock. His real aim was to advance the party organisation—but he was grossly inept. Valder says: 'We were in opposition, not government, and people expected a more assertive Federal President. I was no closer to Howard than I was hostile to Peacock. I was never involved in any conspiracy. But I wasn't prepared to ignore the fact that the leader was rating at an extraordinary low level and the entire party knew it.'[10]

Despite the destabilisation, which was deliberate by Howard and accidental by Valder, it was hard to see how Howard could replace Peacock. Few in the Liberal Party doubted that Peacock retained majority support. The appropriate strategy for Peacock was obvious—to champion dry economics, ignore Howard and attack Hawke—but Peacock was losing his nerve.

Peacock's main advisers, staffers Alistair Drysdale and Petro Georgiou and confidant Reg Withers, warned Peacock that the Howard camp, if unchecked, would create a spectacle of public division that would damage Peacock's leadership and the Opposition's standing. In August Liberal research showed for the first time that party divisions had become a vote loser. This reinforced Peacock's instinct to confront Howard. In late August the final provocation occurred which pushed Peacock to retribution.

On 28 August, Howard appeared at the National Press Club as shadow treasurer in a powerful performance which demonstrated that he was the policy and philosophical leader of the Liberal Party. He identified the priorities of the next Liberal government and, in so doing, implicitly raised the question: whose Liberal government?

Howard said labour market deregulation was the 'first priority' for the coalition; he pledged a broadly-based indirect tax, despite Keating's defeat on this plank a few months earlier; he pushed the privatisation program and suggested that conditions be attached to dole payments. Howard was asked several times about the leadership and refused to modify his position. After this appearance I summarised the situation:

> The Howard challenge is unique. It is conducted in public, not secret, thereby denying the law of clandestinity; yet by being so open, the audacity of the challenge is more naked . . . John Howard is frank, accessible and intelligent and few other politicians meet these criteria. Incredibly, Howard has even earned praise for his honesty as he sets about destabilising the leadership of Peacock.

How can Peacock offer himself as a credible alternative to Hawke when, within the Party, his own deputy offers himself as an alternative to Peacock? Yet it is inescapable that Howard has widespread support from within the party for his own tactics. Some Liberals would prefer to see him as the leader; others who might not recognise his credentials accept his potential as a future leader. Just as the authority of the leader ultimately derives from the party, so does the discretion of a potential challenger . . .

Peacock and Howard are of a more equal stature than most leadership combinations and this gives Howard greater clout than an ordinary deputy. While Peacock is more popular with the wider community, it is Howard who has the credentials with the business and financial establishment . . . it is hard to see how the intensifying Peacock–Howard issue will not be seen to be publicly damaging and hence the need for some form of resolution.[11]

On 29 August, the day after Howard's speech, Peacock's office was moving towards a showdown. Drysdale told Eggleton: 'Andrew is thinking of bringing the issue to a head.'

Peacock found some encouragement from the other leaders. On 30 August, Chaney and his Senate deputy Peter Durack spoke to Peacock from Perth. All were worried by the media's coverage of the leadership issue. Chaney said that Howard should be spoken to and Peacock encouraged him to do so. Chaney and Durack raised the leadership situation with Howard the same day. They stressed the problem which Howard was causing, the speculation he was generating, and argued that it was harming the party. Howard could not lightly dismiss Chaney and Durack—they had both his respect and the stature of party leaders. Howard promised to consider their submissions, but Durack told Peacock he was not hopeful. Meanwhile events generated their own momentum.

The same night, the story broke on television that Howard had said privately that Jim Carlton would be treasurer in a Howard government. These comments had been made a few weeks earlier when Howard was socialising after delivering a speech to the Economics Society in Canberra. The remark circulated on the Canberra grapevine and reached Laurie Oakes, who put it on the television news. That night Drysdale told Eggleton: 'It's the last straw for Andrew.'

However, Peacock had always been a faulty tactician, a defect which would dominate the coming events. The Peacock camp was too aggressive and badly misjudged Howard. It briefed the media that Peacock would confront Howard. Such tactics had only one purpose: to intimidate Howard and force him to retreat. In fact, they produced the opposite result and the briefings given by Peacock's office over the weekend of 31 August–1 September produced the final leadership confrontation.

The *Sunday Telegraph* reported under the headlines 'Peacock Comes Out Fighting' that the Liberal leader had decided to confront Howard and demand complete loyalty. The Peacock supporters went public in a futile bid to pressure Howard. Michael Hodgman declared: 'No leader should have to worry about press speculation over his leadership once a week.' He would support Peacock 150 per cent if he acted to end leadership speculation. Howard now resolved to defy Peacock.

The Peacock camp made two mistakes—they expected either that Howard would retreat when put under pressure or that he might challenge Peacock for the leadership directly. But Howard and Henderson had decided on a third course much earlier—that Howard would neither retreat from his public stance nor challenge Peacock. He would simply defend his own position as deputy. This meant that in any confrontation Peacock had to try to remove Howard as deputy, a task he had not properly assessed. Meanwhile Howard was starting a week's holiday in the Snowy Mountains with his family and travelled south on Sunday, 1 September.

The risk for Peacock lay in overreaction; in making a mountain out of a molehill. The Howard camp said with validity that no matter what formula Howard adopted, speculation would continue because of Peacock's intrinsic defects as leader.

Howard pulled on his snow gear at the Cooba Holiday Ranch near Berridale on Monday 2 September, hoping to improve his ski performance. But at breakfast he was faced with headlines: 'Peacock's men confront Howard', and 'Peacock set to take on Howard'. Howard, his wife Janette and the three children set out for the nursery slopes at Smiggins Hole. But Howard's attention was distracted; he knew Peacock could not back off now. So did the media. It headed south from Canberra by road and air to find the ski-suited deputy. Peacock had to recall Howard for the showdown. Chaney, destined to play a paradoxical role over the next few days, was appalled by Howard's behaviour. Their friendship would never recover from the looming showdown. Chaney believed Howard had an obligation of loyalty to Peacock which he was refusing to accept.

Howard's day started badly and got worse. The snow was fine, but the wind was wretched and showers threatened. Howard was a plodder on skis. By late morning the Howards left Smiggins and drove down the mountain towards Berridale and an afternoon of high farce. The media was thick on the ground. The Cooba Holiday Ranch, halfway between Jindabyne and Cooma at the end of a three kilometre dirt road, had pet joeys and paper-thin walls. Howard met the media and gave his interviews. At 2.39 pm Peacock rang Howard at the Ranch. Howard took the call in a small room off the main lounge. The door had a 'private' sign, but the journalists in the lounge heard every word Howard spoke during this strained 12 minute phone call.

Howard told Peacock he wanted to make three points. First, he had not been plotting against Peacock; he had never lobbied a single person against Peacock. There was nobody in the parliamentary Liberal Party who could claim that he had been plotting since Peacock had been leader. Second,

Howard had an apology to make. He had embarrassed both Peacock and Carlton over the treasurer story. It originated from a quite benign source and did not reflect any discussion Howard had had with Liberal politicians. Howard regretted the story and wanted Peacock to know that suggestions about ministry lists were absolute bunkum. Third, and most important, Howard told Peacock he was not able to alter the substance of his response on the leadership. He had told this to both Fred (Chaney) and to Peter (Durack). 'I do not believe I have been disloyal to you,' Howard told Peacock. 'I really do resent very deeply some of the things that have been in the press in the last couple of days suggesting I have been disloyal.'

Peacock said he had not accused Howard of disloyalty and Howard replied: 'I accept that it did not come from you.' Peacock told Howard he wanted the leadership issue discussed as soon as possible and asked Howard to attend the shadow ministry meeting the next day. Howard agreed.[12]

Howard spent the next few hours talking to the media. He was emotional and the intensity of the gathering storm was captured in the tone of his remarks.

> I am not plotting, I have not been plotting. I have not drawn up lists of shadow Ministers. I have not made any approaches to people . . . The response I have given on the possibility of any leadership challenge is fair and reasonable. This response does not represent any disloyalty or treachery to Mr Peacock. I have spent half my life serving the Liberal Party and I am willing to match my record of loyalty to its leaders, present and past, with that of anybody else in the party.[13]

The Liberals were heading for a crisis—but a crisis that Peacock was not controlling. Peacock was creating a trap for himself—he was making the test of his own authority the deputy's job and not the leader's. Peacock had the numbers against Howard as leader. But Howard was not challenging Peacock; Peacock was challenging Howard's right to stay as deputy.

On Tuesday morning, 3 September, Howard drove to Canberra in his holiday attire and the four leaders had a meeting, joined by Eggleton. They tried to find a form of words acceptable to both Peacock and Howard; and they almost succeeded. Howard drafted a statement, the critical parts of which read:

> As Deputy Leader, I will continue to give my loyalty and support to Andrew Peacock . . . As I have frequently said in the past, both publicly and privately, it is not possible or indeed reasonable for a person in my position to state or be required to state categorically that there are no circumstances in the future in which he would ever seek the leadership of his party. I stand by those comments.

Howard, at the urging of Chaney, agreed to add another paragraph:

> However, these comments should not be interpreted as any attempt on

my part to keep alive speculation about a leadership challenge. I can only repeat that as Deputy Leader I will give full support to Mr Peacock.

But Howard, despite the urging of Chaney, refused to agree to an extra seven critical words: 'and I will not challenge his leadership'.[14]

Ultimately, this is what the Peacock–Howard crisis boiled down to— seven words—so little yet so much. Howard would not budge—because it was so much. It was the final test of loyalty; a pledge not to challenge. Howard refused for one reason only: he wanted to keep his options open and did not fancy being a hypocrite. Peacock told Howard his position was a 'contradiction in terms'. He complained to Eggleton: 'We're wasting our time. This is no solution.'

Eggleton realised that Peacock wanted a showdown, not a compromise. While Chaney urged a compromise on Howard, Peacock doubted whether any compromise would work. Eggleton saw that Peacock was moving towards an 'all or nothing' position—his fatal mistake.

The shadow ministry met at 2 pm and heard both Peacock and Howard explain their remarkable impasse. Peacock said Howard's position was unacceptable to him and he would call a party meeting on Thursday to resolve the matter. Peacock's intention was to seek Howard's removal as deputy.

Howard called a press conference, still in casual clothing, to defend himself and said he would fight 'tenaciously' to stay deputy. In the next forty hours he fulfilled this promise to the letter. Peacock saw the media briefly during the afternoon. As the politician who forced the situation he appeared tentative. Having put Howard into a fight for survival, Peacock seemed unable to grasp that Howard would now fight for his life:

Q: If he's [Howard's] re-elected, will you continue as Leader?

A: A lot of these 'ifs'! As far as I'm concerned, I have the full support of the Party . . .

Q: Why do you say you expect a new Deputy, Sir? Have you done some head counting on that?

A: No. But I would expect in the circumstances the Party would accept the fundamental element . . . a Leader expects that a Deputy Leader must give full and total support and rule out that vital element of a challenge.[15]

The defect in Peacock's tactic was the absence of a candidate to run against Howard. Chaney had been briefly considered but not seriously entertained. Peacock's confusion was revealed that evening when he gave a background briefing to a small group of journalists. Peacock had already asked Peter Shack to run against Howard but Shack had declined, saying a more senior figure was needed. Peacock told the journalists that he was thinking of running John Moore, Jim Carlton or Wal Fife—but he hadn't decided.

Peacock's suggested deputies were extraordinary. Carlton and Fife, both from NSW, were close to Howard; neither would run against him. Peacock had dropped both Carlton and Fife from his shadow ministry nine months earlier. He was desperate to get somebody from NSW yet he had alienated the NSW Liberals over a long period. By elimination, Peacock had only one candidate—John Moore. The method of Moore's recruitment was fascinating.

Before Moore left Canberra that afternoon, he told Peacock he did not want to run against Howard. Moore said he had enough extra duty being Queensland Liberal Party president. That night Moore dined with friends at Brisbane's Sheraton Hotel and flicked on the television in time to see Richard Carleton name him as odds-on to become the Peacock candidate. Moore recalled: 'I came back to the table, had a grog, then rang Peacock to see what was going on. He confirmed the story and I flew back to Canberra the next morning.'[16] Moore was drafted because Peacock had nobody else.

The message Howard gave colleagues on the phone was the message he conveyed to the media. He wasn't challenging Peacock as leader; he could work with Peacock; he was the best deputy and he would fight for his job. Howard argued that in politics there are no absolute guarantees; that position depends upon performance. He said it was Peacock, not himself, who was unreasonable.

Howard had only one major tactical decision which he took late on Tuesday afternoon, 3 September, after talking to Janette. He decided to retire to the backbench if defeated. This was a courageous and a critical decision. It was the turning point in the struggle—the move which delivered Howard the leadership. It turned the heat onto Peacock.

The party would have voted Howard out as deputy as Peacock requested if it knew that Howard would remain in the shadow Cabinet. But Howard cancelled any such easy option. He told the party, 'vote against me as deputy and you consign me to the backbench.' This would be an absurd decision for the Liberals: the man with the best credentials as economic spokesman and deputy would be lost to these jobs when there was no obvious candidate for either of them. Howard realised that the shadow Cabinet was not credible without his presence—so his flight to the backbench would keep his honour and weaken Peacock. Howard briefed journalists and this story appeared the next day, 4 September.

Most Liberals were incredulous at the crisis which had erupted so rapidly. Their terrible dilemma was obvious—voting Peacock's way and losing Howard or voting for Howard and repudiating Peacock as leader.

The problem for Peacock is that his strategy, not just his tactics, was flawed. What would Peacock gain by winning? He would force Howard onto the backbench. But this would not reflect well on Peacock's leadership because it would gravely weaken the Opposition. Peacock wanted to protect his own position as leader. But if Howard went to the backbench, he would have a licence to campaign against Peacock and, in conjunction with Carlton and Spender, he would form a mini Cabinet-in-exile. Such a situation would become intolerable for the Liberals, particularly with the ongoing media attention it would attract. Howard was the senior NSW Liberal, the pivot for the business community, the policy leader for the party and the most respected Liberal with the opinion-making elite. By forcing Howard to the backbench, Peacock would look weak, not strong, and his new shadow ministry would appear faintly ludicrous.

John Moore sat in his office throughout Wednesday telling any journalist who dropped in of how Peacock had drafted him. He had no real wish to be deputy, declaring: 'I'm not much of a performer, not much good at speechmaking. I have spent most of my professional life in the financial world . . . you keep your mouth shut and do your job.'[17]

Moore was no match for Howard on merit. But Peacock asked the party to forget merit. The party's preference was Howard. Peacock was saying to the party, 'respect me as your leader by giving me the deputy I want, not the best candidate.'

Peacock had his own fateful decision to make: what would he do if Howard were reelected? This would be tantamount to a vote of 'no confidence' in Peacock. However, it would be qualified to the extent that the vote was not on the leadership itself and few disputed that Peacock would outpoll Howard in such a contest. Peacock decided that if Howard won, he would resign as leader. He told Eggleton late on Tuesday that this was his intention. It was a noble decision, but also a fantastic conclusion to the events which Peacock himself had triggered.

Peacock had elevated bad tactics into an art form. It surely required special skill for a leader to face the option of resignation over the contest for deputy, a contest forced by his own hand, when he still enjoyed majority support as leader. However, Peacock, unlike Howard, kept the fateful decision to himself. Why did he stay silent if he was prepared to resign? This was absurd. It was logical to tell the party its real choice. Peacock, by refusing to reveal his own position, forfeited the chance to solidify support by making his own leadership the real issue. Peacock was too complacent.

By contrast Howard rang every Liberal apart from core Peacock supporters. He seized every media chance—print, ratio and television—and there were many. Every Liberal must have seen Howard on the media at one stage or another. He staged a forty-hour media blitz and under pressure performed better than ever. Peacock, by contrast, was invisible and office-bound. The Peacock camp offered the facade of controlled calm. In retrospect, it was obvious that it did very little. Peacock only did a limited amount of personal lobbying—a severe blunder.

Peacock relied heavily upon Reg Withers as his numbers man. Yet

Withers was isolated from much of the party and most of the lower House. Moore did not work for himself. Shack did a little for Peacock. The leader's camp assumed that Chaney was also organising the numbers, but Chaney, in fact, did not lobby a single person.

Chaney had his own agenda—finding a compromise and halting the crisis. When the initial talks with Howard failed on Tuesday Chaney sought and secured Peacock's permission to keep working to find a compromise. Chaney assumed that Peacock's numbers were secure. This is what he was informed by Peacock, Shack and Withers. So Chaney as the most senior Liberal on Peacock's side worked not for Peacock but for a compromise—an insight into the lack of organisation of the Peacock camp. Chaney spent all Wednesday drafting and redrafting compromise positions and talking with Howard and Henderson. Chaney was always hopeful the contest could be avoided and in this sense he was the harbinger of false hopes.

Chaney found a pattern in his talks with Howard. They would reach a tentative settlement on a form of words with which Howard seemed happy. Howard would then tell Chaney that he needed to talk to his supporters. But after these talks Howard would refuse the compromise. Howard's main advisers—his wife Janette, Henderson and John Carrick—helped to keep him solid.

Gerard Henderson says: 'Chaney put psychological pressure on Howard. Howard believes in the Liberal Party and to tell him he's harming the party is a psychologically disturbing accusation.'[18] But Chaney was offset by John Carrick, Howard's mentor. Carrick told Howard that Peacock's approach was 'monstrous', that Peacock was endangering the party and that Howard's obligation to the party was to fight.

Chaney's compromise was a statement from Howard that he would not challenge Peacock while deputy. If Howard gave the undertaking he would have to resign as deputy before making any challenge. So Howard would avoid the label of hypocrite in this situation and Peacock would get the declaration he wanted. Chaney believed that he had Howard to the point of acceptance—but it was never sealed.

Janette told Howard that if Peacock was so keen to compromise, it was a sign of weakness. She argued with insight that the more frantic they got, the more pressure Chaney applied, then the more fragile was Peacock's position.

Chaney's compromise was doomed completely when a bunch of reporters arrived in Howard's office about 4 pm, the afternoon before the ballot, wanting to know if he had signed the deal. Howard was furious because the leaking of the negotiations before their conclusion could only damage him. If Howard was seen to be faltering or about to compromise, then his own supporters would quickly melt away. So Howard slammed shut the door on any compromise.

The day before the ballot Westpac chairman Sir Noel Foley openly declared that it would be a tragedy if Howard's ability was lost to the

Liberals—an intervention Howard believed was significant. The night before some Howard backers predicted 33 votes out of 70—just short of victory. Feedback from the party rank and file and the business community was strong for Howard. In Peacock's home state of Victoria an active group of Howard backers had emerged.

Just before midnight Howard went to Chaney's office for another talk, lasting about ninety minutes. Howard knew better than anybody else the mood of the party—it didn't want a bloodletting. Howard again rejected Chaney's plea for compromise. Howard believed, wrongly, that he would be defeated in the morning; he decided, in effect, to stand on strength and lose the deputy's position rather than make a concession in order to save his job. Howard had contacted about fifty Liberals by the time he left the building that night. Peacock, by contrast, had not spoken to more than fifteen. Howard went to the Commonwealth Club to catch a few hours of fitful sleep.

On the morning of the vote, 5 September 1985, Max Walsh wrote an article that had the ring of truth for Liberal doubters:

> The situation is absurd, because John Howard is simply the most indispensable member of the Opposition front-bench. He is the only person there who even pretends to stay on top of the key function of contemporary government—economic management.
>
> For the Liberals to put this rare nugget of talent on the backbench would be the ultimate triumph of the politics of personality—in this case Andrew Peacock's—over considerations of total Party welfare.[19]

Howard walked into the party room at 10 am believing that he was a beaten man. Howard needed 36 votes to stay deputy and his own estimate put his support in the high 20s, at least six votes short. Howard says: 'The prospect of finishing leader did not enter my head.'[20] Peacock was confident; but it was a confidence bred of ignorance. Withers and Shack had told him Howard could not muster more than twenty votes—a bad misreading. Peacock had broken every rule in the book of political survival.

Peacock opened the meeting by explaining why he required the written assurance from Howard. But Peacock failed to convey to the party room that he saw the contest as a 'life or death' vote on his own leadership. Some Liberals assumed it, but many did not reach this position. Chaney spoke next after circulating a letter to all members in which he said the crisis stemmed from 'the quite narrow point of difference' between the two men. Howard then spoke, emphasising his loyalty and saying that no deputy in the party's history had been asked to make the pledge that Peacock was demanding from him.

The Peacock camp blundered when its supporters moved to spill the leadership, only to withdraw when it became apparent that Peacock did not want such a motion. The spill was then moved on the deputy's position—the first Peacock–Howard test of strength; it was to declare the deputy's job vacant as a prelude to replacing Howard. The spill was carried only 35–34, evidence that Peacock was tottering. But the vote was not read out.

Moore and Howard nominated for the vacant deputy's post and Howard won 38–31. When the announcement was made a shaken Peacock rose, told the party he would consider his position and left the room with Howard, Chaney and Durack.

The four leaders went to Peacock's office. Peacock told the other three leaders that his position was untenable—a pointer to resignation. Chaney tried to dissuade him: 'I think that's a mistake. I don't think you should. You should take advice from your people, Shack and Withers.' But Peacock hardly bothered to respond. He had made up his mind.

On their return it was Howard who opened the party room door and entered first, a sign that he was taking charge. Peacock announced briefly that in the light of the vote he would resign. At this point three or four members called out 'No, don't go' and 'Don't be silly', some only now realising the significance of the vote. There were two nominations for leader, Howard and Carlton—the two leading drys in the Liberal Party. Howard won easily 57–6, but there were seven informal votes, Peacock supporters disillusioned with the triumph of the drys.

A total of 12 candidates then stood for deputy, a contest without a form guide. The vote in the final round was: Neil Brown 36, Ian Macphee 15, John Moore 11 and Peter Shack 8. Peacock gave a generous speech appealing to the party to support Howard. Chaney privately told Howard that he would stand aside as Senate leader if Howard wanted a clean sweep. But Howard declined the offer.

The Liberals left their party room just before 1 pm after a momentous meeting which began a new era. They left with a Howard–Brown leadership team, a result which nobody in Australia, not even the Liberals, could have predicted three hours earlier.

Peacock's aid, Graham Morris, and wife Margaret St George were waiting for the results in the Opposition leader's press office. Peacock walked in. 'What happened?' Margaret asked. Peacock replied, 'Neil Brown won.' 'But what happened to you,' she asked. Peacock replied, 'I quit.' Margaret went white.

The Liberal federal executive had been meeting in Canberra the same day while waiting for the news from Parliament House. Just after 12.30 pm Eggleton's secretary entered to say that Howard was leader. Eggleton noted later, 'The executive was stunned and there was disbelief.' Eggleton asked his secretary to check again—but there was no mistake.

Peacock had achieved a remarkable defeat. A majority of Liberals wanted him as leader, yet he had resigned during the meeting. The mood of the party was obvious; it had wanted the status quo—Peacock as leader and Howard as deputy—and an end to the stupid contest of pride between them. The vote for Howard over Moore was a triumph of commonsense.

Howard later praised the four people who had helped to sustain him through the pressure—his wife Janette, Carrick, Henderson, and his brother Stan.[21]

Many Liberals did not realise the deputy's vote was a confidence vote in Peacock's leadership. It is true that some did realise and voted for Howard in an effort to destroy Peacock—but not many. Far more Liberals believed that they could still have the Peacock–Howard team—that the party room could impose its own resolution on the crisis.

Peacock's strategic failure was to think that he could gain from trying to break the Peacock–Howard team which the party preferred. Peacock's tactical failure—once he had launched the strike—was his refusal to take a decisive stand. He had two choices: he could abort the contest by reaching a compromise with Howard or announcing to the world that it was an issue of confidence on which he would resign. Peacock did neither, and this is the origin of the claim that Howard became leader by accident. This claim is largely correct. It was an accident for which Peacock was responsible.

Howard beat Moore by seven votes; this means if four Liberals had voted the other way, then Howard would have lost. There were certainly more than four Liberals who would have switched votes if told that by voting for Howard they were terminating Peacock's leadership. But they didn't know. Peacock forgot that the party while supporting him as leader might not permit him to remove Howard as deputy. By pressing to remove Howard, Peacock lost his position, even when a majority of the party still wanted him as leader.

At his press conference later, Peacock deployed the guise of honourable resignation to disguise the collapse of political will. But Peacock lacked the tenacity and skill to command the jungles and byways of Australian politics. His most famous admission, with a wry grin, was that he may never have wanted to be prime minister. Perhaps his enemy was pride; the sense of pride which propelled him to confront Howard but prevented him from asking his colleagues to vote for him.

Asked at his media conference if he had expected the spill motion to be so close Peacock replied: 'No, I didn't.' He said that 'over the last few days I, in fact, spent very little time on the phone talking to people about how they would vote.' Why? Because, he said, he was interested in a compromise and 'I really didn't pay much attention to numbers'.

The following exchange then occurred:

Q: Mr Peacock, did you tell Mr Howard that you would resign if he was elected Deputy?

A: No.

Q: Did you tell anyone in the Party?

A: No. Yes, sorry, I told one person.[22]

This entire process reflected the political amateurism of the Liberal

Party. It had an element of farce from start to finish. The Liberals changed leaders in a few days of bedlam with most of the parliamentary party caught by surprise and the result being more accidental than deliberate. If this was a measure of their political skills then it was just as well the Liberals were not running the country.

This contest inaugurated a political theme of the 1980s—the superior political professionalism of Labor over the Liberals. Leadership was an issue within the Liberal Party, not the Labor Party. Hawke, in fact, had never faced a leader's ballot and was unlikely to face such a ballot for years. Despite Labor's many faults, it was inconceivable that the ALP might change leaders by accident. The ALP's political, factional and organisational skills made Labor a formidable force when it was united and, when it was divided, they offered a method and process for conflict resolution.

The Liberals, by contrast, had revealed in this contest their lack of leadership depth, a consistently shallow attitude towards the leadership issue, an ineptitude with numbers, a lack of sophistication in internal party debate, all of which produced a Howard–Brown leadership team to the surprise of the party. The Liberals had exposed themselves as political amateurs.

Although stunned by his election as leader, Howard behaved like a politician who was ready. He had escaped from the ridiculous and achieved the sublime. Howard was euphoric and for the first, and possibly only time in his leadership, he was inspiring. The content and fluency he displayed at his first press conference left few journalists with any doubt that the Liberals had snatched victory from the jaws of defeat.

The keys to Howard's success were philosophy and tactics. He won because of the perception that he was the spearhead of economic rationalism inside the party, that he was a figure of substance. In the three days of struggle, Howard displayed greater inner strength than Peacock. The Liberals, in effect, decided that Howard's presence as deputy was more important than Peacock's pride as leader.

The Liberals had emerged stronger when it appeared that they would finish weaker. Peacock's ineptitude had delivered the leadership to Howard—a success Howard would probably not have achieved during this parliament on his own efforts. Peacock had solved for Howard his insurmountable difficulty—the act of assassination.

Howard became leader in very favourable circumstances for himself and the Liberal Party. The Hawke government had completed nearly a year of its second term with two years before the next election, and was facing severe political and economic difficulties. The previous six months had seen an increase in ALP factionalism, evidence of Cabinet disunity, the fiasco of the Tax Summit, and advancing political attrition in the marketplace. Far worse news was coming—the currency crisis and an export price collapse.

The Peacock surrender

It was apparent at the time of Howard's election that the economic adjustments being forced on the Hawke government might break it politically.

For many Liberals, Howard was the man for the times. He was Australia's most prominent neo-conservative politician; an admirer of the Thatcher and the Reagan revolutions. Howard's strategy was to harden the choices and sharpen the contrast in politics. He would replace the smooth pragmatism of Peacock with ideology. Howard won others through his personal qualities. Chaney rang his wife Angela to tell her that Howard would make an excellent leader.

Howard's elevation gave the coalition a new opportunity. Politics in Australia was moving decisively towards the right and Howard would establish the pace of change. The non-Labor parties had begun a new march. Only later would the Liberals grasp that they had exaggerated Howard's ability to inspire a sense of confidence in himself and his policies.

On Saturday evening, 7 September, the Howards held celebratory drinks at their Sydney home. Friends, local Liberals and media associates attended this enjoyable event. They spilled through the living areas and into the back garden. But everyone crowded inside when Janette Howard kicked off her shoes, climbed on a table, and delivered a little speech. She applauded her husband's win and, being the most confident in a confident gathering, finished with a ringing declaration: 'Next stop, the Lodge!'

11
The banana republic

We must let Australians know truthfully, honestly, earnestly, just what sort of international hole Australia is in . . . if this government cannot get the adjustment, get manufacturing going again and keep moderate wage outcomes and a sensible economic policy then Australia is basically done for. We will just end up being a third rate economy . . . a banana republic.

Paul Keating, 14 May 1986

The fortunes of the Hawke government and the course of Australian life were transformed in the mid-1980s by the 40 per cent depreciation of the dollar between February 1985 and August 1986. At one stage the value of the exchange rate, adjusted for inflation, reached its lowest point this century. The depreciation was a response to the collapse in the balance of payments—Australia's ability to pay its way in the world—and the rise in net foreign debt.

This crisis in Australia's external accounts represented a confluence of short-term economic policy and long-term cultural traditions. It forced a dramatic change in Labor's policies; it inaugurated a new era in Australian economics and politics which will endure far into the 1990s; and it was a turning point—the stage at which the balance moved decisively towards the free market economic rationalist agenda and against the Australian policy tradition. It is the symbolic point at which the dimensions of the 1980s emerged—namely, that the decade would inaugurate the third phase in modern Australian history after the nineteenth century establishment of a Western civilisation and the twentieth century experiment of the Australian Settlement's ideas and structures.

The flashpoint was Paul Keating's warning in May 1986 that Australia faced the risk of becoming a banana republic. This facilitated the demise of the old order and the advance towards a new one. It is also proof that history is made as much by accident as by design. Keating's remark was inadvertent but it became a psychological pivot. It lifted community consciousness about Australia's economic predicament to an unprecedented level and it changed the limits of political tolerance.

The banana republic

Keating's 'banana republic' statement was converted by the media and the treasurer into an appeal to the Cabinet, the ALP and the community to recognise a national dilemma. It also required the assumption of responsibility by the government for combating the crisis; it provided a benchmark by which the Hawke government would be judged for the rest of its life. It is the source of the ambivalence about Keating's record as treasurer—whether he was a success as the prophet of the new order or a failure because he was unable to confront the crisis he defined.

The spectre of the banana republic was seen in Australia at the time and afterwards as a warning that the country's underlying institutions and ideas required drastic revision. These ideas were those embodied in the Australian Settlement—protection, regulation, introspection, arbitration, commodity reliance—which, as the 1980s unfolded, came under irresistible demolition pressures.[1]

From 1986 onwards the leadership within both the Labor Party and the coalition was driven, in policy terms, by this sense of economic crisis. While Labor and coalition fought over many issues, they both saw the economic solution as lying in a new radical market-oriented direction which involved the destruction of the old order and the fashioning of a new Australian ideology to improve economic performance and to fit the competitive realities of the 1980s and beyond.

Keating's 'banana republic' warning was an admission that Labor's economic approach during its first term had hit an immovable obstacle. It meant that the policy structure arising from the 1983 National Economic Summit was not a solution to Australia's problems. At this point the Hawke government confronted the central policy problem of its existence—how to reconcile strong growth with the limitations imposed by the balance of payments. There had been some early recognition of a potential problem but it was not taken seriously. For instance, in his first ministerial speech Peter Walsh had warned that 'the state of our overseas current account is, like the impending domestic deficit, one of the most serious problems confronting the new Government'. But as Walsh later admitted, 'I then, more or less, forgot about it; I think we all did.'[2]

The problem was that strong domestic growth was spilling into a level of imports which Australia was unable to finance through its exports. The nation was importing too much and exporting too little, which meant that Australia was having trouble paying its way in the world. The nation was living beyond its means.

The magnitude of the depreciation was a measure of the severity with which the markets saw Australia's plight. For a while the $A behaved as a Pacific peso. It was a demonstration of how the markets, through a floating exchange rate, could impose a severe adjustment upon Australia, the theory of which Keating had recognised when he floated the dollar. The depreciation was a response to Australia's mounting current account deficit which would dominate economic policy during the decade. The current account deficit is a measure of the extent to which Australia draws upon overseas resources in excess of its capacity to earn such resources through exports and other credits.

Australia has been a capital importing nation throughout its history. As a consequence it has typically run a current account deficit—drawing upon overseas savings beyond its capacity to earn such resources through trade, tourism and dividends. This is what being a capital importing nation means. For the post-war period until 1980 the current account deficit averaged 2.5 per cent of GDP. But around 1980 two important changes occurred.

The underlying current account deficit rose to about 4.5 per cent of GDP and stayed at this level during the 1980s which meant that Australia was drawing upon overseas resources significantly beyond its own means. It was, in short, spending far beyond its own level of production. The second change occurred in the way this higher current account deficit was financed each year. There were two basic sources of finance—foreign equity investment and foreign borrowings. During the post-World War II period the deficit had been financed by foreign investment in Australian enterprises which returned a steady stream of overseas dividends for the foreign owner and advanced local industry. The result was a debate during the 1960s and 1970s about foreign ownership of Australia and publicity about the danger of 'selling off the farm'.

Foreign investment was the price Australia had to pay to fund its current account deficit and develop the nation. There was nothing remarkable about this process, since Australia had never been able to fund its investment requirements from its own national savings.

However, just before 1980, the method of funding began to switch from foreign equity investment to foreign borrowings. This was the start of an international fashion in which debt was preferred to equity. The switch was partly because of the size of capital required and partly because the funds were being mobilised within financial institutions. This meant that instead of paying dividends overseas, Australia had to meet the interest costs on the borrowings. In the process Australia began to incur a significant foreign debt—the accumulation of the financing of annual current accounts largely through overseas borrowing. From the start of the 1980s when Malcolm Fraser was prime minister, these two trends—overseas borrowing and growing foreign debt—were established.

In the 1980–86 period there were three factors underlying the initial widening of the current account deficit to around 4.5 per cent of GDP. First, there were extensive overseas borrowings to finance mineral processing and electricity generation associated with the resources boom of the early 1980s which followed the second OPEC oil price shock. It was assumed at the time that the higher current account was no cause for concern because it involved the financing of projects which would produce a sharp lift in

The banana republic

Australia's export income. But this hope was undermined by the early 1980s wages explosion, an example of the benefits of the resources boom being taken in higher wages before the export gains had been achieved.

The second factor was the speed of economic growth during the recovery from the early 1980s recession which witnessed a surge in demand fed by both public and private spending. This was hailed by the Hawke government as its finest achievement—the powerful recovery from the sterility of recession. But in fact the budgetary expansion of both the Fraser and the Hawke governments helped to create the overspending problem. Demand spilt over into an excess of imports which by 1985–86 turned into an alarming deterioration in Australia's trade account.

The sharpness of this deterioration in 1985–86 was attributable in large measure to the third factor, the collapse in the terms of trade (that is, export prices in relation to import prices) which between March 1985 and March 1987 fell by 14 per cent. This was more than just bad luck. It was a dramatic reminder of the structural weakness of the Australian economy. It revealed the contradiction between Australia's first world living standards and its third world export structure. It was a fracture between the national lifestyle and the inability of Australia's export base to continue to produce sufficient revenue to sustain that lifestyle.

A US observer visiting Australia in 1986, David Hale, a Chicago economist, wrote: 'The Australians are increasingly uncomfortable about their economy's split personality, but after decades of depending upon raw material exports to sustain one of the world's highest standards of living there is no easy way to restructure.'[3]

In 1986 the current account deficit blew out to 6 per cent of GDP and the alarms were rung in Australia's main economic institutions. This meant that Australia was spending 6 per cent more than it was earning and was obtaining the difference in borrowings from the rest of the world, an unsustainable process.

The convulsions of the 1980s represented the collision of long pent-up forces, most notably the deterioration in Australia's competitive position in relation to its trading partners. Australia was in danger of being left behind in a tougher, harder world. The country had responded too slowly to the forces transforming the international economy during the previous generation. It was a victim of its political tradition: the protectionist mindset of the Australian Settlement. Australia was a young nation with geriatric arteries.

The three factors responsible for the rapid deterioration in the current account deficit—the resources boom, excessive domestic spending, and the terms of trade decline—merely reflected deeper structural issues. These highlighted the need for a national reassessment including a drastic policy shift which would be tantamount to a new phase in Australian history.

The most obvious issue was Australia's failure post-war to move

199

towards a more diversified export base with more raw material processing. After World War II the greatest burst of wealth generation in history occurred, built upon the unprecedented expansion in international trade. This was a phenomenon from which Australia had all but excluded itself, clinging to its border protection and fatalistic import substitution at the cost of efficiency. In the period from 1960 to 1987 when world trade exploded, Australia's share of total world exports fell from 1.7 to 1.1 per cent. The so-called Menzian Golden Age of the fifties and sixties was the last great Australian slumber: a period when the international community was gearing to dash past a lazy Australia. In most industrialised nations in this period the export/GDP ratio doubled, but Australia's remained static at about 14 per cent.

The long-term risk for Australia of remaining locked into a raw material export base was revealed by international trends in 1986. This was the year that raw materials prices, excluding petroleum, fell to their lowest levels in recorded history in relation to the prices of manufactured goods and services. Despite the collapse of the raw materials economy there was little apparent fallout for the industrialised world. The reason, according to US business management analyst Peter Drucker, was that for the developed nations 'the primary–products sector has become marginal where it had always been central before'. But for Australia the story was different since its export revenue was dependent upon the collapsed prices for raw materials.[4]

The industrial world was using a diminished supply of raw materials for each unit of manufacturing output. This meant that wealth would accrue to those nations which applied added value to raw materials rather than to those which exported the simple raw materials. Drucker argued: 'The raw-materials economy has thus become uncoupled from the industrial economy. This is a major structural change in the world economy.' There were many ways this change could be dramatised. Drucker explained: 'If raw-materials prices in relation to manufactured goods prices had remained at the 1973 or even the 1979 level, there would be no crisis for most debtor countries, especially in Latin America.' Using the same figures Australia would have faced no balance of payments crisis in 1986.[5]

The moral for Australia was not just its bad luck over the fall in commodity prices; it was rather the inflexibility and incapacity of the previous generation to respond to the changing international economic system, largely the result of McEwenism.

The two further underlying issues for Australia at the core of its current account deficit crisis were its lack of international competitiveness and its inability to generate higher national savings to reduce its call upon overseas savings. These questions would dominate economic policy and the political agenda for the rest of the 1980s and into the 1990s.

Much of the economic debate in Australia from this point onwards focused upon a series of measures to improve the country's international competitiveness, a compulsion which drove both government and opposition. It was under this heading that inflation reduction, wage restraint, protection cuts, micro-economic reforms and the shift to an enterprise bargaining wages system were promoted over the next five years. Such changes were major ingredients in securing a better export performance and a more efficient economy.

The associated campaign was to reduce Australia's consumption and increase its savings. The more Australia could fund its economic development from its own resources the less it would be dependent upon overseas borrowings. Associated with this, a related and overlapping agenda was fashioned in the late 1980s, extending into the 1990s, which involved turning the public sector from a net borrower into a net saver, lower inflation, and changes to the taxation system which encouraged savings, not consumption, along with the use of superannuation as a savings vehicle. These two agendas, in fact, constituted a redesign of Australia's governing ideas and institutions.

Australia's high current account deficit in 1986 raised a fundamental question about the wisdom and viability of the growth strategy pursued by the Hawke government since 1983. The result was that Australia grew faster than the rest of the world since most OECD nations had adopted a more cautious strategy. Paul Keating's boast in 1984 and 1985 about Australia's growth leading the world was true, partly because the industrialised nations chose a different option—slower recovery, higher unemployment, lower inflation. While Australia reflated many other nations gave deflation a priority. This meant that there was less overseas demand for Australia's exports but plenty of Australian demand for imports.

A major issue posed by the Hawke–Keating post-1983 growth strategy was whether it was viable for Australia to sustain a growth trajectory higher than its trading partners. Could Australia grow faster than the rest of the world? The risk was that Australia's high growth would hit the balance of payments constraint because of a massive spillover into imports. This is precisely what happened in 1985–86.

The balance of payments—the measure of Australia's ability to pay its way in the world—has traditionally been a preoccupation of Australian governments and economists. In 1965 the Committee of Economic Inquiry (the famous Vernon Committee) declared: 'In the long run the rate of growth that can be sustained by the economy will be governed by, perhaps more than anything else, the extent of the good fortune and good management that attends the balance of payments.' The delusion of the next generation was that the balance of payments had been 'cured' in the 1965–80 era, a period which saw the export benefits of large-scale mining and energy projects. For example, in November 1979 John Stone was warning about the need for economic action to respond to the expected surge in export income.

It is not surprising that when Hawke took office he gave little attention to the balance of payments constraint. After all, it had not been a major problem for two decades, despite signs of deterioration at the end of Fraser's regime. Labor's growth policies soaked up domestic demand and boosted spending in both the private and public sectors. The budgetary expansions of the early 1980s under Fraser and Hawke saw the government sector become a substantial net borrower. While this helped to keep activity and employment higher than otherwise, such pump-priming undermined the country's balance of payments position.

The year 1986 brought a full-scale recognition that Australia was back in the position of two decades before, 'when our balance of payments placed very tight constraints on our internal economic growth and on the development of our economy.'[6] A series of successive current account deficits funded by foreign borrowings caused a rapid accumulation in net overseas debt.

Net foreign debt as a proportion of GDP rose from 6 per cent in 1980 to almost 30 per cent by mid-1986. This was also a reflection of the depreciation of the $A value of the foreign currency component of the debt. By 1985–86 Australia's debt was divided nearly equally, with the public sector incurring 45 per cent and the private sector 55 per cent.[7] A significant proportion of the debt, about one-third, was incurred through Australia's banks and financial institutions for lending to companies and entrepreneurs. Another feature of foreign borrowings—a bonus point—was that they were utilised to fund the historic surge in Australian equity investment abroad during the 1980s, a process made possible by financial deregulation. By the end of the decade these overseas investments were worth nearly $50 billion, giving Australian corporations a diversity of assets and income earning structures never previously realised.

However by 1986 the burden of foreign debt had become the overwhelming concern, behind Australia's current account deficit. It was the driving force behind the two economic imperatives of the late 1980s and early 1990s—a more competitive economy and a better savings performance.

The start of the foreign debt debate was signalled by John Stone's swansong speech of August 1984 titled '1929 And All That . . .', which raised a parallel between conditions before the Great Depression and those of the early 1980s. Stone said these periods had shared a rapid growth in debt, a fragile world financial situation, and risks to international commodity prices on which Australia was dependent. He warned that 'in many cases—increasingly at State level and for some time now at Federal level—the debts being incurred are not even being used to finance works at all but merely to maintain, and indeed increase, current expenditures'.[8]

Stone noted that over the previous fifteen years there had been a fourfold increase in the size of Australia's total public sector borrowings

The banana republic

relative to GDP, from 2 per cent in 1969–70 to 8 per cent in 1983–84. He described this trend as one of fundamental failure, warning that public borrowing would defer, not hasten, a lasting solution to unemployment. He quoted Thomas Jefferson's warning 'that public debt is the greatest of the dangers to be feared . . . [to] preserve our independence we must not let our leaders load us with perpetual debt'.[9]

Finally Stone recalled the January 1931 statement by economists which had identified three goals for the post-Depression recovery—reduction of labour costs, balancing of budgets and the improvement of internal and external prices. These should be achieved respectively by a 10 per cent cut in real wages, cuts in public spending, and allowing the currency to find its natural price. Stone's point was that fifty years later Australia was still struggling to effect these policies. He cautioned that there was 'a great deal of ruin' to be had by a nation as rich as Australia before it might be called to account.

All debt, public and private, had to be serviced, which meant that as the debt mounted a growing proportion of export income had to be diverted from covering import costs to debt servicing. By 1985–86 interest payments on the net debt were taking an equivalent of 16 per cent of export income. This was the origin of the 'debt trap', the crippling process by which new overseas borrowings were financing the interest repayments on earlier borrowings.

There is nothing wrong with foreign debt as such. The issue is whether the foreign debt is incurred in the financing of projects which will generate an income stream in future years to repay the interest and leave an enhanced national income. It was obvious by 1986 that such was not the case. An influential EPAC discussion paper prepared for the government noted:

The increased external borrowings in the 1980s has not been supporting higher levels of capital investment . . . While there was a brief investment revival in 1979–81 [the resources boom], the level of business investment has been low and the effect of Australia's recent foreign borrowing has been to finance a higher proportion of this investment from overseas thereby supporting correspondingly higher domestic consumption.[10]

This was the most dangerous aspect of foreign debt. The more such debt was incurred for consumption, not income-producing investment, the more it represented an indulgency by the current generation at the expense of its children. Such a conclusion about Australia's foreign debt during the 1980s was inescapable. The above-mentioned EPAC paper examined the potential for Australia to stabilise its foreign debt, concluding, on optimistic settings, that stabilisation might occur at a debt level equivalent to 40 per cent of GDP by 1990.

It was against this backdrop that economic policy evolved during 1985

203

The end of certainty

and 1986. In February 1985 the protracted depreciation of the $A began—the transmission of Australia's trading weakness—inaugurating an 18 month saga which culminated in political crisis and the start of an enduring economic revolution which would drive the thinking of all senior politicians—Hawke, Keating, Howard and Hewson. By late 1986 the legacy from the dollar's collapse threatened to finish the Hawke government.

The initial fall was provoked by a mixture of economic and political factors—the abandonment by the Reserve Bank of monetary targets in the wake of financial deregulation suggesting an easier and less predictable monetary stance, and uncertainty about Labor's decision-making stemming from Hawke's ineptitude in handling the MX missile crisis. The government welcomed the initial depreciation. It was widely accepted that the $A had been overvalued. Hawke's main economic adviser, Ross Garnaut, had believed from the start that the success of Labor's growth strategy was dependent upon a major depreciation to reconcile domestic growth with a sustainable balance of payments outcome.

There are three keys to grasping Labor's economic policy during Hawke's second term. Its style was shaped by Keating and its substance came from Hawke and Keating who shared the same outlook but whose personal rivalry provoked competition between them over initiatives; the policy was adopted by Hawke and Keating as an ongoing response to Australia's currency crisis and weak external accounts; and it meant that Keating was prepared ultimately to impose upon the government a tough-minded treasury-inspired economic rationalist direction because he accepted and believed the theoretical propositions advanced by his senior advisers that this prescription would solve Australia's problems.

The story of the second Hawke government is the story of how the Keating–treasury alliance underwritten by Hawke spearheaded a new economic direction in response to the current account deficit crisis. This was made possible by several factors—Hawke–Keating agreement on the approach; the pervasive influence of the economic ministers through Cabinet's Expenditure Review Committee (ERC), which saw both the centre-left ministers and the senior left-wing minister, Brian Howe, endorse this outlook; the consensus within most of the Canberra economic advisory elite over the policy; and the cooperation, sometimes reluctant, of the ACTU leaders, Bill Kelty, in particular.

The new direction was fashioned over 18 months and was a unique marriage of the treasury line with Labor's Accord-driven penchant for economic growth.

The depreciation marked down the value of Australian assets which made Australian products cheaper and more competitive on world markets; imports were dearer, exports were cheaper. Economic theory said that depreciation should correct the current account deficit because the price effects would produce fewer imports and a surge in exports. The trouble was that in the short-term the external deficit worsened because only the price effect was obvious before volumes were adjusted. This phenomenon was known as the J-curve, a piece of economic jargon which Keating made famous in 1985–86 when he tried to explain to the party and public why economic deliverance would take some time.

Since a depreciation was a cut in Australia's international value, its assets and its living standards, it was imperative that it be shared throughout the community and that its competitive advantages be transmitted throughout the economy. The government's task was to ensure that the benefits were not lost in higher inflation and higher wages. Labor responded to the depreciation from February 1985 and over the next six months began to tighten policy. Interest rates were lifted from February, budget cuts were announced in May and the Accord was renegotiated in September.

The government was heading in the right direction because of the trilogy commitment made before the 1984 election. In his May 1985 economic Statement Keating announced spending cuts of $1259 million across a range of programs. It was a modest check on public spending and the start of Labor's policy of public sector contraction after two years of expansion.

When Keating's third budget was framed in July 1985 the depreciation was hefty—18 per cent against the trade-weighted index (TWI) which gave an overall measure. In this setting Labor took its trailblazing first steps towards a tough economic policy, unveiled in the 1985–86 budget which further tightened spending, reinforced in September 1985 when the government negotiated a more flexible Accord Mark II with a 2 per cent real wage cut to retain the competitive benefits of the depreciation.

Keating was the driving force behind these tighter budgetary and wages policies, but they were also backed by Hawke and his advisers. Keating expended much political capital in their achievement, a cardinal point in grasping the crisis of 1986, the next year. Keating had no inkling of the extent to which the $A would plummet during 1986 nor any conception that the restraint which he had delivered in August and September 1985, far from being sufficient, was merely a down-payment.

In his 1985–86 budget Keating restrained spending to an increase of 1.3 per cent in real terms compared with 6.1 per cent the previous year. The budget deficit was cut to 2.1 per cent of GDP compared with 3.1 per cent the previous year. This was achieved by spending cuts, not tax increases. Keating boasted about being a responsible treasurer and keeping the trilogy commitments. But his budget was set for growth; it put the brakes on the public sector to permit a private sector expansion. Keating now delivered the famous line exhorting people to 'set their sails for growth'.

There was no sense of crisis in Keating's 1985–86 budget speech, just an optimism that the policy changes would guarantee Labor's future. Keating predicted 'many more years of consistently high growth and economic

The end of certainty

discipline', growth which would be required 'for the rest of this decade to restore full employment'. Keating still defined the return to full employment as 'the greatest challenge of our administration, of the labour movement and of the nation'.[11]

But Keating's confidence was undercut by scepticism in the treasury's own analysis in the budget papers. It agreed with Keating that 'in many respects the economic fundamentals are stronger now than they have been for some time'.[12] But it said that durable prosperity lay in policies which delivered low inflation, wage restraint, adequate profits and international competitiveness. The treasury suggested that Keating's growth model might be flawed:

> If exports are responding to slow world growth while imports are responding to strong demand in Australia, the current account will continue under pressure and external indebtedness increase. With slow world growth, world commodity prices are unlikely to recover and Australia's terms of trade are likely to remain weak . . . Provided Australia's improvement in competitiveness is maintained, our external accounts will move over time towards a historically more normal and sustainable pattern. The balance of payments constraint therefore really comes back to the inflation constraint . . .[13]

The risk inherent in Keating's high growth policy was high inflation. The inflation differential between Australia and the world was starting to widen significantly. The average OECD inflation rate was predicted to remain under 5 per cent while Australia's would rise to around 8 per cent as the depreciation forced up prices.

The Accord Mark II of September 1985 was born from the recognition that full wage indexation was incompatible with the balance of payments slump. Put simply, the depreciation was a blowtorch to the Accord. It would make or break the Accord as a wages policy. Keating's challenge was to persuade the unions to take a real wage cut to hold the competitive gains from the depreciation. The Accord Mark II was Keating's greatest achievement in 1985 and was concluded only after a seven hour bargaining session which reached a famous compromise.

In the Accord Mark II the ACTU consented to a 2 per cent real wage cut in the autumn 1986 wage case. Keating agreed that to maintain living standards income tax cuts would apply from 1 September 1986 to compensate workers for the real wage cut. Keating and Kelty further agreed that the government would support an ACTU sponsored 3 per cent increase for productivity which employers would pay not through wages but as occupational superannuation benefits during the 1986–88 period, a reform which Labor would later embrace with enthusiasm. This negotiation stretched the tolerance of the Accord partners to the limit.

There are two judgements on the Accord Mark II—it was a tribute to

206

the realism of the unions that wage indexation was modified; but within months the agreement had been exposed as inadequate, made obsolete by the escalating current account deficit which would reveal that both the process and results of such a wage system were no longer suitable to the national predicament.

The government's late 1985 post-budget mood was fragile because the $A was jittery and financial markets had not been comforted by Keating's budgetary and wage restraints. In this period a significant reassessment of Australia's outlook was made by a growing number of economists, analysts and institutions developing dire scenarios about Australia's external accounts and foreign debt. The economic opinion making elite began to warn of a possible national crisis. The sentiment of the times is captured by two assessments from different quarters.

The prominent economist and friend of the ALP, Professor Fred Gruen, warned of:

> . . . the frightening increase in our external indebtedness over the past three years, the doubling in the debt-servicing ratio over the past four years, the fact that our current account deficit is now the third highest in the OECD world, partly produced by the Government's excellent growth performance. Given the marked deterioration in our terms of trade, given the poor prospects for world trade . . . prudence demands that we reduce money wage growth. Otherwise the longer-term danger of continuing devaluation (and perhaps ultimately some IMF supervision of our affairs) is by no means unthinkable.[14]

This was a sobering assessment from an economist known for his measured judgements.

The analysis by the financial advisory service Syntex, prepared by its principals, the economists Alan Wood and David Love, noted the:

> . . . sheer audacity of the high-growth strategy embodied in Labor's [1985] budget . . . the IMF without doubt would demand from Australia an internal policy vastly different from that now being pursued by Labor. The IMF would demand for starters the end of wage indexation and a specific cut in real wages. It would demand an internal deflation severe enough to force Australian producers either to export or collapse. As part of all this, unemployment would have to leap far higher than it is at present. Real interest rates would have to average around 10 per cent. Because the Labor Government approach is novel and unconventional and the antithesis of what the IMF would apply doesn't necessarily mean that it won't succeed. What it does mean is that the rest of the world will be watching with fascination to see how this experiment in unorthodox economics works out in Australia.[15]

Syntec had propounded an orthodox position—that Australia might need a recession to correct the deficit in its external accounts; that the economy might need to be 'closed down' to stem the haemorrhage; that this was a harder but surer means than to continue Labor's growth strategy with the risk that the imbalance became much worse before it improved. Keating scorned such defeatism. But Keating, as Syntec claimed, was pioneering a risky course. This conflict between Keating's growth strategy and orthodox economic theory would shape much of the debate for the rest of the decade.

In late 1985 the jury—the financial market—voted against Keating by forcing another major depreciation of the $A. It meant that Keating had failed in his attempts through both the 1985 budget and the Accord Mark II to restore confidence. The proof that confidence would not hold came in October–November 1985, just three months after the budget, when there was a dramatic $A fall. The message for Keating was unmistakable—a bigger depreciation meant a further policy tightening and this meant higher interest rates.

Keating and the Reserve Bank had been tightening monetary conditions during 1985. Now they lifted interest rates to their highest levels under Labor. The squeeze became severe with 90 day bank bill yields and prime lending rates peaking at about 20 and 21 per cent respectively. Keating's hope was that this monetary crunch would be short-term since these interest rates over a longer period would deliver the recession which he had promised above all to avoid. But Keating's hopes were frustrated.

Exports prices just kept falling and the current account deficit kept rising through early 1986. This meant that foreign debt would continue to rise; that inflation would rise due to the depreciations; that living standards would have to be cut to ensure, again, that the competitive advantages were kept. It also meant, without offsetting action, that interest rates would remain at unacceptably high levels.

Keating knew that if the exchange rate stayed weak then a further policy change would be required.[16] But he was never a treasurer to rush to hard options. From early 1986 the options were obvious. In February the *Sydney Morning Herald*'s economic editor, Ross Gittins, said:

> Although Paul Keating doesn't seem to have realised it yet, the fate of the Hawke government could be sealed within the next month or two . . . Interest rates have been so high for so long that if monetary policy isn't eased within the next month or two, the likelihood of the economy dropping into recession in the second half of this year seems very high . . . Mr Keating needs to announce, first, that he will be bringing down a May mini-budget and to specify the size of the cuts in government spending and the size of the reduction in the budget deficit . . . Second, he needs to announce that the government will be seeking further wage discounting in the September wage case . . .[17]

Gittins was outlining the orthodoxy within the economic establishment. Unless Keating put more of the burden on fiscal and wages policy then high interest rates would cause a recession. Labor had to tell the people and the unions that more restraint was essential since Australia was living beyond its means. But Keating faced an acute problem—the Labor Party did not understand the nature of Australia's economic trouble and was reluctant to learn.

The story of 1986 for the Labor Party was the smashing of its icons. Labor embraced an economic rationalist agenda not by choice but by compulsion. It was driven throughout by a mounting currency crisis. Labor's policy was reshaped against a backdrop of falling electoral support, internal disputes, fear of recession and a growing undercurrent of Hawke–Keating tensions.

Keating faced opponents on either side—from the right, an economic establishment which insisted on the traditional response to a balance of payments crisis, even if that risked a recession, and, on the left, the old-fashioned ALP pump-primers suspicious of the modest policy tightening that he implemented.

The treasurer repudiated the pessimists who wanted the economy shut down: 'They do not have any credible explanation of how to handle wages policy after the demise of the Accord—for to abandon our growth objective would be to kill the Accord and its basis for agreed wage restraint.'[18] Here was an honest admission about the nature of the Accord: it committed Labor to solving the current account deficit within a growth framework.

Within the party Keating was warring with both the left and the right. The left, spearheaded by social security minister Brian Howe, attacked Keating's fiscal 'deficit fetish' while the NSW right, Keating's base, complained that its once favourite son had 'a fetish about economic rationalism which blinds him to political realities'. Keating had not spoken to his factional colleague, Graham Richardson, for months.

On 4 March 1986 Keating won in-principle agreement from Cabinet to cut $1.4 billion from spending in the next budget as part of a fiscal tightening. But getting the cuts from sullen ministers was another matter. Keating conceded, years later, that he should not have waited until the August budget; that he should have pushed for a cost cutting economic statement in May 1986. But that would have necessitated an internal party showdown.[19]

The next month, April, Keating persuaded the Cabinet to accept partial deregulation of the home loan rate to ensure that his tight monetary policy did not kill off home lending. This exercise was a classic study in the changing nature of 1980s politics. In this decision Keating kept the 13.5 per cent ceiling for home loans taken before April 1986, but future bank loans would attract a deregulated rate, then about 15.5 per cent. He had struck a deal with the banks: in return for having the ceiling lifted they would boost their home lending for 1986–87 from $3 to $6 billion and examine flexible repayment schemes.

This was Keating's solution to the dilemma in which the home loan rate was still regulated in a deregulated financial system which meant that banks had no incentive to lend money at 13.5 per cent when they could get a better return elsewhere. The risk was that housing finance would evaporate, the housing sector contract and jobless numbers rocket. Keating offered the banks a subsidy in return for getting more funds into housing, and introduced a system of partial home loan deregulation.

Home loan deregulation had been the proposal on which Labor had savaged Howard the year before. During preliminary talks with Keating, Hawke had rejected Keating's proposal for total deregulation on political, not economic grounds, acting on advice from Richardson and Barron. This was old-fashioned politics: Labor couldn't take a decision to lift home rates. But Keating in his dedication to new politics had found a solution which would persuade Hawke and avoid Howard's pitfalls.

One of Keating's media critics, the *Sydney Morning Herald*'s political correspondent Mike Steketee wrote:

> He encountered so much resistance that the Cabinet meeting scheduled for 9.30 am did not start until 2.30 pm. By then, he had neutralised the prime minister, his strong-willed staff, key members of caucus, and, to a lesser extent, the housing minister, Stewart West. It took another four and a half hours to demolish the opposition in Cabinet from Tom Uren, Bill Hayden and others. Keating . . . once again has proved to be the dynamo in the Hawke government. No dogma and no political boundaries can contain him. A setback to him is not a loss; it is a postponement of victory.[20]

Keating was smashing many traditional ALP positions but also dinting many political egos. Each success bred greater hostility. Keating believed that he had outgrown the reflex politics by which the NSW right still lived. He began to sell his famous dictum that 'good economics is good politics', an idea foreign to the Labor right. Richardson believed that Keating was heavily into self-delusion, isolated from the party and a growing victim of office.

As fascination grew with Keating doubts mounted about Hawke. The trust and friendship between Hawke and Keating, prejudiced at the 1984 election, fractured at the 1985 Tax Summit, would be further undermined during the 1986 economic crisis. The days of weekend gatherings at the Lodge and of social contact between Hazel and Annita were over. Hawke was a disciplined, efficient leader, harnessed to the task, but since the 1984 election, with the exception of foreign relations where he hoped to leave an international imprint, he was remarkably passionless and passive.

His biographer, Blanche d'Alpuget, revisited Hawke in office in autumn 1986 and reported:

> The room was quiet and felt empty. Hawke was distant . . . Menzies used to get drunk when he was Prime Minister. Holt had a mistress.

210

The banana republic

Gorton was a larrikin. Hawke has defined his Prime Ministership as super-respectable. He said repeatedly that physically he was on top of the world. Indeed, his skin tone and colour looked excellent. But . . . my overwhelming impression was of a lack of vitality, that he was vanishing.[21]

Hawke was on the Pritikin diet, proud of his capacity for work, praising the quality of his ministers and settling into an active but comfortable lifestyle at the Lodge and at Kirribilli House. Hawke felt comfortable as prime minister; his appeal was as Australia's natural prime minister. But it was threatened by an economic convulsion.

In autumn 1986 the Labor Party came face-to-face with its fundamental political dilemma of the 1980s. How did Labor address the current account deficit crisis while avoiding a recession? Keating knew the answer. Labor must move from public sector expansion to contraction. The Accord must become an instrument to secure not real wage gains, but real wage cuts. In March 1986 Keating told the parliament that the collapse in Australia's terms of trade was 'disastrous'.

In April 1986 the Reserve Bank finalised a long-term and pessimistic balance of payments projection into the 1990s. The treasury was sceptical but the projection was pushed by the Reserve's head of research, Peter Jonson, and endorsed by the Governor, Bob Johnston. The Reserve's officers briefed Keating on 24 April and 13 May. One session was very long with the bank advocating a major policy change—the options were either an interest rate tightening or a tightening in fiscal and wage policy. Jonson argued that the debt and current account were more serious than Keating had admitted and there was a long and testy exchange between them. Bob Johnston told Keating: 'We can't keep going the way we are now. People know our policies aren't working. You'll score marks if you say this. I think people will thank you.' The Reserve believed that this advice was basic to the subsequent events.

The turning point came in mid-May with the $1.48 billion current account deficit for April 1986, far worse than expectations. It was discussed in Cabinet before Hawke's departure to Japan and China with agreement that the tough spending line must be enforced at the Premiers' Conference. The treasury was shocked by the figures which it saw as evidence of a structural deterioration. 'We're buggered,' David Morgan told Keating. 'Yes, we're buggered,' Keating agreed. Treasury conceded the deterioration was far more serious than it had believed and adopted the bank's pessimism. Hawke was stamping his feet in Tokyo while Keating faced the music at home and, like a conductor without an orchestra, began to improvise.

After a breakfast function in Neil O'Keefe's seat in Victoria the next morning, 14 May 1986, Keating agreed to an impromptu radio interview with John Laws. He conducted the interview from a wall phone after the

211

breakfast with plates and dishes rattling in the background. Keating, warmed up and hyped up, gave the interview of the decade:

> **Keating**: We are importing about $12 billion more than we are exporting on an annual basis. What it means is that we are living beyond our capacity to meet our obligations by $12 billion . . . we must let Australians know truthfully, honestly, earnestly, just what sort of international hole Australia is in. It's the prices of our commodities— they are as bad in real terms since the Depression . . . and if we don't make it this time we never will make it. If this government cannot get the adjustment, get manufacturing going again and keep moderate wage outcomes and a sensible economy policy, then Australia is basically done for. We will just end up being a third-rate economy . . . If in the final analysis Australia is so undisciplined, so disinterested in its salvation and its economic well being, that it doesn't deal with these fundamental problems, then the fallback solution is inevitable because you can't fund $12 billion a year in perpetuity every year . . . the only thing to do is to slow the growth down to a canter. Once you slow the growth under 3 per cent, unemployment starts to rise again.
>
> **Laws**: And then you have really induced a depression.
>
> **Keating**: Then you are gone. You are a banana republic.

The words hit the financial markets like a thunderclap. The dollar fell US 3 cents. The message was stark: Keating had warned of a national crisis. In one interview he had transformed the climate of politics. Despite subsequent rationalisation, the 'banana republic' statement was testimony to the truth that politics is a traffic in symbols and that history is made as much by accident as by design.

This was not a calculated, measured effort by Keating to shift the political parameters. Keating was being spontaneous, urgent, concerned—selling a warning about the severity of the position after the April figures. He didn't intend to deliver a dose of national shock therapy. Keating told David Morgan later that it had been a mistake. For weeks Keating became the target of intense party criticism. ANOP research revealed that people were shocked and bewildered by the 'banana republic' warning which to them was a bolt from the blue. The content of Keating's warning was not new—it merely reflected his recent comments in parliament—but the rhetoric was dramatic. The media paid close attention because this was Keating's first response to the April BOP figures and it was natural that his 'banana republic' warning became page one headlines.

The fall in the $A left the impression of a Keating miscalculation, even a disaster. Obviously he had not foreseen this reaction. At first he was thrown onto the defensive. Hawke was stunned, then furious. The ALP was rocked and mainly dismayed. The community was confused by the volte-face: here was the treasurer who had been boasting about economic growth

212

The banana republic

now saying that Australia might become a banana republic. The spontaneity of Keating's remarks was obvious from their arithmetic absurdity: his warning was entirely valid but he didn't really believe that growth below 3 per cent meant 'banana republic' status. The declaration put Keating himself in a perilous position by its admission of economic crisis. But it had another effect—having declared a crisis Keating was imposing an onus upon himself to address the crisis. Henceforth his challenge was manifest: to deny the banana republic. This was Keating's burden for the rest of his treasurership.

A few hours later at a Melbourne lunch, Keating tried to modify his earlier remarks: 'Far from being on the skids, the economy has last month produced 60 000 jobs.' The treasurer stressed that policy adjustments would come from spending restraint, not renegotiating the Accord Mark II. Keating was not seeking a change in policy beyond what had already been discussed. He was seeking greater community awareness of Australia's plight. In his many interviews over the next few days Keating never repeated the phrase 'banana republic'. It became taboo.

But the banana republic would become the next great issue dividing Hawke and Keating. It offered an insight into their contrasting styles and temperaments. Hawke's initial response to the April figures en route to Tokyo was cautious. They were 'disturbing' but did not suggest 'some major change'. Wages policy would be reviewed but Hawke said of the trade account, 'I think we've seen the worst of it.' Hawke and Keating, separated by the Pacific Ocean, were operating in different political constellations. As the Hawke party received the full details of Keating's remarks and the market reaction, they were appalled.

The next day, 15 May, Hawke tried to calm the waters from Tokyo's Imperial Hotel. After a phone call with Keating, Hawke was reassuring: 'This is not a time for panic.' Asked if he believed Australia was heading towards a banana republic he said: 'No. I don't'. Hawke conceded that Keating's remarks, if taken out of context, could be 'rather horrific', but he agreed that the recent trade figures were a 'devastating turnaround'. Hawke endorsed Keating's policy prescription of more spending cuts but keeping wages policy intact. His message was that 'we don't want any basic new policy directions'. But within 24 hours Hawke's statement was overtaken by events and Keating's opportunism.

Keating's fear about his warning was turned into confidence by the favourable response of the quality media the morning after. The *Financial Review* said it was 'rare and refreshing' and called upon the Cabinet to back Keating to get the policy changes. It criticised the markets for dropping the dollar when Keating's message was exactly what the markets had wanted to hear—a basis for tougher policy. The *Sydney Morning Herald* said Keating had hit 'exactly the right response . . . [and] has begun the task of preparing party and public opinion for the decisions ahead'. Keating in his follow-up interviews warned that living standards would be cut, temporarily.

213

He coined the line: 'the economy wasn't sick, it was too strong'. Keating was encouraged by the praise he had received.

The Advisory Council on Prices and Incomes held a long scheduled meeting on 16 May, attended by Keating, Willis, union and employers' representatives. Tempers frayed when the employers complained that they were too isolated from decision-making. But ACTU president Simon Crean made an important concession at this meeting—he said the trade unions might agree to have some elements of the Accord Mark II changed while retaining its integrity. Keating seized upon this opening. The subsequent Keating–Willis media conference sent shock waves rolling all the way to Tokyo.

Keating saw that the effect of banana republic shock therapy had given him an opening—that the employers and unions would consider policy changes to meet the crisis. He now moved to lock in the new sentiment for policy progress. He publicly hardened-up a series of issues canvassed at the meeting. First, there would be another meeting of government, unions and employers which would examine all issues relating to the balance of payments. Second, the Accord Mark II would be reexamined, which implied a tougher wages policy. Third, the timing of the September 1 tax cuts and the productivity deal would be reassessed, another pointer to budgetary and wage policy tightening. After a good day's work Keating rang Hawke to inform a startled prime minister.

Hawke's trip to Japan was being engulfed in this upheaval from which he was removed. At his evening media conference in Tokyo the same day, Hawke was weak and isolated. He was neither consulted about Keating's initiatives nor pleased afterwards and he refused to endorse any policy change. Having said the previous day that there would be no major policy switch, Hawke faced a bevy of questions about the policies which would emerge from the meeting—tagged a 'summit' by the media—which he had had no part in calling and about which he knew nothing. Hawke, of course, would be in the Chinese provinces when the meeting's preparations were occurring. Would Hawke chair the meeting? He didn't know, but thought he should be there! No, the meeting was not a summit. Yes, it was important. No, it was not 'a drastic new change' of direction. Hawke's advisers went into white fury mode. Their target was Keating. Their accusation: that Keating had set up Hawke. Their fear: what would Keating try next?

But the media went for Hawke, who was resisting the policy changes. Michelle Grattan's column began: ' "Well, it just reinforces what we all knew," said a highly placed Canberra official at the weekend. "Keating is running the country." '[22] My comment in *The Australian* was: 'Hawke is a fast thinker, an excellent salesman, an astute judge, intellectually and physically sharp, relaxed and confident in office. But he cannot lead. Leadership by definition means striking out alone. But Hawke seems to find this psychologically impossible.'[23]

The impression of the Cabinet, the party and the media was that Keating, not Hawke, was running the country. This was certainly the impression of Hawke's political adviser, Peter Barron, who could smell a repeat of 1985, when Keating bolted from Hawke on tax reform. Barron had an earthy but refined nose for leadership psychology. He knew this perception of Keating dominance was poison for Hawke—indeed, it was this quality, above all others, which became the basis of Keating's subsequent leadership push. Barron felt that Hawke's leadership was on the line. If Hawke didn't act to reclaim his leadership authority and control the government, then his days as prime minister were numbered. Barron felt that if Hawke didn't nail Keating now Keating would soon nail Hawke. He believed that Keating was putting a crisis straightjacket on the nation. Barron knew there was only one way to handle Keating: stop him dead in his tracks.

Barron had no intention of working for a leader who refused to lead. After the 1984 campaign and the 1985 tax debate, he refused to accept a repeat in 1986. He gave Hawke his advice and said: 'This is it, sport, unless you take charge now, then I'm off.'

After a series of consultations Hawke rang his deputy, Lionel Bowen, just before midnight on 16 May from Tokyo. He gave Bowen a series of instructions which could have fitted under the title 'Hawke's reassertion strategy'. On Sunday 18 May the party flew to Beijing with the media demanding access to Hawke over ongoing economic policy change. On arrival in Beijing the party went to the Great Wall Hotel and the media went to the communications centre to file their reports. But within ten minutes the drama began: the word spread among the journalists that Hawke would give a briefing. Barron had carried the day.

Hawke and his advisers arrived in a reversal of practice: this time Hawke visited the media. The prime minister sat at the head of a large table strewn with papers, typewriters and tapes, surrounded by the Australian media, behind whom sat a long row of Chinese teleprinter operators. Hawke announced that he would be giving a strictly non-attributable background briefing. He was breaking his practice as prime minister—this would be a major news story by which Hawke would seek to regain his ascendancy over Keating.

Hawke told the media that he had rung Bowen before leaving Tokyo and given him a number of instructions. He told Bowen to assume control of preparations for the economic meeting, an obvious humiliation for Keating. He asked Bowen to arrange a meeting of senior ministers in Canberra for the next day to whom Hawke could speak on a phone hook-up from China. The planned economic meeting was not a summit, not a decision-making meeting and would not be held for a fortnight. Hawke might still chair the meeting but he was concerned to downgrade its significance. The meeting was not to renegotiate the Accord; Hawke had clarified this with Crean the previous day. Any minister who wanted an input into the meeting should act through Bowen. The meeting would focus on deferring the September tax cuts and the productivity deal with the ACTU. Hawke said he had not spoken to Keating for two days.

Hawke was controlled and determined. He had dropped a political rock on Keating. As Hawke left the room, Barron, wearing a big smile, cigarette in one hand, patted Hawke on the back. Sometimes advisers have big wins too.[24]

Hawke had downsized the meeting which Keating described as 'the most comprehensive discussion of the issues since the summit'. This could have been mistaken for schoolboy rivalry between Hawke and Keating. In fact, it was a battle over which man ran the government and the country.

The Chinese teleprinter operators had a busy night and the newspapers carried banner headlines the next day typified by 'Hawke pushes Keating aside' and 'Hawke moves against Keating'. When the ministers met that morning in Canberra for the phone hook-up Hawke's remarks were hardly necessary. He merely confirmed with the same phrases the reports in the press. Keating sat, newspaper on lap, ticking off the points as Hawke made them. After Hawke had finished Keating angrily accused him of inspiring the newspaper reports.

The ministers saw Keating's temper flaring. 'Be careful, the Chinese will be listening,' they cautioned. 'Fuck the Chinese,' Keating replied. 'Just what's the point of this bullshit, Bob?' Keating demanded. 'Who's that?' Hawke asked. 'Who the fuck do you think it is?' replied Keating. 'We've got problems here and we're trying to solve them. Just what the hell do you think you're playing at.' The Chinese listeners received a graphic insight into ALP politics.

After his return to Australia Hawke admitted that he was the source for the Beijing briefing but denied that he had sought to undermine Keating. Keating, in turn, unable to attack Hawke openly, seized upon his staff as a substitute, branding them the 'Manchu court', the derogatory term he had been using privately ever since the Tax Summit. 'They're always my trouble,' Keating said. 'They've never been elected but they think they have . . . mostly I beat them.' It was a crack at Barron and Garnaut, the latter by then Ambassador to China.[25] Barron later quipped to Keating, 'Mate, I stopped you from running the country.'

There were two lessons from this bitter Hawke–Keating fracas. First, they were competitors in the contest to dominate the government; second, despite their rivalry and contrasting styles, they shared the same policy positions. This ambivalence would prevail for most of the government's life. When the Opposition tried to divide them in parliament Keating would perform a political pirouette and declare brazenly that he and Hawke were 'the greatest partnership of economic achievement in half a century'[26] and the Labor backbench would roar with delight.

Upon Hawke's return to Australia he and Keating held two long meetings in late May. The upshot was that personal pride was submerged in the interests of their common need—reshaping economic policy to meet the ongoing currency depreciation and export price collapse. The risks for Labor in ignoring the economic challenge were far worse than the unpopularity involved in facing it. In late May the Cabinet agreed to adopt harsher policy settings. It terminated Hawke's political strategy of 'good news', and Hawke now sought to exploit and build upon the tougher political climate which Keating had generated by his banana republic stance.

Hawke announced, without reference to Keating, that he intended to make a prime ministerial address to the nation. On 30 May he puffed out his chest before the television cameras and fell into the assertion mode which only Keating could provoke: 'The government's position is determined in the Cabinet room under my leadership.' Having established this point, Hawke declared that he would tap national 'guts and determination' and any other quality required to secure economic policy adjustments. Of course, just a fortnight before, Hawke had insisted that 'we don't want some drastic new policy directions'.[27]

The nation's greatest communicator had decided, belatedly, to utilise his unique status to reconcile the nation to tough times. This is exactly what senior ministers—Button, Hayden, Dawkins and Walsh—had wanted to see. They believed that Hawke's prestige had to be associated with the shift towards a harsher economic policy, and had been complaining for months about his 'Pollyanna syndrome'. They knew that a policy change could only be successful if backed by Hawke's office and popularity.

Hawke was driven now by several factors: he couldn't let Keating control the process; he recognised that major policy change was necessary; and he had no option but to lead this move. Trust between Hawke and Keating was poor but divorce was not imminent. They were married by their self-interest in the government's fate.

The trouble for Hawke was that his decision to give a national address was inspired by politics, not economics. It created huge expectations which were accentuated by another run on the $A in early June. This prompted calls for draconian solutions ranging from a twelve months wage freeze to a massive slashing of the public sector spending. Hawke was trapped, unable to meet the expectations fed by a climate of ongoing crisis.

In his 11 June address to the nation Hawke depicted the crisis solely as a function of the collapse in commodity export prices (thereby absolving Labor of any blame)—the world was paying Australia less so Australia must accept a cut in living standards. It was a 'bad luck' scenario which downgraded the extent of the changes required. Hawke had one substantial announcement—the government would seek another round of wage discounting—sowing the seeds for an Accord Mark III. It was a determined gamble to persuade the ACTU to more sacrifice. Hawke finished by invoking the names of outstanding Australians—Robert de Castella, Joan Sutherland,

Ben Lexcen and John Bertrand—to sell a message of success. He pledged: 'I will not shirk the hard decisions that are necessary to ensure a bright future for us and our children.' But the reaction was unfairly adverse, often damning. Hawke was strong on rhetoric, weak on solutions, yet he did tackle the fundamental issue of wages.

At a meeting with the ACTU wages committee the previous week, Hawke had led the way in pressing for another round of wage discounting. This was a necessary risk which provoked a threat from Kelty to 'cut and run' with a defiant wages campaign, if necessary. The Accord was shaking. It was a measure of Hawke's switch: within a few weeks he had moved from rejecting any wages tightening to a necessary push for another wages discount. The result was later embodied in Keating's 1986 budget as another 2 per cent discount which the ACTU grudgingly accepted, not without bitterness.

The background documentation to Hawke's address explained the national dilemma clearly: the collapse in export prices meant that Australia had lost 3 per cent of national income over the previous year. This cut in living standards had to be shared. Wage earners were not entitled to be exempted, hence the need for a further wage discount.

The economic crisis had tilted the political pendulum towards the right wing with growing, often strident calls for wage freezes and public sector cuts. Analysis of Australia's condition was heavy with foreboding, typified by the popular financial commentator Terry McCrann's view that Hawke's fate was to 'preside over a full-blown disaster or merely an old-fashioned economic crash'. It was far from an isolated opinion. But it was an outsider, the US economist David Hale, after a three week visit to Australia, who offered a wider appraisal:

> Australia today is a country where all the economic traumas of the 1980s appear to be converging. As the country approaches the bicentenary of European settlement in 1988, it is confronted with a crisis in its export prices typical of countries in the third world and an inertia in its capacity for domestic price adjustment comparable to old industrial societies in the first world.
>
> Fortunately Australians appear to be waking up to the fact that they are no longer living in a lucky country . . . they have embarked upon a form of economic self-examination comparable to that which preceded the election of the Thatcher Government in 1979. The chairman of a large mining house (Sir Roderick Carnegie) has publicly stated that Australians will become 'the poor white trash of Asia' if the country does not become more competitive . . . [but] Australia remains a very comfortable country and, unfortunately, Australians still tend to make favourable comparisons between themselves and their poorer cousins in Britain and New Zealand rather than with more successful countries. But not even the most complacent Australian can avoid noticing symptoms of economic decline in his everyday life . . .

The banana republic

The eclectic and pragmatic nature of Australia's current policy mix (the Keating model) is a reaction to the high unemployment of the 1970s as well as to memories of the savage deflation which occurred in Australia during the 1930s. It is an attempt to nudge the economy in the direction of re-structuring while avoiding the shocks which the Labor Party identifies with the early years of Thatcher and Reagan. It is not clear how long Australia can sustain a gradualist policy, though . . . Australian policy is a waiting game, an attempt to play for time in the hope that a commodity price recovery will eliminate the need for greater austerity or at least postpone it until after the next election.[28]

At this point, mid-1986, the historic challenge facing the Hawke government became obvious. It was quite different from the expectations of 1983 when Hawke was elected to end Australia's recession through a new compact. This had been accomplished faster than anybody had predicted. But the recovery had contained a nasty shock for Labor. It betrayed the extent of the structural and competitive deterioration of the economy— namely, poor productivity, reliance upon raw materials exports, and inadequate national savings to fund investment. This legacy of decades confronted Labor with electoral and philosophical challenges as severe as any in its history.

The 1986 crisis changed the nature of the Hawke–Keating government. It saw the creation of a new policy framework based upon two principles: real wage cuts sanctioned through the Accord, and a public sector contraction through spending cuts, a squeeze upon the states, and a tighter rein on borrowings. Labor was driven to these policies; it acted not from desire but compulsion. The new approach was anathema to the ALP tradition and had not been envisaged by Hawke and Keating when they assumed office. It involved a belief in the 'twin deficits' theory, that increasing public sector saving should cut the external deficit.

The instrument which had imposed these adjustments upon the Australian government was the float of the dollar, which had transmitted the impact of the depreciation. The trauma of the sharp depreciation had produced a period of improvisation within the Cabinet. Ultimately, Labor accepted the logic of the financial markets, the advice from its central economic departments and the prescriptions of the OECD. It became a government of severe wage restraint and serious public sector contraction. The aim of such policies was to secure a shift in resources to the traded goods sector of the economy and to boost national savings at the cost of consumption—an attack on the current account deficit.

Keating had been conditioning the market for a $5 billion plus budget deficit in 1986–87. The budget processes were close to finalisation with a deficit of just under $5 billion when, late in the week ending July 25, 1986, there were signs of another dramatic collapse in the currency. This crisis—the most severe in the depreciation saga—was triggered by market alarm about the current account and Keating's 1 July decision to tax dividends and interest paid to parent companies by their Australian subsidiaries (technically the removal of the interest withholding tax exemption). Keating later confided this was the one decision as treasurer which he made with genuine reservations. The reaction of the markets confirmed to Keating that his judgement on these issues was superior to the treasury's.[29]

On Keating's initiative, over the weekend of July 26–27 his officials laid the ground for two moves to restore confidence by encouraging further foreign investment. The first involved freeing up foreign investment restrictions, particularly in property, by eliminating a half-share local equity rule. The second was the reversal of the withholding tax decision—a backdown which would make it easier for companies to send untaxed profits to their overseas parent. These proposals revealed the extent to which Australia had to underwrite foreign capital to fund its excessive consumption and investment.

The currency crisis hit Australia on Monday 28 July when the ERC ministers were finalising the budget. Keating had his little Reuters screen on the Cabinet table and kept pointing to the falling $A rate. An exchange rate of US 60 cents was seen as a psychological barrier but on this day the dollar fell from around 63 to 57.2 cents. The slide was arrested only by Reserve Bank intervention. The Cabinet was infiltrated by a distinct mood of panic. Keating's banana republic warning had never seemed so real. It was probably the single worst day in the first three terms of the Hawke government. During the Cabinet committee meeting Keating kept calling out the rate. It is doubtful if any budget meeting in the last twenty-five years has been subjected to such pressure. Hawke cancelled an overseas trip to the South Pacific. There was a palpable feeling of national crisis. The response took two forms—immediate and budgetary.

It was fortunate that Keating's officials had been reviewing emergency measures since the sheer magnitude of events left many participants dazed. Reserve Bank governor Bob Johnston was involved in a phone hook-up to Hawke, Keating, senior ministers and advisers. But they were alarmed when Johnston confessed at one point that he didn't know what to do. Finally, it was decided that Keating would announce his more liberal foreign investment policy, ease the withholding tax provision, and that the Reserve would throw a lot of money to hold the dollar rate. It was Keating who synthesised these responses. The upshot was a stabilisation of the currency and a gradual rise. The label 'panic' dominated the newspaper accounts the next morning. But the process was unmistakable: Labor had no choice but to 'sell off the farm' to meet Australia's immediate obligations.

At the same time the crisis led Hawke and Keating and their senior officials to reopen the budget deliberations to tighten fiscal policy even further. Peter Walsh recalls: 'The ERC ministers meeting that day were shell-shocked. It was on this day that the decision was made to bring down a budget which had zero real growth in spending.'[30]

The power bestowed by the float on the currency markets was never more manifest. The market place was imposing upon Australia a regime of fiscal severity which the Labor Party had never remotely entertained. It was a demonstration of the consequences of Keating's internationalisation of the economy and a shattering reminder that the old Australia, protected and uncompetitive, could not survive within this environment. This day, 28 July 1986, the leadership elite of the Hawke government began to confront the true policy imperatives that would be required to refashion Australia's economic lifelines. It was a turning point for the Labor Party and for the nation.

The decision to reopen the budget discussions was taken in Hawke's office by Hawke and Keating. The upshot was another round of spending cuts and tax hikes through the ERC which took the budget deficit to $3.5 billion, far below market expectations. Keating and Hawke kept the deficit figure a secret—not even the finance department was told. Hawke and Keating were the only ministers who knew the bottom line. It was part of Keating's technique—to surprise the financial markets with a greater degree of fiscal restraint than they expected, thereby winning greater support for the currency.

In his August budget for 1986–87 Keating reduced the deficit to 1.4 per cent of GDP, compared with 2.5 and 3.2 per cent in the previous two years. Federal spending was cut by nearly $3 billion to zero real growth, the same rate as inflation—a tight spending stance only achieved three times in the last thirty years. It signalled a change in the structure of federal accounts which would result three years later in the greatest ever federal budget surplus.

Keating also announced that the government would seek a further 2 per cent wage discount—the first and only such declaration during the Hawke era made without prior ACTU approval. It was proof of the sense of desperation within the Cabinet to secure greater wage restraint but it reflected a political calculation of what the ACTU would wear. Keating said in the budget that wage costs would rise about 6 per cent, just above the level of Australia's trading partners. His speech declared that 'with the world having slashed our national income by over $6 billion we could not continue as though nothing had happened . . . we believe that Australia must maintain control over its own destiny and that this can be done by facing the problem squarely and making the remedial changes quickly and decisively'. Keating argued that the tight budget and wage positions would allow an easing in interest rates, a better policy balance which would avoid any recession. Meanwhile Hawke declared Australia's economic situation was equivalent to a 'crisis of war' which presumably demanded wartime austerity.

Post-budget Keating's primary aim was to underwrite the dollar and prevent another currency crisis, an event which would demolish the government. His most revealing remarks came in September when he noted that the financial market had stabilised 'due to its more contemplative reaction to the budget' and partly because the market believed there was a floor under the dollar. 'It is not an assumption I would disabuse them of,' Keating said.[31] The policy of the Reserve was to hold a minimum value just above US 60 cents; before the year's end the dollar had firmed dramatically to US 67 cents.

However, on 11 September 1986 one of the world's main credit rating agencies, Moody's Investor Services, downgraded the federal government's credit rating from AAA to AA1, an event which received great publicity. The Moody's statement was that while Australia's credit quality remained 'strong' there was 'a variety of economic and structural weaknesses' which 'cloud the nation's flexibility for servicing long-term external debt over a 5 to 10 year horizon'. It noted that more than 75 per cent of external earnings were farm and mineral receipts that would suffer from weak world prices and that there was little prospect of rapid structural change in the short-term. Keating said the government rejected the Moody's judgement; that more than any post-war administration the Labor government was advancing the internationalisation and long-term competitive position of the Australian economy.[32]

But treasury's own budget analysis offered more sober insights than Keating into Australia's predicament: a reduction in living standards was unavoidable; the scale of Australia's economic adjustment meant that improvements would be gradual and 'substantial improvements' would lie beyond 1986–87. In the coming year the economy would slow and unemployment would rise a little. But the current account deficit as a proportion of GDP, the measure of Australia's problem, would remain at about 5.8 per cent, an historically high level. That meant that foreign debt would continue to mount. Australia's economic malaise required long-range solutions and that suggested difficulties for Labor's reelection.

The treasury had both praise and a warning for the Accord. It said that the Accord was expected to deliver 'more acceptable [lower] wage outcomes than any practical alternative'. It placed great responsibility upon the trade union leadership. Their discharge of that responsibility over the previous three years had led to the creation of 630 000 new jobs. The going was getting tougher but failure 'would make virtually inevitable the path of serious recession as the sole remaining means of correcting Australia's external imbalance'.

While Labor used orthodox tools its economic strategy was unorthodox. The orthodox response to Australia's problem was to slow the economy and induce a mild recession. The chairman of the Business Council of Australia, Bob White, said that the government 'might have to help to push the Australian economy into recession . . . as a long-term solution of its growing trade problems'. The much practised method of beating a current account deficit—chloroforming the economy—was rejected by Hawke and Keating in favour of the unorthodox.

Hawke and Keating had always been 'economic growth' politicians. Indeed, Keating had developed during the 1970s the belief that Labor's future success depended upon being a superior growth party to the Liberals. But Labor's adherence to the growth model in 1986 transcended personal philosophy and entered the realm of political necessity. Labor governed through the Accord; the Accord's essence was growth or 'jobs, jobs, jobs'; so Hawke and Keating had to find solutions to economic problems within a growth model.

The IMF, OECD and traditional treasury prescriptions for a slowing of the economy were accepted by Hawke and Keating but the harder option favoured by these same institutions, a mild recession at the cost of steadily rising unemployment, was rejected. In 1983 Hawke had pledged to fight inflation and unemployment simultaneously. In 1986 Keating was trying to fight inflation, unemployment and the current account deficit simultaneously. Something had to give.

Keating said the difference between Labor and Liberal lay in the Accord; the Accord could secure wage restraint which meant that Labor put less reliance upon high interest rates and was therefore able to let the economy grow faster than its opponents. Recessions were Liberal politics; Labor politics was more skilful. Labor didn't need a recession because it had coopted the trade unions into a tight wages policy. This was the Keating litany. He propounded this model at scores of press conferences, dozens of financial dinners and within the parliament for the next three years.

In a paradoxical fashion, the banana republic made Paul Keating as treasurer. Before this, his three main achievements were the economic recovery, financial deregulation and the taxation package. But in 1986 Keating presided over a decisive change in economic direction designed to increase national savings and competitiveness. The tough decisions after the banana republic declaration left Keating with two assets—honesty and authority—and his tragedy was to expend them too easily and too quickly.

Of course, Keating's transition owed more to improvisation than to planning. He had to be driven to these harsher policies by the exchange markets but, once driven, he responded to the lash.

The result was that Keating slowly came to be seen as the dominant figure within the government, much to Hawke's incredulity and frustration. In private Keating was damning of Hawke, whom he characterised as a weak leader whose chief assets were popularity, consensus and a preparedness to be manipulated on most policies by Keating himself. Keating told people to their faces that he was the 'real prime minister'; Hawke was merely a frontman. Keating was awaiting the time when his status would match his self-image.

By this time Keating was a manifest threat to Hawke. Barron once said to Keating: 'Do a deal with Hawke, that he stand aside for three months and you be PM. You've wanted this job since you were a kid and you need to get it out of your system.' Barron was joking, but his point was serious.

After trying to hijack tax policy in 1985, Keating succeeded in 1986 in hijacking economic policy. He was a more fascinating figure than Hawke. Why? Because Keating exuded a sense of political power unmatched within the government. Hawke kept his unique popularity with the people but he was not the dominating figure inside his own government.

Hawke's resentment of Keating was reflected in a public patronising of his treasurer. Just before the 1986 Budget, interviewed on Channel Nine's *60 Minutes*, Hawke said he believed that Keating wished he had never made his banana republic remark. Hawke added that it would be churlish of him to 'have a go' at Keating simply because 'under pressure he drops a phrase'.[33]

The banana republic episode liberated Keating from his past. He was driven by the dollar crisis to champion a series of policies that were historically anti-Labor but which he slotted into a new Labor framework. In the process Keating was ruthless in breaking with political allies, discarding much of the electoral orthodoxy of his NSW right origins and constructing new alliances. But this was not a solo effort. It was possible only because Keating had three sources of internal support—Hawke, the small group of ERC Cabinet ministers that became the policy vanguard (Walsh, Dawkins, Button and Willis being the main figures) and, thirdly, the ACTU led by Bill Kelty.

Within the wider community the government's credibility rested upon three other institutional pillars—a grudging respect from financial markets which became associated with Keating's own persona; the quality print media and its leading commentators, the majority of whom were influenced intellectually by Keating rather than Hawke; and business, where Hawke and Keating enjoyed the qualified confidence of the major chief executives and the enthusiastic backing of Australia's famous entrepreneurs, ranging from cowboys like Alan Bond to sophisticates in new money such as Robert Holmes a'Court to the media baron Kerry Packer.

Labor's survival through the 1986 crisis was also a function of Hawke's ongoing popularity. During 1985 and 1986 a new phenomenon began to emerge—Hawke as a leader above politics. Labor fell behind the coalition and the polls pointed towards a change of government. But Hawke was always above Peacock and Howard as a preferred prime minister. Hawke kept leadership as an electoral asset for Labor. He was seen partly as a de facto president whose popularity transcended Labor's electoral woes.

At the end of 1986 Keating was approaching the zenith of his treasurership—blooded by economic crisis yet unbroken by the business cycle. Keating, a power addict, had found the international power domain. He dealt with the treasury in Canberra, the Reserve Bank in Sydney, Paul Volker in the US, Carl Otto Pohl in Germany, Rupert Murdoch in New York, and his three friends, Bill Kelty, Robert Holmes a'Court and Warren Anderson anywhere. Keating's passion became almost the rhythm by which Labor's mood sank and swelled. Keating in late 1986 was a man enraged by his enemies, obsessive with his confidants and persuasive with his colleagues. Yet his friends were worried by his passion and his opponents whispered that there was a touch of madness in Keating. In October 1986 during Keating's IMF trip, he delivered without notes a panoramic lecture on the international economy with panache which left other finance ministers wondering from what jungle this hybrid, so arrogant yet so charming, had originated.

But Keating's flaws were about to exposed—elitism and lack of organisation. In late 1986 Keating's failure to file his 1985 and 1986 tax returns broke in the parliament. It revealed a treasurer preoccupied by office, disorganised in his personal affairs and reluctant to admit a mistake when caught. While Keating conceded his error he fought the issue instead of burying it. The public saw the treasurer who had spent two years closing off tax loopholes failing to meet his own obligations as a taxpayer to submit his return on time.

The second issue, Keating's travel allowance, was a greater political burden. The allowance was to assist politicians travelling from home base to Canberra for sittings. When Keating became treasurer he moved his family to Canberra, away from his Sydney base, into rented quarters. Keating claimed the travel allowance and met the requirements for it. But he invited criticism for defying in his personal life the exact standards which as treasurer he was imposing on others by closing tax rorts and special perks. The more Keating was criticised the more he railed against the terrible conditions and sacrifices he endured as treasurer. It was the start of Keating's public fantasy about quitting politics to make a fortune.

The crisis of 1986 changed the focus of economic policy to the current account deficit. It became the major constraint upon employment creation and had to be contained before Labor could deliver its ultimate promise of sustained growth. It revealed the underlying weakness of the Australian economy in a cultural and institutional sense, a perception which remains today. It inaugurated the era of fiscal restraint in which spending in each year from 1986–87 until 1989–90 was cut in real terms by 0.2, 2.9, 4.6 and 0.2 per cent respectively. In overall terms this was equivalent to a 7 percentage points shift in GDP from the public sector. It also triggered an era of wage restraint in which the ACTU sanctioned a reduction in national income and thereby a new role for the Accord in combating the current account deficit.

In terms of power politics this period entrenched the future Hawke–Keating disputation over leadership, power and history: notably, whose government was it?

Hawke was offended by Keating's audacity in claiming to be the real leader. Hawke's entire life had been dedicated to achieving the prime ministership and he could not comprehend or tolerate Keating's threat to his legitimacy. The timing of Keating's threat—after Hawke's legitimacy had been validated by the party and the people at elections—just made his claim seem fantastic to Hawke. The key to Hawke's psychology was that he had fused his own prime ministership, the messiah mentality with which he had pursued Hayden for the leadership, with Labor's self-interest. Hawke's psychology was bound to the axiom: Hawke had delivered Labor to power and only Hawke would keep Labor in power—Keating's claims, therefore, were those of an imposter. Hawke and Keating were united as political professionals by the government's interest but divided as men by their personal rivalry.

Keating's worst public relations mistake—and Hawke was an even greater offender—was to oversell the rapidity with which his reforms would solve Australia's problems. The treasurer sold a message of restraint but, always optimistic and impatient, he was too anxious to declare a victory. In October 1986 he declared that the economic reforms were basically completed! While warning that 'Australians understand that this is the start of a long road out', Keating then told the Press Gallery that 'you will never live through, while ever you are in this parliament I'm sure, changes greater in both magnitude and quality than you are reporting now'.[34] Herein lay the origins of an epic delusion.

Those critics of the Hawke government who bemoan its so-called economic rationalist ideology are too remote from the action. Virtually every economic milestone in the early years was a response to a crisis. The currency crisis of 1983 produced the float; the terms of trade collapse of 1986 produced a new Accord based upon real wage cuts and the drive to a public sector surplus. Hawke and Keating were improvisers, using Labor's policy tools, their economic advisers and individual instincts. The story of their government, typified by the 1986 experience, is that of managers having to combat huge shocks imposed from abroad. Their policies revealed economic management as an experiment with old-fashioned data to predict the future; this is a truism of the government which Hawke–Keating ego and optimism nearly always obscured.

The 1986 reforms, in their psychology and substance, were a decisive step towards the dismantling of the Australian Settlement. The enduring message was that the old Australia could no longer endure—that raw material exports did not guarantee prosperity; that reliance upon the public sector was of declining utility; that wage rates could not be determined independent of the exchange rate; that Australia had to internationalise its economy and terminate its history of protection and introspection. This was the message which Hawke and Keating delivered without respite and with conviction during 1986–87.

The banana republic

The 'banana republic' was a dose of shock therapy for the nation which for a while left a legacy of crisis which Labor could have utilised to impose far tougher policies upon the nation. The Opposition gave Labor plenty of room. Howard called for a freeze of wages and public spending; the New Right was mugging unions from Robe River to Mudginberri. Keating's authority was as potent as Hawke's popularity. The prime minister declared the crisis the equivalent of war. The historical judgement in terms of the public mood and the depth of the problem is that the Hawke–Keating team failed to seize the full magnitude of the moment. Labor could have gone further but lacked the courage and imagination.

Labor felt it was heroic enough—its decisions were draconian by orthodox standards and its advisers were pleased. Labor was also frightened by the demons of revolt from its base and a community backlash. Hawke and Keating depicted themselves as bold warriors. But history will record that the times demanded more and would have given more.

12
The Howard leadership

*In politics it is more important to be right than popular. In time
correct policies will become accepted.*

John Howard, January 1985

John Howard was a new type of Liberal leader—the first free market
reformer to hold this post. This meant that he aspired to the greatest changes
in the party's nature since its foundation. Howard's dilemma was that his
ability as a politician did not match the historic objectives he sought.
Howard, in short, was no Menzies. The challenge he encountered in the
mid-1980s required a leader of authority and flair—sincerity and diligence
were not enough.

Howard fell victim to the 'strong man' leadership mythology of the
Liberal Party. He was never able to establish a commanding presence in the
community or unite his own party—a fatal defect. A popular leader can
prevail despite a divided party and a leader with a united party can prevail
despite his unpopularity. But the leader who has neither unity nor popularity
is the leader doomed to perpetual crisis. This was Howard's fate during his
four long, bitter, frustrating years as leader; a situation for which the party
must share equal culpability with Howard himself.

Howard's difficulty as a political tactician, like the batsman from the
second eleven, was that he was always playing the previous delivery. He
was applying today the lesson from yesterday, failing to grasp the dynamic
of tomorrow. The contrast with his opponents was revealing: Howard could
not match Hawke's community appeal and he could not combat Keating's
will to power. This meant that even when economic events dictated a change
of government Howard was always vulnerable to Labor's political clout.

As Liberal leader Howard stood for four main ideas—free market
economics, traditional social values centred upon the primacy of the family,
upholding the post-war foreign policy based upon the Australian–American

228

alliance, and support for the Liberal–National coalition as the vehicle of non-Labor rule. The first of these ideas was the most important because it enunciated a revolution. The other three were faithful genuflections before the Menzian edifice.

But Howard's mixture of radicalism or orthodoxy, depending upon the issue, excited his opponents. They attacked his economics for being too libertarian or 'heartless', and his social agenda for being too reactionary or 'out of date'.

Howard's tragedy was that the main position he tried to advance—an Australia with smaller government, lower taxation, much less regulation and control, greater choice, more competition, less union power, more freedom for workers, cheaper imports, more exports, greater scope for business, and a harder line on welfare and unemployment benefits—was a natural majority position within the 1980s community. The polls confirm that the people recognised the new economic realities and were prepared to adapt. Howard's pitch was to Middle Australia, beyond big unions and big business, an updated appeal along the lines of Menzies' 'forgotten people' of the 1940s. Sometimes Howard tried to communicate this message, but it was neither often nor successful.

Howard's central proposition was to reverse the trend towards greater regulation. One estimate showed that in the 1966–80 period, Australian parliaments had passed 2612 pieces of legislation and had promulgated 25 986 regulations—about a 50 per cent increase on the previous decade.[1]

The judgement on Howard is that he lacked the institutional support and personal qualities which had secured past Liberal success. Menzies had enjoyed four immense advantages—a split Labor Party, a magnificent leadership projection, a political skill superior to that of his opponents, and a strong and cooperative Country Party coalition partner. Fraser was denied the first but he had aspects of the second and enjoyed the third and fourth for most of his period. Howard, by contrast, had a unified Labor Party, a weak leadership projection to the community, distinctly inferior political skills to those of his opponents, and a coalition partner that was neither strong nor cooperative.

In power terms, Howard had too many opponents during his leadership years and not enough allies. This was partly the result of forces beyond his control but also a function of personal failing. He had to combat not just a still-formidable Hawke–Keating government but a crisis within non-Labor politics as profound as any which it had undergone.

It was under Howard that the tensions from the free market political revolution engulfed the Liberals, the coalition, and virtually every interest group within non-Labor politics. Howard was a shock absorber for a combination of identity crisis, culture trauma and leadership rivalry.

The 1980s saw the social base of the major parties begin to erode. Progressive Liberals went to the Democrats; business was disillusioned with non-Labor politics and less hostile towards Labor; a larger proportion of women was working, which promoted the disintegration of the Liberal command of the female vote; young people were more attracted to Labor than to the Liberals; and farmers were agitated and engaged in another periodic speculation about a new party.

Howard's attempt to identify an ideological position was not a new phenomenon. History showed that the Liberals did best when they injected ideology into politics, notably anti-communism at home and abroad. Menzies and Fraser were complex politicians. They would deploy ideology where it was necessary but they were experts in the art of political expediency. They could pinch ALP policy or change their own—for example, Menzies' 1963 embrace of state aid, an electoral masterstroke. The difference is that Howard's ideology did not necessarily promote electoral success. Nor was Howard able to dictate the terms of political debate in the fashion of Menzies and Fraser, although he often led Labor on policy.

It was Hawke, not Howard, who refined the Menzian technique; Menzies had stayed in the middle ground and pushed Labor to the left, so Hawke kept the middle ground and pushed Howard to the right.

Within his own spectrum there were three forces which gravely undermined Howard—the Peacock camp, which never accepted the legitimacy of the 1985 leadership change and plotted a coup; the Liberal 'wets', who refused to accept Howard's economic libertarianism or social conservatism; and the 'New Right' in both its serious and populist dimensions, symbolised by Ian McLachlan and Joh Bjelke-Petersen, which felt a compulsion to brand Howard a wimp and attack the Liberal Party for being an unreconstructed relic of failed Fraserism.

This trilogy provided a formidable set of domestic tensions. It meant that Howard was under internal attack from the left, the right and the rear. Peacock, the resident opportunist, waited to mobilise the wreckage into a leadership putsch.

Howard and Peacock taunted each other for years. It became the worst sort of leadership competition: compulsive but unresolved. It was a psychological and political war which exhausted the party and diminished the contenders. They were personality opposites whose mutual antagonism nourished the battle, while they were politicians too evenly matched to enable a convincing resolution. From March 1983 until March 1990 Peacock and Howard occupied the Liberal leadership in three extraordinary phases—Peacock under threat from Howard; Howard under threat from Peacock; and Peacock weakened after his coup against Howard. After the 1990 election the party would rush towards John Hewson and liberation from this torment.

The pressure upon Howard from Peacock, the wets, and the New Right meant that his leadership became too defensive and too reactive. Howard spent too much time on domestic repairs and too little on either his alternative program or the demolition of the Labor government. The consequences were lethal—he grew too cautious and developed an image as a reliable but weak leader. The worst quality for any leader is weakness; it spells electoral death. But an inability to resolve internal tensions leads inexorably to this perception. The irony is that the policy recasting to which Howard was pledged revealed him as a strong, not a weak, leader.

Howard's problems as leader were compounded by two of the major influences on contemporary politics—the media and the opinion polls. Howard received a hostile media for much of his leadership, despite his courtesy and accessibility. It was a function of Liberal enemies, Labor onslaught and media bloodlust. The opinion polls were Howard's protracted agony: their regularity, publicity and frequent misinterpretation made them one of the worst features of Australian politics in the 1980s and handy weapons for destabilisation.

In this environment Howard became a victim of a vicious circle—his poor public standing weakened his party position and his weak party position made his public standing even poorer.

Howard strove to improve his media performance—capped teeth, new glasses, steel grey suits. He did talkback radio, anytime, any hour. He gave the print media his greatest asset—time. He became a media junkie but never mastered its back alleys. He fell from being a media favourite as deputy to whipping boy as leader. Howard's finest performance was during the 1987 campaign, when he showed not just ability, but began to communicate an image as a direct, dedicated, honest leader in touch with Middle Australia. Such glimpses were all too rare during his embattled tenure.

While Howard was an experienced politician with a grasp of Liberal tradition, his leadership was handicapped by inadequate man-management. Howard was a poor chairman who was afflicted by a hearing defect and a weak organisational capacity that provoked shadow treasurer Jim Carlton into trying to bring management techniques to his office. The shadow Cabinet was badly run with little definition of priorities. Howard found himself on the losing side more often than was wise or necessary. He tried to conduct his shadow Cabinet on the Menzian model but was unable to inspire, persuade or organise his colleagues sufficiently. He was friendly but never close, too distant to be persuasive and too decent to be intimidating. The result was a leader with too little influence—over his shadow Cabinet, the federal party, his state divisions and his coalition partners.

Howard had an authority problem. His own supporters complained about their inability to help him, about the influence of his wife Janette, which assumed notoriety within the party, and of his indecision under pressure. His office was faithful to Liberal social practice—most staff called him Mr Howard, not John.

Howard was leader when Australia's economic troubles led the Opposition to conclude that it should win an election. Yet the economic crisis had a double impact; it shook the government but it destabilised the Opposition even more.

Despite this litany of traumas, Howard presided over an historic transition in Liberal Party ideology. It is no surprise that the party suffered an identity crisis since its identity was in transition. Howard has a unique place in the story of the 1980s. It was under his leadership that the non-Labor side began to redefine its future as a political force, embrace and explore the ramifications of free market economics, and begin the process of rethinking its political tactics and appeal in a new era with a new ideology. The heartburn involved was immense. It was Howard's leadership which absorbed the damage; it was John Hewson's leadership after 1990 that inherited the benefits.

Howard was unlucky because he had four years as Opposition leader, the bulk of two parliamentary terms but, like Bill Hayden, had only one election campaign to become prime minister. Howard's leadership was a failure measured against this test of ultimate ambition—he lost the 1987 election. But Howard's leadership must also be judged against other criteria: he led the party during its time of greatest internal division and most important philosophical recasting. The mid-1980s witnessed an explosion of ideas, theory, ideology and a lot of nonsense from the non-Labor side. Discernment was not the quality of the era. The non-Labor side was unable to manage the consequences of its own internal revolution.

The Liberals, compared with Labor, looked political amateurs—inferior in most aspects of politics including performance, tactics, discipline, media skills and election fighting. The Liberals were further handicapped by the decline of the National Party, a malaise which could prelude its ultimate death throes.

After his election Howard appointed Jim Carlton as shadow treasurer, Neil Brown to industrial relations, Peacock to foreign affairs, Fred Chaney to industry and commerce and Ian Macphee to communications. The drys won more power but Howard still believed in power-sharing between drys and wets, labels that he refused to acknowledge.

A vulnerable Opposition leader needs a busy and loyal deputy and a shadow treasurer with firepower. Howard had neither. His deputy, Neil Brown, was brainy and witty but a loner. A working class boy from Mooney Ponds who had made good, he had acquired a refined voice and a disdain for less gifted colleagues. Brown was loyal though he flirted with disloyalty; he had no inclination to mend Howard's broken fences.

Carlton was a foundation dry but a rare bird. An intellectual whose formative years were spent in British management and delving into political theory, Carlton was a soft politician in the Australian context, a gentle but purist ideologue with a global view, a touch of romanticism and a penchant for solutions that fell into his universal schema.

Carlton saw Australia as 'a self-indulgent nation with ageing and rigid institutions'. The salvation of which he dreamed was a liberalism which would achieve a once-in-a-generation change by bringing all the elements together in the perfect production which Carlton likened to an opera; to be precise, it would be exactly as he remembered when on 7 March 1961 he was at Covent Garden for 'Beethoven's only opera, *Fidelio*, produced and conducted by Otto Klemperer . . . with the gnarled and crippled hands of that old refugee from Hitler drawing out from pit and stage Beethoven's incomparable message of triumph of the human spirit . . . Beethoven's message in *Fidelio* is the message of liberalism'. Carlton would mark Keating, another admirer of art. But Keating, unlike Carlton, was a savage by day, connoisseur by night.[2]

The upshot was that Brown never acted as a traditional deputy; Carlton was an easy target for Keating; and Howard distrusted Chaney too much to rely upon him.

As leader Howard failed to match the expectations he had created as deputy—the politician of conviction offering ideology, zeal and honesty. Howard came not to praise Fraserism but to bury it, a hard but essential task. Neil Brown explains the problem of Fraser legacy: 'We found that nobody would believe us. When we tried to outline our policies people wouldn't listen. Then they would say, "What about Fraser? Why should we believe you?" '[3]

Howard's gospel was delivered in January 1985 to the Young Liberals, in a speech written by his aide, Gerard Henderson:

> We must do more than feed off Labor's mistakes. We must present ourselves in a positive sense as an effective alternative government with the correct policies to overcome Australia's social and economic problems. There will be no shortage of those who advocate a compromise, a blurred approach to difficult issues. Government, we will be told, is just around the corner, so we should avoid antagonising any part of the electorate by taking a definitive stand on sensitive questions. Such thinking is not only political cowardice, it also displays dubious political wisdom. Many people deserted the former Liberal government because they felt it had lost its philosophic clarity towards the end of its term of office . . .
>
> If the middle ground means that we must automatically adopt the mid-point between the opposing sides of the argument on any given issue then I am totally opposed to such a concept. Such an approach will produce mediocre, lowest-common-denominator solutions . . . In politics, it is more important to be right than popular. In time correct policies will become accepted.[4]

Brave words, but difficult to implement. This appeal was redolent of a Churchill or de Gaulle or, closer to home, Fraser himself in his famous 1971 Deakin lecture, when he declared that 'life is not meant to be easy'. Political strength is a synthesis between the man and the situation. Howard was not the man; it is debatable if Liberal politics in 1985 was the situation.

It was probably inevitable the Howard as leader would be forced into regular compromises, given the party's internal policy and power rifts. But Howard fell victim to the demands and perceptions of both the left and the right. For instance, his pragmatic advisers, Tony Eggleton and Graham Morris, believed that Howard courted trouble by being too ideological. Yet his more ideological advisers such as Henderson drew the opposite conclusion—that Howard's problem lay in his propensity for indecision and compromise under pressure which was destroying his previous image of strength.

In fact, Howard was losing on both counts—and this is the paradox of his leadership. The Liberal moderates and wets attacked him for free market extremism and appeasement of the New Right. The message came from Peacock that Howard was too narrow to win. The right-wing ideologues, by contrast, accused Howard of flirting with betrayal of their cause. The word was despatched from Melbourne: Hugh Morgan felt that Howard was going soft on free market beliefs. This was Henderson's fear, which culminated with his quitting in late 1986, feeling he had no influence. 'This party's too indecisive,' Henderson said, meaning that Howard was too indecisive. 'All I've done since the middle of the year is change the lock on the door, so there's no point in staying.' They had a blazing row.

Howard, in fact, found in his first several months as Opposition leader that being 'right' can carry a heavy penalty. He was taught devastating lessons about tactics, communications and power in three incidents in his early months as leader, incidents focused on tax, financial deregulation, and privatisation, all central to the new free market Liberal Party.

The first retreat Howard made as leader was from tax rationalist to tax populist. It was a fundamental shift because it determined the course of politics up to his 1987 election defeat. It was the first intimation of the 'tax trap' into which the coalition sank during the 1985–87 period. Howard's comments as deputy suggested that as leader he would try to win the next election by offering an economic model superior to that of the Hawke government. In fact, Howard was sucked down the path of trying to win the 1987 election on taxation, a mistake he later conceded. He made tax, not economic management, the issue. The tax package which he devised owed more to radical right populism than to tax reform principles of efficiency and equity.

Howard said on the day he became leader, 5 September 1985, that he would support decent Labor policy. When Keating announced his tax package on 19 September Howard opposed only the capital gains tax and kept his options open on the rest, saying this was the 'sensible' course. As a former treasurer he knew many of these reforms were desirable in terms of tax efficiency, elimination of avoidance and equity. The logic of Labor's package was manifest—the financing of a lower rate scale through a crackdown on tax shelters and the imposition of a capital gains tax, fringe benefits tax, abolition of entertainment expenses, a national identification card and closing of other rural and property deductions.[5]

But Howard's responsibility was swamped in a tide of hostility towards Labor's package from the coalition's voting base—business, farmers and employers—who demanded coalition action. He was shocked at the way Peacock and his backers exploited the tax issue to depict him as vacillating. He was horrified at a torrent of leaks from the shadow Cabinet, including documents which depicted a party in disarray. Howard was forced to change and in November 1985 he turned on the Keating package with a vengeance, a process which culminated in late 1986 with the coalition's decision to block the Australia Card—which gave Hawke the constitutional grounds for a double dissolution.

But Howard's conversion won little thanks from his cynical critics. They said that he'd taken too long, that he had failed from the start to seize the national leadership of conservative Australia to launch a crusade against Keating's tax crackdown. Howard absorbed this criticism and spent the rest of his term trying to do just that—lead the grassroots tax revolt. Howard felt that he had no choice and he was probably correct.

Those calling for a comprehensive attack on the Labor package included Peacock and many wets who argued on straight political grounds, the federal National Party, Joh Bjelke-Petersen, the NFF, small and big business, many Liberals including several drys, and a grassroots movement of farmers and small business for whom the commentator Katherine West had become the chief propagandist. This small business and farmer constituency was the electoral heartland to which Howard was pitching his main policy—deregulation of the labour market and the attack on the Accord and union power. This was *his* constituency; the new grassroots movement that he needed desperately. So Howard surrendered to it on taxation.

He denied his treasurer's conscience and assumed the mantle of tax hero. He probably had no choice. Why be reluctant? Here was the easy road to success, even to the prime ministership.

Of course, there were minor embarrassments. The leaked memo from his shadow taxation minister, Tony Messner, who had written of the Keating package: 'The four main "nasty" issues are central to the package and are the main sources of funds for the "goodies". By appearing to oppose the "nasties" while supporting the "goodies" opens us to the charge at the very least of inconsistency and more likely of irresponsibility.'[6]

During 1986 the more political trouble Howard faced, the more he sank his teeth into the Keating package and the more he saw taxation as his salvation. Labor's new taxes were deeply unpopular. The decisive policy pattern of Howard's first leadership term was established: the bias towards tax populism before tax rationality. First, Howard opposed Keating's crackdown on tax shelters; second, he was forced to abandon his cherished plans for an indirect tax since that was too unpopular; third, he still offered large personal income tax cuts since this was demanded by the tax-cut populists and the coalition opportunists; fourth, he declined to identify exactly what spending cuts would be made to finance these tax cuts since that was too unpopular; finally, he tried to win the 1987 election on his tax package, not on economic management superiority.

This was a sequence of events which Howard had never envisaged when he became leader. He was a victim, then a willing victim, finally an enthusiastic victim of these events. Howard was pulled along in a political current which he rarely controlled and to which he succumbed. The evidence is clear from the comments he made the day he became leader. He said that the major issue dividing government and Opposition was deregulation of the labour market and the reduction of union power and predicted that the nation wanted this reform. But it was too hard to sell.

Howard's tax strategy was a popular recourse to vote winning in the name of incentive and Reaganomics at the cost of recorrupting the tax system. Howard fashioned a mid-1986 political strategy to reverse Labor's assets test, abolish its taxes on superannuation lump sums, capital gains and fringe benefits. But the restoration of tax perks and shelters for the better off was hardly a pointer to a Liberal government that would possess the fortitude and skill to tackle the difficult economic issues facing Australia. There was an old-fashioned reflex in Howard's tax campaign which recalled the Liberal tax bribes of the 1970s and Fraser's fistful of dollars. Howard's pitch was popular and applauded within non-Labor ranks but he paid a price.

Many political and economic commentators who had supported Howard's leadership and philosophy repudiated his embrace of tax populism. In fact, Howard's tax populism began to bring into disrepute his credibility on free market economics and this was political poison. In July 1986 Max Walsh wrote:

> The man we used to call Honest John has decided that cynicism in the clothes of evangelism is the route to office. As Howard was, for many years, Treasurer of this country he does not even have, as his predecessors had, the excuse of ignorance . . . Howard is a politician promising salvation without pain, riches without effort, government without taxes and industrial peace by crushing the unions . . . There is not one skerrick of evidence to suggest that John Howard has a policy with which to govern this country. He has a tried and true formula for entering office—wait for the economic downturn and promise the earth. We have in the past been able to afford such opportunism, such cynicism. Not now.[7]

Howard's dilemma was that his free market agenda was a collection of policy items—it had never assumed a coherent framework. This had two consequences. First, he was not able to market to the voters his alternative economic model. Second, he was unable to explain sufficiently how his programs would operate from office and even his own side was confused over how a program of free market economics might actually work.

Howard had the same problems as Peacock had at the 1984 election: how did the coalition sell free market economics to the voters? In 1984 Peacock just attacked Hawke's record. In 1987 Howard went for the big tax cut. The Liberals had a new philosophy which nobody wanted to buy and which they couldn't sell.

This was verified in the second and third areas where Howard encountered difficulty immediately upon becoming leader—his appeals for greater financial deregulation and privatisation. Both approaches were touchstones of his hard-headed economic realism. Both resulted in political fiascos which damaged him severely. Both coincided with the first election in Australia after Howard's elevation: the December 1985 South Australian election, a milestone.

The South Australian Liberals led by John Olsen planned to centre their campaign against the Bannon ALP government by offering tax cuts financed by the first major privatisation program of any Australian government. As a bonus they hoped for a backlash from Keating's high interest rate policy which was hurting home buyers.

Howard, at this time, supported full financial deregulation, including the abolition of the 13.5 per cent ceiling on the bank home loan rate. The economic theory was obvious: abolish the ceiling and the banks would attract more funds for home lending. Howard was articulating his brave new world, in which financial deregulation played an integral part. But the practice was fatal—the market was far above 13.5 per cent, so his policy meant a further lift in bank home loan rates. Olsen refused to support Howard's position, producing a Howard–Olsen policy split. Howard had achieved the near impossible, turning Labor's high interest rates into a Liberal negative.

On the final weekend of the South Australian campaign, John Bannon called upon the voters to make interest rates the issue and send a message to Howard rejecting his deregulation. Behind the scenes there were terrible brawls and shouting matches between the Howard and Olsen camps and the two leaders. Howard was trapped between two views of politics—the one based upon long-range commitment and the other on the short-term hip-pocket nerve. It is the perennial dilemma for all politicians unless they are pure ideologues or cynics. Howard felt unable to retreat on a basic tenet of his philosophy but he had been caught preaching his philosophy in the wrong square at a bad time.

If Howard was guilty of naivety over interest rates, the Liberals collectively were naive over privatisation. In late 1985 the Labor Party in Canberra and Adelaide waged a brutal and effective anti-privatisation campaign which had an effect on Australian politics for several years. It intimidated the Liberals on privatisation and contributed to Hawke's own failure post-1987 when he tried to reverse the ALP's hostility towards privatisation.

John Olsen declared that the state election was a national test for privatisation. His remarks were akin to poking a tiger in the eye because Labor wanted exactly such a test. Olsen pledged tax cuts from revenue raised by the sale of 49 per cent of the State Oil and Gas Corporation and other bodies.

The Western Australian Liberals were also planning a privatisation onslaught. They had invited to Australia the world's leading privatisation expert, Dr Madsen Pirie, adviser to the Thatcher government, a bow-tied zealot who declared that privatisation 'is not a fad but history itself', and who entertained his Australian audiences with amazing anecdotes, such as the one about the cliff-watcher appointed to the public payroll during the Napoleonic wars to watch for the French in the Channel, a post abolished only in 1948! It was Pirie's approach which provoked the famous lament from former British prime minister Harold Macmillan that under Thatcher, 'first of all the Georgian silver goes, and then the nice furniture . . . then the Canalettos'.

While Pirie preached in Perth, the ideological swords were flashing under Howard's leadership in Canberra; privatisation was a shining weapon. Howard and Carlton wanted to extend the public enterprises for sale to include the Commonwealth Bank and Qantas, and they said that Telecom was under review.

But Howard hadn't yet formulated his policy details or tactics. He wasn't ready to fight. The Liberals were split on privatisation; two senior figures, Senator Alan Missen and Steele Hall, both wets, publicly criticised the party for seeing privatisation as a panacea. Labor saw its opening and deployed its heavyweights for the kill.

The Labor anti-privatisation campaign involved Hawke, Keating, communications minister Michael Duffy, Mick Young, Bannon and the South Australian government, the ACTU, the Australian Telecommunications Employees Association, and the entire SA union movement. It dominated the state election and was designed to destroy Olsen's campaign and derail Howard's leadership. It was an attack on the politics and economics of privatisation—and it worked.

Labor's thrust, notably over Telecom, was to show that privatisation would destroy the hidden subsidies built into public ownership on the basis of social equity. For example, Duffy said the Telecom cross-subsidisation was worth about $500 million, mostly to rural Australia, and that if Telecom were sold then such people 'will simply not get a modern telephone system'. When Howard pledged to keep this subsidy but pay it from the budget, Duffy retorted: '$500 million from Mr Small Government, pigs might fly.' The National Party fell into a panic with its leaders Ian Sinclair and Bruce

Lloyd launching veto messages to city and country media, a sure sign that they knew Labor had a winner.

Mick Young said the argument that what had happened in Britain or America would necessarily happen in Australia was ideological claptrap, about as relevant as the fact that governments ran steel mills in Russia. Hawke hammered the wider picture—privatisation meant higher costs, charges and fares, less employment, greater rationalisation. It was a fertile field for an electoral scare.

But Labor also challenged privatisation on economic efficiency grounds. Hawke and finance minister Peter Walsh attacked Olsen's plan for using a one-off sale of a public asset to finance ongoing tax cuts, and Hawke quoted Howard, who had described such techniques in a different context as a 'fiscal fool's paradise'. The *Economist* had slated Thatcher's program on these exact grounds—'selling to provide for current spending—in business a sure way to go bankrupt'.

Peter Walsh warned that Thatcher's privatisation had been at the cost of competition; that Thatcher had sold enterprises but often increased regulation in the affected industries. He identified the conflict between 'achieving efficiency through competition and achieving a high price for a government firm', that is, that privatisation could be the enemy of deregulation. Walsh told the Liberals that they had made a tactical error in examining Telecom, since full cost recovery of rural phone and postal services was impossible and that a profit-maximising company, if acting rationally, would close such services because they were 'innately unprofitable'. The Liberals never seriously considered selling Telecom; in the list of asset sales they subsequently compiled for the 1987 election neither Telecom nor Australia Post was included. But their sloppiness gave Labor an opening.

Towards the end of the campaign Howard went to Adelaide for an ear operation. For years he had been handicapped by being deaf in one ear. But asked during a street walk who was going to win the election, he replied, 'John Bannon'. It was the most human of mistakes but a terrible embarrassment which symbolised his wretched campaign. Then a few days later his staff let a photographer into his hospital room—the result showed Howard in pyjamas, ear bandaged, hairy leg dangling, the way a leader should never be photographed.

Bannon won the election with a swing of about 2 per cent to Labor. The Liberals, needing two seats to win, lost four. Howard knew that he had made himself a political bunny. It was a savage initiation from which Howard never recovered.

The consequences were that privatisation became a political negative and Howard's leadership was destabilised, in the end irreversibly. His critics had a surplus of weapons. Steele Hall said that 'by loose-lipped policy declarations and vague references to some ultimate privatisation position we have sown the seeds for a political dragon we cannot now control . . . by formalising years ahead of office, a sledge-hammer approach to government utilities and institutions, we have formalised a means of keeping ourselves out of office'. Michael Hodgman warned on the floor of parliament that the Liberals might sit in Opposition for a decade 'clothed in the robes of economic purity' and that the Liberals might 'literally debate ourselves out of government at the next election'. South Australian party president and future Liberal Senate leader, Robert Hill, another wet, said the federal party was 'electorally unreal' and called for 'a change in direction'. Deputy leader Neil Brown said that privatisation should be about competition, not sell-offs.

The Western Australian Liberals threw their privatisation plans into reverse. Their state leader, Bill Hassell, said he would never use the word again. Privatisation was ditched as their spearhead in their coming election. The Liberals had made three mistakes. First, they had failed to grasp that as reformers they would be subject to the attacks from vested interests to which reformers are always prey. The Liberals were trapped between a reformist economic program and a 'status quo' political consciousness. They hadn't yet grasped the consequence of their economic rethink—that it meant a change in Australia's political culture from a philosophy of regulation to competition which would deliver a profound shock to much of the community. The Liberals had not learnt that they had to persuade, propagandise and market their entire program—indirect taxation, labour market deregulation, small government, and privatisation.

Second, they were complacent in assuming that ideas which Thatcher and Reagan had made popular in Britain and America would automatically become popular in Australia. Privatisation in Britain was an ideology—an end in itself, a political as well as a financial objective. Under Thatcher it served several purposes—providing revenue for tax cuts, boosting enterprise productivity, breaking the power of the public sector unions and creating a new generation of shareholding capitalists. But there were many differences between Britain and Australia. In Australia there was a more formidable Labor Party, a less nationalised industry structure, a less aggressive union movement against which the idea of privatisation could be mounted, and a tradition of equality of services between regions and states to combat cost difficulties created by distance.

Finally, the Liberals underestimated the capacity of the ALP to inflict damage with its authority, money, government resources and media skill. A battered Howard decided that he needed a tough communications strategy and hired a former journalist from the party headquarters, Graham Morris, as his political minder.

The Liberals knew that their policies on financial deregulation and privatisation had been distorted. Howard explained that Liberal policy was to deregulate interest rates when they were falling, not rising. Howard,

Carlton and Chaney all clarified the principles of privatisation—market competition after any sales; a sale management program to avoid any debacle with a float; the use of sale proceeds not for tax cuts but for debt reduction; and the involvement of the employees as small shareholders. The irony is that this was the very program which Hawke would try unsuccessfully to embrace post-1987.

The damage to Howard from the three issues—tax, interest rates and privatisation—was devastating. There was a whiff of madness in the air. No recent federal leader has sustained so much damage so quickly, so soon after his elevation. Howard never had a honeymoon; he was threatened instead with divorce.

The rapidity of the deterioration is revealed by the fact that by November 1985, Peacock—who had resigned only ten weeks before—was entertaining hopes of a return, and his backers were working to this end. The believability of a Peacock threat was a disastrous development for Howard. The media warned that Howard was in danger, though a challenge was not imminent. Peacock smirked when asked about Howard's performance: 'He's doing his best . . . that's all you can ask.'

This was a game Peacock played from memory, a Liberal ritual. Yes, Howard had his support as leader. But Peacock 'sometime down the track' would 'like to offer myself again'. The party, the media, the public, got the message. Peacock was tracking Howard.[8]

The failure of Howard to established a firm grip as leader unleashed a series of intersecting tensions. His internal critics were driven by three motives—hostility towards his economic policy, hostility towards his social policy, or a belief that Peacock was a superior leader—and often they were driven by all three. Once Howard faltered his opponents grew bold. Many of them were wets, Howard's natural opponents and Peacock's party base, while others were Peacock's mates or Howard haters—Michael Hodgman, Max Burr, Ian Macphee, Steele Hall, Chris Puplick, John Moore, Robert Hill, Peter Shack and Wilson Tuckey, among others.

The ongoing problems Howard faced from virtually his first fortnight involved betrayal, opinion polls and 'illegitimacy'.

The destabilisation was conducted through the traditional rituals of leaks, rumours, group rebellion, public criticism. The mood of chaotic betrayal was captured by Henderson, Howard's chief of staff:

> It became mayhem in a way . . . within days the tax position found its way from the shadow Cabinet to Richard Carleton. That happened just after the shadow Cabinet meeting . . . there were other documents that went straight to Ministers. In that kind of environment you couldn't put anything on paper. Neil Brown did but Neil was quite neurotic about his policy document and almost slept with it under his bed. Anything that went as a working paper to the shadow Cabinet was just away . . . when things went to the party room it had to be arranged for them to

be read in the Whip's office under some form of security. The problem was the very effective use the government made of the documents in Parliament by saying 'you're all an incompetent rabble, here's another document that's been leaked' . . . and this continued all the way until the end of 1986.[9]

Neil Brown said of the leaks: 'It shows that we can't trust each other'. It was a poison in the party.[10]

The polls, some public, others leaked private polls, became another of the anti-Howard devices. By the end of 1986 the Morgan poll for preferred Opposition leader had Peacock leading Howard 43 to 18 per cent, a margin which had been established the previous autumn. The same poll on the preferred prime minister question had Hawke leading Howard 63 to 22 per cent. These results were typical of most polls being published on a regular basis. For most of 1986, the Morgan poll showed the coalition winning an election but towards the end of the year the situation had become closer. Former Australian Democrat leader Don Chipp said that if Howard stayed leader then it was certain that more Democrat second preferences would be directed to Labor.

The most spectacular poll was a private survey commissioned by a Perth businessman, Michael Sweet, from a well known Melbourne company, Quantum, run by George Camakaris, at a cost of about $50 000. For anybody remotely involved in politics, it was a classic set-up. Sweet was acting for a group of businessmen targeting Howard because of his tax avoidance crackdown as treasurer. The exercise was remarkably similar to an event in 1982, when Camakaris conducted a survey which, when leaked to the media, showed that Labor needed to change from Hayden to Hawke to beat Fraser. It became a benchmark in Hayden's demise. Sweet's poll was leaked to the *Financial Review*, which gave its findings publicity on 16 June 1986, the morning of Howard's television address to the nation on the economy.

The survey, based upon 1000 households, found that Howard was the coalition's greatest weakness. Peacock was preferred as leader to Howard by a 2:1 plus ratio. Most damaging for Howard was that the voters did not perceive him as prime ministerial material. The June leak was seen as a high point in the destabilisation of Howard and the manipulation of the media to this end.[11]

A subtle ploy in the undermining of Howard was the 'illegitimacy' argument. In mid-1986, Macphee spoke at a Liberal meeting in Alexander Downer's electorate in Adelaide and argued that because Howard had never beaten Peacock in a ballot his leadership credentials were dubious. It was a frequent line from the critics: Peacock had resigned as leader; Howard never had the numbers to beat him; therefore Howard's mandate was flawed.

The anti-Howard campaign was conducted with a passion, a sure sign of events beyond any individual's control. It was a political cannibalism that was bitchy and personalised and betrayed the Liberal Party's loss of sophistication as a political instrument.

In this battle, social and economic policy was an issue of dispute and a tool with which to promote Peacock against Howard. Howard's critics were offended by his style as much as by his substance. Howard, in fact, was almost bereft of persuasiveness—too formal, too distant, too uncommunicative. When it came to substance, his critics were probably more offended by his social conservatism than his economic libertarianism. An examination of Howard's leadership reveals that the single issue which most damaged him within the party was social, not economic—his position on multiculturalism and Asian immigration.

Howard's critics made spasmodic forays against him on economics. In March 1986, Steele Hall, Hodgman and Burr staged a revolt against his 'hands-off' stance on the Holmes a'Court BHP takeover bid. On the industrial front, Macphee never forgave Howard for his advocacy of labour market deregulation. But the most comprehensive economic assault in the battle over ideas came from Malcolm Fraser who warned that 'deregulation alone leads only to 19th century laissez-faire'.

In his main contribution for 1986, Fraser attacked the 'level-playing field' in tax policy and advocated the use of tax incentives for exports. He warned that deregulation and tax policy had 'encouraged the takeover of healthy companies with little debt'. In America $160 billion of equity had been replaced by debt and 'a large part of it has been as a result of corporations retiring their own equity and replacing it by debt, so that they would not be targets for takeover'. He attacked the market concentration created by the Coles–Myer merger, saying it would not have been permitted in Britain or America. He warned of the dangers if BHP were taken over by 'a predatory and aggressive firm'. Fraser said that 'a good deal of the deregulation that had happened has been ill thought out . . . the debate on deregulation in general in Australia has been unbalanced, and unhelpful to good government, because too many people have got away with depicting deregulation as an end in itself'.[12]

Much of the anti-Howard sting was a backlash against Howard's declaration that he was the most 'conservative' ever Liberal leader. It was provoked by his scepticism about multiculturalism, his opposition to South African sanctions, his campaign to retain all the British symbols of nationhood, his opposition to affirmative action, his distaste for feminism, and his apparent backing for most aspects of the Thatcher and Reagan experiments. The Fraser–Macphee axis emerged as a counterpoint with Macphee the standard-bearer of a late 1980s Fraserism. Another touchstone of these differences was media policy. Fraser and Macphee called for government action to stop Rupert Murdoch's takeover of The Herald and Weekly Times group on grounds of media ownership concentration, an intervention Howard rejected.

The end of certainty

One of the prominent wets, Chris Puplick, says that Howard's problems
with the wets were more in social than economic policy. He says

> I argued back in 1974 for the breaking of the two airline policy and
> government sanctioned monopolies. I've always supported a strict needs
> based welfare system. I've believed in lower tariffs and I've sought a
> competitive market place in which your primary tool of management
> should be the Trade Practices Act. The entry of foreign banks and the
> floating of the currency were policies I supported. But I've taken the
> view that if you get government out of the boardroom you also get it
> out of the bedroom. I've found it difficult sometimes to cope with
> those who believe that everything should be deregulated except
> personal liberty.[13]

The mid-1980s revealed that Labor was more skilful than the Liberals
at handling ideas. The policy divisions within the ALP were as great if not
greater than those within the Liberals, yet Labor was far more successful
in their containment, through many techniques: government and party
patronage, internal power-sharing, dialogue, factional discipline, and peer
group pressure.

Howard could neither persuade nor discipline the rebels, nor could the
shadow ministry. The party organisation was too weak. Liberal MPs had no
factions to impose peer group pressure or channel debates. To whom were
Liberal MPs responsible? Their so-called freedom became in this climate a
licence for destruction.

The judgement upon Howard is that he failed to make a successful
transition from the most prominent dry to Liberal leader. His efforts to make
power-sharing work between drys and wets were unsatisfactory to both
sides. The wets felt he was not sympathetic to or understanding of their
positions; too often the right felt he was too soft on the wets. Howard's
trouble was his inability to rise above these often petty squabbles and
persuade the party to put the benefit of doubt his way rather than always
against him. A dangerous mood of intolerance was given rein, described by
Neil Brown: 'The feeling grew that people in another group with different
opinions almost had no right to hold them.'[14] This was a party that magnified
its internal differences.

There were many Liberals steeped in the Deakin tradition who believed
that a Liberal government should play a strong role in welfare, Aboriginal
affairs, human rights, the arts, education and promoting equality of opportunity. They feared that the free market zealots would deny such roles.
Chaney reflected on Howard's inability to manage the party as a coalition
of forces, unlike Menzies and Fraser: 'Fraser understood and appreciated
that the Liberal Party is a coalition of a whole range of people, interests
and ideologies and he was prepared to have Alan Missen at one end and
God knows who at the other.'[15]

The most interesting effort to resolve this wet–dry dilemma came from the NSW Liberal leader Nick Greiner, who in August 1985 offered a third course—a fusion between dry economics and social compassion. Greiner declared as Opposition leader:

A dry wind is blowing through Australian politics . . . But it is essential, I believe, that the Liberal Party emerges from these changes dry and warm, rather than dry and cold . . . In our understandable enthusiasm for economic rationalism let us never forget that the one and only purpose of all this political activity is people. Preoccupation with increasing profits; blind commitment to balancing the books; ideological dedication for its own sake; ordinary men and women are chilled by such a message. I do not believe that the Liberal Party can succeed with such a platform.

Greiner called for Liberals to have 'a warm heart and a hard head'.[16] (Warm and dry worked for Greiner initially but his own personality failed to match this philosophy in office.)

In December 1986 the wets sought to dramatise an intellectual counter-attack through their book launch of 'The Continuing Vision' by the Liberal Forum group. These essays were presented as the start of a campaign to claw back the ground lost in the public debate to the combined influence of the drys, the think-tanks, and the New Right. The group, formed in February 1985, was seen as an intellectual vanguard for the wets to propagandise for that mainstream liberalism originating with Deakin and reinvigorated by Menzies and Fraser.

The wet campaign sought to appropriate to themselves the Menzian mantle in an effort to re-establish their legitimacy. They recalled the Menzian appeal of the 1940s and 1950s, in particularly, Menzies' famous 'forgotten people' broadcasts, when he outlined the social ethos on which the Liberal Party was established. The Liberal lobbies rang with a Menzies echo as the politicians of the 1980s studied the master communicator.

In his 1940s exposition Menzies said the 'middle class' was 'the backbone of the nation' and issued his declaration:

It has a stake in the country. It has responsibilities for homes—homes material, homes human, homes spiritual. I do not believe that the great life of the nation is to be found either in great luxury hotels and the petty gossip of so-called fashionable suburbs, or in the officialdom of organised masses. It is to be found in the homes of people who are nameless and unadvertised, and who, whatever their individual religious conviction or dogma, see in their children their greatest contribution to the immortality of their race. The home is the foundation of sanity and sobriety; it is the indispensable condition of continuity; its health determines the health of society as a whole.

For an hilarious interlude the Liberals fought over whether Menzies was a dry or a wet and whether J.S. Mill was a feminist. Macphee said that feminism was essentially liberal. Henderson mocked the wets for arguing that the slave trade and child labour were free market products.

Menzies, in fact, had been a believer in both individualism and state power, and had been pragmatic in his application of these concepts. This meant that both drys and wets could use him to find precedents for their causes. The real point, however, was that in the 1980s Australia's social base, its economic conditions and its intellectual climate were fundamentally different from the Menzian period.

The historic message of the 1980s, which the drys realised and the wets rejected, was that the age of Menzian stability had been the long blissful twilight of the Australian Settlement; it was the last period of Australia's history when political success would be based upon the certitudes of protection, regulation, intervention and Empire bonds. It was an age departed, never to return. The internationalisation of the economy in the 1980s was destroying the political basis of 1950s liberalism. The challenge for the Liberals in the 1980s and beyond was to synthesise free market economics with a political ethic of caring, responsible liberalism, a synthesis which they failed to achieve then and had still not reached in the early 1990s.

During this mid-1980s crisis three long-term scenarios were proposed for the Liberals—death, a libertarian future, or a revitalised Fraserism; their respective authors being B.A. Santamaria, Howard on behalf of the drys, and the Fraser–Macphee wets.

Santamaria's prediction reflected his experience and began with this insight: 'The Liberal Party's essential weakness lies in its lack of a cohesive social foundation with its own particular philosophical frame of reference.' Santamaria argued that Menzies founded the party on the property-aspiring rising middle class but that this social factor 'would not automatically have produced its own party had it not been for the chance of events and the simultaneous flowering of Menzies' undoubted political genius'. The Liberal Party, in fact, was an example of the great man theory of history. But great men die and, being great, aren't replaced. So the 'party of everybody' became the 'party of nothing'.

Santamaria, who visited Menzies regularly during his long illness, says that Menzies 'had ceased to vote for the Liberal Party' during the late sixties and early seventies. Santamaria says: 'As he came to the end of his life, Menzies was prepared more than once to state that the Liberal Party had probably run its course, and that its end was merely delayed rather than ultimately averted by the election of Malcolm Fraser'; in short, a party without a future. Santamaria, a critic of dry economics, predicted that the free market, small government gospel with a dash of feminism would take the Liberal Party into a dead-end.[17]

The historic importance of Howard's leadership is manifest in the second scenario: it was Howard who aspired to chart a new position for the

Liberal Party that would endure into the twenty-first century—to create a model beyond the Menzies mould, a task the Liberals had never attempted. This was the position of the drys. For all Howard's faults as communicator, manager and politician, he possessed a redeeming virtue—he had a Liberal vision and the courage to articulate it.

Howard's vision assumed the disintegration of the Australian Settlement. It postulated a new Liberal Party, beyond Menzies' vision, operating in an internationalised Australian economy with a market philosophy that asked individuals to assume greater responsibility to match their freedoms. This was a party that would operate in a post-Arbitration, post-Protection, post-Accord climate where class, union power and corporate privilege were being eroded as determinants of economics and politics. The Liberals would be the party of individual initiative, not sectional privilege.

Howard failed to sell this vision. He was a weak advertising man, his party was divided, and his opponents were too strong. Howard united his party opponents by trying to marry social conservatism with his free market liberalism; he was caricatured as a throwback agent of social Darwinism.

But Howard's view of the Liberal Party had a final sanction: if the Liberals refused to implement a free market agenda then another non-Labor party would be established to do the job. Public warnings to this effect were given by Ian McLachlan, Gerard Henderson and Andrew Hay. There were enough Liberals who would not tolerate another era of lost opportunity. The Liberals had a choice: reform or irrelevance.

This is why the third scenario, reversion to Fraserism, was unsaleable. The weakness of the wets during the 1980s was that they looked to the failed past to find their future. The wets watched immobilised for much of the 1980s until Howard's leadership provoked them into belated retaliation. As Australian politics moved to the right, they fought the tide.

Hawke and Keating were sophisticated and ruthless in keeping the pressure upon Howard. The transformation of Keating, the decisive political figure during Howard's leadership, into an implacable enemy was a milestone. It happened in February 1986 as a result of an aggressive parliamentary strategy Howard had approved involving the chief Liberal 'hit man' Wilson Tuckey. Tuckey raised the name of a woman who was plaintiff in a breach of promise action against Keating 13 years before, and hurled a confusing barb: 'Kristine had a little girl called Paul.' Keating interpreted the comment as falsely implying that he had had an illegitimate child by the woman. He descended into biblical mood—but this was old testament law, not new testament forgiveness.

Keating announced on the stairs of Parliament House his quest for revenge: 'From this day onwards Mr Howard will wear his leadership like a crown of thorns and in the Parliament I will do everything I can to crucify him . . . to obliterate him from the leadership.' Then he went into his office, rang Howard and delivered the same threat—just to make the message personal.[18] This event changed the atmosphere of national politics. It was a rationalisation of Keating's anti-Liberal political needs but it had a material effect on Howard's leadership.

It was the end, not just of the Keating–Howard joint late night parties, but of any meaningful cooperation between the most important policy architects on either side of national politics during the 1980s. It turned Keating into a savage enemy. He pursued a passionate vendetta every day of Howard's leadership.

Howard's micro-dilemma within the Liberal Party was reflected as a macro-dilemma within the wider community: how did Howard intend to beat the Labor government?

By mid-1986 Howard was convinced he had the answer. The sense of national economic crisis was palpable. Keating's banana republic warning, Australia's credit downgrading and the currency collapse had generated an unusual climate in which the voters were prepared to listen to radical solutions. Howard believed that the projection of a tough economic line, his natural policy, would succeed in this atmosphere. He knew the people wanted leadership and answers. During an interview in America with Anne Summers he delivered his famous line: 'The times will suit me.'[19] Howard said:

> I think there's an enormous sense of disappointment developing in Middle Australia about Hawke. For the first time since I've been in politics there is a realisation that we have fundamental problems and we're not going to be saved by another minerals discovery. I'm picking it up through the Liberal branches and it's coming through in our research work . . . If there's a realisation that things are crook and that changes are needed, there can be quite a significant change in public opinion. Governments on our side in the past have been too timid about change. I think that's wrong. You've got to be willing to hang on very hard to certain things but be willing to radically change other institutions.

Howard tried to capture the mood which John Hewson briefly exploited in the early 1990s. In 1986 Howard said that he wanted to be portrayed as a radical in the Thatcher and Reagan mould. Warning of the need for radical economics Howard pledged, 'I am absolutely determined to say over the next 18 months the things that I think are right.'[20]

The strategy was launched in Howard's June 1986 national television address, replying to Hawke during the 'banana republic' phase, when Howard beat Hawke on substance and presentation. It was a result essential to protecting his leadership, and it emboldened Howard. He spoke to the nation in clear and strong terms:

> The economic difficulties facing Australia today are more serious than at any time since the Great Depression. And yet, until last month Mr

> Hawke and Mr Keating continually told us that all was well and that
> our economy was robust and healthy . . . Australia has reached a stage
> where a basic change of attitude and direction is needed. And it's
> needed right now. Tinkering at the edges, hoping that something will
> turn up, it just not good enough. The longer hard decisions are put off
> the greater will be the fall in all our living standards.[21]

Howard proposed a series of immediate steps—a mini-budget to tighten
fiscal policy; abandonment of the 3 per cent ALP–ACTU superannuation
deal; a six month wages pause; abandonment of the new taxes in the Keating
tax package; and the relaxation of foreign investment restrictions. In the
medium-term Howard called for implementation of the dry agenda—labour
market reform, a three year freeze in real government spending levels, a
reduction in union power, and greater incentive for the private sector.
Howard, unlike Hawke, fired real bullets. He looked, briefly, like a winner
and a leader with a mission.

The high tide of Howard's leadership came at the Adelaide Liberal
Federal Council in mid 1986, a meeting which saw the rekindling of the
old Liberal lust for power. The Liberals were hungry and cynical as Howard
dumped on Labor and offered a radical alternative. In an election rehearsal
Howard identified his four principles—a government spending freeze, a new
two-step tax scale which substituted incentive for progressivity, industrial
reform including a reduction in union power, and a comprehensive program
of micro-economic reform.

The psychological key to this approach was the belief that Australia,
in a desperate search for solutions, would adopt such radicalism. It was a
violation of several of the country's political traditions—egalitarianism,
moderation, gradualism. Howard proposed to solve not just the economic
problem. His proposition involved a major redistribution of wealth towards
the better off, the risk of a confrontation with the unions and a repudiation
of state intervention. In truth, Howard hadn't mastered his ideas. He was
flying on hope and instinct, confident of direction, fixated on strength, but
carrying explosives whose chemistry he scarcely knew.

The Liberals produced at this 1986 meeting a 'Policies For Business'
document—the predecessor of the 1989 Economic Action Plan and the 1991
Hewson *Fightback* strategy. It was mainly the work of David Trebeck at
the Liberal Secretariat, with input from Carlton and Chaney. It sought to
integrate the main economic reforms into a new philosophy for Australian
enterprise. The document asserted:

> It is now beyond argument that efficiency and prosperity come most
> abundantly from private initiative and enterprise, private ownership and
> a competitive market place operating within a secure legal
> framework—reinvigorating the Australian economy requires more than
> economic policies. Attitudinal change is the necessary complement to
> institutional change. The next Coalition Government will encourage

positive community attitudes towards competition, enterprise, excellence
and reward for effort . . . outdated, destructive and divisive notions of
class conflict impoverish us and disguise the fact that everyone in
Australia has a joint interest in prosperity.

The document identified a series of macro-economic reforms—a new
labour market system; a program of protection reduction; a program of
privatisation; an attack on inefficiency in transport, communication, coastal
shipping and the waterfront; and the abolition of the two-airline policy. It
was a blueprint for a comprehensive alternative governing model for Australia. It should have provided the basis for the 1987 Howard campaign—but
that required clear thinking.

In July 1986 Howard looked an election winner and the Hawke government appeared in disarray, beaten by the economic crisis. Howard's
tragedy is that he failed to maintain this mid-1986 momentum. The combined forces of Peacock, the wets, the ALP, and more self-inflicted blunders,
saw his problems return and his confidence collapse.

In late 1986 speculation about a leadership challenge from Peacock
reached a new pitch. Hawke told the Labor caucus Peacock's return was
merely a question of timing. Howard was damaged by the bad media
reaction to the Opposition decisions to oppose the Australia Card and the
proposed ABC–SBS merger. Tony Eggleton was forced to deny reports that
Liberal research showed that Howard couldn't win an election. In mid-
November the Morgan polls showed a clear narrowing in the Opposition's
lead over the government, now down to a very tight 46 to 44 per cent.
Keating said that Howard was 'spooked'. The Peacock camp grew excited
and Peacock's wife Margaret, interviewing Hawke on her radio program,
said: 'I don't think I will redecorate the Lodge . . .' Howard had become
the butt of jokes.

In late 1986 Howard unveiled his marketing formula: 'Incentive is the
concept I'll be heavily developing in 1987. It's a concept for the times.' He
called the philosophic direction 'individual liberty, family security, smaller
government, less tax, less regulation and a strong commitment to national
security and defence'.[22] But this concept, launched in early 1987 in a
package called 'incentivation', was undermined by one of the spectacular
advertising failures of the decade. Journalists laughed at the 'incentivation'
slogan and many Liberals were appalled. It was an omen of Liberal campaign inadequacy.

The Howard leadership in the 1980s was tied to the fate of Liberal
economic rationalism. Its failure was one of strategy and communication.
The believers did not explain properly their own position, consequently they
were judged by the old standards: they were rejected as heartless 'value in
the dollar' men because they failed to convey the moral or spiritual dimension of the greater freedom and responsibility which they envisaged for

individuals. Too often the effect of their 'incentive' policies was to assist the rich at the expense of the poor, a feature Labor ruthlessly exploited. Howard fell victim of that axiom of Australian politics, that ALP governments on the right maximise their electoral chances by holding the middle ground. Howard was attacked by the New Right for not joining its cause; then he was attacked by the wets for being a right-wing extremist.

Some drys put their case with commonsense, merely noting that they wanted less economic regulation, not more regulation—a statement most people would have endorsed. Others sought to dramatise the philosophical crossroads that Australia had reached, declaring that they wanted to reverse the entire direction of the twentieth century which had been towards greater state regulation. This far transcended economics; it was a new philosophical basis for Australian Liberalism which was still rejected by much of the party. Carlton, for instance, put the issue in the terms outlined by the theorist F.A. Hayek, declaring that the non-Labor parties 'are being transformed from parties of intervention to parties of freedom'. Hayek's liberalism was not interested in the twentieth century battle by conservatives to resist the latest extension of state power proposed by socialists or progressives. Hayek proposed an alternative theory—a substitution of the idea of individual freedom for state authority as the central idea of politics. In Australia this was almost a revolutionary notion, given the country's tradition.

The drys were trying to change a political culture and a national identity. But their alternative vision was not necessarily appealing—many Australians saw privatisation as asset-stripping, interest rate deregulation as bank profiteering, lower protection as a loss of job security, public spending cuts as threatening their quality of life, and labour market deregulation as giving the boss too much power.

It required one of the biggest campaigns in Australian political history to change this thinking, but the Liberals relied upon ineffective gimmicks. The drys rarely grasped that the economic revolution they proposed would only be carried by a corresponding political transformation of the Australian electorate and national institutions. Above all, they failed to sell the moral basis of their economic policy and to grasp the cultural transformation required to make it succeed. Meanwhile Howard warned that only disunity could defeat the Liberals—an exact prediction of the future.

13
The New Right

I and 170 000 farmers think Australia is coming apart at the seams. So those parts of it that we can fix, we are going to fix.
National Farmers' Federation President, Ian McLachlan, August 1986

The clash between competing visions of Australia's future reached its zenith in 1986 in the phenomenon of the New Right and its challenge to the Hawke government's consensus model. The New Right was a revolt against Hawke's corporate state and the chief institutional force in Australian history, the arbitration system. It was inspired by the insight that the logic of the Accord—a culmination of this historical legacy—would hasten the destruction of arbitration. The New Right lay outside the political party framework and this was the key to its character. It was utopian in its hopes, confrontationalist in its methods, religious in its fervour. Such traits were taboo in the media-induced mediocrity of party politics, where the search for majorities too often degenerated into 'lowest common denominator' solutions.

The New Right was a small group of influential figures who sought to change the industrial system from within, an industrial guerilla group using the law as its weapon. The New Right was encouraged by the Liberal Party's drive to embrace a policy of labour market deregulation, but it declined to wait upon politics. As lawyers, employers, producers and polemicists, its members worked to achieve changes in industrial practice. In its most primitive form it assaulted the power of trade unions. But its ultimate target was the demolition of the arbitration system—its laws, tribunals, employer and union structures.

The New Right believed that history was on its side. Its bedrock assumption was that those Australian institutions created to resolve the class conflict and income redistribution arising from Australia's nineteenth century industrialisation were now obsolete and, more seriously, were throttling

252

Australia's efforts to create a productive society for the late twentieth century.

In looking to the future the New Right resurrected the past. It believed that trade unions exploited workers, not helped them, that employer organisations crippled enterprise, not protected it. Finally, it believed that unless Australia killed arbitration then arbitration would most certainly kill Australia.

While Hawke governed through consensus the New Right said that the era of decision-making through big government, big unions and big business was dying. It saw corporatism and the Accord as the last hurrah of industrial institutions. The next phase—or Alvin Toffler's 'third wave'—would be a of celebration of individuality: an industrial system where the people, not organisations, were dominant; this new culture would provide the key to greater productivity. These were dangerous ideas which excited resentments bred by their threats to vested interests. The New Right supported deregulation and the free market economy and sensed, correctly, that the greatest battle for these principles would centre on the labour market.

In one sense the New Right was created by the Labor Party and the media, the name being popularised when they discovered the existence of the H.R. Nicholls Society, a group formed to reform the industrial system. The New Right was a generic term which referred to a movement rather than to a single organisation. There was never a New Right charter; just the actions of individuals from Ian McLachlan to Charles Copeman, from Peter Costello to Joh Bjelke-Petersen. They were united by their rejection of Hawke's consensus and their search for reforms which weakened unions and empowered individuals.

Many of the New Right figureheads were or became Liberals—Hugh Morgan, Peter Costello, Charles Copeman, Ian McLachlan. But the New Right was never hostage to the tactical requirements of the Liberal Party. Herein lies the key to the ambivalent impact which the New Right had on Australian politics during the mid-1980s. Its influence damaged the Opposition in electoral terms, but the New Right's pyrotechnics were successful in moving the debate in favour of labour market deregulation. Its success was reflected in the fact that in 1990 there was no New Right; the 1985 extremists had become the 1990 Liberal Party mainstreamers.

No individual embodied the New Right but the best approximation in 1986 was Ian McLachlan, then 49, Australia's pastoral iconoclast. McLachlan was a natural leader and a startling political commodity—appealing, intelligent and very rich. The four years McLachlan spent as National Farmers' Federation (NFF) president made him a national figure and the focus of the most intense recruitment campaign for the prime ministership since the Hawke push.

McLachlan, like Hawke, was a natural television performer. Like Hawke he had a political heritage, his father being a former South Australian Liberal president. The NFF was his power base just as Hawke had had the ACTU. But there was a basic difference—McLachlan was devoid of messianic delusions. McLachlan wanted power but hated blood on his hands. He was a dilettante, drawn to politics but too lofty to be a politician. McLachlan was the archetype of New Right romanticism—the noble farmer or businessman who might briefly enter politics to restore national order before returning to his true calling.

The rise of McLachlan coincided with the rise of the NFF in the 1984–88 period. It was driven by three factors. First, a tide of small business and larger corporate support for the NFF's aggressive industrial strategy. Second, the creation of an NFF 'fighting fund' of more than $10 million, which gave the farm lobby a financial clout commensurate with those of the ALP or Liberal federal secretariats. Third, the conjunction of the McLachlan image — appeal and strength — with a time of national economic crisis.

The landmark in the NFF's rise was McLachlan's speech to the 25 October 1985 meeting of the National Party Federal Council. McLachlan came as usurper, a more powerful farm leader than anybody within the National Party, whose own leaders he humiliated. McLachlan's speech deserves a special place in the history of the National Party's decline. He explained that the NFF was 'the single federal voice of Australia's 170 000 farmers on issues which affect more than one commodity'. Its constitution bound the NFF to a strict 'non-party' stance. 'We will treat them all even-handedly,' McLachlan said of the parties. His message—if you want farm support then you must earn it.

He continued: 'We have had enough of political posturing which masquerades as philosophical commitment . . . we need fixed directions, not fixers . . . There is great dissatisfaction with your performance in the bush. Your credibility has been diminished because your policy research has been inadequate. You have not provided new directions but have relied on the same, tired rhetoric we have all heard thousands of times before.' He continued for page after page, outlining the philosophical position of the NFF and the policy criteria it followed. Ian Sinclair was furious but impotent, an unfortunate political combination.

The NFF aims identified by McLachlan were the exposure of all Australian industry to market forces; the creation of an internationally competitive economy; a deregulated labour market; equality of all interests before the law; and reward for initiative and incentive for risk-taking.

The NFF's tactic was to mobilise its constituency and use farm power for policy ends. During the mid-1980s David Trebeck, after establishing the NFF's policy framework for the decade, went on contract as policy adviser to the Liberal secretariat. He was replaced at the NFF by Andrew Robb who in turn was assisted by Rick Farley (called by McLachlan his 'stiletto man' for the tight political work). Both Robb and Farley had vast experience in rural politics.

As the 1980s unfolded industrial reform replaced protection as the NFF's priority. The two were inexorably linked, but as protection began to fracture the NFF turned its sights towards the industrial battle. David Trebeck explains:

> The protection debate—in which NFF and its predecessors, along with many others, were so heavily involved—was 'won' during the 1980s. It was won largely because manufacturers, government and the community generally came to understand that protection was a one-sided response to a deeper problem—competitiveness. Competitiveness was and is the real issue; protection is a way of treating its symptoms as far as import competing industries are concerned, but doing so in a way which imposes a tax on exporters.[1]

Once the farm sector embraced the cause of low protection to assist its competitiveness, it was inevitable that it would also address the industrial system.

The New Right's momentum came from four industrial disputes in the mid-1980s—Mudginberri, the Queensland power dispute, Dollar Sweets, and Robe River. The first three had several common features—renegade unions breaking from ACTU discipline and grossly misjudging their strength; a split between the workers and their militant leaders; the determination of the employer in each case to fight rather than succumb to union intimidation; and the successful resort to legal remedies to break the unions.

The ACTU dismissed these disputes as mere industrial hiccups. In fact, their significance was immense—it lay in the demonstration to employers that they didn't have to remain prisoners of the arbitration machinery. They helped to persuade employers that a shift to enterprise bargaining was possible without exposing themselves to union blackmail. The conversion of the Business Council of Australia, representing the country's eighty biggest corporations, to enterprise bargaining a short time later would have been inconceivable without these proven successes and the intellectual climate to which the New Right contributed.

Mudginberri was the main victory for the strategy upon which the NFF embarked at the start of the decade—to break union power in tandem with smashing protection. In both struggles it assumed the need for direct action; waiting for politicians meant waiting forever. Paul Houlihan, a former union official and farmer, was hired as NFF industrial director to organise the NFF's assault. The NFF had enjoyed earlier victories in the live sheep export dispute and wide combs dispute, both of which had given McLachlan national status. (Indeed, it is doubtful if McLachlan would have emerged as NFF president without the wide combs dispute). However, in the mid-1980s it was Mudginberri which became a landmark.

This was the first occasion on which the Trade Practices Act was used successfully against a trade union. It made s45D of the Act into a powerful instrument for reweighting the legal balance towards employers. But Mudginberri had another role—it was the making of the NFF.

The NFF became involved at Mudginberri as a result of economic analysis that showed extreme inefficiencies in the meat industry due to the influence of the Australasian Meat Industry Employees Union (AMIEU) and because of the piecework method used, the unity tally system. The Commission brought down a decision that was satisfactory to the workers and management at Mudginberri but not to AMIEU—it allowed employees and employers to negotiate their own piecework arrangements.

The union voted to sabotage the Commission's decision. It dishonoured its pledge to abide by the Bench, expelled its Mudginberri members, defied return to work orders, and maintained a picket line which the Commonwealth meat inspectors refused to cross, thereby halting Mudginberri's export shipments. The responsible minister, John Kerin, refused to order the meat inspectors to do their job, a refusal which the NFF branded 'craven cowardice . . . a complete surrender of governmental authority to the AMIEU'.

The Mudginberri owner, Jay Pendarvis, took action under s45D of the Trade Practices Act which resulted, finally, in the union being fined $144 000 and incurring $2 million in legal costs. He was funded mainly by the NFF, after making a personal appeal to McLachlan and to the Northern Territory government. The AMIEU's action was a costly misjudgement of changing power relativities. Its defeat was achieved by a combination of the Commission's decision, the employer's courage, the NFF's clout and the Trade Practices Act amendments introduced by John Howard during the Fraser era. But the NFF's public relations and a campaign by *The Australian* turned Mudginberri into a national symbol.

The NFF depicted it as proof that small business could prevail, ultimately, against a union bent on sabotage. The farm lobby saw Mudginberri as altering the employer–union power balance and Houlihan said that 'our society is in the process of reassessing the rights and obligations that it will demand from trade unions in the future'.[2]

Hawke made two efforts to negotiate Mudginberri with McLachlan— both times he was rebuffed, as McLachlan felt that any talks involving Hawke, the union and the NFF would be stacked against him. At one point when McLachlan told Hawke he would send him a list of the NFF's concerns, Hawke replied, 'What do you think I am, a fucking post office!'

It was on Mudginberri's success that the $10 million plus NFF 'fighting fund' was built. 'Without Mudginberri we couldn't have done it,' McLachlan said. About 60 per cent of the fund came from farmers; the rest from large and small business. Professional fund raisers were employed but McLachlan still made many personal approaches to business. He sought the monies from companies on a specific basis—fund the NFF to spearhead the ongoing national industrial reform campaign—that is, the NFF would fire the bullets to change the system.

These NFF donations were funds that to some extent would normally have gone to the Liberal and National Parties—proof of business doubts about the non-Labor parties. The NFF kept its fighting fund intact throughout the 1980s. It is administered by a separate trust whose principles stipulate that the funds are to be used mainly for industrial issues and projects which set a national precedent. Before the 1990 rural recession the NFF ran a national headquarters in Canberra stronger than either the ALP or Liberal Secretariats, with a $2.3 million budget and a big policy research staff.

The rise of the NFF symbolised a cultural resurgence within rural Australia—an assertion of individuality and rural pride against the agrarian socialism of organised parties. It was a claim by rural Australia for a greater stake in decision-making based upon its export contribution; an assertion of its moral right as an export earner to impose micro-economic efficiencies upon the nation. It was also a repudiation of urban Australia's complacency in taking the living standards which exports delivered but declining to make the sacrifices to sustain them. McLachlan used the NFF to establish a national profile but the NFF used McLachlan's charismatic image to promote its cause.

Eventually McLachlan's profile worked against the NFF's interests. Hawke and Keating decided to treat McLachlan for what he was—a political enemy. The climax came on 9 December 1986 when McLachlan met Hawke and Keating to put the NFF's view on economic policy. The meeting was delayed, so McLachlan spoke to the media before it began (to catch the evening television bulletins). When ushered inside he took with him a 'banana republic' T-shirt, since it was Hawke's birthday. But McLachlan found Hawke in a cold fury, holding a transcript of his media criticism. Hawke savaged McLachlan and said that meetings with the prime minister weren't held as media stunts. Told that he was putting politics before farm interests, McLachlan was abruptly dismissed. 'Well done chaps', he muttered. The shutters went down.

The Queensland power dispute the year before (1985) was a demonstration of the power that government was able to apply against a renegade union; it left Joh Bjelke-Petersen with enhanced status as the only political leader who would confront and defeat union power, a status which Bjelke-Petersen would later exploit unpredictably.

This dispute, between the militant Electrical Trade Union (ETU) and the South-East Queensland Electricity Board (SEQEB) was over the Board's push for contract labour. The ETU had thrown out a previous agreement and resorted to extreme strike action which denied electricity to hundreds of thousands of consumers and forced standdowns in many industries. The Bjelke-Petersen government moved to withdraw the electricity industry from the jurisdiction of the State Industrial Commission. It established a new legal framework for the industry which made strikes illegal under threat of dismissal, prohibited picketing, abolished compulsory unionism and set up a separate industrial tribunal for the electricity industry. Those employees who defied the ETU and kept working were subjected to threats and often frightening intimidation.

The dispute was a disaster for the union movement within Queensland. Many workers who followed the ETU tactics were left jobless and in serious financial hardship. Bjelke-Petersen's action was popular, a symbol of the anti-union line which small business was demanding around the nation. It was the most dramatic government intervention in any of the industrial disputes of the 1980s until the pilots' dispute in 1989. It helped to entrench Bjelke-Petersen's hero's status among the rising tide of farmer and small business opinion. Even Bjelke-Petersen's critics from the right, notably John Hyde, had to admit the effectiveness of his action.

The third case involved the Melbourne Dollar Sweets company, which was famous for the 'hundreds and thousands' much loved by Australian children. It fell victim to union ideologues who took control of the small Federated Confectioners' Association, which became part of Victoria's 'tomato left', so-called for the tomatoes it threw at right-wing unionists. The union repudiated the Arbitration Commission's wage principles and in 1985 began strike action for a 36-hour week. The workforce was split, some remaining, those striking setting up a continuous picket.

Dollar Sweets was subjected to bomb and arson threats, its management to death threats. A driver was assaulted and his truck vandalised. The union ignored settlement recommendations by the Commission.

The company took the case to the Melbourne industrial barrister, Peter Costello who in turn discussed it with Andrew Hay, president of the Chamber of Commerce. The upshot was a campaign for funds to finance legal action in the Victorian Supreme Court. Costello, representing the company, won the case on common law grounds. The strike was ended and the union paid the company $175 000 as compensation. It was a legal and political coup.

Costello and Hay were spearheads of a tougher Liberal Party. Costello was a future Liberal frontbencher and a friend of the future Victorian president, Michael Kroger, who would become renowned for severing Liberal deadwood. Costello had excited attention even before his pre-selection as a 'future prime minister'. Hay's prime ministerial ambitions, by contrast, were almost yesterday's news. As a former senior adviser to Phillip Lynch (Malcolm Fraser's treasurer before Howard) and principal in exposing the Khemlani loans affair, Hay was one of the best political operators the Liberals had put into the Parliament House field. Back in Melbourne, Hay was impatient and ambitious and used the newly formed Australian Federation of Employers to promote both himself and small business. Costello and Hay proved that unions could be sued at common law.

Costello says:

The number of occasions on which successful action had been taken against unions at common law was so negligible that, for all practical purposes, the law was extinct. Moreover, in 1985 everybody was still in bed with the Hawke government. One of the reasons common law actions were not taken was a fear of the possible reaction to the ending of the unions' privileged exemption from the law. For Dollar Sweets the exercise was expensive and the personal cost high. But it turned out to be less expensive and less costly than the nightmare of intimidation which the Court action ended . . . Far from becoming an example of the folly of tackling unions in the Courts, it became an example of the reverse. Psychologically it was part of the break in the mid-1980s against consensus.[3]

These disputes didn't affect most companies since suing a union was always a last resort, costly and time-consuming. Bill Kelty said: 'There will never be a thousand Mudginberris. That simply is in no one's interests. For every Mudginberri there would be 50 negotiations through which people get improvements in wages and working conditions.'[4] Kelty was right but this didn't diminish the significance of these cases. They changed the underlying employer–union power balance and the psychology within the system precisely because such a 'last resort' option was now available.

These cases were powerful deterrents to militant union action. The Queensland dispute showed that state power, when mobilised with popular support, was highly effective against rebel unions. Hawke would later provide even more dramatic evidence of this during the 1989 pilots' dispute. But the value of the common law and Trade Practices Act as revealed by Dollar Sweets and Mudginberri was that they gave a recourse to employers even when governments declined to protect them.

The assertion of rights by small business and farmers had struck a chord within the Liberal Party; the election of John Howard as its leader in September 1985 had seemed to reflect the spirit of the times. Within hours of his election Howard issued a rallying call to the small capitalists of Australia. He had concluded in the two years since Fraser's defeat and Hawke's victory that industrial reform was the key to unlocking Australia's productivity improvement. As an aspiring prime minister Howard saw this as his greatest challenge and Australia's main long-range gain.

Howard was trying to mobilise small business and farmers behind his leadership. They were the grassroots agitators against the Accord and consensus, unlike big business, which in 1985 was divided and frightened over challenging Hawke on industrial policy. Howard declared 'let a thousand Mudginberris bloom'. His gospel was that the Accord would fail Australia and fail the Labor Party. It would become the deepest intellectual conviction within non-Labor politics during the decade.

The evening of his elevation to leader Howard declared:

I think the biggest single economic challenge over the next five to ten years, is to free up the labour market and, in doing so, to alter the balance in our industrial relations system. It does involve a winding back of certain elements of trade union power, not the destruction of the trade union movement and not some mindless union bash . . . that is the biggest single difference that will exist in the Australian political battle ground over the next few years.[5]

Howard's immediate fear was whether his deputy and shadow industrial relations minister, Neil Brown, would share his position. This prompted some serious Howard–Brown talks and then confirmation that Brown would build upon, not retreat from, the established Howard position.

By early 1986 the rising confidence among Arbitration's opponents was celebrated in the formation of the H.R. Nicholls Society, which was to achieve an infamy beyond the wildest hopes of its sponsors. It originated with Western Mining Corporation's (WMC's) Ray Evans, who served as Hugh Morgan's 'brains trust' in their mutual collaboration against arbitration, Aboriginal land rights, the Green Movement and Australia's dismal productivity. Evans discussed the idea with three mutual friends—John Stone, Peter Costello and Barrie Purvis from the Australian Woolbrokers Employers Federation.

Evans knew that industrial relations was being transformed by landmark cases such as Dollar Sweets and Mudginberri and that the unfolding debate would signal an historic change in Australia's outlook. They agreed to establish a forum; it was Evans who proposed that it be called the H.R. Nicholls Society after the former editor of the *Hobart Mercury*.

The excellent biography of Justice Henry Bournes Higgins by John Rickard had just been published; Evans' fancy was taken by the story of Higgins' attempt to convict the 82-year-old Nicholls for contempt of court. As editor of the *Mercury* Nicholls had described Higgins as 'a political judge' but had the satisfaction of seeing the case which Higgins inspired against him being dismissed. Evans says: 'having discovered this octogenarian newspaper man of delightful character we decided that he should be brought back into contemporary debate as a symbol of what was right against Higgins in Higgins' own time'.[6]

The letter of invitation signed by Evans, Stone, Costello and Purvis said:

We would probably have to go back to the early days of Federation, and the debates leading up to the passing of the Conciliation and Arbitration Act, to find a precedent for this debate. Its outcome will have very great significance indeed for Australia's future economic growth, political development and ultimately, perhaps, territorial integrity . . . there needs to be an increase both in the tempo of the debate and of its depth and breadth of intellectual content. Although it has started off well there is a risk that it may slow down and perhaps peter out.[7]

The New Right

It is a commentary upon Labor's manipulation of public opinion that the organisation which it persuaded the media to depict as a right-wing conspiracy held its innocuous inaugural meeting at a Country Women's Association house in Toorak in February 1986. The list of attendees, which excluded politicians, is an honour roll of the free market counter-establishment of the 1980s, together with participants from the main industrial clashes.

It included Morgan and Evans (WMC); McLachlan and Houlihan (NFF); Gerard Henderson (Howard's office); John Hyde; the rising Liberals Peter Costello, David Kemp and Rod Kemp; John Stone; Michael Porter (Monash University); David Trebeck and Geoff Carmody (later a principal of Access Economics); Charles Copeman (Peko Wallsend); Wayne Gilbert (SEQEB); Bert Kelly; Andrew Hay; Dr Ian Spry (barrister); the businessman Neville Kennard; and Sir John Kerr, an old industrial warrior. Stone accepted nomination as the inaugural president. The Society's aims, identified in its charter, were to promote a debate on industrial relations and to promote the system's reform.

In his opening address Hugh Morgan complained that the great export industries had been divorced from the consciousness of most Australians—an assessment that was indisputably true. Morgan said: 'The farmers and miners today feel that the rest of the country regards their present struggle with unconcern. For the rest of Australia, it seems to be business and borrowing, as usual.' Morgan complained that the union leaders and the arbitral bureaucracy seemed unconcerned 'for our front line troops in the world market place'.[8]

The antagonism towards the system was revealed in Ray Evans' remark that Justice Higgins was 'a nut who, to the great detriment of his country, found himself able to give legal form and substance to his fantasies'. Morgan declared that the unions, in effect, ran Australia: 'They are our masters. Can you name any other country in the world that has to take its budget to the trade union movement and get approval before putting it to the House?'[9]

John Hyde delivered a paper debunking the orthodox view that S.M. Bruce lost the 1929 election because he attacked arbitration. Hyde denied that assaulting the industrial system meant electoral suicide for politicians. The entire seminar concerned the possibilities, opportunities and tactics for the demolition of the arbitration system.

The society was a rallying point for participants involved in the attempt to transform the industrial system. It produced over the years a valuable collection of case studies from its seminars. But its first meeting was significant for another reason. Charles Copeman said later that it gave him the 'inspiration' he needed to prosecute the Robe Rover crisis—the biggest and most political dispute of 1986.

As Chief Executive of Peko Wallsend, which had acquired a controlling interest in Robe River, a Pilbara iron ore operation, Copeman decided to confront serious overmanning, chronic industrial disputes and a list of 284 restrictive work practices, appalling even by Australia's standards. The more exotic involved $12 000 a month on special 'smoko' needs—pink salmon, tuna and smoked oysters. On other occasions strikes were held when the canteen ran out of ice-cream flavours. Copeman said he faced 'blatant extortion and corrupt practices' and produced evidence to substantiate his claims. He sacked the local management, announced a crackdown on working conditions, a redundancy scheme, and the intention to seek federal award coverage to replace the state award. When the WA Industrial Commission ordered a return to the status quo, Peko refused and sacked the entire 1180 workforce, lodged an appeal against the order and then began to rehire people on its own terms.

These actions, which coincided with the atmosphere of crisis arising from the banana republic declaration, made Copeman a national figure. He publicised the dispute, the inefficient work practices, and upheld Robe River as an issue of national political significance. Copeman, subsequently an unsuccessful Liberal candidate for federal parliament, tried to use the crisis as a practical symbol of the changing power balance in industrial relations. He declared that 'there can be no sanitised distinction between industrial relations and the polarised politics we have in Australia'. The unions were shocked that an employer accepted the logic of the Accord—its fusion of industrial and political power—and fought it on exactly the same basis.[10]

Copeman, in fact, had made the same political judgement which Howard had made—that Australia's economic crisis offered a unique chance to force through radical change. Howard backed Copeman, declaring: 'The Robe River dispute is of great importance to Australia. What is at stake is the right of Australian management to manage.' Hawke said the best solution to inefficient work practices came through dialogue, not confrontation. At this point the media broke the story of the H.R. Nicholls Society and Copeman's membership.

New Right polemicist Des Keegan said that 'generations of men are falling like leaves . . . yet Charles Copeman may leave a mark on our century'.[11] Hawke went for the jugular with a denunciation of the New Right as 'political troglodytes and lunatics' in a campaign to split the business community and keep the majority locked into his system. John Dawkins said the Nicholls Society tactics were 'closely aligned with the word treasonable' because they shot overseas investor confidence in Australia. Most businessmen had no wish to become martyrs for a better industrial system. They happily wished Copeman well but would never have assumed such risk themselves. However, the Business Council of Australia (BCA) warned Hawke not to underestimate 'mainstream business sympathy' for Copeman.[12]

Copeman eliminated the offending work practices but Peko was forced by the Commission to pay compensation to workers and then sustained another strike before reaching a negotiated settlement in January 1987. In the interim Copeman's actions had dramatised inefficient work practices on a national scale. Hawke responded by calling a meeting of major employer groups in an effort to secure improvements.

The New Right's emergence exposed the division among employer groups which reached its apogee in the mid-1980s. The main employers, the Confederation of Australian Industry (CAI) and the Metal Trades Industry Association (MTIA), were appalled by the New Right's tactics. The radicals, in turn, saw the CAI and MTIA as prisoners of Hawke's centralised system. In fact, the real wages cuts which the Accord and the centralised system had delivered to employers gave them plenty of financial incentive to support Hawke. The employers were cautious men now taking some of their best profits for years.

The CAI chief, Bryan Noakes, attacked the principle being advocated by the industrial reformers: 'The notion that industrial relations should be a matter for the individual employer and individual employee is . . . so far removed from reality that it is a dangerous distraction.'[13] Noakes repeated the case against deregulation—that wage rises in one part of the workforce would flow through to other parts. He feared that deregulation might fuel a wages explosion. His CAI colleague, David Nolan, argued that a move to decentralisation of wage fixation would only 'make matters here worse'. America and Britain had gone down these roads and finished with higher unemployment than Australia for no better inflation result. But Chamber of Manufacturers Director Brian Powell went further, saying the New Right was showing 'truly fascist tendencies that make it harder and harder for us to negotiate change'.[14]

The small business spokesmen Peter Boyle and Andrew Hay went with the radicals. Hay said: 'I would like to see the Conciliation and Arbitration system abolished. I don't believe we have time on our side which will allow us to take an evolutionary route over a 10 year period.'[15]

The Liberal deputy, Neil Brown, rewrote the Opposition's industrial policy against this backdrop. Within the Opposition Macphee was still the chief opponent of a freer labour market. As shadow communications minister in a dry-dominated shadow Cabinet he was reduced to harassment rather than defiance, but Macphee knew how to harass Brown. The agony of the industrial policy rethink for business and the Opposition was revealed in two meetings in early 1986.

On 3 February the shadow Cabinet dined with the Business Council of Australia (BCA), the forum of the big business elite, at Melbourne's Regent Hotel, with presentations from Howard, Carlton and Brown. Brown's exposition of industrial policy did not impress, and an around-the-table debate ensued. It was a good discussion but there was criticism, notably from Bill Dix (Ford).

Dix argued the incompatibility between a free market for wages and strong trade unions. He said that when he went to work the next day he'd be dealing with 19 different unions; the Opposition had to grasp the reality. It was pie in the sky to believe that a brave new world would appear. Australia's union power was different from that of America (57 per cent of Australia's workforce was unionised compared with 19 per cent in the US). Dix was sceptical about the Liberal's ability to make their policy work. The risk was that the result might be worse, not better. He said the Liberal provision for opting out of the centralised system was 'not sensible and in need of a re-think'.

Others speakers criticised the Opposition for depicting Australia as a corporate state and in particular for trying to drive a wedge between large and small business. After much discussion Jim Carlton, impatient with such narrow vision, told Australia's business elite that ultimately it had no choice. The Liberals wanted to free the labour market and weaken union power. Business must realise that the union hold over the economy would be retained only at the cost of further economic decline.

An account of this meeting was leaked to the *Australian Financial Review* in a report which cast doubt on Howard's ability to carry business behind his policy. There was uproar within the party. Howard's backers called the leak 'an act of treachery'. The BCA chairman, Westpac chief Bob White, trying to reflect the balance among his members, declared: 'There is a great deal of concern that too sudden a change will cause chaos . . . there's no philosophical opposition. But there's a worry that if we don't have the centralised system then what's going to take its place. Is it just going to be the law of the jungle?'[16]

CRA's chief, John Ralph, identified the fracture among the chief executives. Exporters had to face overseas competition and could not tolerate an excessive domestic cost structure while firms selling to the local protected market had more fat. Second, heavily unionised industries feared the transition far more than low unionised industries. So farmers and miners favoured reform while manufacturers were apprehensive.

The second encounter with the BCA was far more revealing—it was a window into the Liberal convulsions during the decade. On 25 February 1986, Howard, Brown, Chaney, Macphee and Carlton met the BCA industrial committee chaired by Stan Wallis (Amcor) for a thorough policy review. Brown began his exposition but the participants became aware of Macphee, edgy and agitated.

Macphee interrupted, asking Howard: 'What is the status of this meeting?' After Howard explained Macphee exploded: 'I've got to say something. I want you to know that I abhor what's been said here. This is not Liberal policy and it has no relation to Liberal policy. Our policy is not a union bash and the Liberal Party doesn't believe in what Neil has just said.' Macphee was attacking Brown directly and Howard by implication in front of the BCA industrial committee. In an extraordinary performance Macphee sabotaged the meeting.

When the BCA left Howard invited the Liberals into his room. 'Why can't you be loyal to your deputy?' Howard asked Macphee. 'How can you undermine us so blatantly?' Macphee replied: 'Neil was saying outrageous things. I clarified the situation with you before I spoke. That's not our policy and it's different from the drafts that Neil has shown me. I know those businessmen. If I stayed silent they'd think I agreed with Neil.' Brown told Howard that Macphee was intolerable and should be sacked from the frontbench. Macphee in turn accused Brown of leaking the earlier BCA meeting to the press. Brown said it was an 'outrageous' accusation. Macphee said if it wasn't Brown then it was his staff. Howard was shocked—he had asked Macphee to this meeting to involve him in the industrial policy. But his conciliatory gesture had backfired.

The final humiliation was another leak—this time Trebeck's strategy paper to Brown on selling the industrial policy, drafted in Liberal headquarters and containing material that should never have been put on paper. Tabled in parliament by Ralph Willis, it devastated Howard. An internal memo dated 18 February 1986, it was an insight into Liberal thinking, an admission by the party that its industrial policy had powerful opponents in business and the media who must be 'neutralised' to win its acceptance.

Trebeck said that Joh Bjelke-Petersen was 'a key ally if favourably disposed', but that Tasmanian Liberal premier Robin Gray, who had made 'awful comments' on the principle of a freer labour market, must be neutralised. The 'potential supporters' among business were John Leard (formerly ANI), Hugh Morgan, Charles Copeman, John Ralph (CRA), John Spalvins (Adelaide Steamship), Rupert Murdoch, John Elliott (Elders) and Sir Arvi Parbo (WMC). But those under the 'need to neutralise' heading included Bill Dix (Ford), Sir Peter Abeles (TNT), Brian Loton (BHP), Chuck Chapman (GMH), John Utz (Wormald) and Brian Kelman (CSR). The next page contained a list of senior journalists divided into supporters and opponents.

Labor created havoc with Trebeck's memo while Howard cringed. It was a cruel attack from within. Despite these disasters the Opposition industrial policy was still launched successfully. Brown knew its significance—'the major area under the Howard leadership where our credentials would be tested'.

The industrial policy released on 11 May 1986 was the first comprehensive attempt by a major political party for more than half a century to reform fundamentally the conciliation and arbitration system. There was no compromise this time between Howard and Macphee as there had been on the 1984 policy. Macphee told the shadow Cabinet that he disagreed with the policy, but he had no influence. It represented a complete victory for the free market lobby; for Howard as leader, for Brown as industrial spokesman. It is this document upon which all subsequent coalition industrial policy was built. It is this document which is the basis for industrial reforms of the next coalition government. It was the single most important policy advance under Howard's leadership.

The policy sought to reform the centralised system and create an alternative system based upon voluntary contracts. Such contracts would begin with businesses employing fewer than fifty people, the 'soft end' of union power, and be extended progressively. The minimum agreed wage would be the award hourly rate. Such agreements between employers and employees could cover any or all work conditions and would be encouraged by the government. They would have the status of awards and would be legally enforceable but would fall completely outside the Commission's ambit or authority. The law would be amended to prevent flow-ons from such agreements into Commission decisions.

Within the mainstream system the Full Bench would be required to determine national wage cases according to the criteria of capacity to pay and the competitive condition of the economy, not wage indexation.

The use of the common law as a means of obtaining redress would be encouraged where appropriate. The secondary boycott provisions in the Trade Practices Act would be kept and strengthened. Essential services legislation would be passed and voluntary unionism upheld. Employee share ownership schemes would be encouraged. The philosophy overall was to transfer power from unions to employers, employees and the public. The 1980s quest for greater freedom for individuals was reflected in the policy. It was an assault upon the Accord, Hawke's corporate state and arbitration.

Brown summarised his policy: 'The thrust was to allow the Arbitration Commission and those who wanted to use it to continue to operate but to allow others who did not want to use it to "opt out" and to make agreements over which the Arbitration Commission had no control.'[17] From day one, an employer and employees by majority consent could seal a contract outside the system.

The change in the political climate in just two years was hardly recognisable. In 1984 Howard had battled Macphee without any outside support to win the opting out concession. In 1986 the national debate was dominated by precedent-setting disputes, a mood of economic crisis and the demands of the New Right for the Liberals to become much tougher; overall, a rapid move in the national debate towards the dismantling of a pillar of the Deakin Settlement.

The policy, ironically, won a better reception than its 1984 counterpart. It seemed tame compared with the New Right's rhetoric but in substance it reflected the New Right philosophy. Howard and Brown found that virtually all business groups, large and small, from the CAI to the small business lobbies, strongly supported the Opposition's thrust and were prepared to minimise their differences over its extent. Public opinion had also moved;

polls showed that 78 per cent believed that unions had too much power—this included more than 50 per cent who said the unions had 'far too much power'.[18]

Brown was sensitive over his policy authorship: 'The idea at the time that the so-called New Right was hovering over my shoulder and holding my quivering hand and writing my words was a lot of nonsense. They did no such thing. They controlled neither the concept nor the provisions of the policy.'[19]

In fact, Brown had consulted widely in the drafting phase—Peter Boyle from the Small Business Association, Andrew Hay, Peter Costello, Paul Houlihan and a Melbourne barrister, I.F.C. Spry, also from the H.R. Nicholls Society, as well as the main employer groups. He did not speak to the ACTU—'there was no point, we were dismantling the system'. Brown showed the policy to Joh Bjelke-Petersen who said: 'It's very good if it helps to get rid of this Whitlam man.'

Brown told the New Right it was his policy, not theirs, while Labor claimed the Liberals had been captured by the New Right. Howard replied that his 1984 policy had pre-dated the New Right. The 1986 policy was a streamlined version. Brown and Howard had got the balance right this time—the proof was the attacks from conflicting sides, the wets and the New Right.

Realising the extent of policy overlap between the Liberals and the New Right, Macphee launched a last ditch assault upon the New Right in November 1986. He warned that the New Right was debauching the Liberal Party. He said that liberalism as a philosophy had to be distinguished from conservatism and libertarianism. The conservatives upheld the status quo but libertarianism, the creed of the New Right, was 'the antithesis of the just society'. It elevated selfishness and denied the role of government in favour of markets. It was marked by a 'social heartlessness' where 'strong dominate the weak'. Macphee's loathing of the New Right was mutual, but he was beaten within the Liberal Party.

In late 1986 Brown commissioned work on a draft industrial bill for a coalition government from Costello and other Victorian lawyers. Getting wind of this, the media depicted the Liberals as a shopfront for the New Right. Industrial reporter Pamela Williams wrote: 'The New Right has a firm grip on the Liberals . . . members of the H.R. Nicholls Society are quietly drafting the policy.'[20]

Such reports were understandable when the Small Business Association president, Peter Boyle, declared: 'We say to Brown, "How's that policy going? Have you toughened up the wimps in the party room yet?" I go to Brown's office and he comes to mine. And I talk to Howard if I think Brown's not helping us.'[21] But the truth was quite different. As the year turned, Howard was failing to land the 'big men' of the New Right.

The New Right was distrustful of party politics, sceptical of professional politicians, self-righteous and moralistic. It believed that Australia had been betrayed by leaders such as Fraser and Hawke. The New Right was a mixture of rural revivalism, contemporary neo-conservatism and a cultural assertion of Australian individualism. It was rooted in the economic truth of farm and mining efficiency which urban Australia often ignored. It was distinctly short on political brainpower and, despite its claims to the contrary, it had a distorted view of public sentiment. It had become as obsessed about the Liberal wets as the wets were obsessed by the New Right. It missed the main point about non-Labor politics — that it was being transformed and that support for Howard, rather than criticism of Howard, was the path to deliverance. Ultimately, the New Right refused to accept the validity of the dry revolution within the Liberal Party.

The mood of fatalism was captured by David Barnett, a journalist attuned to non-Labor politics: '1987 will be the year of the New Right. It may be Bob Hawke's last year as prime minister. If it is not, it could be the last year of the Liberal Party as it now exists and the same can be said for the National Party.'[22]

The talk within small business and at the corporate dinner tables of Sydney and Melbourne was of money, agitation and upheaval. The glue which had held the old Establishment together was coming unstuck. The revolution within the domains of finance and business, the lifelines of non-Labor support, was spilling over into a destabilisation of the non-Labor parties. It was a time when the old rules were being smashed. The technique of creative destruction was the fashion; noone, and no institution, was immune — not BHP, not the Liberal Party, not the prime ministership.

Howard defended the integrity of his party but supported the New Right: 'We're not beholden to any group. We'll never be beholden to any group . . . but I'm certainly not going to walk away from people like Ian McLachlan, Andrew Hay, Charles Copeman and Peter Boyle—who are making a very intelligent contribution.'[23] But Howard's efforts at conciliation were not reciprocated.

The greatest disappointment to Howard was McLachlan, whose prestige was denied to the Liberals. McLachlan became the leading spokesman for rural and business disillusionment with Australia's political establishment. He captured the growing disgust towards politicians and parties: 'I don't see myself as a Liberal or anything much. I mean not anything. I think all this party political bullshit had got us into a lot of trouble.' McLachlan condemned McEwenism, Fraserism, Hawke, the National Party and Howard. He was a loner. He blamed careerist politicians for many of Australia's problems: 'retention of job becomes more important to them than doing the job'.

'I'll be honest with you: I think the Liberal Party's not going to do the job even if they get back in,' McLachlan said. 'They say they will but I don't think they will.' McLachlan said of the Liberals: 'They will not be allowed by their parliamentarians to fix it.' This was the vote of 'no confidence' which Howard found so debilitating.[24] It was the Fraser legacy: the more Howard tried to escape from Fraser, the more Fraser's ghost rose up to haunt him.

The prominent wet Chris Puplick attributed the influence of the New Right to external factors:

> the New Right ideas gained a high degree of acceptance within the Liberal Party because the Thatcher and Reagan models appeared to be working. The stories you read were about the US economy booming and everything coming up roses in London. When people went to the United Kingdom, they went to London, not Glasgow, Liverpool or Merseyside to see the human cost of Thatcherism. Everybody went to New York but nobody went north of Central Park or saw what was happening in the American cities under Reagan.[25]

The Liberals and the New Right forgot that the reasons for the reelections of Thatcher and Reagan lay primarily outside their economic ideology. Thatcher was reelected overwhelmingly on the 'Falklands factor', while Reagan won on a mixture of authority against the Soviets, social conservatism and prosperity, not on economic reform. But the main factor driving New Right policies within Australia was not the experience of overseas models, it was an interpretation of Australia's own history.

The economic rationalists within the Liberal Party and the New Right were correct in their fundamental insight—once Labor decided to internationalise the economy and abolish protectionism, the institutions and ideas of arbitration were doomed. The timing of the New Right's attack was perfect. The mentality of the banana republic crisis only encouraged the embrace of radical solutions. The victories won in the workplace by the New Right along with the entrenchment of the federal Opposition's new industrial policy suggests that 1986 may have been the turning point in the history of Australia's industrial system. It was the year when the forces of change became manifestly stronger than the forces of resistance. The irony for Labor is monumental—its own internationalist policies were undermining arbitration and centralised wage fixation.

The New Right was not popular but it was not interested in popularity. Howard's problem was that he could not alienate the New Right; they were his people and his issues. He had to persuade them to work with him, not against him. This enabled Hawke to depict Howard as a New Right sympathiser and confrontationalist, although the New Right had never accepted Howard's legitimacy nor taken him seriously.

The Liberals and the New Right, despite their differences, won the intellectual debate but lost the political war in 1986 and 1987. Hawke, Keating and Kelty were too smart for them. Union power did not become an issue in Australia the way it did in Britain. In Australia the moderates of the labour movement were in command while in Britain it was the left-wing radicals who sought to confront Thatcher and played into her hands.

Labor's consensus had reached its zenith in 1986 and the New Right, seen through this prism, was a fantastic distortion of reality. But consensus is a political vehicle whose utility cannot endure. Once Hawke's consensus failed the New Right would be rehabilitated. Before this occurred, however, in the 1987 election the New Right would reveal its own flawed vision, in embracing Joh Bjelke-Petersen the destroyer as saviour.

The national crisis was breeding a new animal, a mixture of old-fashioned Australian individualism, nationalist xenophobia and economic populism. A familiar but threatening form was silhouetted at sunset slouching towards Canberra.

14
Consensus, business and unions

I think my relationship with the union movement is as strong as any Labor treasurer has ever enjoyed.

Paul Keating, September 1985

There was a distinct convergence in the latter half of the 1980s between the Labor government and the coalition Opposition over the future national direction. The decade, while marked by calls to ideological warfare, still possessed an underlying unity. Hawke strove to hold the centre of political gravity in Menzian fashion—and he succeeded. The Hawke consensus—which involved Labor, unions, business, and Canberra's policy-advising elite—was so remarkable that its durability had to be brief.

But the nature of Hawke's consensus underwent dramatic change in 1986–87, when Australia was compelled by external shocks to reform its habits. At this point the Hawke consensus was transformed. Its original purpose, to promote recovery from the early 1980s recession, had been accomplished. Its new challenge, defined by Hawke and Keating, was to provide an ethos for the severe domestic reforms demanded by the current account deficit crisis. Consensus assumed a new and unexpected role: to facilitate the transition to a more competitive economy. History shows that its success was only partial, and the consensus model was undermined by the early 1990s recession.

Australia's political debate during the late 1980s saw Labor and Coalition, business and unions, opinion makers and economic institutions, agreed upon the direction—the need for a more competitive, flexible, high saving economy, less reliant upon state regulation, border protection and arbitral machinery. The real division was about the timing, income redistribution and methodology of the transformation.

Against Hawke's consensus the coalition demanded a faster pace of change. It said that consensus might be a luxury that Australia could not afford. In the early 1990s the new Liberal leader, John Hewson, campaigned as a 'consensus buster', claiming that Labor's consensus had failed the nation.

The value of consensus is that it mobilised so many interests behind the 'economic rationalist' path—party, business, unions, economic advisers and, briefly, even the voters. The weakness of consensus ultimately is that it limited the pace of economic reform when urgency was required given Australia's international predicaments.

Consensus was integral to Hawke's conception of his unique relationship with the Australian people. Hawke felt he governed for all society, so he maximised his appeal. Consensus was a symbol of comfort for those who feared change and a method by which change could be made more orderly. It was the antithesis of Whitlam's 'crash through or crash'—the slogan of the crazy brave.

Hawke's consensus was the bridge which united his two dominant yet conflicting images—the strong leader and common man. Their fusion was the key to his popularity. Hawke exploited consensus to depict himself as a natural leader for the entire nation but consensus had another purpose—to reveal Hawke as a man of compassion. Consensus was a political idea which Hawke used as a substitute for the Labor ideology of class conflict which he, along with most of the modern ALP, repudiated.

Hawke was never a passionate reformer; his political style was centred in his self-obsession. The narcissist in Hawke was addicted to securing the approval and love of others hence his spectacular love affair with the people. In office Hawke projected the emotions of his personal life to the national stage—he sought the approval of unions and business, he aspired to cure child poverty, repay the debt to the Aboriginal community, look after his mates. Hawke was often incapable of distinguishing between the responsibilities of office and obligations to his friends. His inability to insist upon Brian Burke's resignation as Ambassador to Ireland during the WA Royal Commission hearings was the ultimate example of this confusion.

Hawke saw each election win as a vindication of his relationship with the voters, not just a victory for Labor politics. Before he became leader he refused to accept the leadership legitimacy of Hayden and Whitlam; as a successful prime minister he refused to accept the leadership legitimacy of his rivals—Howard, Peacock and then Keating.

Hawke used television not just to communicate with the people but to maintain his emotional links with them. The feedback came when he visited the shopping centres to touch people, shake their hands, stare into their eyes, utter a sincere cliché. Whenever Hawke was depressed in Canberra because of political blunders or adverse print media coverage, he would take flight to the shopping centres to restore his spirits and replenish his self-image. He was an emotional leader whose relationship with the people was more complex than those of his predecessors. Because Hawke's consensus was rooted in his search for community applause it was his constant companion, deployed too often and for too long.

After Labor submitted to Hawke's leadership in 1983, Hawke forgave the party its past sins of rejection and enshrined consensus in his dealings with the party as well as the public. This coincided exactly with his self-interest. Before Hawke became ALP leader he was a leadership pretender—a brilliant but divisive influence within the party. Labor, in turn, was ambivalent about Hawke, seeing him as both saviour and betrayer, and comparing him unfairly with Billy Hughes, Labor's greatest rat. Hawke's relationship with Labor in the 1980s saw a decisive transition from impatient outsider to consensus leader.

As leader Hawke applied the techniques of dialogue and consultation to flatter individuals and pacify the caucus. This was reinforced by cunning in his handling of the factions. Hawke enjoyed the support of the right wing as his power base, but he also pacified the centre-left, the Hayden faction, and promoted its senior ministers so that Button, Dawkins and Walsh became very influential. Finally and most significantly, Hawke sued the left faction for peace after his second election victory in 1984. In his second term he incorporated the left into his government; he moved from being a leader for two-thirds of the party to a leader for the whole party.

There were three keys to the left's incorporation. First, a generational change in the left's senior ministers from Tom Uren, Arthur Gietzelt and Stewart West to Brian Howe and Gerry Hand, followed by Nick Bolkus and Peter Baldwin, a move towards a more pragmatic group. Second, Hawke opted for a power-sharing strategy when he promoted Howe into Cabinet after the 1984 election as social security minister and then, in early 1987, when he put Howe onto Cabinet's Expenditure Review Committee (ERC) despite Keating's vehement protest. Hawke's aim was to tie the left into Cabinet's economic discipline. His gameplan worked so well that he finished by tying the left into his own leadership. Thirdly, the left leadership reassessed its own aspirations and tactics after its assumption of real power. Howe symbolised the change when, as an ERC minister, he confronted the current account deficit crisis, accepted the Hawke–Keating economic direction and in turn devised his own needs-based welfare strategy to advance Labor's social justice platform.

While Hawke was influential with the public and the party, Keating's influence was geared more to policy making. The pillars of Keating's power were the Cabinet, the economic institutions (treasury and the Reserve Bank) and the ACTU, a combination which made him the most powerful treasurer since Ben Chifley. For a while Keating achieved a synthesis between these three diverse domains which represented a consensus between the organs of institutional power.

The 1984–87 term saw the growth of a Cabinet collegiality within the ERC whose ministers bore the punishing hours and applied the intellectual rigour. Keating as treasurer established an alliance which dominated the ERC based upon his policy concord with Hawke, his intimacy with Dawkins, his respect for Walsh and his cultivation of Howe. These ministers came to believe with a passion in their economic model. But Keating's authority within Cabinet was based also upon the treasury's revival, a process which followed Bernie Fraser's elevation to replace Stone as secretary to the treasury in late 1984.

Keating knew his man. Hawke and the Cabinet had wanted to appoint another treasury deputy, Chris Higgins, an outstanding academic economist, but Keating insisted upon Fraser. Fraser was also Stone's choice and the preference of former treasurer Howard. In his life and values Bernie Fraser could hardly have been more remote from the 1980s fashionable stereotyping of Canberra's economic elite as aloof and mediocre careerists. Fraser came from a poor working class family of seven in rural NSW, secured a pass degree at Armidale and joined the old National Development Department in 1962.

Three elements shaped Fraser's approach as treasury secretary.[1] Fraser was a product of his background, bringing to economic policy a belief in social justice which had a decisive consequence: it made him a monetary policy dove. Some said superdove; others, like his deputy David Morgan, called him a wimp. Fraser shared the Keating philosophy; he believed that the main economic problem of the decade, the current account deficit, had to be tackled gradually, not at the cost of 'massive rises in unemployment and destroying business confidence'. Fraser believed that a monetary policy squeeze risked killing the patient to cure the disease. Like Keating, Fraser believed in economic growth and job creation. He tied his treasury to Keating's model and repudiated the shock therapy of hard-liners like Stone.

Second, Fraser had seen first-hand the mistakes of the treasury over the previous twenty years, the rupture of its relations with both the Whitlam and Fraser governments, the ridicule and policy eclipse which had befallen his department, and he concluded that a change in approach was demanded. Fraser repudiated the absolutism of the 'Stone Age'; he substituted practicality for purism. He decided that part of the problem rested with treasury's excessive dogmatism, that too often it was not 'prepared to shape advice within the general framework' of the government. Fraser decided that the treasury must work with government, not against it; he believed in trying to secure second-best solutions if politicians refused to accept first-best solutions.

Finally, Fraser was self-effacing, accommodating and responsive, in contrast to Stone's arrogant, combative and dogmatic disposition. Fraser forged an intimate relationship with Keating based upon trust, helping Keating to achieve his objectives. Keating and Fraser brought the treasury in from the cold and restored its influence within the heart of power. It was a complex process of cross-fertilisation. The treasury shaped Keating's views to its economic philosophy but Keating reshaped the treasury to Labor's Accord. From the start Fraser had a firm view of Keating's value: 'I've worked with other treasurers who were persuaded about the need for change. But they couldn't deliver. That's where Keating was different. It was his ability to deliver that marked him out. That made him the engine room of the reforms.'

Fraser was open about the historic synthesis that had occurred, saying: 'What this government has tried to do with some success is to keep the economy going, to make some gradual progress on inflation and the current account deficit but at the same time maintain employment and reduce unemployment. I think that's the distinguishing feature of this government. I think it's also the distinguishing feature of the kind of advice that's being going forward from the Treasury.'[2]

In his speeches Fraser argued that the Accord was promoting rational economics. But treasury acceptance of the new Labor–treasury model was never universal. There was worry within the department that its soul had been half-mortgaged to Keating. It was reflected in warnings from former senior officers who resigned in the 1980s, some of whom were disillusioned.

The personal dimension in the Keating–treasury relationship was vital. Keating broke the sense of institutional formality, bringing intimacy to his links with his department. He fashioned in the senior ranks a mood of loyalty that was redolent of the NSW right's tribalism. This intimacy went beyond Fraser and included the three new deputy secretaries, Chris Higgins, Ted Evans and David Morgan—friendly rivals dedicated to advancing the treasury agenda with Keating. The official family circle extended to include the Reserve Bank Governor Bob Johnston who, since the 1983 float and financial deregulation, was an unabashed Keating fan.

The power realities that underpinned Keating's ties with the economic institutions were twofold—Keating was a winner in Cabinet and he was pushing the treasury agenda. For fifteen years the treasury had been plagued by weak ministers, overruled by prime ministers and unable to achieve sustained policy dominance. Now Keating was its minister and Hawke sought largely to work with Keating, not against him. He had little inclination to use the prime minister's department against treasury in the style that Malcolm Fraser had perfected, an inclination further lessened when Ross Garnaut, Hawke's influential economic adviser, left his office in 1986. Keating's return of the treasury to policy dominance is fundamental to the 1980s story. The heroes and villains of the decade were carried on the back of this remarkable Labor–treasury alliance.

While the Accord was the chief instrument of consensus, Hawke also sought to tie business, not just unions, to the wheels of his chariot. Despite the tensions between government, unions and business, there was still a loose consensus for a new order. From 1986 onwards the seeds were sown for a shift in the wages system towards enterprise bargaining and towards substantial cuts in industry protection. This revolution reflected a reappraisal within both capital and labour; it was the stirrings of the 'productive culture' of which John Button was chief proselytiser.

The Hawke–Keating team followed a dual approach towards business. They cultivated a number of informal friendships, particularly Hawke, who was more active and less discerning than Keating. Hawke also tried to promote a reorganisation of business groups to enable business to participate in his 'corporate state' dialogue. He influenced the formation of the most influential business group of the decade, the Business Council of Australia (BCA).

Business was outmanoeuvred at the 1983 National Economic Summit; it welcomed Hawke but worried about the Accord to which it was not a party. The 'gang of 18' chief executives decided on the morning after the Summit to fast-track an earlier proposal which led in September 1983 to the creation of the BCA, which initially involved around sixty of the nation's chief executives. Peter McLaughlin, later BCA director, said that Hawke 'was neither father nor mid-wife but had some role in inducing the child'.[3]

Despite Sir Peter Abeles' appeal at the Summit for the Accord to expand from a bilateral into a trilateral agreement, the business chiefs never sought such a role. They repudiated the notion of collective decision-making throughout the Hawke era, although many manufacturing leaders applauded the professionalism of the Crean–Kelty team. They were also impressed by the quality of the Hawke Cabinet, many saying it was the best they had encountered. But there was tension between Hawke's addiction to formal backing for his policies from business groups and the determination of the chief executives to remain independent.

Many chief executives rejected small business's campaign against Labor and its propagandists such as Katherine West who ranted against a Mussolini-style corporate state. Nor did most chief executives appreciate Labor's embrace of the high flyers—Abeles, Alan Bond, Kerry Packer and Robert Holmes a'Court. Such romances were too special to be either typical or representative.

The futility of Labor's efforts to incorporate business within its schema was exposed in successive events—the 1985 Tax Summit, the Accord Mark II, and the 1988 campaign for executive remuneration restraint. The Tax Summit was a failure for business because it was obsessed about avoiding any repeat of its seduction at the 1983 Summit. The upshot was that BCA chief Bob White (Westpac) delivered an exaggerated rejection of Keating's package at the Summit and Labor's deal-making over tax reform. Business lost the consumption tax which it wanted but incurred a series of new taxes which it had opposed.[4]

Keating finished the tax debate with a conviction that the ACTU, not business, was the hope for decent policy and he acted on this belief. Business, in turn, saw Keating's final tax package as anti-business, a manifesto constructed by the ALP, public servants and the ACTU.

Hawke and Keating were dismayed in September 1985 at the BCA's refusal to endorse the Accord Mark II, their new agreement with the unions which provided for a 2 per cent wage discount. The ACTU had accepted this real wage cut as part of a package—including compensatory tax cuts and a superannuation provision—to maintain overall living standards. The commentator Richard Farmer wrote: 'If the Tax Summit saw the beginning of the end of the "corporate state" involving an alliance of government, unions and business, the reaction of the BCA to the renewal of the Accord saw the conclusion. Hawke and Keating were stunned at the initial reaction of Council members.'[5]

The intellectual roots of business disaffection were twofold—a worry, despite the wage discount, that Labor was soft on inflation, and a feeling of exclusion, that the new deal was negotiated between the ALP and ACTU but that business paid the bill.[6]

However, a frustrated Keating blamed business for its failure to grasp the magnitude of his pioneering economic reforms. According to his senior aide, Keating believed that 'ALP administrations are judged more harshly than their political opponents', particularly by business.[7] Keating's frustration would erupt periodically, sometimes in immortal hyperbole. Most notable was this outburst: 'If this was any other country in the world, looking at the quality of the policy settings in place, I think we'd have businessmen lighting candles to us in cathedrals . . . Here the broad business community is such a rednecked society that the sophistication of these policies had just not yet sunk in.' But Keating's prophet and pagans analogy meant little to voters.[8]

The final incident which demonstrated that business would not 'cut a deal' was Labor's 1988 push for restraint in executive remuneration, which had become an emotional issue within both the ACTU and the Cabinet. The upshot was a mini-summit convened in early 1988 between representatives from the BCA, the CAI, small business, the Council of Professions and the ACTU, chaired by Ralph Willis. It saw a protracted, intense, sometimes bitter argument which finished in deadlock. The Accord partners wanted an agreement to restrain executive income increases to the increase in wages— to secure equality of sacrifice.

This approach was rejected by business and the BCA, which was aggressive in pushing the line that executive remuneration was market driven, unlike wages; that the market was partly an international one; that historical relativities had no special validity for the present or future; and that executives operated with greater risk as well as greater reward.[9]

However the most symbolic victory of business over Labor was its campaign against the 1987 proposals to abolish the secondary boycotts provision of the Trade Practices Act, the provision touted by the New Right as essential to reducing union power. It was killed by a television advertising campaign in 1987 organised by the NFF, produced by The Campaign Palace and backed by employer groups on the theme of legal privilege for unions. With a federal election looming Hawke ditched the bill, for which the ACTU had been pressing since 1983.

Labor's proposal to protect the unions had come from the report into the industrial system headed by Professor Keith Hancock which was a defence of arbitration, centralised wage fixation and, by implication, the Accord. The report was criticised by Howard as a 'product of the IR Club, by the IR Club, for the IR Club'. Hancock's report led to the creation of a new Industrial Relations Commission, but its effort to bolster the legal position of unions foundered upon business and community opinion.

The most contentious element of Labor's approach to business was the personal association between Keating and Hawke and senior businessmen. By 1986 Keating had become convinced that the corporate establishment was incompetent and riddled with Liberal Party prejudice. Feeling that Australia's entrepreneurial class had failed, he looked to the new generation of active entrepreneurs, of whom Robert Holmes a'Court was his favourite and with whom he developed close ties. His instincts were captured when Holmes a'Court launched his takeover bid for BHP, a bid which Keating determined to back against the bulk of the ALP.

NSW premier Neville Wran, president of the NSW ALP John MacBean, sentiment within the right and left wings, and much of the union movement, were antagonistic towards the Holmes a'Court bid. The interloper was seen as a paper-shuffler: smart, unreliable, self-interested. Keating was unequivocal in his dismissal of such sentiment. He was not prepared to compromise his market policies to sanction a federal inquiry to halt Holmes a'Court, as sections of the ALP demanded. Keating asked his critics: why should Labor protect BHP when it had never helped Labor and its corporate performance was so dubious?

Hawke, alive to party pressures, flagged the option of an inquiry into the BHP takeover bid but never pursued it. In March 1986 the Cabinet followed Keating (supported by Kelty) and left the door open for Holmes a'Court, an opportunity he was unable to realise.

Later the same year Keating, with Hawke's acquiescence, hijacked media policy, enlarged the limits on television ownership, promoted the cross-media ownership law to break joint television-newspaper holdings and laid the basis for Rupert Murdoch's takeover of the Herald and Weekly Times (HWT) group. Hawke and Keating loathed this group, which they saw as the banner of a failed and reactionary corporate establishment. They hoped to strengthen Packer or Murdoch or Holmes a'Court, proprietors whom they saw as modern, tough and pragmatic and with whom they could deal. In a caucus meeting Keating said that Packer was a 'friend of Labor', Murdoch was a pragmatist and the Herald and Weekly Times group would always oppose Labor. While the Fairfax press tended to support Keating's economic policy, both Hawke and Keating were profoundly suspicious of Fairfax. Hawke told me of the Fairfax group: 'If I find them engaged in something which is inimical to the interests of the Labor Party, then they'll find me there as a tough opponent.'

Keating was critical of Fairfax, inspired by its hostility to ALP right-wing governments and a personal sentiment after the *National Times* launched a minute investigation of his personal affairs. The paper tried to nail Keating as a corrupt politician but failed to find any evidence. Its chief line of inquiry was that Keating had given his friend, Warren Anderson, special tax exemption, a suggestion that stung Keating. He concluded that the paper had embarked upon a calculated effort to destroy his career.

The upshot was that Keating devised a complex media policy which could be endorsed on intellectual grounds, supported by the Labor Party but would tilt the balance for and against different players. The policy had three effects: it would abolish the absurd two station rule which would help Packer; it would facilitate the breakup of the HWT group; it would force players to choose between television and papers and limit any Fairfax gain from the HWT breakup. The final result was a new media structure with two newspaper groups, Murdoch and Fairfax, and a national network for television owners—a situation which the owners misjudged, some with fatal consequences, incurring excessive debt and paying absurd prices.

Hawke's closest business associate was Peter Abeles, a family intimate of twenty years. When Rosslyn completed her rehabilitation she worked for Ansett in Canberra. It was a 'given' within the Cabinet that Abeles had a personal link to Hawke, not just on aviation policy, but virtually any issue, political or personal. Their relationship had a history in which Abeles had cared for and looked after Hawke. In office it was assumed by the Cabinet, perhaps unfairly to Hawke, that this relationship underwrote Ansett's position vis-a-vis Qantas and Australian Airlines and protected Ansett during domestic aviation deregulation.

Some of Hawke's associates like Abeles and Frank Lowy reflected his search for intimate ties among men of wealth. Others such as his transitory meetings with Alan Bond and Laurie Connell were facilitated by ALP colleagues like Brian Burke and Graham Richardson. In 1987 Hawke launched a strong defence of Bond: 'There's a lot of sloppy talk going around this country at the moment that somehow there should be no place in the concerns of a federal Labor government for the Alan Bonds of this world. Now I want to repudiate that nonsense unequivocally. It would be an entirely perverse concept if we didn't recognise the enormous contribution of the Alan Bonds and the other great entrepreneurs and risk-takers of our country.'[10]

Hawke wanted his government to be associated with the success of the entrepreneurs. He felt, correctly, that his policies had influenced their emergence. Later ALP advisers told Hawke that his image in a bow-tie mixing with Alan Bond and fishing with Laurie Connell was disastrous. That was when the entrepreneurs had become as popular as rat poison. Bond eventually did severe damage to Australia's international reputation and became a taboo figure among politicians.

The two policy issues on which Australia's business leadership would focus in the late 1980s and early 1990s were a more competitive economy and a new industrial system.

In 1987 BCA president Sir Roderick Carnegie and the BCA's executive director initiated a thorough survey of the eighty member companies. The conclusion was that 'the broad corporate leadership was overwhelmingly concerned with two major issues for themselves and for Australia . . . the national debt arising from problems in competitiveness; the other was employee relations, seen to be arising from the centralised and adversarial nature of our industrial relations system'.[11]

This reflected a gradual transformation of the corporate sector and Australia's business culture. The BCA pushed for a tight fiscal policy, more savings, and faster micro-economic reform to tackle the national debt. Its enduring contribution, however, was the pioneering of the new industrial culture. It was a turning point, a long delayed admission by business that poor management lay at the heart of Australia's weak economic performance.

The first fruit was the 24 March 1987 BCA statement, 'Towards an Enterprise Based Industrial Relations System', which pledged Australia's major companies for the first time to a deregulated labour market. This policy called for a 'fundamental re-orientation' of the system away from arbitration to individual enterprises. It proposed that companies negotiate to achieve legally binding enterprise agreements either annually or biennially. Employees could be represented by a union or group of unions. Outside union officials could attend but not control workplace negotiations. The BCA's aim was an eventual dismantling of the craft union structure in favour of single-union enterprises, a revolutionary concept.

This policy was the product of intense work led by Stan Wallis (Amcor), Jim Layt (Blue Circle Southern Cement) and Ian Webber (Mayne Nickless) among others, backed by the BCA Secretariat headed by Geoff Allen. It revealed the broad front on which support for industrial reform was mounting. It had been less than three years since Howard first got 'voluntary agreements' into coalition policy. The previous year had seen Keating's 'banana republic' policy circuit-breaker and the coalition endorsement of Neil Brown's comprehensive shift towards enterprise agreements. But a rethink of equal magnitude was underway within the heartland of industrial orthodoxy, the ACTU.

The wage discipline Hawke and Keating imposed upon the ACTU to combat the 1986 current account deficit produced a startling legacy—a search by the ACTU leaders for a new wage system. As Bill Kelty explained it:

We had already given a wage discount, effectively, in relation to Medicare (1983). We accepted there had to be a discount in relation to the terms of trade (1985). The government was lining up again for more discounts (1986) and at this point we said the wages system had got to change. We couldn't stick by a centralised system that was just going to cut our wage rates. So we decided to change. We decided we wanted greater flexibility and we developed the concept of the two tier system.[12]

It was the break in the dam wall, the point at which the ACTU conceded the principle that wages had to be based more on productivity than price compensation. The two-tier wages system was a direct legacy of Keating's banana republic politics.

The ACTU would now outsmart its critics. Ever since 1983 business had been obsessed with the question: how long could the Accord survive? Kelty's riposte was that the Accord would adapt; the child would grow to adolescence. Keating offered the insight that the Accord was 'not so much a document—more a state of mind'. It would endure as long as the meeting of minds prevailed.

The meeting of minds reached its peak in the Keating–Kelty intimacy, a decisive relationship of the Hawke era. By 1985 the Accord had assumed a unique symmetry, controlled in each domain, political and industrial, by a craftsman who had mastered his own powerbase. Keating and Kelty, inspired by their sense of national vision and intoxicated by personal achievement, ran the Accord. It was a natural fit—Keating dominated the Cabinet and Kelty dominated the unions; their alliance reinforced their individual power; they delighted in their rapport. Keating and Kelty began to talk the same language; they were 'big picture' addicts with a severe dose of egomania. They formed an enduring partnership which shaped Australia's economic path.

The foundation stone of their alliance was trust; their word to each other was their bond. Keating and Kelty spoke as individuals and on behalf of institutions—the Cabinet and the unions. They gave the institutional alliance of the Accord a new dimension, the seal of personal trust. History reveals the value of such trust; it can unite nations and institutions. In the 1980s it helped the Accord to realise its finest moments; but the origins of the 1990s recession cannot be grasped without an understanding of this trust, which finished as a liability that denied Labor essential policy options.

The Keating–Kelty alliance was rooted in a tribal loyalty that was the bedrock of labourism and the essence of mateship. When Kelty was asked to explain the key to his attitude towards Keating he replied:

It was trust and mutual confidence. Our people finally came to the view—and some of them still don't like him—that they could trust him. And they did trust him. He'd say 'this is my position', or he'd say, 'if you do this I will support you in Cabinet and you know that I will

281

support you'. And he always delivered. I mean, you never had the slightest doubt. You'd walk away from a meeting and every one of our people would be totally committed to the arrangement because they always knew that Keating would deliver. He always delivered the tax cuts; he always delivered the superannuation commitments; he always delivered the family income supplement. When the Accord had to be reviewed he always came back to talk to us. He told us plainly and openly. And he had a vision about where he was going.[13]

Such trust was not an exclusive Keating–Kelty commodity—it arose from the trust between Labor and the ACTU. But their personal intimacy gave the Accord more intensity.

Keating and Kelty influenced each other's vision. The Accord gave Kelty access to the inner sanctum of power as a member of the Reserve Bank board, ally of Keating, chief ACTU negotiator. Kelty, an economics graduate, came to support Keating's economic policy adjustments and Keating, in turn, came to support Kelty's major trade union reforms. Kelty nominates superannuation as the first issue on which their trust was established. He says:

I think on superannuation we partly changed Paul. Some of our people were very committed to it—Simon [Crean], Laurie Carmichael, Gary Weaven, myself . . . we said we'd put this on the agenda, that it'll be the number one issue for us. We said that we'd trade off wage increases for it. Now the union movement had never said that before; never contemplated that before. As soon as we said we were prepared to trade it off against wages Keating said that we must be serious. Keating then agreed to examine it closely and we were on our way. When we did the first agreement with Keating on 'super' there was a feeling in the unions that this was a real achievement; it was for future generations. It wasn't just a 2 or 3 per cent wage increase. It was changing the nation. It was a bit historic and if we are going to talk about history our people walked away from that with tremendous respect for Paul because Paul pushed it. That's not to say Ralph [Willis] didn't support us but Ralph was slower to take decisions, less an enthusiast for change. Paul's always been prepared to make decisions and once he decides on a course he's very enthusiastic for change; and, you know, that gets a bit infectious.[14]

The superannuation deal was incorporated into the Accord Mark II in 1985 but broad agreement between Keating and Kelty had been reached long before. In January 1985, at the initiative of Ross Garnaut, there had been a remarkable meeting at Kirribilli House involving Hawke, Keating, Kelty and Garnaut, where Garnaut had attacked Keating's and Kelty's initial productivity deal as too generous, in terms of superannuation. Garnaut's complaint was that Hawke and the Cabinet had been pre-empted, that the productivity deal was premature. He tried to break the Keating–Kelty deal and force a tougher line. Keating and Kelty were incredulous and Garnaut was kicked around the Kirribilli lounge room before being dumped. The incident, like the 1985 Tax Summit, showed that Garnaut would defy Keating. The end result was that the 'super' deal incorporated into the Accord Mark II was not to come into force until 1986–88. The 'super' policy was embraced by Hawke and Keating partly to kill the left's push for a national superannuation scheme.

The incident was an insight into the nature of power. The Accord was an institution outside the Cabinet which was manipulated by Keating and Kelty in a way that pre-empted the Cabinet itself and denied true Cabinet sovereignty.

The Accord, of course, was an institutional link, not just a Keating–Kelty operation. Kelty declared:

> A national collective bargain can't work between Kelty, Crean, Hawke and Keating. What people fail to understand is that the task the ACTU faces is to obtain the involvement of our key unions. That's our task. Therefore the Carmichaels, the Halfpennys, the Harrisons so far as the metal workers are concerned, the Ivan Hodgsons and Harry Quinns of the Transport Workers Union, the finance unions, the Storeman and Packers union, the Tom McDonalds and others of the building workers, they become the people and organisations which have to become committed. You have to deliver them collectively.[15]

At an early stage of their government Hawke and Keating adopted the basic position that a successful Labor government had to be grounded in the trade union movement. Their core belief was that benefits for the unions had to be delivered through the political process, not by unions taking industrial action. The strategy had to be political, not industrial; a strategy of governance, not the politics of impotence. This meant the unions had a vested interest in helping Labor govern in the national interest and staying in office. It was a belief shared by Kelty and it required compromise on both sides to be sustained.

The record offers its own testimony: during the entire eight-year Hawke–Keating partnership 'there was an acceptance by the trade unions of the economic strategy of the government'.[16] Keating's senior aide, Don Russell, explains the process:

> The commitment to the Accord was also strengthened by the Government's support for arbitrated superannuation, supplementary payments for lower paid workers, tax cuts centred upon the lower paid, the training levy, family allowance supplement and changes to family allowance along with tax initiatives designed to broaden the income tax base such as the capital gains, the fringe benefits tax and the abolition of entertainment as a deduction.[17]

The Accord, as Kelty said, was about 'the politics of achievement'. He explained the dialogue with Keating as a process in which the unions said, 'This is what we can deliver and this is what we can't deliver.' The upshot was that 'Keating has accepted it'. Kelty continued: 'He hasn't come back to quibble about a cent. He's said, "All right, this is as far as you can go." Politics is about that.' Keating confirmed the accuracy of Kelty's account. In 1985 he, in turn, said of the Kelty-led ACTU that 'when they say they can't deliver something I believe them'.[18]

While the financial markets made Keating their darling, the treasurer had another relationship of greater priority, a fact evident (but not appreciated) as early as 1985. Keating said: 'I think my relationship with the union movement is as strong as any Labor Treasurer has ever enjoyed. It doesn't stand comparability . . . no other Labor Treasurer has come within eons of this relationship. But that's come out of the whole operation of the Accord.'[19]

Keating said that as an economist Kelty was 'tip top' and that the ACTU was superior to both the corporate and financial sectors in grasping the nature of Labor's economic reforms. Keating praised individual businessmen but unlike Hawke had no time for corporate politics. He attacked the employer groups, notably the BCA, as sub-standard. His fear was not a desertion by the unions of the Accord but an ascendancy within business of the 'rednecks' over the 'sophisticates'.[20]

The decisive event for the Accord in the 1980s was the unions' recognition that the current account crisis would lead to the collapse of the existing wage system based on the principle of indexation. The ACTU faced an institutionalised cut in real wages or the leap towards a new system. The findings of a representative ACTU delegation to Sweden and other parts of Europe at this time helped to clarify a new course. The upshot was ACTU support for a two-tier system in which wage rises at the second stage were based upon productivity and could vary across industries.

The transition towards the two-tier system, 'a product of true consensus between the ACTU, government and the CAI, was handled as skilfully as the adversarial history of Australia's industrial relations would allow'.[21] The Commission brought indexation to an end on 23 December 1986, closing a three year experiment.

The new two-tier system, which had the broad support of the three main parties, was ratified by the Commission on 10 March 1987. It took the form of a flat $10 a week across-the-board rise plus a deferred 1.5 per cent first tier for all workers. The second tier, not to exceed 4 per cent, was to be negotiated between individual unions and employers on the basis of efficiency gains and improved productivity.

This deal, known as the Accord Mark III, represented the abandonment of full wage indexation without equal offsetting benefits. The Accord's principal managers—Keating, Willis, Kelty and Crean—scuttled their old boat and jumped into a new one. The partners outsmarted the New Right and the Howard Liberals by moving to the two-tier wage system, the prelude to enterprise bargaining and award restructuring.

This rethink was driven by three factors—the external economic crisis; the union movement's fear of the New Right, which made it more prepared to make concessions to Hawke (who exploited this situation with skill); and the ALP's and ACTU's mutual recognition that they had to stick together or be hung separately.

Accord Mark III represented a shift towards decentralised wage bargaining while allowing the Commission to impose a national wages ceiling. It was a compromise; but the concessions by the ACTU were unmistakable and must be seen in the context of the overall industrial debate as an initial step towards a decentralised wages system where the unions accepted a link between pay and productivity. It was a recognition of the need for macroeconomic gains through the wages system if Australia's problems were to be solved. The new system enabled Hawke and Keating to argue at the 1987 election that the Accord had adapted to Australia's trading crisis. It was a reapplication of consensus politics to the national dilemma.

The ACTU had recognised that unless a more flexible wages system were introduced the consequence, as Hawke warned, would be greater unemployment. Kelty sold the system to the unions relying heavily upon the protection for low income earners and the industrially weak given by the first tier. But delivery of the entire union movement to the new system reflected the ethos of solidarity bred by the Accord, the confidence of the ACTU elite in its strategic judgements and, among the most farsighted, the fear that unless the unions adapted then the national economic crisis would annihilate them.

Here was a terribly irony for the ACTU. In 1983 it endorsed the Accord to prevent a domestic wage explosion killing growth, the chief problem of the previous fifteen years. But from 1986 onwards the Accord faced a different challenge: preventing a balance of payments crisis from killing growth, a situation which had never entered the heads of its originators. This would take the Accord into a new dimension where its utility was more suspect—the need to improve productivity and competitiveness and to promote rapid structural change.

The situation in early 1987 was that Hawke and Keating had modified the Accord and, despite tensions with the business and financial community, still enjoyed the respect of corporate Australia and the financial markets. They were just holding the electoral middle ground as Australia's centre of political gravity moved to the right.

In economic terms the government faced two great dilemmas. First, it was decoupled from the inflation cycle of the rest of the world. Australia had put growth before inflation, with the result that the country was locked into a higher inflation rate than the OECD average. In late 1986 Australia's inflation was 8 per cent plus, where the OECD's deflation orthodoxy had produced negative inflation in Japan and West Germany and annual inflation rates for the United States of 1.8 per cent, Britain 2.4 per cent, Canada 3.7 per cent and France 2 per cent. The inflation differential was unsustainable.

The second dilemma was Labor's greatest policy conundrum of the 1980s—how to reconcile its internationalisation of the economy with its belief in the Accord. These were its two primary policy philosophies, established in the first term. The story of Labor's second term was the battle to keep them in harmony. How did Labor make Australia internationally competitive while honouring an agreement with the ACTU to keep its reforms acceptable to the unions?

There were many examples of the same conundrum. How did Labor reconcile its belief in having the price of its own currency set by a floating exchange rate with its equal belief in having much of the domestic price structure determined by prices and incomes negotiated through the Accord? Was the dynamic of a deregulated exchange rate compatible with a regulated labour market? The float would force pressure for domestic reform. Yet it was within this 'clearing house' that the momentum of the float collided with the mechanism of the Accord. It was a meeting between an instrument of the market and an instrument of politics.

The proof of the political nature of the Accord was Keating's declaration the day after the 1986 Budget that the 2 per cent wage discount was merely 'what the traffic would bear'—in short, the maximum political concession he dared to demand from the ACTU.

Hawke and Keating said that the Accord promoted an internationally competitive Australia; that reforms could best be made by cutting deals with the ACTU on wages, tax and spending. They were right, but only up to the point where the unions refused to budge or moved too slowly. That point depended upon the depth of Australia's problem and the flexibility or 'pain threshold' of the unions.

The Opposition interpreted the process as a clash between the irresistible force (exchange rate) and the immovable object (Accord). Howard said that politics must submit to the market; therefore the dismantling of the Accord, deregulation of the labour market and reduction of union power would be the inevitable consequences of the deregulation of the financial system. Keating's reply was that the coalition had ends but no means to achieving them; that the Liberals were 'strong on objectives and short on process'; that the essence of power was implementation but the Opposition had no idea how to run Australia to reach its ambitious objectives.[22]

Labor was committed to proving a practical alternative proposition: that the float and Accord could mesh together, that the Accord could serve as a 'clearing house' for the competitive pressures applied through exchange rate adjustment. The unions were loyal, equipped with astute leaders; they tried to assist the government, displaying in the process a rare maturity. But when vital concessions were needed Labor made them to the Accord, not the business community since its primary bond was always to the unions and the workforce. The Labor model of consensus worked well until 1986–87, and helped to win Hawke an historic third election. Beyond this, however, stretched an unbroken series of further challenges which would test the utility of consensus on the way towards a new labour system and a new business culture. The conundrum of consensus remained—it slowed the pace of reform yet it meant that reforms, when introduced, were deeply implanted.

PART III

CONSERVATIVES IN CRISIS

15
Joh for Canberra: the false prophet

I am determined to turn politics upside down in Australia . . . I am Joh Bjelke-Petersen of Queensland with a lot of experience and I know what I am doing.

Sir Joh Bjelke-Petersen, February 1987

Brian Ray was a Gold Coast businessman, friend of Kerry Packer, a target of the Costigan Royal Commission, and one of the closest confidants of Joh Bjelke-Petersen. Ray had fought the Taxation Commissioner and socialist politicians and in 1987 was charged, tried and then acquitted of conspiracy to defraud the Tax Office over a bottom-of-the-harbour operation. Ray had first met Bjelke-Petersen about 1971 and the two men had grown close. It was in Ray's Gold Coast home in autumn 1986 that Ray and Bjelke-Petersen first talked about an idea that would rock Australia—that Joh would become prime minister.[1]

At the time Ray was involved in a project just north of Surfers Paradise. It was near the vast Sanctuary Cove development which was being pioneered by a smalltime businessman with big dreams, the burly Queenslander Mike Gore. Gore was a phenomenon of the Gold Coast, where the spirit of US capitalism thrived. He started as a car dealer, escaped bankruptcy, fought the Taxation Commissioner, engaged Hawke's personal lawyer, Peter Redlich, to negotiate his tax truce, and boasted a range of mates including the gargantuan Queensland minister Russ Hinze, and the Sydney advertising man John Singleton. Gore was the living embodiment of the Coast's legendary 'white shoe brigade'.

Ray and Gore were business acquaintances, not mates. But Ray told Gore about Bjelke-Petersen's dream and Gore was enthusiastic. Gore was driven by two forces—his support for Bjelke-Petersen and his hostility towards the Hawke government. The Joh-for-Canberra push had its origins in the culture of Gold Coast capitalism. Years afterwards Gore had no doubt how it happened—Ray and Joh had put the idea on the table and Gore produced the plan to make it work.

The inspiration came from Bjelke-Petersen himself: the final crusade of the aged warrior. Ray insisted that Joh had persuaded him, not vice versa as Gore believed. During the initial Joh–Ray talks, Ray was worried about Joh's capacity to translate nationally since he calculated that Bjelke-Petersen's success was a Queensland phenomenon. But Ray's conversion to the Joh cause was based on the rationale which others would later employ— Joh was determined so he must be supported. Ray told Gore: 'Joh can become a white knight in Canberra.' He said that Joh needed an organised campaign and he was talking to the right man.[2]

Mike Gore was a friendly buccaneer and a gambler. He had attempted to transform with only a few million dollars a mosquito-infested swamp into one of the world's prestigious resorts. Gore was sufficiently angry with Hawke, beholden to Joh, and naive about politics to seize the Joh-for-Canberra push.

Gore owed a debt to Bjelke-Petersen because the premier had saved the Sanctuary Cove project. At the start the state government had passed a special law to make the project possible. Later, when the banks were about to close on Gore, the premier met with Gore, subsequently ordering his officials to lend him $10 million through a public agency for several months. This assisted Gore to secure Ariadne Australia as a majority partner.[3] Sanctuary Cove was a visionary concept devised by Gore which Joh helped him to realise.

Bjelke-Petersen later dismissed the roles of Gore and Ray: 'Mike Gore never gave me a cent and he got me into a lot of trouble. He was no help at all. Brian Ray was a good friend but he wasn't involved.' Despite these remarks it is clear that Gore was the initial backer of Joh's push and that Gore was influenced by Ray.[4]

The Joh campaign's origins lie deep within the transforming impact of 1980s politics. Bjelke-Petersen grasped that conventional wisdoms, ideas and institutions were being destroyed. He was an opportunist, ready to seize the cards that fell his way, aware that the 1980s was a time for political entrepreneurs.

In autumn 1986 Gore had his first talk with Bjelke-Petersen about the Canberra push—at least eight months before it become a public issue. Joh talked about destroying Hawke just as he had destroyed Whitlam through his notorious appointment of Albert Patrick Field to the Senate in 1975. Gore told Bjelke-Petersen that through his business links in North America he knew people who could help. He meant the market research company International Strategies, whose subsidiary Decima was run by a Canadian, Alan Gregg. They had been involved in the Reagan campaigns and in the election of Canadian prime minister Brian Mulroney. From the start Gore saw the Joh push in marketing terms, just as he was marketing Sanctuary Cove. He never grasped the complex political issues involved.

Gore went to Toronto to meet Gregg, brief him and organise his support. Gregg agreed to come to Australia to meet the messiah. Gore rang Joh from Vancouver and felt a discreet warning about Gregg might be appropriate: 'You should know Joh that he's 33 years old, has hair down to his shoulders, wears a T-shirt under his coat and calls everybody a mother-fucker.' But Joh didn't complain.

In mid-1986 a three hour meeting in Brisbane involving Bjelke-Petersen, Ray, Gore and Gregg reviewed the strategy. A hugh research program was agreed upon in the prelude to and during the upcoming Queensland state election. Gregg told Ray: 'We had trouble getting Reagan to burn the midday oil. Compared to Reagan, this one's a boy.' Gore, who was bankrolling this operation, wanted Gregg's assessment. He recalls Gregg replying: 'I think Joh's an old fart but it doesn't matter if that's what you want.'[5]

But Gregg gives a slightly different version: 'This was a very odd assignment. It's not one that we've taken since. I met Joh a few times; a mean Ronald Reagan, I'd call him. Most of my work was in connection with the state election and the prospect of Joh as PM was somewhat whimsical.'[6]

From the start Gore confided in his best mate, the late Russ Hinze. For years Gore and Hinze had hit the race track together at 4 am; they drank, played and schemed together. Hinze was an immediate backer of the Joh-for-Canberra push. If Bjelke-Petersen went to Canberra then the Queensland premiership would fall vacant with the chance for Hinze to realise his long-held dream. Hinze was representative of an important characteristic of the Joh push: it was embraced by a collection of individuals who had a diverse range of self-interests.

It was through Hinze that Andrew Peacock was linked with the Joh push. Hinze and Peacock had been associates for years and shared a passion for horses. Hinze introduced Peacock to Gore. Peacock never made pledges to Bjelke-Petersen or his backers, but he spoke with the Joh forces who initially saw him as a partner in the Joh-for-Canberra exercise.

Gregg's early results showed that Bjelke-Petersen's instinct was correct—Howard and Sinclair were an uninspiring team to lead the coalition. Peacock and Bjelke-Petersen were far more appealing; they were winners. According to Gregg, the testing of the Joh–Peacock team was 'part of our focus'.[7] So Peacock became the target of a periodic several-month campaign of persuasion, seduction and recruitment by Hinze and Gore.[8]

It was during the July 1986 Queensland National Party Convention at the Conrad Hilton Hotel that Gore as the self-appointed organiser of the Joh campaign briefed the Queensland National Party organisation on his plans. The meeting in the premier's suite involved Bjelke-Petersen, Gore, the president of the Queensland Party, Sir Robert Sparkes, the vice-president, Charlie Holm, and campaign organiser Fred Maybury. It was the first meeting between Joh's private business backers and National Party strategists. From the start the split emerged which would plague and finally destroy the Joh push. It was over two issues: would there be a Joh push and, if so, who would control it?

Gore outlined the Joh-for-Canberra strategy to a startled group. Joh would run for prime minister in tandem with Peacock. The research he had commissioned from a Canadian firm showed it was viable. The Howard–Sinclair team could not win an election; only the Bjelke-Petersen–Peacock team could win. Gore's theories seemed fantastic but it was obvious that Joh was obsessed by them. Sparkes was alarmed, sensing a grand delusion of unpredictable consequences. Joh's 'kitchen Cabinet' was enthusiastic about his becoming prime minister, especially his pilot Beryl Young and the manager of his personal financial affairs, Sir Edward 'Top Level Ted' Lyons. Sparkes could see that Gore had sold Joh on the idea.

Sparkes told Gore that he was proposing an enormous exercise in logistics, structure and funding. He suggested that as much as $25 million might be needed. 'Personally I don't think it's viable,' Sparkes said of the campaign he would later run. He argued that the National Party leader, Ian Sinclair, would not resign for Joh. Sparkes put the arguments that would later be mounted by the federal coalition against the Joh push. Yet Gore was a zealot for the idea, confident the funds could be raised and uninterested in the difficulties. Sparkes saw Gore as a big talker, with a touch of plausibility.[9]

At the same conference, Hinze called Queensland health minister and future premier Mike Ahern to his hotel suite. 'You're not going to believe this son but the old bloke is going federal,' Hinze said. He had a message: 'Let the bastard go. Don't interfere. Don't oppose him for God's sake.' When Ahern kept professing disbelief, Hinze said: 'I'm telling you this is going to happen. There's a lot of money and a lot of support. Some of the biggest people in Australia are backing this. I've had Andrew Peacock in my home talking about it.'[10]

Sparkes was alarmed because the priority for the Queensland Nationals was the imminent state election, not some federal romance. The first challenge for Bjelke-Petersen would be to retain government in his own right, thereby keeping both the Liberals and Labor in Opposition. It had been after the 1983 state election, when he enjoyed the benefits of two Liberal defectors, that Joh had transformed his Nationals-dominated coalition government into an exclusively National Party government. It was on the tide of such electoral success that Joh could delude himself into thinking that he was invincible; that he could impose the Queensland model—the only state where the National Party was dominant—on the nation.

In 1986, while Bjelke-Petersen appeared to be at his zenith, fatal cracks were opening in the National Party power structure. Joh was starting to drift; infatuated with dreams of going federal he had ignored his own base. Sparkes was worried about the state election. He had difficulty getting Joh to concentrate on his own backyard and forget distant horizons. Relations between Bjelke-Petersen and Sparkes had deteriorated. It was widely accepted that Bjelke-Petersen faced a struggle to retain power in his own right in Queensland.

At the July 1986 state conference Bjelke-Petersen declared his intentions, but they were dismissed as typical Joh ramblings. Joh said that he intended to take over conservative politics in Australia. He said that the Australian people would only vote for a federal leader they trusted—a reference to himself. In the final hours of the conference, Joh loyalist and Brisbane lawyer, David Russell, appealed to the party:

> Maintain your love; your love for our nation, our party, our Premier and Senator who have been a light in the darkness . . . And in that love go into the shires, the towns and cities of our State and ensure in this election that we light a fire that will never be put out.[11]

Here was a great paradox—the elevation of Bjelke-Petersen to the status of national saviour when his Queensland powerbase was starting to fracture. The National Party machine that had run Queensland for so long had already begun its decline, although this was not yet conceded. Joh's popularity was starting to disintegrate, with the Morgan poll showing his disapproval rating higher than his approval rating. Joh was 75 years old and the upcoming poll was seen as his last hurrah. But a strange star was hovering over the political twilight of Bjelke-Petersen, shining on him as the messiah for a new nationwide constituency.[12]

This constituency was broader than the National Party's old electoral base in Queensland. It sprang from an intersecting collection of influences— new money, redneck entrepreneurs, Gold Coast clout, the rise of aggressive businessmen in Queensland and the West anxious to control both state and federal politicians, corporate disillusionment with the Howard–Sinclair team, profound hostility towards Howard over his retrospective 'bottom of the harbour' tax laws as Fraser's treasurer, resentment towards Keating's capital gains and fringe benefits taxes, and the demand for a faster, tougher, anti-union, low tax leadership to liberate free enterprise.

This was combined with a grass-roots movement in provincial Australia supporting Joh, combining strands of religion, nationalism and rural assertion. The extreme League of Rights was fuelling the Joh push, enjoying a spin-off from the rise of the National Farmers' Federation under the charismatic leadership of Ian McLachlan. These forces were given respectability by the pen—the espousal of Bjelke-Petersen by aggressive and, within their domain, influential columnists based in the national broadsheet, *The Australian*, led by Katherine West and Des Keegan.

295

The Gold Coast businessmen backing the project were a floating population but the main figures were Gore, Ray, the managing director of PRD Real Estate in Surfers Paradise, Gordon Douglas, and the executive director of Ariadne Corporation, Geoff Wilson, who later formed his own development company in Brisbane. Lang Hancock from Western Australia was a Joh loyalist, with a thick bankroll and his own links to the premier.

Before the November state election Gore went to Hinze's home for a meeting with Hinze and Peacock. Gore's priority was to convince Peacock about the professionalism of the exercise. He briefed Peacock about Alan Gregg's role, the poor ratings of Howard and Sinclair, and the superior ratings of Peacock and Bjelke-Petersen. Peacock was cautious; he listened but said little. He knew that such theories were both wild and lethal. Gore left the political scheming to Hinze, who continued his talks with Peacock after Gore left.[13]

Hinze was serving as the link man to Peacock with Joh's full approval. Later he boasted about this role: 'Peacock was calling on me . . . nobody in Australia knows this. He [Peacock] had nothing to do with it [publicly]. He didn't criticise it. But he would have been part of the package if Joh was successful.'[14]

In August 1986 Joh's senior political adviser, Ken Crook, held a long discussion with the premier, urging him to refocus on the state election. Finally Crook found the right formula: 'If you can't win in Queensland first then how can you expect to get elected nationally?' During the state campaign Crook ridiculed media inquiries about Joh's federal ambitions, terrified the story would take off.

Bjelke-Petersen himself had no such inhibitions. He attended private functions for businessmen before and during the campaign where he revealed his post-election plans to run for prime minister on an anti-union low tax manifesto. At one function businessmen were expected to donate $25 000 a head for their intimate dinner and access to the premier's thinking. His message was that those Liberals and Nationals who refused to back his federal push would be opposed by Joh candidates. He would fix the country in three years and then retire to Kingaroy before he turned eighty.[15] Joh's long-standing friend, Lang Hancock, said that Bjelke-Petersen would go to Canberra because 'he's the only man who can lead Australia'. In his policy speech for the state election Sir Joh declared that his victory over the socialists in Queensland must become the 'signal for what will soon happen to their comrades in Canberra'.

The 1986 Queensland election therefore had a dual significance. It would determine not just the fate of the state government but whether Joh had sufficient momentum to launch his bid for national office. A poor state result would have killed the Joh-for-Canberra push.

Joh, in fact, snatched a win from the jaws of defeat. He was saved by two factors—a furious last-week big spending drive by the Nationals and a blunder by the Liberals, who drove voters to Joh by raising the prospect of a hung parliament. Election night, 1 November, became a triumph for Bjelke-Petersen who entered the Brisbane tally room radiating vindication and alluding to a federal crusade. Watching Joh on television John Howard said to Janette: 'We'll have trouble with this lunatic now.'

Bjelke-Petersen's win was a perverse result. It exaggerated Joh's strength, concealed his weakness, propelled him to the strike against Hawke and, finally, ensured that his internal critics such as Sparkes could not stop him. Bob Hawke was advised by ANOP's Rod Cameron that the result was achieved despite Joh; that it merely disguised his ongoing decline as a political force.

Joh gave thanks at Kingaroy's Lutheran church, posed outside for the media and declared of the federal coalition: 'They will work by the policies I set or I will work against them.' Joh was beyond restraint, a 75-year-old able to indulge himself in federal fantasies from the safety of office, having cleared his own state election hurdle. Joh had nothing to lose; Howard and Sinclair had an election to lose. Joh says: 'The momentum for me was huge. The phone never stopped. I had businessmen from all over promising to fund me. I told them I'd start a bushfire but the grass was drier than I thought. Howard and Sinclair couldn't win. Nobody in his right mind was going to back them.'[16]

Hinze declared the morning after the state election that a Menzies or a McEwen was needed to lead the nation or 'a type of leader like Sir Joh'. Then he endorsed Peacock to replace Howard. In a prophetic column Katherine West said that Sir Joh's win would weaken Howard and Sinclair; that Sir Joh could go federal using either the National Party or a new party; that he would only make the switch provided he could dominate the subsequent conservative government as prime minister. Most of the federal Liberals and Nationals dismissed any Joh push on Canberra as fantastic.[17]

After the election Gore met Gregg in Canada, where they devised a blueprint for Joh's run. It was based on the intensive research which Gregg had conducted in Australia with the assistance of Spectrum, a local agency. The work was all quantitative, with a sample of 30 000 nationwide and 96 questions. The main result, stronger than ever, was that Peacock and Bjelke-Petersen was the only combination that could beat Hawke. Gore paid from his own pocket for the surveys, a figure he once put at a final total of $400 000. His master-plan was somewhat bracing.

Gore envisaged that Joh would resign and enter federal politics at a by-election, taking the National's leadership from Sinclair. Peacock would resign and then recontest Kooyong as a National. Howard would remain leading the Liberals. The National–Liberal coalition would win the federal election under the leadership of Bjelke-Petersen and Peacock. Peacock would later replace Joh as prime minister with the Nationals being the majority party. Gore organised research in Peacock's seat and claimed the results showed that he would still win as a National.[18]

Despite its absurdity this was the original Gore concept; subsequent adaptations of the Joh-for-Canberra push were only slightly more sensible.

Peacock, a student of North American politics, was impressed that the Joh camp had managed to involve Gregg's company. Peacock never entertained Gore's more fantastic plans, but he was interested enough in their joint ticket to keep talking to Joh's backers. Peacock seems to have been fascinated by these amazing plans, too practical to accept their wilder side but too aware of the bizarre nature of politics to ignore them entirely.

Meanwhile Howard's leadership was taking a pounding in the Liberal Party, the parliament and the media. Hinze's post-election comments had triggered a severe bout of destabilisation of Howard. Wild stories appeared predicting a Peacock challenge. Hawke told the Labor caucus that Howard was finished; it was only a matter of time.

In mid-November 1986 the coalition took a far-reaching decision to oppose in both Houses the Australia Card Bill, a basic element of Keating's tax package. The significance of the coalition decision to reject the Australia Card was that if defeated twice it would provide Hawke with the grounds in 1987 for a double dissolution.

After the Queensland election Sparkes tried to dissuade Bjelke-Petersen from the Canberra campaign. But Joh treated Sparkes with contempt: 'If you don't want to back me then go jump in the lake. I've got plenty of people who will.' Sparkes was put on notice; too weak to resist Joh, he was still reluctant to endorse him.

Joh's senior aide, Ken Crook, tried to put the realities before the premier. What resources and structure did he have? How would Joh handle Sinclair? When Crook finally saw the research he spotted the defect. The research showed that the total non-Labor vote rose with Joh in the federal coalition leadership, but it did *not* show that under Joh's leadership the Nationals could outpoll the Liberals. It never showed that Joh could become prime minister. This point was fundamental, but Gore and Joh ignored it.

Throughout 1986 Joh's plans were made outside the framework of his own office or the National Party structure. He relied upon a collection of friends and the Gore–Ray business backers, the grassroots movement and his own premier's department, whose coordinator general was Sir Sydney Schubert. The department prepared a range of policy options. Joh was clearly hoping that both Schubert and the head of the treasury department, Sir Leo Hielscher, would follow him to Canberra. This unorthodox task for the premier's department was rationalised on the basis that the material could be required for a Premiers' Conference.

Some time before Christmas Gore says that he met Peacock and Hinze at Hinze's farm to discuss the plans at length. Peacock gave no promises, but Gore, a natural enthusiast, was convinced that Peacock would ride with the Joh campaign.[19] The reality was different, as Joh said later: 'The whole thing with Peacock was there in the background . . . and it was talked about . . . but there was nothing really, you know, ah . . . concrete about it . . . Andrew wasn't doing anything he shouldn't have done.'[20]

Andrew Peacock has never given a full account of these events. A spokesman for his office once admitted that Peacock spoke with Hinze on these matters 'about three times' but that he had only gone to Hinze's home in this connection once. This conflicts with Gore's recollection of three meetings with Peacock at Hinze's farm. Peacock says that 'practically every man and his dog supporting Sir Joh . . . including Russ Hinze contacted me and requested my support for Joh. I did not give it.'[21] Peacock later told colleagues that 'Hinze wouldn't take "no" for an answer and wanted to talk to me about it at the office, at the track, at his farm . . . the whole thing was madder than the mad hatter's tea party'.

On Christmas Eve 1986 the 'white shoe brigade'—Mike Gore, Brian Ray and Gordon Douglas—made a famous 'Apocalypse Now' journey in Gore's helicopter to Joh's Bethany property. Here was high symbolism; they flew into Bethany to deliver Bjelke-Petersen their final blueprint for the takeover of the Australian government. It was their Christmas present.

Gore felt the meeting was a triumph, giving Joh the completed strategy which they had bankrolled and which they believed would install their own white knight in the Lodge. Gore told Bjelke-Petersen: 'It's over to you now Joh.' Ray said later: 'We just went to say Happy Christmas!' Gore told Joh he was sure that Peacock would run in tandem with him. Bjelke-Petersen replied, 'Andrew, my goodness, he's a nice boy.'

It would be easy to ridicule Gore but his optimism reflected his life. He was making Sanctuary Cove into one of the world's great resorts from dreams which practical men would have dismissed. Gore believed that Joh could become prime minister because his own success was rooted in defiance of the orthodoxies. When Gore, Ray and Douglas went out to the helicopter they posed with Bjelke-Petersen outside his home, arms around each other, and Flo took the photograph—Joh and his sponsors. Gore put a caption beneath the photograph which caught the crazy optimism of those late 1986 summer days: 'Kirribilli House Christmas 1987'—their target for next Christmas, the prime ministerial residence. Meanwhile Hinze focused on the premier's suite and Peacock was on holidays.[22]

The Gore plan raised the basic tactical questions: would Joh form a new party or would he run as a National? Joh was ambivalent; there was much wild talk about a list of prominent Australians who would flock to his banner. Sparkes was determined to keep Joh inside the National Party and avoid a schism at all costs. Meanwhile Bjelke-Petersen decided to go public. On New Year's Eve, fourteen days short of his 76th birthday, he met Peter Ward from *The Australian* in his Brisbane office to launch 1987 with a splash.

In this interview Joh left no doubt that he was running and declared that one hundred groups were supporting him. He had a platform—flat rate tax. He was ready for an election anytime. He attacked Fraser, Howard and Sinclair. Joh had no truck with the federal Liberals or Nationals. He would launch a crusade and would recruit a series of candidates to his cause; some were National Party but others were prominent Australians prepared to take a stand. The details remained vague; the intent clear. The interview marked a new stage in the campaign—the direct appeal to the people over the party structures.[23] It was a populist crusade.

Joh was the symbol for the new breed of entrepreneurs who detested both parties for their tax rationalism. It was Joh's flat rate tax—more money for the rich—and his repudiation of Howard's 1982 'bottom of the harbour' law and Keating's 1985 tax crackdown which was the essence of his appeal.

Katherine West opened the New Year with a column declaring that 1987 would change the balance of party politics and see a new set of low-tax candidates who would nominate across the nation promising justice to ordinary families. She said that this team would win the federal election—a ludicrous proposition. West was already a recruit to the campaign. She was influential in rural and provincial Australia where she had been drawing large crowds to rallies over the previous two years. So was her colleague Des Keegan, who wrote: 'Sir Joh told me he might come to an accommodation with Mr Howard and Mr Sinclair but only if they established their bona fides with his agenda . . . This remarkable man is clearly going to shift the debate substantially towards personal freedom after 20 years of weak, grasping and undemocratic leadership.'[24]

In the list of possible candidates, about which there was much speculation, one man stood out—National Farmers' Federation president, Ian McLachlan, a natural leader. Many names were given by the Joh forces as possible recruits—surgeon Bruce Shepherd, yacht designer Ben Lexcen, and businessman John Leard, but the real prize was McLachlan. He was an electoral circuit-breaker, a man who just might be able to change voting patterns in the post-banana republic climate. McLachlan was convinced that Australia faced a crisis; like Joh he saw in 1987 an opportunity to use community concern to install a radical government. McLachlan's mind mirrored the turbulence engulfing non-Labor politics. Both Howard and Joh were after him.

The courting of McLachlan reached its peak in Perth in January 1987 during the America's Cup races. Joh told McLachlan that he was going federal and he wanted McLachlan to come too. There was a touch of coercion in his tone which McLachlan resented; he told Joh he'd think about it. But McLachlan had a lot to consider.

Howard had breakfast with McLachlan in Perth and the NFF chief speculated about coming into federal politics as a Liberal. McLachlan was a long-time Liberal Party member who had joined the party about 1970 but didn't attend many meetings. It was logical that he would look to the Liberals. Howard made no pledges but he let McLachlan know that a big job was awaiting. Meanwhile the former Liberal Western Australian premier, Sir Charles Court, warned Howard that Joh's charge towards Canberra was serious. 'I think he's become irrational,' Court said.

But McLachlan was moving into Joh's orbit. The first inkling Howard had came from his brother Stan. 'I had a funny conversation with McLachlan,' he reported. 'He didn't want to talk about you or the Liberal Party.' Later McLachlan rang Sparkes who said: 'Joh's on the end of the fishing line and we can't reel him back in . . .' So McLachlan went north to see Sparkes.

A short time later Howard's mentor, the senior NSW Senator John Carrick, offered to retire early to allow McLachlan's quick entry into parliament as a Liberal. Carrick's motive was to help Howard fend off the Joh push. Howard told McLachlan the seat was hanging; he was sure that NSW could deliver him the Senate vacancy. But McLachlan let the chance perish.

On 1 February 1987 Bjelke-Petersen addressed a much vaunted rally at Wagga Wagga, NSW, organised by one of his backer groups, Grassroots 2000. Joh declared: 'I'm starting the bushfire here today and the media is going to fan it.' Joh said that Howard must accept his agenda or resign. He delivered an ultimatum to the coalition—its policies were too weak and conservative candidates who refused to accept Joh's manifesto would be opposed by a Joh candidate. 'It must be all or nothing, support the candidates who support me,' he declared. Yet the crowd was a disappointing 1200, suggesting that the grassroots was not as enthusiastic as its organisers. This rally was the start of a new phase of Joh's populist crusade—he improvised as he went.

Howard made the obvious political argument—that only a conservative squabble could save the Hawke government—but this was ignored. Howard said that the coalition stood for lower taxes, smaller government, family security, cutting back union power—the very policies Joh wanted. But Howard's commonsense was buried: Joh was hijacking the political airwaves. Joh was immune to influence, even that of his wife, a member of the federal coalition that he was assaulting.

In early February Bjelke-Petersen began to savage Howard and Sinclair. Their policies were no good; nobody knew what their policies were anyway. Howard's team couldn't be trusted. They weren't firm and strong. If Howard wanted to support him, that was okay. 'I'm not interested in John Howard, for goodsake stop talking about John Howard,' Joh told two million listeners on *AM*. Joh would have no trendies or wets. He would run candidates against every sitting member who rejected his policies, regardless of party. He left open the question of whether he would give Howard a job after the election. Joh declared, 'I am determined to turn politics upside down in Australia. I am Joh Bjelke-Petersen of Queensland with a lot of experience and I know what I am doing.'

Joh accused Ian Sinclair of 'cuddling up to the Liberals'. He attacked both Howard and Sinclair as losers who 'mucked it up when they were there'. He promised to 'do a General MacArthur' on Howard and Sinclair and explained: 'we will annihilate them'. Sinclair's call for Joh to support the coalition was merely 'stupid'. Australia's problems were simple, there was no need for detail. Reporters struggled to find exactly what he intended but Joh was elusive.

This was a declaration of internal warfare, a demand that Howard and Sinclair negotiate a surrender. Howard tried to pacify Bjelke-Petersen and pointed to their shared policy goals, but such rationality was futile. Joh's crusade was rooted in a defiance of political commonsense. So Howard lashed back at Joh. Sinclair fluctuated wildly between appeasement and firmness. He declared that Joh risked losing his party membership if he opposed properly endorsed National Party candidates; then Sinclair said he was sure that Joh would abide by the rules. But the same day Joh repudiated Sinclair and declared he would run his own candidates. Howard and Sinclair tried another tack; yes, they would welcome Joh as a federal candidate. But this was hardly the point—Joh wanted to supplant them.

Sinclair's strategy was to channel any federal role for Joh within the constitutional processes of the party while refusing to accept his intimidation or flat rate tax policy—an impossible combination. Sinclair said:

> Joh's intervention could have been a plus for our side by boosting the overall vote. There were several scenarios that would have worked . . . if Joh had announced that he was a candidate for a House of Representatives seat, or announced the seat, or resigned as Premier, or made clear that he would resign before the federal election and worked through the constitutional processes of the National Party. But that didn't happen.[25]

The mood was reflected in the opening remarks by the ABC's presenter Richard Carleton on 3 February: 'The Premier of Queensland, a man who can't string together three words in the English language, a man who believes in water-powered cars and quack cancer cures, this man is stomping the country preaching voodoo economics and flat earth finance and he's being listened to.'

Bjelke-Petersen gave some classic radio interviews; witness this exchange from *AM* on 5 February:

Q: Sir Joh, how can you expect to stay part of the National Party?

A: I'm not interested in staying part of the National Party. I'm only interested in doing what the people of Australia deserve.

Q: You might resign from the National Party?

A: I won't resign from the National Party.

Q: But you just said you're not interested in staying part of the National Party.

A: Well, I can't stay . . .

Q: So if the National Party in Canberra won't do what you want, will you leave the National Party?

A: Lead it, I'll lead it, not leave it.

Q: No. I said leave it, leave it.

A: No. Don't be stupid . . . otherwise I won't talk to you.

Q: When can we meet some of these candidates you were talking about before?

A: Well, they don't grow up like mushrooms.

It was farce as a prelude to tragedy. Liberal president John Valder declared that Joh power 'could sow the seeds of the destruction of the whole non-Labor side of politics'. A few days later Valder called Bjelke-Petersen 'a political terrorist in the Colonel Gaddafi mould'.

But Andrew Peacock took a different stance. In a careful intervention Peacock supported Joh's campaign and called for summit talks to heal the divisions. Peacock said that Sir Joh's campaign was 'a God-driven and abiding duty to drive the Hawke government from power'. He said that Joh's policies were not anti-coalition and he called upon Howard and Sinclair to meet the premier. Peacock was lavish in his praise of the man who had declared war on the federal conservative leaders, saying: 'Sir Joh is a great Australian, a great patriot who always—and I mean always—put his country first.' Peacock said Joh was a good and reasonable man whose policies were not too different from those of the coalition. He moved to the crux: 'He [Bjelke-Petersen] has every right to be in the federal arena. You may have observed there is some respect between Joh and me and I think I know the way the man thinks.'

Howard, who was enraged by Peacock's remarks, offered to meet Sir Joh but said that no self-respecting Liberal leader would go cap-in-hand to him. Bjelke-Petersen then put the blowtorch on Howard, predicting that he could be deposed and calling him a 'silly little boy'. Joh said that Peacock would challenge Howard for the Liberal leadership—'I knew it when I was in Melbourne the other day.' Peacock had to deny any challenge and Joh retreated when Howard rang him.

Joh's next announcement was that his son John would accompany him to Canberra. Howard asked if Joh had any daughters and Bill Hayden promptly called upon Joh to appoint his horse to the Senate.

Bjelke-Petersen appeared beyond any dialogue with Howard and Sinclair short of their humiliation. Meanwhile Australia's only Liberal premier, Tasmania's Robin Gray, criticised Howard's handling of the situation; he favoured Joh and Peacock.

The Joh push won extra momentum with a series of favourable polls. A Channel Nine phone-in poll (popular but unreliable) showed 72 per cent of 204 000 callers supported Sir Joh's drive, with the backing in NSW at 84 per cent. This poll received saturation publicity despite its worthless methodology. In mid-February, Newspoll in *The Australian* showed that Bjelke-Petersen was seen as the best leader of the conservative side, polling 33 per cent, with Peacock on 30 per cent and Howard on 17 per cent. The methodology of some polls was highly dubious along with the reliability of all such polls as pointers to the support Joh would win in a federal campaign.

In technical terms Joh's push involved two fundamental issues—his pledge to break the Liberal–National coalition and his belief that by breaking the coalition the Nationals could emerge as the major non-Labor party. This belief revealed a lack of understanding within non-Labor politics about its own history, structure, and tactics.

Howard grasped the magnitude of the disaster which Joh was unleashing. As a NSW Liberal Howard understood that the instrument of the coalition was essential to conservative election victories and successful conservative government. He knew that without a coalition the conservatives could not govern and probably could not win an election. He reminded people of Menzies' remarks when he retired twenty years before, that his two greatest political achievements were the formation of the Liberal Party and the maintenance of the Liberal–National coalition. Howard declared correctly that this was as relevant in 1987 as it was in 1966.

Joh's electoral success in Queensland had unleashed National Party scepticism about the coalition, and delusions of grandeur. Joh was the only National Party leader to govern in his own right. Queensland had broken the mould of conservative politics when the Nationals had become the dominant partner over the Liberals and then dispensed with them. In Queensland there had been no coalition since 1983. Joh fought the Liberals as well as the ALP. The Queensland National Party saw no special value in the federal coalition. In Queensland Joh was king; invocations of Menzies fell on deaf ears. This was a clash of political cultures and rival ideas about the future of conservative politics.

Joh's push introduced a new issue into the politics of 1987: how should the conservatives govern?

The facts, which were almost entirely missing from the upheaval, were that the Nationals at the previous federal poll had won 21 out of 148 seats and had representation in only three states. Their strength was less than half the 45 seats held by the Liberals and just over a quarter of the 82 held by Labor. The Nationals had polled only 10.6 per cent of the primary vote at the previous election. The party's highest vote since 1949 had been 11.2 per cent in 1975. The feature of the National Party vote was its stability.

There was absolutely no evidence that the next federal election would see any change in this historical experience. The idea that the Nationals could replace the Liberals as the major non-Labor party at the coming election was pure fantasy. In the web of delusions within the Joh push this was the greatest and the most important.

History showed that it was the coalition which had given the Nationals a power in government and politics beyond their numerical strength. The famous phrase about the 'Nationals' tail wagging the Liberal dog' described the excessive influence which the Nationals had enjoyed in Australia's public policy process—typified by past leaders such as Earle Page, Arthur Fadden, McEwen and Anthony. Bjelke-Petersen could not have been more mistaken: the coalition was a source of strength, not weakness, for the National Party.[26]

But Bjelke-Petersen was exploiting the absence of a real authority figure in the federal coalition, feeding on the weakness of Howard and Sinclair. The three previous federal National leaders—Fadden, McEwen and Anthony—had each possessed a better leadership profile than Sinclair. Such a strike would have been inconceivable against McEwen. Fadden and Anthony had always commanded the backing of their party, but Sinclair had lost the respect of his own troops. He had never been able to fill Anthony's shoes.

The crisis revealed yet again the organisational defect in non-Labor politics—weak central authority. Power in the Nationals, even more than in the Liberals, existed in a collection of state-based accumulations. The conservatives talked about modernising Australia yet clung to their anachronistic party structures.

Sinclair said: 'The National Party's organisation is State based. No federal member receives public funding. The federal party is quite dependent upon the States.' The Joh-for-Canberra push split the Nationals at their base.[27] The Joh war was conducted state-by-state. Joh's real opposition was the NSW National Party which had no intention of falling for Joh-power and was appalled by his tactics. The NSW party was Sinclair's power base, the home of a successful state level coalition which aspired to win the next state election and had a firm and competent state chairman, Doug Moppett.

From the start Moppett spoke for the NSW party in saying that coalition unity was essential, that outside pressure on the party would be resisted, that proper constitutional process would be followed in preselection, and that NSW would not tolerate Queensland disruption of the federal coalition. In the war that would engulf the National Party, the attack of the Queenslanders would be met with an equally determined defence in NSW. This would prove fundamental in breaking the Joh push. Moppett was backed by National Party federal president Shirley McKerrow.

At the leadership level Sinclair found that Bjelke-Petersen was too elusive. His drive was an experiment in grassroots anarchy. Whenever he was asked questions Joh had a simple reply—details didn't matter. He was beyond the limitations imposed by structure, form and party discipline. Joh was creating mayhem not merely because of unbridled ambition but because of his disregard of political form. He was playing a double game, threatening to outflank the National Party while trying to steal the party from Sinclair.

In mid-February Mike Gore announced there was $25 million to bank-roll the Joh push, a claim which infuriated Sparkes who knew of no such funds. Gore predicted that when Joh became prime minister the action would be dramatic: 'Tear all this shit up. He'll whip through it,' Gore exclaimed with effect but little detail.

There were two decisive meetings in February 1987 where the Joh push triumphed in a fashion which stunned the professional observers of Australian politics. The first was the inaugural 1987 meeting of the Federal National Parliamentary Party on 16 February. This was the first test for Sinclair against Bjelke-Petersen. It was imperative for Sinclair to win the full backing of his own parliamentarians against Joh's drive to depose him. The second was a Queensland National Party Central Council meeting at Hervey Bay in late February where the state division would have to formulate a formal position on Joh's push.

A few days before the federal party meeting, Sinclair saw Joh in Brisbane in an effort to reach a settlement. Joh says: 'Sinclair told me I wouldn't take the leading role. Then he said I might get a ministry. But Sinclair was bonkers. Why would I leave Queensland to become a junior minister?'[28] Their truce talks collapsed when Joh walked out after ten minutes and a blazing row. This proved that any peace was remote. 'I had very little communication with Joh after that aborted attempt to resolve our differences,' Sinclair conceded. But Sinclair failed to heed the warning: he had to lock Joh out of the federal party room—to teach Joh that that was his domain.

But Sinclair, incredibly, was overconfident. He failed to make the necessary calls and relied upon his deputy Ralph Hunt, who was also too confident. They misjudged the mood of the Queenslanders. Hunt told Howard before the meeting: 'Don't worry. Everything will be okay.' It betrayed the paralysis of the federal Nationals.

The day before the party meeting, Joh flashed his ruthless streak; he called upon the 26 federal Nationals to quit the coalition and asked them to convince Sinclair that he must submit to Joh. Of this 26, 12 were from Queensland. Joh now threatened the 12 Queenslanders with cancellation of their endorsement unless they backed his move to split the coalition. This threat was published on page 1 of *The Australian* the morning of the meeting; it would have been read by the entire Queensland contingent. It was brazen intimidation. Bjelke-Petersen said he would attend the Hervey Bay Central Council meeting and would oppose the nomination of any

Queensland National who refused to back him. Joh had put a political gun at the head of each Queenslander: a threat to finish their careers.

His wife, a confused Senator Bjelke-Petersen, decided it would be discreet to miss the Canberra federal party meeting.

It was at this party meeting on 16 February that the federal Nationals lost their only chance to deny Bjelke-Petersen—by defeating him at the start. They had no will and no clarity. The Nationals betrayed their own weakness as a party and their own fears as individuals by seeking to appease Bjelke-Petersen. The meeting was a failure for Ian Sinclair from which neither Sinclair nor Howard nor the federal coalition ever recovered. Joh smashed into the federal party room with the first swing of his political axe.

The Nationals passed a motion which was tantamount to legitimating mayhem. They condemned themselves as an institution and as a party. The core values of any party—its ideology, courage and principles—come from its caucus. But this party meeting surrendered all three; it is a milestone in the decline of the National Party.

After a ninety-minute debate and examination of four motions, a consensus motion was adopted with which Sinclair was involved but which he did not initiate. It was based upon respect for and fear of Joh, regard for his vote-winning capacity, and the view that he was well equipped to lead the campaign against Hawke. The motion, much weaker than Sinclair wanted, correctly captured the mood of the meeting:

> That this party, recognising the crisis in the Australian economy and the need to defeat the Hawke government, states its accord with the thrust of that which the Premier of Queensland seeks to achieve and supports his general philosophy.
>
> This party proposes that the benefits which the Premier would bring to such a united effort be harnessed by requesting the Premier to become fully involved with the Federal National Party in the campaign to remove the Hawke government from office and thereby gain the maximum benefit of the electoral support the Premier of Queensland has within Australia.

The motion revealed the failings of the federal National Party—bedrock weakness and lack of direction. It was heavily into wish fulfilment. It was designed to accommodate Joh without putting any obligations upon him. It included no support for Sinclair or the coalition. Its purpose was to keep Joh within the family of the National Party and stop him from creating a breakaway. It endorsed Joh's intention to move into federal politics without addressing the essence of that campaign—that Joh was demanding that the coalition be broken, that his own policies be accepted, that Ian Sinclair be deposed, that he was prepared to destroy the careers of any federal National who resisted him, and that those resisting Nationals whose endorsements he could not cancel would be opposed by his own candidates at an election.

This was political blackmail, pure and simple, of which Sinclair had accused Joh before he went into the meeting. When it finished Sinclair was left with a policy of appeasement. He was humiliated, reduced to platitudes at a press conference and nonsense about how a reconciliation was possible. Anxious to defend his position, Sinclair said that support for the coalition had been unanimous. The Nationals called the motion an 'olive branch'. So they pleaded for peace with their blackmailer. Joh's response was totally predictable. He called Sinclair 'very weak', dismissed Howard and Sinclair as 'an absolute liability', described the motion as recognition of the 'cold hard facts', and said the result was a 100 per cent victory for himself and his ideas. When told that Sinclair's supporters saw the motion as a victory for Sinclair because the Nationals had not agreed to split the coalition, Joh replied with deadly accuracy: 'Let them fool themselves a bit longer. But they're on the skids.'

That night at a coalition dinner to celebrate the opening of the session, Sinclair showed Howard the approved motion. Howard was shocked. 'This is going to create problems,' he warned. 'The media will write this as a win for Joh.' Sinclair said the decision was to try to harness Joh's popularity. Howard was dismayed and upset; he realised that the federal Nationals were nearly broken. Howard told Sinclair that he could not support the coalition unless the federal Nationals supported it. He wanted a stronger resolution. In private Howard was appalled at Sinclair's tactics. 'He's operating on the principle that if you feed the crocodile you're the last to get eaten,' he told a colleague.

Howard's prediction about the next day's media reaction was accurate. The meaning of the party room decision was obvious yet it eluded many Nationals—Sinclair had lost his authority. Some federal Nationals did see Joh as a saviour; they preferred him to Sinclair and they believed that Joh was a winner, not a wrecker. Queensland Nationals Tom McVeigh, Peter Slipper and Clarrie Millar praised Joh. But any vote-winning ability of Joh's would be overwhelmed by the disunity he was creating.

Power in the National Party was now split between Joh and Sinclair— and Joh had the upper hand. The old Country Party had always operated on the principle of the führer and the family. The leader—Page, Fadden, McEwen—was the führer, and business was always settled within the family. But Sinclair had lost his führer's coat and the family was being torn apart.

As a result of Howard's request, the Nationals met again the next day and passed a motion supporting the coalition. But they rejected a move from Ralph Hunt for a vote endorsing Sinclair's leadership. The federal party was broken and confused.

After this opening victory for Joh the focus shifted to Sir Robert Sparkes, who now faced a decision of some historic magnitude at the 27 February Central Council meeting at Hervey Bay: what form would the Joh-for-Canberra push assume?

Joh for Canberra: the false prophet

Sparkes was bitter about Gore and the grassroots enthusiasts who had seduced Bjelke-Petersen. But Sparkes was also surprised by the progress Joh had made in humiliating Sinclair and his performance in the polls. Sparkes was trapped between two unpalatable choices. If he opposed Joh's push the Queensland party would be split down the middle between Sparkes and Joh. In this situation Joh had said that he would move outside the formal party structure to mount his Canberra assault. Sparkes would be blamed and lose his influence. The alternative for Sparkes was to take over the Joh push and bring it firmly under the control and direction of the Queensland National Party—which would terminate any possibility of a rival force being created.

For nearly three weeks before the Hervey Bay meeting, Sparkes said nothing. At the federal management committee meeting in early February he had supported the coalition. But at Hervey Bay Sparkes crossed the Rubicon and joined Joh. There should be no doubt: Sparkes chose the easy option. He rationalised it as the lesser of two evils; he bowed before the need to preserve the unity of the Queensland National Party to which he had dedicated his public life. By this decision Sparkes cast himself as Joh's campaign manager. Bjelke-Petersen says: 'At first Sparkes just watched and told me that it was impossible. Finally he came forward and said he wanted to make it official, that he'd run the campaign. I wasn't keen but I agreed. This was the trouble—if Sparkes hadn't gummed it up, then it would have worked.'[29]

Sparkes did not believe that the Nationals would outpoll the Liberals; he did not believe that Joh would become prime minister. But he allowed the Queensland National Party to become the vehicle for these endeavours. Sparkes was prepared to surrender the Queensland National Party to Joh to prevent him from splitting it. Sparkes took the wrong decision. Like the federal Nationals he chose appeasement. The result was that the entire Queensland National Party became discredited through Joh's reckless pursuit of power. Sparkes signed a political death warrant for his party's integrity in the name of its self-preservation.

Sparkes was deeply influenced by his own fight with the 'white shoe brigade'. Early in 1987 when Sparkes and Gore clashed Sparkes said: 'We don't want amateurs and overseas people. It's no business of yours. If there's going to be a campaign then we'll run it, not you.' When Sparkes took over Gore pulled out, complaining that Sparkes had ruined his scheme. He offered no money and no help. Sparkes, in turn, would always blame Gore's big mouth for turning away donors: if you've got $25 million then you don't need any more.

Sinclair came to the Hervey Bay meeting to put his views, but he was humiliated and left a beaten man. A final plea from Howard was dismissed. The tactics employed by Joh and Sparkes were brutal—the federal Queensland parliamentarians had their endorsements put on the line. Sparkes put it politely: 'Our parliamentary representatives are agents of the party organisation and their endorsement imposes on them certain responsibilities and obligations. One of them is that they must accept the direction of the party on important issues of this nature.'

The fight was carried by Ray Braithwaite, the frontbench member for Dawson. Mike Ahern, future state premier, walked out of the meeting in disgust. Every federal parliamentarian was required to give a specific guarantee of support for the motion to break the coalition. Sparkes told the parliamentarians in front of the 250 delegates that their endorsements would be withdrawn unless they implemented the motion. It was intimidation that recalled the railroading tactics of the old Labor Party.

The resolution carefully drafted by Sparkes was a gun at the Howard–Sinclair coalition. It was serious in its intent and methodical in its exposition of the battle plan. It said:

That the National Party of Australia (Qld) fully supports the move by Sir Joh Bjelke-Petersen to attain the Prime Ministership so that he can put in place an anti-socialist federal government equipped with appropriate policies and the will to implement those policies . . .

1. Recognising that no great battle can be won by great and charismatic generalship alone, and hence that a vital prerequisite for the success of the Joh for PM campaign is adequate efficient organisational structure, we strongly recommend that, wherever practicable, existing National Party structure be used because: (a) time does not permit the establishment of an adequate alternative structure right across the nation; and (b) attempted operation outside existing National Party structures, and probably in conflict with it, could have serious adverse repercussions on our State National Party—something that must be avoided at all times.

2. As the instrument for overall control and coordination of the Joh for PM campaign, we recommend the establishment of the National Joh for PM committee, appointed jointly by the Premier and the State President . . . It is envisaged that the committee would utilise the existing National Party headquarters and facilities at Bjelke-Petersen House supplemented by additional staff and equipment as required . . .

3. The Council asserts that it is the right of the party organisation to determine whether or not its parliamentary representatives enter into or remain in any coalition arrangement . . . We request that the National Party federal parliamentary leader, Mr Sinclair, immediately withdraw the National Party from the federal Opposition coalition because of basic difference in taxation and other philosophies and policies. Failing that, we request the Queensland delegation to the next National Party federal council meeting to put forward a motion to the effect that the Federal Opposition coalition be terminated immediately. Failing that, we request that our Queensland National Party federal shadow Ministers immediately withdraw from the federal shadow Ministry and all Queensland National Party federal parliamentarians

who are members of joint policy committees to withdraw from those committees.

Sparkes knew that Sinclair was unlikely to quit the coalition on this directive. But he believed that the Queensland position would prevail at the Federal Council meeting in March and would force the severing of the coalition. Even if that failed the resolution meant that the 12 Queenslanders in the 26-strong federal National caucus would withdraw from the coalition—enough to wreck it.

The Hervey Bay resolution, the product of a night of political intimidation that lasted until 4 am, was the death-warrant for the coalition. Howard and Sinclair would keep fighting but could not deny the sentence. In the early hours of Saturday morning, 28 February, on the central Queensland coast, the coalition—the instrument which had sustained every federal conservative government for half a century—was slated for demolition. It was done—here was the ultimate irony—on the basis that this was the only way the conservatives could beat Labor. Howard and Sinclair said it might become the only basis on which Hawke could beat them.

Bjelke-Petersen was honest enough to call the decision 'a type of hijack'; then he said 'takeover' was a better word. He said everyone knew he would be prime minister after the election. Sparkes, who had spent months trying to stop Joh, now predicted that he would become prime minister. Sparkes recalled that one of the world's greatest post-war leaders, Konrad Adenauer, became Chancellor of Germany at 76. Sparkes denied that he was pushed into supporting Bjelke-Petersen, saying there was growing support for the premier and 'in politics like anything else, if you see an opportunity, grab it'.

Joh had managed to attract support from a number of prominent Australians. John Stone declared that Sir Joh was driving the Hawke government into facing fiscal reality and declared: 'More power to his paddle!'[30] Queensland academic Dr Joe Siracusa compared Joh and Ronald Reagan with the Tom Sawyer legend. Mining chief and Joh's old mate, Lang Hancock, said Joh would build the railway of his dreams—between Queensland and the iron ore province of north-western Australia. The chief executive of Peko Wallsend, Charles Copeman, said Sir Joh's move was 'very helpful' for the conservative forces. The retired former chief of ANI, John Leard, took out full page advertisements under the heading 'Where Sir Joh Is Right' and attacked the Labor government. Joh nominated AMA heavyweight, Dr Bruce Shepherd as one of his strongest backers.

However, the NSW National Party had no intention of being intimidated by Joh and Sparkes. Its chairman Doug Moppett called on the 11 NSW Nationals to support the coalition—with or without the Queenslanders—saying that what had begun as an intriguing idea was now assuming preposterous dimensions. Moppett's resolution and the unanimous support for his stance in NSW would become fundamental in breaking Joh power. Just as Sinclair had initially underestimated the Queenslanders so the Queenslanders would underestimate the determination of the NSW Nationals to resist them. There sprang up an alliance which embraced the Greiner–Murray team at state level and the Howard–Sinclair team at federal level.

Howard and Sinclair were fighting for their political lives. Howard declared that Joh's campaign was a power grab, pure and simple: 'Power, nothing else. It's got nothing to do with philosophy, it's power, naked power, nothing else. It's nothing to do with reviving Australia.' Howard was determined to ensure that if the coalition split Joh should carry the responsibility. He now began to refer to Joh as 'Petersen' and branded him a hypocrite. Howard said that Joh had never been interested in small government, that he always wanted a special deal for Queensland when Howard was treasurer, and that his attitude about the deficit was 'let it rip'. He said Joh 'will go down in history as the great wrecker of the conservative side of politics', that the fight was for the 'rational soul of the conservative side of politics'.

Sinclair pledged to fight 'the faceless group of power brokers' who were deploying a 'sort of blackmail' against the parliamentary wing to split the coalition. He left the implication that the Queensland resolution was unconstitutional because it sought to dictate to the parliamentary wing how it should conduct itself in the parliament.

The former federal leader, Doug Anthony, came down from his farm to accuse Joh of being on a course of 'destruction and fantasy'. He said that there was a 'plague of political madness spreading across the nation from Queensland'. He defended Sinclair, expressed disgust at his humiliation by the Queenslanders, and said that it was inconceivable that their electoral tactics could work.

Meanwhile Sparkes had struck an arrangement with the organiser of Bjelke-Petersen's state campaigns, Fred Maybury. It was agreed that Maybury would work from party headquarters as the national coordinator of the Joh-for-Canberra push. Maybury was a trusted colleague of Sparkes, and his wife Helen had worked for years as Sparkes' secretary. Joh had full confidence in Maybury.

The basic electoral question in evaluating the Joh push was whether Joh was an asset or a liability for the conservative side. Sparkes pointed to the late February Morgan poll in *The Bulletin* which showed that Joh would increase the overall non-Labor vote. But this was part of the early 'Joh novelty' factor evident in all the polls. For instance, in 1977, when Don Chipp quit the Liberals, he rated higher than Fraser or Whitlam—but at the election his party, the Democrats, won only 11 per cent of the vote. It was obvious that as the election neared Joh's high ratings would almost inevitably be overwhelmed by other political factors. If Joh had united with the federal coalition leaders a different assessment would be demanded. But there was never any prospect of this.

Joh's push had split the National Party, created a war between the Liberal and National parties, and by seeking to destroy the coalition made it impossible for the Opposition to offer a united policy program at the federal election. The voters had a recorded distrust of disunity. The answer was unmistakable—the Joh push could only hurt the conservative cause.

The second claim, that the Joh push would enable the Nationals to become the major non-Labor party, was extraordinary and always without foundation. The further claim mounted as its original justification—that only the Joh push could beat Hawke—is one of the greatest delusions ever entertained in Australian politics. The Joh push offered indisputable evidence of profound problems on the non-Labor side.

It was years of Liberal appeasement of Joh which had helped to make him strong. Despite this, the Liberal Party would not acquiesce in his federal push. The rotten Queensland electoral system and a high level of corruption, later documented in the Fitzgerald Report, made Joh a candidate whom significant elements within the Liberal Party would not tolerate.

Joh's campaign thrived upon a perceived weakness, the absence of an authoritative conservative leader. The Liberals had produced only two, Menzies and Fraser, in the previous forty years of federal politics. History shows that the conservatives need a messiah. If they don't have such a leader within their own ranks they will recruit him from Labor, from business, from anywhere—even the National Party—a factor Joh tried to exploit.

The Joh push made it clear that the Nationals had become a liability for the conservative forces. They were divided over strategy, leadership and the coalition. The Nationals had misplaced the central lesson of their existence—the power which their sectional party had obtained over decades was derived from the coalition. The Joh crisis was only a part of a deeper crisis within the Nationals, which would be resolved after their 1987 election failure with a repudiation of Joh's strategy and an admission of the National Party's weakness.

The Joh push exposed the major philosophical conflict in the conservative politics of the 1980s—the struggle between free market economics and the radical or sleazy populism of which Bjelke-Petersen was the arch exponent. While these positions overlapped there were also sharp differences between them. Howard and Bjelke-Petersen both supported lower tax, smaller government, family security and reduced union power. But Joh's flat rate tax was dismissed by Howard as voodoo economics; Howard wanted an indirect tax which Joh repudiated. Joh was a political fixer, an interventionist, who distrusted free markets in areas as diverse as labour and agriculture where Howard aspired to free these markets.

The parallel with Joh was Jack Lang's 1930s assault on the federal

Labor Party. Joh's success derived from his exploitation of Australian insularity, xenophobia and selfishness. He was a prophet preaching easy solutions—the 'let it rip' school—with overtones of religious revivalism, not a strong force in Australia. Joh appealed both to people frightened of change and to those who wanted easy change. His rhetoric was hostile to state power, but in office he exploited public institutions for his own ends.

Joh's content and style was antithetic to many of the changes in Australia's culture which the Liberal economic drys had been promulgating since the early 1980s. They wanted an open, rational, tolerant, more internationalised Australia, but the Liberal reformers had failed to persuade the spectrum of conservative opinion to their views. In the turbulence of the late 1980s Joh was a false prophet only likely to divide and discredit the conservative reformers.

16
The conservative crisis

Joh Bjelke-Petersen will go down in history as the coalition wrecker.
John Howard, 28 April 1987

In the autumn of 1987, Joh Bjelke-Petersen's anarchistic influence helped to restore Labor's credibility and expose the fragilities of the non-Labor side. The Joh factor's domination of politics—leadership, policy and strategy—culminated in Hawke's decision to call a July 1987 winter election.

The Bjelke-Petersen push helped to trigger several explosions—a revival of the Howard–Peacock leadership tensions, leading to Howard's dismissal of Peacock from shadow Cabinet; a climax to the wet–dry ideological dispute which left both Ian Macphee and Peter Baume on the Liberal backbench; a paralysis of policy which forced the abandonment of Howard's plan for an indirect tax; and finally, the breaking of the coalition, which saw the Liberal and National Parties enter the election under separate banners for only the second time since 1949. Non-Labor politics was about to enter one of its worst seasons for fifty years. The Hawke–Keating triumph in their third election can only be grasped in this context.

The crisis of 1987 became a turning point in the history of the National Party. Sparkes now gave his rationale for the Joh campaign: 'The Premier and his party are just trying to save the nation . . . the coalition would still be in government if Malcolm Fraser and the people with him had made the decisions the people wanted. We cannot risk another weak government like that.'[1] Sparkes told Sinclair to 'accept the inevitable'. But Sinclair likened Sparkes to 'Norm Gallagher and the union thugs', the worst insult he could summon.[2]

Sparkes said the breaking of the coalition would enable the National Party to campaign on its own policies. He envisaged a radical break with past policies—a small government, anti-union power, low tax blueprint. He intended to promote a flat rate tax policy drafted by John Stone. Sparkes invoked section 18 of the National Party's constitution, which he said empowered the Federal Council to direct the Parliamentary Party to break the coalition.[3] This was a highly dubious assertion. Sinclair said that only the Parliamentary Party could vote on the coalition issue; this had been the position since 1949 and it would continue to be the position.

However, as early as February 1987 the polls revealed a new trend—a Labor revival. For the first time in eight months the Morgan poll in *The Bulletin* showed Labor leading the coalition by 47 to 45 per cent, in a survey taken on 21–22 February 1987—suggesting that Labor might be the final winner from Joh's upheaval.

There were four factors which would deny and then destroy Joh power. First, the Joh Nationals failed in their first election, the Northern Territory poll. Second, some state National Party divisions, spearheaded by NSW, refused to endorse Joh. Third, even while the federal parliamentarians were being 'blackmailed' to support Joh and break the coalition, they had little faith in his crusade. Finally, the 'white shoe brigade' seemed to have developed paralysis of the pocket.[4] The campaign would cost in the $15–$20 million range—but the bankroll never arrived.

The Northern Territory chief minister, Steve Hatton, celebrated on election night, 7 March 1987, when he reduced the Joh Nationals to a modest 17 per cent. They won only one seat when their leader and former chief minister, Ian Tuxworth, barely survived. There was no rise in the total non-Labor vote. Hatton, who headed the Liberal–Country League (LCL), mocked Joh by waving a lavatory brush for him to remove the egg. Howard and Sinclair chortled. 'Joh, you made it a test, nobody else. You failed that test very badly,' Howard declared.[5]

Joh's failure to reverse the pattern of Australian politics in the Territory election meant he would also fail in the capital cities. Beyond Queensland he was an outsider, an old man, competing against established national leaders.

Meanwhile Sinclair was establishing the defence that would break the Bjelke-Petersen push. On 6 March the NSW National Party central executive supported Sinclair's leadership, the federal coalition, and the independence of the federal National Party. It was the NSW party which would eventually smash Joh.

The Victorian party was divided but took a similar position. The South Australian branch went for a compromise—it opposed the coalition but said the decision rested with the federal parliamentary party, a concession to Sinclair. Only the Western Australian branch supported Queensland.

The parliamentary National Party met on 17 March, the first such meeting since the Hervey Bay resolution. Sinclair had the numbers 14–12 on a vote to keep the coalition, relying upon the 11 NSW and three Victorian parliamentarians against the 12 Queenslanders. He had planned to use these numbers but changed his tactics before the party meeting when he realised his victory would be only pyrrhic. If Sinclair won this vote, the 12 Queenslanders would be obliged to follow their orders and quit the coalition. That would split the National Party down the middle: a Sinclair group in coalition and a Joh group outside the coalition.

At this point Sinclair's impotence was revealed. Joh didn't have the numbers in the federal party room but that didn't matter because Sinclair was unable to defeat him.

Sinclair opened the party meeting in a conciliatory stance but put his office on the line by inviting challenges to his leadership. There was no challenge but his implacable enemy, Queensland MP and Joh loyalist Tom McVeigh, launched a bitter assault, telling Sinclair he should resign. McVeigh announced his immediate withdrawal from the coalition. After a three hour debate the meeting finished in a stalemate of tears, accusations and confusion.

Joh predicted that the coalition would be broken at the approaching National Party Federal Council on 27–29 March—the timetable he had set with Sparkes.[6]

Meanwhile the limited nature of Joh's appeal was revealed on Saturday 21 March 1987 by a modest turnout of 1500 at a rally in the southern border town of Albury, where no 'Joh for PM' banners were seen. The Nationals' Albury organiser, Bill Pickles, said he had expected 3000. Bjelke-Petersen was undaunted: 'The day Hawke announces the election I'll resign as Premier, give up the jet and the car . . . and I'll tell you what seat I'm standing for too . . . Poor old John Howard. He's on his knees. He's the greatest tax-happy man we have ever seen. And now he's planning this 8 per cent consumption tax.' Joh was supported by Ben Lexcen and John Leard.

But the interesting aspect of this rally was the cries for unity, the demand for Joh and Sinclair to get together. The local member, shadow minister and future Nationals leader, Tim Fischer, part of the pro-coalition group, told the crowd he supported Sir Joh's policies 'but not his methodology'.[7]

The Liberal Party now sank into a leadership crisis superimposed upon the coalition crisis. It was conducted according to the rhythm of the polls and Joh's mayhem. While Joh attacked the Liberal wets, he supported Peacock, the wet candidate against Howard! The Peacock camp could smell Howard's vulnerability. On 19 February Reg Withers said that Bjelke-Petersen and Peacock were the two most popular non-Labor politicians and the polls should not be ignored. The next day Liberal backbencher Paul Everingham declared that Peacock was within 'shooting distance' of leadership and predicted a challenge to Howard.

An *Age–Sydney Morning Herald* survey published on 10 March 1987 and based upon a 2000 sample across all federal seats showed Peacock leading Howard 47 to 17 per cent as the preferred Liberal leader, a majority of nearly three to one. Peacock said he would not challenge Howard but he wanted to be Liberal leader again—sometime. It was part of the destabilisation ritual. A week later, on 18 March, the Morgan poll in *The Bulletin* showed a Peacock–Joh team would score 52 per cent of the vote compared with 42 per cent for the Howard–Sinclair team. On his arrival at Parliament House Peacock announced that these results were 'important, of course, and interesting'. The next day the *Sydney Morning Herald*'s Mike Steketee reported fresh manoeuvring to make Peacock leader. Howard was now under assault from three quarters—Hawke, Peacock and Bjelke-Petersen.

Meanwhile the Peacock forces had opened up a new front—they claimed that the Liberal Party should terminate the coalition of its own volition. Peacock asked his colleagues: why wait until the Nationals wreck our coalition? Peacock was presenting himself as the champion of Liberal integrity, demanding that the divided Nationals be left to their own 'house-wrecking'.

Howard's approach to this point had been correct, but his objective was probably unattainable. Howard knew that the fight was for control of the National Party. If Joh won he would sever the coalition, destroy any hopes of re-establishing unity on the conservative side, and deliver Hawke the election. Howard wanted to deny Joh control of the Nationals, not to cast the Nationals aside. That meant keeping the coalition together to help the anti-Joh NSW National Party defeat the Queensland push.

On 19 March the Liberal federal president, John Valder, called upon Peacock to 'put up or shut up'. Another Howard loyalist, shadow attorney-general John Spender, said, 'If Peacock wants to challenge, let him.' On 20 March Howard put the issue before a special meeting of the shadow ministry. He confronted Peacock over the media destabilisation campaign and demanded an end to undermining of his leadership. Peacock, in turn, lashed Howard and his supporters. Peacock said he was happy to have a leadership vote, but argued that it would not solve the party's problems. He said there was no challenge and that he hadn't invented the polls. Howard announced that he would dismiss shadow ministers who broke solidarity or engaged in disloyalty.

The truth was that Howard and Peacock were both defective: a flawed leader and a flawed challenger. Howard had grit and substance; Peacock had style and poise. Each man's strength was his opponent's weakness. They were too different to tolerate each other and too equal to resolve their conflict.

Peacock was willing to wound but afraid to strike. Howard was unable to persuade either his party or the voters to his flag. Peacock was exploiting the Australian addiction to opinion polls. Like Hawke, Peacock was a master of the art of 'polls and pose'. But Peacock had no policy framework to bring to Australia's national economic problems and this defect was recognised. The drys, the small business lobby and the NFF had no faith in Peacock. McLachlan said that if Peacock became leader there would be a grassroots revolt against the Liberals.

A Peacock elevation would be a victory for Joh power, a blow for the coalition, a new trigger for internal dissension, and a confirmation of the Hawke–Keating line that the Liberals had abandoned economic responsibility. Yet the Liberals were incapable of uniting behind Howard.

The Howard–Peacock issue boiled over during the weekend of 21–22 March 1987 after Peacock's friend, Victorian Liberal leader Jeff Kennett, rose above the Liberal squabble to win a state by-election. That night Peacock and Kennett had a conversation on a car phone. The conversation was tapped by a member of the group People for Equality not Institutionalisation (PENI), and extracts were quoted in the *Melbourne Sun* newspaper on Monday, 23 March 1987.

Kennett began by describing to Peacock his earlier phone call to Howard. Kennett said that he told Howard: 'Tomorrow I'm going to bucket the whole lot of you. Tomorrow, John.' Peacock urged him not to do this. According to Kennett, Howard had said, 'I know where your sympathies lie.' Kennett continued: 'I said, "I couldn't give a fuck. I've got no sympathies anymore. You're all a pile of shit. And tomorrow I'm going berserk." Well, he went off his brain and at the end of it I said to him, "Howard you're a cunt, you haven't got my support, you never will have. And I'm not going to rubbish you or the party tomorrow but I feel a lot better having told you, you're a cunt . . . And the poor little fella didn't know whether he was Arthur or Martha." '

After Peacock praised Kennett for the by-election result, Kennett said: 'I thought I should let you know where I ended up with your little mate.' Peacock replied: 'Well, fuck him. I'm not worried . . . I almost bloody cried . . . I was terribly worried. My fuckin' anger yesterday as Margaret knows . . . the first thing I came in last night I said, Aah fuckin' cunts! I said the whole fuckin' thing could upset tomorrow . . . and she said, 'What's Jeffrey done?" I said, "It's not what Jeffrey's done, it's what everyone's fuckin' done to Jeffrey." '

Referring to the next day's state conference Peacock said: 'I've got to sit in a chair about four or five rows back from the front and allow Howard after he's had his tumultuous reception to come down sit next to me and be photographed together smiling.' Kennett replied, 'How pathetic.' They rang off. Kennett said, 'See you then. Give my regards to your good lady.'[8]

Confronted with the publication of the Kennett–Peacock exchange on the Monday morning Howard decided to dismiss Peacock from the shadow Cabinet. He secured the agreement of the other three Liberal leaders and Sinclair.

At a lunchtime press conference Howard announced: 'I found that story not only very damaging to the Liberal Party but also implying disloyalty to me on the part of a shadow minister.' He said that Peacock had confirmed the substance of the newspaper account. Howard said: 'For me to have done anything less today would have been to surrender any claim at all to authority within the Liberal Party.'

Peacock was 'hung' without proof but justice was served. It was unfair to condemn Peacock for comments made during a private discussion with a friend which he had never intended to become public and in which his criticism of Howard was mild. But Peacock was really sacked because of his sustained destabilisation of Howard's leadership. The phone call was the hook.

Three days later Howard lost another shadow minister, the prominent wet from NSW, Senator Peter Baume, who resigned to the backbench after the coalition parties decided to oppose the government's affirmative action bill in relation to federal instrumentalities. Baume told Howard he could not accept the decision on grounds of conscience. Howard admitted that in deciding its attitude the shadow Cabinet had considered the coalition issue. The National Party opposed the affirmative action provisions and it would have been damaging for Howard's pro-coalition strategy to force approval of the bill against the wishes of the National Party. Hawke virtually accused Howard of putting his coalition before the interests of women.

The Liberals were taken to the knife-edge when Ian Macphee came close to resignation on the same grounds. Macphee was persuaded against the move by his colleagues—Baume himself, Senator Robert Hill and Senator Chris Puplick. Hill told Macphee, 'One sacrifice is enough—nothing further can be achieved.'

The Baume resignation revealed another spin-off from Joh's campaign—it was intensifying the wet–dry divisions within the Liberal Party. From early January, the wets had been under intensive attack, with New Right figures including Bjelke-Petersen, Ian McLachlan and president of the Small Business Association, Peter Boyle, calling for action against them. Macphee, Steele Hall, Max Burr and Chris Puplick were the targets. Steele Hall had warned that these attacks risked 'ripping the guts out of the Liberal Party with a butcher's knife of extremes'. Hall claimed there was a campaign to eliminate the Liberal moderates.[9]

All this coincided with a Howard–Macphee crisis in January 1987 over Rupert Murdoch's takeover of the Herald and Weekly Times group. Howard had told Murdoch at the time that the Opposition would remain neutral and allow the market to decide the result. Howard informed Macphee of his position and instructed him to adhere to it, but Macphee was a passionate opponent of the Murdoch takeover. He gave an interview to *The Times-On-Sunday* published on 11 January 1987 which criticised the Murdoch bid, saying its success 'would appear contrary to the national interest' on ownership concentration grounds and that Labor had an obligation to block the bid. Howard, on holidays, was furious. He summoned Macphee to a Sydney meeting and Macphee assumed that he would be dismissed.

Before the meeting Macphee spoke to Malcolm Fraser who in turn rang Eggleton and the Victorian president, Eda Ritchie, both of whom tried to save Macphee. The message was that Fraser would defend Macphee and attack Howard—he believed that Macphee was correct and courageous. Macphee was forced to recant yet he survived. But the rift between Macphee and the shadow Cabinet pointed towards an inevitable rupture.[10]

On 3 March Macphee warned that Bjelke-Petersen threatened not just the coalition, but the Liberal Party. The wets were alarmed at Howard's declaration that he was the 'most conservative leader the Liberal Party had ever had'.[11] Macphee told Howard not to move the Liberal Party to the right just to protect himself against Joh.[12]

In Howard's April frontbench reshuffle he decided to dump Macphee to the backbench, concluding that Macphee had transgressed too much and that he was irredeemably disruptive. He rejected Tony Eggleton's effort to save Macphee, Eggleton arguing the need to keep a wet–dry balance and pointing to Macphee's symbolic position as the leader of the Liberal wets. But Howard felt the times called for tough action—against Bjelke-Petersen, against Peacock, against Macphee. Macphee joined Peacock and Baume on the backbench. The Liberals wets, consigned to impotence, nursed their hatred for Howard.

Howard had reason to sack Macphee but it only accentuated internal tensions. Howard was desperate to achieve a united Liberal Party yet he forfeited the credentials for unity, under pressure abandoning the Menzian technique of balancing moderates and conservatives. Howard met the challenge from the political right by making the Liberal Party drier than before. Macphee would not recover from his dumping—but he would ensure later that Howard paid the price. Macphee now accused Howard of betrayal, while Peacock rattled his sabre. It was the age of the phoney tough within the Liberal Party.

As the conservative crisis unfolded, Hawke reexamined his election timetable. On 9 March Cabinet decided to reintroduce the Australia Card bill, which had already been blocked once in the Senate, in exactly the same form as before—proof that Hawke wanted a double dissolution option. If the same bill was blocked twice then Hawke had the constitutional right to call a double dissolution election.

Labor, in fact, was taking out insurance. Neither Hawke nor Keating was pushing for an autumn 1987 election. Hawke believed the government should 'bed down' its economic credentials and hold an election in the 1988 bicentennial year. But Hawke wanted to maximise the pressure upon the Opposition. Hawke was sure that Peacock would replace Howard as Liberal leader and was anxious to force the change sooner rather than later.

However, there was a two-man 'early election lobby' within the government—Hawke's political aide Bob Sorby, and the Canberra personality and ALP election consultant, Richard Farmer. They argued for a May 1987 election on the grounds that Labor had a 'window of opportunity' created by a unique coalition crisis.

On Sunday 22 March, the day before Howard sacked Peacock, Hawke stoked up the May election speculation when he said that the Opposition crisis was creating economic uncertainties. 'I do want the government to go its full term,' Hawke said. 'But the Opposition is making it very difficult, as business itself is saying and the financial press is saying.' Hawke was enjoying his torture of the Liberals.

The Press Gallery was reporting that Labor was assessing the May option—the possible date was 9 May. The overwhelming view within the ALP's senior ranks was against a May election, opponents including Hawke, Keating, virtually the whole Cabinet, Bob McMullan, and most state secretaries. The risk was too severe; Labor had not recovered sufficiently in the polls. But Labor decided to 'go to the wire' with the May option. It booked the Opera House for an April policy speech, just in case.

In the interim Labor settled down to watch the upshot of the long awaited National Party Federal Council in Canberra over the weekend of 26–27 March 1987. On Council eve Doug Anthony tried to lance the agents of instability. Anthony said that Peacock had played his game and should retire from politics. He predicted that Bjelke-Petersen's divisive tactics would lead to his destruction. Anthony stated the obvious: 'What the nation is crying for is unity between the Liberal Party and the National Party so they can beat the Hawke government.'[13] Meanwhile Flo Bjelke-Petersen said she wanted her husband to stay premier of Queensland, not to go to the Lodge—evidence of domestic disharmony.[14]

The apostles of the new Australia arrived in style in Canberra: Sparkes drove from Queensland in his gold Rolls-Royce and Joh flew down in his private jet, arriving in a white Mercedes. But they were worried men, fearful of an early election. At lunchtime on Friday 27 March, just a few hours before the Federal Council began, Joh, Sparkes and their advisers held an urgent meeting in Canberra's Lakeside Hotel. Sparkes gave an exposition of their dilemma.

The Joh forces were totally unprepared to fight a snap federal election, Sparkes explained. The coalition was still in place and a fight lay ahead to break it; the Joh candidates were not endorsed; the funds for the Joh campaign had not arrived; the Joh tax policy did not exist. It was imperative, therefore, to try to prevent Hawke calling a snap poll. If Hawke called the election he would catch Joh with his pants down.

Sparkes recommended a tactical retreat at the Federal Council meeting and postponement of the breaking of the coalition. The reason was the need to deny Hawke an election pretext. He said, 'Let's get working on campaign preparations and get the flat rate tax policy clear—and then press ahead.' Sparkes said the Queensland National Party Executive meeting on 10 April

322

was probably the time to implement the Hervey Bay resolution to break the coalition.

They decided that Queensland would support a South Australian compromise resolution at the Federal Council, the motion Sinclair was backing. The Queenslanders were buying a fortnight's truce, but the impression after Joh's 'huff and puff' was that they were beaten.

Sparkes wanted to ensure that people realised the Queenslanders were postponing their breaking of the coalition, not cancelling it. That evening, after 6 pm, Joh's media aide Ken Crook began to brief the media just off the main conference area at the Lakeside. Crook said the Nationals wouldn't fall into Hawke's election trap. There was a large media crowd around Crook struggling to get the gist of his comments and it was close to Friday night deadlines. In the ensuing scramble only one message hit home—Joh's retreat. It was a very big story.

There was unrelieved jubilation in the Sinclair camp. Joh was finally breaking. Sinclair felt that he had found his miracle. The word spread like a bushfire from the Lakeside and jumped Lake Burley Griffin to Parliament House. Howard broke open the champagne, saying: 'I told you to put your money on Sinkers.' Sinclair's deputy, Ralph Hunt, quipped, 'A minute is a long time in politics.' The Saturday newspapers declared that Joh was running from Hawke's election threat. Bjelke-Petersen hated the reports; the Liberals deluded themselves that the Joh push was dead. But cunning old Joh was playing the fox.

On Saturday morning the lion from the north rose to address his minions. Joh had plenty of roar but little bite. In an extraordinary speech Bjelke-Petersen lifted his arms, gave the victory signal and told a startled assembly of delegates: 'I have some very very good news for you—the coalition is finished.' The silence was deafening. His speech was arrogant, confused and deluded. It was inconceivable after watching this performance that Bjelke-Petersen could handle the pressure of a federal campaign as a serious candidate for prime minister. It was an idea that could have credibility only because it was so fantastic.

On Saturday evening in a suite of the Lakeside, Sparkes spent an hour giving a detailed briefing to *The Australian* newspaper:

> It's totally wrong when people assert that Joh's not serious, that the movement's not serious. We will implement the Hervey Bay decision—withdrawal from the coalition—it's highly probable that we would implement that resolution at the April 10 State executive meeting . . . The only problem would arise if Hawke moved for an election within a day or two of that meeting . . . the last thing we want is to help Hawke get back . . . If there's ample time, say, a July election, then we'd be running candidates, I think in all seats.
>
> Probably the linchpin of the whole Canberra exercise will be the single-rate tax policy. Not only will it become an election winner but I

believe it will play a major contribution in getting this country out of
its economic stagnation . . . The ideal is to be the major party in
government. Alternatively, we want to hold the balance of power. We
have to work with the Liberals after the election.

Sparkes then offered a rationalisation for the entire Joh push: 'We took
the view we couldn't rely upon the present Opposition leadership to win
the election or, having won, have the right policies to put into effect . . .
Joh took the view that he had to go into Federal Parliament for the first
100 days so he could put these things into place.'[15]
Ian Sinclair failed to grasp the tactical nature of Joh's retreat and fell
into a dreamy euphoria; he likened Joh to the boy who cried wolf too often
and predicted that the Queenslanders would now defy him. Sparkes, in turn,
was provoked into a public repudiation of Sinclair; he left Canberra determined to break the coalition at the 10 April State Executive meeting.
The same day, Sunday 29 March, when the Sinclair–Sparkes spat
occurred, Hawke received a briefing on the economic outlook from treasury
and prime minister's department officials. They said that economic conditions would firm throughout the year: interest rates were easing, activity
was rising and the fundamentals would improve.
With the coalition still intact and economic advice that 'time is on your
side' Hawke decided against the Sorby–Farmer option of a May election, a
decision supported by the ALP 'brains trust'—Keating, Mick Young, Richardson, McMullan and ANOP's Rod Cameron. Cameron advised Hawke that
Labor's position, while recovering, was still vulnerable; it was not in a
strong position to win a May poll.
Keating argued that the key to Labor's reelection was a successful May
Economic Statement. Keating, in fact, was planning the biggest public sector
savings of the Hawke years to secure a reduced current account deficit.
During the talks in Hawke's office Keating said that provided Labor's May
Statement was a success, it could have the best of all worlds—a mid-winter
1987 election when the coalition crisis was still alive. But Hawke's advisers
ridiculed any winter election option. They were now set upon a 1988
bicentennial election, to exploit the surge of pride in Australian achievement
after 200 years.
Hawke chose April Fool's Day to announce before a full press conference that he had abandoned the option of a May election—having created
the election speculation, he now killed it. Hawke rejected not just a May
election but any early election. He said the election would be held at its
normal time, which would be 'towards the end of this year or early next
year'. This was an unwise statement since prime ministers have the discretion to call elections when they wish, the double dissolution provision was
established on the Australia Card bill and the Opposition remained in

The conservative crisis

ongoing crisis. Howard said that Hawke would have lost any May election—but Howard's own worst fears were about to be realised.

On 10 April, under the direction of Sparkes, the Queensland National Party executive authorised the implementation of the Hervey Bay decision—the 12 Queenslanders would leave the coalition.

This left the Nationals in a condition fluctuating between farce and tragedy. The Liberals could not remain in a coalition with half the National Party while the other half was out of it. Sinclair wanted to keep the coalition alive—but he couldn't split the National Party to achieve this. How could the circle be squared?

Howard and Sinclair, refusing to accept the coalition's death, applied a life support system. They devised a new coalition agreement to thwart the Queensland wreckers. It was, in effect, designed to achieve the impossible: keep the coalition but avoid any National Party split. It was endorsed by the shadow Cabinet at Lilydale on 14 April and achieved a unique status: it was both the most bizarre and the shortest lived coalition agreement in Australian history.

The new coalition comprised the Liberals and the National Party without the 12 Queenslanders. All coalition members had to support coalition (not Joh's) policies at the federal election. Joint party meetings would continue as usual. The crux for Sinclair was the provision that banned the Queensland Nationals from attending regular meetings of the National Party dealing with policy, tactics and election strategies. In short, the Nationals were to become a two-tier party; one tier coalitionist, the second isolationist.

Bjelke-Petersen saw through this farce: 'As soon as the sun comes up, it's not an agreement between everybody.' Howard had asked Sinclair: 'Ian, are you sure all your people approve this? Why not call a party meeting and put this arrangement through it now?' Sinclair assured Howard that the arrangement would work—but Sinclair had made another misjudgement.

At the first National Party meeting after this new agreement was made Sinclair failed to carry its terms. The Queenslanders had the support of two NSW defectors to reject the critical provisions of the agreement that banned full and regular meetings of the whole National Party. Sinclair tried to persuade Howard to make more concessions to hold the coalition but Howard sensibly refused. Howard did not break the coalition, he just buried it.

The National Party decision was clear—it had to choose between unity or coalition and it chose unity before coalition. It chose to leave the coalition en masse rather than exist in an ambivalent condition, half-coalition, half-free. The coalition ended at 7.28 pm on 28 April when the shadow Cabinet endorsed a recommendation from Howard for a break.

It was a smashing victory for Joh Bjelke-Petersen. Joh crushed Sinclair after a four month battle and destroyed the coalition just as he had pledged. Sinclair had suffered a humiliation which demanded his resignation as leader, on grounds of honour if not self-interest. But Sinclair had no

325

intention of resignation. The real loser was manifest—the once-formidable National Party, the party of Page, Fadden, McEwen and Anthony. If there is a turning point in the modern history of the National Party then this is it.

The Nationals broke the coalition in a prolonged fit of deluded grandeur and bedrock weakness. Joh Bjelke-Petersen was a corrupting influence in the National Party. He promised the Nationals the ultimate prize in politics—an absurdity given their structure, base and sophistication as a political vehicle. But Joh was strong enough to intimidate those Nationals who should have known better, notably Sparkes. Howard was right when he slammed those Queensland Nationals 'who did not have the guts' to confront Joh. Ultimately Joh helped to achieve the reelection of Hawke—the opposite to his intent.

In a characteristic comment Malcolm Fraser said: 'The ending of the coalition is an evil day for the Liberal side of politics. Queensland is solely responsible for its destruction. Whatever some with short memories and less knowledge of history may say of "separateness", it has not worked and experience suggests it will not work in Australian politics . . . Only the Liberal Party will be able to achieve the change of direction Australia requires.'[16]

The failure of Joh and his strategy in the 1987 general election would lead in several years to a revised National Party outlook of humility, coalition obedience and acceptance of its subservient place in politics—Hewson's benefit from Howard's pain.

The tragedy was Ian Sinclair's, a man once dressed for a prime ministerial career. He had stayed too long. His fellow travellers (Fraser, Anthony and Nixon) had gone, but Sinclair remained, an old bullock to be driven but not to lead. The truth is that Joh did very little to win—he huffed and he puffed, but his prime ministerial cart had already hit the quicksand. He was dying politically when the coalition broke.

At this juncture the politics of 1987 moved into a three-way split: Labor, Liberal and National. Howard had the consolation of knowing that it was the Nationals, not the Liberals, who had finished the coalition. He said that after the election he would seek to negotiate a new coalition agreement and form a Liberal–National government. But Hawke, lucky man, now faced a divided opposition in the election. The conservative side would enter the campaign without a coalition agreement, which had been the only successful instrument for conservative rule in the last sixty years of Australian politics.

The broken coalition saw a tactical tiff between Hawke and Keating. An excited Keating advocated a parliamentary onslaught, arguing that a broken coalition meant that the Opposition was no longer in a condition to rule. Hawke and Mick Young disagreed. They felt the Opposition was destroying itself and needed no help from Labor. Keating was overruled and went home disgusted.[17]

The final humiliation for Howard was the defeat of his preferred tax policy, the move to a broadly based indirect tax, which fell victim to assaults from Keating and Joh.

On 11 February 1987 Keating performed his famous volte face on the indirect tax for which he had campaigned at the 1985 Tax Summit. Keating said: 'I believed that building a more secure base in consumption to sit beside the direct tax system was a desirable thing. I still do, but only in a safe economic environment.' Keating insisted that the climate of 1987—a devalued dollar, a current account deficit, rising inflationary expectations and a real wage cut—made the introduction of an indirect tax too dangerous. He put Howard on notice that Labor would try to win any election on a Liberal indirect tax policy.[18]

Joh Bjelke-Petersen's tax campaign closed the circle against Howard. In the 1984 election Howard had persuaded the Opposition to support a broadening of the indirect base, a euphemism for a consumption tax. But three years on it was impossible for Howard to carry this policy, which would be sold through large personal income tax cuts. The reason was the crisis of belief within non-Labor politics. Joh power did more than create mayhem; it undermined faith in the Opposition among its own grassroots.

The moment when Bjelke-Petersen derailed Howard's tax policy can be identified exactly—the evening of Sunday 15 February 1987, just before parliament resumed. That night in Canberra the coalition leadership group, including Howard, Brown, Chaney, Carlton, Sinclair, Hunt, Durack and Tony Messner, gathered for a four hour meeting to establish the parameters of the policy. Messner, who was responsible for the tax details, gave a briefing and tax papers were issued. But Hunt asked the obvious question: what did the group think about the consequences of Bjelke-Petersen's activities? They fell into a long discussion and the tax papers were pushed aside. Jim Carlton, then shadow treasurer, tells the story:

> 1987 was dreadful, the worst year I've been through . . . we had all the basic tax work done. We had one discussion in the leadership group in February. That was supposed to be before it went to shadow Cabinet. But nothing was ever finalised. From that time the entire decision-making apparatus at the top of the Liberal and National parties was completely paralysed. We had to bring everyone along but the National Party people only had time for their crisis. It was just total turmoil. The National Party which had been rock solid all the time we could remember had suddenly become totally unstable. To get them to sit down and spend hours going through complicated material about the tax system was impossible. You can't exaggerate the atmosphere of crisis, almost hysteria, going on. You couldn't have a sensible conversation with anybody from the National Party.[19]

From mid-February until the coalition broke apart in late April there was no study by the shadow Cabinet of the Opposition's tax package. But

Carlton's analysis needs to be extended. Howard's indirect tax package was killed not just by a policy paralysis; it was killed because Howard lacked the credibility within the non-Labor constituency that would enable him successfully to bring down a radical package whose centrepiece was a new indirect tax.

David Trebeck, coordinating the tax package from the Liberal Secretariat, says: 'The trouble was that post-Fraser the credibility wasn't there to convince people that if the indirect tax was introduced then government spending would be cut as well.'[20]

This was the core point. It was the argument which John Stone mounted against the indirect tax: don't trust the Liberals to cut spending if you allow them a new tax from the start. Carlton concedes the point:

> Even without Joh I am profoundly sceptical whether it would have been possible to get such a policy [an indirect tax] in place. I thought the economic arguments were substantial. But I was sceptical as to whether we could ever get an amalgamation of political forces to support it. There was no guarantee that National Party candidates in the field would support it. Within the Liberal Party there were quite a few people who were worried about it.[21]

As May 1987 broke over Canberra the Liberal disarray was profound. Howard had lost his coalition and his favoured tax package, and had consigned his wets to the backbench. Hawke's reply was to strike with a snap winter election.

17
Hawke strikes

Tonight I can report that Australia is winning . . . for the first time in its history Australia now stands on the verge of breaking away from it precarious dependence on a narrow range of primary exports.

Paul Keating, 13 May 1987

It was Paul Keating's Economic Statement of 13 May 1987 which gave Labor the confidence to dash to a July federal election and an historic third election victory. The destruction wrought by Joh Bjelke-Petersen had boosted Labor's confidence—but the Keating Statement was the tonic of successful governance which allowed Labor to dictate the politics of the 1987 campaign.

This Statement is a milestone of the 1980s—it triggered the mid-1987 election, it represents the zenith of Labor's macro-economic policy efforts, and it introduced a false optimism into the Hawke government that contaminated its fourth parliament.

Hawke's 1987 election victory was founded as much on Labor positives as on Opposition negatives, a point not grasped in most analyses of the time. The two milestones in the pre-election period on which the election victory was based were the breaking of the federal coalition on 28 April and Labor's Economic Statement on 13 May.

The economics of the May Statement involved a large reduction in federal spending and a re-ordering of federal priorities as part of Labor's attack on the current account deficit. It brought to its hightide the Cabinet's faith in the 'twin deficit' theory; that is, as Keating explained, by reducing the public sector's call on national savings those savings are 'freed up to go where Australia now really needs them, into plant and equipment for export expansion and import replacement'.[1]

The centrepiece of the Statement was a $4 billion public sector savings, achieved by spending cuts and assets sales which Keating inelegantly called his 'shit sandwich'. This package had its deepest impact within the Reserve

329

Bank. It convinced the monetary authorities that such budgetary restraint permitted a generous easing of interest rates—a conclusion that was basic to the miscalculations behind the 1990s recession.

The politics of the package were to depict Labor as the managers during a national economic crisis. Keating wanted to satisfy three conditions. First, to solidify the currency markets after the 1986 shock and Moody's downgrading and prevent any dollar crisis during a 1987 campaign. Second, to convince Australia's opinion-making elite in the media, business and banks that Labor had the courage to face the nation's economic problems. Third, to embody Labor's belief in equity and job growth as simultaneous objectives in making Australia more efficient.

The reception given Keating's Statement was the best accorded any economic document during the Hawke era. Each of these political objectives was achieved. Indeed, the reception was so overwhelming that it swept Hawke into a July election which had been Keating's objective.

When Hawke's advisers, Richard Farmer and Bob Sorby, had argued for a May election they assumed that Labor was safe from another currency crisis. But Keating said, 'We need another down-payment on fiscal policy. We'll introduce a mini-budget in May to secure the dollar and our credentials and then have an election in winter.'

The evolution of the May Statement is testimony to the durability of the Hawke–Keating partnership. It revealed, again, that despite some differences, Hawke and Keating were a team too formidable for the Opposition. Hawke allowed Keating to chair the ERC (Cabinet) process which produced the May decisions. Hawke devoted his energies during a time of conservative crisis to cultivating his popularity and selling Labor's message.

The May Statement within the ERC was carried by three ministers—Keating, Walsh and Dawkins. As finance minister with overseeing responsibility for federal programs, Walsh made a special contribution. From an early stage Keating was aiming for a $4 billion savings target which was twice the initial expectation of $2 billion. Hawke endorsed the strategy at every point. But Keating said later: 'We could never have got this result with Hawke in the room.'

This assessment was probably too severe on Hawke.

A more balanced judgement of the entire ERC process of the 1980s—typified by this 1987 exercise—comes from Peter Walsh:

> For the first two terms in government Hawke was a much better Prime
> Minister than I or, I suspect, some members of his cheer squad
> expected him to be. His application to the enormous burdens of office,
> his self-discipline, his ability to grasp very quickly the essential points
> of all issues and to summarise them could scarcely be faulted. He was
> a good Cabinet chairman, although, especially in the ERC, inclined to
> allow debates to meander and replicate while hoping for consensus to
> emerge.[2]

The truth is that Hawke endorsed the strategy but would sometimes infuriate Keating and Walsh within the ERC by his caution over the electoral consequences of decisions. He always examined the issue from the perspective of the spending program ministers as well as that of the economic ministers.

In Hawke's 1 April statement rejecting a May election he said that before any election Labor had to address the economic challenge: 'Through paying drastically lower prices for many of our exports the world has cut more than $6 billion off the nation's income; that is, we are poorer to the tune of $1500 per Australian family.'[3]

Hawke saw the historic challenge facing his era. He believed that each ALP government had confronted a unique task and that:

the unique challenge of our time is to carry out the most sweeping reform in our history of our national economic institutions and attitudes . . . Let me just read you the list of Australia's top 10 exports today. They are coal, wheat, wool, iron ore and concentrates, alumina, beef and veal, crude petroleum oils, refined petroleum products, aluminium and gold . . . we must not be so heavily dependent [in future] as we are today on what we can dig up, or grow or shear . . . economic reconstruction is the principal task which my government is pledged to fulfil, not just in the lead-up to the next election but as the country enters the 1990s.[4]

Having defined the task Hawke let Keating, Walsh and the ERC ministers devise the immediate response. The May Statement was a defensive attacking strategy. The Cabinet broke plenty of ALP political axioms but there was still an overall electoral caution about the package.

The $4 billion savings was achieved through recurrent spending cuts of $2.6 billion, of which $1 billion was taken from the states. There were extra taxes worth $400 million and one-off asset sales worth another $1 billion. Keating declared that these decisions amounted to a real cut of 2 per cent in government spending—the biggest fall in thirty years. This laid the basis for the elimination of the federal budget deficit the following year.

The decisions involved the abolition of unemployment benefits for 16 and 17-year-olds to encourage better school retention, and other measures to keep youths at school and away from welfare; abolition of the Community Employment Program; a crackdown on welfare fraud and abuse; the application of an assets test to unemployment and sickness beneficiaries; the application of an income test starting at a joint parental income of $50 000 for receipt of the family allowance, thereby applying to the family allowance the same needs principle applied to other social security payments; a tightening in health and Medicare benefits; a shift from funded child care to family day care; and a squeeze on defence spending on the manpower side, as distinct from capital equipment.

These changes were proof of Labor's commitment to needs-based welfare, a tougher approach to unemployment benefits, and incentives to boost school retention. But the National ALP left issued a statement saying that 'the overall impact of the cuts poses serious economic and employment problems, particularly at State and local level'.

Keating extracted substantial savings with only a modicum of pain, notably, about $650 million from the sale of part of the Tokyo embassy site and other property as well as by demanding severe disciplines from the states. Overall, the ERC won its savings with a minimum of political fallout.

In his follow-up National Press Club speech Keating reflected the belief of his advisers in the treasury and Reserve Bank in the 'twin deficits' theory: that the public sector discipline would enable resources to flow into the private sector and hence the trading sector of the economy. This proposition was accepted implicitly in the favourable response from business and financial markets to Keating's Statement.

It was a measure of the changing nature of the economic debate that the biggest selling tabloid in Australia, *The Melbourne Sun*, covered the Statement with a huge page one headline, 'Grim but Fair'. The *Australian Financial Review* called it 'A Carefully Crafted Election Mini Budget'. *The Australian*'s commentator and Joh backer, Des Keegan, declared: 'Mr Keating has won his spurs with the first significant rollback in government spending since World War Two. Modern Labor has come of age.'[5] Max Walsh proclaimed: 'The Government. Cabinet and the caucus has passed an important psychological milestone. Welfarism, perhaps Whitlamism . . . now looks like going into reverse, mugged by reality.'[6] The *Financial Review*'s Ian Cassie wrote: 'There is little risk that last night's spending cuts will not satisfy the international investment community.'[7]

The *Sydney Morning Herald* saw the political caution behind the audacity. It wanted more action and asked: 'Why continue to excuse the goldminers from company tax? Why leave superannuation tax concessions untouched? Why still only nominal fees for tertiary education?' Its economics editor, Ross Gittins, said:

> The money market reaction to the mini-budget has been remarkably complacent with most observers accepting Paul Keating's $4 billion worth of savings at face value and failing to discount for the $1 billion of asset sales . . . do asset sales reduce consumption and increase savings? No. Do they reduce upward pressure on interest rates? No . . . though the word is out that the mini-budget was the last of the hard decisions, we must pray for more spending cuts in the August budget.[8]

The May Statement, above all, was an assertion of Labor's control of the political agenda, a decisive shift of the centre of political gravity towards the right and a bid to doom the Opposition parties to irrelevance.[9] The favourable reception was fundamental to Hawke's decision 14 days later to call an election.

The telling voter survey was Newspoll's question whether the Opposition could have produced a better mini-budget—a result 58 to 20 per cent Labor's way. A total of 35 per cent of Opposition voters said they believed their own side could not have done better: proof that Keating's strategy had worked.[10]

For a while Keating had won the markets and the punters. The best insight into Labor's emotions came from Alan Ramsey: 'Caucus is fairly fatalistic about what happens from here on. A senior government member described it: "There is now a necessary element of economic faith in that caucus knows that Keating is in absolute charge of economic policy . . . the destiny of this government and their own personal political futures are synonymous with Keating's success." '[11]

It was Hawke who took Labor's message to the people. He promised lower interest rates, more business investment, and said the package was proof of his 1986 'restraint with equity' pledge; that Labor would take the hard decisions to get Australia right. Hawke showered praise upon Keating: 'I have an undiminished continuing respect for Paul Keating's intellectual capacities, for his toughness and, above all, for his unwavering commitment [to] . . . the great Australian tradition of a fair go.' Earlier Hawke said that Keating was 'the best Treasurer in the history of this country'.[12]

During late April when Keating pressed Hawke on a July poll Hawke was unequivocally against it.[13] But on 15 May Hawke said an early election depended partly upon what the 'rabble of an Opposition does'; on 20 May he said 'there is a temptation'. On 21 May he refused to rule out an early election. After a week in which Hawke campaigned around the nation in shopping centres, old people's homes, ethnic social clubs and at business lunches, he was smelling an election victory.

ANOP's Rod Cameron advised Hawke that 'the trend line of government support is running 3.5 to 4 per cent higher than during the government's 1986 slump' and that 'Labor has enjoyed six months of a steadily upward trend'.[14] Cameron said that before the Statement Labor's rise was based upon Opposition disunity; after May it was based upon Labor's performance as well as on Opposition divisions. It was evidence that the May Statement had changed perceptions of the government. Cameron said that Labor was rising about a percentage point a month and if the trend were maintained then Labor would win a July election.

Early in the week starting 25 May the groundswell for an early poll was overwhelming. Hawke's advisers were united for July—national secretary Bob McMullan, national president Mick Young, Hawke's staff, Bob Sorby and Barrie Cassidy, and of course Keating, who had been the winter election enthusiast.

They were influenced by three factors: a belief that Labor had neu-

The end of certainty

tralised any campaign currency crisis; the prospect of fighting a broken coalition with institutionalised divisions; and the May Statement-induced boost to Labor's governing credentials. Labor's campaign professionals— McMullan and Cameron—did not assert that the government's position was strong; just that if Labor won the campaign then it would win the election.

But Hawke and Keating were supremely confident, euphoric about Labor's recovery, convinced of their superiority over the Opposition in every sense—policy, campaigning, presentation. Hawke and Keating would not countenance any result but an historic victory.

The early election was easily justified, despite Hawke's absurd dismissal of the mid-year option on 1 April. This is because the grounds for a double dissolution existed on the Australia Card bill, a substantial measure to assist tax collection and halt welfare fraud, designed to save an estimated $725 million a year. The bill was littered with defects but the requirements of section 57 were met—the bill had been refused a second reading in the Senate on 10 December 1986 and again on 2 April 1987. The prime minister was entitled to seek a double dissolution.

However, at the penultimate moment there was a mini-drama. Keating now told Hawke that he wanted an early August poll. His reason was an insight into the looming struggle.

Keating had been given wrong advice by the attorney-general, Lionel Bowen, that if a double dissolution were called before 1 July then the next half Senate election would be required before 1 July 1989, just two years away. Keating was violently opposed to this situation. At one stage he said: 'I don't want to have to be fighting a Senate election in 18 months time.' It was a Freudian slip; Keating was assuming that at the next election he, not Hawke, would be prime minister.[15]

Hawke noted the slip. Keating was later told that Bowen's advice was faulty. An 11 July election meant that the next half Senate poll was not due until mid-1990. That was plenty of time for Keating to settle into the Lodge. But Hawke had no moving plans for the next three years.

In announcing the July 11 winter election Hawke pledged to campaign on 'certainty, stability, continuity'. But he fumbled when quizzed on why he had changed his mind on an early election. Howard in an aggressive reply declared that Hawke 'has made the biggest mistake of his political career'.

Howard was relieved that Hawke had struck—finally. The urgency of the contest would subsume many of the Opposition's problems. In truth, Howard wasn't ready. But the man Hawke had caught with his pants down was Howard's nemesis, Joh Bjelke-Petersen. Howard would begin the 1987 campaign with a triumph: the negotiation of a remarkable truce with Joh Bjelke-Petersen which gave Howard a chance to win the election.

Joh was guest speaker at a black tie dinner for Californian business leaders at a Los Angeles hotel when told that Hawke was en route to

334

Government House. A stunned Joh exclaimed: 'You mean to tell me they have called an election!'[16] Upon his urgent return home there was an intense series of talks and negotiations which culminated in Joh's withdrawal as a candidate for federal parliament and the effective end of the Joh push. The origins of Joh's federal ambitions were startling, but the inside story of how those ambitions were finally buried is even more remarkable.

As soon as Hawke called the election Sparkes knew that Joh had to revive his campaign or retreat. Joh needed allies, desperately and quickly. There were two contenders, neither of whom belonged to the National Party but who were potential recruits—John Stone and Ian McLachlan.

Bjelke-Petersen had previously invited Stone to Kingaroy to speak at the dinner celebrating his fortieth anniversary as an MP. Stone had gone to Joh's home for tea with Joh and Flo and had fed the possums. He had agreed to Sparkes' invitation to write Joh's tax policy. It was one of the strangest alliances of the 1980s: Stone advising Bjelke-Petersen. Sparkes wanted to shoehorn Stone into politics as a Queensland Senator, a temptation which Stone found irresistible. Stone declared that neither the Labor nor Liberal parties had 'the people, the energy or the policies . . . to repair Australia . . . that is why I am working for Sir Joh'.[17]

But the 'big play' centred upon McLachlan. Sceptical about the Howard–Sinclair team, McLachlan, his nose close to rural Australia, believed that Joh might put together a viable package. Years later McLachlan reflected: 'We had a bit of euphoria going. We didn't think that Labor or the Liberals had it right.'

McLachlan was influenced by the prospects that Joh might increase the overall non-Labor vote and deliver election victory—an analysis made by his advisers at the NFF, Andrew Robb and Rick Farley; the dream was an alliance of red-necked ALP votes and the traditional non-Labor vote.

McLachlan was trapped in a net of conflicting emotions. He didn't want to enter politics but he was being told he had an obligation to do so by many people. Hugh Morgan advised McLachlan to commit himself. McLachlan was tempted and flattered by the attention he received. He had lost his faith in the Liberals and he saw that the Nationals were ripe for a takeover. Finally, he believed that urgent policy action was required to save the country. McLachlan was drawn by Joh's magnet.

An illuminating contrast is provided by John Hyde, the founder of the Liberal free market lobby. Hyde was never swayed by the Joh caravan. He complained that politics was assuming the surreality of the Rocky Horror Show and that 'Sir Joh's policies, identified best by looking north, are as irrelevant to Australia's difficulties as those of the wets he so despises'. Hyde felt that Joh was a fraud.[18]

Joh and Sparkes had courted McLachlan in early 1987; the premier had seen him in Brisbane 'three or four times'.[19] Stone had briefed McLachlan on Joh's tax policy. McLachlan had established his own working party with the Joh camp to assess whether Joh's policies were consistent with those of the NFF. He had held talks with Joh, Sparkes, Maybury and Crook as well as Stone. Bjelke-Petersen says: 'We had our own Queensland officials working on the tax policy and all our policies. I let McLachlan bring his own people up to study our plans. They spent days with my people.'[20]

A list of possible new National Party candidates had been prepared—McLachlan, Stone, yacht designer Ben Lexcen, the AMA's Bruce Shepherd, Andrew Hay, former ANI chief John Leard, and John Hay from the Australian Enterprise Group. Joh saw McLachlan initially as his running mate, then gradually as the key to his campaign—an admission of his own weakness.

Joh's weakness was induced partly by a secret deal struck in Howard's office between the NSW National and Liberal parties, finalised on 7 May and formally embodied in a two-page signed document. Its effect was to lock Joh out of the biggest state.

Its main provision was to bind the Liberal and National parties to support each other's candidate against any declared Joh National. That is, the NSW Nationals were pledged to support a Liberal before a Joh National and vice-versa. Bronwyn Bishop and Doug Moppett signed on behalf of their respective parties. Howard and Sinclair knew that in terms of running viable candidates that they had isolated Joh to Queensland.

The story of Joh's 1987 push was his attempted seduction of and then rejection by McLachlan. It was McLachlan's dalliance with Joh that gave hope to Joh's federal delusions but finally it was McLachlan's desertion which destroyed them. This allowed McLachlan a smoother entry into Liberal politics which he would exercise at the subsequent 1990 election.

The personal journey of McLachlan from 1985 to 1990 reflected the story of non-Labor politics; first he embodied the split between radical and mainstream liberalism which reached its zenith in 1987; then he symbolised their reconciliation post-1990 when he became a senior frontbench coalitionist.

On 28 May, the day after Hawke's election announcement, McLachlan met Sparkes in Brisbane for talks over two days. Sparkes realised that Joh would only be a federal election candidate if he could restore his momentum by recruiting McLachlan to his banner. Joh needed McLachlan for four reasons which Sparkes had itemised carefully. McLachlan, unlike Joh, was a serious contender as prime minister; McLachlan's arrival as a National Party candidate would overwhelm Sinclair and finish him as a force; McLachlan was the 'big domino' to impel the other dominoes and persuade the Joh candidates to run; finally, since Joh had no money, he needed the $10 million NFF fighting fund, about ten times as much as the Joh campaign had raised, plus access to the NFF's grassroots organisation that could be mobilised on behalf of any transformed National Party crusade. In other words, McLachlan was the linch-pin.

Sparkes and McLachlan had a natural affinity. They were both very rich men, controllers of huge agricultural interests, compelled to the world of politics and convinced that Australia faced a crisis which demanded radical solutions. In his long career Sparkes had never attempted a political manoeuvre so spectacular in import or so desperate as this bid to secure McLachlan.

McLachlan said there were three conditions necessary for him to join the Joh push—Joh's policies had to be consistent with those of the NFF; Sinclair and the federal National Party would have to support them so the disunity problem would be solved; and McLachlan must be convinced that Bjelke-Petersen was stable and would not undermine their efforts during the campaign.

McLachlan said that he was largely satisfied about policy compatibility. On condition two, Sparkes told McLachlan that if he committed then Sinclair would have no choice but to support them. The combination of Joh and McLachlan would swamp any resistance by Sinclair. Sparkes' plan was to spring the Joh–McLachlan–NFF union on a surprised Sinclair.

Sparkes told McLachlan that the prime ministership was in his sights. Not only would McLachlan become the eventual leader of the National Party but he was the only leader in Australia capable of restructuring the conservative side by bringing the right-wing Liberals and the Nationals together into a new majority party, a restructuring over which Sparkes had ruminated for years.

In relation to McLachlan's third condition, Sparkes could only offer encouragement about Joh; in recent weeks Joh had been very disciplined. McLachlan had little experience of Bjelke-Petersen and Sparkes felt it was best to keep it that way.

A confident Sparkes now told Joh: 'We've got McLachlan.' Bjelke-Petersen was delighted. A summit conference was organised in Melbourne the following Monday to thrash out the policies, the plans, and finalise the deal. McLachlan had not committed but Sparkes believed that he would. Joh felt excited; he was going to ace Hawke. Joh would snatch victory from the jaws of defeat.

But Sparkes had misread his man.

Over the weekend 30–31 May McLachlan asked Farley to attend the summit. He told Farley that he hadn't made up his mind. McLachlan was reluctant—but he was under pressure.

It was in the heartland of the Melbourne establishment at the Windsor Hotel where on 1 June 1987, one of the most bizarre meetings in the politics of the 1980s occurred. It is where McLachlan, the object of Joh's seduction, finished by slaying Joh.

The Queenslanders rose early and travelled to Melbourne in optimism. The meeting took place in the Churchill Room of the Windsor beneath a large portrait of the great man—the main participants were Joh, McLachlan, Sparkes, Stone, Holm, Crook, Maybury, Maybury's aide Jenny Russell and

McLachlan's adviser Farley. With the media assembled in the foyer the participants found a secret passage from the Churchill room to their own rooms in the hotel. They could remove a wall panel only doorhandle high, climb through into a broom cupboard, exit into the kitchen, then catch the service lift upstairs to their rooms.

Sparkes opened the meeting with an important statement—he would advise Joh not to run unless McLachlan and other candidates came aboard. The meeting then reached agreement on a common policy framework. Then Joh offered a deal. McLachlan would become Joh's deputy but Joh said he only wanted to stay a short time, one term at most and probably less. McLachlan would succeed him as the National Party leader.[21]

McLachlan then began to explore the conditions he had required. From the start McLachlan was very tough; so tough that he may have had another motive—the need to find an escape route. McLachlan said that the National Party must be united with the Joh–Sinclair issue resolved: 'I won't join a divided rabble.' McLachlan also wanted the Nationals to get behind Howard and to back him as prime minister. McLachlan bluntly declared that unless the right-wing forces were united then Hawke would win the election—a belatedly correct assessment. McLachlan told Joh that unless there was unity there would be no money, support or decent candidates.

Sparkes agreed with the position put by McLachlan. He said the meeting should endorse McLachlan's approach as the basis for their actions. Sparkes said he believed there was enough common ground for an agreement.

But McLachlan was not satisfied about his conditions. Here was a man who wanted power but didn't want to get his hands dirty. McLachlan told Joh that he must resolve the Sinclair issue. Joh replied: 'Okay Ian, but we've tried to get rid of Sinclair. We can't. If you just come with us we'll have added strength knowing that you'll take his place.' Here was Joh's first problem: he had never been able to finish Sinclair; he needed McLachlan for that.

But McLachlan was unyielding: 'No Joh. You mucked it up. You fix it. I won't help you to fix it up. I'm not going to be involved in anything with you until you clean up your party.' Bjelke-Petersen now appealed to McLachlan. Just assume, he asked, that the Sinclair problem is sorted out, would McLachlan come then? Now McLachlan shifted ground: 'I'll make the judgement after I see how you perform and what sort of support you give Howard.' McLachlan was slipping away. Then it got bitter. Joh said: 'You want me to give up my plans, my staff, my cars. But what you are going to give up?' He looked like a petulant old man. Then Joh made his fatal error and McLachlan went out the door.

As McLachlan pressed, the pilot Beryl Young went into a whispered conversation with Joh; there was a long pause. Then the mask was torn off and the real Joh spoke: 'I'm not going to give up the premiership to be number two. You must understand that. I'll be prime minister, even if we don't win more seats than the Liberals I'll be prime minister. That's why I'm running.' There was a silence; a political abyss.

It was an assertion of ego and an act of stupidity. Joh was telling McLachlan that regardless of whether the Nationals outpolled the Liberals that he would be prime minister. He wanted the top job; it didn't matter what the voters said. McLachlan replied coldly, 'If that's the case then there's no point us staying here.'

McLachlan saw the premier in his true nature—the egocentric loner who underestimated his dependence upon others.

Sparkes knew it was the end. With one lethal sentence Joh convinced McLachlan that it was political folly to strike an alliance with him. McLachlan had his excuse to terminate the charade. McLachlan told Sparkes: 'You've satisfied me on most things but you can't control Joh.' Sparkes said later: 'It was that remark by Joh at the Windsor that killed the Joh-for-Canberra exercise.'[22]

Towards the end Joh and McLachlan were on their feet speaking in raised voices. McLachlan's final words were: 'It's best to proceed on the basis that I will not enter politics at this election.' The Joh-for-Canberra campaign was killed by a mixture of Sinclair's tenacity and McLachlan's rebuff of Joh.

Two days later Bjelke-Petersen lashed McLachlan:

He called us all for real suckers . . . but I guess we were. I said, 'Ian, tell us now if we do exactly what you want will you then come.' He said, 'No. I won't. I'm not coming.' It was quite straight, hard. That was it . . . I said, 'But you indicated to us that you'd be prepared to consider it . . . You want me to be the sacrificial lamb, to forgo everything . . . but you won't forgo that' . . . One thing I hate is having a man who pulls your leg.[23]

McLachlan was returning to the Liberals. He rang Howard: 'I think he's mad. He's just mad. He's got nothing organised. There's no structure and no organisation. He can't work with anyone. He's just hopeless. I told them the best thing they can do for conservative politics is to support you.' But McLachlan had been flirting with Joh for months.

McLachlan told Howard that he would not be a Liberal or a National candidate, and that Howard and Joh must close ranks for the election. Sparkes rang Howard with the message 'we want a meeting'. 'We're trying to get him out,' Sparkes said, 'But it's very difficult.' The Joh camp headed for a Sydney meeting with Howard. A reluctant Joh had agreed to make peace. McLachlan went to dinner with Howard's mentor John Carrick and loyalist Wal Fife.

McLachlan had had three other problems with Joh's offer. First, if McLachlan agreed then he had to be a National Party Senate candidate in South Australia, in defiance of his South Australian Liberal heritage. It was too great a family and social break. Second, there was hardly a South Australian National Party. Third, McLachlan would be a Senator, not the place from which to run for high office.

Meanwhile, at 30 000 feet above Victoria, Joh changed his mind. He told Sparkes in the plane: 'I'm not going out there [Howard's home] . . . There's nothing in it for me to go and see Howard. I don't run after anybody.'[24] So Joh sulked at the Airport Hilton, leaving Sparkes, Holm and Maybury to visit Howard's home.

Janette was polite to the visitors and the Queenslanders were models of civility. Howard had called Eggleton and his aide Graham Morris to the meeting. It was time for Howard's vindication. Agreement was reached that during the campaign the Joh forces would not attack Howard or the Liberals. It was a non-aggression pact—a major advance.

But the Queenslanders made a final bid. They told Howard the best way to beat Hawke was through a Joh-for-Canberra push to maximise the anti-Labor vote. Maybury produced his research, the latest commissioned from McNair–Anderson during the period 10–22 April, the material they had given McLachlan at the Windsor. But the research indicated, above all, Hawke's strength. The 3400 nationwide sample showed: Hawke Labor 48 per cent, Howard Liberal 28.5 per cent, Sinclair National 6.3 per cent and Australian Democrats 8.5 per cent. When Joh was substituted for Sinclair the figures were respectively: 47.6 per cent, 22.7 per cent, 16.9 per cent and 6.4 per cent. Joh did boost the total non-Labor vote but Hawke won the election either way.

Howard and Eggleton made the obvious point—the Joh campaign had caused such divisions it would alienate voters from the non-Labor side.[25]

The Queenslanders complained bitterly to Howard about the NSW National Party which had locked them out. The Joh push had met only an official wall of opposition from the NSW party. Howard listened to these laments with satisfaction. The written agreement between the NSW Liberals and Nationals against Joh had been finalised and signed in his own office. Sparkes had not realised the extent of Howard's complicity in the NSW plan to thwart him.

Finally, Sparkes surrendered; he suggested a Howard–Joh meeting in the context of Joh's withdrawal from any federal election candidacy. The Queenslanders landed in Brisbane at midnight, utterly vanquished.

The next day at Bjelke-Petersen House Joh agreed to meet Howard only if Howard came to Brisbane to extend the hand of friendship! But Howard feared a humiliation by Joh on election eve, so Sparkes asked Stone to act as mediator. Stone spoke to Howard several times, assured him that Joh was genuine, pointed out that Howard had an opportunity to mend the rift and that he had to come to Brisbane.

The plan involved a package deal—Joh's decision not to nominate as a federal candidate, his announcement to remain as premier, the use of

Hawke's early election as the excuse for Joh's backdown, and the joint declaration to fight Hawke.

Bjelke-Petersen was making peace with Howard but not with Sinclair. Neither Sparkes nor Joh was prepared to settle with Sinclair. They saw no need. The internal National Party war was merely postponed.

Howard's premonitions were confirmed at 6.30 am on Wednesday 3 June, just before he was supposed to leave Canberra. Maybury rang Eggleton to tell him that Joh had had second thoughts. Eggleton smelt a crisis. He said they would not leave Canberra until they spoke to Sparkes. When Howard, Eggleton and Morris arrived at Canberra airport it was heavy with fog—a nice excuse for their delay.

Howard was busy in the RAAF base from just after 7 pm with a series of agonising phone calls. He told Sparkes he could not tolerate arriving in Brisbane only to find that Joh had done a backflip which made Howard look a fool. Sparkes had to get assurances from Joh otherwise Howard would cancel. Sparkes replied: 'You must come, John, it's your presence that will bring all this to an end.' Sparkes spoke to Joh and then Ken Crook read out to Howard the text of Joh's media statement. Only then did Howard board the Mystère jet; the fog had lifted and they took off into a blue sky.

Howard and Joh met in the premier's office, first with Sparkes, Holm and Maybury, then alone. They were models of politeness towards each other. There was no mention of 'wreckers' or 'silly little boys'. Howard asked for a photograph; Bjelke-Petersen declined: 'You don't want to kill me do you John?' The non-aggression pact was sealed; the war was over. Howard felt no euphoria, just relief.

It was a meeting between professionals but Howard felt its surreality. He saw no trace of regret in Bjelke-Petersen, no remorse, no apology. Bjelke-Petersen offered no excuse for six months of mayhem. Joh believed he was right; it was Sinclair and McLachlan whom he blamed, anybody but himself. When the ritual was finished Howard was prepared to forget Joh forever. Howard flew out of Brisbane for the battle with Hawke—but he was a long way behind.[26]

Howard had united, belatedly, the non-Labor side for the campaign. But the damage was done. He needed a political ace desperately. There was just one option—a stunning tax package that would win middle Australia. Howard decided to base his campaign on a tax cut killing.

18
Hawke—Labor's greatest winner

I would rather risk electoral defeat than take the soft options that would mean we mortgage our great future.

Bob Hawke's 1987 election policy speech

The 1987 campaign brought to its zenith the phenomenon of the new Labor Party as superior election performer and propagandist of economic credibility. Labor was victorious because it was seen as a better alternative on the basic criteria: leadership, unity, credibility and political professionalism. The campaign was dominated by the collective firepower of Hawke and Keating, a combination the Liberals were unable to match.

The 1987 election was the first to be shaped by Australia's historic transition from a closed to an open economy. This makes the 1987 poll unique and is the reason why the alignments behind government and Opposition were so unusual.

The election was driven by the force of external economic events and the globalisation of financial and product markets. The platform on which Labor sought reelection was unprecedented in the annals of the party. Labor sought to deliver more than social justice; it sought to deliver more than economic management competence; it depicted itself as the party best able to secure Australia's transition from a protected to an internationalised economy.

An insight into the election backdrop was provided by a Japanese investment mission led by a friend of Australia, the former head of Japan's Ministry of International Trade and Industry (MITI), Mr Naohiro Amaya. In response to requests for better directed investment into Australia the mission reported on election eve that:

> if Australia remains entrenched in its traditional economic structure . . .
> its current account deficit will remain high and the standard of
> Australian living may have to fall considerably in the near future. The

"lucky country" good life, "take-it-easy" motto and 'happy-go-lucky" solutions must be overhauled.[1]

When Hawke went to the polls, unemployment had fallen from the 10.2 per cent he had inherited in 1983 to 8 per cent, which had involved the creation of more than 850 000 jobs, 85 per cent of them being in the private sector—an impressive achievement. Inflation over the same period had fallen from 11.5 to 9.4 per cent after briefly reaching 5 per cent. But Australia's inflation performance had deteriorated in relation to its trading partners—they had reduced inflation far more, the differential being an alarming 7.4 percentage points. Despite severe real wage cuts, wages were rising faster at home than abroad and productivity was weaker.

Australia's dilemma was its current account deficit and net foreign debt which had risen from $23 billion in 1983 (14 per cent of GDP) to $81 billion (33 per cent of GDP), a function of low savings and poor competitiveness. The crisis was the result of international trends being imposed upon Australia and the country's structural inability to cope. These trends—failing commodity prices and low overseas inflation—meant that Labor's post-1983 growth strategy had produced a balance of payments crisis of historic dimensions. The moral was that Australia had to adjust to international 'first-best' practice or face a rapid decline.[2]

In this climate Hawke and Keating fought a campaign which above all else was an assertion of their right to manage Australia's transition; it flowed directly from the economic policy adjustments they had pioneered over the three previous years. Their campaign was a testimony to the tenacity of their vision of Labor as a governing party. The government entered the campaign in a stronger position than did its divided opponents. Labor had more money, more business backing, more marginal seat expertise and far greater media support—the tests of a governing party.

Labor's two greatest assets were its perception as a competent government by the opinion-making elite and the popular belief that the Opposition lacked the unity, credibility and authority to govern effectively. Hawke won on a roughly equal mix of Labor positives and Opposition negatives.

The campaign maximised the complementary skills of Hawke as presidential populist and Keating as treasury demolitionist. But this had a comical aftermath: Hawke and Keating each interpreted the victory as being primarily the result of his own respective efforts within the team. Labor finished the campaign with two leaders, not one, each claiming the success had legitimised his own position against his rival.

The 1987 election reveals the extent to which the destruction of the old order was creating new and unstable alignments. Labor's victory was established on its depiction of the contest as one between the new establishment (Labor) and the radical right (Liberals); between Hawke the cautious reformist leader and Howard the reckless radical. Labor was supported

343

by a remarkable alliance: financial markets, big business, the quality media, the trade union movement, Hawke cultists, the ALP traditional vote (though ragged), and the 1960s Whitlam generation, now the middle class fashion setters. The Opposition was backed by small business, farmers, the low tax and anti-union legions, the swingers who voted by their hip-pocket, Joh devotees, and the Liberal traditionalists (though slightly disillusioned).

A symbol of the chaotic realignments was the appointment, after the election was announced, of John Singleton Advertising as the ALP advertising agency. Singleton, a leader of the right-wing Workers Party of the 1970s, owned the agency with stockbroker Rene Rivkin, who declared that he had never voted Labor in his life. The move, imposed by Hawke personally, was a reflection of both NSW right powerbroking and the changes generated by Hawke–Keating economics. Singleton, buoyed by his Top 40 hit 'Geez Ya Hopeless' announced that Fraser and Howard had wrecked the country last time and 'if the Liberals get back it will be a total disaster'.

A further symbol of Labor's clout was the support Hawke enjoyed from Kerry Packer and Alan Bond. On 15 June Hawke attended a Perth lunch hosted by his friend, Western Australian premier Brian Burke, and attended by 'last resort' Laurie Connell and several figures associated with WA Inc. The Bond Corporation was prominently represented and nearly $1 million was pledged to the ALP. It was later claimed (without evidence) that the funds came on the condition that Labor kept the gold tax exemption. The meeting reflected an informal alliance between the new ALP and the 'new money' entrepreneurs.

Labor had satisfied the three necessary requirements for a sound campaign: financial market confidence preventing any run on the currency; the shift from monetary to fiscal policy setting the scene for falling interest rates; and an attack on the current account deficit that had avoided a recession.

From this position Labor erected a campaign strategy drawing upon the 'most researched and best researched' effort ever conducted by Rod Cameron's ANOP for the ALP.[3] The 1987 campaign is seen as a classic by the ALP professionals because Labor had to overcome the fall in living standards experienced by most Australians and John Howard's offer of the biggest tax cut in election history, a daunting mixture.

From the start Hawke's ANOP-driven message of 'certainty, stability, continuity' was coupled with a decision to offer only very modest election promises. Labor ran on its record—but this was not a conventional record. Labor depicted itself as the party best able to manage Australia's economic transition. Hawke embraced the research-driven jingle 'Let's Stick Together, Let's See It Through'. Labor's selling point was superior credibility and governance to that of the Liberals.

It was a finely crafted and superbly executed position. But it carried a legacy. The price of Labor's 1987 reelection was the selling of its conviction to the people that Australia's economic transition, though not easy, would be relatively swift. Hawke and Keating had convinced themselves on this point. Although they accepted the challenge they misjudged its magnitude. The combination of Hawke's and Keating's egocentric outlooks and electoral necessity meant that Labor was offering to achieve in a few years the type of change that would require a decade to deliver, a time-bomb for the fourth term.

The key to John Howard's campaign is that he started from behind and had to catch Hawke. Under pressure he succumbed to a 'second best' strategy—he tried to win the election by offering a massive tax cut. During 1987 Howard had been happy to delay the finalisation of the Liberal tax package because he believed that the chronic non-Labor disunity could be countered only by a major circuit-breaker close to the poll. The tax package was that circuit-breaker.

A strange fate befell Howard: the leader who had pledged to transform politics and who had declared 'the times will suit me' now entered the campaign with the oldest of all slogans—an appeal to the hip pocket. After six months of mayhem Howard was unable to mount a 'first best' campaign which would have depicted the Opposition as superior managers of the national economic challenge. Thus he offered a big tax cut and a return to traditional values.

Howard, the underdog, presented himself as 'honest John'. The day after Hawke called the election Howard declared that Labor 'has presided over the biggest fall in living standards for the last forty years'. Howard's campaign was to exploit voter anxiety and falling real incomes with a hefty tax cut bait. His election slogan, 'Get in Front Again', was unashamedly pitched at the hip pocket, and his economic rationale was that more incentive would deliver greater productivity.

But Howard was undermined initially by the Opposition's failure over the previous three years to devise a proper health policy. Howard had even declared that $3 billion could be saved from Medicare to finance his tax cuts. But the work was never done, the policy was never constructed and the Liberals were scrambling after the election had been called to finalise a health policy. It was a disgraceful shambles which had two consequences: it meant Medicare was a plus for Labor and it left Howard with few savings for his tax package.

The decisive event of the 1987 campaign was the launch of the Liberal tax policy at Box Hill in Melbourne on 10 June, before the official policy launch. This was Howard's bid to seize back the initiative. He had been under pressure for months to release the policy; he did so as soon as it was finalised. The tax policy was designed to seize the campaign initiative from Labor, bring wavering voters to the Liberals and provide a favourable product differentiation between the two sides. The tax policy would make or break Howard; it confounded campaign orthodoxy by making the Opposition, rather than the government, the central election issue.

The policy was redolent of Ronald Reagan's supply side economics. Howard offered a total tax cut package of $7.3 billion which was constituted in four ways: personal tax cuts worth $5 billion which introduced a new two-tier rate scale of 25 per cent in the $5901–$20 000 range and 38 per cent from $20 000; a 'child care allowance' of $800 a year, additional to the family allowance, paid to assist one-income families; a cut in the corporate rate in two stages from 49 to 38 per cent; the abolition of Labor's assets test on the pension, abolition of the capital gains tax, a severe modification of its fringe benefits tax, a return to negative gearing and a weakening of Labor's crackdown on business deductions for tax purposes.

In addition Howard offered a $4.2 billion three year asset-selling program which included Australian Airlines, Qantas, AIDC, OTC, Aussat, Medibank Private and the domestic airport terminals. He pledged that the proceeds would be used to retire debt, not finance the tax cuts on a one-off windfall basis.

Howard's pitch was to suburbia and the boardroom. It had great potential and was a sharp break from Labor. For a single income two-parent family on an average weekly income of about $500—the Howard model—the tax cut was worth $26 a week, which was a 25 per cent reduction in taxation. It was roughly double the extent of tax relief provided from the phased-in Keating cuts unveiled in 1986.

Labor was nowhere within striking distance of the magnitude of Howard's tax relief. Howard offered a decisive shift towards a lower taxation and smaller government philosophy. The critical feature was Howard's pledge that the entire package would be financed from spending cuts that would total $7.8 billion over three years and involve a reduction in size of the public sector from 43 per cent plus to 38 per cent of GDP. Liberal research consistently showed a favourable response to their tax cuts throughout the campaign, notably in the target middle income group.

Yet Howard's tax package had two severe flaws—credibility and relevance. The missing link in the package was the consumption tax. Howard had kept his big tax cuts but he had no consumption tax to finance them. His insistence that the package would be financed entirely from public sector cuts was openly questioned. He went further than previous Opposition leaders in identifying where these cuts would be made but, given the climate and the doubts about the Opposition's credibility, he should have gone further. Only about $2.3 billion from total promised cuts of $7.8 billion was identified specifically. Much of the remaining $5.5 billion cuts had to come from programs, benefits or services but Howard lacked the time or political capital to say exactly where.

If tax cuts are to be responsible and financed without blowing the budget deficit then, as one election analyst said, 'There is only one reform that counts—spending cuts. There is no real tax reform without spending cuts. Whenever you hear a politician talking about tax cuts without spending cuts then you're being conned. The missing element in the Howard package is obvious—a consumption tax.'[4]

Howard was pledged to cutting taxes first and then finding the spending cuts. If there were an internal revolt or a loss of nerve within a Howard government then Howard would have two choices: blow out the budget deficit or commit political suicide by cancelling the tax cut.

Shadow treasurer Jim Carlton claimed that more details of the spending cuts would have 'alerted every single pressure group in the country', including 'highly articulate middle class pressure groups whose voices would have drowned out the interests of the ordinary taxpayer'.[5]

This was an insight into Howard's problem. The Liberal free market lobby had risen to prominence attacking Malcolm Fraser for timidity. But in the 1987 election it pledged a tax/spending switch in which it refused to identify the bulk of the spending cuts. The Liberals asked to be taken on trust after two years of bitter internal dissension and a coalition split. The test was a simple one: if the Liberals lacked the electoral courage to identify the spending cuts before the election why should anybody believe they would implement the spending cuts after the election?

Keating ran throughout the campaign on the question which Howard found impossible to answer: where will the $7.8 billion spending cuts fall? Keating's refrain was: Howard can't deliver. Howard, facing a credibility problem before the campaign, accentuated this problem during the campaign.

Three days after the launch Howard boasted that 'the government has been unable to find any holes in the arithmetic'. But Labor had found a hole and it was sizeable. Keating used it to pulverise Howard in an attack from which the Liberal campaign never recovered.

The Opposition's tax documents contained a 'double counting' error identified by the treasury, which Keating in a comprehensive reply on 17 June estimated at $1634 million. The treasurer called upon Howard to admit his mistake and either reduce his tax cuts or increase his spending cuts to retain his integrity with the voters. The Opposition's advisers realised the mistake at once, though they disputed the figure.

Four days later Howard and Carlton conducted a Sydney media conference at which they conceded the mistake and estimated the error at $534 million. Howard said the error was 'technical' and that delivery of the tax cuts was unconditional. He refused to identify any extra spending cuts to compensate for the error, which meant he had tried to 'cut the same dollar twice'. In response to questions Carlton declined to accept responsibility for the mistake, a stance which dismayed Howard and hurt the party. Howard, defiant but defensive, refused to change his tactics and respond to media pressure to provide more details on the spending cuts.

The mistake was David Trebeck's, working at the Liberal Secretariat, but the fault lay with the inadequate Opposition policy process over the previous six months. The management failure was Howard's, the policy failure was Carlton's, and their excuse was Bjelke-Petersen's disruption. If the tax policy had been prepared in more time and vetted by more experts, the mistake would not have occurred.

The second defect in the Howard tax package was its relevance to the national problem: Australia's crisis lay within its balance of payments deficit. How would the tax package assist its solution?

The *Sydney Morning Herald*'s Max Walsh attacked Howard's package as 'economic vandalism', claiming that it would boost domestic demand and provoke a new balance of payments crisis. Walsh said the spending cuts envisaged a reduction in the public sector from 43 to 38 per cent of GDP at a time when virtually no other OECD nation had managed even a shift in this direction, let alone a 5 percentage point shift. The *Financial Review* summarised Howard's package as 'bribery and wild guesses—but it might appeal'. The paper's senior editor, Peter Robinson, said, 'The ascendancy of the 'dries'—the economic rationalists—has been shown to be nothing more than a sham.'[6]

Howard was experimenting with a king hit, but he converted himself into a bigger target. *The Age*'s Michelle Grattan asked where was the old Howard who had talked tough and supported an indirect tax, a lower deficit, real wage cuts and lower living standards to fight the current account deficit and foreign debt. In *The Australian* I wrote: 'It is a package for opposition, not government. It is about winning votes, not running the economy. As Prime Minister Howard would be burdened by its legacy.'

The most hurtful critique came from the former leader of the drys, John Hyde, in his pre-election blueprint. Hyde said that Australia's problem was a function of the twin deficit effect: the budget deficit reinforcing the trade deficit. He said, 'Substantial expenditure cuts are needed just to stabilise our current economic situation . . . a lower deficit should allow lower interest rates and lower inflation (which in some ways would count as tax cuts). Massive tax cuts are not required as part of this short-to-medium term macro-strategy although massive spending cuts are.'[7] Hyde thus repudiated the centrepiece of Howard's strategy. He said the election tax debate was 'trivial' and that the real issues should be labour market deregulation, lower protection, a tighter fiscal policy and macro-economic reform.

This illuminates Howard's failure to win the support of the opinion-making elite in the media, business community and financial sector. Much of this elite was sceptical of the Liberals before the campaign began, based upon their performance over the previous two years. It interpreted the tax package in a critical, even hostile fashion, partly because it seemed at odds with the stance Howard had taken in the past.

The scepticism extended to the Business Council of Australia (BCA) whose priority was a lower deficit and lower interest rates. Within the financial sector Westpac's chief currency dealer in New York declared that a Liberal win 'would probably be a disaster' for the currency. A newspaper survey found that 90 per cent of dollar and interest rate dealers backed Labor!

The media coverage was lethal for Howard, probably for three reasons. The media was convinced that Labor was a superior outfit, a judgement shared by unions and business. There was a feeling that Labor, as Hawke and Keating insisted, deserved to win on its record. The Labor team, extending to Button, Kerin, Evans, Dawkins and Walsh, was widely seen as superior.

Secondly, the media saw Howard's tax strategy as an attempt to 'steal' the election. Australia was not a high tax nation, ranking only 18th at the time out of 23 OECD nations in terms of its tax take. Giving tax reform the primary focus was seen as a false priority. There was a suspicion that Howard had succumbed to Ronald Reagan's model, called 'voodoo economics' among policy advisers in Canberra, where it was blamed for transforming the US in six years from the world's greatest creditor to the world's greatest debtor power.

Finally, the media both reflected and was influenced by Labor's superior political management skills after months of watching the non-Labor side devour itself, a judgement confirmed by Howard's arithmetic blunder.

Alarmed, Liberal director Tony Eggleton tried to halt the media rot by warning that the coverage of the Liberal tax policy was 'one of the most jaundiced periods in reporting of campaigns that I have seen in my 25 years in Australian politics'.[8] A bitter sense of injustice pervaded the non-Labor parties.

Howard's package was both an election bait and a bid to dominate the non-Labor side which had three separate teams in the field—Liberals, Sinclair Nationals and Joh Nationals, though Joh was not a candidate. Bjelke-Petersen was still offering a 25 per cent flat rate tax phased in over three years and financed by massive spending cuts of $17 billion plus. While Howard's rhetoric was dominated by incentive, the irony is that his marginal tax rate in the $20 000–$35 000 range was only two percentage points below Labor's (38 in contrast to 40 per cent), a difference which hardly offered great incentive.

Howard's claims to serious tax reform were undermined by the fact that he sought to lower the rates while simultaneously contracting the taxation base. Howard not only rejected an indirect tax; he opposed the bulk of Keating's direct base broadening on assets, capital gains, fringe benefits and property, thereby reopening a series of loopholes heavily geared towards the better off.

In summary, the Howard package was rejected by elite opinion while the swinging voters were shaken by the symbolism of the arithmetic error, a mistake which reinforced doubts about the Opposition's credibility.

ANOP's Rod Cameron now found in his qualitative research that 'people liked the tax cuts but they didn't really believe that Howard would deliver. They would say that if the sums aren't accurate then what else will go wrong'.[9] Cameron found a fortnight after the Howard package that Labor led the Liberals by 12 percentage points when asked which side would deliver the best tax system. When swinging voters were asked whether Howard would deliver his tax cuts 49 per cent said 'no', 33 per cent said 'yes', 12 per cent were undecided and another 12 per cent said it depended upon circumstances.[10]

A month after Howard's tax launch a Morgan poll showed a 51 to 42 per cent majority for the existing tax system rather than Howard's low tax government/spending cuts alternative—a damning outcome.[11]

Howard's mistake was obvious in retrospect. He should have released his package several months before, made the tax cuts more modest and identified all the spending cuts. That would have weakened Labor's attack and eliminated the credibility issue.

The evidence is overwhelming that Howard's great tax gamble failed to persuade enough swinging voters and was unable to repair the credibility damage sustained by the non-Labor side over the latter part of the parliamentary term. This was a necessary condition for Hawke's 1987 election victory.

Hawke's policy speech on 23 June was a superb blend of television craft, research based politics and a touch of indulgence. Hawke arrived at the Opera House by barge from Kirribilli while inside Roger Woodward played Chopin and Julie Anthony sang the national anthem in a two-hour show orchestrated by Peter Faiman of Crocodile Dundee fame.

Hawke made one pledge above all others: that his government would continue 'the great task of national renewal, reconstruction and revitalisation'. He depicted the Liberals as the agents of economic vandalism and social devastation. Labor, by contrast, was dedicated but measured; it 'would not shirk the hard decisions' nor succumb to 'the soft options'.

The essence of Hawke's speech was to kindle emotions of confidence in his government since he had no major promises. Hawke's main initiative, devised with Howe and Keating, was an unfunded $400 million program centred upon a new family allowance supplement. The full entitlement would be made where the family income was below $300 a week. A total of 500 000 families and one million children would benefit. The scheme was an example of Labor's orientation of the welfare system towards the needy and it won wide support. It was also designed to reinvigorate the ALP's working class base. The accompanying documents said that under this scheme 'no child will need to live in poverty'. But this was converted in Hawke's televised policy speech to read: 'By 1990 no Australian child will be living in poverty.'

No pledge made by Hawke during his prime ministership attracted more ridicule and contempt. But few promises have been associated with a more

350

worthy initiative. It was a political blunder but symptomatic of Labor's need to win an election on rhetoric since it had few dollars on offer. Hawke and Keating paraded their virtue: while Howard offered a $7.3 billion tax cut for the middle class they offered $400 million for poor children. Labor's electoral fears were understandable.

They were reflected by Bob McMullan in his post-election report as Labor's campaign director: 'The biggest problem for the Government and party in the campaign was to overcome the adverse reaction to the fall in living standards which had taken place as a result of the international economic situation.'

Hawke and Keating showed courage in fighting a 'no major pledges' election and relying upon unity, management and leadership. Hawke's pitch was honed on the research brief from ANOP which sought an election win on Labor's perceived superiority as a governing party. The professionals saw Hawke's launch as a triumph but the policy analysts were unhappy. One commentator said Hawke's speech 'is short on vision, fails to address the ongoing economic challenge and is unable to spell out an agenda for Labor's third term.'[12]

Such criticism stung Hawke into a response which became a milestone. In his 6 July 1987 speech at Ballarat Hawke sought—for the first and only time in the election—to identify a third term agenda for his government. It was, in effect, the next stage of the battle to make Australia a more productive country. It was this speech which marked the origin of Labor's micro-economic reform program which became fundamental to its third and fourth terms.[13] Later Keating announced his plan to make tariff cuts a priority in the next term. These were the most important policy contributions from Labor's reelection campaign, although they received little campaign attention and did not affect the result.

The atmospherics of the campaign changed with Howard's policy speech on 25 June, when he seized the chance partially to relaunch his platform. In a television address and separate live launch at Sydney's art deco State Theatre—a cross between matinee nostalgia and religious revivalism—Howard projected himself as the homespun hero. He made the absence of campaign razzamatazz into a virtue. Introduced as the leader who 'believes in the values of Middle Australia—God, Queen and country', Howard began: 'We all agree on at least one thing in this election campaign: our country's in a big economic mess . . . I believe the one and only way Australia can get on top of its economic problems is to become more productive. That means giving everyone—you, me, your friends, your family, everybody else—more incentive, more encouragement and more reason to work harder. Because if we all work harder then our country will produce more.' This was the marketing position on which Howard ran for the final three weeks.

The Howard message was strong, clear and simple—incentive was the brand name. Howard said the 'fundamental difference' between himself and Hawke was that 'I'm not asking you to trust me, I'm trusting you'. In his effort to project a new value system Howard declared a 'work for the dole' scheme and the principle that people who have children should carry the financial responsibility of looking after them. Howard savaged the Hawke record as high inflation, high interest rates, record overseas debt, high taxation and massive spending—the start of an effective onslaught against Labor's negatives.

The myth of the 1987 election is that Hawke outcampaigned Howard. It is a judgement not shared by ALP headquarters, whose members realised that Howard's personal effort was excellent. Howard's campaign was undermined by poor strategy, weak organisation, blunders, disunity and the arithmetic error (the areas of Howard's real weakness).

The Age's Michelle Grattan, who saw the campaign as closely as anybody, concluded:

> Howard is a good campaigner. That Young Liberal debating experience stands him in good stead . . . The area in which Howard has won the campaign is in campaigning itself, especially the launch, where his no-frills approach outshone the more staged Hawke effort . . . Howard had to wear the disaster of wrong figures. Interestingly, Howard's revival came after these disasters. His strength is his tenacity, his evenness . . . there's none of the up-and-down indulgence of Bob Hawke. His greatest asset has probably been his wife Janette, who, as one senior Liberal says, is without doubt his best staffer.[14]

Howard, unlike Hawke, tried to project a program for the next parliament, its paradox being that 'Honest John' needed to be 'Super John' to implement the agenda. Despite the traumas within non-Labor politics, Howard's 1987 platform was further evidence of the transformation of Liberal politics since the early 1980s. His platform was radical in content and sweeping in scope: a massive tax–spending switch; deregulation of the labour market which allowed voluntary contracts outside the central system; a large scale privatisation program; deregulation of the communications and transport industries; and the gradual dismantling of Australia's trade protection system. It was a testimony to the triumph of the free market theorists within the Liberal Party.

But Howard never sought to explain how his radical agenda would work. How would he prevent a wages break-out? What guarantees could he offer about funding the tax cuts? What timetable did he have to cut protection? Were more real wages cuts required? Howard, contrary to his claims, asked people to take him on trust.

Neither Hawke nor Howard had the courage to tell people the true dimension of the national malaise or that living standards must fall in the transition towards to a more competitive economy. The *Sydney Morning*

Herald's economics editor Ross Gittins summarised: 'Both sides are seeking to mislead unthinking voters about the prospects for living standards . . . initially Labor managed to avoid an explicit claim that "the worst is over". But first Mr Hawke yielded to temptation, then Paul Keating did.'[15]

Hawke and Howard were doomed by the traditions of Australian politics to make promises that were irrelevant in the new phase of history over which they were presiding. I wrote:

> They cannot promise to hold or lift our living standards because no Australian Prime Minister today has this power. Nobody, therefore, should believe such promises. Domestic economic policy is driven by external forces . . . this means that past practice is no guide to the future. There is no longer any natural party of government. Australia's direction is clear. It is not going to be changed by this election. Australia is moving to the right and the trend will continue. The agenda must be spending restraint, wage restraint, more efficient industrial and work practices, a better skilled workforce, a greater store by market forces to produce a more dynamic private sector, a lesser tax burden . . . Australia has just started the big adjustment. It might be a 10 year process, or, if initially mishandled, a 20 year exercise. Hawke and Howard would have done better this election to come clean. Perhaps the voters suspect the truth.[16]

In technical terms the Labor campaign was more broadly based in its appeal than that of the Liberals. The ALP targeted working women, migrants and above all the emerging environmental movement. Labor put in place a 'green' strategy which helped its win on preferences, influenced by Graham Richardson who declared that the environmental lobby was an alienated group that Labor had to win back. The 1987 strategy was a prelude to Labor's spectacular 'preference strategy' which Richardson would mastermind as a minister in the 1990 election.

Before the 1987 election the government listed its environmental priorities in three areas—the Tasmanian forests, the North Queensland rainforests, and Kakadu National Park.

In a meeting facilitated by Richardson between Hawke and Tasmanian activist Dr Bob Brown, Hawke promised that the federal government would preserve national estate values on the question of logging in national estate areas. Hawke's action led to direct clashes between the federal government and the Tasmanian Liberal government, and to the establishment of the Helsham Inquiry into the Tasmanian forests.

The most important stand taken by the Hawke government pre-election was its pledge to seek World Heritage Listing of the North Queensland rainforests. This reversed an earlier stance of non-interference from the federal minister, Barry Cohen. Hawke agreed to the new policy at a meeting with Australian Conservation Foundation (ACF) director Phillip Toyne, and its consultant Simon Balderstone, later Richardson's and Hawke's environ-mental adviser. The announcement was made on election eve.

Kakadu National Park also saw another win for the Toyne–Balderstone ACF team. They persuaded Hawke and his resources minister, Gareth Evans, to proclaim, immediately before the election, Stage III of Kakadu National Park, on which the Cabinet had agreed in principle in December 1986. The exact Stage III boundaries were still subject to debate over conservation and resource use. Cabinet decided on 4 June 1987, without a formal submission, to declare Stage III of Kakadu, although surveys were not completed. It was a straight political decision.

If Labor were reelected, the Cabinet Decision provided for a final clarification of the boundaries on the basis that the area for mineral explo-ration would not be increased. The Decision said that 'any change should, as far as practicable, maximise the area of the Park around sites of particular environmental and heritage value'. So the ACF had secured the prospect of a further expansion of Stage III later. Its superior influence was revealed in the wording of the Cabinet Decision, which said the minister would endeav-our to settle the final boundaries within ten weeks 'in consultation with the ACF and other relevant interests'.

The ACF and the other main lobby, The Wilderness Society, run by Jonathon West, a former ALP adviser, announced during the campaign that they favoured a vote for the ALP in the House of Representatives and for the Australian Democrats in the Senate. The Liberals only alienated the greens by pledging to eliminate all government grants to the ACF, attacking the use of the external affairs power to secure World Heritage Listings, and saying that they would abolish the department. The environmental lobby ran a series of television commercials and put hundreds of workers into the field to defeat the Liberals and return Hawke. The greens later made an exaggerated claim that they delivered a Labor victory—yet they did help Labor to win some seats and they contributed to its margin overall.

The inside story of the ALP campaign was the tension between Hawke and his campaign HQ dominated by McMullan, Bob Hogg and Rod Cam-eron. The professionals recognised Hawke's leadership superiority over Howard as fundamental to Labor's success. But they believed that Hawke was a poor campaigner; that he lacked the discipline to adhere to a strategy; that his suggestions for television commercials and his insistence on more polls showing a Labor win were counter-productive; that he was a good front-runner but performed badly from behind.

During the last week a worried ALP resorted to the politics of fear. Singleton recorded his 'Wendy Woods' commercials, showing a housewife complaining about Howard's spending cuts. Relations between Hawke and McMullan almost collapsed. Cameron ended the campaign vowing that he would never work on a campaign for Hawke again. 'He thinks he knows but in fact he knows nothing about the swinging voter,' Cameron said. The

ALP professionals finished the election sceptical about Hawke as a campaigner and more impressed with Keating's demolition of Howard's credibility.[17] The most passionate figure on the election trail was always Keating—fighting for his policies, his power and, in Keating's mind, his government.

The victory gave Hawke a unique place in Labor's pantheon—the only ALP leader to win three elections. The triumph was fulfilment of his manifest destiny. Hawke's belief in his own invincibility was confirmed and deepened. Bob and Hazel assumed the intimations of a genuine 'first family'. An ANU study concluded that Hawke's popularity had been the decisive factor: 'If Hawke had been no more popular than his party; if the Liberal and National leaders had been at least as popular as theirs; and if nothing else had changed, then Labor would probably have lost the election by at least four seats.'[18]

But after the election Hawke's former aide, Peter Barron, rang Keating: 'You did a great job. My mate [Hawke] never laid a glove on Howard.' Keating believed that he had destroyed Howard and that his reward would be the prime ministership. But Keating was deluded; Hawke had secured a unique victory which neither Keating nor the ALP team could qualify. Hawke, in his own mind, had compensated for his poor 1984 campaign and success had recharged his batteries.

Labor was just shaded on the primary vote, winning 45.8 per cent against a total of 46.1 per cent for the Liberal and National parties. The Mackerras two-party preferred analysis (assuming a full distribution of preferences) shows a two-party preferred winning margin for Labor of 50.8 per cent to 49.2 per cent—a close result. Labor won on preferences. The national swing to the Opposition was 1 per cent compared with the 1984 election. But the story is more complex. Despite the swing to the Opposition the ALP increased its majority from 16 to 24 seats. Labor lost two seats but won six, four of them in Queensland. The Liberals lost four seats and won two while the Nationals lost two seats and won none.

Australia did not vote as a whole and regional differences were prominent. The anti-ALP swing was greatest in NSW at 2.6 per cent where there was an unpopular ALP state government. But in Queensland there was a 1.6 per cent pro-ALP swing, a bonus from Joh mayhem. The government kept the anti-Labor swing in Victoria to 0.8 per cent and lost only one seat in the state; this was fundamental to its win since half Labor's marginal seats were in Victoria.

Of the 148 seats, 96 saw a swing to non-Labor while 52 recorded a pro-ALP swing. The variation ranged from a 7.9 per cent Liberal swing in Fowler (NSW) to a 4.7 per cent swing to Labor in Denison (Tasmania). The real story of the result is that Labor got the swing where it mattered. The Liberals won huge swings in safe ALP seats but still failed to win those seats, while they made little impression in many of Labor's marginal seats.

355

The ALP tacticians claimed this showed the genius of their targeted campaign. In fact, it probably reflected the nature of the Hawke–Keating government, whose policies over several years had hurt much of Labor's traditional base vote but whose occupation of the electoral 'middle ground' combined with Hawke's appeal was effective in retaining the low to average middle class swinging voters.

Liberal director Tony Eggleton identified five factors which he believed denied the Opposition victory: lack of confidence in the alternative government; Labor's strong marginal seats campaign; the role of special interest groups, notably the greens; fluctuating demographic patterns which helped Labor in rural seats; and the blunders during the Liberal campaign.[19]

As campaign director Bob McMullan put the result into perspective: 'The main reason we didn't lose had nothing to do with targeting. Even if the swing had been uniform it wasn't big enough to beat us. That's why we didn't lose. The reason why we got a bigger majority was because of targeting.'[20]

McMullan ranked the factors which he believed had been responsible for Labor's reelection in order of importance: a vote of confidence in the government and the prime minister; the targeting of marginal seats; regional factors; and the support of pressure groups such as environmentalists.[21] But this list is limited to Labor's positives; it is obvious that the Opposition's negatives were also vital.

I summarised the dynamics of Labor's success the day after the election:

> The Labor victory is a campaign classic . . . in technical terms,
> probably the finest campaign waged in recent memory . . . Labor
> focused the campaign on the swinging voter and it got the swing where
> it mattered. [The result] reminds one that there is no longer any natural
> party of government . . . the basis of victory represents a fundamental
> change in the nature of the Labor Party. This time it was Labor that
> was reelected during the economic crisis. By contrast the old Labor
> Party would have lost by default, by dozens of seats. This historical
> pattern has been broken. This is the ultimate significance of the
> election for Labor.[22]

Simply, Labor won because it was seen as a better government than the non-Labor alternative, a perception which had developed during most of the previous two years. The result was a significant achievement given the severity of Australia's balance of payments problem during this time and the harsh remedies employed by the government. During the election period Labor waged a more skilful campaign than the Liberals and this enabled the government to counter the Opposition's greatest weapon: the fall in living standards which, by objective criteria, should have created a climate for a Labor defeat.

The Liberal campaign was strategically defective but Howard, from the time of his launch, fought with courage and commitment, a fact not fully grasped within his own party. Despite the coalition split, months of division and a tax policy that didn't compute, Howard came within a remote sniff of a remarkable victory. Ian Sinclair says: 'The amazing thing about the 1987 election is not that our side lost but that we came so close to winning'.[23]

But the National Party was humiliated. The 1987 result was a repudiation of the delusions of grandeur which had invaded the party. The swing against the Nationals in Queensland was 2.8 per cent, a result which helped to doom Howard and fatally undermined Bjelke-Petersen.

The defeat prompted the Nationals to commission a review prepared by their toughest veteran, Peter Nixon, which concluded of the Joh–Sparkes push:

> The effort was a failure . . . Not only was it completely unable to attract high calibre candidates to stand for House of Representatives seats, but also it was seen as divisive to the conservative cause . . . If the National Party is to remain an independent political force then it seems logical that it should concentrate its federal ambitions on (1) retaining and building on existing electoral support in rural areas and (2) widening its electoral appeal in provincial Australia.

The report said that after the 1987 poll the 61 rural and provincial seats were held as follows: 23 ALP, 16 Liberal and 18 National. In short, the Nationals were weak at their core and their survival as a party was at risk.[24]

The experience of 1987 reveals a failure to comprehend history within the non-Labor side, notably the National Party. The period since Federation shows that non-Labor success is a direct function of coalition solidarity and leadership intimacy. There are four such periods: S.M. Bruce and Earle Page in the 1920s; J.A. Lyons and Page in the 1930s; R.G. Menzies supported by Arthur Fadden and then John McEwen in the 1950s and 1960s; and finally, Fraser and Anthony in the 1970s. The entire reputation of the great National Party leaders were based upon their ability to win through the coalition an influence beyond their numbers. The notion that breaking the coalition was a route to National Party influence defied history, identity and contemporary trends. It was the action of a party that had lost grip on its own identity.

Nationals leader Ian Sinclair had an erratic election highlighted by some excessive rhetoric—suggesting at various times that Labor had some responsibility for the rape and murder of Anita Cobby and comparing Hawke with Charles Manson.

Howard's defeat involved two personal tragedies. The first was his failure to persuade the non-Labor side to believe in him. The second was his tactical failure to get the balance right in his tax package between economic credibility and electoral appeal.

The end of certainty

The Opposition was unready for the election and was unprepared to govern. Eggleton's post-election report virtually admitted as much. The campaign gaffes exposed the decline of professional skills within non-Labor politics and its subservience to Labor in terms of ministerial quality. These deficiencies would have translated into defects in office if Howard had prevailed. Victory would have left Howard with a narrow majority, a divided party, a hostile Senate, four antagonistic Labor premiers, a sniping trade union movement, a Cabinet of dubious quality, sceptical media and a business community with reservations. It was scarcely the climate for a successful non-Labor reformist government.

Howard's defeat had an historic significance for the free market lobby. It revealed that, while this force now dominated the Liberal Party, the free market political movement had failed comprehensively to formulate the necessary conditions to win an election. The free market ideologues had failed to unite their own side; they had failed to devise an electoral strategy which successfully marketed their program; they had failed to grasp either the weaknesses in their 'radical right' agenda which Labor could exploit, or to develop a consciousness as genuine reformers trying to propagate an agenda for change. They had failed to win elite opinion to their side, with the major broadsheets, the *Sydney Morning Herald* and *The Age*, backing Labor and the *Financial Review* staying neutral. (*The Australian* supported the Liberals.) While they won many swinging voters this was the result of hostility towards Labor and the Liberal's tax bait—not because grassroots Australia shared the free market vision of the new generation Liberals.

Malcolm Fraser challenged much of the free market orthodoxy in his post-election assessment: 'The movement of Bob Hawke and Paul Keating into the middle ground should not dismay any Liberal. It does not mean that the Liberals should move further to the right to seek new and exclusive ground. If the Hawke/Keating changes in the Labor Party come to be permanent, the political debate will more than ever be about competence. It will be less and less about ideology. That is healthy for Australia.'[25]

Many Liberals disagreed, convinced that their free market philosophy was not just correct but would eventually find Labor wanting.

But the 1987 election campaign—the first under Australia's new political rules—had gone to Labor. The new rules, a function of the inevitable internationalisation of the economy, boiled down to two premises: that Australia was facing economic decline and that the solution was a structural and cultural change in the economy and society. Hawke and Keating, after their victory, depicted themselves as figures of destiny: the times had brought forth the leaders. But history is a cruel practical joker for those who pretend to be its master: this would become the moral for Labor's third term.

PART IV

BOOM AND BUST

19
The 1980s boom

He who would be rich in a day will be hanged in a year.
Leonardo Da Vinci, as quoted by Reserve Bank deputy
governor, John Phillips, June 1990

The Labor Party's victory at the 1987 election saw the Hawke government succumb to a euphoria which generated a complacency about its ability to manage Australia's economic difficulties. Labor fell victim, in about equal measure, to its own misjudgements and a series of surprise events, of which the most surprising was a consumption and investment boom. Hawke's third term was dominated by this boom, one of the strongest in Australian history, whose power and longevity confounded all official and private prognostications. Its momentum was maintained despite high real interest rates, the greatest sharemarket crash since the 1930s, and a series of downgradings of Australia's international credit rating.

Labor had waited a long time for the investment surge which began seriously in 1987–88. Its policy settings for several years had been geared to produce this effect—an early fiscal stimulus, high profits, low wages, financial deregulation and then fiscal restraint. In early 1987 a frustrated Cabinet asked for a study on why there had been no investment surge—but then it arrived with a thump.

The 1980s boom had the power of a crazy rollercoaster. Just as quickly stopping a car travelling at 150 kilometres will damage the driver more than halting from a 50-kilometre speed, so the power of the 1980s boom meant that its termination was a high risk exercise. It was the boom's power that made a recession so likely. The Hawke government made two great mistakes in its third term: it allowed the boom to get out of control, and its application of the brakes through monetary policy caused a sharp recession.

This was a failure of both ministerial judgement and the Reserve Bank's application of monetary policy. The recession was the turning point in the

361

history of the Hawke government. It discredited Keating and it led finally to Hawke's overthrow as prime minister.

The boom was caused by a series of self-reinforcing factors—a surge in national income from strong commodity prices, a reckless expansion of bank lending without proper credit risk assessment, a sustained shift in national income from wages to profits, a strong international economy, the entrepreneurial psychology of perpetual expansion, and a failure in the conduct of monetary policy. It is obvious that domestic mistakes occurred but they must be viewed within the context of greater global phenomena, notably the explosion in world liquidity and the shift in captital towards the Anglo-Saxon nations. It is doubtful whether any Australian government would have been able to avoid a boom and subsequent recession. This is the judgement against which domestic policy should be assessed.

The Hawke Government failed in the precision with which it conducted monetary policy—but precision and monetary policy are rarely companions. The real defect within Labor's approach was its substitution of risk for prudence in the overall settings of economic policy after the 1987 election. Labor ran both fiscal and monetary policy too soft, given the economic conditions. This was a function of a deeper mistake—Labor's complacency about Australia's trading and debt crisis, the 'banana republic' legacy. Hawke and Keating fell into the trap, after the 1987 election, of underestimating the national challenge. Hawke, buoyed by three election wins and deceived by his own success, went soft. Keating, dazzled by his economic progress and the spectre of the prime ministership, became infatuated with the myth of his own invincibility. Having survived the 1986 exchange rate crisis, Keating believed that he could pull the economic levers with an exactitude that defied the contemporary experience.

Hawke and Keating declared in the first half of this term, their third, that Australia's problems were solved. Hawke pledged sustained rises in living standards; Keating declared the banana republic economic management was 'bringing home the bacon'. They announced a false dawn and then had to endure humiliation, a legacy from which the Hawke government would not recover its public esteem.

The recession represented the negation of the Labor model, since Hawke and Keating had pledged from 1986 that Labor would solve the external payments crisis without a recession. The coalition was the recession specialist, Keating had trumpeted. Labor's failure was stark, since the early 1990s recession was domestically induced: the first domestically induced downturn since the 1960s credit squeeze in the Menzies period.

Three election wins bred an arrogance within Hawke and Keating counter-productive to effective government. They were irked by any analysis suggesting that it was the Opposition's failure rather than Labor's genius which was responsible for their 1987 election victory. Hawke lost his sense of priorities and ineptly attempted to implement his ideals of an Aboriginal

Treaty, large-scale constitutional reforms and international diplomatic rec-ognition, while Keating began to spin a psychology of economic infallibility.

After their election win Hawke and Keating were impatient to claim the spoils of success, but were uncertain of their exact location. The irony of the September 1987 budget, brought down two months after the election, is that its excellent reception disguised its masterly inactivity. Keating went into a holding pattern and where Keating went the government followed.

The key to the 1987–88 budget's ecstatic reception was the reduction of the deficit to just on zero, a mere $27 million. Keating, for all practical purposes, had brought down a balanced budget. With one exception it was the lowest deficit result in thirty years. For a nation that had lived with the psychology of budget deficits for as long as Australia had, this result enhanced Keating's credentials with finance, business and the media. By this stage even the ALP left had half-accepted that tight fiscal policy was one of the essential ingredients in Australia's economic restructuring. On the first page of his budget speech, Keating hailed the elimination of the virtual $10 billion Fraser deficit inheritance over five years as a 'monumen-tal achievement'.

Keating was able to produce a superb set of figures—a 2.4 per cent real reduction in spending, which meant that the 1987–88 budget was the toughest spending budget for thirty years. Spending, taxation receipts, and the deficit were all falling relative to GDP—only the third time in thirty years that a budget had achieved such an outcome. It was tempting to see this budget as establishing the foundations for three years of a public sector surplus under Labor which, by improving Australia's savings, would combat the call on overseas savings at the heart of the balance of payments problem. Keating became the hero of the bourse—a mantle which he gratefully accepted.

The absolute dominance which Keating exercised over the Cabinet is revealed by the fact that finance minister Peter Walsh did not know until the day before the budget that the deficit had been abolished, and other senior Cabinet ministers were told only an hour before Keating delivered his speech. 'You bastard', John Kerin muttered through clenched teeth. Keating, in fact, treated his colleagues with contempt. Peter Walsh reports: 'There was no surplus target or even explicit ERC [Cabinet] decision to take the budget into surplus. The surplus was residual, a function of growth and other policy decisions.'[1] Cabinet was kept ignorant of the exact fiscal policy projections when the budget was being framed and was not trusted with knowledge of the outcome. Formal Cabinet approval of a balanced budget never even arose. The Cabinet was hostage to Keating's tactics of manipulation of the markets with a final figure far below their expectations.

Three days after the budget, Keating unveiled for *Midday* show host Ray Martin a new vision: 'the great coming age of Australia . . . the golden age of economic change'. Keating said he would have to take 'a very large part' of the credit. It was a blue skies future. He told the National Press Club that these changes would take Australia through to the next century.

There were many hardheads who were unpersuaded. John Stone called the budget 'a total abdication of economic responsibility' and said Labor's policy 'constituted not a strategy but a high-risk on-going accident waiting for somewhere to happen'.[2] But the most notable sceptic was Peter Walsh, who broke from Keating's strategy in the most public budget policy Cabinet split of the Hawke era.

Walsh drew two elementary conclusions after the election victory. First, the time for a government to impose the harsh economic medicine is at its first budget in the new parliamentary term. Second, it was a statistical fact that Australia's foreign debt problem was still deepening and that more urgent measures were required to address it.

Within a month of the election Walsh tried to prepare the government and the public for a tougher policy by taking the unusual step of identifying 13 major spending programs in areas of welfare, education and veterans' assistance as targets for greater restraint. Walsh warned that in addressing its foreign debt, the central national problem, Australia had three options: imposing upon itself a catastrophic depression of the 1930s variety; ignoring the problem until such a depression was imposed from outside; or the balanced approach of seeking to stabilise and then reverse foreign debt through a combination of consumption restraint, economic restructuring and productivity growth. While Labor had correctly chosen the third approach Walsh warned 'we have not been moving as quickly as the externally imposed circumstances demand'.

Walsh believed that the reconstruction of the Australian economy would take longer than did Keating, a judgement which lay at the heart of their differences. It was more a function of personality than intellect; Keating was as resolute an optimist as Walsh was a pessimist. Walsh said: 'The comprador ethos of Australian capitalism and the traditional anti-productivity ethos of Australian unionism are still too common to accommodate the adjustment required. And, regarding the public sector, a subliminal community belief that services can be delivered without being paid for, persists.'[3]

But Walsh was swept aside in the budget process. Keating was now utterly dominant. Labor was in no mood to recast its policy post-election onto a tighter footing. Keating pointed to the balanced budget and mocked such an idea. But most of the fiscal restraint in the 1987–88 budget represented the impact of decisions taken before the election, not in the post-election budget process. Post-election, Labor had a dizzy head from its celebratory champagne.

On 19 September 1987, four days after the budget, in a speech to Labor lawyers Walsh attacked Keating's strategy, claiming that the budget was 'oversold' and that it ran the risk of making the public 'complacent'. Walsh recalled an anecdote from 1986, saying that he knew of two hundred programs unjustified on equity or social grounds which the government had lacked the courage to scrap. He said if commodity prices fell again then 'the IMF will be knocking on the door'. Walsh attacked one of his favourite targets—the middle-class demand for non-profit, taxpayer-subsidised child care—and volunteered that 'if we don't challenge most of the absurd notions that the majority of Australians have about what they are entitled to . . . then we are going down the Argentinian road'.[4]

Hawke and Keating sank into a scarcely repressed fury. Hawke censured Walsh in private and Keating repudiated him in public. Walsh told Hawke he hadn't known that the media was present when he made his remarks. Hawke claimed in public that Walsh's remarks had not breached Cabinet solidarity. Keating blamed Walsh for undermining his budget. Howard asked the government how it reconciled Keating's new 'golden age' with Walsh's 'Argentinian road'. John Stone said Walsh should be praised not buried. Walsh, in fact, had exposed a conflict at the heart of the government.

Walsh now sees the period after the 1987 election as the turning point for the Hawke government. He says: 'I think there was a watershed around that period and that partly through fatigue in the budget which followed the 1987 election there was little, if any, will to make significant changes . . . the government was either too complacent or too exhausted or a mixture of both . . . we missed an opportunity at a budget after an election which we had won.'[5]

The case against the budget was summarised by one of its few media critics, the *Sydney Morning Herald*'s economic editor, Ross Gittins: 'Hidden behind Mr Keating's apparent good-housekeeping is a complacency born of fatigue. This is the "she'll-be-right" budget . . . the budget of a government which has tired of wielding the razor and which could use a long holiday . . . Mr Keating runs the risk that the economy will grow more quickly than he expects with consumer spending spilling into imports and limiting the improvement in the current account deficit.'[6]

Such scepticism reflected the fears among the policy advisers about the high risks inherent in Labor's strategy. An exposition of this position came from the former head of treasury's economic policy division and director of the Business Council of Australia, Peter McLaughlin, who said in September 1987:

> The government faced two clear alternatives in finalising this budget: (1) To take advantage of its re-election . . . to bring down a very tough budget now. The argument for this is that it would reduce the risks a year or two out if the world economy hits the rough patch being predicted by many; or (2) To stick basically with its May 1987 statement and continue the gradual approach which involves higher growth now but great risks down the track.
> They have opted for the latter mainly I suspect because of sheer fatigue and because they locked themselves in during the election

campaign . . . In fact, there is a significant chance that two or three years from now this budget will be seen as a lost opportunity.[7]

The options McLaughlin identified were, in fact, the positions taken by Walsh and Keating respectively. In retrospect, McLaughlin says: 'At that time we were around year eight of a very extended period of current account deficits that were way above average. The corporate sector was worried about the build-up in foreign debt and the Business Council was looking for a budget which would slow the economy quite significantly and even bring on a mild recession. The 1987 budget was seen at the time by some people as an economic and political mistake.'[8]

Another former senior economic adviser, Shell's economist and later principal with Access Economics, Ed Shann, said:

Is it appropriate for Australia to have the highest GDP growth after Turkey in 1987 and 1988—as I believe is likely? If you consider Australia still has an external debt problem—and I do—the answer is obvious. No . . . I am not suggesting Australia should have a recession. I am suggesting that we will be better off in the long run having a lower, but sustainable growth rate for several years, until our external debt has been lowered, rather than having a boomlet that runs the risk of bust.[9]

The 1987–88 budget was pivotal because its settings and its psychology established the framework for Labor's third term, which finished in recession. In this budget Keating maintained the economics of his banana republic stance from 1986 but effectively abandoned the politics. It is hard to institutionalise a crisis mentality, particularly when the fickle markets had declared Australia the new fashion.

In 1987 commodity prices rose, the $A began to appreciate strongly, the world economy was buoyant, the current account fell from 6 to 4 per cent of GDP, capital inflow began to surge, and the recent mood of pessimism died amid booming share and property markets. After a whiff of panic in 1986 the nation was chasing some fast money. Australia was about to enter a new phase over the following 21 months—a false dawn. It was a time of intense danger for a nation that was still taking more from the world than it was returning.

The crisis of 1986 had surrendered to the false optimism of 1987. Most of this change in climate was attributable to factors beyond Labor's control although it is true that Keating's wage and fiscal restraint left the distinct impression of a properly managed economy which further boosed confidence. In one sense this gathering boom was symptomatic of the Australian malaise; it was a mini version of the old cargo cult facilitated by sophisticated financial instruments; a variation of the resource-based 'free ride' which Australia could enjoy today and forget tomorrow. The underlying crisis facing Australia, which Keating had identified in 1986, still remained—Australia had to stabilise its foreign debt, move resources into the traded goods sector to improve its trading position and run a more productive economy.

The historic choice Keating made in the 1987–88 budget was that the Labor government would continue to solve these problems through a growth strategy, which defied the orthodoxy. For Keating orthodoxies existed to be smashed. The orthodox response in this situation was to lean towards prudent economics, particularly just after an election. That meant slowing the economy, cutting imports, dampening debt accumulation even at the cost of higher unemployment. This was the message from the critics: post-election is the time to err on the side of being too tough rather than too slack. But Keating was driven by other factors which revealed the government's character.

First, Keating was honouring Labor's 1987 election pledges that there would be no major spending cuts in its next budget—so it was part of the price of reelection. Second, he was confirming that the Accord pledged Labor to the economics of growth, and the trade-off for the real wages cuts borne by the unions was the creation of new jobs. Keating's growth strategy originated within the institutional imperative of the Accord. He promised the creation of another 100 000 jobs in 1987–88 which would keep unemployment steady at 8.3 per cent—in short, Keating refused to set tighter policies which would lift the unemployment rate. Third, Keating wanted to switch Labor's political priorities to consolidate its electoral base after two years of tough wages and fiscal policies. People had borne a lot of pain and it was time for Labor to offer some dividend, not just sacrifice. The Keating strategy was higher growth, higher risk and slower structural adjustment within the economy. Hawke agreed.

Keating was taking a calculated gamble but the economic professionals had no doubt that it was a gamble. The treasury ventilated its fears in the budget papers in a long discussion about Australia's 'pace of adjustment' to combat its foreign debt, inspired by the head of its economic division, David Morgan. It was couched in equivocal terms, since Keating would not allow the treasury to insert an explicit critique of government policy. Morgan says: 'We had two objectives. We wanted to say that the budget strategy could work but we also wanted people to grasp this was a high-risk strategy which contained no margin for error.'[10]

However a contrary perspective is provided by then treasury secretary, Bernie Fraser, who defends Keating's strategy:

A feature of the 1980s was that employment creation was excellent. In Australia growth was strong and this objective was pursued, rightly in my opinion. Of course, you can avoid the risks of excessive growth by not having any prosperity. But there's not much future in that. At the same time, there must be speed limits on growth.[11]

The mistake Keating made in the late 1980s was to take out insufficient policy insurance against the risks of excessive growth. Yet this was the time when such insurance was more necessary than ever, since the imbalances in the international economy were severe and the English-speaking democracies had embarked upon a grand but unpredictable experiment in financial deregulation. Keating's defence was that his fiscal policy, judged by historical standards, was very tight — yet the extraordinary climate of the 1980s boom was undermining such historical comparisons.

Keating forgot that a minister trying to manage an economy held a humble post; the array of levers he had at his disposal offered a deceptive picture of control when nobody could predict the exact consequences once the levers were moved into different positions.

At this point the nature of Labor's economic model, driven by its political imperatives, became fundamental to the mistakes that followed. This was the Keating–Accord–treasury model, a trinity in conception and influence. In tackling Australia's current account deficit the model had three prescriptions: fiscal policy was pitched towards the medium-term objective of increasing the level of national savings; wages policy through the Accord was designed to restrain wage costs; and monetary policy as implemented by the Reserve was the 'swing' instrument designed to fine-tune the economy. If the economy was running too fast or too slow then interest rates would be raised or lowered respectively to fine-tune economic activity. This was the approach of, among others, influential treasury deputy Chris Higgins, who later succeeded Fraser as head of the department, and it was the model championed by Keating. It placed a great onus on monetary policy.

However a fundamental aspect of power in the Hawke government was that the Cabinet did not take monetary policy decisions. Changes in monetary policy were not referred to Cabinet or to a monetary policy committee of Cabinet, which had been the practice during Fraser's government. Keating made monetary policy himself, in conjunction with his advisers in the treasury and the Reserve Bank, which had official responsibility for the conduct of a monetary policy. But Keating's practice was to consult with Hawke, always. There is no record of Hawke ever overruling Keating on a monetary policy recommendation. The Cabinet was just not involved.

Peter Walsh says 'In the first budget and possibly the second, Cabinet decisions were made about a monetary growth target, but when we abandoned targeting monetary growth I do not recall any specific Cabinet decision being made on monetary policy. There were discussions about the economy which touched on monetary policy from time to time. But formal decisions were outside the Cabinet.'[12]

This was an extraordinary situation and provides an insight into the nature of power within the Hawke government. Monetary policy dictated the level of interest rates, the cost of capital for investment and returns on investments for lenders. There was no more important tool of economic management and none with the same direct impact on households and business. One of the consequences was that 'Keating as Treasurer bore the political responsibility for the conduct of monetary policy and it is a responsibility he acknowledges and accepts'.[13]

During the late 1980s there was an intense intellectual debate about the making of monetary policy. The Opposition finally adopted the position that a new Reserve Bank charter was required to allow the Bank to set monetary policy on an independent basis according to the re-weighted objectives in its charter in favour of low inflation. Keating attacked this line, insisting that interest rate policy must remain the responsibility of the government and that removing this responsibility to non-elected officials was a diminution of democracy. It is clear, however, that the Opposition (and the media) overlooked a central element in decision-making in the Hawke era—the absence of a proper Cabinet approach to interest rate and monetary policy.

Keating's outlook was obvious: that monetary policy was far too sensitive and lethal to expose to the vagaries of a Cabinet discussion.

The issue of Cabinet access to economic data had first erupted in 1985–86 when Bill Hayden, a former treasurer, demanded that the quarterly economic forecasts be provided to the Cabinet. An intense Keating–Hayden brawl over two days promptly ensued. Keating refused, insisted the material was too technical and claimed it was unnecessary. Hayden replied that these arguments were similar to those once put to him by John Stone. Finally Keating relented—'you can have them if you want to'—but a few months later the sub-committee of ministers supposed to review the forecasts stopped meeting. Hayden reflected later that Keating had won.

The message was that Keating used the Cabinet when he wanted collective responsibility for decisions but often kept other decisions away from Cabinet lest it interfere with his own policy. For example, Keating used Cabinet to build consensus for his fiscal policy through the ERC, but never trusted monetary policy to Cabinet.

The first casualty of the gigantic swings in the economic cycle from late 1986 to early 1988 was the Reserve Bank. Its prime responsibility is the management of monetary policy and it made manifestly faulty judgements. This was not just a circumstantial failure. It was a failure of economic theory on a global scale. Financial deregulation had destroyed the 1970s orthodoxies in monetary policy and left the central banks around the world bereft of any new approach to guide their conduct. The economic and political history of the 1980s is indissolubly linked to the inability of central banks, typified by the Reserve Bank, to identify a new star to guide their monetary management during the initial years of deregulation. It was not just a failure of practice or courage; it was a comprehensive failure of economic theory virtually worldwide.

It arose from the abject confusion post-1984 as the authorities had great trouble making much sense of the monetary and credit aggregates. This was a departure from the previous decade where money supply was targeted on the Friedmanite assumption of a close link between money supply and inflation. Such relative certitudes were now destroyed. Monetary policy in the mid-1980s became an exercise in chaos management. It is important to grasp that there was a double confusion: it was difficult to measure the monetary aggregates as a result of deregulation but, more significantly, there was confusion over the precise objectives of monetary policy.

The keys to the 1990s recession in Australia and globally lie in this confusion. Its most universal consequence was the tolerance of excessive money and credit expansion which contributed to an overheated global economy by 1987. It was not just an Australian problem; it was an international problem. It is accurate but easy to criticise the Reserve Bank. A more balanced assessment is that the Bundesbank was probably the only major central bank to emerge from the 1980s with its reputation relatively intact.[14]

Following deregulation the Reserve Bank opted for compromise and announced in 1985 that monetary policy would be determined according to a checklist of factors that involved six main variables: interest rates, the exchange rate, the balance of payments, economic activity, inflation, and money and credit aggregates. It became a moveable feast for priorities from one season to the next. It has been described as 'a piece of political subterfuge of which Sir Humphrey Appleby would be proud'.[15]

The result was that the Reserve Bank changed monetary policy many times during the decade with a lack of consistency. Former treasury deputy, now Westpac director, David Morgan, offers this critique: 'The checklist approach tends to encourage a "steady as she goes" approach whereby monetary policy is merely dragged along in the wake of a market sentiment. Because the checklist approach is a mishmash of ultimate targets, intermediate targets and instruments, it clouds the ultimate objective of monetary policy.'[16]

Former Reserve Bank governor Bob Johnston admits that the checklist was used until somebody thought of a better idea. Former deputy governor John Phillips cautions against seeing the adoption of the checklist as a 'sharp break', saying it was 'only a modest change in approach'.[17] Johnston agrees that most nations put a higher priority on price stability than Australia during this period. He also concedes that the Reserve pursued different objectives in this period—including promotion of private investment through low rates and trying to kickstart the economy.

The first important mistake made by the Reserve and Keating was to ease monetary policy too much in the year before the October 1987 sharemarket crash. Contrary to subsequent Opposition claims, this was not an easing imposed by Keating on the Reserve for political reasons. It was rather a policy advocated by the Reserve for a series of economic reasons. Starting in late 1986 the Reserve began to cut interest rates—a stance that was followed, with variations, for the next year. In the process the Reserve was unconsciously and unknowingly preparing the terrain for the boom—a boom which it then had to kill in 1989.

The Reserve adopted its late 1986 policy of cutting interest rates for three reasons. First, there was concern that ongoing high interest rates would flatten the economy or cause a mild recession in 1987. Keating wanted lower interest rates in 1987 after the high interest rates which had been used to slow the economy during the 1985–86 banana republic crisis.

Second, the low interest rate policy appeared economically responsible, since Keating had tightened fiscal policy and cut real wages with the objective of transferring the burden of policy from interest rates to the budget. The thrust of Keating's 1986 policy and his May 1987 package with its \$4 billion fiscal tightening foreshadowed in February that year was to establish the basis for lower interest rates and restore economic confidence. The Reserve was even more enthusiastic than Keating about the fiscal/monetary policy trade-off involved. The Reserve told Keating that lower interest rates were the result of his fiscal discipline—'the fruits of your hard work', they said. 'It's the price of fiscal success,' Bob Johnston advised Keating.

Finally, from late 1986 there was a dramatic change in sentiment towards the \$A, which now began to appreciate sharply, a surprise development. This was the result of rising commodity prices, capital inflows and better speculative returns in Australia given relative world interest rates. The Reserve was alarmed that a rising \$A would undermine the strategy of a low exchange rate to make Australian exports competitive. It began to target the exchange rate to limit the appreciation by weakening monetary conditions and cutting interest rates. Bob Johnston points out that 'we were getting lots of complaints from the resource exporters about how they were killed by the rising exchange rate'.[18]

Australia, in fact, experienced a commodity price surge during 1987–89, a complete reversal of its commodity price collapse in 1985–86. The nation, still reeling from the 1986 shock, hardly realised that a booming world economy was lifting commodity prices, so that Australia's terms of trade rose by 27 per cent, equivalent to a rise in national income of 4.3 per cent over the 1987–89 period. But Keating and the Reserve knew; they had to cope with the spending demands from such a rapid income boost.

The incident is a reminder of a fundamental feature of the 1980s almost universally downplayed—that many of the wild fluctuations during the decade were a function of the price the international market paid for Australian commodities. Paul Keating's economic policy was not just about a basic reorientation of Australia during the decade. It was simultaneously trying to handle these two great overseas induced income shocks—a commodity price collapse, and then boom—which forced swift change in national spending and the exchange rate.[19]

The effect of the above three trends was a falling interest rate climate

371

during the 1987 general election. The irony, which never occurred at the time to Labor or the Reserve, was that interest rates had fallen too far.

Keating continued this strategy with his post-election 1987–88 budget which was greeted with immediate falls in interest rates as the banks slashed their prime rates and home loan rates. He boasted that the 90-day bill rate had fallen from 19 per cent to 12.5 per cent in the year to September 1987. On the night of the 1987 budget he predicted more interest rate cuts, saying he would be happy to tighten rates later if they fell too much.[20]

Reserve governor Bob Johnston defended his monetary philosophy, saying that the objective of 'exchange rate stability' was not inconsistent with the 'checklist indicators'. In his public remarks at the time Johnston said the easing in interest rates was justified by the fiscal tightening.[21] But as 1987 advanced a deep reassessment was underway at the Reserve, with the conclusion that monetary policy was too loose.

The economy, in fact, was like a growing avalanche fed by disparate sources—world growth, commodity prices, bank lending, asset price inflation and high profits. It possessed a gathering momentum which nobody had fully grasped. Long afterwards Bob Johnston said: 'It wasn't very long before we recognised that the policy was threatening to become too loose and it's almost certain that we would have been taking some restrictive action that would have lifted interest rates around July/August/September 1987.'[22]

This is confirmed by John Phillips: 'We had started in September 1987 to reverse policy. We were contemplating at that point a tightening of monetary policy.'[23]

The truth is that monetary policy should have been tightened before mid-1987. John Phillips says: 'Around March 1987 there were signs that the easing should have been slowed and come to an end.'[24] This view was put in mid-1987 by leading analysts, typified by Ed Shann:

> Monetary policy is too lax at present and will have to be tightened . . . Monetary policy has been relaxed over the last six months and by early 1988 domestic demand is likely to be growing strongly. Since January long rates have fallen 1 per cent and short rates by 5 per cent . . . This suggests that Australian investment is likely to be much stronger in 1987–88 than some are suggesting . . . the government needs to tighten fiscal and monetary policy.[25]

The extent · to which officials and government underestimated the economy's momentum was enormous. The 1987–88 budget predicted gross national expenditure would rise by 1.8 per cent during the year but the final result was growth of 4.1 per cent. The consequence of such excessive demand was that, contrary to budget expectations, imports grew faster than exports and the scene was set for a fatal deterioration in the current account

372

deficit. This, in turn, would demand that the boom be halted as soon as possible.

Before Keating went to the IMF in October 1987, he caught a whiff of the momentum and sensed it was time to tighten monetary policy. 'When I get back we're going to lift interest rates,' he told his staff.

Such action was urgent but it was not taken—not for another seven months. Why? Because of the greatest sharemarket crash since 1929, an event whose timing was fateful for the Hawke government.

Keating returned to Australia on the weekend before the sharemarket crash, which came on 'Black Monday', 19 October 1987, just a month after the budget. The Australian sharemarket collapsed, with $9 billion knocked off values during the day. It was part of the greatest crash since 1929, a crash which had triggered a chain of events that caused the Great Depression.

The question in 1987 was whether the inevitable bankruptcies and collapse in confidence would be transmitted throughout the global economy. Australia with its high foreign debt was vulnerable to any chill contracted by the overseas economy. P. P. McGuinness wrote on 28 October 1987 in the *Australian Financial Review*: 'It [the crash] is almost inevitably the harbinger of a world depression.' Everybody expected demand to slow; it was a question of degree. Most Australian pundits merely warned that the risk of a world recession had grown. The Australian market fell further than markets in the rest of the world, and the loss of confidence spilled into the currency markets. Hawke, speaking from the sublime irrelevance of Tipperary, appealed for calm.

Warwick Fairfax saw his attempted privatisation of the Fairfax company fatally undermined, Robert Homes a'Court lost most of his fortune and his mystique, while Laurie Connell's merchant bank Rothwells was subjected to an ill-fated misconceived bail-out. But the world's major central banks had been reconstituted since the 1930s and understood the causes of that Depression. The US Federal Reserve led the way by ensuring that there was sufficient liquidity in the financial system that the sharemarket crash did not threaten financial institutions. The international economy held together in another proof of the theory that history never repeats itself.

The treasury explained the fateful juxtaposition of events in Australia: 'At about the same time as the October sharemarket decline, economic indicators becoming available were suggesting considerable strength in domestic demand. Any concern that this may have raised was overtaken by the considerable uncertainty and threat to activity generated by stock market events.'[26]

After the crash Bob Johnston told Keating, 'That's the end of our worries about excess demand.' There was no need to tighten interest rates to dampen the economy—the crash had guaranteed that.

When business grasped that the crash had not provoked a world depression it reacted with a presumption of immortality. Corporate psychology believed that it had survived the millennium; investors refused to perceive the warning and increased the tempo of the boom.

Bob Johnston says: 'The fact that we got through the sharemarket crash simply emboldened some people to go further. They started to say, "We can live through anything . . . This is a great country. Let's keep expanding." '27

In Australia, the treasury, isolated in Canberra and poor speculators almost to a man, soon picked the trend: the crash would not cause a recession or depression in the real economy. It was a reversal, not a repeat, of 1929. But it took time to be sure and, in the interim, the primary responsibility of the Reserve was to 'ensure adequate liquidity in the system'. This was the international orthodoxy being passed around the globe. It was not a time to be tightening monetary policy.

The key to monetary policy over the next 12 months is that the Reserve stayed cautious about sharp lifts in interest rates. It was close to the financial institutions, aware of corporate over-leveraging and fearful that interest rate shock therapy might precipitate corporate crashes.

The complexity of the Australian situation was captured, a year later, in the Reserve's 1987–88 annual report:

> The first half of 1987–88—both before and after the share market crash—was characterised by an almost universal failure to recognise the underlying strength of world economic growth. In retrospect, the share-market crash seems to have had only a modest and temporary effect on the real economy . . . buoyed in part by good news from abroad, consumer and investor confidence quickly recovered. The upward trend in commodity prices accelerated, promising more buoyancy in mineral and resource industries. Very strong growth in private domestic demand, both for consumption and investment was recorded in the year. Net exports, however, did not contribute to growth
> . . .
> The stock-market collapse led to a flight by investors to assets regarded as safer. The banks were major recipients of investors' funds. These banks were able to replace high-cost with low-cost funds and to boost to very high levels their lending for real estate, mainly housing, where activity rose to boom levels. Following the collapse of the share market, conditions were conducive to takeover and other forms of rationalisation of ownership. Equity finance, however, became difficult to raise. Emphasis turned increasingly to intermediaries for finance. As a result, credit growth picked up strongly.

The sharemarket crash had two effects upon Australia's monetary policy. The Reserve describes them and admits its guilt: 'The first was a decision to underpin adequate system liquidity to avoid disorder and instability. The second was a preliminary assessment that the size of the market fall would check growth in demand and credit and remove the need for any

Bill Hayden and Paul Keating at the ALP press conference during the October 1980
Federal election campaign (News Limited).

Treasurer, John Howard, on the election trail at the Lane Cove shops, February 1983
(David Motte, News Limited).

Opposition Leader, Andrew Peacock, and National Party Leader, Doug Anthony, displaying their riding skills outside Parliament House, August 1983 (News Limited).

Opposition Leader, Andrew Peacock, checks the race form at the Bondi Hotel during the 1984 Federal election campaign (Peter Bardos, News Limited).

Bob Hawke, Prime Minister and
sports fanatic, tries his hand at
the America's Cup Trials
(News Limited).

Opposition Leader, Andrew Peacock, addresses a Melbourne rally during the
1984 election campaign (News Limited).

Treasurer, Paul Keating, handles demonstrators against his tax package,
26 September 1985 (News Limited).

The ACTU Brains Trust, Bill Kelty and Simon Crean, at an ACTU press conference on 27 May 1986 (News Limited).

Queensland Premier, Sir Joh Bjelke-Petersen, reads his own ads flying above his own state during the 1986 State campaign (David Sproule, News Limited).

Queensland Premier, Sir Joh Bjelke-Petersen, gives the victory sign at a Newcastle rally in May 1987 (News Limited).

Janette and John Howard at a Liberal Party rally in Parramatta during the 1987
Federal election campaign (Anthony Weate, News Limited).

Malcolm Fraser and John Elliott share a joke at the launch of Fraser's biography in October 1987 (John Feder, News Limited).

John Elliott and Nick Greiner at Sydney University, 28 October 1987 (Anthony Weate, News Limited).

Opposition Leader, John Howard, meets British Prime Minister, Mrs Thatcher, at
No. 10 Downing Street, July 1988 (News Limited).

Prime Minister, Bob Hawke, and Opposition Treasury Spokesman, John Hewson, cut the cake at the first birthday party in the Press Gallery of the new Parliament House, 27 August 1989 (Alan Porritt, News Limited).

Prime Minister, Bob Hawke, during a press conference at Parliament House, 1 June 1989 (Graeme Thomson, News Limited).

ACTU Secretary, Bill Kelty, addressing a trade union conference in September 1989 (Christopher Pavlich, News Limited).

Treasurer, Paul Keating, and Employment Minister, John Dawkins, after the swearing in of ministers at Government House, 4 April 1990 (Alan Porritt, News Limited).

Opposition Leader, Dr John Hewson, during his address to the National Press Club on 25 September 1991 (Michael Jones, News Limited).

John Elliott and Paul Keating making a strange lunch pair at a Carlton–Collingwood clash in July 1990 (News Limited).

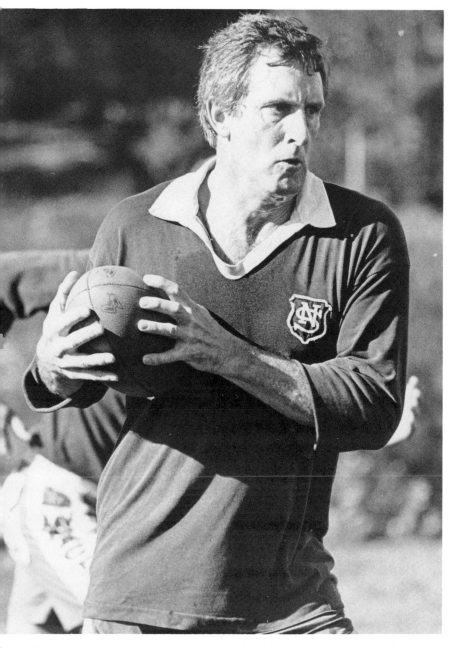

Opposition Leader, Dr John Hewson, playing in a Government vs Opposition touch football match outside Parliament House, 4 June 1991 (Michael Jones, News Limited).

Paul Keating as a backbencher appearing on Channel 9 on 17 September 1991 (Bob Barker, News Limited).

Just deposed Prime Minister, Bob Hawke, embraces Hazel in the corridor before entering his press conference on 19 December 1991 (Christopher Pavlich, News Limited).

Paul Keating at his swearing in ceremony as Prime Minister with Governor General, Bill Hayden, on 20 December 1991 (Anthony Weate, News Limited).

re-tightening of monetary conditions. That assessment proved to be wrong.'[28]

The sharemarket crash delayed for a full seven months a much needed tightening of monetary policy. The crash had another effect—it helped to create an even stronger credit and investment surge. Its timing could hardly have been worse for the conduct of monetary policy in Australia by the Reserve. It was not until May 1988 that interest rates began to rise in a policy response whose delay proved to be fatal. By this stage the economy, like a runaway train, needed to be derailed to be stopped.

The Reserve was guilty of a double failure—an excessive easing of monetary policy for a year from late 1986 until the crash, and a delay of six months after the crash until autumn 1988 before it tightened conditions. The second mistake was far more understandable than the first. The standard critique of the Reserve's monetary policy during the six months after the sharemarket crash is unfair, as the Reserve was following the dictum of all central banks, keeping the system liquid. The priority was to prevent any international depression or recession. The risk was that excess liquidity might overheat the economy but this was really no choice at all—certainly in the early months post-crash.

John Phillips offers the best summation:

> I think the explosion of credit really crept up on people. I think where the authorities including the Reserve Bank dropped their guard was in the early part of 1987 when monetary policy was eased too much . . . I probably rate this misjudgement higher than some other people. You see, because of circumstances [the October sharemarket crash] this misjudgement wasn't picked up for quite some time. It took a full 12 months from March/April 1987 to March/April 1988 to put in place the policy we should have been following. I think it was a costly misjudgement. It meant that when we started to tighten we had to take the interest rates higher for a longer period than otherwise. All the hard searching I've done about policy after the sharemarket crash doesn't lead me to think that we could have done things any differently. I don't think there were major mistakes in this period immediately after the crash.[29]

In fact, Keating and the authorities were in the vanguard of international opinion in thinking, soon afterwards, that the crash would have only a marginal impact on the real economy. Keating was keen to avoid what he called a 'knee-jerk response'. The treasurer, in fact, rejected pleas from prominent figures within the Opposition and the business community that the crash be used as a circuit-breaker to impose more restraint upon Australia in case the overseas economy slowed and Australia's current account deficit deteriorated sharply. For instance, the BCA chief, Rod Carnegie, called for a faster pace of adjustment, complained about a 'disturbing complacency' within government, and wrote to Hawke seeking a mini-budget to tighten fiscal policy and postpone the national wages case. Keating dismissed such appeals as unnecessary.

But the official forecasters—along with the private forecasters—failed to predict the strength of the emerging boom in 1987–88. The reason, above all, was a conjunction of several factors contributing to the boom. The world economic outlook was far stronger than expected; commodity prices rose significantly and Australia's national income surged from higher export prices; the combination of greater national income and lower interest rates stimulated private demand; retail sales, the property and housing sector and business investment all developed healthy momentum; private employment expanded rapidly and unemployment fell; and when the sharemarket crash failed to smash confidence the business climate grew more frantic and the financial sector underwrote lending on a scale that defied rationality.

During his summer break Keating went to Sydney and then to Noosa. In January 1988 after his own anecdotal snapshot of the country Keating called Bob Johnston from the Sunshine coast. 'Look, it's going gangbusters everywhere. The joint is jumping. Sydney property is skyrocketing. We're going to have to move. We can't wait for a recession that isn't happening.' Keating's instincts told him to tighten monetary policy; that the fears of the world's central bankers about a recession were being mocked in the mar- ketplace.

From early 1988 there was an intense debate within the treasury and the Reserve over interest rate policy. Both institutions were split into hawks and doves. Within the treasury the chief hawk was the officer in charge of monetary policy, David Morgan, and the main dove was treasury secretary Bernie Fraser. From January 1988 Morgan wanted policy tightened while Fraser, suspicious of the adverse impact on jobs and investment, resisted such a move. Within the Reserve, Johnston was on the doveish side while officers beneath him were more hawkish. In short, Keating's two principal advisers, Fraser and Johnston, were doves, reluctant to tighten policy.

In February 1988 Morgan told Keating that monetary policy should be tightened. Keating waited; the bulk of official advice was still to delay. Keating waited until after the March 1988 NSW state election and then he switched.

The Reserve Bank board met on 29 March 1988 and a summary of its deliberations described the economy as characterised by strong activity, rising commodity prices and firm housing demand. The board was coming close to urging a policy tightening, but not quite. At the debriefing meeting the next day involving Keating, Reserve and treasury officials, the treasurer was firm on the need to tighten immediately and said it should have occurred earlier. The minutes show that Keating wanted immediate action and said that 'such a tightening could not wait until the content of the May Statement [1988] was clearer'. But a majority said a lift in rates should still wait and Keating accepted this sentiment.

The decision to change policy was finally taken at the next month's meeting—a reversal in the direction of monetary policy that had been first mooted nine months before and should have occurred in mid-1987.

Despite the decision, the Reserve waited a fortnight before taking any action, causing consternation in Keating's office which made a series of phone calls to the Bank. The upshot was a tightening from April/May through June with cash rates rising from 10.85 to 13 per cent. America was the first OECD nation to tighten monetary policy after the sharemarket crash and Australia, which followed immediately, was the second. But this comparative speed must be offset against the fact that Australia's policy settings had been too loose for too long. Morgan says of the tightening that it was 'too gradual, too small, too unacknowledged'.[30]

This inaugurated the most painful and debilitating phase in the history of the Hawke government—a 21 month period from April/May 1988 in which interest rates were tightened progressively and belatedly until cash rates peaked at 18.5 per cent and home loan rates were around 17 per cent. These high interest rates dominated Hawke's third term and cast a political shadow over the government from which it was fortunate to emerge. Interest rates remained at these levels until January 1990, when Keating began the policy easing. The real consequences of the mismanagement of monetary policy became apparent only after Labor's 1990 reelection, when the economy succumbed to a bitter recession.

In a revealing analysis of these two periods—early 1987 and then early 1988—Bob Johnston, the Reserve Bank governor says:

It wasn't a question of people being stupid or failing to be informed. There were a number of things happening. In early 1987 we had the change of government policy to ease the weight on monetary policy. There was suddenly this paradoxical euphoria that Australia was the place to be. We all failed to see the strength of the upswing in commodity prices. We were in the middle of financial deregulation and it wasn't helpful if we showed that the immediate effects of deregulation were that interest rates and the exchange rates went through the roof. Maybe we should have just let it rise. If we had then the early 1987 fall in interest rates may not have been as marked as it was. Then maybe we should have moved to tighten in 1988 earlier than we did. But it wasn't easy to see through the veil of the stockmarket crash and be sure that it wasn't affecting the real economy.

We could probably have dealt with any of these factors singly. But they all came together—we were in the mid-stream of financial deregulation, the government was changing policy, Australia had become flavour of the month which was an abrupt change after the 'banana republic' episode, and stockmarkets collapsed around the world. I think the factor which gets downplayed these days is the 1987 sharemarket crash. It came at a very difficult time for Australia. Without that, I think we would have managed much better. Overall it was a substantial menu to have to deal with. But the responsibility is with the Reserve Bank. We must be judged by the results, even if we were well intentioned. We never tried to disguise what happened. We've said bluntly that we were wrong.[31]

Johnston's successor, Bernie Fraser, argues that the monetary policy mistakes have been exaggerated:

> Monetary policy itself did not *cause* the boom. There were other factors at work. First, the world economy grew faster than anybody expected in 1988–89 and the effect of the sharemarket crash was smaller than everybody thought. In this climate Australia's terms of trade (export prices relative to imports) rose by about 25 per cent from the low of 1986. That was a strong boost from outside Australia that was expansionary and inflationary. Second, we had a high profit share brought about by wage restraint and this helped to generate a very bullish trend in investment. Finally, deregulated financial markets meant there was always enough credit to satisfy demand for expansion by business, even if the interest rates were high.

On the precise criticism of monetary policy Fraser says: 'I believe that it was correct to ease monetary policy in 1987 because the economy had flattened. Interest rates were very high in 1985–86 and by early 1987 this could no longer be justified. In hindsight it can be argued that the easing went too far but *some* easing was required. Monetary policy was also eased after the 1987 sharemarket crash and I believe this was also appropriate. What would have been the effect of tightening at this time? It was right to err on the side of ease, even if the cost of being wrong was a bigger boom. The cost of erring on the tight side and being wrong might have been catastrophic.'[32] In short, Fraser comes close to arguing that monetary policy was not mishandled and that the 'boom–bust' was caused more by a coincidence of events.

John Phillips, former deputy governor, assesses the extent to which the Reserve should have known better at the time:

> I don't think we could have foreseen what was about to happen to the world economy. The judgements we made about the world were the same as the IMF and OECD—that the US economy would weaken, that Japan and Europe would be weak and that commodity prices would fall. All these things proved to be dead wrong. What should have been seen at the time was our over-sensitivity about the exchange rate and the actual connection between fiscal and monetary policy . . . I keep jumping on people who talk about mistakes made after the sharemarket crash. I think all the mistakes were made before the crash.[33]

Despite such self-laceration the Reserve cannot be held solely responsible for the miscalculation. It is likely that history will allocate a greater blame to the banks. One of the advisers responsible for deregulation, Ross Garnaut, says:

> Deregulation caught established Australian banks unprepared professionally for large-scale corporate lending in a competitive environment. Too many Australian bankers, having grown up professionally in the gentle times of official controls on credit, were poorly equipped to assess risk in the new circumstances. The foreign banks, seeking to attract new business, took risks on the fringes of Australian practice and, with few exceptions, suffered numbing losses when bad loans began to be brought to account.[34]

The Australian banks were alarmed by the entry of foreign banks and responded with an aggressive pursuit of market share. They took both very thin margins and accepted risks which would have previously been unacceptable. Financial deregulation proceeded in Australia as quickly as in any country in the world. There were 15 foreign banks issued with licences and the number of foreign-owned merchant banks rose from about thirty in 1983 to over seventy in 1990. The established banks fought to defend their territory.

Bank executives and branch managers who had lived their careers in a regulated risk-exempt environment were called upon to chase market share and make judgements in an asset boom and high-leveraged feeding frenzy which they had never before encountered. Mistakes were made by many bank officers, most of whom had a perfect record in the old regulated system. It was a case of troops trained for a regimental charge being asked to fight a mobile armoured division.

In its retrospective analysis of banking in the 1980s, James Capel Australia says:

> Many of these loans were being made for the purpose of buying companies rather than assets. Bankers had experience in valuing factories and office blocks but now they had to value a business . . . How do you value a company? Essentially you try to value the growth prospects of a company. The share market was prepared to value companies at 20 times their 1986 earnings and now values them at nine times their expected 1981 earnings. Why should bankers be expected to be exempt from this mass hysteria?[35]

The reality is that the proper risk assessment and traditional bank–client relationships were being dissolved in this climate. A combination of global financial deregulation, excess global liquidity, entrenched inflationary expectations and taxation incentives which favoured debt over equity was feeding the 1980s sharemarket booms. Successful companies without debt became prime takeover victims. In Australia the greatest takeover battle centred upon the biggest company, BHP. The old business establishment was being destroyed in the rise of a new generation of entrepreneurs whose hallmark was the takeover and whose leaders were Alan Bond, Robert Holmes a'Court, Sir Ronald Brierley, John Elliott and John Spalvins. The managing director of BT Australia, Rob Ferguson, says:

> The penny dropped after the Bond Corporation bid for the Castlemaine Tooheys Group in 1985 when, at face value, it seemed a very high price earnings multiple had been paid. From then on, pricing power in the stock market began to move out of the institutional investors' hands into those of the entrepreneurs whose gospel was private company value. At its extreme this became a euphemism for infinite leverage . . . the entrepreneurs kept buying, dealing and raiding, as lenders continued to facilitate their expanding asset base.[36]

The takeover kings were financed by a new generation of bankers who sought to exploit the new rules and instruments at their disposal. The 1970s had been dominated by the adventurism of the US institutions, led by Citibank, who recycled their petrodollars into Third World and in particular Latin American nations, with cavalier disregard of credit standards, thereby dooming that hemisphere to a decade of bankruptcy, repayment rescheduling and depression during the 1980s. Meanwhile the banks redirected their own activities and created, in effect, a new series of corporate Argentinas, a process in which Australia went conspicuously far beyond its modest share of world GDP.

The stockmarket boom fed bank lending which in turn refuelled the stockmarket boom. The takeover raiders used the inflated share values as security for more borrowings to launch yet another sharemarket raid. In this process, credit distorted true asset value. Between 1983 and 1988 business credit expanded at an average annual rate of 25 plus per cent, testimony to the optimism of borrowers and lenders. The most famous price distortion was Alan Bond's purchase of Kerry Packer's television and radio interests for around $1 billion, prompting Packer's crack, 'You only get one Bond in your lifetime and I've had mine.' Packer repurchased three years later for about a quarter of Bond's price.

The most illustrious loan of this period was the ANZ's $2 billion to Warwick Fairfax's takeover vehicle Tryart to buy his family company and some of the greatest newspaper titles in the nation. As V. J. Carroll observes in his book on the affair, the ANZ made its first commitment without even meeting Fairfax. Carroll says:

> The market valued the company at around $2 billion. A year previously it had been $560 million and the year before that also $560 million. There was nothing in the recent trading performance to justify that share price. Operating profits after tax had been flat for three years . . . to the ANZ bank, funding the Tryart takeover was a straight assets deal: the bank lent Tryart funds [eventually about $2 billion] for the takeover. Tryart sold off Fairfax assets to repay the bank and the bank

got a fat fee, interest and the continuing Fairfax–Syme business. It was probably the bank's biggest single commitment, ever.[37]

A fundamental factor underpinning the outlook of the banks was the abolition of credit rationing by volume and its replacement with credit control by price. Financial deregulation had changed the mechanism for the implementation of monetary policy by the Reserve from quantity to price. The Reserve no longer applied quantitative controls; it merely used interest rates—the price of money—to influence activity. Loans funds were now always available; it was a matter of the price borrowers would bear. In this climate the banks, chasing market share, began to allocate credit without proper regard to risk. One of the more successful foreign owned banks, BT Australia, offers this analysis:

> Once released from the cage of credit rationing, our banks pursued market share. This was an entirely inappropriate motivation. It obliterated the natural conservatism that is the foundation of good banking. At the extreme, loans were advanced to borrowers who put up little in the way of equity. The borrowers were taking an options bet with the banks' money. Heads I win a lot and you win a bit; tails you lose. The banks thought they were making loans but often they were investing in equity with a return capped at the loan rate.[38]

It is obvious that the prudential supervision of the Reserve was deficient. But it is equally obvious that the Reserve's function is not to prevent bad loans. There can be no law to ban incompetent lending decisions or to guarantee loan prudence. Prudential supervision is far more rigorous in the United States than in Australia yet the US was unable to address the same problems. The Reserve's competence, in turn, cannot be judged according to the number of bad loans written by the banks. The Reserve's approach is that 'ultimate responsibility for sound management of a bank resides with that bank's board and management'.[39]

Bob Johnston, and his successor at the Reserve, Bernie Fraser, concede that the central Bank could have done a better job, that under deregulation the supervisors 'required a learning phase'. The tightening of the prudential mechanisms occurred only late in the decade, after the bad loans were well downstream.

Reviewing these oversights Johnston says: 'In retrospect it is true the Bank should have done more. The main concerns are to ensure the information coming to the Reserve from the banks is reliable and timely . . . but my very strong view is that each bank is responsible for its own actions and the bank boards must be held responsible for the actions of their employees.'[40]

The current governor, Bernie Fraser, says: '[the Reserve's] primary concerns are to preserve the stability of the financial system as a whole and to protect—but not guarantee—bank deposits. The stability of the financial system is not in question and no bank depositor has lost any money.'[41]

On the supervisory front the Reserve gave warnings to the banks, but they were ignored. Fraser's defence—that the Reserve should protect the depositor, not the shareholders' funds—is correct. But it is also far from the full story.

The ultimate enforcement power of the Reserve Bank is monetary policy, not prudential mechanisms. The Reserve failed to apply the proper monetary policy to check credit growth which was running at 20 per cent. This is the Bank's failure but the government's responsibility and Keating's direct responsibility as the treasurer who boasted about his personal control of interest rate policy.

The consequences of the explosion in credit and reckless bank lending were damaging not just to the entrepreneurs and to the banks' books. It did severe damage to Australia's national interest—it created an asset price explosion, expanded the foreign debt and hurt Australia's overseas reputation such that its lending attracted a further risk premium.

The truth is that the financial excesses of the 1980s were embraced by many different institutions and industries. When assessments are made of the loss of $8 billion of investors' funds by the entrepreneurs, the money trail involves the provisions of loans and debts by the leading banks, support from many institutional investors, legal advice and audit approval from the nation's leading law and accountancy firms, and promotion from the main public relations firms. This process was underwritten by the inadequacy of corporate law provisions and the abandonment by directors of their responsibilities.[42]

It is a systemic failure within which the main responsibility falls upon four parties—the banks, the borrowers, the auditors and the monetary authorities for underwriting excess credit and liquidity. In a wider sense the problem was an institutional and theoretical failure to cope with the new demands and opportunities thrown up by financial deregulation. This reform cast into some confusion the theoretical basis underpinning monetary policy. However, it is also true that the 1987–88 policy settings of the Hawke–Keating government were not as firm as the economy demanded at the time, despite the impressive tightening of fiscal policy by historical standards.

In one of his few statements conceding mistakes Keating says: 'With regard to monetary policy itself, there are things that I would now do differently with the benefit of hindsight. I would have been less accommodating in the second half of 1987 to the monetary authorities' willingness to cut interest rates in the face of a substantial fiscal policy tightening.' He said that the monetary authorities—the Reserve Bank—were arguing in 1986–87 'that a large cut in the PSBR [total public sector borrowing] would solve the current account and allow for an easier monetary policy'.[43]

The misjudgement of monetary policy in 1986 and 1987 had three dimensions. First, there was a failure in economic theory: the trade-off the officials expected between fiscal and monetary policy did not eventuate. The Reserve and treasury felt that Keating's tighter fiscal policy justified an easier monetary policy. In fact, the public sector savings from a tighter fiscal policy were offset by the private sector dissavings—borrowings—during the boom. This meant a higher instead of a lower current account deficit. The treasury admitted subsequently that in the 1980s the two deficits theory didn't work.

Years later Keating and then treasury secretary, Chris Higgins, reflected at Keating's Red Hill home. 'We did it like the textbooks say, Chris. We tightened fiscal policy but it hasn't worked, has it? It just hasn't worked,' Keating said. There was a long pause, then Higgins answered: 'I know, Treasurer, but it [fiscal restraint] will work. It will.'

Second, at a more technical level a defect in Labor's model was the reliance upon monetary policy as the 'swing' instrument to manage the economy. Given the huge national income fluctuations from commodity price movements, this required too much from monetary policy. Keating was an ardent defender of the model, insisting that monetary policy was the correct instrument to be applied in regulating economic activity. But in the 1980s climate this was a high risk tactic, given the asset price boom which meant that a high proportion of the corporate and household sector had borrowed excessively and would face a severe crunch with a sustained high interest rate policy. John Phillips says that monetary policy should 'not be used to balance for deficiencies in fiscal or wages policy because of the sheer damage it can do'.[44]

Third, the impact of monetary policy is hard to gauge accurately because of the great time lag involved between a change in interest rates and its impact, a lag of at least 12 months which can reach two years.

One myth from this period was that in a deregulated environment monetary policy would be ineffective, a claim exploded by the monetary policy induced recession of the 1990s. Another myth cherished by the Opposition was that Keating was overruling official advice on monetary policy. In fact, the reverse was true. The conduct of monetary policy during 1986 and 1987 when the foundations for the boom were laid reflected the majority position among the family of treasury–Reserve senior advisers.

In a wider sense the mistake made by the Labor government and the Reserve during 1987 and 1988 was to favour, on balance, a policy of growth rather than restraint. Labor was determined to err on the side of economic expansion rather than economic contraction; it preferred to tolerate inflation rather than unemployment; it wanted monetary policy to encourage investor confidence rather than price stability; it sought a gradual solution to the external payments crisis, not a faster solution. As an instinctive political animal Keating had always aspired to achieve economic growth superior to the somewhat mediocre levels of past coalition governments.

Bob Johnston says: 'I think if we'd run the economy at a slower level domestically we wouldn't necessarily be in the mess we're in now . . . We had the economy running at a high rate of knots, a deliberate policy of trying to boost investment, a growing economy with guaranteed wage levels and a willingness to spend—that was the demand side—and on the supply side you had a deregulated financial system standing ready to finance that spending.'[45]

As 1987 closed this intersection of monetary, banking and sharemarket miscalculations was an event beneath the surface. Premonitions of danger were apparent but the consequences were grasped by very few. In December 1987 Keating's optimism was palpable. The 1987–88 budget had been revised and was now showing a surplus, an improvement on its earlier $27 million deficit.

Keating and Walsh released forward estimates showing that spending would decline in real terms for the next three years. Keating was burning with his 'golden age' rhetoric; it was the dawn of a new era of Labor-induced surplus. The treasurer intoned: 'No other group of journalists who have lived in this building have ever cast their eyes on anything as important or significant as that.' Keating matched his lyricism by offering to autograph the release—incredibly, some scribes accepted.

At the same time Keating won Cabinet agreement to a May 1988 Statement of spending cuts. The aim was to tighten fiscal policy, reassure business and finance and prove that Labor had kept its nerve. Keating reported that the economic fallout from the crash was adverse but marginal. Labor needed to harden its policy as an insurance against international uncertainty.

The upshot was that in May 1988, seven months after the crash, Keating brought down a further but modest tightening of fiscal policy plus a series of industry reforms. The budget surplus for the coming 1988–89 year would rise to $3 billion plus, with another round of spending cuts yielding $1 billion in savings, the bulk coming from the states. Keating, the architect of policy during this period, had chosen a gradual response to the sharemarket crash. He never utilised the crash as a circuit-breaker. He chose to ride out the late 1987 climate of uncertainty rather than exploit it.

The truth is that the Reserve, the treasury and the private forecasters were baffled by the wild gyrations in the domestic and overseas economy in this period. It was the most unpredictable period in an unpredictable decade. Nobody can reread the treasury and Reserve documents of this time without being awakened to the essentially hazardous nature of the economic forecasting which is the basis for policy making.

The sharp and massive external shocks imposed upon Australia made economic management a high risk exercise. In 1986 the dollar collapsed while in 1987 it was too strong. In 1986 commodity prices free-fell while in 1987 they rose strongly. In 1986 Keating was worried that interest rates were too high and in 1987 he made the mistake of keeping them too low. In 1987 the sharemarket crash was expected to damage the economy but 1988 revealed a boom of alarming proportions. Keating had to deal with a sharp fall and then a sharp rise in Australia's terms of trade. The one certainty was uncertainty and that meant that the risk of policy miscalculation was high.

The defect in Labor's approach in this climate is that its policy was too ambitious. In trying to satisfy too many constituencies, Labor ran the risk that it would satisfy none properly. Finally, this is exactly what happened. Keating was trying to deliver jobs for the unions, beat inflation for the financial markets, promote investment for the business community and stabilise the foreign debt for the nation's future, objectives too often in conflict. They were rooted in Labor's belief that it could beat the current account deficit within a growth strategy and without embracing even a mild recession.

Keating sensed the danger but he was compelled to the challenge. He once likened his economic management to a 'Houdini trick', a revealing remark because treasurers can't run the economy like Houdini engineered his tricks. Miracle escapes had a limited shelf-life in economic management in the Australia of the 1980s.

20
A competitive economy

*We're on the way to transforming the nation from the complacent
Lucky Country to the Productive Country, the Innovative and
Hard-Working Country.*

Bob Hawke, 6 July 1987

After the 1987 election the Hawke government moved to tackle Australia's
economic crisis at one of its sources—the need for more efficient workers,
firms and industries. It was a recognition more that economic policy had to
be supported by a change in work habits and company practice. This idea
was bipartisan and was put on Labor's agenda by Bob Hawke. It was the
declaration of a new benchmark against which Australian institutions and
practice would be measured—the benchmark of international competition.
It was a repudiation of the values of Fortress Australia.

The new benchmark would affect ultimately every enterprise in the
nation. It derived from the realisation that lack of international competitiveness lay at the core of Australia's malaise. Australia's competitiveness had
declined over the previous two decades, a legacy of cultural attitudes dating
back to the post-Federation Settlement and more recent economic policy
failures. Hawke's initiative was an attack on the habits of protection,
regulation and national introspection. It meant changes in how people
worked, their motives, their outlook and their relations with fellow workers
and managers.

Hawke's aim was to resolve the paradox identified by the analyst Fred
Hilmer:

> Australians are achievers, but not, it seems, when working in large
> organisations . . . Australian individuals have excelled in their
> contributions to sport, literature, films, music, medicine, science and
> technology . . . prospectors have found mines and oil, technologists
> have found ways to convert remote and often difficult ore bodies into
> mines and even industries . . . [but] a negative attitude towards work

386

within large organisations seems to develop early . . . if the large majority of Australians working in organisations were more satisfied by their work and thus added more value, the pot of gold for both individuals and the nation would be a large one.[1]

The bedrock purpose was to generate the growth of the 'productive culture' to which industry minister John Button often referred. In the 1980s this strategy fell under the ugly and obscure heading of 'micro-economic reform', a phrase which mystified much of the nation. In previous decades 'micro-economic reform' had been called 'structural adjustment'—which was probably just as conceptually inaccessible.

For people micro-economic reform meant working smarter, and for companies it meant greater productivity. It also meant a more efficient infrastructure—in areas such as energy, transport, shipping, ports and tele-communications. The micro-economic reform program flowed inevitably from the government's internationalisation of the Australian economy. It was designed to turn that policy into a grassroots reality.

The reason it was so difficult to implement, for both employers and employees, was that micro-reform was the cutting edge of genuine change; being internationally competitive would change the lives of waterside workers, university lecturers, airline executives and small businesspeople.

There were, broadly, four areas in the micro-reform agenda of the 1980s—financial deregulation; the reduction of protection; labour market deregulation; and market pricing and privatisation in telecommunications, transport and energy. There was a furious debate about the reforms covering each sector. At the end of the 1980s there was another furious debate about the sequence in which these areas should have been reformed. Finally, in each sector micro-reform was a shock therapy which delivered a multitude of winners and losers within the outcome of greater national progress.

The origins of Labor's micro-economic reform agenda are found in Hawke's speech in Ballarat on 6 July 1987, during the federal election campaign. Stung by claims that his campaign agenda was devoid of vision, Hawke identified a new theme for his third term—transforming 'the complacent Lucky Country to the Productive Country'. His twelve-point program, primitive and piecemeal, was still a milestone for the ALP.

Hawke promised to reform the transport lifelines, terminate the two airline agreement, promote competition and lower airfares, improve the waterfront, grain handling and the rail freight network. He pledged to deregulate crude oil marketing, treble the size of the computer and communications industry, pursue trade union amalgamation, eliminate unnecessary business regulation, promote greater research and development, eliminate inefficient work practices and give priority to value-added mining and farm products as well as expanding the tourism industry. The program was vague and quite inferior to the Liberal business strategy unveiled in July 1986.

But it was a landmark for the Labor Party. The technical meaning of micro-economic reform was to allow prices to change relative to each other—for products, wages and services—thereby using the price mechanism to re-allocate resources on a more efficient basis.

This was the true meaning of supply side economics which had been damaged in Australia by the assumption that it was little more than a Ronald Reagan tax redistribution in favour of the rich. In fact, micro-economic reform shifted Labor's traditional focus from the Keynesian orientated demand side of the economy towards the supply side. It was a recognition that Keynesian demand management which had been dominant since the Great Depression did not have the exclusive solution to Australia's problems in the 1980s. In its purest form micro-economic reform was a liberation of the supply side, an embrace made far easier for conservative parties than for social democratic parties which were more tied to the Keynesian chariot.

After the election Hawke established Cabinet's Structural Adjustment Committee (SAC) which became the clearing house for Labor's micro-economic reform program.

There are two views about Labor's embrace of micro-economic reform, both valid in their own right. John Button says:

> Micro-economic reform only became an issue because this government made it one. If you look back through the 1970s these issues—waterfront and labour market reform—weren't discussed. Why? Because the entire nation, industry and finance, was protected. It was very cosy. Australia was a nice little closed shop. But once you started to move on financial deregulation, and then protection, it became obvious that you had to extend you reforms throughout the economy.[2]

An overseas observer of Australia, the Chicago economist David Hale, provides a more sceptical and international evaluation:

> The missing ingredient in Australia's economic experiment of the 1980s was micro-economic flexibility . . . the Hawke government dragged its feet on the privatisation of government enterprises and rationalisation of low productivity state controlled sectors, such as the docks and railways . . . In retrospect, the Hawke government's decision to pursue rapid financial deregulation while moving slowly to deregulate the real economy was a major blunder. The surge in bank lending produced a boom and bust cycle in asset prices which helped to set the stage for one of the most severe recessions in modern Australian history . . . Because prices within the Australian economy were still distorted by wage controls and poor public sector productivity, the country did not have a proper micro-economic framework for encouraging efficient resource allocation.[3]

In short, Hale suggests Australia's problem stemmed from a hungry financial system seeking to maximise its returns but finding that inefficiencies in the real economy directed its investment options towards asset speculation and property.

There is, however, a point of reconciliation between the Button and Hale perspectives. Button was correct in saying that the Hawke government was the first to tackle the micro-economic reform agenda. Hale is correct in saying that Australia did not move fast enough. The difference is the test of measurement; it is whether Australia is judged by its own historical standard or by an international standard. There is no dispute that Australia has made advances; but those advances are not sufficient unless they are advances in relation to Australia's trading partners, all of whom have their own micro-reform programs. This is the conundrum which bedevilled Australia's micro-economic reform debate of the 1980s.

The agenda was subject to hundreds of variations, alterations and modifications since micro-reform involved just about every interest group. The upshot during the rest of the Hawke years was a program that involved protection reductions, linking wage rises more closely to workplace productivity, establishing the transport, aviation and communication industries on a more efficient market-orientated basis, increasing research and development, and securing more value-added exports. These ideas were driven by the international economic orthodoxy of the decade, best represented in OECD reports that a more flexible economy with more freedom for prices would deliver the best productivity.

Micro-economic reform was a direct consequence of the internationalisation of the Australian economy. This process was described by treasury:

> In many respects the floating of the exchange rate is the pivotal policy decision of the last decade. It has imposed a discipline on all players . . . these ramifications will continue to spread throughout the economy and ultimately influence economic decision-making in every nook and cranny. The greater internationalisation of the Australian economy, the depth and dynamism of its financial markets and the imputation system are already spurring management to improve performance.[4]

Keating cut through the jargon to say that micro-reform meant 'we've got to clear all the bloody crap from the pipes, we're blowing the pipes out'.

Labor's approach to micro-reform was sincere but flawed; it was driven by the recognition that macro-economic policy or fiscal/wage/monetary solutions were not enough given the depth of Australia's problems. Both the ALP and the ACTU recognised that greater productivity, not institutionalised real wage cuts, had to be the objective. So micro-reform was based upon an implicit trade-off: that structural change could ease the squeeze on real wages. This represented a new implicit dimension to the Accord—not necessarily universally endorsed by the union movement.

There are two hallmarks of Labor's approach to the micro agenda. First, the conviction which sprang from the Accord that reform had to be based on consensus, not confrontation or government fiat. So Labor usually implemented micro-reform on a gradual basis and accepted a pace of change largely dictated by the union movement. Consensus bred only gradual changes, largely because micro-reform was an attack on union power which necessitated job losses as feather-bedding was eliminated. During the early 1990s recession ALP politicians around the nation confronted the harsh reality that the short-term result of micro-reform was higher unemployment since it involved a shift in resources between firms, industries and states.

Second, Labor's approach to micro-reform was somewhat hypocritical. It was based on consensus when dealing with its own constituents, notably the public sector and the trade unions, but it was more audacious when dealing with business and finance. Labor scarcely worried about consensus when it deregulated the financial system in 1984 or cut protection in 1988 and again, more dramatically, in 1991. The government was almost heroic in dealing with capital but reduced to caution when facing the unions. Labor was too slow in the imposition of change on the unions in telecommunications, shipping and the waterfront during its 1987–90 term. It would display more courage in the fourth term but progress, again, was necessarily incremental.

The story of the 1980s is that Labor had much more difficulty dealing with micro-economic than with macro-economic reform. Micro-reform posed a direct challenge to work practices, union influence and ALP ideology. Labor's difficulty is proved by the diffidence of its 1989 three-year waterfront reform package, by its acquiescence to the ACTU's deciding the pace and shape of the move towards enterprise bargaining during the late 1980s, by the four-year delay between 1987 and 1991 before Labor could begin privatisation of major government enterprises and by the same delay before it was able to break Telecom's monopoly position. Both these latter initiatives were banned by the ALP platform and required major platform revision before the Hawke Cabinet could advance.

Characteristic of Labor's third term was Hawke's lack of skill in implementing micro-economic reform and Keating's very selective interest in the area.

Hawke began his third term with a surge of zeal which promised much and delivered little. His first move was to announce the greatest reform of federal government administration for thirty years: the creation of a series of 'mega' departments with senior and junior ministers. The main new departments were foreign affairs and trade (Hayden), transport and communications (Evans) and employment, education and training (Dawkins). The post-election ministry included three women, saw the full integration of the left wing into the government, and the elevation to the ministry of three faction chiefs—Graham Richardson and Robert Ray from the right and Gerry Hand from the left.

Hawke then went into aggressive mode, likened by one minister to Toad: 'He threw open the garage door, donned goggles and driving coat and then set about terrorising the neighbourhood.'[5] In August he launched an appeal for a new agenda—reduced industry protection, deregulation in transport, elimination of inefficient work practices, and privatisation of major public enterprises. Hawke politely called privatisation 'asset sales', saying the test to be used was efficiency, 'not some ideological debate about appropriate levels of public ownership'.

But Hawke and his Cabinet faced stiffer internal resistance to these reforms than they anticipated. Their main failure lay in the ALP's refusal to sanction privatisation, while their chief success was formulation of a new industry policy based upon reductions in protection levels.

During his third term Hawke tried to persuade the party to accept privatisation but was repudiated. A feature of this term was Hawke's limited ability to translate his election victories into party support for new economic reforms. Indeed, by the end of 1989 defeatism had gripped a majority of the economic ministers, generated partly by shame over their micro-reform failures.

There was poetic justice in Hawke's frustrations over privatisation—only two years earlier he and his ministers had campaigned as anti-privatisation zealots to undermine Howard's leadership. In his 1985 Chifley Lecture Hawke had asked: 'What in the name of reason is the justification for breaking up and selling off the great and efficient national assets, like the Commonwealth Bank, Telecom, TAA, Qantas? The fact is that this recipe for disaster represents the height of economic irrationality . . . it is based on a blind and mindless commitment to a narrow, dogmatic and discredited ideology.'

In 1987–88 Hawke reaped the harvest when his own privatisation program for the airlines was denied by the ALP for another three years. It was a costly delay. In the interim the market price for public assets fell sharply.[6]

The 1987 informal Cabinet position favoured a float of 49 per cent of both Australian Airlines and Qantas. Papers commissioned by Gareth Evans showed both airlines in an unsustainable financial position. The overseas trend was towards 'mega' airlines and alliances between carriers. The issue was whether Qantas would remain an international carrier or shrink to regional status. Cabinet told the party that Labor's spending priorities had to be welfare, education and health, not government-owned airlines and businesses. Hawke now branded his party opponents as 'total conservatives' who refused to accept change.

But the ALP was falling victim to a psychological craving for a victory over the Cabinet free marketeers. The party was incapable of confronting

391

the long-term future of Qantas or the financial projections Evans produced. The party wanted to teach Cabinet a lesson for being too well disposed towards the finance sector, the banks and the entrepreneurs, and for supporting a deregulation ideology.

While the party denied aviation privatisation, the Cabinet prevailed on domestic aviation deregulation. The major advance in policy was the 7 October 1987 announcement by Gareth Evans that Australia's two airline policy would be terminated from 1990 in favour of partial deregulation. It was a cautious step in the right direction.

Evans rejected any 'open skies' approach by keeping the barrier between domestic and international aviation markets. The experts assumed that Ansett would dominate the market post deregulation and the government was attacked for its restrictive terminals policy which contradicted deregulation and posed a barrier to market entry.

Hawke's privatisation campaign was buried officially on 7 June 1988 at the ALP National Conference when eight months of effort produced a political lemon—a new committee to study privatisation. It was Labor's way of saying 'no' to Hawke while saving his face. Hawke sat through the Conference's privatisation debate in silence; a leader who had tried to persuade the party at the wrong time and was now too weak to persuade them in the right forum. He renewed his efforts inside the parliamentary party in 1989 but again was unable to break Labor's mindset. It was classic ALP dogmatism: the public was prepared to accept the airline privatisation but the party felt its icons were being discarded and clung to public ownership.

The issue revealed Hawke's limitations as a leader attempting to secure a formal change in ALP policy. But it also offered an insight into Keating: he took a calculated decision to leave Hawke with his failure. Hawke's mistake after the 1987 election was Whitlamesque: he lectured the party but forgot the technique of private persuasion. The upshot was that Evans, Button and Keating all complained that Hawke's unilateralism was only undermining the cause of reform—a reminder that Hawke's primary relationship was with the people, not the party. Hawke had more faith in his ability to carry the country than in his ability to carry the party. Hawke won elections for Labor but unlike Whitlam was never a hero to the party.

The centrepiece of Labor's third term micro-reform was its May 1988 Statement, delivered by Keating in a blaze of exaggerated rhetoric. Keating, in fact, had been disdainful about micro-reform although it had been at the initiative of treasury chief Bernie Fraser that Keating had assumed the main responsibility for the Industries Assistance Commission (IAC) after the 1987 election. Fraser was initially disappointed at Keating's lackadaisical attitude towards the IAC and the nuts and bolts of structural change. But Keating, as usual, seized the decision-making process when an economic statement loomed.

Keating, Button and Hawke worked together to ensure that the May 1988 Statement was a substantial initial foray into micro-reform. Labor cut the company tax rate from 49 to 39 per cent by broadening the corporate tax base, consistent with treasury's 'level playing field' philosophy. It abolished many tax concessions, including depreciation for plant and equipment and the gold mining exemption. Keating announced a 15 per cent tax on superannuation fund earnings but allowed the funds, by using the imputation system, to receive offsetting tax credits by investing in Australian companies. Under a four-year plan tariffs would be reduced to two new benchmarks, 15 and 10 per cent. This was equivalent to a 20 per cent cut in average protection levels for manufacturing. In separate changes for the car industry, protective quotas were abolished and a program to cut tariffs to 35 per cent by 1992 put in place. Protection still remained high for cars and for the most inefficient manufacturing sector—textiles, clothing and footwear—where, under a late 1986 plan, protective quotas would be abolished only in 1995. Keating announced that the average effective rate of assistance for industry would fall from 19 per cent in 1986–87 to 14 per cent in 1992–93.

The government moved to put Qantas, Australian Airlines, Telecom, OTC and Australia Post on a more effective commercial footing, designed to secure rates of return comparable with the private sector. The book value of the main enterprises was more than $20 billion; separate reforms were made for each body to underwrite a more competitive performance. These changes, of course, were only third-best reforms. There was no private equity injection into the airlines; Telecom and OTC kept their monopolies in telephone services; competition in telecommunications was permitted only at the margin. This was a win for the Australian Telecommunications Employees Association (ATEA) and its caucus backers. The direction was clear: make me competitive but not just yet. A new regulatory body, AUSTEL, was established to oversee the introduction of competition in the next decade. Labor had succumbed to caution, ideology and sectional interest in the public enterprise reforms, thereby mocking the urgency of its economic reform message.

In his Statement Keating identified micro-economic reform as an indispensable priority, saying that Labor's philosophy of change must be transmitted into 'the heart of the nation—to where individual firms and businesses operate . . . if we cannot get these things right, we will never really get the big picture right. What we have been after is a full picture, not something half finished.'

In this May 1988 Statement the Hawke government enshrined greater national productivity as a test of its credentials. In historical terms the extent of change was dramatic. No previous government had asked to be assessed by the extent of its protection cuts, public enterprise reform, corporate tax cuts and its overall capacity to deliver a more efficient infrastructure. The micro-economic reform agenda, once established, would endure for many years. By 1991 Nick Greiner's NSW Liberal government would be seeking reelection essentially on the basis of its first term fiscal and micro-economic reform program.

The Statement was the turning point in the Hawke government's industry policy. The first five years, from 1983 to 1988, had been shaped by a series of industry plans, pioneered by John Button, in cars, steel, textiles, clothing, footwear and heavy engineering. They were corporatist in outlook, inspired by the early 1980s recession and designed to consolidate jobs and investment and promote gradual change. By 1987–88 the Cabinet accepted that Australia's manufacturing industry required greater international competition rather than protection.

This was a courageous move given the heavy current account deficit, a problem which would have encouraged many nations into greater protection. It was a testimony to the intellectual penetration of the low protection philosophy into Australia's governmental elite over the previous decade. The hallmark of the 1988 decisions was that protection would be cut, not across the board, but 'tops down' (high rates were cut to a benchmark leaving lower rates unchanged).

The Business Council of Australia (BCA), representing the top eighty companies, accepted the tariff cuts but asked as a quid pro quo for a better attack on inefficiencies in transport, ports, shipping and telecommunications. This revealed that the politics of protection had been transformed by several forces. Australia's international campaign for freer world trade in agriculture demanded cuts in its own industrial protection; the expansion of the services sector instead of manufacturing would absorb many new job market entrants; and with a floating system the exchange rate rather than tariff cuts had the potential to exercise a greater influence on competitiveness.

The BCA's executive director, Peter McLaughlin, called for a better effort in shipping, waterfront and telecommunications, saying the new public enterprise guidelines were the first step in a long journey: 'My guess is that if efficiency improvements of 100 were achievable in our public authorities then something like 5 of that 100 would be achieved as the result of guidelines, 65 from the introduction of competition, and 30 from the introduction of private ownership.' Labor had scored 5 out of 100.

McLaughlin was correct in saying that 'it's quite clear senior Ministers wanted to go further on economic grounds and, in fact, know that they must ultimately go further to maintain the credibility of the reforms'. McLaughlin said the two keys to more efficient government business enterprise were the introduction of competition and the introduction of private capital and private owners 'who can vote with their feet'.[7]

The basic equation of Australian economic history was being unwound. This was described by the overseas analyst David Hale: 'In the past many business commentators blamed Australia's low productivity and high inflation on militant trade union leaders. But the trade union leaders could not have engaged in successful wage push without trade protection. In the absence of tariffs, they simply would have pushed unemployment to higher levels.'

The immensity of Labor's micro-reform difficulties was revealed in 1989 in three areas widely seen as critical—the third runway for Sydney Airport, the waterfront, and coastal shipping. In each case the forces resisting change occupied a place of power within the ALP. They were the NSW party, especially the NSW right, which saw the third runway as electoral death in Sydney's inner south-west; the Waterside Workers Federation (WWF), whose bargaining power had entrenched massive inefficiencies which helped to make Australian ports some of the world's worst; and a union–industry alliance in shipping to uphold cabotage, the policy which protected the coastal trade from foreign ship entry and competition.

The key to the 1989 Sydney Airport decision was its political transformation from a provincial to a national issue; from one of local environmental protection to national micro-economic reform. This was a tussle between old and new politics. It involved disadvantaging some people in the cause of improving the air links to Australia's main city which, given the rise of tourism as one of the country's major export earners, was directly related to Australia's export performance and national efficiency.

Hawke and Keating, after early prevarication, particularly from Hawke, whose indecision was greater than usual, decided for national economic interest. The Cabinet split was between the economic ministers and the political pragmatists. Keating led the former group while his right-wing colleagues, Richardson and Ray, led the pragmatists. The debate was about maximising Sydney's capacity from its existing airport and the timetable for the second airport near Badgery's Creek outside Sydney.

Labor had partly created its own problems by cancelling the Fraser government's decision for a third runway, and in Hawke's appointment of the irrepressible Gary Punch, an anti-runway local politician, as aviation support minister. The NSW Party argued against the third runway on grounds of airport noise, environmental protection and property values. After a protracted Cabinet debate the government accepted the economic imperative and put national progress before provincial politics. Gary Punch resigned, transport minister Ralph Willis was criticised for being too faint-hearted but Hawke and Keating, despite the political agony, had forced through a transition in Labor's outlook.

The affair was typical of Labor's piecemeal approach—too little, too late. The government had taken the correct decision, finally. But the statutory requirement for environmental impact statements meant that years would elapse before third runway construction could begin.

Labor's limitations were exposed more clearly on the waterfront and coastal shipping. In 1988 Hawke declared: 'I can think of no reasonable argument why employers and unions in our manufacturing and export sectors must adjust to international trading conditions while stevedoring and shipping remain shielded.' Yet Labor delayed and deferred, reluctant to redeem that pledge.

In April 1989 a comprehensive report from the Inter-State Commission documented waterfront inefficiency and estimated a net $620 million gain a year if the waterfront were reformed. The report showed that the average age of waterfront workers was 50, that many had disabilities, that wages were close to $800 a week for little more than 35 hours work. Additionally, WWF membership had fallen from 80 000 in the 1930s to less than 8000 in the 1980s.

The report said: 'The evidence to the Commission on many matters such as inefficient work practices, unsatisfactory industrial relations, ineffective supervision and management, high costs and wide-spread unreliability, all indicate that fundamental rather than incremental change is required.' It recommended generous redundancy proposals that would cost government and employers $145 million each over three years. The WWF rejected these recommendations immediately, thus verifying the Commission's belief that 'it is abundantly clear that the waterfront industry will not reform itself'.

From the start Labor's approach was based on a consensus with the WWF. This was demanded by Bill Kelty; the WWF chief, Tas Bull, had been an Accord loyalist. On 1 June 1989 Cabinet endorsed a compromise giving the industry and unions the chance to negotiate a three-year agreement to establish enterprise-based employment and more efficient work practices including training, job redesign and redundancy payments. Hawke told Cabinet that reform through confrontation would be counterproductive. It is a measure of Australia's national decline that such a negotiating process was needed to enable the parties to agree on a $300 million redundancy package, half of which would be funded by taxpayers, to create employment conditions which would be merely the norm in the rest of the country.

The final agreement was authorised by Cabinet on 10 October 1989 and rejected any 'conditional acceptance'—the withholding of the government's $150 million subject to delivery. The agreement was specific on the benefits for the WWF but vague on the WWF's concessions. There would be a three-year process involving a transition to enterprise-based employment. The full spirit and letter of the Inter-State Commission report was not embraced. The WWF's monopoly was not tackled and compulsory redundancies were still banned. Labor put vested political interest rationalised by the need to avoid confrontation before the imposition of international transport standards.

The irony is that after the 1990 election the waterfront became a litmus test by which Labor's micro-reform credentials were measured. The chairman of Conaust, one of the main employers, warned that Australia suffered 'the disability of gradualism' and that 'the heart of the inadequacy of the present reform program is its short-sightedness; it looks only at our own domestic standards for its measures, it does not facilitate change or even a capacity to cope with change'. Meanwhile Britain and New Zealand implemented much faster waterfront reform with massive labour shedding.[8]

In its coastal shipping reform Labor rejected the chief recommendation from the IAC—to scrap the 'cabotage' system and allow foreign ship entry. For a Cabinet that boasted about imposing foreign competition in industry and finance the idea of extending this to shipping was far too dangerous. Labor commissioned a second report, dominated by the shipowners and unions, which allowed them to determine their own pace of reform. Cabinet endorsed a proposal to cut the average crew size from 29 to 21 and subsidise voluntary redundancies, claiming that manning would be reduced to OECD levels by 1992.

The day before Ralph Willis announced Labor's decision on shipping and the waterfront, Australia's foreign debt passed $100 billion, a reminder that Labor was pledged to gradual change when the economic indicators demanded an urgent response.

The waterfront issue exposed the deepest flaw in Hawke's micro-reform agenda—his test of success. During his third term Hawke's refrain was that 'no government had achieved more on micro-economic reform than this government'. His point was right but his conclusion was wrong. The test of Australia's progress was not improvement against its own historical record, but whether it was advancing or declining relative to the rest of the world.

Labor's failure at the 'micro' level was to use the historical standard of comparison, not an international standard of 'first-best' practice. It betrays the central flaw of the Hawke years, although Hawke would say that Australia had to mend its ways before challenging the rest of the world.

This forces two different judgements about Australia's late 1980s boom. First, blame must attach to the banks and entrepreneurs who made foolish investment decisions along with the authorities who mishandled monetary policy. Second, blame must also attach to the Hawke government for its delay in following financial deregulation with matching deregulation in other sectors of the economy to improve the efficiency of the body overall. The financial arteries were racing, but the economic body was still unfit. Australia's micro-economic inefficiencies were fundamental in the distortion of investment flows during the 1980s into the non-trading side of the economy. This was a defect in the implementation phase—but the final destination was clear.

In Australia financial deregulation came in the 1983–85 period. It led to the historic scaling back in protection announced in 1988 and then in 1991. The next pillar to fall would be that of labour market regulation, despite Labor's own timidity; this move to a more flexible enterprise based wages system loomed as the main reform of the 1990s.

Years later John Button reflected: 'There was a world bank study recently and what it says, in effect, is that you should deregulate your labour market first. Second, you reduce protection. And third, you free up your financial sector. That's exactly the opposite way to Australia in the 1980s.'[9]

But governments cannot operate from textbooks, as Button knows. Micro-economic reform was about changing Australia's work culture and destroying the mindset that produced the Australian Settlement. That meant seizing whatever opportunities arose to implant the seeds for a replacement culture. Labor's sequence of reform may not have been perfect and its progress was gradual. But its redeeming grace was that as the party of labour, it tried to introduce the cultural change into the heart of the workforce.

21
The Elliott emergence

Disunity is death.

John Howard, after his election defeat in July 1987

John Elliott believed in business, politics and football in that order. Elliott was a ruthless exponent of the new money creed—the takeover code of the 1980s based on choice of an undervalued victim, the high debt buyout, tax minimisation, the cultivation of patrons and winning the confidence of creditors. While turning Elders–IXL into an international corporation, Elliott remained a creature of his roots. He loved Melbourne—its football, its beer and its Liberal Party, and he assumed a proprietorial control over all three.

Elliott was Carlton football club president, controller of an overseas empire with Foster's as its spearhead, and federal treasurer of the Liberal Party. Elliott was ruthless but friendly, an international businessman with the tastes of an ocker; he was a believer in the philosophy of Margaret Thatcher, and his authentic hero was Winston Churchill. He devoured companies, became a media celebrity and a cult figure in Melbourne. Elliott embodied and exploited the 1980s obsession with the entrepreneur as the pinnacle of achievement—and fell victim to it. Public fascination with money and power, and the extravagant worship of material excess guaranteed him a status beyond the reach of normal chief executive. For Elliott it was not enough—and this is the key to his downfall.

Elliott's ambition to become prime minister was common knowledge though underestimated. Elliott would become prime minister on his own conditions, provided events suited him. The mountain would come to him. Despite some similarities to Hawke, the great difference was that Elliott displayed little apparent belief in public service or political idealism— beliefs which eventually forced Hawke to gamble to fulfil his destiny.

Elliott smelled the weakness in the parliamentary Liberal Party as keenly as he could locate a takeover victim. He supported Howard's economic policy and saw Peacock as devoid of policy conviction. To Elliott, Howard was a 'little man' and Peacock an aged dandy. He scarcely knew either of them but felt their superior. The message the Liberal Party drew from defeat was the imperative for unity—but unity would defy the Liberals during the entire 1987–90 term. It would be dominated by a three-way power struggle involving Howard, Peacock, and Elliott. The Liberals were to spend another three years plagued by intrigue, disloyalty and political assassination.

On the day after the 1987 election defeat, five men gathered at Sydney's Intercontinental Hotel to lay the basis for a new order of Liberal stability— Howard, Chaney, Elliott, Valder and Eggleton—but their efforts were soon shot.

They agreed that Howard would stay leader and that Howard and Peacock must bury their differences. Chaney came with an uncompromising message about the need for a final Howard–Peacock settlement. Valder told Elliott that he was resigning as federal president and urged an enthusiastic Elliott to take his place. Elliott and Eggleton reviewed plans to revive the Liberal Party and increase the authority of its organisational wing. Valder and Elliott were convinced that a Howard–Chaney team was the best and Chaney decided to nominate as deputy and announce that he would eventually move to the lower House.

Howard depicted himself as an 'honest' victim of the Joh frenzy, which he used to disguise his own leadership failures. For the party Howard's fighting quality had shown in adversity. His inadequate personal skills, weakness as a team leader and faulty strategic judgement could be partly exonerated by the extraordinary pressures under which he had operated. Howard, Chaney and Elliott symbolised the new Liberal elite which denied Peacock's effort to return to the leadership.

Peacock, whose power base was still intact, hit out at Elliott: 'He doesn't like standing for positions, he likes them handed to him'—the first volley in a spiteful firestorm between Peacock and Elliott which would rage for months. An impulsive Malcolm Fraser rang Elliott to warn him that Howard's mythology (that the defeat was Joh's work) must be exposed. Liberal rebel Steele Hall spoke up for the anti-Howard wets and declared that even if Howard were reelected, 'there is an inevitability that he cannot lead the Liberals into the next election'.

Within three days of the defeat Elliott announced his availability to succeed Valder as federal president. He offered his drive, his profile, his financial power and his big fist. Most Liberals welcomed the Elliott emergence but some were terrified. Elliott was blatant and patronising. His announced candidature for the presidency was coupled with an announced interest in seeking pre-selection in the seat of Higgins in 18 months time. Elliott was shaking the trees, a man close to intoxication with success.

The Elliott emergence

At this point the Liberal wets, still led by Ian Macphee, rallied and prevailed against the emerging power structure. Since 1983 the wets had voted as a bloc on leadership ballots and they remained the core of Peacock's power base. A few evenings after the election the wets dined in Melbourne at a long-planned Liberal Forum with Peacock as their guest.

Peacock was campaigning for the leadership, but Macphee, aware that Howard would prevail as leader, wanted to deny control of the party to the emerging Howard–Chaney–Elliott structure. Macphee and Chris Puplick told Peacock he must run as deputy if beaten by Howard in the leader's ballot. They saw a powerful Elliott as even more terrible than an incumbent Howard.[1] From the start Macphee believed that Elliott might try to seize the leadership.

The evening before the vote, Janette Howard said on television that her husband's best qualities were honesty, loyalty and courage. Asked if Peacock had them all she replied, 'No.' She said, 'A leader is someone that shouldn't be judged on the ability to smile at a TV camera.'

Howard beat Peacock 41–28 as predicted, his first win against Peacock in a leadership contest. The surprise was that Peacock nominated and won the deputy's ballot in a field of 11, beating Chaney 36–24 in the final count. It was Peacock's second party room spur-of-the-moment shock in the two years since his 1985 performance. There was a second message in this result—the endurance of the Peacock power base. Peacock had resigned the leadership in 1985, flirted with the Joh push in 1987, been dismissed from the shadow ministry by Howard before the 1987 election and had taken no substantial role in the campaign. Yet Peacock fell only seven votes short of beating Howard. The Peacock base was institutionalised, reliant upon long personal association, the loyalty of the wets, the intensity of anti-Howard sentiment and the absence of any other contenders.

The final message from this ballot was that the Liberals were bereft of leadership figures. Howard and Peacock had both lost an election to Hawke, yet there was no one else with the stature to stand for the leadership. Australian history shows that Opposition leaders generally perform best at their first election—a point which would hardly have inspired the Liberals if they had known enough history to realise it. Elliott saw a party becalmed in mediocrity.

The Liberals, tormented by the Howard–Peacock rivalry, produced the solution of an arranged marriage. Howard and Peacock could tolerate each other but could never form a partnership. Neither personality insight nor political experience offered any hope for a constructive partnership. Howard appointed Peacock as shadow treasurer, ditching the hapless Carlton, and gave Chaney the critical industrial portfolio.

Howard in a famous remark said the lesson the Liberals had learnt was 'that disunity is death'. Peacock, looking uncomfortable, admitted that he still wanted to become prime minister but that event might be ten or twenty years away. He ruled out any challenge to Howard, in contrast to Howard's answer from the same position after the previous election. This joint front was quite unconvincing. But the political grenade came from Elliott, who added the gratuitous remark that Peacock 'has no chance in the future of going into the leadership'.

Tony Eggleton had drafted a four-point program for the reform of the Liberal Party structure, designed to boost its election fighting capacity, which became the Elliott program. Its elements were an enhanced power for the federal director in federal election strategy; more accountability of the parliamentary wing to the organisational wing by requiring the Federal Executive to take action against MPs who engaged in serious acts of disloyalty; an expanded Federal Secretariat with a special unit devoted to campaign strategy and implementation; and a new strategy group which linked the parliamentary and organisational wings.

These reforms implied a greater centralisation of party authority, a firmer discipline among Liberal politicians, a greater assertion of central control over federal campaigns and a more powerful Federal Secretariat. They were decisions which the Labor Party had long since taken and which were central to its election victories in the 1980s. The reforms were endorsed by the Federal Executive at its 17 August meeting after the election. The Eggleton blueprint was backed by Elliott and created the misleading impression of an Elliott takeover of the Liberal Party.

Howard reconstructed the coalition with the National Party on the basis of three assurances from the Nationals: that a coalition meant joint policies; a pledge that there would be 'no recurrence of the Queensland problem'; and a requirement that all federal National MPs participate in the coalition arrangement. The Queensland Nationals were too badly burned to fight; National Party separatism was in retreat as the 'Joh for Canberra' push assumed the status of an historical aberration.

Howard had distinct reasons for optimism, since the two great negatives which had plagued the non-Labor side during the previous term had now been reduced or eliminated. The first was the policy conflict embodied in the wet/dry split: the economic direction of the party was settled; the dissidents had surrendered that fight.

The second change was the disintegration of the non-Labor assault on its own federal parliamentary wing. The agents of this revolt were soon vanquished, discredited or apologetic—the Queensland National Party, the National Farmers' Federation, Ian McLachlan, the small business lobby, the New Right industrialists, Katherine West, and flat tax populists.

This meant that the Liberal embrace of free market economics became a virtually undisputed position. The policies of small government, industry deregulation, labour market deregulation, cutting the tax burden and renewing the fight against inflation were largely accepted. Over the next two years the Liberals filled their ranks with many notable drys and perceived 'hard men' of the right—McLachlan, Michael Kroger, Costello and David Kemp. Other symbols of this process were the entry into federal parliament of John Stone (as a National) and the former Howard adviser and economic dry, John Hewson, who won a safe Sydney seat at the 1987 election.

But the coming term would witness further deep divisions inside the party originating in personality and power conflicts. There would be a revival of the Liberal Party's instinctive obsession—the imperative for a powerful leader to guarantee electoral victory. Howard would falter in the coming period because he would fail to satisfy this most deeply rooted of Liberal sentiments, the need to submit to an authority figure.

The next candidate for the messiah's mantle would be John Elliott. In retrospect he may look a wild card but in 1987–88 Elliott was a dominating figure. The next tragedy to befall Howard was a protracted struggle with Elliott, a conflict between Liberal leader and Liberal president. It began slowly but it mounted in intensity until it left Howard exposed and weakened.

Elliott denied Howard the prize he sought after the 1987 election—a genuine leadership authority. But, Elliott would say in his defence, this quality was always lacking in Howard. The Howard–Elliott battle took the party towards a fatal judgement about Howard—that he was doomed to internal fights without ever taking command.

Peacock was alarmed by the Elliott emergence, his indolence stirred because Elliott was a domestic rival, a threat to Peacock's position as the senior Victorian Liberal. If Elliott came into parliament he would destroy Peacock's comfortable self-image. Elliott was too rich, too powerful and too self-confident for Peacock. He was too crude in his beer drinking, pie eating habits, too intimidating in his financial nous, too influential in football, too magnetic in his radiation of raw power.

Elliott was aggressive and a blunderer where Peacock was slippery and clever. Elliott said what he believed when Peacock struggled to find what he believed. Elliott was strong where Peacock wavered. Elliott was a man of the times—fast money, hard politics—where Peacock was an adaptor to the times. Elliott had the killer label stamped on him while Peacock was too soft. So Peacock determined to block Elliott's influence.

But Peacock had a decisive advantage over Elliott—the skills of the professional politician. Peacock was proud of his skills and he correctly saw Elliott as an amateur. Peacock dismissed as fatuous the parallels which some Liberals drew between Hawke and Elliott. Peacock saw Elliott as a bully who was unlikely to surrender his pot of gold or corporate lifestyle to the vagaries of politics—a shrewd assessment. Peacock identified the flaws in Elliott.

Elliott excited the passions of the Liberals just as Hawke had once excited Labor's more flammable passions. At this time Elliott was 45, three years younger than either Howard or Peacock. He was a natural leader and, by mid-1987, a businessman of extraordinary success.

Elliott was the product of a comfortable, middle class childhood in East Kew, Melbourne. His father was a lifelong bank employee and the values imparted to Elliott were a belief in family, private enterprise, the Liberal Party, the competitive spirit, Carlton football club and hard work. At 16 Elliott took his career decision: it was business, not politics. He completed a Commerce degree at Melbourne University and worked briefly for BHP. But Elliott broke away, did an MBA degree and, inspired by a talk given by McKinsey's principal Rod Carnegie, came second in his class and won a rare post with McKinsey and Co.[2]

McKinsey's gave Elliott corporate sophistication and invaluable contacts such as BHP general manager Sir Ian McLennan, soon to become his patron. Six years with McKinsey's gave Elliott an insight into a range of Australian businesses and an analytical capacity to dissect corporations. He had joined the Liberal Party in the run-up to the 1972 election, but he was getting ready for the big leap.

Elliott raised $50 000 and raided the failing Tasmanian jam manufacturer Henry Jones (IXL), which had poor dividends and book assets in the $30–$50 million range. Elliott was backed by the Melbourne establishment—McLennan, Carnegie and Baillieu. The 'jam man' was launched.

His subsequent success was shaped by several factors—boardroom fears of Robert Holmes a'Court ; the ruthless and effective Elliott team comprising the finance guru from McKinsey's, Richard Wiesener, former test cricketer Bob Cowper, and marketing expert Peter Scanlon; and Elliott's technique of borrowing big for the takeover and then relying upon cost savings, asset selling and tax minimisation to generate hefty cash flows. These factors were critical in Elliott's first extraordinary coup—his effective takeover of Elders GM, thus forming Elders–IXL, a modern version of the British East India Company, which became the platform for his domestic and overseas expansion.

Elliott next acquired Carlton United Breweries (CUB) in the biggest takeover in Australian history, with the CUB board partly paralysed and unable to mount an effective defence. Then he consolidated Elders–IXL into five major divisions—pastoral, international trading, finance, brewing and resources. Elliott's strategy was to 'Fosterise' the world—a word coined from the beer he once described as 'an angel crying on your tongue'.

The biggest play came in 1986 with the Holmes a'Court bid for BHP, a move of frightening audacity. Elliott began buying and came to occupy a unique place in Australian business. Initially himself an outsider, he was finally recruited by the Melbourne establishment to become the white knight to save BHP from the true outsider, Holmes a'Court.

The bigger Elliott grew the more irresistible became the rumours of a political career. Years earlier Elliott had turned down two chances to enter politics. The first was in 1975 when John Gorton resigned and the seat of Higgins fell vacant; the second was in 1980 when Tony Staley quit politics and invited Elliott to take his seat of Chisholm. Elliott declined both times due to corporate pressures.

In May 1986, when Elliott and Holmes a'Court were negotiating in Melbourne over the BHP deal, Holmes a'Court said he would make an offer for Elders: 'We'd get to buy the shares and you'd get to be Prime Minister of Australia.' Politics was Elliott's shadow life. If he made politics his real life he would be the most important high level recruit to the Liberals in decades and the most senior businessman to enter federal parliament.

Party opinion about Elliott was sharply divided. His appearance invited divisions—his gruff voice and a touch of intimidation behind his smile. Yet he carried the ring of trust, the 'true blue' open Aussie stamp as well. Jim Carlton, a long-time Elliott friend, declared: 'He's a damn good leader. He has a natural command. People enjoy that, they feel secure . . . he shows no signs of doubt.'[3]

Elliott's economics were heavily on the dry side with overtones of Menzian simplicity: 'My basic beliefs are that you have a strong economy so everyone has a job, you raise the living standards of your citizens, you have the freedom of the individual and welfare that is based upon need, not greed.'[4]

Elliott's third flirtation with politics came before the federal election in early 1987, and this time he was prepared to move. Many Liberals were shocked to hear that Elliott and his local backers were trying to get the Higgins preselection reopened and remove their local member, Roger Shipton, an earnest tryer on the backbench and Peacock's mate.

Shipton was too honest to exploit the forces trying to secure his removal. In the saga of Elliott's thwarted political career, Shipton was destined to achieve his only real fame in politics. He blocked Elliott not once but twice—the second time with great consequences.

Elliott had the support of the president of the Victorian Liberal Party, Eda Ritchie. His momentum was driven by the conviction among intelligent and younger Liberals in Victoria that their parliamentary ranks were manifestly inferior to those of Labor. Many saw Elliott as a symbol of the change needed—the choice between the past and the future. The Elliott push reflected the organisation's disillusionment with the parliamentary party—its self-hate, its brawls, its failure to match Hawke and Keating.[5]

Hawke's swift rise to power in 1983 had exercised a powerful influence within Liberal circles. It revealed Labor as the successful party in recruitment and promotion of the vote winner. The Liberals sought to replicate the Hawke solution, which is why figures such as Elliott and McLachlan were such a focus of attention. Elliott was a call to power. It was the power he radiated that drew the party towards him like a magnet.

The Victorian administrative committee voted in April 1987 against

Elliott by declining to reopen preselection for Higgins, a decision confirmed by the Higgins committee. Howard supported Shipton as the preselected candidate, adding that 'you can never assume that a person who is a whizz in business is a whizz in politics'.[6]

Within weeks, at the start of the 1987 election campaign, Elliott had another chance. Victorian president Ritchie told Elliott, 'We can give you Bruce—but I need to know within 48 hours.' But Elliott declined and the offer was kept a secret. It illuminated the Elliott dilemma: he wanted the right seat at the right time—almost to the hour.

The defeat of the Liberal Party in the 1987 election only increased Elliott's influence within the party. A fortnight later a strong Elliott backer, the thirty-year-old lawyer Michael Kroger, was elected president of the Victorian party. Kroger wanted to shake up the party and reform preselection procedures to get better candidates. His victory was a decisive vote for change.

In July 1987 Elliott confirmed plans to marry Amanda Drummond-Moray, announced a major restructuring of Elders–IXL and won in principle support for his Liberal Party presidency. A company restructuring proposal gave Elliott a hefty equity incentive for staying in business and forgetting parliamentary politics. It was the prelude to his most ambitious move—the effort to secure majority equity in Elders through Harlin Holdings, which was controlled by the Elliott circle.

This was a great step: Elliott's attempted transition from businessman to owner–entrepreneur. Harlin emerged from the wash-up of the Elders/BHP/Holmes a'Court settlement; it was Elliott's vehicle in 1989 for the launch of a fantastic bid for a large slice of Elders. In retrospect the numbers defy logic but Elliott won the backing of international banks for his bid, which has been described as 'the most amazing financial deal of the late 1980s'.[7]

The outline of the Harlin story is known; it was Elliott's ultimate business deal and the instrument of his failure. But the related story is little known; that at the same time Elliott was involved in a series of dramatic political events—he fell out with Howard, he made his own amazing dash towards the prime ministership and, finally, he backed Andrew Peacock as his man in the Lodge.

On 2 August 1987 Howard and Elliott met in Sydney, and Howard signalled tacit support for an Elliott Liberal Party presidency. Howard, like Peacock, had bowed to the inevitable; he knew that to deny Elliott would send a terrible message to the business community.

It was agreed that Elliott would become interim president pending his confirmation at the Federal Council in autumn 1988. Asked on 17 August about his parliamentary ambitions Elliott gave an equivocal reply: 'Hopefully, I won't have to contemplate it because we'll win [the election]. If we were still in opposition—I don't think we will be—you've got to re-look at the situation.'[8]

The Elliott presidency offered much for the Liberals but was also fraught with danger. Elliott's recent career had involved the reshaping of tired and old-fashioned companies and turning them into successful profit makers. The Liberals needed the Elliott treatment. Yet Elliott was an explosive commodity. First, he had ambitions to become prime minister, which meant a degree of rivalry between himself and the parliamentary wing. Second, the realisation of this ambition was a direct function of the performance of the current leaders—if they failed then the party would turn to Elliott—which meant that a potential conflict of interest existed between Elliott and the parliamentary leaders. Third, the president was required to limit his public remarks to support for current policy, yet Elliott had his own policy beliefs (for example, needs-based welfare and a consumption tax) which were not party policy but which Elliott was hardly likely to suppress. Fourth, Elliott saw the presidency not just as a chance to boost the finances, resources and talent of the party but also as a public platform for himself and the ideology which he wanted the party to embrace.

Howard had sought and believed he had won from Elliott an assurance that as federal president he would not comment on policy issues and that he would avoid the controversial public comments which had highlighted the Valder presidency. The principles involved were simple. The parliamentary wing made policy and the party organisation had a right to consultation but had no power over policy, a division of responsibility long understood in the Liberal Party.

But Elliott was a man who gave orders and got his way in business. Politics was very different—authority rested upon influence and persuasion. A leader had to persuade his Cabinet, his party and then the community. Elliott had little grasp of the rules of political institutions and his refusal to accept this new culture lay at the core of the convulsions that followed.

Despite Elliott's conviction about the need for the assets test and a consumption tax, the Liberal Party had campaigned against the assets test at the two previous federal elections and against the consumption tax at the most recent election. Both issues were under review in the post-election policy rethink, but there was no certainty that either would be embraced. Any public campaign by Elliott, particularly for a consumption tax, would only create an upheaval within the party. Yet this is exactly what happened.

From the 'in principle' acceptance of the Elliott presidency until its formal confirmation in April 1988 by the Federal Council, relations between the parliamentary wing and Elliott moved from unease to crisis. In particular, relations between Howard and Elliott deteriorated so badly that the Liberals were faced with the worst clash between a federal leader and federal president in the party's history.

Elliott arrived back in Australia from his honeymoon during the sharemarket crash, made several million dollars in two days and declared Australia needed a leader like Margaret Thatcher, more vision and an indirect tax.[9]

Peacock, the shadow treasurer, opposed the indirect tax and criticised Elliott. Howard, a supporter of the indirect tax, knew that Elliott's advocacy would only make it more difficult to sell the idea to the party. But Elliott just kept talking. A week later he called for both an assets test *and* a consumption tax. Liberals were dismayed and Peacock again criticised Elliott.[10]

It was inevitable, therefore, that the party executive at its 30 October meeting would appoint Elliot as interim president on the condition that he cease to publicise his personal policy views. Agreement was reached at a dinner the night before at the Commonwealth Club in Canberra, attended by Howard, Peacock, Chaney, Elliott and Eggleton. The aim was to secure from Elliott a pledge to abide by party rules. But Peacock launched a withering assault on Elliott which stunned the rest. For ten minutes Peacock attacked Elliott and his public comments on economic policy, a performance which the others later called a Peacock rage. Howard watching this Pea-cock–Elliott stoush could draw only one conclusion—Peacock and Elliott would never combine against him.

Eggleton drafted a letter of understanding to set out the guarantees Elliott had given.

The drive for unity by Howard and the parliamentary leaders was understandable. But within a fortnight Elliott was campaigning for an extra $3 billion spending cut and a lower dollar, around US61 cents. Keating made a killing in parliament, demanding to know who made policy— Howard or Elliott. Howard rang Elliott to remind him of his undertaking. But it made no impression, for Elliott soon repeated the same remarks. On 19 November, speaking to the Institute of Directors in Sydney, Elliott virtually mocked the parliamentary wing declaring: 'I said it in the chairman's address at Elders on Monday and I am certain some of my colleagues would have liked me to have gone further, as chairman's addresses are reviewed by all the Board not by the Liberal Party . . . (loud laughter from the audience) . . . that the Government ought to get up and say we are going to cut expenditure by about $3 billion.'[11]

The next day Howard openly rebuked Elliott: 'You can only have one captain of the political ship and that's the parliamentary leader . . . I run the political side of things. Mr Elliott is the head of the organisation. Any comment he makes on policy matters must reflect the policy of the party.'

On 22 November Peacock publicly warned Elliott, declaring that he, not Elliott, was shadow treasurer. Referring to Elliott's recent remarks as a 'settling in period', Peacock added, 'I trust it's now over.' Howard wrote to Elliott, again spelling out the basis of his appointment as acting president. But it was obvious that Elliott was never going to be bound by Howard.

Elliott's position was similar to that of Hawke when he served as ALP president during the Whitlam years. Both men wore two hats—Hawke the ACTU and ALP presidencies; Elliott the Liberal and Elders–IXL 'presidencies'. The interests of these positions did not necessarily coincide so there was an institutional conflict. Howard was trying to rebuke a man who refused to be rebuked, a dangerous position for any leader.

In early 1988 the Hawke government stumbled badly with an 8.5 per cent two party preferred swing against Labor at the Adelaide by-election. It was the first electoral contest between Hawke and Howard since the 1987 federal election and Howard placed an overwhelming priority on a sound Liberal performance. Yet the Adelaide campaign was notable for another event—the elevation of the Elliott–Howard rift to a more serious level.[12]

The day before the by-election Howard and Elliott were in Adelaide for a federal executive meeting. Elliott addressed a Liberal breakfast at Norwood Football Club, having just arrived, once again, from London. He told them the party machine had been 'moribund' at the 1987 federal election; that the party had only begun to shed its 'born-to-rule attitude'; that it had clung to campaign strategies that were more than a decade old. Elliott said that from the late 1960s, when Menzies quit, the Liberals had started to go bad. Rejuvenation had followed the demise of Whitlam but 'Fraser did not deliver and now we have got Hawke'. He pressed ahead: 'Now we in the Liberal Party have started, as a result of losing at the last election, to get our act together because we haven't had it together. I do believe that in a sense there is a watershed here in Adelaide because what we have done since the election is to sit down and basically face up to the fact that we did not deserve to be in government. We hadn't done a good enough job.'[13]

Elliott's pithy analysis of party history on the day before a critical by-election which would have a direct bearing on Howard's leadership was pure folly. Elliott, by implication, was criticising Howard. Elliott had handed the media a Howard–Elliott split story on the eve of the by-election. It would dominate the Friday night television coverage and newspaper coverage on Saturday morning, voting day. The federal executive was sitting when Howard was informed about Elliott's comments. A furious Howard spoke up: 'John, I believe you've caused us great embarrassment and damage yet again.' Elliott was surprised. 'No I haven't. I didn't say anything that was wrong,' he replied. But Howard refused to be soothed by his protestations. He railed against Elliott, blaming him for the blunder. Peacock backed Howard's criticism.

Elliott, as usual, defended himself aggressively. He claimed to have been misreported; he had meant that the electorate had not thought the party deserved to win. At this meeting some Liberals watching Elliott defend himself felt that the process of political comment, reporting and fall-out, seemed beyond his comprehension. The South Australian Liberal secretary,

Nick Minchin, later suggested to Elliott it might be best if he didn't return to Adelaide at election times.

It was at this point that Howard identified Elliott as the real threat to his position, both as a potential challenger and an agent for destabilisation. The seeds of Howard's obsession with Elliott were deeply planted. Howard asked himself: were Elliott's remarks the product of naivety or inspired by malicious intent? Their impact was obvious—they were undermining the leader.

Howard called for party loyalty: 'I don't as parliamentary leader want to hear any more talk from Liberals in public dumping on their own party. The years of breast-beating and self-criticism in public have got to be put behind us.'[14] But John Elliott was not listening. Inside the parliamentary wing there were mutterings: was Elliott a conspirator or a stumbler?

Elliott was delivering for the organisation and that was generating gossip about an Elliott takeover. The annual budget for the Federal Secretariat had doubled to $2 million. The staff was expanded and boosted with the appointment of a deputy to Eggleton. This was Andrew Robb, who had been director of the National Farmers' Federation for the previous three years. Robb was appointed by Eggleton but was Elliott's own choice. He came because he believed that Elliott's drive combined with a new generation of young Liberals like Kroger and Costello would revitalise the party.

As the April 1988 Federal Council meeting neared, Howard was secure in the leadership and he approached the meeting with great optimism. The win in the Adelaide by-election and the 9 per cent two party preferred swing to the Opposition in the Port Adelaide by-election, along with the smashing NSW state election victory by Nick Greiner, offered the prospect of a sea-change in politics.

Elliott was keen to see the Council meeting advance the consumption tax cause. He spoke to Howard in mid-March and confirmed that Howard would be arguing in favour of the tax. Then Elliott, much to Howard's surprise, spoke out publicly in favour of the consumption tax. Elliott said the tax was 'essential' in terms of running Australia but conceded it was not necessarily 'a major winner in the electorate'. He said he would promote the consumption tax cause at Federal Council although he agreed that the decision rested with the parliamentary party. His comments were in apparent contradiction of his assurances to Howard.

The backlash from the parliamentary wing was enormous. Elliott denied that he was trying to undermine Howard and gave an unequivocal pledge that he would not enter parliament before the next election. Asked by Laurie Oakes if this pledge could 'change for any reasons at all', Elliott replied, 'No. I have no intention to change that.'[15]

One reason that the Federal Council meeting was so sensitive was that the coalition's economic policy group of Howard, Peacock, Sinclair, Stone and Hewson had held talks over several months on tax policy and was divided. The National Party bitterly opposed any consumption tax, fearing the impact on its rural constituency. Peacock was always sceptical for political reasons. Howard and Hewson believed such a tax was inevitable, along with most of the Liberal drys and Elliott.

Howard had tried and failed during the 1980s to persuade the non-Labor side to accept an indirect tax. After the 1987 election he was more convinced than ever, but Howard had never solved the political problems inherent in such a concept. It was a difficult initiative to market from the Opposition benches.

Howard now found a new and formidable opponent of the consumption tax—his shadow finance minister John Stone. Stone was as brazen as Elliott in his campaign against a consumption tax and compromised his shadow Cabinet responsibilities in this exercise. In October 1987 he told the National Party Federal Council that in its tax review the coalition should dismiss a consumption tax. Stone argued, as before, that if implemented it would broaden the revenue base, thereby serving as a substitute for spending cuts, which should have a higher priority. Stone warned that 'he wouldn't be in the coalition' if it embraced the consumption tax, adding that such a tax 'would be so crazy that no sensible person would be part of it'.

Howard was left in an impossible position—a consumption tax, even if he could persuade the Liberals, would break the coalition—a price Howard would never pay.

On 3 December 1987 Stone gave the annual Earle Page memorial lecture and in the context of immigration policy, he declared that the Opposition had not deserved to win the last federal election. The resulting uproar in both Liberal and National Parties ensured that Stone's shadow ministry position became strictly conditional. At a shadow ministry meeting on 7 December Stone was put under intense pressure and warned to toe the line, or else. He did so for three months, until Elliott's efforts to rekindle the consumption tax issue in March 1988. This time the Nationals went for Elliott's throat.

This occurred during the federal by-election in the Queensland seat of Groom where the Nationals were fighting the Liberals. In their desperation to stave off a Liberal Party move to steal the seat, the Queensland Nationals, seizing upon Elliott's comments, began to paint the Liberals as the pro-consumption tax party.

On 27 March Ian Sinclair attacked Elliott: 'A consumption tax has never been part of our National Party policy. Somebody said to me John Elliott could be our secret weapon in the Groom by-election. I'm not sure there's not some truth in that.' Two days later Stone delivered another tax ultimatum by lashing out at 'the business wing of the Liberal Party' for talking 'divisive nonsense' about a consumption tax—an obvious reference to Elliott.

Howard arrived back in Australia on the eve of the Federal Council to confront an uproar: his challenge was to discipline both Elliott and Stone.

He told Stone at a shadow ministry meeting on 5 April that he would be dismissed from the front bench if he refused to support agreed procedures for determining policy. Then he sprang an ambush on Elliott later the same day.

Howard had assembled at Liberal Party HQ in Canberra the elite of the party—himself, Peacock, Chaney, Austin Lewis (the four leaders) and Valder, Eggleton, vice president Joy Mein and the federal treasurer David Clarke. It was Howard's most concerted effort to pull Elliott into line, just three days before the Federal Council would meet.

Elliott arrived more than two hours late, after the others had caucused. They had examined the party constitution and confirmed that the federal executive could remove the party president. Elliott walked into a trap.

Howard began by telling Elliott that his loose tongue had to be curbed and the time for any further concessions had gone. He said: 'You're a straight-shooter, John, so I'll give it to you straight. It's essential that you make a public statement saying you'll abide by the rules. We've been in this situation before and it's happened too many times.' If there was a next time, Howard told Elliott, then 'it will be the last'. In this situation, Howard said, 'If we can't work together then you'll have to resign. I just won't work with you again.'

Elliott was unmoved. He stared down Howard. 'There's no way I'll be resigning,' Elliott said. Pure defiance.[16] If Howard declared war then Elliott would fight.

At this point the Howard–Elliott contest became a struggle of political life and death. It moved from the phase of tension, warning, cajoling, into a deadly struggle. No parliamentary leader had ever threatened a federal president this way; no federal president had ever shown such defiance towards a parliamentary leader. Howard and Elliott, leader and president, were deadlocked in the Menzies room at Liberal HQ.

Howard insisted upon a statement from Elliott or the inclusion in his presidential address to Federal Council of a 'good behaviour' pledge. But Elliott refused point blank. Finally Eggleton suggested that the meeting break and took Elliott to his office for 15 minutes, where he persuaded Elliott to agree to Howard's demand for the 'good behaviour' pledge. After Elliott relented the meeting reassembled with the tension broken. Howard said that when the meeting finished he would issue a press statement saying that Elliott had reaffirmed that he would not comment on policy issues. One point on which Elliott insisted and Howard endorsed was that there was no mention to the media of Elliott's agreement to include the 'good behaviour' pledge in his Council speech. Elliott was firm on this.

John Elliott left the meeting and flew to Hong Kong with the feeling that Howard had ambushed him; that Howard had not played by the rules. Elliott, of course, was wrong. His own self-indulgence had given neither Howard nor the party any other choice. But Howard's authority was running out. Opposition disunity nine months after the election was still the biggest political issue in the media. From Howard's viewpoint, Elliott, and Stone to a lesser extent, were ruining the potentially winning position of the coalition.

Desperate to assert his leadership, Howard made a terrible mistake after the ninety-minute meeting broke. He allowed his staff to background senior correspondents on the meeting. The next morning several major newspapers reported that Howard had threatened to remove Elliott and that Elliott was on notice of dismissal unless he changed his ways. The stories were featured prominently on page one of most papers. There was only one conclusion—the Howard camp had briefed the media in breach of Howard's agreement with Elliott on what would be said. Howard's office could not resist the opportunity to depict Howard as a strong man.

Elliott went into a rage in Hong Kong when he was told about the media coverage, believing that Howard had breached their agreement. Elliott felt that his humiliation was the price Howard demanded to project authority. The trouble for Howard was that the leader who had to manufacture events to display his authority was revealed as having an authority problem. Eggleton had sent Elliott a draft form of words for inclusion in his presidential speech, as Howard had wanted. But Elliott was not interested. He said that Howard had broken their agreement so he was no longer bound by it.

When Eggleton spoke to Elliott he sensed a storm looming. The next day Elliott told Eggleton from Tokyo that he would make a public statement defending himself and criticising Howard. 'I'll write it myself, Tony, because you're too tactful,' Elliott said. Eggleton saw that a Howard–Elliott showdown was inevitable. Howard would not retreat from his insistence on an Elliott 'good behaviour' pledge now his staff had informed the public about it, but Elliott refused to submit. The content of the dispute had become irrelevant; it was a battle of will and authority.

However Howard had problems with Stone as well as Elliott. On the afternoon of 5 April, only hours after his censure by the shadow Cabinet for his remarks about the consumption tax, Stone told the media: 'Nothing that happens in the shadow Cabinet or anywhere else changes my mind about any of the statements I have made in the past.' When asked whether or not a National Party advertisement used in the Groom by-election saying the Liberals backed a consumption tax was misleading, Stone said with contempt: 'If they don't, they can say so, can't they?' This was the very advertisement which Howard had branded as dishonest and about which he had already complained to Sinclair.[17]

The next Friday Liberals gathered in Sydney for the memorial service for their former leader Sir William McMahon. As senior Liberals filled the pews at St Andrew's Cathedral, Eggleton reflected on the continuity of the crises in the party from McMahon to Howard. Eggleton knew his self-appointed role in this crisis—he had to pacify Elliott and save Howard's honour.

After the service Howard flew to Melbourne and the Hyatt Hotel, with its ostentatious marble, huge potplants and media throng. The weekend Federal Council, opening that night, was a very public event. By Howard's side was his wife Janette, his confidant and his steel. Janette was resolute; Elliott had to be beaten in this test of wills; Elliott was a threat to the leader. Valder later described Howard as 'arriving in a rage the like of which I had never seen in him . . . he was physically shaking'. Valder took Howard up to his hotel room in an effort to calm him. But Howard was beyond compromise. Valder found Elliott just as stubborn, declaring: 'Howard's got to come to see me.'

Elliott's statement, released in the afternoon was softer than he had originally intended, but although his criticism of Howard was veiled it was still obvious. The Liberals plunged into crisis in front of a huge array of the national media. Meetings, urgent talks and briefings took place as the media surged back and forth through the large off-conference area. The formal dispute was about Elliott's refusal to include the 'good behaviour' pledge in his speech and Howard's determination to get it inserted. The real dispute was about power.

Howard called a series of meetings—the four parliamentary leaders, and then a shadow Cabinet meeting off-stage to secure its full support for his insistence on the 'good behaviour' pledge from Elliott. Before the shadow Cabinet met Valder asked Howard to back off, telling him that the state presidents supported Elliott. But Howard was in no mood for retreat. Yet when he confronted Elliott he was met with defiance—Elliott would not tolerate another backdown to Howard.

Howard then convened the same group which had met on the Tuesday afternoon at party HQ. At first Elliott declined even to attend, but persuaded by Valder he marched in and confronted Howard. Elliott accused Howard of setting him up. He said the media coverage of the Tuesday meeting was inspired by Howard and directed from his office. It was in breach of their agreement. When Howard denied this Elliott insisted: 'What you're saying is wrong.' But Howard refused to budge. He said that Elliott had agreed to the 'good behaviour' pledge in his speech and this was public knowledge. It was wanted by the parliamentary leaders and the shadow ministry. Howard's face was taut; his emotion was white anger. Elliott said he had made his statement and would say nothing else. Howard repeated his threat of three days earlier: unless Elliott agreed, their relationship was 'unworkable'.

The situation was perilous. Unless Elliott backed off the only solution was the resignation of one of them—clearly Howard would not resign as parliamentary leader.

Outside the room the Hyatt's convention floor was bathed in lights, blue banners on the walls, posters of Howard and Elliott together, the leader and president, in harmony, as though a decorative satirist, aware of the crisis, had come to mock the party.[18]

It was obvious to Valder and Eggleton that the only solution was an Elliott retreat. Valder became an intermediary; he warned Howard of the resentment building towards him within the assembled body of the party and that pushing too hard contained serious dangers for him. Valder and Eggleton told Elliott that he must concede in order to save Howard; that if he refused Howard's leadership of the parliamentary party would be ruined and his authority broken. There was no alternative leader, which meant that the party had an obligation to support Howard.

Eventually Howard, Elliott and Eggleton agreed upon an innocuous form of words. The long planned pre-Council cocktail party took place just after the stand-off broke. Elliott, cigarette and beer in hand, mingled with the media, looking completely unruffled. Eggleton, who had spent so much of his life watching politicians under crisis, was amazed at Elliott's capacity to isolate himself from the pressures. Howard by contrast appeared agitated and excited as he tried to mix with delegates and journalists; he was in post-crisis shock, split between desperation and relief.

The party insiders knew that Elliott had conceded to save Howard from humiliation. Howard's position meant that without Elliott's retreat he would have had to ask the Federal Executive to sack Elliott as federal president at the very Federal Council meeting that was designed to confirm his presidential appointment! Would the Federal Executive have agreed to sack Elliott? Perhaps, but there must be a serious doubt about this. The state presidents were on Elliott's side. If such a point had been reached, Howard's leadership would have been at risk. Howard could scarcely stay leader if he required as a condition of his leadership that Elliott be removed, and the executive had refused him, but this was the position in which Howard had put himself when he threatened Elliott.

Valder and Eggleton told Elliott the political truth—the president could afford to lose face but the leader could not. Elliott retreated to save Howard's position, which meant that Howard prevailed not through his strength but his weakness.

The form of words Elliott actually used in the statement negotiated between Howard, Elliott and Eggleton was hardly a 'good behaviour' pledge. The next morning—the day of the consumption tax debate—Elliott was breezy but Howard was touchy and slower to recover.

The party was split over the indirect tax. Its diehard opponents, notably state leaders, included Kennett in Victoria, Olsen in SA and Mackinnon in WA. The proponent or 'options-open' school included Elliott, David Clarke, Howard and Greiner.

The resolution moved by Elliott was safe and neutral. The real message from the debate was its demonstration of Liberal political failure. The dominant mood of the party was opposition to the indirect tax on political grounds. When the National Party's hostility was considered it became obvious that the coalition would not embrace a consumption tax in its policy review. So what was the point of having such a protracted fight about a tax the coalition was never likely to accept?

The political mistake made by the Liberals was elementary. The existing indirect tax system of the Hawke government was chaotic and badly needed reform. As Greiner explained, there was a consumption tax on ice-cream but not on pornographic magazines; on orange juice but not on mink coats. The Liberals should have been attacking Labor's existing indirect tax system, which was both inefficient and inequitable, as a first step towards the creation of a political climate for its reform and extension. They should have pointed out that Labor over five years had boosted its sales tax revenue by more than 100 per cent. The Liberals forgot that the first step in any reform was to discredit politically the old system. They had no idea of how to mould a climate for change.

During the long, debilitating non-Labor debate on indirect tax, the issue in the public arena was always the Opposition's policy, not the inadequacies of the government's tax system. The consumption tax deadlock inside the Liberal Party during the 1980s was a classic illustration of the limits of its political culture. With the mentality of a party of the status quo, the Liberals had no concept of how to mobilise opinion, win the media, attack the orthodoxy and marshal powerful advocates for the reform it sought.

After the tax debate Jim Carlton went to see Elliott to tell him the politics of the consumption tax issue were too hard and the shadow Cabinet was certain to reject it, the main reason being the absence of coalition unity. After explaining the politics to Elliott he asked whether Elliott would be prepared to live with the decision. Elliott told Carlton that he would and that nobody had analysed the politics of the issue with him before. Carlton left wondering why Howard had never sat down with Elliott to do so.

However Howard did have some good news before the Federal Council broke. The results of the Groom by-election coincided with the Saturday night dinner—the Liberals had taken Groom from the Nationals with a 20 per cent swing to them in the lush Darling Downs countryside. Queensland politics was being remade.

The next day Stone again attacked the consumption tax—an act of defiance in the teeth of the Liberal victory in Groom. When the shadow ministry met on Monday 11 April Howard applied a gag to all shadow ministers, barring them from expressing personal views on the issue. Asked if he would change his mind about the consumption tax Stone told the media: 'If pigs fly!' But Stone did not need to break the gag because he knew he had won the consumption tax battle.

In May the shadow Cabinet agreed to a set of tax principles leading to the next election, which excluded the consumption tax. The idea for which

Howard had been pushing for eight years still eluded him. Few leaders have been so unsuccessful persuading their own side of politics to one of their own basic policies.

In parliament Keating went for the jugular:

> The power has passed from Mr Howard to Mr Elliott. We heard all about the business representatives milling around Mr Elliott as though he was some sort of ageing political rock star . . . We have the case of the shadow Treasurer [Peacock] afraid of power and unable to strike down Mr Howard. So it is a case of the living dead . . . I described the leader of the Opposition the other day as a political carcass. I am saying to Mr Elliott: cut him down and let us get back to a proper basis of politics where the real power of the Liberal Party faces us in the Parliament.

Howard and Elliott had lost their campaign for the consumption tax. The Nationals had prevailed on this issue but that could not halt the progress of their political collapse in Queensland. Beyond the consumption tax question, Howard and Elliott were divided by their personal battle. Both knew that any recurrence would demand an execution—one would lose his job.

Elliott was a new president while Howard looked an old leader. The clash only served to illustrate the depth of Howard's limitations as a leader and Elliott's determination to exercise greater influence over the party.

The manner in which Elliott conducted himself as federal president was ultimately contrary to the interests of the Liberal Party. Elliott represented in extreme form the desire of the party to have a high profile president as part of the organisation's assertion of its position in relation to the parliamentary party. But Elliott only weakened the parliamentary leader and antagonised much of the parliamentary wing by his repeated forays onto its territory.

The same judgement can be passed on Elliott as applied to Bob Hawke during his own ALP presidency—the appointment of such an ambitious and high profile individual only created a rival platform to that of the parliamentary leader. Elliott abandoned the traditional role of the president—working quietly and privately—and substituted publicity for influence.

Howard emerged weaker, not stronger, from this clash. His hopes of achieving unity inside the Liberals and within the coalition after the 1987 election had failed. That failure, although the result of the wilfulness of Elliott, Stone and the Nationals, would ultimately be sheeted back to Howard. That is the nature of leadership. As the 1988 winter closed over Canberra there were two conflicting views of Howard's future—that a leader so scarred was tough enough to survive any future test or that a leader so doomed to internal disputes would not survive much longer.

22
Howard—the social agenda

When I was young my mother told me
As I sat upon her knee
Son, you're Australian
That's enough, for anyone to be.

from the 'Plain Thinking Man' jingle launched with
John Howard's 1988 *Future Directions* blueprint

In 1988 John Howard attempted to achieve a synthesis between economic libertarianism and social conservatism, an audacious blueprint for a new Liberal model. His motive was to fashion a broad appeal to the community to win the next election, projecting the values which were important to Howard's own life: support for the traditional family unit, greater individual responsibility and the idea of 'One Australia'.

The comprehensive statement of Howard's philosophy was released in his *Future Directions* document on 4 December 1988, a bold experiment that failed.

Howard was attempting to address the central challenge for modern liberalism: how to reconcile free market economics with a system of social values that preserved community life. Howard was the first Liberal to grasp that free market economics required a moral dimension and that the power of free market economics must be offset by an equally powerful theory of social order. The poverty of political debate in Australia was revealed by the response to *Future Directions*. It fell victim to attacks from both economic rationalists and social progressives, neither group comprehending the nature of Australia's unfolding political dialogue.

The issue can be stated simply—free markets have the potential to destroy the social status quo. They can uproot communities, transfer capital and labour from one location to another and demolish long-established social ties and employment habits.

Many consequences flow from this reality—that the more people grasp the meaning of free market economics, the more apprehensive they will become; that free market economics cannot suffice as a complete political

418

philosophy; and that free marketeers must explain the type of society they envisage from their reforms. The Liberals failed to satisfy these tests in the late 1980s and there is little sign that their leaders in the 1990s even understand them, which is a reason for the doubts about John Hewson's leadership.

A pure theory of economic efficiency cannot satisfy most democratic electorates where social, human and moral requirements will often outweigh the economic. The Liberals had to find a political position between government paternalism and unrestrained individualism. They had to address the cultural accusation that their free market policies would destroy a fundamentally good aspect of Australia or even its very national essence. This challenge remained unresolved in 1992. The Liberals had still not projected a view of Australian society based upon a synthesis of free market economics and social values close to the Australian community.

Howard's attempt to address some of these issues in 1988 was primitive, piecemeal and flawed; but it was an attempt. The irony is that its poor execution only weakened his leadership to a terminal stage.

Howard was motivated by three forces. First, the need to avoid the type of single issue campaign which the Liberals had waged in 1987 on taxation. Howard knew that the key to success in 1990 lay in fighting on a broad front against the Hawke government and that meant maximum differentiation from Hawke. Second, Howard knew that he would never become a 'popular' leader so he devised an alternative: he could not sell his persona but he could market his philosophy. Thirdly, Howard grasped that the economic differences between Labor and Liberal were only likely to diminish further during the 1987–90 parliament, since both sides saw the solution to the current account deficit problem in terms of the widely accepted OECD prescription. If economic differences were diminishing, then Howard would maximise the difference on social issues.

In this period Howard made a strong though flawed effort to recast the view of society held by the Liberal Party. His aim was to tap the growing reservoir of people who were worried, fearful and suspicious about the changes in economic power and social values occurring in Australia. He sought to give these people a framework, almost an emotional grid, from which they could draw comfort. Howard replied upon two central ideas. He sought to project the security and reliability of the traditional family as a source of deliverance from social turmoil, and to advance a chauvinistic nationalism which emphasised the responsibility upon minority groups and new arrivals to subscribe to the Australian way and to ensure that cultural diversity did not diminish Australian values, institutions and customs.

Howard's philosophy was a critique of the ideas which had guided Australian conservatism during the Fraser era. He raised a series of basic questions for Australian conservatives. Did they endorse Howard's assault upon the multiculturalism which Malcolm Fraser had nominated as one of his major achievements? Did they agree with Howard's elevation of the traditional family unit, now located in only 25 per cent of households, as a preferred model to be encouraged by public policy? Were they prepared to accept the consequences of Howard's free market economic philosophy, whose application would breed more winners, more losers and more uncertainty as the protected, regulated, paternalistic shield of state power was torn away?

The first manifestation of Howard's new social agenda came in mid-1988 on immigration policy. This was provoked by the release of the Fitzgerald Report, commissioned by the Hawke government to advise on immigration and named after the chairman of the review, Dr Stephen Fitzgerald, academic and ambassador. But Howard failed at this point to market effectively his 'One Australia' policy. Instead of selling his central theme Howard was derailed on the question of Asian immigration, an issue only peripheral to his philosophy. It was Howard who raised the issue and Howard who failed to bury it.

The result was that Howard deeply divided his own party, left himself alienated and vulnerable against the three senior Liberals (Peacock, Chaney and Elliott), disappointed many of his own supporters, and lost the intellectual backing of many of the nation's opinion makers, who believed that Howard had compromised his political reputation. Howard's effort to project a new position on immigration was a turning point in his leadership of the Liberals from which, in retrospect, it appears he never recovered.

The story of Howard's effort to market a social agenda reveals the uncertainty which periodically plagued the conservatives throughout the 1980s over issues of race, immigration and multiculturalism. It revealed that Labor, the political zealot for White Australia in the Federation Settlement, had undergone a deeper transformation of its political culture on these issues than had the non-Labor side.

The tragedy for Howard was that the Fitzgerald Report which sparked the debate was a comprehensive condemnation of the Hawke government's immigration policy and administration, which offered an excellent rationale for his own position.

The shadow immigration minister, Alan Cadman, was aware of the thrust of the Fitzgerald Report in autumn 1988, before its release. The shadow Cabinet was prepared and had endorsed the five principles which would guide Opposition policy. They were announced by Howard on 15 May 1988 when he said the report 'should provide a trigger for a full and open debate on the direction of Australia's immigration policy'. Howard's determination to make immigration an issue was reflected in his remark that the correct policy must prevail over any 'blind pursuit of bipartisanship'.

The five Liberal principles were: Australia's national interest must dominate immigration policy; post-arrival policy must be shaped by the belief that all Australians have a common destiny; the intake must be adjusted to the capacity of Australia to accept and absorb change; a strong level of immigration is essential to economic growth; and acceptance of Australia's responsibilities to receive refugees.[1]

Howard argued that the intake had become unbalanced over the previous five years with family reunion growing at the expense of skilled workers. But there was a notable omission from the five principles—the principle of non-discrimination. This was still Liberal policy but its omission pointed to a subtle shift in emphasis.

The Fitzgerald Report, released on 3 June 1988, was a golden opportunity for the Opposition. It was a repudiation of the ethnic lobby which had such influence with the Hawke government.[2] Fitzgerald argued that community support for immigration was faltering and that reforms were imperative to sustain immigration as a national concept. Existing selection procedures were inadequate and likely to deliver a target overrun of tens of thousands. But the more serious problem was the decline of community confidence in immigration because the program was no longer connected in the public mind to the national interest. The report was resolutely pro-immigration. It supported an increase in the overall intake, but insisted this would be acceptable only with a new rationale for immigration. The old 'populate or perish' rationale was both inappropriate and obsolete.

The Fitzgerald reforms were based on a far sharper economic focus in selection, with a greater emphasis on Australian identity and citizenship in settlement. The report said immigration must serve Australian's national economic needs. The recent trend towards more less skilled, older, higher welfare-dependent migrants should stop. The criteria should be rebalanced to put a greater weighting on skills, entrepreneurship, professional talent, English language skills and youth.

The report did not extrapolate but these criteria would lead to a growing proportion of immigrants from Asia, given the shift in the source of skilled worker applicants. In 1986–87 the Asian component of the program was 34 per cent. Fitzgerald said that the current trend would lead to 7 per cent of the population being Asian-born by 2025. While admitting that racism remained a factor in Australia, the committee concluded from its polling analysis that the real problem was not opposition to Asian migrants but opposition to the immigration program as a whole. It found strong support for the principle of non-discrimination. Fitzgerald said the response to those who thundered about Asian immigration 'is not to halt immigration from Asian countries or abandon the principle of non-discrimination . . . It lies in putting immigration back onto a middle path which gives emphasis to Australia.'

This would come through a recognition that the program was for Australia as a whole and that 'immigration to Australia is about becoming Australian, it is not driven by multiculturalism'. The report called for a renewed emphasis on Australian citizenship and pointed out that 43 per cent of overseas-born people had declined to take out citizenship. The report said that of all the issues, multiculturalism aroused most suspicions—from businesspeople and unionists, Labor and Liberal voters, old and new arrivals. Fitzgerald said: 'It is the Australian identity that matters most in Australia. And if the government will affirm that strongly, multiculturalism might seem less divisive or threatening.'

The government was dismayed. The report was criticised by immigration minister Clyde Holding in public and by Hawke in private. The ethnic groups were in a fury. It was a damning critique of policy administration and appeared far closer to the Opposition position than to Labor's.

During the winter recess Elliott, Howard and Eggleton met in London on overlapping visits and discussed two political issues on which Howard intended to run hard—Bill Hayden's appointment as Governor-General, and immigration policy. Elliott asked if Howard had read the Fitzgerald Report. Howard hadn't. 'Well, it's great stuff,' Elliott said. 'It's what you and I believe in.'

Howard, however, was still glowing from his audience with the Iron Lady. She had just given him the standard Thatcherite lecture on willpower and principle. Howard had enjoyed their meeting and absorbed her message—never retreat, and stand by your beliefs. It was advice that Howard literally took to heart. The shadow of Thatcher would hover over Howard's impending agony. Flying home Howard wrote out a tough speech, launching his 'One Australia' theme in Perth en route to the east.

Howard was fully aware of the contentious immigration debate within non-Labor politics. He knew of the cultural assimilation stance adopted by Geoffrey Blainey and his own shadow finance minister, John Stone. In late 1987 Stone said that non-English speaking migrants should be prevented from coming to Australia. In April 1988 Blainey said that multiculturalism was turning Australia into a 'cluster of tribes'. He warned that Asian immigration could lead to Australia's downfall: 'I know of no nation in history which has positively encouraged such fragmentation and survived.'[3]

The Blainey–Stone line was rooted in a diagnosis of community concerns similar to Fitzgerald's—but they offered conflicting solutions. The Blainey–Stone line sought a concession from the non-discriminatory policy to ease community concerns. Fitzgerald sought an aggressive defence of non-discrimination through restoring national confidence and purpose in immigration overall.

Howard, when interviewed as early as 16 May 1988 about his five principles, said that they were not based on concern about the numbers of Asians coming to Australia. Asked then if racial composition of the program was an issue he said: 'I'm not raising that as an issue and I won't.'[4] After his return from London he said: 'I don't think Asian immigration as such is a problem . . . I would never get into an election campaign on anything that could be remotely related to racial issues.'[5]

Howard—the social agenda

The next day, 1 August, was Howard's first full working day after his return from London and he undertook a series of radio interviews. The events of this day were a perfect demonstration of his predilection for defining policy positions on radio on the run, rather than through the written word.

Before the tyranny of electronic media driven politics, leaders would write out what they intended to say. But in the 1980s they relied upon oral rather than written statements of position. These were less precise, prone to internal contradiction and often made without adequate thought. Howard's experience on 1 August 1988 is a study of the process.

During the interviews Howard grew frustrated with the misinterpretation of his remarks on multiculturalism. He began to draw some inappropriate analogies, suggested that Japanese, Indonesians and Germans 'don't pretend they're a bit of everybody' and that Australians should not either. Just before lunch, interviewed by John Laws, Howard began to take a new direction. Asked if his policy meant fewer Asians, Howard said: 'It could. Because if you have less family reunion, you may have less coming from Asia. It wouldn't be an aim . . . but that could happen. I would never want to see Asian immigration stopped.' Howard, for the first time, was talking about fewer Asians. He was making policy on the run. It made no sense because less family reunion was likely to mean more, not fewer, migrants from Asia over the medium term.

That evening on the *PM* program, Howard, asked if the rate of Asian migration was too fast, said: 'I think there are some people who believe it is.' Asked what he thought, Howard replied: 'I wouldn't like to see it greater, I am not in favour of going back to a White Australia policy. I do believe that if it is in the eyes of some in the community, it's too great, it would be in our immediate term interest and supportive of social cohesion if it were slowed down a little, so that the capacity of the community to absorb was greater.' Howard said it was the legitimate right of a government to cut the level of immigration from any area to limit social tensions and improve social cohesion. But the only area he so nominated was Asia.

Howard made three mistakes in these remarks and his subsequent refusal to change them. First, he had exceeded the terms of his own shadow Cabinet decision which said nothing about a possible cut in the level of Asian migration. It was one thing to assert the legitimate right of government to control the program; it was another to raise the prospect of cutting the number of Asians coming to Australia. Howard was putting a construction on coalition policy which many Liberals resented. Second, his comments inevitably divided his own party. Many senior Liberals did not believe that the level of Asian immigration was too high, opposed any suggestion to trim it and made their views public. Third, by raising the Asian immigration issue Howard effectively launched a new debate. He abandoned the Fitzgerald position which offered such an excellent opportunity for attacking the Hawke government along the lines originally envisaged by the Opposition and moved much closer to the Blainey–Stone position. By introducing a racial component into the argument Howard made it much more difficult to persuade fellow Liberals, let alone the community, about his 'One Australia' philosophy.

It was obvious from the start that this stance would only weaken Howard's leadership and that he should correct himself immediately. This would have caused embarrassment for a day or two at most. But Howard, stung by the criticism, grew stubborn and emotional. His anger at some members of the ethnic lobby was quite justified—they were claiming that Howard was trying to revive the concept of the master race.

The next day an emotional Howard announced that he would never retreat: 'I made some very balanced and moderate remarks speaking the truth as I hear it . . . about what people think on this issue. I'm being kicked from one end of the nation to the other for being a bigot or racist. Now, that's just nonsense, but I expected it and I expect more of it. But I don't intend to change the view that I have adopted.' From the start the issue began to transcend immigration. Howard let emotion cloud his judgement; he felt his honour and authority was at stake; he would never retreat.[6]

Margaret Thatcher was making an official visit to Australia; the Iron Lady who had put steel into Howard in London. So how could Howard retreat? Thatcher arrived in Australia on 1 August, the same day Howard made his remarks, stayed for a week and addressed the coalition parties explaining the secret of her success. Eggleton detected the nuances. He told colleagues later that Thatcher's presence had been important in Howard's stubornness. Howard forgot that a strong leader knows when to admit a mistake.

The coalition's immigration policy document was being finalised at this time. It contained a phrase about the overriding right of any government to vary the composition and level of immigration intake to protect Australia's social cohesion. But shadow minister Cadman had never thought that this phrase, which he had written, might be used to cut Asian immigration. It was Howard, not Cadman, who put this interpretation upon this clause.

In his defence Howard focused on the personal criticism of himself as racist which he rightly repudiated. But he never adequately dealt with the policy and political implications of his position. Howard had raised the prospect—but made no pledge—of cutting the level of Asian immigration. This meant, in effect, racial targeting. Howard repeated and resolutely defended his remarks, over a period of several weeks refusing to modify, adjust or correct. He said he had no wish to fight an election on this issue, but he invited the voters to see him as a strong leader for being tough enough to raise the issue. He denied that the coalition would abandon the policy of non-discrimination or introduce racial targeting. For weeks a protracted and sterile debate raged as Howard recorded countless interviews in which the media tried to force him to elaborate or clarify.

There was no movement in Howard's position—he left on the table the prospect of a cut in Asian immigration, a position which had foreign policy as well as domestic consequences. Meanwhile there was public uproar within the Liberal Party.[7]

The Hungarian-born NSW Liberal premier, Nick Greiner, rejected Howard's stance on multiculturalism and Asian migration—the two issues being now inevitably linked. The Victorian Liberal leader, Jeff Kennett, a former state ethnic affairs minister, also rejected Howard's stance. The LCL Northern Territory chief minister, Marshal Perron, said he wanted more Asian immigration. Malcolm Fraser made a powerful intervention: 'Comments based on race do not belong in the Australian political environment. I don't believe they belong in the Liberal Party.'—a withering criticism of Howard. Elliott was appalled at the mess Howard had made of the situation. Peacock offered ostensible support but kept declaring that he would never accept immigration arguments based on race—leaving the media to infer his difference with Howard.[8]

The two former immigration ministers in the Fraser government, Ian Macphee and Michael MacKellar, and the former shadow immigration minister, Phillip Ruddock, criticised the Howard position. So did the chairman of the coalition backbench immigration committee, Senator Baden Teague. Several backbenchers and former ministers went public expressing their concern, including Ian Wilson, Steele Hall, Peter Baume and Kathy Sullivan. A future shadow foreign minister and Liberal Senate leader, Robert Hill, who had an adopted Asian daughter, declared the priority was for Australia to become more closely integrated with Asia. Shadow minister Cadman, a Howard supporter, tried to support his leader but never used Howard's words himself.[9]

Greiner and Kennett were worried about the electoral harm that was being done to the Liberals in the heavily migrant cities of Sydney and Melbourne. One of the most penetrating comments came from former Fraser government minister, Bob Ellicott, who declared that the Liberal Party had been destabilised for some time because of leadership style, the failure to articulate politics which the public understood, and the tendency to make policy on the run.[10]

Meanwhile Howard became angry and assertive in interviews, talking louder than ever, declaring there were 'no racists in my Party', complaining about media bias, frustrated as almost every day he was under fire from another Liberal. The media began to speculate about his leadership. The internal crisis gave Peacock new heart. He spent a lot of time on the phone in August talking to his colleagues, criticising Howard and complaining about the electoral damage. Peacock had forgotten about Michael Hodgman and the politics of 1984.

Howard claimed that the immigration mix had been changed under Hawke. In fact, the bulk of the change had come under Fraser. In Fraser's last year, 1982–83, the Asian component of the total intake had risen to 26 per cent. Under Hawke it reached 32 per cent by 1987–88. Another dilemma which Howard refused to address was that the intake of Asians was determined chiefly by the size of the overall intake. The Liberals had promised to increase the total numbers. This would increase the numbers of Asians if there were no offsetting action.[11]

However, Howard did have a large number of supporters within the parliamentary party. Any perception that his critics held a majority position would be incorrect. Most of the supporters stayed silent, though, and their motives varied—loyalty to Howard, scepticism about multiculturalism, opposition to the level of Asian immigration, and the need for party unity. Howard also won supporters that he didn't need, including Ian Sinclair and John Stone. On 9 August Stone declared: 'Asian immigration has to be slowed. It's no use dancing around the bushes. Nobody is talking about stopping immigration, just a sensible adjustment in the composition in the program. That's what we are going to have, and don't you make any mistake about it.'[12]

This statement was a severe blow to Howard. His shadow finance minister was confirming as a fact what Howard had raised as a possibility. Labor MPs cynically said that Stone had just told the truth. Why, they asked, would Howard raise the possibility if he didn't intend to act on it? Howard's critics inside the Liberal Party were deeply angered. Here was Stone hijacking immigration policy and Howard had made it possible.

However, two days later Sinclair, the shadow deputy prime minister, took the Stone line. Sinclair said there were too many Asians coming to Australia and that a coalition government would draw more on other sources.[13] By this stage Howard's position was becoming untenable. He censured Sinclair and announced that the coalition had made no decision about altering the intake.[14] Yet Howard himself had spent the previous fortnight raising as a possibility the very issue over whose presentation as a certainty he was censuring Sinclair. Meanwhile Howard kept repeating that he was prepared to cut the flow of Asian immigrants if that were necessary for social cohesion.[15]

On 19 August Malcolm Fraser made his strongest statement since resigning from federal politics—Fraser said the immigration debate was under notice in the region and that the national interest was at stake. Fraser said that Australia's only option as a nation was closer links with Asia. He was speaking out because 'I see fundamental Liberal values being questioned in ways that would seriously alter the complexion of the Party . . . The issues of race and multiculturalism have been important, indeed fundamental to me, in many years of active politics. Those concerns are not new.

426

I believe it tragic that the Liberal Party runs the prospect of being divided on these issues.'[16]

But Howard declared: 'I'm not budging, okay. Definitely not. Is that clear?' Asked if immigration would turn into a leadership issue Howard replied: 'Garbage. It won't. Nobody's going to knock me off.'[17]

The formal policy as endorsed by the shadow Cabinet was approved by the joint party meeting on 22 August, with nearly a third of the parliamentary party in dissent. Howard held a long, tense and futile media conference to announce it.

Meanwhile Hawke had moved to exploit the divisions within the Liberal Party. Hawke's political consciousness was formed during the 1950s and was deeply connected with the commitment to abolish White Australia. Hawke believed that Howard's stance would hurt both Australia and the Liberal Party. From the start Hawke declared that he was prepared to fight an election on the principles in question. He dismissed any suggestion that Howard was racist but attacked him for lending support to the racist minority in the community. Hawke decided to introduce into parliament a motion seeking reaffirmation of the traditional policy.

In one of his strongest speeches as prime minister Hawke had attacked Howard on 21 August:

> The Opposition leader has explicitly called for a slowdown in the rate of Asian immigration . . . The National Party leader has said explicitly: 'Asian immigration has to be slowed' because there are 'too many Asians coming into Australia.' . . . These comments are unprecedented in contemporary Australian politics in their discriminatory references to race. They are as ugly as they are blatant. And yet they stand unretracted by those who uttered them.

Hawke moved his motion on 25 August to the effect that in exercising its sovereign rights over the composition of the immigration intake no Australian government would use race or ethnic origin as a criterion. Howard moved a long amendment with the emphasis on the overriding right of government to determine the size and composition of the intake based on the national interest. The best speech was made by former ALP minister Barry Cohen, who said that Howard should defend the right policy, not apologise for the wrong policy: 'All that is required for evil to triumph is for good men to do nothing.' Four Liberals crossed the floor to vote with the Hawke government against the Opposition—Macphee, Ruddock, Steele Hall and Peter Baume. Two others abstained from the vote in the House, MacKellar and Wilson. Howard used every means to prevent defections. Peter Baume said that in 14 years in the Senate he had voted in 1300 divisions and was now about to cast his second vote against his own side. Baume said he agreed that politics was about compromise and he had made many compromises; on this issue he had to stand on principle. But there was a sequel to the vote.

On 11 September 1988 John Stone declared on television that he stood by his earlier remarks on Asian migration. Howard, having tolerated Stone's transgressions on indirect taxation and immigration for 14 months, felt compelled to act. On 12 September Howard told Sinclair that Stone must accept the discipline of the shadow Cabinet or be removed from the front bench. Howard wanted a statement from Stone which reaffirmed coalition immigration policy (which did not necessarily mean fewer Asians) and a pledge that any future comments would be limited to his portfolio area or in support of agreed coalition policy.

But Sinclair was unable to persuade Stone after a ninety-minute discussion. Knowing that the coalition itself was on the line Sinclair bowed to Howard's demand and dismissed Stone from his front bench with 'deep disappointment'. Stone remained as the National Party Senate leader. Howard told the media that the real issue had been shadow Cabinet discipline, not immigration.

This saga of disastrous events originating with Howard's personal interpretation of the new immigration policy divided the Liberal Party, created new tensions within the coalition and undermined Howard's leadership. The tragedy for Howard is that the injury was self-inflicted and the damage was quite unnecessary. Howard's dogmatism was driven by his own weakness. Howard saw the debate as a test of his own authority. He knew that the party research showed the public perceived him as a weak leader and he was determined to counter this image, not reinforce it.

In one sense Howard's leadership never recovered from this uproar. Howard betrayed the confusion within Australian conservatism over the questions of multiculturalism, Asian immigration and what was actually meant by Australia's integration with the Asia/Pacific. Within the Asia/Pacific his standing as shadow prime minister was distinctly compromised; at home many opinion makers concluded that Howard's blunder pointed to misjudgement on a more serious scale. Too many influential Liberals now turned against Howard, with deep determination. Two years later, during a series of interviews for this book, Liberal after Liberal nominated this issue in the winter of 1988 as fundamental in setting the scene for Howard's removal as leader.

However, in the spring of 1988, after the immigration issue had settled, Howard pressed ahead with plans for a comprehensive statement of his social–economic philosophy. It was written in the Federal Secretariat and drew upon ideas from Howard, his staff, and the party's new advertising agency, George Patterson. The aim was to find a new philosophical appeal for the next election and in the process revive Howard's leadership.

Future Directions was a synthesis of Howard's beliefs with the results of extensive qualitative research for the Liberal Party conducted during

1988. It projected a set of values on which Howard could sell himself.
Values had two advantages: they were cost-free and they could supplement
hard money pledges for the hip-pocket nerve. The essence of Howard's
values was a return to the basics. The sub-title to *Future Directions* was,
'It's time for plain thinking', and the booklet depicted an ideal couple with
two children outside their home with picket fence. The advertising jingle,
'A Plain Thinking Man', was an effort to market Howard as a leader in
touch with ordinary Australians—or in American parlance, the silent majority. It was an identity anchor for Howard whose image had been that of a
weak leader. Howard would now be given a political character which the
voters could grasp—the plain thinking leader who believed in God, family,
nation and freedom.

The 109-page blueprint opened with a dedication to the people and a
declaration that Australia was in decline. Howard offered a five-point
solution—strengthen the family unit; restore individual control and weaken
government control over people's lives; offer more personal incentive;
provide equality of opportunity or a 'fair go'; and build 'One Australia'.
The blueprint was a coalition document, not just a Liberal document.

Future Directions argued that Australia had gone off the rails and had
to be put right. The Labor Party was a symptom of the disease; once it had
been the party of the battler but now it had been stolen by the trade unions.
Howard offered the simplicity of the old values and tapped the deep vein
of nostalgia running through a community apprehensive about the pace and
nature of changes in contemporary society. Howard offered some examples
of the Australia he aspired to recreate—a school system that taught children
how to spell; a sense of personal security that allowed people to sleep on
a hot summer night with their door open; a freedom to allow workers to
negotiate their own wages with employers; an Aboriginal community which
had equal rights with others but was denied any claim to sovereignty through
an Aboriginal Treaty. Howard's message captured the worries of middle
Australia about its life and society. It had the potential to become a
vote-winner.

Future Directions was a milestone for Australian conservatism for two
further reasons. First, it was an explicit acceptance by Howard as the senior
free market Liberal that the agenda of dry economics was not enough to
win an election for the Liberal Party. Second, it was a declaration that the
Liberal Party had to address and provide the answers to the central social
questions in Australian society if the party were to remain viable. Howard
may have provided some of the wrong answers. But his blueprint was a
defiant assertion that the Liberals had to address the basic issues of family
security, multiculturalism and personal freedom if they were to avoid degen-
eration into a party of 'nothingness', obsessed by mere economics and
therefore unable to attract a new generation of party cadres and leaders.

The main political problem lay in Howard's possible underestimation of the social pluralism and secular materialism of Australian life. The images displayed in the television advertisement were strictly the old Australia—lifesavers, Bob Menzies, sheep, diggers and beach kids. Such a powerful appeal to nostalgia might alienate, in turn, the constituencies of the new Australia—migrants, working and professional women, young people, the yuppies, Aboriginals, single parents and students.

In another sense Howard was trying to disprove historian Manning Clark's diagnosis that the current generation of Australians was the first to believe in nothing at all. At a time when the influence of the Christian churches seemed to have reached a new low and secular humanism was almost triumphant, Howard sought to re-arm the state with a firm moral code. There was a touch of evangelical fervour in the Howard pitch. It had pulling power but it also ran a political risk in a country which, unlike America, lacked a 'moral majority' and which disarmed zealots by caricature.

Beyond these considerations *Future Directions* was burdened because the contradiction between its economic and social dimensions was too great. The document revealed Howard's historical significance in terms of Liberal political thought, since it was under his leadership that the foundation tradition of Deakinite Liberalism was abandoned. The economic era against which Howard revolted was the most recent manifestation of this tradition—the period of Menzies, McEwen and Fraser. Yet it was the social stability of the Menzies age which he idealised in *Future Directions* and whose certainty he aspired to recapture. In short, Howard's economic anti-model became his social model.

The link which Howard ignored is that the social stability of the Menzian age was partly a function of the interventionist and patronising state which Menzies declined to dismantle when he defeated Chifley. The contradiction in Howard was his pretence that the transformation of the Australian ethos which deregulation, competition and market forces would bring was consistent with the safe, certain, stable suburbia on the dustcover of his booklet. The economic reforms Howard wanted meant a tougher more competitive climate, a removal of protection and regulation, a new list of winners and losers, the net effect of which meant greater social change. Yet social change was the very factor which worried so many people, accentuated their uncertainties and motivated their search for a nostalgic past.

An assessment of the document's five principles—strengthening the family, more individual and less government control, greater individual incentive, equality of opportunity or a fair go, and 'One Australia'—reveals the strengths and dilemmas of the conservative side during the 1980s and the service Howard performed by putting such issues on the debating table.[18]

Howard's appeal to traditional family life was redolent of Menzies, who achieved much of his success on the back of suburban family stability and the great Australian mum. It might appear that Howard was merely parroting

Menzies but this is not correct. Howard's pitch was more risky than Menzies'. For Menzies the family model was a given and when Menzies made his family appeal in the 1950s it was to the orthodoxy. But when Howard made his family appeal it was contentious. Howard sought to rebalance the social system and recreate his ideal family model. Howard was pitting his version of the family against the pluristic tyranny of the decade, against the multitude of family configurations from the transient heterosexual relationship to the homosexual couple.

Menzies had used his appeal to the family brilliantly during the post-war era to undermine Labor's own appeal on a class basis to the mass of Australian workers. Labor's success depended upon political values being shaped at the workplace; Menzies tried to get political values shaped at home. Labor's political strength was its power as a mass party driven by a class and workingman's consciousness. Menzies rarely tried to confront Labor on its own ground at the workplace. He never presented himself as an agent of class. Menzies outsmarted Labor by going to the family home and stealing the votes at the hearth. Menzies' family appeal was far better based than Howard's.

Howard's problem was that the social change which had transformed the family unit was probably irreversible; 1988 was no longer 1955. People were trying to manage in the new environment and improvise with work sharing, day care, child care, and in numerous other ways. Few were seriously interested in reverting to the traditional model when only 20 per cent of households were now a one-income family with children. In 1988 more than 50 per cent of married women were in the workforce. This was the expectation held by most young women leaving school. Economic pressures, the decline of religious values and the rise of the feminist movement had transformed the social structure. It was never certain that Howard's opponents would not outnumber his backers. It is sobering also to note that many of the areas covered by Howard—school education, crime, neighbourhood safety, law and order—were state, not federal, issues.

Howard's second principle was the need to substitute individual power for government power. This was the essence of dry economics, which in the Australian setting was a revolutionary concept. Contrary to the romantic claims in *Future Directions* that Australia grew on a tradition of rugged individualism, the reverse was the story. From the foundation of the colony with British soldiers and Irish convicts to the Deakin Settlement and the Fraser Consolidation, the ruling elite and the conservative side had relied upon government power.

During the 1980s the drys had persistently misjudged the political challenge of selling their economic policies—on labour, financial and product market deregulation, privatisation, indirect taxation, and even the smaller government–lower taxation trade-off. The lesson of the 1980s was that the rhetoric of smaller government and less regulation was instantaneously popular but inevitably difficult at the point of execution because, like all reforms, it redistributed income and power. It made sense for Howard to market individualism as a personal concept to link with dry economics. But individualism was a double-edged sword in Australia where there was intense belief in individual rights but far less belief in individual responsibility.

The third and fourth principles were intertwined and revealed another dilemma for the economic drys—how to reconcile greater individual incentive with maintenance of income equity and fairness. The market research from both sides during the 1980s often showed the voters anxious to support the party promising a fair go. Whenever a party was lost for a slogan, the fair go position was usually successful. But in policy terms the Liberal economic rationalists had tended to put efficiency before fairness. This was understandable since they were attempting to cut back government intervention, revive individual and private sector dynamism, and secure more competitive and productive results. Their claim was that the best way to lift the living standard of the lowest was to boost the overall size of the economic cake. The upshot was that the coalition was always vulnerable on the issue of fairness and income equity, a point which Labor exploited cleverly.

The concept of 'One Australia' was extremely divisive within the Liberal Party but strongly supported within the National Party. It represented the most concerted effort by Howard to break from the Fraser era on social policy grounds. Howard feared that Australia was being seriously weakened by government multicultural policies which encouraged separate cultures. *Future Directions* took a sweeping prescriptive stand: immigrants should make an 'overwhelming commitment'—not just to Australia's democratic values and its laws but also to its social values, ethical background and national identity. This rule applied not just to immigrants but to minority groups such as Aborigines. The difficulty about this argument is that it boils down to a question of degree; to a degree Howard was right and to a degree Howard was wrong. The balance point is the essence.

Howard tapped a sympathetic vein in the Australian community; he was right in seeking to rebalance immigration and settlement policies to ensure that they were directed to the national interest and not to narrow ethnic interests. But Howard also went too far in two respects.

First, the evidence suggested that his attack on multiculturalism was an electoral negative for the Liberals. The adverse reaction of the Liberal leaders in the main states, Greiner and Kennett, was a pointer to this. The second problem with Howard's 'One Australia' is more important. In the 1980s the Liberals finally decided that they wanted a free market economic policy and an internationalised Australian economy. But they were slow to identify the inevitable social changes which would flow from a more open economy and greater integration with the Asia/Pacific. Those changes would

432

involve a greater Asian presence in Australia—more investment, residents, students, businessmen, joint ventures, tourists and land holders. In short, a much greater dialogue and interaction among the peoples. This would demand change, tolerance, adaptation and discipline on Australia's part.

In this sense Howard had failed to grasp the consequences of his economics. The social issue was how the Australian identity would continue to be changed by the internationalisation of its economy, not how the old Australian identity could be protected. Here was the real defect in 'One Australia'. Labor, in fact, was more relaxed about the social and identity changes which internationalisation of the economy would inevitably bring—multiculturalism, racial diversity and republicanism.

23
The Kirribilli pact

Paul had some view that perhaps he might leave if he was not Prime Minister . . . he thought he should have his turn.
Bob Hawke trying to explain his retirement pledge to Paul Keating

After Labor's 1987 election victory Paul Keating moved to secure a leadership transition at the mid-point of the third term—late 1988 was his target. Keating moved to realise his ambition, unaware that the forces were being unleashed that would create the 1990s recession. The resulting political struggle was subtle, remarkable and largely subterranean: a successful treasurer trying to force the retirement of a successful prime minister.

For Keating the legitimacy of his leadership claim was beyond dispute; he privately called himself the 'real prime minister'. But he found that Hawke's thirst for office after three election victories was unquenched. Hawke was determined to remain prime minister, to take Labor to a fourth election. Hawke regarded his legitimacy as leader as self-evident, verified by three election wins. The result was a fierce leadership struggle between Hawke and Keating during 1988 which culminated in the most secret and sensational deal ever concluded on the prime ministership.

The Hawke–Keating confrontation came to its climax in August 1988 and its reverberations threatened to wreck the government. At this point the pent-up rivalry between the two men, stoked since the 1984 campaign, exploded in verbal pyrotechnics and profound antagonism. Hawke never forgave Keating's audacious assertion of his right to the prime ministership. Keating, in turn, could never purge his frustration at Hawke's determination to remain in power. Their relationship nearly disintegrated and it was salvaged only by the Kirribilli agreement.

The Keating leadership campaign during 1987–88 was performance orientated and devoid of any direct lobbying until the end. It was successful in convincing the party that Keating should be the next prime minister but it failed singularly to persuade Labor that Hawke should be sacrificed for Keating. This was the most difficult outcome for Keating: an acceptance of his credentials but a refusal to act on them.

The central political fact in this struggle was that Hawke's three election wins had earned him the right to decide the timing of his departure. The ALP had a long record of supporting failed leaders; it was not going to execute its most successful leader.

Keating's leadership push in 1987–88 was driven by the conviction that his superior leadership credentials would be obvious to the party—a triumph of egotism over judgement. He conducted his campaign for the prime ministership not in any backroom with whispered tones but as the orchestra conductor on a stage bathed in light, sound and movement.

By 1987 there was a consensus across the three factions—right, left and centre—that Keating was the next leader. Not Kim Beazley, John Dawkins, Brian Burke, Simon Crean or John Bannon, all named at various times. But Keating wanted the office immediately, and for this his support was much smaller, comprising individuals among the senior economic ministers, the centre-left faction and the ACTU leadership.

The public loved Hawke but the scepticism of senior ministers was captured by Button during the 1987 campaign: 'Hawkie? There is always concern within the government about Hawkie's morale . . . he's certainly a bonus in the electoral contest, if he goes well.' Keating's case against Hawke was that he offered the government little overall strategic leadership and that the government lacked any *esprit de corps*.

It was not long after the 1987 victory that Keating began to tell party confidants and journalists that he would leave politics for dazzling horizons unless the party was prepared to support him for the leadership. This was his 'Paris option'—a threat and a serious flirtation.

It is surprising in the light of the Keating campaign that Hawke was so publicly restrained for so long. Asked if he wanted the leadership Keating's public pose was 'No, not yet.' The implication—it was just a question of time. His leadership qualities were praised by an assorted bunch: his ACTU friend, Bill Kelty; radio man John Laws; his Cabinet mate, John Dawkins; former leader Bill Hayden; and the media which grasped that Keating dominated the government. The *Financial Review* suggested as early as March 1988 that 'the time may have arrived for Bob Hawke to stand down as Prime Minister'. On 31 May *The Bulletin* featured a cover story 'Prime Minister Keating—How He'll Run Australia'—much to Hawke's anger. On 30 August the *Sydney Morning Herald* editorialised in favour of a Keating leadership succession during the current term.

Meanwhile Keating was speaking as if he were the prime minister. After the 1987 election it was Keating, rather than Hawke, who defended the Hawke government against claims that it had betrayed Labor's reform tradition. The case against the government was put in newspaper articles by

Gough Whitlam and the social critic Craig McGregor, a dedicated Whitlamite. Keating replied in several forums, notably his 11 November 1987 Fabian Society Lecture. His intention was obvious but grasped by few: Keating aspired to establish an intellectual leadership of Labor in the late 1980s similar to that which Whitlam had enjoyed in the late 1960s.

Keating argued that just as Whitlam had had to discard old baggage, then so did the Hawke government; that just as Whitlam's program was relevant to the real interests of the people, then so was the Hawke government's; that just as Whitlam's program was devised to win an election, so was Hawke's. But Keating then fingered the flaw in circa 1972 Whitlamism—that 'the economic growth upon which the "program" was based was disappearing'. Australia's real challenge had become 'not the distribution of wealth but its creation', yet Whitlam had failed to grasp this.

Keating attacked the 'romantic nostalgia', pointing at Whitlam among others, which led critics to accuse the Hawke government of a sellout. He said the government, by running an efficient growth economy, was attacking the root causes of poverty and inequality. This began at a basic level—the right to work. Labor's job creation was nearly one million, far superior to the OECD average; it had re-established and improved Medicare; taken the pension to nearly 25 per cent of average earnings; lifted school retention rates; reformed the tax system by capital gains and fringe benefit taxes; devised family assistance directed to the needy; and instituted a basis for occupational superannuation throughout the workforce.

He said the key to this process was the collaboration between the government and the unions. The Accord was not 'an itemised shopping list but a state of mind'. Keating then moved to close the circle: 'We hear the critics say—the outcomes are not Labor—but in essence there can be nothing more Labor than an intelligent commitment by the unionised workforce to a common ideal with a conscientious Labor government. It is the very essence of unified and concerted Labor action . . . fixing the economic fundamentals is the reform which underpins all other reforms.'

Keating identified this task as the historic achievement of the Hawke government. It was made possible because the government was flexible about means to achieve its ends—witness financial deregulation, the float and foreign bank entry. These were undertaken 'not to make some foreign exchange dealer a bigger salary' but 'to integrate the Australian economy with the rest of the world because the past policy of introspection had failed us'. Keating said it was the 'broad Labor constituency' which bore the burden of Australia's protracted decline and 'it is turning this tide for the longer term that has become the Hawke government's most unremitting objective'.

But Keating finished with a concession—that the anti-ALP swings (up to 8 per cent in safe seats in the 1987 federal election) meant that Labor voters had become disenchanted and succumbed to the propaganda that the government was somehow 'un-Labor'. Keating called for a national effort within the party and unions to return these deserters to the fold and 'nail every falsehood' about the government.[2]

This speech encapsulated Keating's strengths and flaws. Its analysis was accurate but its tone antagonised the targets. Laurie Oakes wrote:

> Keating may not be wealthy but he flaunts the trappings of wealth—the Italian suits, the antique clocks and art collection . . . his own behaviour and lifestyle have probably done more than anything else to create the feeling among some workers that the Hawke government is not a genuine Labor government. Bob Hawke said a year ago that Keating should get out into the supermarkets and spend more time with ordinary Aussies. It's still good advice.[3]

Keating was a peculiar cross between Jack Kennedy and Jack Lang, contemporary style and vengeful throwback. His fascination and his flaw was his tongue; he used words like tomahawks. Hayden saw a touch of Camelot in the Keatings but Hawke saw Keating as a man who would frighten the horses.

Keating's political strategy for becoming prime minister was to demonstrate that he was Australia's best treasurer and the government's real leader. He had almost convinced himself that his economic policies had laid the basis for enduring prosperity. In late 1987 Keating was predicting that in just a few years Australia would have 'one of the most successful and balanced economies in the world'. Keating said he was playing monetary policy 'like a harp' and the government had a 'Tarzan-like grip' on the economy.[4]

After the 1987 election Hawke assumed the guise of a phoney tough. He launched three initiatives—to persuade Labor to accept privatisation, to mount a series of constitutional referenda, and to support a Treaty with the Aboriginal people. Each initiative finished in political retreat and humiliation, the result of poor preparation and inadequate assessment.

But Hawke never allowed such setbacks to cloud his self-image. He told colleagues that Keating was too elitist, remote and aloof, from the people and from the party. But Hawke's private criticism went further—he believed that Keating was unstable. Hawke identified the stridency within Keating—the almost irresistible urge towards 'overkill'—as betraying a vein of emotional instability which the public would reject. But Hawke, like Keating, was hoping to complete the bulk of Labor's economic reform agenda during 1988. Hawke's next ambition was to raise his profile as an international figure, an aspiration made manifest during his late 1987 visit to the Soviet Union and his meeting with Gorbachev.

In this psychological battle the first half of 1988 broke Keating's way. It was dominated by three factors—a number of electoral reversals for

Labor, a series of blunders by Hawke, and the successful May Economic Statement.

Hawke was held responsible for the loss of the Adelaide by-election in February 1988. When ANOP's Rod Cameron told Hawke before the campaign that Adelaide was at risk Hawke laughed at him. During the campaign Hawke raised the possibility of charging local phone calls on a timed basis, and turned a non-issue into the main issue. Labor lost in a swing of nearly 9 per cent.

This was followed by a series of convulsions for the ALP: Mick Young's retirement from politics, the confirmation of Bill Hayden's elevation to Governor-General, Hawke's efforts to help Young establish his new consultancy, Young's appointment as a Qantas consultant, and the defeat of the NSW ALP government during a campaign dominated by adverse federal news. It was a time of utterly bizarre revelations and events which left Hawke seriously weakened.

Hawke called Young's departure his most personal setback as prime minister. But Hawke suffered one of his worst political setbacks with the 'jobs for the boys' electoral legacy from the Young and Hayden appointments. Hawke's efforts to find clients for Young betrayed his inability to distinguish between his role as prime minister and his role as Mick's mate. Hawke hit back at criticism, saying 'I repudiate any suggestion of arrogance' and that 'if I were arrogant I wouldn't have the communication that I have with the ordinary people of Australia'.[5]

The subsequent by-elections in Port Adelaide and Oxley saw huge swings against the ALP.

After these events Rod Cameron found in his ANOP surveys that a 'trigger mechanism' of anti-Labor hostility had been released around the nation. He warned in Autumn 1988 that this was the sharpest decline in ALP fortunes since the Whitlam era in 1975. The lower living standards being imposed on the community by the Hawke government were generating a backlash. This was combined with hostility towards perceived ALP hypocrisy, centred upon a 'jobs for the boys' image, the type of double standard which disgusted the electorate.

Hawke's popularity remained a phenomenon, but his faulty judgement was imperiling the government. Hawke, of course, asserted that his popularity kept the government afloat. But the 19 March 1988 NSW election loss, with a massive 10 per cent swing against Labor running through its voting heartland, held federal as well as state messages. Hawke conceded that a rethink was needed. Keating, meanwhile, became patronising, saying that '[on the economy] for which I'm responsible, we're leading the world'.

On 9 March Hayden had anointed Keating as successor and described him as one of the greatest economic managers 'either at this time or anywhere around the world, or at any time in the post-war history [of Australia]'. Hayden declared Keating 'a great human being'. Surveying the outlook in March 1988, the *Sydney Morning Herald*'s political correspondent, Mike Steketee, said, 'The brutal reality is that Hawke's star is falling and Keating's is still in the ascendant. To many in the Labor caucus their paths have already crossed.'[6]

The May 1988 Statement brought the Keating tide to a new high with a series of micro-economic reforms and protection cuts. One of Keating's subsequent critics, P.P. McGuinness, said that the Statement 'certainly represents the most courageous set of initiatives presented to the Parliament for many years'. A few months later Max Walsh said 'there would not be one Liberal voting inhabitant of the central business districts who would seriously claim that John Howard or Andrew Peacock were superior economic managers to Paul Keating'.[7]

Keating's momentum provoked a backlash. Former Whitlam minister Jim McClelland complained that the self-educated Keating lacked 'genuine erudition'. (This prompted Keating's famous call to McClelland: 'That you Jim? Just because you swallowed a fucking dictionary when you were 15 doesn't give you the right to pour a bucket of shit over the rest of us.') The commentator Craig McGregor said Keating would be Labor's next leader 'not because he deserves to be but because nobody can stop him', an analysis that was wrong on both counts. McGregor said that Keating 'epitomises the sense of betrayal' by the Hawke government of Labor principles.

But Bill Kelty said it would be a 'tragedy' if Keating left politics before becoming prime minister and implied that Hawke should retire. 'After five or six years you start to see people have run their race in a particular endeavour and want a change of job,' Kelty said. 'It's a long time to be Prime Minister or even a Treasurer.' Kelty expressed concern about the 'vacuum of ideas' within the government—the Keating text for leadership. Keating believed he would recharge an ailing team. Kelty was patronising of Hawke and laudatory of Keating, trying to prepare the ground.[8] ACTU president Simon Crean took private soundings on a change of leadership. The ACTU liked Keating; it wanted the shift sooner rather than later.

After six months of irritation fielding questions about Keating, Hawke lost his nerve. He made a mistake and announced that he would serve the full term, face a fourth election campaign and retire midway through the next term.

Hawke told the ABC's Michael Schildberger that in the next term 'I would stand down'. He spoke to Brian White about 'a significant life after politics'. In March 1988 during a series of interviews Hawke said he expected to retire during the next term. He told *New Idea* he doubted that he would be staying another term and planned to conduct a series of television interviews in retirement. These remarks, just nine months after the 1987 election, had only one result: they threatened to make Hawke into a lame duck.[9]

A *Business Review Weekly* magazine poll published in mid-August 1988 showed that Keating was the preferred prime minister from both sides of politics among 120 chief executives in Australia's 500 biggest companies. The results were Keating 19 per cent, Elliott 17 per cent, Howard 13 per cent, Chaney 13 per cent and Hawke 9 per cent. Meanwhile Keating's approval rating as treasurer hit 66 per cent.[10]

In August 1988 the political earth began to move for Labor's 'big three', Hawke, Keating and Hayden. At a poignant Cabinet meeting on the night of 17 August, Hayden made his farewells after 27 years in politics. Hayden, the victim from 1983, was being rewarded by Hawke, the victor. Hayden was leaving for Yarralumla and vice-regal isolation where he must secretly have hoped he would endure as head of state beyond Hawke's tenure as head of government. It was a strained Cabinet meeting, with Hayden's colleagues sharing emotions of regret, nostalgia and incredulity.

The next night, August 18, Keating went to farewell Hayden personally. The Hayden–Keating relationship, which had been plagued by misunderstanding for years, was ending in peace. Hayden had long since recognised that in 1982 Keating had wanted to support him against Hawke and had sought to make Hayden, not Hawke, the prime minister. Hayden now wanted to see Keating in turn succeed Hawke. Hayden had already publicly anointed Keating: 'When Bob decides he wants to move on, I should have thought Paul had a pre-eminent claim.'[11]

But Hawke was determined to stay, and this was both a political and a family decision. Hawke and Hazel liked the Lodge, the lifestyle, the publicity and the challenge. Hawke and Keating had no agreement that Hawke would retire after three elections and Hawke denied that he had ever given a 'three terms' pledge to Keating. But Hawke had said before, publicly, that three terms was probably enough for him, and Keating had drawn this impression from comments made to him by Hawke at different times. Now Hawke was staying and Keating had convinced himself that Hawke was ratting on a pledge.[12]

Keating made three points to his friends—he was not interested in a lifetime political career and would not return to Opposition; his ambition was to succeed Hawke in the near future to revitalise the government; and finally, that if he were thwarted then he might as well leave politics.

But the Hawke camp, alive to the Keating threat, had the challenger beaten before he began. Hawke and his advisers had operated on the assumption that Keating might mount some form of challenge. Hawke, in fact, was broadening his support within the party; in particular, his tactic was to keep the loyalty of the dominant NSW right faction, Keating's own base. Hawke's political aide Bob Sorby, appointed on the advice of Graham Richardson, worked closely with Richardson during 1988 to ensure that there was no defection to Keating on the leadership issue. The Hawke–Keating struggle would be fought out in the right wing before it reached the wider party.

The key to the right wing was its NSW and Victorian powerbrokers, Richardson and Robert Ray. Hawke could rely upon Ray, who disliked Keating, but Richardson had been Keating's friend for many years in the most tribal of all ALP branches. While Richardson stayed with Hawke, Keating was stymied.

The centrepiece of Keating's drive for the Lodge was his sixth budget, delivered on 23 August 1988. Keating hoped it would be his last budget and he tried to make it his best—it was his 'bringing home the bacon' budget which, unbeknown at the time, would crash-land the next year. It was presented by Keating as his swansong, a point scarcely grasped at the time. On page one of his speech Keating said, 'I can report to the people of Australia that the nation is successfully emerging from its most severe economic crisis in a generation . . . we are now well on the way back to prosperity.' Thus Keating tried to close the book on a successful treasurership.

The key to the 1988–89 budget is that it was designed by Keating to win the next election—for himself, not for Hawke. Keating operated in the hope that Hawke would be gone and that he would become the leader. Keating hoped he was putting together a strategy which would deliver a smashing election victory on which to establish his prime ministership. This psychological factor shaped the extent of Keating's budget's miscalculation.

Keating misjudged Australia's progress. He was too keen to announce a victory over the historic economic challenge which he had defined two years before. He said:

Our foreign debt burden has already stabilised and begun to fall. Inflation is down. Real wage increases are in prospect. Our rate of job growth is unmatched in the Western world. Business investment is rising rapidly. On the export front, new manufacturing activities and tourism have blossomed . . . Unquestionably, a dramatically better state of affairs now exists than when I warned in 1986 of the threat of Australia degenerating to the status of a banana republic.

When Keating designed the 1988–89 budget the signs of a powerful economic recovery seemed irresistible. It was obvious that the October 1987 sharemarket crash had been only a hiccough on the growth curve. In mid-1988 the world economy was strong, in turn delivering rising commodity prices and buoyant Australian exports. There was a surge of income from high commodity prices. Domestic demand, notably for housing, was very firm. The long-awaited business investment had arrived in a mounting tidal wave. The economy had grown far more powerfully over the previous 12 months than the government had expected. Total national spending in 1987–88 had risen by 4.1 per cent, compared with only 0.8 per cent in 1986–87. Herein lay the trap—the economy was far too hot.

It is an extraordinary feature of the 1988 budget that the seeds of miscalculation at its heart were evident at the time. The budget papers noted that in the growing boom of 1987–88 the level of national spending had exceeded the level of national production. The consequence was that imports were growing faster than exports — a reversal of the previous two years of net export gains. In short, Australia was living beyond its means yet again. It was both consuming and producing more — but consumption was running ahead of production. It was an unsustainable position. It could only lead to a resurgence in Australia's current account deficit and net foreign debt.

The budget papers revealed an alarming link between local demand and import penetration; any rise in demand meant a magnified lift in imports. The treasury warned that Australia must not repeat its past mistakes of allowing excess demand to rekindle inflation and undermine the balance of payments. Yet the treasury acquiesced in figures which undermined its warning.

Keating's 1988 budget estimated national spending to run at 4 per cent, which was again ahead of national production at 3.5 per cent. It predicted that import growth would again outpace export growth. Yet it produced an optimistic estimate for a further reduction in the current account deficit to 3 per cent. This was the cutting edge—the budget predicted a level of economic growth that would strain Australia's external deficit.

The then head of treasury's economic policy division, David Morgan, says: 'It was clear from the spending estimate that the economy was projected to grow too fast. If the estimates were correct the budget on its own numbers was too loose. In the event the numbers seriously underestimated the level of national spending.'[13]

So what was Keating doing?

Keating knew that he was running a risk; but he misjudged the odds. The centrepiece of his strategy was an audacious wage–tax deal which Keating hoped would break Australia's inflation rate to the same level as its OECD trading partners.

This would become one of Labor's greatest achievements. Keating believed that its delivery within the budget parameters would establish the basis not just for Labor's reelection, but for a 1990 election victory which would redeem the meagre 1984 result. Keating was looking for a virtual Wranslide, an election win which would increase Labor's majority and set up the Keating government for many years.

The Accord and the Keating–Kelty partnership were at the heart of this strategy. In his budget speech Keating said: 'While the balance of payments deficit is Australia's number one economic problem, inflation remains Australia's number one economic disease. It has infected our economic system for two decades . . . we have inflation locked into single digits. Now we have the opportunity to drive it lower.'

Keating used two mechanisms: a $400 million indirect tax to shave the CPI, and a personal income tax cut effective from 1 July 1989. The key was the tax cut. Keating's plan was to provide the biggest tax cut ever, about $5 billion, which could be funded from his mounting budget surplus. He envisaged a deal with Kelty in which the ACTU would substitute the tax cut for the 1989 wage case. Keating aimed to secure a zero or close to zero wage rise by paying wages from the budget through the tax system. He said that 'the size of the tax cut to be provided will be dependent on wages growth during 1988–89 and the quality of the wage/tax trade-offs to be negotiated'. In other words, Keating planned a massive economic fix.

This strategy derived from the Accord which Labor saw as a unique mechanism to lower inflation. The price Keating paid was the same as before—the delivery of a growth economy to strike the deal with Kelty and the ACTU. Keating was trying to use the Accord, not monetary policy, to attack inflation. The fiscal discipline which created the budget surplus merely generated a pool of money for a responsible tax cut to 'buy down' the inflation rate.

As usual, Keating erred on the side of growth, not discipline. This time the consequences were disastrous. He wanted a strong economy, but he was overwhelmed by a boom.

Keating predicted an inflation rate of 3 to 4 per cent in 1990. He called it 'an achievement which has eluded us for a generation'. But Keating, in fact, had reached for the stars. If Hawke adjusted his aspirations to the economy then Keating adjusted the economy to his aspirations. Hawke was a man skilled at exploiting history; Keating was a man anxious to bend history.

In 1988 Keating sought to maintain activity, promote jobs, bed-down the investment surge, stabilise the foreign debt and break inflation. The critics said he was experiencing delusions of grandeur. But Keating did not fabricate the economic forecasts on which the budget was based. They came from the treasury and the treasury, in turn, far from being too optimistic on commodity price forecasts, underestimated their increase, the income they generated and the growth of the overseas and domestic economy.

At this point, Hawke ignited the leadership crisis. Acting from a position of strength, he moved to exploit Keating's private threats about leaving politics unless he secured the prime ministership. Hawke would signal to Labor that there was 'life after Keating'; that the government could still prosper without Keating.

The day after the budget, Hawke goaded Keating on three separate occasions—in a prerecorded interview for the ABC's *7.30 Report*, in a radio interview, and that night at the annual *Financial Review* budget dinner. Hawke said he didn't want Keating to leave but conceded 'it's a possibility . . . I don't discount that he could go'. Hawke said that 'we would miss him'. While he was 58 and Keating only 44 Hawke said, 'I still feel young, only feel about 44 . . . don't get upset by that, Paul.' Hawke agreed that John Dawkins could be treasurer. 'There are people of very considerable talent in the Ministry and the position would be filled,' he noted. At the dinner Hawke, pointing out that he had given six post-budget speeches, said: 'I'm looking forward to addressing another six. That may be good news for some and bad news for others.' Hawke said that while Keating had prime ministerial ambitions, he 'knows what the realities are in terms of time . . . it's clear that the party and the people want me as Prime Minister . . . I think their judgement is the correct one'.[14]

Hawke had been buoyed by the Morgan poll published that morning showing Labor heading the coalition 47 to 42 per cent and Hawke heading Howard as leader by a huge 69 to 18 per cent. Hawke, as usual, was poll driven. His comments were a calculated tactic. Why say this of your treasurer the day after his budget? It was an assertion of Hawke's determination to stay as prime minister, even if that meant Keating would leave. Hawke was teaching Keating a lesson.

The next day the papers were filled with the story and graphic headlines: 'Hawke casts doubt on future of Keating' and 'PM takes shot at Keating'. The budget's momentum was terminated immediately.

Keating, who had watched Hawke's television appearance, was furious. He spoke separately with Beazley and Howe, who agreed that Hawke's remarks had been unnecessarily provocative. Keating called National Secretary Bob Hogg, who went public the same night saying that Hawke's comments were 'unwise'. Many other senior Labor figures used sharper terms in private. Hawke had miscalculated.

Taking stock of the situation on 25 August, two days after the budget, Keating spoke separately with Bowen, Button, Dawkins and Beazley. Bowen and Button told him to see Hawke. Dawkins told Keating: 'I've just seen Hawke, who said "I hope you're not too embarrassed by the flattery I'm giving you".' Keating went to Richardson's office where he met Richardson, Leo McLeay and Stephen Loosley, a trio of the NSW right. 'It's an obvious attempt to undermine me,' he told them. 'Hawke's a bastard and I'll confront him.'

He went to Hawke's office at 1.45 pm on 25 August where Hawke was busy writing a speech. But Keating was short and brutal.

'You've made a thoroughgoing bastard of yourself,' Keating said. 'You think I'm dispensable. What you're really saying is the relationship between you and me is finished. I'm telling you, you're dead right. As far as I'm concerned, you and I are finished. The relationship is over, dead and buried.'

Hawke replied: 'I see that you're in an inflammatory mood. You even rang the *Financial Review*, I'm told, to complain about the Budget coverage.' Keating shot back, 'Of course I did. They stuffed it up.' Keating was most upset over Hawke's speculation that he might leave federal politics, saying that he had never made any public suggestion of resignation, indeed, that he had said precisely the opposite at the National Press Club when asked the previous day. Keating told Hawke he was sick of hearing the prime minister say he needed to 'broaden out'. He told Hawke: 'You've decided to put the drip on me just like you did on Hayden and (Clyde) Holding before they went. I've just presented the most important budget in the nation's history with the first surplus in 35 years and you've stuffed it in one go.'

Keating would now stalk Hawke on the leadership.

But Keating had other problems besides Hawke. The Opposition was attacking him in Parliament for having travelled to Japan on an expired passport. Keating slammed the coalition frontbencher, Jim Carlton, who raised the issue as a 'snide underhand little man', a 'sanctimonious and obsequious' Uriah Heep. Labor members joked that Carlton got off more lightly than Hawke.

Richardson now moved into damage control. He went to Hawke's office at 5.30 pm, nearly four hours after Keating. Richardson told Hawke it was time to retreat. If Hawke thought Keating was dispensable, he was wrong. Hawke had indulged himself. Now it was time to recant, in public. Hawke should know, Richardson said, that the party, including Hawke's strongest backers, thought Keating essential to the government.

Richardson told Hawke to get back on television as fast as possible. His message was blunt—fix the damage. Finally Richardson told Hawke that he should remember that Hawke himself was not indispensable. Eventually Hawke was persuaded and his office went straight for Channel Nine. That night Hawke went live on *A Current Affair*. Hawke didn't just praise Keating; he gushed over him.[15]

Hawke said that Keating had made a 'magnificent contribution'; he was 'the best Treasurer this country has had'; indeed, he was 'the best Treasurer in the world'. Hawke looked at Ray Martin: 'I really mean that.' As for Keating's ambition to become PM, it was 'totally legitimate'. Hawke said that nobody was indispensable, not even himself. 'If I went under a bus . . . I think Paul Keating would make an admirable Prime Minister.' Hawke hoped desperately that Keating would stay. No, he didn't believe that Keating would go.

Keating listened to the Hawke interview but he wasn't buying this bill of goods. He wasn't letting Hawke off the hook.

Richardson rang Keating: 'I've got him to square off, now you go and see Hawke to fix things.' But Keating refused: 'No. Why should I go and see him? I won't.' Keating said Hawke's performance was insincere, then savaged Hawke, attacking his character and competence. He complained that Hawke had undermined the budget, which Keating regarded as unforgivable. Then Richardson told Keating he was talking on a car phone. Keating exploded: 'You must be mad.' The discussion had, in fact, been intercepted.

Keating provided a progress report on his exchanges with Hawke to Bowen, Button and Dawkins. Bowen said: 'Sit it out until early next year. We can't afford a brawl between the two of you.' Button said: 'You've done the right thing.' Dawkins was enthusiastic: 'Good. We should tell him to leave right now.'

Meanwhile Keating's old antagonist, Tom Uren, had offered him praise and advice. 'He's the Jack Dempsey of Australian politics,' Uren said of Keating. 'You can put him on the canvas, but then he will get off that canvas and achieve victory . . . there are very few visionaries but Keating is one . . . but he is an elitist and he is arrogant . . . if I could give Paul just a little advice, one word of advice—patience.'[16]

On the evening of Friday 26 August Hawke was provided with a detailed account of Keating's car phone remarks to Richardson. It was being offered to the press gallery—for a price. Hawke read the details on a flight to Sydney and upon arriving for a function at the NSW parliament he rang Keating immediately. According to Hawke's press secretary, Barrie Cassidy: 'About 200 guests waited for 45 minutes while Hawke delivered a tirade that would have cleared the bar of the John Curtin Hotel in Hawke's younger days.'[17] It was perhaps the most bitter phone exchange between Hawke and Keating. They engaged in mutual criticism and condemnation of each other's values. Keating said that Hawke's comments to Ray Martin were insincere. 'You've decided to stay for a fourth election and I can go to buggery as far as you're concerned,' Keating said. Hawke warned Keating that he would defend himself if the car tape leaked. The upshot in a second conversation later that night was that Hawke offered Keating a meeting on Sunday afternoon, August 28, at the Lodge. The subject was obvious—the leadership.

Beazley spoke to both men before the meeting and Keating assured him it would be civil, no abuse, just straight talking. But Keating went, determined to reject Hawke's timetable and insist on a transition of the prime ministership in late 1988 or early 1989.

On Sunday morning, on Channel 10's *Face to Face* program, Button said that Keating should be the next leader and it would be desirable for Hawke to reach an agreement with Keating on a handover. Button declined to say when the transition should occur but did not rule out Keating's elevation in the current term. In fact, this was Button's preference. Button had put the idea of a leadership deal into the marketplace. His remarks reflected the alarm with which senior ministers viewed the collision between Hawke and Keating. Beazley believed a solution should now be negotiated between the two men which would allow a transition in the next term. An unusual event had occurred before Button's interview. Hawke had called him to discuss what he might say and during the conversation had complained about Keating's destabilisation. Hawke did not ask Button directly to criticise Keating but Button felt that this option was implied.

Keating went to the Lodge at 3.15 pm. It was a civil meeting, with Hawke saying: 'I don't resent the events of last week and I don't bear any ill-will towards you.' Keating put his case: 'This government has probably got a seven-to-ten year life expectancy. Even if we win the fourth election, the fifth election can probably only come to us in very difficult circumstances. Post-1993 [after the fifth election] is strictly a never-never land. You want eight and a half of this 10 years. All you want to give me is the last 18 months of the fourth Parliament . . . I don't think the Liberals are as institutionally weak as you believe.'

Keating warned Hawke that the government was getting weak and tired. It would struggle to win the fourth election, let alone the fifth. Hawke had an obligation to leave with a smooth and effective transition of the leadership. He could leave in the near future as a three-election winning success. Keating's approach was made in the belief that he was the driving force within the government, the major determinant of its overall strategy and that he therefore had a legitimate claim to lead it soon—a position Hawke rejected at every point.

Hawke told Keating that he didn't accept his analysis. He said the government could be reconstructed around Dawkins as treasurer, Robert Ray as finance minister, Gareth Evans as foreign minister and Michael Duffy as trade minister. Hawke said that he'd recently talked to John Elliott at a Governor-General's dinner and Elliott had said it would take ten years to rebuild the Liberal Party. Hawke said that he didn't know of any election since 1949 in which the people had made the wrong decision, with the possible exception of 1980. 'So why would the people choose the Liberals in 1993?' he asked. 'It will take them much longer than that to repair themselves.' Hawke was telling Keating to be patient. But he also revealed the depth of his optimistic view of politics.

He then outlined his ambitions on the world stage, allowing Keating another insight into the extent of those ambitions. Hawke said that in his five and a half years as prime minister he had established the credentials and contacts that now enabled him to play a more important role in world affairs. People abroad were now putting proposals to him, 'things on which I might be able to help'.

Hawke said Keating didn't grasp that a leader needed time to establish himself abroad and reach the stage where he was asked to make contributions in international diplomacy. It was obvious that Hawke shared in greater measure than normal the penchant of Australian prime ministers to leave their mark abroad. Hawke made it obvious that he intended to focus more intensely then ever on international affairs. He said his scenario was to play a stronger role internationally over the next two or three years before organising a transition.

But Keating was unyielding. He said that the Cabinet, notably the Expenditure Review Committee (ERC) ministers, thought that Hawke did not provide 'nourishment' for the government. Keating said the government needed 'spiritual uplift'; it lacked 'enthusiasm and drive'. In short, it lacked leadership. Keating believed that Hawke had failed to lead the Cabinet and that, in fact, the Cabinet was looking to Keating.

Keating told Hawke there was more to leadership than just setting the agenda for the Structural Adjustment Committee of Cabinet, the implication being that Hawke's role was limited to listing items for discussion. Labor needed enthusiasm to win an election, Keating argued. It required a revitalisation. Keating then asked Hawke to broaden the discussion. He wanted to reconvene their review of leadership—both its quality and its transition—within the senior Cabinet committee to find what senior ministers believed. Hawke said at once any such move would be unwise.

Keating said he wanted a leadership resolution in the current term, the third term, under which he would lead the party to the fourth election, the next, in 1989 or 1990. He told Hawke that he reserved his position on the leadership. He believed that the party was entitled to know his views and it was entitled to choose between them for the leadership at the next election. Keating's fear, of course, was that when he got the leadership it would be too late and Labor's batteries would be exhausted, which is why he wanted a third-term rather than a fourth-term transition. Keating said that it was 'unlikely that I'll be staying around to accept a probable defeat at the end of the next term at a fifth election'.

Hawke remained resolute and unsympathetic. He told Keating that he was Labor's best reelection hope, that nobody else had his electoral ability. His intention was to remain to fight the next election and he would probably stay at least a year after that. Keating said that was probably up to Christmas 1990 and Hawke agreed. 'That's two and a half years away. If I have to keep doing this job until then, I'll be going gaga,' Keating replied.

Although the meeting was deadlocked on the leadership the discussion had helped to create the basis for an arrangement. Both men agreed to say publicly they had an ongoing working relationship—to keep the party happy and maintain a public front.

The next morning Dawkins went on the *AM* program calling upon Hawke to set a timetable for the transition. 'I think certainly the question of the succession has to be sorted out and the sooner the better,' Dawkins said, aligning himself with Button. But many Hawke supporters rejected both the need for any timetable and the assumption that Keating should become leader.

Dawkins, a passionate believer in the need for Hawke to surrender to Keating, planned a more dramatic intervention. He was convinced that Keating would be a great leader and feared he might quit politics if Hawke stayed. Since Dawkins was putting this view within the party he felt obliged to give Hawke its benefit too. It was about 29 August that Dawkins went into Hawke's office and asked him to resign in Keating's favour, an action he took without reference to Keating.

The conversation lasted more than an hour, but Dawkins was blunt: leaders should know when to go and Hawke's time had come.

Dawkins won full marks for courage but sustained a lot of damage. The Hawke camp was enraged and wrote him off. Hawke realised that his 'alternative Treasurer' was a Keating zealot. He told Dawkins he was staying because he was Labor's best winner, because the party and the Australian people wanted him, not Keating, as leader and, finally, because Hawke had obligations to the international community and opportunities which he wanted to discharge. Dawkins was as incredulous at Hawke's pomposity as Hawke was at Dawkins' hide.[18]

Hawke could never complain that Keating was trying to stab him in the back. Keating and Dawkins carried their daggers openly. Their technique was to assault Hawke front-on and keep hacking.

The next day Hawke publicly repudiated any suggestions that he devise a retirement timetable and criticised the media, especially the print media, for bias. His complaint was that the leading journalists were pro-Keating. This was an instinctive Hawke response which would reappear whenever the Keating issue flared and which culminated in late 1991 when Hawke lost the leadership. At that point his relations with the main print journalists virtually collapsed.

The irony is that Hawke's media strategy for some time had been to ignore, largely, the broadsheet newspapers as organs of influence and focus almost totally on the electronic media, particularly television. It was Hawke's own strategy which isolated him from the print media. Its effect was to cripple any influence Hawke may have enjoyed with the quality press. Keating, by contrast, treated the senior print journalists with a seriousness and attention that was rare for any federal politician. His aim was to persuade them to accept his economic agenda and his view of politics.

However Keating's real problem was that the right-wing powerbrokers, Richardson and Ray, refused to back him against Hawke. Keating did not expect Ray's support but was bitterly disappointed that Richardson stayed with Hawke. The two right-wing figures with whom Keating dealt were his friends Leo MacLeay and Laurie Brereton, but they drew a blank with Richardson. Meanwhile a left-wing delegation visited Hawke to declare its factional support for him. This closed the political circle: Hawke had the right-wing and left-wing powerbrokers. Keating found his strongest backing came from within the centre-left faction (the smallest), and among the Cabinet's economic ministers.

Keating had failed to prepare the political ground against Hawke. His mistake was to think the party would share his own perception of his dominance within the government and seek a leadership change on this basis. He never organised against Hawke and was too busy being treasurer. The sentiment within the caucus was: we don't usually dispose of failed leaders so how can we ditch our most successful leader?[19]

The challenger's argument was too presumptuous for the party—that Keating's own leadership would be maximised if he became leader this term, not next term. Keating told Labor MPs the issue was not winning the fourth election; it was about winning the fifth election. Unless Labor went for new leadership blood now, it would be dead meat in 1992–93. Hawke would be too old and Keating would be denied time to establish himself. The conclusion: elect Keating now! When the caucus pointed to Hawke's winning record, Keating shot back: 'He blew the 1984 campaign, lost ground in 1987, and has stuffed up the 1988 by-elections.'

Keating's ambition for the Lodge was just as deep as Hawke's. One ALP wit quipped, 'It's a contest between an egomaniac [Hawke] and a megalomaniac [Keating].' The impatience Keating displayed after his 1988 budget reflected his belief that the budget strategy would deliver low inflation, economic growth and foreign debt stabilisation: the trifecta which meant political success. Keating hated the thought that his strategy would be appropriated by Hawke to remain leader and win another election.

Hawke was shaken by the brazen nature of Keating's assault yet smug about his superiority within the caucus. Hawke was now very close to the view that he didn't want Keating to succeed him. Hawke was affronted by Keating's refusal to accept his legitimacy as prime minister and by Keating's claim to a greater legitimacy. He doubted Keating's judgement, temper and volatility. Above all, Hawke was almost paranoid about Keating's claim to dominate the government. The Hawke–Keating struggle was about power and history; it was a contest heavy with psychological trapdoors.

Keating aspired to replace Hawke on the grounds that he was the real prime minister, not on grounds of popularity. Keating said the Hawke–Keating government was really a Keating government, not a Hawke government. He conceded Hawke one point—the consensus doctrine. For the rest, Keating claimed, if not political copyright, then chief weight in dual authorship. The potency of the Keating challenge was twofold—it threatened not just to seize Hawke's prime ministership but to steal his place in history.

The nature of the Keating challenge meant that Hawke could not allow Keating to succeed him. Hawke knew that if Keating followed him then Keating would attempt to appropriate the entire period of the Labor government as his own political monument. It was too risky for Hawke to permit a Keating succession, particularly if Keating was a success and, most particularly, if Keating won an election thereby casting doubt on the uniqueness of Hawke's own election-winning ability. Hawke had let the dull Cliff Dolan succeed him as ACTU president nearly a decade earlier—the perfect successor for the historical record. Hawke knew that even if he held Keating out he faced another challenge—proving before history that he, not Keating, had shaped the government and its policies.

Hawke felt confident that his superior electoral record was a complete justification of his determination to remain as prime minister. Moreover

Hawke had organised his entire personal life around the prime ministership. Hawke's extended family lived just near the Lodge. Bob and Hazel had sold their Melbourne home and had made no new purchase for themselves. The Lodge was their home and Kirribilli House in Sydney their holiday house. Hazel had found Bob's prime ministership the most personally rewarding years of her life.

On 4 September 1988 Bill Kelty tried to lower the curtain on his friend's ambitions. Kelty said: 'Paul Keating will succeed Bob Hawke. They will work that out together and the party will vote unanimously for Paul Keating to be leader at the right time.' But Kelty said the right time was after the next election.[20]

As Keating saw his hopes turn into dust he grew furious towards the right wing, withdrew from its faction meetings and complained because his Cabinet colleagues didn't make a collective approach to seek Hawke's resignation. Keating had to decide whether to remain in politics now that he was being denied a leadership transition in the third term. But there was another reason for Keating's anger; it was located in the treasury.

Keating's budget set the stage for an immediate fight over monetary policy. David Morgan, head of treasury's monetary policy area, was worried before the budget and alarmed afterwards. Morgan launched a push for a monetary policy tightening within a fortnight of the budget. In his debrief minute to Keating for the September 1988 Reserve Bank board meeting, Morgan argued for a further lift in interest rates. Morgan said the level of demand was too strong to hold inflation and the foreign debt. Even worse, demand was likely to be stronger than projected in the budget. Urgent and firm action was required. The senior deputy and next treasury secretary, Chris Higgins, also signed Morgan's minute but the third deputy, Ted Evans, refused because he disliked its tenor though approving its substance.

The note was given to Keating on 8 September, ten minutes before the meeting with senior treasury and Reserve officers. Morgan's advice was that the budget forecasts were in jeopardy—'the balance of risks is that growth in earnings, inflation, the current account deficit and imports will be higher than forecast in the budget'. He warned that the economy had 'a considerable head of steam going into 88–89', with expenditure running ahead of production. His prescription: 'A further tightening of monetary policy would be useful to minimise these upside risks'. In particular, Morgan said, 'We should all be mindful that the large income tax reductions foreshadowed from next year will represent a significant change in the stance of fiscal policy . . . and will almost certainly require adjustments elsewhere, particularly in monetary policy.'

In a departure from practice Keating savaged Morgan at the meeting in front of his peers and promised to reply in writing. Keating was furious because the treasury was telling him to change policy a fortnight after delivering his budget; if it was this serious, Keating demanded, then why hadn't treasury been so agitated when the budget was framed?

Morgan returned to the treasury and complained that Keating had been listening to monetary policy 'wimps' for too long. The wimps were readily identifiable—Bernie Fraser and Bob Johnston—head of treasury and the Reserve Bank respectively, Keating's two closest advisers.

In his reply to Morgan, Keating said the gravity of the situation was that 'Treasury is saying three weeks after the budget that the forecasts might be wrong and the structure of policy is wrong'.

Keating reminded Morgan that as treasurer he had said in the budget that 'monetary policy will play its vital balancing role. I wrote those words myself and know what they mean'.

But this Morgan–Higgins advice was a forewarning of the gathering storm. Keating said he found Morgan's advice that fiscal policy should be tightened as well as monetary policy, 'bizarre', since the budget surplus had risen from $2 to $5.5 billion. Keating attacked Morgan's claim that there were 'presentational difficulties' with fiscal policy, asking rhetorically: 'Presentational difficulties with whom, Des Moore?'[21]

The upshot is that monetary policy was tightened again not in September but November 1988. This was done to prepare for the following July 1 tax cuts which would inject an extra $5 billion in the economy. The government was attacked for not tightening earlier but the advisers were divided. The bulk of advice from both treasury and the Reserve Bank favoured higher interest rates but the institutional chiefs, Fraser and Johnston were reluctant. The three treasury deputies, Higgins, Evans and Morgan, all wanted policy to be tightened. Bernie Fraser, the monetary policy 'dove', was isolated. Meanwhile the economy continued to steamroll ahead.

At a senior officers meeting in treasury in December Fraser said that monetary policy was a matter of judgement and he believed it was tight enough. At this point Ted Evans told Fraser that he believed that this judgement was wrong. Fraser hit back subsequently: 'I haven't been arguing that we don't tighten interest rates at all. I have been resisting suggestions that we go for a big hit on interest rates.'[22] Later Fraser defended himself against the 'wimp' accusation: 'These people ought to be holding their heads in bloody shame. In 1989 I was trying to persuade people to desist from putting up interest rates even higher. What sort of employment consequences would that produce?'[23]

In fact monetary policy had been run too loose for two years. Keating, the treasury and the Reserve had misjudged — all three. A short time before Keating had asked Morgan rhetorically who was his most experienced associate, only to answer his own question: 'Me. I've been involved in more economic statements than anybody you've got in Treasury.' But neither Keating's judgement, nor treasury's, nor the Reserve's, was remotely correct.

In its 1988–89 report the Reserve was forced to admit that 'the strength of demand was underestimated for much of the year'. This meant 'the gap between domestic spending and production which began to widen in 1987–88, grew further in 1988–89'. This set Australia upon a path which ran counter to Keating's budget. Keating predicted lower inflation and a lower current account deficit but inflation was rising and the current account deficit was rising.

When Keating left in September for his annual trip to the International Monetary Fund (IMF) he carried these premonitions about his budget. But Keating's preoccupation at this point was with power, not policy. Hawke had blocked his run and it was an unhappy and frustrated Keating who left Australia knowing that during the trip he must decide his political future. While overseas he delivered a hardsell on the 'end of Australia's insularity' and its new role within the fast-growing economies of the Asia/Pacific. But Keating was deciding whether he should retire from politics in early 1989 and leave Labor with the consequences of sticking by Hawke's leadership.

Dawkins had a wretched time as acting treasurer, plagued by poor performance in parliament, the revelation of his 'retirement' request to Hawke coupled with ridicule as 'Keating's failed campaign manager'. When Dawkins spoke to Keating by phone, he found a treasurer moody, despondent and talking about resignation. Keating was frustrated with the ALP, with Hawke and with his political life. He was unable to reconcile his self-image with the political situation. Hawke had Keating beaten on the leadership because Keating has misjudged him and the party.

On returning to Australia in October, Keating reviewed his position. One of his advisers, Shamus Dawes, advised him to retire but the others were neutral or told him to stay. Keating's wife Annita said she would let Keating decide. Keating went to see Hawke. 'While some people have advised me to resign now, I've decided against that,' he said. 'I've decided to stay and fight the next election with you. But if I do this, I want a commitment. I want a specific commitment from you to stand down next term and I want that commitment witnessed.'

Keating didn't have the numbers but he didn't want to resign. He still believed that his economic strategy would win Labor the next election. So he took the fallback option—the promise of the prime ministership next term. Keating was offering Hawke another three years of a working partnership.

Hawke was prepared to accept this arrangement, despite some doubt. He agreed to Keating's request. At a subsequent meeting, they discussed the witnesses. Keating suggested somebody from caucus but Hawke raised his finger, saying: 'No. Nobody from the caucus.'

Hawke said he wanted his friend Sir Peter Abeles, and Keating agreed. Keating knew Abeles and respected him. He returned to his office but Keating's staff in whom he confided told him to get his own witness. Keating decided he should have somebody from the Labor movement. So he rang Bill Kelty and got his agreement. Keating then returned to Hawke's office and asked for Kelty's attendance too. Hawke paused, then agreed.

After Hawke agreed, there was a six week delay which involved a series of phone calls between the four participants. Keating felt that Hawke was reluctant to convene the meeting and told Kelty so. The upshot was that Kelty, Keating's strongest supporter, actually organised the meeting. It was held at Kirribilli House about 6 pm on 25 November 1988, and involved only Hawke, Keating, Abeles and Kelty.[24]

When they met, Hawke got straight to business. He wanted to lead Labor to the fourth election. If it was won, then he would serve a suitable time, stand down and 'hand over to Paul'. Keating, in return, would serve the current term and fight the next election with Hawke. It was considered important for Labor's chances that Hawke and Keating be together. Hawke's resignation pledge was subject only to one proviso: if the story leaked, it was null and void. The pact was understood by both men and both witnesses. The deal had to be kept secret at the coming election since it was recognised that such a transition pact would hurt Labor if revealed. Overall, it provided for a smooth transition of the Labor leadership in the next term. The deal was oral and was not put on paper.

At the conclusion Hawke lectured Keating: 'I want to say to Paul that he can't keep coming late to Cabinet meetings. It doesn't show much respect for the colleagues. Secondly you've got to be more agreeable with the colleagues.' Keating told Hawke that if he was late for Cabinet there was always a reason. If he wasn't always agreeable it was because he was the fiscal sentry. Keating said he respected the spirit in which Hawke made the agreement. He just wanted to record the point that the transition next term had to give him sufficient time to become established as prime minister. There was never any intention to pre-empt the caucus. Both men knew that the caucus would have to elect any new leader.

Hawke said three years later that he was 'reluctant' to make this agreement. He had a 'profound belief' that he 'would continue to be the one best able to lead this government to victory'. He promised to leave after the 1990 election but hoped Keating would 'come to understand' Hawke was Labor's best election winner and thereby release Hawke from the pact.[25]

Despite this, Hawke still did the deal. It had lots of pluses for him. It got Keating off his back, buried the leadership issue before the fourth election, guaranteed a united Hawke–Keating front, gave Keating great incentive to stay on in politics and, finally, it meant that Hawke didn't have to meet his obligation and resign until 1991. Hawke got his benefits upfront and paid later.

Hawke says he 'desperately' wanted Keating to stay and fight the 1991 election with him: 'Paul had some view that perhaps he might leave if he was not Prime Minister . . . he thought he should have his turn.'[26] The deal locked in Keating, at least for three years.

The Kirribilli pact

This secret pact was unique. It revealed the deal-making character of the Hawke government and its principal architects. It demonstrated both their faith in deals and their lack of personal trust. Keating sought confidence in Hawke's promise yet refused to trust him. Abeles and Kelty were present because the deepest secrets could not be entrusted to Labor ministers. Hawke and Keating felt the pact would never be disclosed. It was political therapy at three levels—it solved the 1988 leadership crisis; it kept the Hawke–Keating team intact for the 1990 election, which was the wish of the Labor Party; and it gave Keating the promise of a smooth transition to the Lodge.

Did Hawke mean to honour his agreement with Keating? Hawke knew it was a moral, not a legal agreement. He could easily have persuaded himself that his promise was genuine while realising it might never be delivered. Hawke knew that circumstances change and that three years in Australian politics is a long time. It was inevitable once Hawke made this pact that Keating would challenge if Hawke broke it. But Keating felt at the time that a challenge would not be necessary.

In summary, Hawke had denied Keating the prime ministership in 1988 but Keating had obtained a witnessed pledge from him to resign in the next term. Keating felt that his transition to the prime ministership had been delayed three years—not terminated. Neither Keating nor a majority of the Labor Party felt that Hawke would want to hang on for a fifth election in 1992–93.

But Keating knew in November 1988 that his prospects of enjoying a successful prime ministership had been severely compromised. Hawke had denied him the transition for the fourth election which was the optimum timing for a successful Keating prime ministership. If Keating prevailed in the next term the government would be older, battle weary and defeat-prone. The party was doubtful of Keating's ability to win a fourth election, let alone a fifth. So what guarantee did Keating really have? Hawke, in fact, had boxed him in.

Recent history suggested that the treasury portfolio always damaged its incumbent, sooner or later. Keating's tenure at treasury was lengthening, the economy was overheating, Keating wanted no other portfolio except the prime ministership. He had missed his optimum time to replace Hawke and Hawke might prove more politically durable than Keating. Hawke had called Keating's bluff about quitting politics, but few in the ALP had believed the bluff.

In December 1988 Keating signalled his reconciliation to his pact with Hawke by a vivid attack upon Howard, declaring that he and Hawke were 'spinning a web that will ensnare Mr Howard . . . we'll crawl across the web like a couple of black widow spiders'. Keating delivered a hymn of praise to Dawkins, saying that he could be treasurer 'anytime'. In a famous line, declaring that he could adapt to the popularity demands of the leader-

455

ship, Keating said, 'If I want to throw the switch to vaudeville I'll do that at the appropriate moment.'[27]

The leadership issue was put into cold storage, frozen until after the fourth election—if Labor won. The economy would make that remote but the Liberals, as usual, would give Labor fresh hope.

24
Elliott denied

*The more people spoke to Roger Shipton, the more determined he
got to stay in politics.*

> John Elliott, July 1990, reflecting on the man who
> blocked his path to power

While Hawke and Keating fought over the prime ministership John Elliott
made his own decision to pursue the ultimate prize. In late 1988 one of the
strangest and least known events of the decade unfolded in a series of secret
meetings—a campaign to make John Elliott prime minister. Elliott found
that many Liberals shared his own view, that John Howard could not win
an election. He became the willing target for a 'draft Elliott' leadership
campaign.[1]

Elliott had lost his respect for Howard as a result of their battle of wills
and Howard's blunder on Asian migration. Disillusionment with Howard
was profound inside the parliamentary party but it was greatest inside the
shadow ministry, where it was most dangerous. Howard had succumbed to
paranoia, the natural malaise of leaders under threat. The paranoid leader
cannot trust anyone and thereby runs the risk of alienating everyone.

A typical remark made about Howard at this time was that he listened
only to his wife and to his top aide, Graham Morris. Howard became
isolated, a danger for a leader who lacked man management skills. As the
party lost confidence in Howard it looked for an alternative.

The Liberals were reluctant to return to Peacock. He was not performing; he inspired no enthusiasm; and between Peacock and any return as
leader lay a psychological hurdle. Some Liberals saw Peacock as lacking
in political steel; others dismissed him as yesterday's man. Peter Shack, a
Peacock man for ten years, visited Elliott, asked his intentions and suggested
that he run. Many Liberals wanted a new candidate—there was only Elliott.

A pattern of informal but systematic contact grew in the August–
November 1988 period between Elliott and the parliamentary party. Central

457

to this dialogue was Alistair Drysdale, Elliott's political minder, who had excellent contacts inside the party and with the media. Drysdale's main job was to keep Elliott out of political trouble.

But from the day Drysdale started he had a second agenda—an Elliott move into politics. Drysdale knew all about political coups—he had helped Fraser beat Snedden in 1975, Fraser thwart Peacock in 1982, and had seen Peacock succumb to Howard in 1985. Elliott and Drysdale organised their own seduction. Drysdale was an Eggleton appointment; he would tell Eggleton what he needed to know but protect him from embarrassing information. When Drysdale started with Elliott he rang Peacock to tell him. 'Elliott's only got five votes,' Peacock said. But Peacock was wrong.

In the next few months half the shadow ministry and some back-benchers made their own political pilgrimages to see Elliott. They came to woo, persuade, explore, or just talk; they included Peter Shack, Fred Chaney, David Connolly, Jim Carlton, John Spender, Richard Alston and Bronwyn Bishop. The list, crossing the old Peacock–Howard factional lines, had the potential for a new power structure.

Shack made three or four visits to Elliott's Melbourne office, once taking Wilson Tuckey with him to meet Elliott. Shack told Elliott: 'I was Peacock's key supporter but we can't go back to Andrew.' Chaney told Elliott that the leadership was a major problem and that he should enter politics. Carlton, an old friend of Elliott, told Elliott that Howard's weakness, management and persuasion, was Elliott's strength. Carlton even told Elliott that another senior NSW Liberal, Wal Fife, would back Elliott if he came. In the interim Carlton said the strategy must be to 'prop up Howard' until Elliott arrived.

Within the parliamentary party Elliott only had about ten 'hard' votes overall, but the mood was volatile, as events later proved. There were 'core' Elliott backers such as Bronwyn Bishop and Richard Alston. The Elliott draft, in fact, was taking people from Howard who were not prepared to shift to Peacock. Elliott also had strong support within the party organisation, notably among the state presidents. The assumption of his supporters was that once Elliott entered politics support for Howard's leadership would disintegrate.

Howard's tribulations were reflected in the collapse of his relationship with Fred Chaney, his Senate leader. Chaney felt he had been frozen out by Howard, and Howard in turn was suspicious of Chaney. When John Valder pleaded with Howard to work properly with Chaney and take him into his confidence Howard delivered his final reply: 'Janette says you can't trust Fred.'

Early in 1988 Chaney told Howard that his public image was terrible, that he must reassess his standing as a leader. He advised Eggleton that the Federal Secretariat should respond to Howard's image problems with a clothing and entertainment allowance. Chaney said that Howard's opponents were jeering at his parsimony. Eggleton made some arrangements.

Chaney saw Howard as a solo performer, skilled at articulating a policy position for the Opposition on the media or attacking the government in the parliament. But he was a poor team leader, a bad chairman of shadow Cabinet and, as time progressed, his relations with his colleagues fell into disrepair. Finally, a Howard confidant, Tony Messner, told Chaney: 'You'll have to stop criticising John to his face. There's no point and it's counter-productive.' But Chaney blamed Howard, not himself, for the coolness in their relationship.

When Howard was overseas in mid-1988 Chaney gave an interview on 13 July in which he declared his support for Howard but confirmed that if the opportunity arose then Chaney himself would be a leadership candidate. Chaney's remarks were qualified but his declaration of firm interest in the leadership provoked intense speculation in the Liberal Party.

Howard returned to Australia via Western Australia to attend a state council meeting at Esperance. That night Howard, Janette and Chaney had a very difficult dinner together, with Howard venting his anger and telling Chaney that he had been disloyal. Chaney defended himself and told Howard the text of the interview did not sustain the interpretations placed on his remarks. Chaney assured Howard and Janette that he was not just a trust-worthy colleague but their friend. He said that he would work to regain their trust and demonstrate that the accusation of disloyalty was wrong. This conversation became central to Howard's later conviction that Chaney, as a fellow leader, was disloyal and untrustworthy.

The entire purpose of the Elliott push was to make Elliott the leader before the election and have the voters install him as prime minister. Elliott was going to 'do a Hawke'—crash through the parliamentary party and with this momentum win the election. This required a by-election and Elliott knew the seat he wanted—Higgins, still held by Roger Shipton.

The tactics, as defined by Elliott and Drysdale, were that Elliott would win Liberal endorsement, win the by-election and enter parliament in a blaze of national publicity. Elliott's arrival would destabilise Howard. Like Hawke, his arrival would occasion the leadership push. Elliot was coy about the plan but passionate in his political ambition.

Elliott no longer ran Elders on a daily basis. He was a rich man, prepared to seize the chance to become prime minister, and he believed the next election was just waiting for the Liberals to win. But Elliott had a responsibility to his board. In August 1988, as Elliott's plans reached a new intensity, Elliott asked the board to give him a six month period of grace in which to decide between politics and business. That meant until the end of January 1989. Elliott promised that his situation would be resolved by that stage.

In September 1988 specific plans were laid for Elliott's move. Drysdale convened a meeting at Clemenger advertising agency in Sydney involving Clemenger principal Greg Daniel, a Greiner strategist, Ian Kortlang, and Liberal backbencher Richard Alston. The announcement Drysdale made was brief but electric: 'We have a candidate; he has agreed to run.'

Drysdale outline the plan. Roger Shipton was to be convinced to resign in Higgins. That task was being managed by WMC boss Hugh Morgan, an Elliott associate. Clemenger, under Daniel's direction, would prepare a multi-million dollar corporate campaign to market Elders without Elliott to protect its share price on Elliott's departure into politics. Elliott would enter parliament at a Higgins by-election in early 1989. He would depose Howard as fast as possible—hopefully at the first party meeting he attended in 1989.

Drysdale admitted that Elliott was vulnerable on claims of tax minimisation, but he had a plan to address this issue. He said that Elliott would agree to have a firm of independent auditors scrutinise his tax return and make a public 'sanctioning' statement.

Drysdale had picked the team carefully. Kortlang and Daniel were seen as winners, key players in Greiner's triumph six months earlier. Kortlang was wanted for his political planning skills, Daniel to repackage Elders but with the prospect of taking the federal Liberal Party's advertising account if Elliott became leader. Alston was the link into the parliamentary party. While the political columnists still said that Elliott would never come, the plans to make him prime minister were being coordinated from his South Yarra headquarters.

On 21 September Drysdale organised a small meeting at the jam factory in South Yarra, a mini-brief for Elliott. It was not a complete success. Sitting around the conference room were Drysdale, Kortlang, Alston and the next Victorian Liberal director, Petro Georgiou, all keen to see an Elliott led Liberal revival. Elliott implied that running Australia would be easy. He said that Australia was being mismanaged and it wouldn't be too hard to do better than the existing politicians. 'What would you say if I reckoned that running Elders was easy?' asked Kortlang. 'Bullshit,' replied Elliott. 'Well, don't kid yourself that running the country will be easy,' Kortlang said. Elliott was riding high but his arrogance was a risky political commodity.

Howard's problem in 1988 was that despite heavy anti-Labor sentiment he was unable to purge the doubts about his leadership. The Liberals won the Adelaide by-election; they secured a major swing at the Port Adelaide and Oxley by-elections. A momentum was building, but Howard never convinced his party that he was a winner and the Liberals refused to let Howard convince them.

There were three elements in Howard's defensive fortifications. First, he was determined to project an image of strength, a plan which foundered disastrously on the Asian immigration issue. Second, Howard announced a late 1988 reshuffle in a bid to strengthen his team which elevated John

Hewson from the backbench to finance and Peter Reith into industrial relations; it also involved promotions for Neil Brown, Peter Shack and Robert Hill. Howard had fired Carlton and then asked him about Elliott. 'I've told you before, I'm sceptical about whether he'll ever come,' Carlton replied. 'If he did come would you support him for leader?' Howard pressed. 'I might well do so, John,' Carlton said crisply.

Third, Howard was planning the most comprehensive statement of Liberal ideology for decades, an ambitious attempt to synthesise dry economics and social conservatism. The manifesto *Future Directions* would give a powerful ideological profile to the Liberal Party and it would market Howard to swinging voters.

The heartland of disillusionment towards Howard was Victoria, whose two most senior Liberals were Peacock and Elliott. Peacock was Howard's old enemy and Elliott had become his new enemy. They symbolised the old and new Victorian Liberal establishments. While Peacock and Elliott were Howard's chief opponents, they were themselves rivals. The Liberal Party was filled with Howard defectors, Peacock disillusionists and Elliott romantics.

The moment a Peacock–Elliott alliance was sealed then Howard would be doomed. Howard had been protected because of the long-standing Elliott–Peacock animosity. This is where Alistair Drysdale's role become so important. Drysdale was close to Peacock, whom he had known for nearly twenty years and for whom he had worked when Peacock had been Opposition leader. Now Drysdale as Elliott's chief political adviser worked to secure a rapport between Elliott and Peacock. He realised their animosity was based on ignorance; they had never got to know each other. So Drysdale arranged a series of meetings in which Elliott and Peacock broke the deep freeze.

Drysdale told Elliott that he would only become leader on the basis of some arrangement with Peacock. Before the first meeting Peacock and Drysdale had lunch. Peacock was profoundly pessimistic about his chance of returning as leader but professional enough not to dismiss it. Then Peacock came to see Elliott at the jam factory where they talked some policy and politics; it was shadow boxing. But the dialogue developed and they dined out and had several discussions. Elliott never told Peacock directly that he wanted to enter politics; but Peacock knew the seriousness of such an option. Shack had already informed Peacock that he had defected to Elliott. Liberal treasurer, Ron Walker, had spoken to Peacock about Elliott as the new leader.

Peacock advised Elliott that Elliott didn't have the numbers; that he would only ever have the numbers against Howard with the Peacock supporters. Peacock said that Elliott's support base lay in the Howard camp. The conclusion Elliott drew was that Peacock would be kingmaker, if Elliott was to be king.

The truth about these strange Elliott–Peacock talks is that the two men

461

put different interpretations upon them, partly because they were not completely frank with each other.

Elliott convinced himself that Peacock had given him a signal—that Peacock would back an Elliott run on the leadership. Elliott believed that Peacock had used words along the lines: 'If you run then I'm with you and we'll carry the vote.' The upshot was that Elliott felt the leadership and the prime ministership was within his grasp.

When asked about these discussions, Peacock said: 'At no stage did I really believe that John would go into federal parliament. Although I was pressed to make a deal with Elliott on the leadership I never did.'[2] Peacock finished the talks certain that no deal had been done; that no signal had been given. In fact, Peacock's position was complex. Peacock knew that Elliott was a wild card, that his tactics might destabilise Howard so much that Peacock himself would have a fresh chance to regain the mantle.

Elliott's game plan was to rely upon senior party figures—Shack, Carlton and finally Peacock—to develop a steamroller effect. But Elliott never put his cards on the table with these men; he never categorically said that he was coming. Elliott always wanted a special deal or 'fast-track' entry into politics. Peacock realised this and he always doubted that Elliott would come or that he would be a success.

The extent of anti-Howard feeling within the Victorian Liberal Party reached its peak during the September 1988 state campaign, which saw ALP premier John Cain narrowly defeat the Liberal leader, Jeff Kennett, in a contest dominated by splits within the federal party. The swing against Cain at his third election victory was only one per cent, a condemnation of Kennett and the Liberals. The message was that Labor would keep running professional campaigns. Labor's national secretary, Bob Hogg, said, 'The discontent is there. The Liberals tapped it but we managed to contain it.' The Victorian Liberals blamed Howard for the fall in their ethnic vote due to his Asian migration comments.

Howard had few friends in Victoria, with Peacock, Elliott and Kennett aligned against him. Melbourne business saw Howard as weak and without real clout. Opinion makers, once his supporters, used his Asian migration comments to erode his standing. The Melbourne based editor of *Business Review Weekly* (BRW) magazine Stuart Simson, said: 'There is a very serious level of discontent that exists among the higher echelons of the Liberal Party in Victoria towards John Howard. It really is acute. They are turning on Howard in a way that hasn't happened before.'[3]

The Howard crisis was set in the context of a dramatic upheaval within the Victorian Liberal Party. Its focal point was the young Victorian president, Michael Kroger, a clean break from the old Victorian–Liberal culture. Kroger grasped the Liberal dilemma in the 1980s—that the successful selling of free market economics depended upon a thorough internal reform of the party and the preselection process to secure better candidates. Kroger was dismissive of the outdated party practices and attracted by Elliott's drive. Influenced by Labor's success in the 1980s Kroger wanted the Liberals to move in the same direction—greater party professionalism, a strong party machine, and a willingness to 'kingmake' leaders.

Kroger declared:

> I cannot think of a single reason which better explains the Liberal Party's continued electoral failures in recent decades than the outdated preselection system . . . Perhaps the most resounding argument against a totally localised preselection system is the fact that it is almost impossible to encourage outstanding Australians on the conservative side of politics to nominate . . . where there is little or no chance of them winning. . . . It is time all of this nonsense stopped and senior office bearers of the Liberal Party in all state divisions being the Presidents, Vice Presidents, Treasurers and other high-ranking individuals, have a direct say in the outcome of preselections.[4]

Kroger was creating a climate in which support for Elliott and other high flyers could thrive. He was most offended by the situation in Higgins, a seat Shipton had held since 1974, yet Shipton was on the backbench. This seat was a prize, a seat made for Liberal prime ministers. The Kroger-led reform forces were determined to beat Shipton at the next preselection. The two most likely candidates in Kroger's mind were Elliott and his old university mate, Peter Costello. He saw both as prime ministerial material. Kroger facilitated a climate in which support grew for Elliott—but Kroger was never told of the secret plans of the Elliott camp.

The most significant business figure backing Elliott was WMC's Hugh Morgan, who believed that Elliott was the closest figure to an Australian Thatcher. Morgan, a mixture of nous and romanticism, believed that the professional politicians had failed Australia. Morgan was the principal figure in an interesting group of Elliott sympathisers.

Morgan and Elliott reached an understanding. Morgan would talk to Shipton in an effort to persuade him to retire and create the by-election which Elliott wanted. Elliott was not told the full details; it was better that he did not know. Morgan spoke to Shipton on several occasions. He was offered a position outside politics at a very generous salary, a package Shipton would not expect to match in any normal political retirement. Within the Elliott camp there was intense speculation about how much Shipton was offered but no figure was ever confirmed. Morgan saw Shipton about September 1988. But Shipton was playing it tough, despite his bleak future in politics where he faced defeat in the next round of preselections.[5]

The Elliott camp believed that several people spoke to Shipton in an effort to secure a resolution. But they had misjudged Shipton's stubbornness. Logic suggested that he take the offer—but Shipton was not governed by logic. Shipton was a product of the political culture which Kroger wanted to destroy. Kroger, in retrospect, was unsurprised that Shipton had decided to stay. Kroger pointed out that no sitting Liberal, state or federal, had lost his endorsement in Victoria since 1973, so history suggested that a Liberal seat was a permanent job. Shipton could be forgiven for thinking that he could survive. Elliott reflected later, 'The more people spoke to Roger Shipton, the more determined he got to stay in politics.'

On 26 October, *The Bulletin* appeared with a cover story headed 'Prime Minister Elliott—how he'd lead the Liberals from the wilderness'. Inside was a nine-page spread and a poll specially commissioned for the magazine from Gary Morgan, comparing Howard, Peacock and Elliott. The result for preferred Opposition leader split Peacock 32, Howard 14 and Elliott 12 per cent.

Elliott, not yet in politics surpassed the others on measures of political strength. Gary Morgan made a speech, saying:

Mr Howard is the most unwanted leader of the Liberal Party since my father began polling in the early 1940s . . . If the Liberal Party wants a leader who is honest but who, after three years as their leader, is still seen as indecisive, not having clear policies, being weak and changing his mind too often, then they should stay with Mr Howard . . .
However if the Liberal Party wants a strong, capable, positive leader with clear plans and policies then they should select Mr Elliott.[6]

Peacock drew another conclusion. He noted that he was far ahead of both Howard and Elliott. Meanwhile Howard grew more agitated about the leadership destabilisation. About this time Howard demanded of Eggleton: 'I want names. I want the names of the politicians and businessmen working against me. I want the names.'

The day after the *Bulletin* article, the *Melbourne Sun* reported that Elliott was planning to enter politics. It was the final twist that snapped Howard's nerve. Howard was frustrated because he could not pinpoint the source of the problem—he didn't know what Elliott was doing. An enraged Howard called Eggleton demanding that the Elliott speculation be terminated. His mood was white hot. Eggleton rang Drysdale and briefed him on Howard's anger. That afternoon Drysdale spoke to Elliott at the Sydney Opera House just before he went to give an interview to 2UE. The upshot was that Elliott, on Drysdale's advice, felt he had no option but to make a public declaration denying any intention to enter politics. Drysdale told Elliott that Howard had been 'nearly off the planet' and that the issue must be defused. So Elliott said: 'I would only consider entering after the next election if we didn't win . . . and I do believe we'll win and I do believe John Howard will be Prime Minister.'[7]

This statement was tactical. Elliott was still planning to move, provided that Hugh Morgan could reach a settlement with Shipton. His denial, necessary to avert a crisis, was misleading as a guide to his intentions.

Indeed, it was designed to mislead. Drysdale told Elliott that if he entered politics at a by-election the statement would pose a problem—but it would be forgotten within 24 hours.

Howard after speaking with Eggleton was scheduled to appear on Channel 9s *Midday Show* with Ray Martin. The interview revealed a leader under psychological siege. Howard was reliant on military metaphors: 'I've been to the equivalent of political hell and back . . . the arrows now not only of outrageous fortune but of personal polls bounce off me as though they were hitting armour plate . . . Sherman tank-like.'

But when Elliott publicly backed off Howard became cocky, taunting Elliott, saying that he'd 'love to come in and take over the show, I'm sure'. The Howard camp briefed the media that Elliott would be a political liability because of his companies' tax practices.

The next week Elliott held his company's pre-Melbourne Cup party at his Mount Macedon Sefton estate. Business and political figures mingled; it was time for champagne, gambling and anticipation. The media stories kept flowing but the rock began to turn dry. Hugh Morgan had still failed to move Shipton.

Shipton was a stubborn fellow and he was an old family friend of Peacock. Shipton had attended the funeral of Peacock's mother and Peacock had gone to Shipton's wedding. Peacock knew that Shipton had been under pressure to quit. He talked to Shipton about his future and joked about the rumours of offers to Shipton to leave—'make certain you ask for a Rolls, mate.' Peacock called this banter with Shipton 'cuddle therapy'. Drysdale's theory—only a theory—was that Peacock would have encouraged Shipton to stay. That would block Elliott—indeed it would finish Elliott—and it would leave Peacock as the alternative to Howard.[8] It is a fascinating speculation but unsubstantiated. Peacock told colleagues that Shipton would never confide in him about what offer he had received and Peacock later felt guilty in joking about Shipton's agonising decision.

Meanwhile the Liberal Party stayed on edge, unsure about its leader, uncertain if it had a challenger. Fred Chaney said high profile candidates like Elliott should enter politics—and was attacked by a sensitive Shipton in the party room. As the meeting of the Victorian State Council to vote on Kroger's preselection reforms loomed, Hugh Morgan made an appeal on Kroger's behalf.

Morgan complained about the decline of the doctrinal foundations of conservatism since Menzies and the need for a new concept of political representation. Taking as his model the great Roman soldier–statesman Cincinnatus, a man who answered his country's call to power but then retired to his farm, Morgan said:

> Our side of politics can never compete with a Keating, a Richardson or a Kelty . . . they are professionals in a game which we do not believe

is part of our culture . . . the ideal political representative from a conservative point of view is one who finds Canberra burdensome and who goes there out of a sense of duty . . . who is pleased to serve for four or five years and then . . . return fulltime to his business, farm, professional or corporate activities.[9]

It was a noble, romantic and unreal view of Australian politics. It was also a recipe for defeat. The irony is that political deals were required to make it a reality, as both Elliott and Morgan knew. Elliott had been Morgan's prime candidate yet Elliott has been thwarted by the political system.

A fortnight later Kroger had most of his demands met when the Victorian party changed the preselection system to give a 60/40 weight between the branches and head office in preselections.[10] But that made no difference to Elliott. He still couldn't settle a deal with Shipton.

Over his Christmas break Elliott made up his mind and closed the window on politics. He rationalised his decision in terms of Howard's electoral boost from *Future Directions* and his own takeover bid for the giant UK Scottish and Newcastle operation.[11]

The truth is that Elliott was beaten by Roger Shipton, the man who never made it in politics. Shipton's place in history is that he stopped Elliott on the brink of a charge towards the Lodge. And that opened the door for Andrew Peacock.

25
The Peacock coup

*The loyalties which centre upon number one are enormous. If he
trips he must be sustained. If he makes mistakes he must be
covered. If he sleeps he must not be wantonly disturbed. If he is no
good he must be pole-axed.*

Winston Churchill on the political leader

It was over the two days 9–10 February 1989 in Adelaide that John Elliott
told Andrew Peacock that he should depose Howard and lead the Liberals
into the next election. Elliott informed Peacock that he had abandoned his
plans to enter politics and that the decision was final. Elliott would now
support a Peacock move against Howard. The torch had passed from the
new pretender to the old pretender.[1]

This established the Elliott–Peacock alliance to replace Howard, and
gave Peacock new confidence to mount a challenge. It was a deadly alliance
despite the momentum Howard had gained from *Future Directions*. Elliott
told Peacock that Howard had no managerial or organisational capacity; that
Howard would fail as prime minister if he won an election. Elliott had
always known Peacock's weakness, his inability to handle policy issues.
Now he discerned a strength—that Peacock could bring out the best in the
people beneath him.

This meeting was a milestone in Peacock's return as leader. Elliott was
federal president and—at the time—a businessman of great standing. Peacock was nourished by Elliott's support which boosted his personal confidence. From this point Peacock would appease Elliott but not surrender to
him.

The meeting occurred in a hotel room where Elliott destroyed most of
a bottle of scotch. The surprise for Peacock was the depth of emotion with
which Elliott discussed his own ambition and his antagonism towards
Howard. Elliott reflected at length on why 'I'll never be prime minister',
and Peacock despite their talks the previous year, only realised at this point

the obsession which the prime ministership had been for Elliott. As they talked Peacock knew that this was a dramatic moment.

Elliott's decision destroyed the fragile stability which had sustained Howard's leadership. Howard's position had rested upon a basic premise—that Peacock and Elliott would never join forces. Howard had seen at first hand their mutual antagonism, but his own weakness had helped to forge their alliance. Once it was sealed Howard's position was in peril.

Elliott was not involved in delivering numbers for Peacock, but he was fundamental in delivering legitimacy and business approval. These two qualities were central for Peacock, not just in staging a coup but in making a successful transition. Elliott's status as president gave a respectability to the challenge.

In early February Elliott and Jim Carlton had held a ninety-minute meeting in Sydney. Elliott, aware that Carlton as an economic dry had never respected Peacock, asked: 'What's your view about Peacock running for the leadership?' Carlton specified the conditions which would be necessary—Peacock must give a firm commitment to free market economics; Hewson should be shadow treasurer; Peacock must delegate to his team and select the team wisely; he must have a competent chief of staff. Elliott asked: 'If we can get these kind of commitments from Peacock will you support him?' Carlton said that he would; his defection to Peacock was a symbol. If such a theoretician of dry economics was backing Peacock then ideology was no barrier to his election.

Elliott supported Peacock on certain conditions: that Peacock as prime minister implement the tough economic and industrial policies already in Liberal policy documents. There would be no backsliding to the wet agenda of Peacock's traditional base.

Elliott had clout but he was outside the cauldron of the parliamentary party where any coup had to be planned, organised and mounted. However the push for a Peacock challenge had predated this Peacock–Elliott deal.

From late 1988 the Peacock loyalists within the parliamentary wing, known as the 'gang of five' or 'the cardinal's group', had been seriously discussing a Peacock challenge. This group was Peacock's parliamentary vanguard—John Moore, Peter Shack, David Jull, Wilson Tuckey and Chris Puplick. They met regularly at Moore's apartment in the Canberra suburb of Kingston.

But in late 1988 this had been an unhappy group because its candidate appeared disinterested in the leadership. Peacock was flattered by media speculation that he would return as leader but he didn't believe it. Peacock, in fact, had confided in close friends that he didn't want to be leader again—a psychological key to the course of politics in 1989–90. The story of the Peacock coup is that Peacock was pushed, cajoled and drafted to the challenge by Elliott, by the 'gang of five' and by the media.

The first sign that Peacock was turning came at the 1 December 1988

468

meeting of the group, minus Tuckey, which was told by Peacock in response to their urgings that he was thinking of a challenge to Howard the following March. Peacock said that he preferred Moore as his deputy given the importance of Queensland in the federal election. In the days before this meeting there had been a series of separate talks involving Puplick, Neil Brown, Don Dobie and Warwick Smith about the prospects of a leadership change.

In the first meeting of the group for 1989, held on the evening of 28 February, Peacock's mood was more intense. Peacock reported that Elliott was backing him and that Hugh Morgan was ready to help. The gang was heartened. It was at this meeting that a decision was taken to aim for a challenge in the second sitting week in May and to meet on a weekly basis to discuss progress. Drysdale would be Elliott's link to this group and to the parliamentary party. But Peacock's ambivalence was obvious—he told the colleagues that while he would be a candidate he would not lobby. This was tactically smart; but it was symptomatic of his psychological reluctance to return to the leadership. But a deal was made—the gang would deliver the leadership.

The Peacock group, tied by self-interest, was more anti-Howard than pro-Peacock, reflecting in its ambitions and histories the instability of Liberal politics.

John Moore was an old Peacock mate, a Fraser minister who had to resign over the 'colour TV' affair, a bitter opponent of the Queensland Nationals, a tennis buff and former stockbroker. Moore had a touch of style and a distaste for Howard who, in turn, had tried to court Moore but had failed, thereupon concluding that Moore was the most bitter and twisted figure in the party. Moore had prepared a blueprint for the coalition's privatisation program (the greatest sell-off in Australia's history) yet he was disappointed that Howard had never bothered to discuss the document with him as shadow minister, even after he leaked the policy draft to the *Financial Review*.

Peter Shack was young and ambitious and had returned from Elliott to Peacock via a flirtation with himself as a leadership candidate, an experience he found to be solitary. One of the foundation drys, Shack had always seen Peacock as a better election winner than Howard and a better colleague. But Howard had promoted Shack in the late 1988 reshuffle and Shack had become convinced that the Peacock challenge would never materialise, so he had tried to boost Howard, pledging his personal support and preparing strategy papers.[2] Shack was a bitter critic of Howard, dismissing his claims to policy substance but playing both sides of the street until he saw some iron in Peacock's intent.

Wilson Tuckey was a wild man, detested by Labor, weak on self-control, jointly a horse owner with Peacock—and testimony to Howard's misjudgement. Howard had promoted and defended Tuckey, without grasping that

Tuckey saw him as a loser and was strictly a Peacock man. In late 1988 Tuckey lobbied Fred Chaney for a switch from Howard to Peacock. Chaney rejected the offer and reported back the exchange to Howard.

Senator Chris Puplick was a long-time factional opponent of Howard in NSW and in Canberra, a wet who had always backed Peacock and seen Howard as a weak leader and a narrow man. Puplick's judgement of Howard hardened when Howard failed to support Puplick as a frontbencher against Brownyn Bishop when she marshalled party support in NSW, Howard's power base, to demote Puplick on the Senate ticket. This move led to Puplick's departure from politics after the 1990 poll. The final figure in the group, David Jull, a big, burly Queenslander, was another long-standing Peacock backer who felt that Howard had never recognised his talents. Jull, an under-rated politician, was the only member of the gang to survive and prosper in the 1990s.

One reason for the deadline for a leadership coup before the winter recess was the group's fear that Hawke might catch Howard with a winter election. But the truth is that while Howard was a weak leader, Peacock was also a weak challenger.

As 1989 unfolded Howard was undermined by a documented failure to turn a strong anti-Labor swing into primary votes for the coalition. The monthly evidence revealed that Labor's budget strategy was failing and that the economy was growing at unsustainable levels which were forcing higher and higher interest rates. A decisive change of public opinion was underway, but Howard was unable to establish a firm opinion poll lead. His position was similar to that of Bill Hayden in 1982 when the ALP was never convinced that his lead over Malcolm Fraser was enough to ensure a victory.

Howard's problem was revealed in the February 1989 reelection of the Western Australian ALP government of Peter Dowding which occurred despite the burden of WA Inc. It was an election that Labor deserved to lose; its record was inexcusable, a judgement conceded even by senior Hawke ministers. There was a strong anti-Labor swing of 10.4 per cent on the primary vote, easily enough to defeat Labor, but less than 2 per cent of these first preferences went to the Liberals—an extraordinary failure. The bulk went to minor parties, independents or informal votes, and then returned to Labor through preferences.

The campaign was fought exclusively on state, not federal issues, but the media and the Liberals unfairly turned the result back on Howard. Labor won the election on the leadership appeal of premier Dowding and by exploiting the Opposition's weakness, the strategy which Hawke would run. The lesson was that a failed government with attractive leadership did not necessarily lose office. The voters had to be persuaded by a credible alternative to reject Labor. It was once again the message of 1980s politics writ large. Central to Dowding's win had been the superiority of Labor's campaign and the superiority of its leader—Dowding against the inept WA

470

Liberal leader, Barry Mackinnon. Hawke promptly predicted his government would win the next federal poll.[3]

In early March, Greiner's team, Ian Kortlang and Gary Sturgess, lunched in Brisbane with John Moore. Kortlang sensed that a move was afoot. Later he rang Moore: 'If something's happening then I want to be part of it,' he said. 'I want to stop Howard from becoming Prime Minister.' Moore rang back ten minutes later: 'Feathers and I will be in Sydney on Sunday. Perhaps we can talk.' Kortlang arranged a room at the Airport Hilton.

At the Hilton Kortlang told Peacock: 'I don't think Howard should be Prime Minister. I'll level with you and say I was involved last year in the Elliott push which didn't come off. If you're going to stage a challenge then a lot of planning and organisation is required and I can help there.' Peacock was non-committal. The next day Moore rang Kortlang: 'Peacock loved it; he likes the idea of planning. We should meet Drysdale soon.'

A week later Drysdale hosted a lunch for Kortlang and Moore at his Mosman home. This was the origin of Kortlang's role as coup planner and note keeper. Kortlang would keep the lists; he would prepare plans covering the takeover, before and after. He tried to apply some management consultancy to a political bloodbath.

The Kingston group met on 7 March and had a long discussion about the numbers. One of them made a diary note—they were optimistically predicting a 44–28 vote for Peacock. This was almost exactly the final result, proof of their early confidence. At its 4 April dinner meeting, the group reaffirmed the plan for a strike on 9 May. Peacock reported on further talks with Elliott—in particular, Elliott wanted senior positions in the new regime for Carlton, Bishop and Alston.

By this time Moore and Drysdale had sent Kortlang a draft planning document for the coup. It dealt with the critical three days, D minus 1, D-day, and D plus 1 (D-day being the day of the coup). Although rudimentary, it provided for Eggleton to move into Peacock's office to manage the transition, the immediate announcement on D day of the shadow Cabinet, a statement by Peacock returning to bipartisanship on immigration, and a list of the key businessmen to be contacted immediately—Dean Wills, Arvi Parbo, Will Bailey, Hugh Morgan, Ken Cowley, Kerry Packer, Christopher Skase, Frank Lowy and Warren Jones.

Kortlang and his assistant Sue Cato then went to work drafting a tally sheet of Liberals under three headings—the Good, the Bad, the Waverers. It was this list which Peacock had with him at the challenge. Kortlang would feed this material to Moore who would distribute the plans at the Tuesday meetings with Peacock and the cardinals in Moore's flat.

When Moore and Shack told Peacock in April he had 35 or 36 certain votes, Peacock had one comment: 'I want more than forty.' The organisers were divided over whether this would be possible. As the challenge loomed

Peacock grew cautious; he wanted the leadership but he wanted to avoid a repeat of the 1985 fiasco when he had misread the party's mood disastrously.

The irony for Howard is that while his enemies plotted he began to win some victories. Howard, in fact, had moved into a 'crash through or crash' mode. The autumn 1989 session saw him achieve two far-reaching results. First, he forced through the shadow Cabinet, against National Party resistance, an endorsement of Labor's domestic deregulation of the wheat market. Second, with Michael Kroger's assistance, he won a joint Liberal–National Senate ticket in Victoria. Both decisions illustrated the precise brand of political reform which was necessary for non-Labor politics. They were classic 'new politics' versus 'old politics' issues.

The coalition had no right to claim a micro-economic reform superiority over Labor unless it was prepared to tackle the inefficiencies within rural markets which the Nationals had protected for decades. In addition, the coalition would stay susceptible to Labor's campaign professionalism unless it achieved a far tighter Liberal–National alliance at state level. Howard delivered on both counts—but got curt media recognition and little credit from his party. It was symptomatic of a party that had lost patience with its leader.[4]

In April a political tornado erupted from nowhere to strip Howard's defences. It was a crazy, irrational firestorm beyond the domain of any individual, centred upon Ian Macphee who, in his exile from politics, must ponder that in his last performance he played Howard's nemesis.

In April 1989 Macphee fell victim to the aggressive attitude towards preselection which Kroger had been injecting into the Victorian branches. After his 1987 sacking from the shadow ministry Macphee had pursued his own agenda and his profile had grown as an internal party critic, always a dangerous position. The man who creates trouble over the running of the household may find himself evicted. In the process Macphee grew distant from his own branches, and lost some of them when the boundaries of his Goldstein seat were altered in the redistribution. The net result was that at the time of Liberal preselection Macphee was extremely vulnerable.

Kroger had three Liberal incumbents slated for execution—Shipton in Higgins, Ken Aldred in Bruce, and David Hamer in the Senate—and he expected they would be peaceful executions. He never conceived of any central office plan to finish Macphee. But when the climate of the party opinion which Kroger had fostered led to his friend David Kemp challenging Macphee, then Kroger could only back Kemp.

On 11 March a delegation from Goldstein visited Kroger to tell him they wanted to depose Macphee. They were sick of him, claiming that he was disloyal to the party and to Howard whom they strongly supported. Kroger refused to help, but the delegation told him that if he couldn't find a new candidate then they would recruit one.

The Goldstein grassroots revolt soon found a likely candidate, Professor

The Peacock coup

David Kemp, academic, former Victorian director, Fraser's chief of staff, Liberal theoretician and son of C.D. Kemp, whose pioneering work in the 1940s gave Menzies the intellectual framework for his new Liberal Party. Kemp was just turning his mind to a political career and had been thinking about Bruce. But the Goldstein people invited Kemp to run, and said that he would defeat Macphee. Their concerns were primarily about Macphee's conduct and only secondly about his ideology. Kemp, a cautious man, made his own inquiries, discovered that Macphee was sinking and decided to nominate.

When Eggleton found out he was alarmed and incredulous. He told Kroger that the political storm would be tremendous, that Macphee would give the challenge national prominence and that the media would provide vast coverage. Eggleton said it would cause a lot of electoral damage at the soft end of the Liberal Party and its voting support where Macphee was a popular symbol. He warned from the start that 'it could also do immense damage to the leader'.

Kemp, a Howard supporter, rang to get Eggleton's assessment first hand. 'Is this really going to be a big story, Tony?' he queried. Eggleton told Kemp that it would. Eggleton's advice to Howard was to keep Macphee intact and try to shift Kemp into another seat, sound but belated advice. Eggleton felt that Howard was too slow to move, probably because he liked the idea of Macphee's demise. But Macphee was not an easy man to help. On 7 April Howard raised with Macphee the prospect that Kemp might run against him, but Macphee dismissed it—'Kemp wouldn't be silly enough,' Maphee said. A fortnight later he was demanding that Howard save him.

Kemp was a man of determination whose experience of political leaders meant that he was resistant to their intimidation. Having given a commitment to his backers in Goldstein, Kemp would not withdraw. He was merely exercising his right under the party's constitution. Kemp believed Macphee had been disloyal to the party. The time for compromise had been lost before the need for compromise was ever recognised. The irony is that Howard and Macphee, political enemies for so long, would become the joint victims of the battle for Goldstein.

From the start Macphee chose to wage a public fight, a decision which inflamed the party and damaged his cause. He launched a torrent of denunciation against Kroger, and the young Victorian president hit back. The media fell upon the Macphee story like starved lions on a carcass. Within one weekend the Victorian Liberal Party was plunged into a spectacular orgy of recrimination which held the national stage and left non-Victorian Liberals stunned at its venom. Howard, the leader who preached that 'disunity is death', saw his party burning fiercely for weeks.

Macphee accused his opponents within Goldstein of being inspired by hostility to his stand on immigration and of being supporters of Bruce Ruxton, a claim which was untrue in relation to Kemp. He accused Kroger of plotting to destroy him and of abusing his post as state president. Finally, Macphee said that Howard should act as Fraser or Menzies would in this position and use his leadership to intervene to save Macphee. Maphee put these propositions with a notable lack of restraint. On 17 April he declared: 'The legacy of the Kroger years will be chaos and self-destruction and a defeat for what was a once great party.' Elevating the stakes, he declared: 'I win the swinging voters the party needs to win government. If I were removed the party would lose voters in other marginal seats and not win government.'

Central to this crisis was the media's uncritical acceptance of Macphee's position. This was most notable in the ABC and *The Age*, two institutions Macphee had prominently supported over recent years, particularly when *The Age* was threatened with a takeover by Robert Maxwell. The Canberra Press Gallery, where Macphee had many friends, was heavily disposed to accept his claims. The media, in summary, tended to agree that Howard should intervene to protect him. Such perceptions missed the trigger for the crisis—Macphee's loss of support in his own seat. Macphee was victim not of a plot hatched by the hierarchy but of the hostility he had generated in his branches.

But Howard was caught in a deadly trap. He was being called upon by Macphee and the editorialists to solve a problem which had no solution. Contrary to the trumpeted claims, Menzies and Fraser had been extremely cautious in intervening in preselections; evidence for such intervention is virtually non-existent. Howard came from NSW where challenges to long-serving members were commonplace; it was this practice which Kroger wanted to establish in Victoria. Macphee was not the only Victorian member under challenge.

The only basis on which Howard could intervene would be to persuade Kemp to run in another seat, a course Eggleton urged. Eggleton's view that Howard moved too slowly is probably correct but Howard's position is understandable: Howard was being asked to intervene in a highly risky fashion to save a man whose problems were self-generated and who had been Howard's most bitter internal party critic for years. But the real catch was that Kemp would not concede.

When Malcolm Fraser rang Kemp and asked him to withdraw in the party's interest, Kemp refused. Kemp, in fact, had already decided that even if Howard did approach him and request that he stand aside he would refuse. It is Kemp who was responsible for the political consequences of the challenge. If, as former senior party figure Dame Beryl Beaurepaire asserted, the loss of Macphee would cost the Liberals 2 to 3 per cent across metropolitan Melbourne, then Kemp had to carry that responsibility. Kemp rejected such claims, although it was inconceivable that Macphee's defeat would not hurt the Liberals. If the sole criterion for action were the maximisation of the Liberal vote then the challenge to Macphee was a negative. But Eggleton realised in his talks with Kroger and Kemp that the new Victorian hierarchy had other priorities. It was obsessed about rebuilding the party in the medium term, not necessarily winning the next federal election.

The Macphee issue soon settled into a leadership question. Alan Ramsey from the *Sydney Morning Herald* attacked Howard for being weak and inept and said the issue was now 'Howard's paralysis of leadership'. A desperate Roger Shipton, for whom the reality of defeat had only just dawned, lashed Howard for allowing Victoria to fall into 'shambles and crisis'. A trio of old politicians came out of retirement to back Macphee—John Gorton, Peter Nixon and Jim Killen. In NSW Macphee's friend Peter Baume predicted that if Macphee lost preselection the Liberals were doomed at the election. By late April the Liberal Party was a public shambles.

The great beneficiary would be Andrew Peacock, for whom the timing was exquisite given the 9 May coup deadline. Peacock got the tone just right; he said the entire Maphee incident should never have occurred, in an indirect slap at Howard; but he angrily denied he would exploit it to stage a leadership coup—the guise of reassurance. Asked about a coup, Peacock said, 'It is unfounded, there is no truth in it.'

But Peacock was briefing the media, selling the message of Howard's failure—a claim which overlooked the fact that as deputy and the senior Victorian it should have been impossible for Peacock to blame Howard without also blaming himself. Such logic had no place in the party's mood in late April, nor in the media's analysis, with most of the media adopting an anti-Howard mindset driven to a large extent by bloodlust.

On 23 April Macphee played his big card—the Fraser declaration. In a television interview recorded in Washington, Fraser said: 'If Ian Macphee does not have pre-selection as a Liberal for the election, there will inevitably be a perception that the Liberal Party as a party has rejected the kind of image that he represents. That in my view would be very damaging in electoral terms.' Fraser enraged Howard by saying there was a 'perception' arising from the contest that the party had 'narrowed its approach' and was too far to the right. Fraser was reflecting adversely on Howard's leadership; it gave a challenge further legitimacy.

Howard branded as 'pure drivel' Fraser's claim that the party was seen as too right-wing. He attacked Fraser, saying there was ample room within the party for people holding Macphee's views, that some such members in NSW had won preselection ballots, that his shadow ministry contained people of progressive views such as Fred Chaney, Chris Puplick and Robert Hill. Howard said the Liberal Party was proud of its diversity which he was determined to uphold. But the perception was that of a leader under siege. The irony is that the Liberal rank and file was behind Howard and neither Fraser nor Macphee cut any ice with the branches.

In his wild attacks Macphee failed to substantiate properly his claim of branch stacking and in his political death throes failed to do justice to his fine years of service to the Liberals. He had three options if defeated in the preselection—retire from politics; resign from the party and contest Goldstein as an independent; or seek preselection in another seat or on the Senate ticket. In the week before the Goldstein contest on 6 May, moves were afoot to find an alternative for Macphee and to keep him in the party after Kemp's expected victory.

Meanwhile on Anzac Day, at the height of the Macphee crisis, Elliott convened a fascinating meeting in Melbourne. It was attended by Elliott, Peacock, Hugh Morgan, businessman and party treasurer Ron Walker, John Moore and Drysdale, and was designed to clarify the terms on which Peacock would become leader and prime minister. Elliott wanted to ensure that Peacock gave guarantees on policy and personnel before he became leader. It was the first and only meeting between the old Elliott push and the new Peacock push. It was to clarify Peacock's *quid pro quo* in return for the influence commanded by Elliott and the business backers.

Elliott gave Peacock two messages—his leadership bid must rely upon supporters from both the dry and the wet sides of the party; secondly, he must give policy guarantees for a tough minded dry agenda. Elliott called it later a 'let's hear it from Andrew meeting', although Elliott had plenty to say. It was assumed that Hewson would get treasury; Elliott said Carlton's management skills made him a natural for defence; Elliott wanted both Alston and Bishop on the front bench. But Elliott told Peacock that he had to govern the party on a broad base and give senior positions to Howard people as well as to his own supporters. Elliott told Peacock bluntly, 'You have to bridge the gap', meaning bring both sides of the party together. Peacock gave specific policy assurances—no capital gains tax, labour market deregulation and heavy spending cuts.

The two businessmen Elliott saw as very important were Morgan, given his role in non-Labor politics, and Rupert Murdoch, given his newspaper assets. Elliott had spoken to Murdoch earlier, and had informed him about the Peacock push. Elliott's argument was that the Liberals had to change leaders to win the election. But Elliott knew that Murdoch was more interested in economic results than personalities. In the interim there was no change of attitude within News Limited's publications. Elliott, in fact, was in the process of convincing himself that Peacock would make a competent prime minister. He told Peacock later: 'Andrew, if you win this election I think you'll become one of our great Prime Ministers.'

The Peacock numbers men believed that for some months Peacock had been sitting on a majority of 37 in the 72-strong party room. But in the first week of May the tension began to show. Peacock told the group at its 2 May meeting that he wanted the timetable put on hold and the operation suspended. He was worried about slippage of support and 'overkill' from the Macphee issue. It was another sign of Peacock's reluctance as the moment of decision arrived. But the 'gang of five' felt the situation was ripe. They said, correctly, that the Macphee affair only facilitated Howard's demise. They sought to 'steamroll' Peacock's doubts.

By mid-week Moore told Peacock they had at least 37 or 38 votes but Peacock was still not satisfied. He told Moore, Shack and then Drysdale: 'Forty is not enough. I want 41.' Peacock was making his organisers work to the limit. He wanted the biggest possible winning margin. But the 'cardinals group' knew that there was a deeper problem: did Peacock have the nerve? Did Peacock have the will to power required for leadership? Peacock knew from his track record—a failed strike against Fraser in 1982, discarding the leadership in 1985, forcing Howard to sack him in 1987—that a failed putsch now would be a catastrophic curtain to his career.

Drysdale spoke to Peacock on the Wednesday: 'We've got to do it next week.' He said it would be fatal to let the parliament adjourn without exploiting the party's mood. The chance might never come again.

On Thursday 4 May, Shack and Moore felt they had a firm forty, with good prospects of winning more. Moore said it was 40 'rolled gold'. Some Howard defectors told Shack, 'Do it, just do it.' The group met on 4 May without Peacock who was absent in Melbourne and they put the coup back on the agenda. They confirmed the strike for the next Tuesday, 9 May. The group was forcing a reluctant Peacock to the coup.

Shack prepared a draft letter for the party meeting to enable him to get the required signatures to thwart any bid by the Howard camp to postpone the meeting. Then Shack took a fateful decision. He informed his Canberra house companion and best friend in politics, the National Party's Charles Blunt, about the coup. Blunt had told Shack several weeks before that he had the numbers to depose Ian Sinclair as National Party leader. He was waiting for a hook on which to hang his challenge. Shack now gave Blunt the hook.

But Peacock was still reluctant and unsure of himself. Shack knew he needed a final push and its source was obvious—the deputy leadership. Peacock was now deputy so his ascension to the leadership necessitated a new deputy. Moore, Shack and Tuckey all coveted this position. They were about to remake the Liberal Party and personal ambition was not absent from their deliberations. Yet it was obvious that Peacock's best deputy was Senate leader Fred Chaney.

By every measure Chaney was the number three Liberal after Howard and Peacock. In terms of national recognition, personal appeal and ministerial experience, Chaney easily outranked any other Liberal. The aim of Moore and Shack was to secure a successful Peacock coup and this led them to accept a Peacock–Chaney ticket. Shack pushed the idea, Moore was extremely reluctant and Tuckey wanted to run himself.

Peacock said later he never needed Chaney; that he only approached Chaney after the challenge was launched. This is true yet it is also true that the group and Peacock wanted Chaney to seal the challenge and a successful transition. If Chaney was left hanging there was always a risk that in the final hours before the ballot Howard might stitch together a Howard–Chaney ticket to beat Peacock. The truth is that Peacock needed Chaney to give him confidence. Once Peacock got Chaney then Howard was finished. Chaney also delivered a certain vote—his deputy Austin Lewis. But Chaney had another importance. By winning Chaney, Peacock transformed the nature of the challenge; it became the other three leaders against Howard, not Howard uniting the other leaders against Peacock.

Chaney was disillusioned with Howard and had considered both Elliott and himself as alternatives. He was inclined to believe that Howard would survive by default. Chaney felt that television was Howard's destroyer. With confidants in his office Chaney would point to the box and declare that it was crucifying Howard. This point was understood by Howard himself. He had met too many people who expressed surprise at the firmness and sincerity he displayed in person; surprise because that impression of Howard was so different from the drone who nightly invaded the living room. This image was a perpetual frustration to Howard.

In early May Chaney had a conversation with his Western Australian friend and Senate colleague, Peter Durack, about the party's prospects. Durack, a dedicated Howard man who would never shift, was pessimistic. 'I think we'll lose this election,' he said. Durack said that post-election Chaney would become Liberal leader, a sound basis on which to rebuild. This exchange left its imprint on Chaney for he realised that defeatism had infiltrated the core Howard backers. Chaney may have been flattered by Durack's remarks but he rejected their logic. He wanted to become a senior minister in a coalition government at the next election, not Opposition leader.

Chaney spoke to Eggleton about his worries, in particular asking Eggleton about the recent party research. Eggleton was appropriately frank with the Senate leader: 'Fred, the research bears out what you say. It's now moved from a position of leadership unpopularity to active dislike.' Chaney mused, 'John's hardly the sort of bloke you can ask to stand down in the party's best interests.'

The Liberal Secretariat had qualitative research from its commissioned company, Brian Sweeney and Associates, showing that Howard wasn't rating as a leader and that *Future Directions* had made little difference. Ron Klein who handled the Liberal research for Sweeney's started another round of research from 24 April. This time his conclusion after group interviews was worse than before—the Liberals were unlikely to win with Howard; the anti-Howard trend was deepening and the view was that 'Howard was terminal'.

This is puzzling because Howard was performing better than before and Labor's polling agency, ANOP, had a more subtle assessment. ANOP found that Howard remained a weak leader but that a redeeming quality was emerging—he was seen as standing for something—the values of *Future Directions*. Meanwhile Klein gave Eggleton a verbal report on his research in early May, the prelude to a major briefing that was never needed.

On 4 May Moore told Kortlang that Peacock was going soft and Kortlang volunteered to see Peacock on Saturday to settle him. Moore made the arrangements. Meanwhile the Peacock camp agreed that Shack should approach Chaney en route back to Perth on the Friday. Yet Shack would take no risks with Chaney. He spoke to Drysdale to find out where Elliott was in the south of France; 'Fred's been in bed with Elliott for months,' a Peacock man declared. Shack wanted Elliott to lock-in Chaney. At Perth airport Shack and Chaney agreed to talk the next day.

On Saturday morning Chaney was stunned when Shack told him that Peacock would challenge Howard for the leadership on Tuesday, that he would win and that the numbers were certain. Shack told Chaney the test was to make the leadership change as successful as possible. He asked Chaney to support Peacock in the interests of the party. He told Chaney that both Peacock and Elliott would be talking to him. He asked Chaney to maintain the secrecy of this information.

Chaney's surprise quickly turned to agony at the terrible dilemma which he now faced. Shack and Chaney agreed to have breakfast on Sunday. Meanwhile, the night before in Melbourne, Roger Shipton, the man who stopped Elliott's run just six months earlier, was defeated by Peter Costello in the Higgins preselection.

This was a bad omen for Macphee whose own ballot was on Saturday 6 May, the morning Kortlang flew into town and went to Peacock's East Melbourne terrace. Peacock, a model bachelor, was doing his laundry when Kortlang arrived. They yarned for a few hours and Kortlang got Peacock talking about the future; got his mind into the leadership groove. Peacock wanted Chaney as deputy and Macphee as foreign minister, so Macphee had to be saved. Shack rang to report on his initial talk with Chaney. Peacock and Shack agreed that Elliott must talk to Chaney. Peacock rang Drysdale to confirm this; yes, Elliott would make the call. Peacock knew that Elliott would deliver Chaney. When Kortlang and Peacock left the house to walk across the park for lunch Peacock knew he was the emperor elect. The fix was set. Andrew was on the verge of his greatest triumph in politics.

After their pasta lunch Peacock went to the football and Kortlang flew back to Sydney. Late in the afternoon Peacock rang Chaney to tell him that the party's mood was against Howard. Peacock said a number of people had approached him and that the feeling was widespread. He explained that Elliott was supporting him. He pointed out that the deputy's job would fall vacant. Chaney was left with two decisions to make. The first was whether to support Peacock against Howard. The second was whether to run for deputy, which would mean a Peacock–Chaney ticket. Being a Senator was no problem since Chaney had already secured preselection to run for a lower house seat at the next poll.

When Elliott rang he had the impression that Chaney was still in a state of shock. It was not easy for him to change political gears and support Peacock, to whom Chaney had been saying for years the party could never return. In the Peacock coup Elliott lobbied just one politician—Chaney. Elliott, talking from the Riviera, informed Chaney there was strong business backing for the move. In a script that could have come from the satirist Max Gillies, he assured Chaney 'my view is that there's a place for you in the new shop'. Elliott explained to Chaney it had been a deliberate policy to keep the move secret from him. He finished up, 'You'd better talk to your friends but ring me back when you've decided.' Elliott was taking no chances.

The only people in whom Chaney confided were his wife Angela, his parents, and his top aide Keith Kessell. On Saturday evening Kessell and Chaney talked the issue through. Chaney said that he had always supported the leader—Snedden against Fraser, Peacock in 1985 against Howard, and Howard ever since. He had rejected leadership approaches to him; he had asked John and Janette Howard to trust him. But the Liberal Party imperative was to win the election and Howard was not working. Chaney had an obligation to be loyal but he also had an obligation to act in the party's interest. Kessell gave firm advice—Chaney had no real option; it was time for the tough decision; Peacock would win; it made sense for Chaney to make that victory as complete as possible. A Peacock–Moore combination was untenable. But Chaney was worried about how his action would be perceived.

Although Chaney was sceptical about Peacock he realised that Howard's weakness had led to Peacock's rehabilitation. Chaney favoured the Peacock option, but that meant he had to betray Howard.

While Chaney fought with the issues of loyalty and power, 3000 kilometres away Macphee was broken in Goldstein, ditched after 16 years in parliament. Macphee saw defeat as a commentary on the reaction and racism of party branches rather than on his own indulgence. 'Politics is a tough game and even Neutral Bay boys don't cry,' he said while pledging to keep fighting 'to make this country a more liberal one'. Then Macphee and his wife put an answering machine on their phone and headed for the hills. Before he left Macphee told a friendly journalist, Peter Bowers from the *Sydney Morning Herald*, that he would fight Goldstein as an independent, a horror scenario for the Liberals. Bowers began his page one article the next day saying that Macphee 'is determined to quit the Liberal Party and strike out as an independent'.[5] Meanwhile Howard decided to call a press conference for Sunday to combat the Macphee issue head-on.

Pauline and Peter Shack came to Chaney's home for breakfast on Sunday. Over fruit, muffins and croissants, Chaney kept agonising, the

Catholic conscience under torture; Chaney was coming but he wanted the move sanctified. Shack's approach was psychologically sound: 'We don't need your vote. We're going to do this whether you come or not. We've got the numbers.' Shack encouraged Chaney to run for deputy, saying Chaney was the best candidate. He made it easier for Chaney's conscience by saying his vote was not essential and he made it harder for Chaney to say no by depicting Peacock as a certain winner.

After breakfast Fred and Angela went for a walk together to settle the decision. They also spoke to Fred's parents who lived next door. The Shacks waited at Chaney's home. Fred returned, ready to rationalise his betrayal of Howard. Then he rang Peacock.

Chaney told Peacock that he would support him against Howard in the party's interest. This decision was unconditional; it stood on its merits. He wanted no deal on any job. Chaney's fear was manifest; he wanted to avoid the accusation that he backed Peacock and betrayed Howard as part of a deal to become deputy. Chaney wanted to convince himself and others that he was not trading Howard's blood for his own gain.

Chaney then said he was interested in running for deputy but this decision rested with Peacock. He told Peacock there were other individuals with whom he would be more comfortable. He said Peacock would be happier with somebody like Shack with whom he had been closely associated. Chaney ensured the onus was totally with Peacock on the question of the deputy leadership. Peacock had to decide whether he wanted Chaney and could work with him and Chaney would only run on this basis. That is, Chaney wanted Peacock to invite him to become deputy.

Peacock obliged. He was happy to have Chaney; Peacock was inviting Chaney. But Chaney left the offer on the table. He did not accept until that evening in Canberra. But from this point his acceptance was almost inevitable.

The circle of mutual self-interest was closed. Chaney could accept with an easier conscience. Peacock had what he wanted—a Peacock–Chaney team against Howard. Peacock started his challenge by winning Elliott and finished it by winning Chaney. Elliott, who had launched Peacock on the challenge, now put Chaney on board. Chaney had both Peacock and Elliott legitimising his betrayal of Howard in the party's name.

This was a Peacock–Chaney deal despite any denials. Chaney kept the challenge secret from Howard. He became the last and most significant addition to the Peacock conspirators. The upshot was that Peacock and Chaney were running on a ticket against Howard. It was the most formidable team and Howard was finished. Chaney was aware that from the time he committed to Peacock and kept the challenge a secret from Howard then the charge of disloyalty could be laid against him.

Chaney knew that in his personal relationship with Howard he had gone far beyond the formality of his obligations as a fellow leader. He had assured

John and Janette Howard that he was a friend, that he could be trusted, that he wanted to help Howard. Chaney had offered personal assurances to Howard which Peacock had never pretended and which Howard would never have expected from Peacock. Chaney, unlike Peacock, presented himself as a trusted friend to Howard and to his wife. Now he was breaking the trust.

Chaney's justification was party interest—he had an obligation to ensure the leadership transition was effective, fast and as clean as possible. Chaney remembered that Howard had always said, 'I'll have to be blasted out of this job.' Chaney knew that an efficient transition meant secrecy—this was a political reality, an inescapable part of Chaney's decision. It was his toughest decision in politics.

However, it was a decision which was to virtually terminate Chaney's career because he was seen by most of the party—Howard and Peacock backers alike—as untrustworthy. It was especially damaging as Chaney had always presented himself as a politician for whom morality was important. Politicians respect an opponent who can confront them face to face. Chaney was inviting a severe judgement upon himself by not informing Howard that he had withdrawn his support for his leadership. When Peacock lost the 1990 federal election it guaranteed the death of Chaney's own leadership aspirations, his loss of the deputy leadership, his political decline and finally, his resignation from politics.

Howard said later that at the very least Chaney should have called him and said: 'John, you've got a big problem. There's a move against you and I can't help.'

On the Sunday Howard, unaware of any challenge, held a media conference to deny the received orthodoxy that Macphee's defeat was the work of the New Right. He declared: 'I reject that in some way the Liberal Party has become a "New Right" Party or has moved too far to the right in the political spectrum. The term "New Right" is a political smear invented by the Labor Party.'

Howard said he wanted Macphee to stay within the Liberal fold. Howard spoke to Peacock twice on Sunday about how to keep Macphee within the party; he rang Puplick, who confirmed that he had spoken to Macphee on Saturday and Macphee had said he would make no rash statements about his future. They pretended to help while plotting Howard's execution. On Sunday afternoon Moore, Drysdale, Kortlang and Greg Daniel met in Sydney to review the numbers and the planning documents.

On Sunday evening Howard, Peacock and Chaney met in Howard's Parliament House office to discuss how best to contain the Macphee issue. It was a bizarre gathering, the leader and his two senior deputies who had entered a secret pact as his executioners. They talked at great length and Howard detected no sense of unease in Peacock or Chaney. The secrecy of the coup was profoundly embarrassing in its efficiency. Peacock wanted to persuade Macphee to run for Deakin where the preselection ballot was still a month away; it was agreed that Peacock should speak to Macphee. Howard arrived at his Canberra flat about 10.40 pm; Chris Puplick called to review further the Macphee situation. The Peacock gang had made their deception into an art form. Howard went to bed for his last night's sleep as a safe Liberal leader. His innocence was testimony to his personal failure with his colleagues and his insensitivity as a politician. The dream of Howard's life was about to be detonated.

As Howard slept Peacock, Moore, Shack and Chaney met in Moore's Canberra apartment. It was at this meeting that the deal for Chaney to become the deputy was finalised. For the first time Chaney entered the plotters' den—and at this point the curious nature of the Peacock forces became obvious. Moore now denounced Chaney bitterly, saying he distrusted Chaney and that this view was widely held. Chaney was being pushed as deputy, the job Moore had wanted, out of sheer pragmatism, not affection. Moore resented Chaney's elevation from the coup which the 'gang of five' had organised.

Howard rose early to appear on morning television, but down the corridor in Moore's office, a room Howard had never visited, an extraordinary 7 am meeting took place. For the first time all the main Peacock backers met—Moore, Shack, Tuckey, Jull, Puplick, Carlton, Bishop and Alston. It was a strange group, drys and wets meeting to bury Howard and elevate Peacock. They appointed booth captains on the basis of personal and state affiliation: Bishop, Shack, Alston, Carlton, Jull, David Hawker and Puplick. Peacock had four people to canvass—Hewson, Fife, Lewis and David Hamer.

A few hours later there was the normal leaders' meeting before the shadow Cabinet. As it broke, Senate deputy Austin Lewis, ignorant of the moves, but impressed by Howard's firmness over Macphee, told Howard, 'John, I want you to know that so many more people think you are acting and sounding like a Prime Minister. You're above the ruck. You've turned the corner.' Chaney and Peacock cringed. When shadow Cabinet finished Peacock went to give a stunned Lewis the news of the challenge.

During the day the booth captains did their work. Peacock spoke personally to several MPs. Peacock saw Macphee after Question Time and told him of the challenge and of his plans for Macphee to become shadow foreign minister. Macphee was elated, but anxious: he wanted a better seat than Deakin.

The first Monday of each session, Howard hosted a leader's dinner attended by the four Liberal leaders, the National Party's two leaders and the two party secretaries. But this dinner was a feast before execution. The conspirators had the decency to stay away. Lewis told Chaney he couldn't sit at Howard's table and dine with the leader he was betraying. Peacock had rung Howard in the afternoon to say he would be dining with Macphee to discuss the Deakin option. Later Howard's personal secretary took a call from Chaney's office. The message was that 'something has just cropped up and neither Chaney nor Lewis can make dinner tonight'. Chaney was taking Lewis outside the building to convince his distraught deputy.

Howard now grew a little edgy. He had just read the transcript of an unusual interview Peacock had given on Melbourne radio that morning. Laurie Oakes had reported on the 6 pm Channel Nine news that there was leadership trouble afoot. Channel Nine's Peter Harvey told Howard's PR, John Wells, that two Peacock backers had broken a tennis appointment for an urgent meeting. So it was dinner for five, not eight—Howard, Sinclair, Lloyd, Eggleton and Paul Davy. They even joked about 'absent friends'.

Peacock did not have dinner with Macphee; he had more pressing business. Peacock, Moore, Drysdale and Kortlang met at Moore's flat during the dinner break to rehearse the post-coup agenda. This involved the media conference where Peacock would need to explain and justify the coup and take questions from a potentially hostile Press Gallery. Drysdale and Kortlang put Peacock through a mock media conference, firing questions at him. They hammered out the words, themes and lines Peacock would use. Peacock would open his press conference accepting his responsibility to the party and nation and reaffirming the spirit of liberalism for every family and every battler. He would announce a return to bipartisanship on immigration. Kortlang had formula answers drafted for the trick questions—a response to Keating's line that 'soufflés don't rise twice', and Peacock's 1985 remark about never wanting to be prime minister. After dinner Kortlang and Drysdale finalised the D-day document and Moore collected it from the Hyatt Hotel.

At 8.28 pm Howard was told that Chaney and Lewis had sought an appointment in a couple of minutes. He smelled trouble now; it was too formal an approach, too unusual, after missing the dinner. Howard knew when Peacock arrived with them. Peacock said to Howard: 'This is very difficult. But an overwhelming number, more than forty, want the leadership raised tomorrow. There will be a spill motion.' Howard shot back: 'Who wants it? Give me examples, names.' Howard knew that Peacock had a core vote of thirty. He was shocked at a claim of more than forty. He turned to Chaney: 'Do you agree?' Chaney said: 'Yes, we agree and we are joining the movement.' This is where Howard was rocked; the political dagger through the heart. Howard's only instinct was to dismiss them. But they almost lingered, as if hoping Howard would relent. As they left Howard irresistibly asked Lewis to stay. He reminded Lewis of the comment he had made that morning in praise of Howard. 'What has changed since this morning, Austin?' he asked. Lewis confessed: 'They've convinced me. They've shown me a list.' Lewis was squirming, a man caught by his victim in betrayal, captured in the execution of a leader he had praised.

Howard now acted in a mixture of desperation and shock. But it was too late; he was calling upon his friends and supporters, people he had not seen sufficiently over the past year. They gathered in the bunker which Howard's office had become and the news of the terrible defections became clear. Around him Howard had Messner, Reith, Fife, Hewson, Michael Baume, Durack, Margaret Reid, Ewen Cameron, Neil Andrew, Warwick Parer, Alexander Downer, Shirley Walters. But they were staring at defeat. Howard rang Carlton. 'You know that Peacock will be an economic disaster,' he began. 'John, it's just too late,' Carlton told Howard. Then Howard called Lewis again and asked: 'Austin, are you really sure you want to do this?' Lewis replied: 'John, it's tearing me apart. But the die is cast.' Howard rang Chaney and asked if he was running for deputy. 'Yes,' Chaney replied. 'That's all I need to know,' said Howard.

The Peacock camp was very thorough and accurate in its reading of individuals in the party. They had a number of defections which Howard had assumed to be his votes—Bishop, Carlton, Connolly, Hawker, Lewis, Alston, Vanstone, Porter, Pratt, Chaney, Prosser, Panizza, Knowles and Crichton-Browne. Facing defeat, it was appropriate that Howard should call a midnight press conference. He would revisit his 1985 tactic; but it was too late. The Gallery was full, since the story had broken after the Peacock delegation visited Howard at 8.30 pm. Howard performed admirably but it made no difference. His last call that night was to Janette, telling her he was beaten.

In the morning Howard rang Greiner to report that he had heard a rumour that the state leaders were backing Peacock. Greiner denied it. At 8 am a furious Greiner assembled his staff: 'If any of you are involved in this I want to know now. If you are then you are sacked.' Greiner's staff were innocent; Kortlang was a NSW departmental head.

In the party room the preliminaries were kept tight and the Peacock–Chaney ticket held firm. Peacock beat Howard by the convincing margin of 44 to 27 and Chaney defeated Reith, the Howard candidate for deputy, by the same margin. Peacock, like Menzies, had returned from his earlier leadership humiliation.

Charles Blunt acted on the information supplied by Shack, the result being a remarkable double coup which saw the demise of the warhorse Ian Sinclair, taken by surprise by his own MPs. Sinclair says: 'I had previously come very close to sacking Blunt. But I decided after a discussion with him that we should avoid that. The coalition was doing quite well at the time. Blunt wouldn't have made his move if the Peacock backers hadn't come to him saying, "It's best to have a clean sweep." On the night it was a total surprise. A few weeks earlier I would have been expecting it.'

Howard's chief complaint was about Chaney, whom he accused of 'an act of treachery'. Howard told colleagues that he should have listened more to his wife's advice about Chaney; she had told him never to trust him. 'Chaney is the Kim Philby of this affair,' Howard declared to his loyalists.

Peacock was impressive at his victory press conference, stressing the bipartisan pledge to a non-discriminatory immigration policy and invoking the fall and rise of R. G. Menzies when asked whether his return to the Liberal leadership should be taken seriously.

So the coalition had three new leaders—Peacock, Blunt and Chaney. It was the best executed transition of power in recent Liberal history—fast, sharp, ruthless, a classic ambush and an unusual coup. The margin was commanding and the mood of the party decisive. It was exactly what Peacock had intended. The momentum generated had the potential to change dramatically the pattern of federal politics.

Howard was not alone in being caught by surprise. So were the media and the Labor Party. It suggested a professionalism and toughness in Peacock not before apparent. The victory disguised the self-doubts which had plagued Peacock on the leadership. It was Peacock's finest week in politics; a golden opportunity for him to revive Liberal fortunes and exploit Labor's woes to return the coalition to office.

26
Towards the recession

This government has the stink of decay and I don't want to be part of it.

Peter Walsh, March 1989

The worst blunder of the Hawke government was to underestimate the power of the late 1980s speculative boom and its second worst was to underestimate the depth of the bust. From autumn 1988 until January 1990, when Paul Keating was using an interest rate crunch to puncture the boom, he predicted a 'soft landing' instead of a recession. This was a failure of judgement: Keating was afflicted by the 'great man' theory of history. He exaggerated his ability to fine tune economic instruments in an entirely new environment.

The 1990s recession was not caused by the factors at work in the two previous recessions in the 1970s and early 1980s—an international downturn and trade union greed. It was the direct result of government policy which was designed to halt the boom and which finished in overkill.

By the summer of 1988–89 it was obvious that Keating's audacious strategy from the previous August—the 'bringing home the bacon' budget—had collapsed. The power of the boom led directly to another blowout in Australia's current account deficit which, in turn, fed the deterioration in net foreign debt—the precise issues on which Keating had declared the banana republic in 1986.

The current account deficit in 1988–89, forecast at $9.5 billion, finished at $17.4 billion or 5.2 per cent of GDP. It was Australia's external payments fragility which drove Keating, his advisers and the government to a path of austerity. Unless they halted the haemorrhage in the current account deficit, the markets would impose a greater and more draconian shake-out upon Australia. So the early 1990s recession was a function of the balance of payments problem which had plagued Australia throughout the decade. It was a 'banana republic' legacy.

At the same time Keating's effort to return Australia to a path of low inflation—a cardinal objective in the August 1988 budget—was blown away with the CPI rising 7.4 per cent in 1988–89.[1] The killing of the low inflation hopes was symbolised by the release on 31 January 1989 of the 2.1 per cent December quarter CPI which Keating later claimed poisoned the climate for the next six months.[2] The *Sydney Morning Herald*'s economic editor, Ross Gittins, reflected the reevaluation of the government: 'This appalling inflation result has broken completely the government's budget strategy. Paul Keating should now go back to the drawing board. Sooner or later he will. Sooner or later he'll unveil banana republic Mark II.'[3]

But Keating felt that crying 'banana republic' twice would condemn the government. He tried another option, an old-fashioned interest rate squeeze to slow the economy short of killing it. He hoped to solve the problem without terrifying the voters.

The truth, admitted more easily post-recession, was that the power of the 1980s boom was so great that an interest rate crunch was always likely to finish in a severe contraction. The Reserve's new deputy governor, Ian Macfarlane, said in May 1992: 'The dynamics of a modern capitalist economy are such that it is hard to believe that this excess [the boom] could be followed by a gentle slowing; it was far more likely that it would be followed by an absolute contraction. Some people think that if only the instrument of monetary policy had been adjusted in a more skilful and timely manner we might have avoided a recession. But I very much doubt it.'[4]

This assessment of course, is made with the luxury of hindsight. There is no evidence that the Reserve or the treasury believed at the time that a recession was inevitable. In the August 1989 budget papers the treasury said that policy 'should lead to a rebalancing in the economy while avoiding the risks of a recession'. Keating's entire strategy was to prove Labor's mastery by slowing the economy without a recession. But Keating was an explorer of unique terrain—sustained high interest rates operating in a deregulated financial system, a debt-heavy corporate sector, and the bursting of an asset price boom. He was not alone.

The misjudgements Keating made had a universal aspect, as his former adviser Barry Hughes said: 'About 95 per cent of economists didn't see the strength of the Australian economy in 1988. I might add that's true of Britain, it's true of America, it's true of most countries.'[5]

In tightening monetary policy and then easing policy from early 1990, Keating worked closely with the Reserve Bank and followed, broadly, the Bank's advice. The accusation from the coalition—notably from John Hewson—that Keating had corrupted the process or politicised the Reserve, does not stand scrutiny. This claim was rebutted by the former governor,

Bob Johnston, his deputy governor, John Phillips and, in turn, the new deputy, Ian Macfarlane. The recession was a blunder, not a conspiracy.

On his retirement Bob Johnston said: 'Throughout more than six years in office, this government [Labor] has been very correct in its dealings with the Bank. Relations personally have been harmonious and very fruitful. There has been no interference in matters that are the responsibility of the bank. Only an "insider" can known that that has not always been so!'[6]

But Johnston had been personally shaken by Keating's aggressive rhetoric, notably his infamous 1989 line on the Reserve—'They do as I say'—a propaganda coup for the coalition. At the time Johnston was appalled; he didn't know whether to correct Keating publicly or resign—but he did neither. His successor Bernie Fraser later called Keating's remark 'inaccurate and intemperate'.

Finally Ian Macfarlane in his early days as deputy governor declared: 'All the decisions . . . have occurred because they have been recommended by the board of the Reserve Bank and the size of the changes has been determined by the Reserve Bank. So if you don't like how monetary policy has turned out, if you think it is a terrible mess, blame us. Blame Martin Place.'[7]

The recession was caused not by a politicised Reserve Bank but by forecasting failures within the official family, the Reserve and the treasury. Keating's policy mirrored these defects—as far as interest rates are concerned. It was a failure of both economic theory and monetary policy practice.

During and after his application of the monetary policy squeeze, Keating was accused of four mistakes which contributed to its severity. First, he tried to pretend in 1988 that monetary policy was not being tightened; second, he refused to tighten fiscal policy further in 1988–89 in an effort to ease the load on interest rates; third, he injected a massive tax cut into the economy in 1989 which worked to offset the impact of high interest rates; and fourth, that he eventually tightened the monetary screws too much.

In 1988 Keating sought the best of all worlds—he wanted to tighten policy but deny responsibility for high interest rates. Keating spent much time in parliament denying that policy was being tightened. This undermined the impact of the tightening by destroying its 'announcement' value: a conspiracy of silence to deny the obvious. Keating only adopted this technique because he misjudged the clout that was needed to halt the boom. Keating blundered—but he was urged to this tactic by the Reserve's governor, Bob Johnston. Johnston offers a *mea culpa*:

> I have to take a lot of the responsibility. I wasn't advocating a public explanation of the tightening of interest rates. I was beguiled by the view of allowing markets to have more say in what happened and I was really urging markets to tell us what they thought should happen with interest rates. But the markets had gone to water and they were

The end of certainty

looking for leadership. In hindsight I should have been open and bolder and said we were putting rates up.'[8]

Johnston's own deputy governor, John Phillips, oblivious to the advice of his chief, offers a withering condemnation of Keating for this behaviour: 'If you're going to tighten monetary policy then it doesn't make any sense to tell people the opposite because you lose the effect. This has one of two consequences—rates will have to rise even higher or they will have to remain high for longer in order to have the same impact.'

Phillips says that Keating's misleading remarks were important in two respects: 'It meant that investment in assets and asset inflation was not getting the shake which a tightening in monetary policy should have delivered. Our attempts to prick the bubble were undone because Keating pretended that we weren't trying. It also helped to prolong that period of madness in the property market which contributed to the poor mixture of investment which we got.'[9]

Throughout the period of interest rate increases Keating was attacked by the Opposition, the media and Labor's fiscal policy hawk, Peter Walsh, for failing to tighten fiscal policy further. Walsh grew so discouraged that he tried to resign in 1989 before being talked around. Walsh said: 'It would have been irresponsible for the government to ignore the demand/current account blow-out. But almost all the policy response was loaded onto monetary policy, casing business rates to hover around 20 per cent for a year or more, leading ultimately and inevitably to the present recession. Over-reliance on monetary policy was a mistake . . . the alternative was tighter fiscal policy.'[10]

Keating described fiscal policy as 'tight as a drum' and rejected more fiscal action for several reasons. He argued with justice that interest rates, not fiscal policy, was the best way to halt the boom and that 'monetary policy is being employed in the role designed for it'.

Moreover fiscal policy had been tightened such that Keating's 1989–90 budget projected a $9 billion-plus surplus with federal spending falling to 23.7 per cent of GDP, the lowest level since the 1960s, and a total public sector surplus equivalent to 1.2 per cent of GDP. 'What more can we do?' Keating asked rhetorically, and pointed to thirty years of coalition budget deficits as opposed to his lift of 7 percentage points in total public sector savings.

Keating grew hostile towards further spending cuts, asking critics why he should cut the single parent benefit to ease the interest burden for yuppies. He began to question openly not just the political sustainability of the surplus but its economic utility. In addition, Keating wanted to preserve the 'social wage' benefits of the Accord and that meant adequate provision for health, welfare and labour market programs in the budget to maintain the public sector policy distinction between Labor and the coalition. Finally,

490

Keating was influenced by the failure of the 'two deficits' theory after the 'banana republic' phase. He found that his attack on the budget deficit had not similarly improved the external deficit. Keating had improved public sector savings by an equivalent of 7 per cent of GDP but private sector investment rose to offset any net gain in Australia's savings position. The theory had not worked. Another conclusion drawn by Keating and the treasury from 1987 and the boom was that the trade-off between fiscal and monetary policy was much less than expected. The logic of this conclusion was to dispute the extent to which even tighter fiscal policy in 1988 and 1989 would allow any significant relaxation of interest rates.

In this situation Keating insisted that monetary policy was the appropriate 'swing' instrument. This meant the greater the forecasting miscalculation, the more interest rates had to swing upwards.

The third area of criticism concerned the 1989 tax cuts. They were a function of the Accord which, by the late 1980s, offered a fresh insight into Keating's view of economics and power. The Accord had become inseparable from Keating's conception of economic policy and his own powerbase within the labour movement. Keating, in fact, had become a true Labor treasurer in the traditional sense; working to implement reforms in unison with the trade unions. He grasped that if Labor had no Accord then it was no different from the Liberals. The irony is that as the utility of the Accord declined, Keating's commitment to it deepened.

Bill Kelty had repackaged the Accord as a vehicle to deliver enhanced productivity while retaining its original benefits. This had inspired the Accord Mark III which saw the decisive shift to a two-tier wages system in 1987, the second tier supposedly based on productivity. It was maintained during 1988 for the Accord Mark IV, which was an elaboration of its predecessor with the Industrial Relations Commission beating the new path. In its historic August 1988 decision the IRC opened the way for unions and employers to reform their award structure to promote greater efficiency. This is the origin of the enterprise bargaining philosophy as understood within the evolving new approach of the Accord partners.

Kelty's grandest objective, however, was the Accord Mark V, whose principles were backed by a special unions conference on 9 February 1989 in which Kelty, though he had the numbers, felt compelled to deliver an extraordinary speech of hysterical magnetism. Under this deal the government gave the unions a hefty tax cut and better welfare benefits and, in turn, the unions pledged their efforts to an award restructuring process instead of exploiting the boom to chase market wage rates. In April 1989 Keating was delivering his side of the deal.[11]

Keating's original August 1988 plan was to use the Accord to lock-in low inflation by offering a massive tax cut from 1 July 1989, largely in place of a general wage rise. In October 1988 Keating had said heroically that a 'zero wage outcome is a possibility' for the coming year—a sign that

491

he was planning a massive wage/tax trade-off to change the inflation trajectory. But by autumn 1989 the boom had exploded these hopes. The challenge facing Keating was to halt a runaway economy and prevent inflation from skyrocketing.

A number of commentators urged Keating to cancel the promised 1989 tax cuts since they would only fuel the animal spirits that he was trying to control with high interest rates.

But Keating had no intention of cancelling the tax cuts for two reasons—economics and politics. Keating now felt that he had to use the tax cuts for another purpose—to halt a wages break-out during the boom. On 12 April 1989 Keating honoured the Accord: he announced his most contentious autumn economic package; a $4.9 billion tax cut and $710 million welfare bonus based on a deal with the ACTU that the wage increase for 1989–90 would be limited to 6.5 per cent. In effect, for a total cost to the budget of $5.7 billion, Keating was providing a wage equivalent increase of 12 per cent for which employers would pay only 6.5 per cent.

Keating said the package was 'affordable, paid for from the surplus and would keep wages growth moderate'. The cuts were directed at the $18 000–$30 000 income range. The package injected $5.7 billion into an overstrong economy that Keating wanted to slow, which meant that it acted to hold up interest rates. Keating was a politician who offered contradictory policy stances; he was a car driver who used interest rates as a brake and tax cuts as an accelerator. The immediate aim of the package was to deny a wages explosion. But this was not the real test of the Statement—that would be determined by whether the policy was sustainable, whether final demand fell fast enough to avoid a recession despite this cash injection.

The centrality of the Accord remained; only its rationale was being changed in this package. The prosecution of this wage/tax deal in the climate of 1989 was driven by politics. It was the ultimate proof that Labor would live or die by the Accord.

There were reservations within the treasury which examined the option of cancelling the tax cuts. Chris Higgins and David Morgan reviewed this, but they knew that Keating was committed in a political sense. At the Reserve Bank, according to John Phillips, 'We were troubled about their size and timing, but it seemed that the government was locked-in.' The same conclusion was made within the Cabinet.[12]

Peter Walsh reports: 'We should have tightened fiscal policy by a cancellation of the 1 July 1989 tax cuts. But I never did propose that to Cabinet. I don't think there was any chance of it being accepted. It was the most appropriate action but only if one operated in a political vacuum.'[13]

The April Statement was a tribute to the power of institutional and personal alliances. The trust between the government and the unions was deep; they were hostages to each other. Their institutional strategies had grown mutually dependent. It was not just an economic issue; Keating had given his word to Kelty. They had cut a deal—and Keating's career as treasurer had been based upon Kelty delivering on such deals. Kelty's ability to deliver the unions, in turn, depended upon Keating honouring his own promises.

Kelty had spent the previous two months fighting off a union push for a return to cost-of-living adjustments. He says the tax cuts were more than just a pledge—they were basic to halting a wage inferno. Kelty used Keating's promised tax cuts to persuade the unions to accept a wage rise below the rates that were available in the market. Reflecting on this period from the vantage point of 1991, Kelty defended the tax cuts as a viable policy weapon:

> I think most people thought that we were going to have some form of wage explosion. You had a wage explosion already at the top, for chief executives who were getting 10, 20, 30, 100 per cent wage increases. It was a wages explosion coming down the escalator. We thought that with a combination of tax cuts and restructuring that we might, for the first time in this situation, prevent it. I think we won. But the ACTU leadership was under considerable pressure. We were not the advocates of a wages explosion; we were the advocates of a rational wages system. Many people felt it was time to get whatever they could out of the system. At one stage I think most people felt the ACTU leadership would be swamped and we would get beaten, but we didn't. It was a combination of Simon Crean, myself, Laurie Carmichael, Tas Bull and others.
>
> One of our objectives had always been to get Australia into a low inflation period without burning the heart out of the economy. It's true that the economy got away from people and commodity prices went up. But we [ACTU] held firm and it would have been impossible to get today's [1991] historic low rate of inflation without that 1989 decision which bought off a wages explosion.[14]

Many economists felt the risk of a wages blow-out was overstated; that the unions understood the link between wages and jobs; that such an option was unlikely because it was suicidal for employment. This is rational but it ignores politics. The unions, watching the greatest explosion of executive salaries, would have sanctified their recklessness on the altar of equity.

The judgement about the 1989 tax cuts, as BT's André Morony conceded, was that the Keating–Kelty deal was probably the best available for the economy. It wasn't good enough, as Keating's former adviser Barry Hughes said. But it was 'the lesser of two evils'. The coalition complained but the coalition had no mechanism which would have delivered a lower wage result at such a time.

Like most items of unfortunate economic news, this outcome had been predicted by John Stone. As early as September 1988 in a major address Stone identified the central dilemma: how did the government reconcile the growing foreign debt problem with the aspirations of Australians for rising real disposable incomes? Stone put the hard question: unless the boost to living standards through the tax cuts came from higher productivity, cutting the government's call on resources or extra national income, then it had to come from higher foreign debt or selling Australian assets to foreigners.[15]

Peter Walsh read Stone's speech and told him, 'Put that away for 12 months, I fear you're going to be right.' Walsh was losing his faith. For a short time he accepted the main forecasts in Keating's August 1988 budget—a current account deficit of 3 per cent of GDP and inflation trending to 5 per cent by mid-1989. Walsh says: 'By November I don't think any dispassionate observer could have believed either of these critical forecasts. By December 1988 I came to the conclusion that the economic strategy could not possibly work.'[16]

Keating had tried to convince Walsh but he failed. Walsh was sinking into pessimism about the government and Australia. But his rage was reserved for Hawke's incurable optimism.

In late 1988 Hawke was pledging both wage rises and tax cuts, prompting *The Age*'s Michelle Grattan to declare that 'whenever Hawke opens his mouth these days his name is Pollyanna . . . the bad times are over; the community is to be rewarded for restraint.' When Keating nearly went as far as Hawke, Walsh chided him, 'What the hell are you doing?' Keating told Walsh he had three options with Hawke—to agree, disagree or modify.[17]

Walsh, in fact, was getting ready to resign. He was demoralised by the blowout in the current account deficit and felt that only a severe recession could tackle the foreign debt. He was also disillusioned at the lack of Cabinet support for a firmer fiscal stance. Walsh believed that Labor was doomed.

He painted a sombre picture: Labor's fiscal policy was static; it was using tight monetary policy to slow the economy; the Accord was condemning Australia to high inflation and slow micro-economic reform; Australia's comparative advantage in mining and agriculture was not being utilised; Cabinet government was being 'debauched'; the 10 day rule for lodgement of submissions was not followed; and ministers arrived not having read their submissions.

The weekend of Walsh's birthday, around 11 March 1989, a month before Keating's Statement, Walsh's family gathered at Alice Springs. Walsh decided to resign and rang to tell his staff and departmental head, Mike Keating. When Walsh got to Canberra Hawke asked him to wait a few days—but Hawke didn't try to change his mind. However Keating, Dawkins and Beazley launched a campaign to turn Walsh around. He was wavering when he had lunch with Dawkins. Asked why he was resigning Walsh said, 'This government has the stink of decay and I don't want to be part of it.' But Dawkins gave the perfect reply—'The most obvious sign of decay will

be your departure.' Walsh didn't want to be depicted as a Labor rat; leaving the sinking ship. So Walsh stayed—but he couldn't dishonour his intellectual belief that Labor was doomed; even worse, that it deserved to go.
Reflecting on Labor's policy Walsh says:

> We ultimately implemented a policy with interest rates running at around 20 per cent for 12 to 18 months. They were inequitable in the way they spread the burden, the pain being taken by home buyers and businesses and ultimately the unemployed. High interest rates did not hurt the majority of the population to any significant extent and some people gained from them. On the economic side, if you hold interest rates at that level for that time I would have thought it was highly predictable that there would be a fairly serious recession. Business that was exporting or competing with imports copped a double whammy—high interest rates and an over valued exchange rate.[18]

Keating's problem in 1989 was that he tightened policy but the economy just kept rolling along. The reason was the lag—probably 12 months before monetary policy had any real impact. In this climate it was easy to succumb to interest rate overkill.

This was the fourth criticism of Keating—that interest rates were taken too high for too long. It is a criticism more prevalent after the recession than before.

Then treasury secretary Bernie Fraser says:

> In hindsight this criticism—that policy should not have been tightened so much—would seem to be obvious. But at the time there were few who put this view (though there were some). That said, we did underestimate the effects that high real interest rates would have on business. This was the calibration problem—the same sort of rates in 1986 had had much smaller effects.
>
> We didn't have the experience before of a slowdown with such a debt overhang. That was a new experience and it contributed to the extent of the recession . . . We were also looking at inflation. In retrospect, we erred on the cautious side because we wanted to seize this opportunity to really make some progress on inflation.
>
> It is noteworthy that we started to ease monetary policy in January 1990 which was earlier than many people advocated. There were another five easings in 1990. Every one of them was criticised by the Opposition and others as premature, as politically inspired and as likely to reignite inflation. In retrospect, of course, we should have eased earlier and faster.[19]

Meanwhile, before these consequences were known, Keating was fighting in mid-1989 to contain the loss of nerve within the Labor Party and maintain his own political persona as the magic faded. He escaped briefly to Paris, Moscow and Leningrad in mid-year, a break during his worst year in politics. Every month Keating had a living hell—the balance of payments figures revealing the magnitude of Australia's slide into debt. Before his departure John Hewson out-debated him for the first time in parliament. Keating was also fighting business, the economics profession and the media—his former captives. He was attacking both the *Australian* and the *Sydney Morning Herald.* He was hostile to many of his colleagues and resentful at the economic deterioration as interest rates kept rising. Asked by a reporter what he planned to do in the Soviet Union, Keating shot back: 'Whatever it is, you won't be knowing about it.'

It was the architect in Keating which led him to call his economic model the 'essence of reason and order'. But the unpredictability of the economy was defying even Keating's flexibility. His penchant for long smooth lines and geometric precision was being mocked. Within parliament Keating could still create his own domain of triumph but when the statistician arrived he wanted his revolver. Keating discovered that the economy was a monster which defied its master. He was fighting for his political career—Keating, the architect of economic policy had dug his own trap.

The intimacy between Keating and the treasury fell victim to the tensions. Keating, hostile towards the Reserve, appointed his favourite 'son', Bernie Fraser, as Reserve governor when Bob Johnston retired. He put Chris Higgins into the top treasury post although his sentimental favourite was Ted Evans. But these changes boosted the influence of his own office chief, Dr Don Russell, and led to a growing strain between Keating's office and the old treasury team, which now began to disintegrate.

The television networks staked out Keating in Paris, much to his fury. Keating had barely checked into his hotel when Hawke rang him. It was early June. Hawke wanted a mini-budget squeezed between Keating's April Statement and his August budget. Keating was incredulous, then alarmed. Hawke proposed savings of around $1 billion through a series of measures including bringing forward company tax collections and hitting luxury imports and using these funds to offer interest rate relief to home buyers.

Labor's nerve had started to crack.

The backbench wanted interest rates concessions, notably a home mortgage subsidy scheme. Hawke had told Graham Richardson that he accepted the arguments for such a scheme. Richardson began to spread the message—home relief in the August budget. Within Hawke's office an intense policy rethink was underway. The political professionals feared that a 17.5 per cent home loan rate was an insurmountable obstacle to Labor's reelection. A swing through marginal seats in Victoria had convinced Hawke that some initiatives were required. Hawke's office talked of an interest relief package similar to that introduced by Malcolm Fraser in 1982. They said it would automatically phase-out as rates fell. But Hawke was opposed by Keating and the economic ministers.

A few days later, on 19 June (during his own overseas trip), Hawke floated the idea of a tax break for savings and an indirect tax on luxury items. This proposal enraged Keating, who knew that luxury items were inconsequential in Australia's import bill.

Hawke, as described by one correspondent, 'desperately wants to be seen as a caring leader. He wants to do something to help ease the pain of his government's policies. He is worried that the sales pitch of his Treasurer, Mr Keating, is too harsh. He is also worried about the political risks of the government's "hang on and hope" strategy.'[20]

In this environment Keating seized back control of economic policy in a major speech on 21 June at Sydney's Menzies Hotel. In the process he established the guidelines for Labor's reelection strategy. Keating, oscillating between humour and anger, administered a clinical demolition of the calls for boosting national savings by a tax break on interest income and lifting the sales tax on luxury imports. He dismissed these ideas as 'embroidery on the fabric of policy'.

In a fiery performance which betrayed his agitation Keating sent a message to the ALP and the country—that while he was treasurer the government would not be 'spooked by economic ratbaggery'. Keating put down the nervous nellies, including Hawke. He made a powerful political statement—Labor had to accept that the political and economic cycles were out of kilter. That was unfortunate but it was now unavoidable. That meant a high interest rate election. Labor's correct response was not to panic or call for 'band-aid' solutions. It was, rather, to recognise that Labor's policy structure could still deliver a victory. This was a view of which the party professionals were sceptical.

Both Bob Hogg and Richardson believed that 'we can't win with interest rates at this level'. Hogg wanted to look at an interest earnings deductions scheme, after being briefed by ANOP's Rod Cameron. But Keating killed these ideas: a rare case of a politician telling the advisers and strategists where their domain ended.

Remarking on his own intervention, Keating says: 'I called the situation back to order and Bob dropped the silly talk. He allowed himself to be led, again, by the ERC and this set up his election victory.' An assessment which, post-election, would have left Hawke incredulous.[21]

These events of June 1989 were decisive in establishing the policy basis on which Labor would enter its fourth election. It meant that despite high interest rates, the threat of recession and criticism about Labor's micro-economic reforms, there remained an identifiable policy strategy on which Keating kept a firm grip.

The result was a 1989–90 August budget in which Keating stuck by his policy mix in the hope that the high interest rates, a $9 billion surplus from the growth surge, and the Accord, would secure a soft landing. The 1989 budget was designed to correct the blunders of the 1988 budget while trying to preserve its benefits. Hawke and Keating, after their winter tiff, were in harmony. The logic of Keating's budget was manifest—Labor

497

wanted to call the election only when it could argue its 'slowdown' strategy from high interest rates was working.

By September 1989 net foreign debt was $112 billion or 32 per cent of GDP. But the budget forecasts were again astray. The current account deficit in 1989–90 blew out to $20.7 billion or 5.6 per cent of GDP, worse than Keating had predicted. The extent of the emerging downswing during the next two years would also be greater than predicted.

The technique of slowing the economic boom was only half of the cure to Australia's current account deficit blow-out in 1988–89. This was recognised in Keating's budget speech and in the 1989 Reserve Bank report. The Reserve declared: 'Monetary policy remains a potent demand management tool . . . it will reduce, or even reverse, a surge in aggregate demand if applied vigorously enough for long enough . . . On its own, monetary policy will not produce the longer-term structural benefits Australia is seeking . . . Australia needs a major shift of resources into the traded goods sector to stimulate increased exports and, more importantly, to replace imports.'

Keating identified the gap between national spending, running at 8 per cent, and gross domestic product, at 4 per cent, as the measure of Australia's current account problem. That was being attacked in two ways: by slowing the economy through interest rates and by lifting production. In order to lift production and win a shift of resources into the tradeable goods sector Australia had to perform more efficiently, which meant the implementation of the micro-economic agenda—better work practices, more skills, greater productivity and more efficient infrastructure.

The tragedy of Australia's late 1980s investment boom was that too much of the boom occurred outside the tradeable goods sector, a point made increasingly by the Reserve Bank in 1989. Keating tried to pretend otherwise:

We are running through the largest investment phase in our history. Investment is higher than we've ever had since we've been keeping the records, and that was from 1948. So we are now re-equipping the place for a much better supply-side response to the current account. This country doesn't have a huge producer goods industry. It doesn't have a major mainframe computer industry. It doesn't own the Boeing aircraft company. All those things have to be imported. At some point the Australian economy had got to take a knock on the current account to re-equip itself. It's been doing that for the last two years. We've got the investment phase now we've been after for two decades.[22]

Keating was only partly right—too much of the new investment went into asset speculation, not the tradeable goods sector which would solve Australia's underlying problem.

As Australia slid into recession, within the advisory structure two intellectual conclusions were drawn from the policy failure of the 1980s which are certain to shape the direction of the 1990s. These are first, that Australia was too sluggish in tackling its micro-economic reforms and second, that it failed to give proper weight to inflation control.

The evidence was manifest—Australia's inability to achieve more flexibility and enterprise efficiency undermined the effort to increase capital investment into tradeable areas. It was a fact that Australian failed in the 1980s to run an inflation rate at internationally competitive levels; accordingly, its investment patterns were corrupted by a high inflation psychology which produced an asset price speculation and 'get rich quick and easy' mentality.

Labor had won the 1983 election on a repudiation of Fraser's so-called 'fight inflation first' policy which, of course, Fraser had abandoned towards the end. When Labor assumed office the electoral constituency for anti-inflationary policies was weak. Labor's mandate at the 1983 election—and at every subsequent election—was to give priority to employment over inflation. This is exactly what it did.

The natural solution to Australia's current account deficit from 1985 onwards was a policy of structural reform within a low growth economy. But Hawke and Keating were compelled by their history, preference, and Labor politics to attempt a reconciliation between a high growth economy and structural change. The upshot was that for the entire 1980s Australia's average GDP growth, domestic spending growth, and inflation rate were high by OECD standards. The inflation rate ran about 3 per cent higher than the OECD average, evidence of different priorities.

While the Accord had been a macro-policy success in securing real wages cuts by voluntary agreement, it was less successful at the micro-policy level because it delayed the elimination of structural and work practice inefficiencies. Senior ministers such as Button, Walsh and Dawkins were upset at the slow pace of micro-reform although they had no solutions within the ALP model. Plagued by conscience, during 1989 they began to lose respect for Hawke and for their government.

The most damaging claim—a chorus from the coalition and Peter Walsh's real worry—was that the Labor model of the 1980s based on the Accord and financial deregulation, might now be obsolete. But Keating saw the Accord as the best solution to Australia's 15 year inflation problem and he hoped that the float of the dollar, by eventually promoting a balance of payments equilibrium, would nullify the external payments constraint on growth.

The major achievement of the Accord was to prevent the type of wages breakout which had provoked much of the higher inflation in 1974–75 and 1982–83. There was no wages breakout in the 1980s despite strong domestic demand. Australia conquered this historical problem and inflation was kept to 7 per cent at a time when, according to past experience, it might have reached double digit figures. But Keating was solving yesterday's problem, not today's, an important achievement but not enough.

In the interim the world had embraced an ever lower inflation regime. While the Accord 'institutionalised' a 6–7 per cent inflation rate, Australia's trading partners had reduced to 3–5 per cent. Australia had improved upon its historical legacy, but it was not matching its international competitors—the test that counted.

Keating argued with justice in his April 1989 Statement that the Accord was delivering an historic advance for Australia: 'In the last six years the Accord has delivered 1.3 million jobs, a phenomenal 20 per cent increase in employment . . . if we leave you with one single thought tonight it is this: if a government cannot run wages in Australia it cannot run the Australian economy.'

Peter Walsh saw the Accord as an asset for the government, but as the 1980s advanced it turned into a liability. 'Around 1987 or 1988 I think it became a far more dubious proposition. For a number of years from this point the government accepted a nominal wage increase of around 7 per cent with little productivity. That made high inflation an inevitability.'[23]

Both these assessments are true: it is the difference between applying a relative standard and an absolute standard; between a judgement based on domestic history and one based on international imperatives.

Kelty, however, was driven to the brink by the reluctance of the Commission (IRC) to ratify these government–ACTU deals. He recalls the IRC's 1989 National Wage Decision on award restructuring:

> For most wage and salary earners there was a real wage reduction . . .
> but for some they could get big increases . . . it was really a tortuous
> decision for the ACTU leadership. We thought the union movement
> would be better off by rejecting it and proceeding with more effective
> bargaining. But the cost would be that perhaps the Labor government
> would disappear. I think of all the decisions I've made during the
> 1980s this was the toughest decision. I was personally tortured by this
> decision. It was the epitome of unfairness. Arising from that assessment
> I put to the government that we had to have a greater flexibility in the
> wages system. So it was planned, arising out of that [1989] decision,
> that we would have much greater flexibility in Accord Mark VI.[24]

From the start Labor assumed that the float would impose a correction on the nation through the price effect of the exchange rate; that a current account deficit would force fiscal and monetary changes to limit imports and boost exports and thereby 'cure' the deficit. But the immediate practice differed from the theory. The revolution of financial deregulation witnessed a credit explosion which overwhelmed such corrective mechanisms.

This prompted two basic questions: Did financial deregulation cause the boom and then the recession? Should the government have been able to prevent the 'boom and bust' syndrome?

Towards the recession

The credit explosion after deregulation is unmistakeable. In the five years to 1983 credit grew at an annual average rate of 16 per cent compared with more than 21 per cent in the five years to 1988. This credit growth was devoted largely to business and saw a lift in business debt to equity ratios post-1983 from 45 to about 100 per cent.[25]

What caused this increase in business debt? The critics of deregulation assert that it was caused by the increased availability of loan funds under the reckless lending policy of the banks and other finance institutions; the pursuit of market share; the fact that post-1983 the Reserve's volume controls on credit no longer existed and credit was rationed by the price at which interest rates were set.

The point, however, is that people were prepared to pay the price. Borrowers were prepared to pay high interest rates for the privilege of access to loan funds. Real interest rates on a bank overdraft averaged 8 per cent for much of this period. Borrowers were incurring very steep liabilities. Demand for loan funds had risen along with the extra supply of such funds from deregulation. Why had demand for loan funds risen? The most persuasive explanation comes from the Reserve's Ian Macfarlane:

> I think the fundamental reason is that after nearly two decades of relatively high inflation, the community had concluded that the road to increased wealth has been to become the owner of assets that increase in value. These assets range from owner-occupied houses to shares and controlling interests in companies, and in between include other forms of real estate, equities and collectables. The way to maximise the rate of return on holding these assets has been to gear up and so the desired extent of borrowing or degree of leverage has increased. The alternative of being a lender of funds whose income depends on interest receipts has lost favour . . .
>
> The main reason that acquiring debt has become more attractive is to be found in the interaction between inflation and the tax system. The deductibility for tax purposes of the full amount of interest costs confers a major tax advantage on debt over equity . . .
>
> This is not a phenomenon that has arisen overnight; the pre-conditions have existed for 15 years. It is more likely that there was a gradual recognition of the advantages of heavier reliance on debt, a recognition which reached its fullest flowering in the economic expansion that followed the world recession of 1982. It was assisted by relatively strong growth in the economy, by the increasing profit share in national income and, importantly, by overseas interest in acquiring Australian assets. It would not have been possible to have had such a large increase in asset prices entirely as a result of the domestic increase in credit; we could not have pulled ourselves up only by our own bootstraps.[26]

The process was unsustainable since the debt/equity ratios could not continue to rise without endangering the financial system. Investor strategies based on a continuation of the asset price boom were condemned to failure and many of Australia's richest corporate figures did fail. The mistake they made was, in essence, quite elementary.

In summary, while financial deregulation assisted the supply of loan funds, the demand for such funds arose as a result of interaction between inflation, the tax system, strong profits and surplus global liquidity. Banks kept lending and credit kept expanding because lenders were competing for market share and because borrowers were successful each year from 1984 to 1989, thereby making these transactions mutually rewarding. The key link was between expanding credit and spiralling asset prices.

This analysis suggests that the underlying factor in the late 1980s boom was the long nourished and lately freely licensed asset price inflation psychology. This is deeply embedded in the Australian culture, both on the individualistic and the corporate level. It will take a lot more than just the early 1990s recession to purge. It is a function of greed, apathy, the tax system and inflation. Financial deregulation enhanced the instinct by providing a ready supply of loan funds, but the diagnosis of the problem transcends the supply side and lies more heavily on the demand side. Attributing the excess to financial deregulation both misses the cause and mistakes the cure.[27]

The government and the Reserve Bank should have done more to pre-empt the crisis, in two ways. First, tighter fiscal and monetary policy to give greater priority to inflation over growth. Second, a faster pace of structural change to deliver a more efficient economy.

A firmer commitment to inflation control throughout the decade would have contained the excesses of the boom. A more rapid rate of micro-economic reform and internal market liberalisation would have assisted investment in the traded goods sector. In short, the two lessons from the late 1980s are the corrosive impact of inflation and the imperative for greater productivity.

By 1990 it was obvious that one of the Hawke government's failures had been its inability to deregulate the real economy fast enough after its deregulation of the financial sector. This left the Australian economy with a split personality—an aggressive financial sector searching for opportunity and an arthritic productive sector still labouring in chains. The financial sector was hungry for action, the real economy was still heavy with poor productivity.

An analysis was offered by Chicago economist David Hale:

In Australia, external borrowing was encouraged by a financial liberalisation program which caused the number of commercial banks to expand from four to 20 and the number of merchant banks to mushroom from 44 to 108. Because of the depression prevailing in many of Australia's traditional primary producing industries during the 1980s, the bankers could not make loans to finance new capital intensive natural resource projects. So they went to work engineering a boom in speculative corporate takeover activity which has since been followed by a wave of bankruptcies . . . it is obvious, in retrospect, that the critical factor which attracted capital to Australia was not a boom in export generating investment; rather, it was the interaction of an overdeveloped financial sector with open asset markets and surplus global liquidity . . . [28]

The boom and bust reflects upon both the quality of Australia's financial institutions and its corporate leaders, the lenders and borrowers respectively. The pretence that the entire responsibility lies with the government is a furphy which was promoted with some success post-1990.

The 'boom and bust' is an insight into the primitive nature of the Australian business culture, nourished in an environment of fast population growth, relatively high inflation, a frontier mentality and weak internal competition in many sectors. The technique adopted during the 1980s relied upon high debt financed takeovers and profits through asset price accumulation, a more sophisticated version of the standard property speculator technique. To blame the boom solely on greed is to mistake the character trait involved for the real cause. People have always been greedy; but in the 1980s there was a conjunction of circumstances which allowed this instinct great licence.

There is a proviso to these arguments, since the story of the 1980s is inevitably a global story. Australia's boom and bust was not unique. It was repeated with variations in both Britain and America. The truth as summarised by David Hale is that: 'The credit problems which developed in Australia as a by-product of financial deregulation were part of a much larger global phenomenon reflecting macro-economic conditions in the leading industrial countries as well as some unique features of Anglo-Saxon culture that influence Australia as well as the US and Britain.'[29]

Within the English-speaking world the longevity of the 1980s expansion led to a growing disregard for equity in favour of credit. There was a new behaviour—negative pledges, few controls on borrowers, a collapse of standards.

The obvious conclusion about the global financial liberalisation of the 1980s is often ignored because it is unfashionable—that it improved the performance of the world economy during the decade. That story cannot match Wall Street for scandal or drama. The developed world enjoyed an unusually sustained period of high economic growth which averaged 3.5 plus per cent in the OECD. America's ability to import capital, for example, allowed her to enjoy 'the longest peacetime expansion in the modern era despite large government deficits and low private savings'.[30] Over time, increased capital mobility should encourage more efficient resource allocation in the world economy although the difficulties thrown up by the recession are substantial. Reviewing the period Bernie Fraser says: 'Financial deregulation was still a plus, for all its perceived failings . . . the financial system is unquestionably more dynamic and responsive than ten or fifteen years ago. The system is strong and well capitalised.'

The consensus view in 1989–90 was that Australia's slowdown would be worse than that of 1986–87 but not as bad as that of 1982–83. For most of Australia this assessment proved to be correct. But these expectations were disrupted by Victoria. Victoria collapsed in the first half of 1990 and the Victorian recession assumed a character qualitatively different from that in the rest of Australia.

Access Economics in its subsequent work placed great emphasis on Victoria in explaining the depth of the recession. Access concluded that from peak to trough the fall in Victorian output was about 10 per cent and that employment fell around 7 per cent. The drop in business investment in Victoria was about 50 per cent greater than elsewhere. By contrast output in the rest of Australia (excluding Victoria) grew slightly or remained even in both 1990–91 and 1991–92. These estimates suggest that the severity of the early 1990s recession is very much a Victorian phenomenon. If Victoria were extracted then the slowdown would have been far closer to the consensus predictions. The poor financial performance of state ALP governments, notably in Victoria, has been fundamental in the depth of the national recession.[31]

The situation was worse in Victoria because it experienced a crisis in financial institutions. Victoria saw the failure of the Victorian Economic Development Corporation (VEDC), Tricontinental, Pyramid Building Society and the collapse of Estate Mortgage. Many people lost money invested in financial institutions. Regional factors were fundamental in determining the depth of the recession, the monetary crunch being accentuated by the collapse of regional confidence.

Bernie Fraser subsequently identified the central problem in the way monetary policy was eased during the 1990s. He says: 'Clearly the forecasts were not picking how deep the recession would be. We did not see how much disinflation was going on. In 1991 the fall in nominal interest rates just kept pace with falling inflation. Had we been better and more confident forecasters we might have eased faster. We might have been able to do more to soften the contraction though I suspect not very much.'[32]

The simplest explanation for Australia's recession came from Paul Keating after the 1990 election, when the indicators revealed two negative quarters of growth—the technical definition. Keating said: 'The most important thing is that this is a recession that Australia had to have: that the spending we had in the two years up to now was unsustainable; that we couldn't go on spending and consuming at the rate we were, carrying the imports we were, and the debt we were, and of course, the erosion of our gains on inflation.'[33]

It is because Keating pledged and swore there would never be a recession and because Hawke and Keating won an election on this sacred promise that the arrival of the recession was greeted as proof of a disastrous mistake. But this is a function of expectations. The truth lies in Keating's statement. It was perhaps the most stupid political remark of his career and it nearly cost him the prime ministership. However, it is largely true—the boom begat the recession. Keating deserves more blame for the boom than for the slowdown.

The mistakes he made during the slowdown—initially disguising the tightening, not leaning more on fiscal policy and keeping the interest rate squeeze for too long—even if they had been avoided, were still unlikely to have averted the recession.

Commentator Alan Wood said: 'Once a decision was taken to correct the excesses, a recession became inevitable and necessary—policy simply cannot fine-tune an economy into a soft landing from such dizzy heights . . . Keating was actually responsible and courageous in hanging onto high interest rates until it was clear that the economy was cooling off; it was essential that all the policy risks be taken in the direction of recession.'[34]

Keating, of course, did not accept that his policy would finish in recession. The week of his 1989 budget Keating launched a propaganda assault claiming that he would avert the recession. Keating was a manipulator but not a cynic. Peter Walsh says: 'In my view Paul Keating was the most brilliant advocate of an argument I have seen in politics. A precondition for that sort of performance is an absolute conviction that the case he is putting is sound. When it is sound, that's a great plus. But when it's flawed, that's a negative.'[35]

PART V

1990—WHY LABOR WON

27
The Liberals falter

Near the end of July 1989 he is a tarnished leader, not a new one.
He is not exciting or inspiring the Australian electorate . . .
[these] are now final judgements.

Rod Cameron's mid-1989 ANOP report on
Andrew Peacock to the ALP

The brilliance of the Peacock coup overwhelmed its plotters, who fell victim to their success. Peacock's tragedy was that the principal advantage to be derived from the change in leadership was destroyed within days of his ascension. The villains were the Peacock coup organisers, whose cleverness in organising the coup was mocked by their ineptitude in celebrating its success.

Within one week of Peacock's return his leadership honeymoon was destroyed, his legitimacy was cast into doubt and John Howard was resurrected as a political martyr. The strategy of using the momentum from Peacock's victory over Howard to generate an ascendancy over Hawke was ruined. The origins of Peacock's defeat at the 1990 election spring from the debacle during this first week of his return.

Rank and file Liberals, albeit often grudgingly, were prepared to back the new leader. They knew the blood rituals of their own party—the leader is dead, long live the leader! But those rituals demanded honour—Howard's political blood had been spilled in the interest of the party and therefore the nation. But the plotters forgot to maintain the facade. They pulled aside the curtain and told the truth. They shattered the hypocrisy by which the party supporters preferred to live. They offended public decency and in so doing they compromised their new leader.

The coup organisers made two fatal mistakes. First, they insisted that Howard should be consigned to the backbench, a serious breach of the merit principle. It would only embitter the NSW division and invite Howard to retaliate. This attitude contrasts with Hawke's approach towards the man he succeeded, Bill Hayden, who became, in turn, foreign minister and Governor-General. The coup organisers' second mistake was to allow the ABC's *Four Corners* reporter Marian Wilkinson to persuade them to appear on television boasting about the plot.

Tony Eggleton, the symbol of permanence amid change, saw Peacock thirty minutes after the coup to urge that Howard be given a senior post. But Peacock, under pressure from the coup organisers to bury Howard, was reluctant.

The night of Peacock's win, Moore, Shack, Drysdale and Kortlang gathered after dinner in Canberra. The subject—the power structure of the party under Peacock. They wanted Howard out and Kortlang in, as Peacock's office chief. Kortlang agreed after Moore negotiated a $170 000 a year deal. Eggleton said he didn't mind Kortlang, with one critical proviso—'providing he knows the federal party doesn't work like NSW'.

Eggleton advised Peacock to put Howard into foreign affairs or defence but Peacock rejected this advice. His team was an amalgamation of old and new alliances, the result of the novel Peacock–Elliot axis. The exception was John Hewson, a prominent Howard backer, who became shadow treasurer. It was a fateful and, for Hewson, a lucky move. (Hewson could not have become leader after the 1990 election without having served as shadow treasurer during the campaign. Peacock, in effect, made possible Hewson's elevation to the leadership by this promotion, which would not have been available to Hewson at this time under Howard's leadership.) Stone was recalled to finance; Carlton, courtesy of Elliott, won defence and Chaney got the industrial portfolio. Macphee was recalled, briefly, to become shadow foreign minister.

Peacock had told Michael Kroger on 11 May that he wanted a seat found for Macphee. But Kroger, in turn, warned Peacock that the rank and file would liquidate Macphee rather than preselect him, a correct prediction.

It was obvious what job Peacock should have offered Howard—defence. This was a post of status; it was safe politically; it kept Howard away from economics and avoided giving him the sensitive foreign affairs position.

On 12 May Peacock had offered Howard the education portfolio and the most senior position in the hierarchy outside the leadership group. Howard, 14 years a frontbencher, five as treasurer, five as leader, could not have accepted this post with honour. It was too subtle a snub. Howard, finally, said that he would take defence—but Peacock said defence was not available; he had offered it to Carlton. Of course, Peacock could easily have rung back Carlton, given him education and retained Howard. Carlton was even prepared to accept education.

So Howard went to the backbench for the first time since 1975 and a new poison entered the Liberal Party.

Relations between Peacock and the NSW division were doomed. There was a groundswell of sentiment for Howard. On Sunday Howard told Channel Nine's *60 Minutes* that it was 'very very regrettable and stupid that

510

it wasn't possible for my fairly modest request to have been accommodated'. His wife Janette said they had been as close to the Lodge as the next election. The tide of sympathy was swelling.

After more pressure from Eggleton, Peacock agreed to explore a reconciliation with Howard to repair the damage. Eggleton knew the party wanted Howard back and he felt that Peacock would compromise. Eggleton made an appointment to see Howard on Tuesday morning to discuss his recall. It proved to be one of the most ill-fated appointments in memory, destroyed by a television program.

The ABC *Four Corners* team had travelled to Canberra the previous week for a program on the coup and Marian Wilkinson had interviewed some of the plotters on the Thursday, two days after the changeover. It had been the night of Peacock's winner's party in John Moore's office, a night of vindication for Peacock. The Peacock torch burnt brightly but the shadow which had always fallen across Peacock's path was about to reappear.

A few hours before the party Moore had taped an interview with Wilkinson, after twice refusing her request. She had interviewed Shack and Puplick but they had been cautious, unlike Moore. Wilkinson interviewed Tuckey at Essendon airport the next day and this last interview was the most lethal.

Thousands of Liberals around the country watched Moore and Tuckey on *Four Corners* talk at length about the plot to remove Howard, the planning, the targeting of 9 May three months ahead, the secrecy, the written timetable, the lobbying. Moore and Tuckey made two blunders. First, they left the impression that they were boasting about their plot, their deceptions and their treachery. Tuckey said: 'We tended to do our best to keep people isolated . . . at times I guess by downright lying . . . I remember one fellow ringing me up to tell me the absolute truth in that regard . . . but I just had to tell him it was a load of rubbish, hadn't heard a word about it.'

It was a classic example of the power of television. The coup leaders had spent two days giving background briefings to the print media and there was nothing they told the ABC which had not already appeared in print courtesy of the principals. But the plotters failed to appreciate the forces that would be unleashed by their television admissions.

Their second mistake was to contradict the version of events which Peacock had given to the media after he became leader. Peacock had called the process a 'draft', yet the coup leaders made it sound like a conspiracy. Peacock said people had approached him only the previous week. But Moore said that Peacock had been aware of the planning document about a fortnight before the coup. The truth, of course, is that Peacock knew and participated from the start, months before. Every successful coup leader is obliged to distance himself from the deed. Yet Peacock's efforts to achieve this were now being undermined by his own organisers.

The next day, 16 May, saw the Liberal Party sink into a convulsion.

When Eggleton arrived at Howard's office the deposed leader told him there was no point in any negotiation. The *Four Corners* program had changed everything. Howard said he would not return to the frontbench unless Moore and Tuckey were sacked by Peacock. But Howard had little time to speak to Eggleton. He was very busy with the Australian media, launching into the first of many interviews he would give over the next two days. His talents on radio were well known and over the next forty-eight hours John Howard, deposed Liberal leader, victim of the internal party conspiracy revealed by *Four Corners*, was heard in every state, city and town in the nation.

Peacock called for unity, censured Moore and Tuckey, saying their remarks were 'stupid and tasteless', but was forced to defend himself. The Howard supporters—Michael Baume, Peter White and Tony Messner—accused Moore and Tuckey of 'gross disloyalty' and 'deliberate treachery'. Baume said that Peacock's honesty had been called into question. 'Who is lying—John Moore and Wilson Tuckey, or Andrew Peacock?' he asked. Baume said that the party was now facing electoral defeat, not victory.

Howard said the coup leaders had been 'foolish in the extreme' to publicise their 'deception'. Under pressure to explain his own role Peacock said that when people came to him 'I dismissed them and told them I didn't agree with what they were putting to me'. But Tuckey was unrepentant and declared, 'I have no regrets . . . if I've done it, I'm not going to say I'm sorry.'

The next day Howard, sensing the license which accompanied his political martyrdom, went harder at Peacock. Asked if he accepted Peacock's denials about his prior knowledge of the coup, Howard said, 'I can't believe that. There is a massive conflict between what Tuckey and Moore said on that program and what Andrew Peacock has said. There is a massive conflict.' As the day advanced Howard accused Peacock of being a liar. Asked if he believed Peacock's denials, Howard said, 'I can't believe that in the face of what transpired on Monday night and what I know now . . . I cannot believe in my heart that he [Peacock] was not privy to the detail of that.' Howard ridiculed the idea that Peacock had been tapped on the arm and told 'Hey chum, we'd like you to be leader'.

Peacock was stunned; he struggled through a series of interviews about his prior knowledge of the coup. Of course, it was all a ritual for the public's benefit. The Liberals, Howard, Peacock and the Press Gallery knew that Peacock had been involved in the coup for months and numerous stories were published to this effect. But the battle on the airwaves was for the public's confidence and Peacock had lost it comprehensively. The hypocrisy of the media was stark: having crucified Howard's leadership for years, they now made him a martyr. Meanwhile Eggleton was being deluged:

In my 15 years as federal director I have never had as much mail or as strong a reaction as I got from the *Four Corners* program. These were solid Liberal voters saying: 'We won't vote for the Liberals at the next election. We're not going to vote for Labor but we won't be giving our preferences to the Liberal Party.' The criticism was very widespread, but especially intense in NSW where we got this sort of message from people who had voted Liberal for 25 years.[1]

Eggleton advised Peacock to persuade Moore and Tuckey to stand down from the front bench, or failing that, dismiss them. The vacancy should be used to recall Howard. But this was too much for Peacock to stomach.

On Thursday 18 May, Peacock held a council of war with his fellow leaders in Melbourne—Chaney, Lewis, Shack and Moore. Nobody at this meeting favoured action against Moore and Tuckey. An agitated Moore said Peacock could have his head but that Peacock was finished unless he fought those calling for their pound of flesh. Peacock was loath to dismiss his mates, without whom he would not again be leader. He was ambivalent—he resented their blunder but he needed them. Chaney later confessed to Eggleton that his advice at this time was wrong and he should have urged Peacock to move against the offenders.

Peacock was trapped between personal loyalty and political necessity. He should have taken some disciplinary action at this point, but his personal psychology made that impossible. Peacock reprimanded Moore and Tuckey but he would not sack them.

The mood inside the party was one of extreme agitation. Baume called upon Peacock to sack all five conspirators to clear the air. Puplick told Peacock this might be the best option. The Newport branch in Jim Carlton's seat called upon him to resign from the front bench for Howard. Moore and Tuckey wrote letters to the parliamentary party by way of apology. Tuckey merely said he had not meant to gloat; Moore regretted the concern caused but then defended himself: 'The course of action in this challenge was similar to others which have taken place over some twenty-five years.' This was the truth.

Eggleton told Peacock on 22 May, the day before the first party meeting since the *Four Corners* program, that the party's mood was as strong as ever; he advised again that Moore and Tuckey be removed and he left believing that Peacock would either demote or dismiss them. But Peacock subsequently retreated; he needed his friends, he could not take their heads.

The party meeting was dominated by an excellent speech from NSW veteran Wal Fife who spoke on 'the party is greater than the man' theme.[2] Although a Howard backer in the coup, Fife was now supporting Peacock as the leader. The speech secured for Fife election as House deputy to Peacock, a position made necessary since the deputy leader, Chaney, was still a Senator.

This ended the immediate phase of politics associated with the Peacock transition. Its significance is much clearer in retrospect—the central rationale behind the leadership change had been denied. Peacock's legitimacy as leader, though validated by the party room vote, was now called into question. His momentum was broken, his personal standing was tainted, and the party was deeply divided.

A fresher, stronger leader could have recovered but Peacock had neither of these qualities. These events, in fact, destroyed Peacock's confidence and his belief in his leadership authority. They ensured that at the next election Hawke would be able to market the line, 'the party that can't govern itself can't govern the country'. Liberals had argued for years about whether Peacock or Howard was their best leader, but nobody doubted that their worst enemy was disunity. Unity was more important to the Liberals than having either Peacock or Howard as leader; neither could function without unity and the leadership transition had replaced one form of disunity with another. The coup had resulted in a new Liberal leader but had failed in its ultimate aim—to improve the coalition's election prospects.

Bob Hawke was relieved that the coup had taken place. His greatest fear was that the Liberals would repeat Labor's 1983 performance and install a new leader on election eve. Hawke says of the Peacock coup: 'On balance I think the Liberals made the right decision.' But Hawke and Keating were confident that they had Peacock's measure. They had known Peacock for a longer time than most of the Liberals who had voted for him. They were convinced in their hearts that they could beat him and they would deserve to beat him. Hawke was determined to avenge his poor 1984 campaign against Peacock. He was soon declaring that 'a leader can be successful if he's bright but lazy; he can be successful if he's not bright but works hard; but it's a fatal combination to be not too bright and lazy'—a reference to Peacock.[3]

Peacock kept telling the press that he was a changed man from 1985, wiser, smarter, cleverer. But he was trying to convince himself because Peacock, in fact, was unable to change. His strength lay in his political professionalism—the smooth pose, the friendly smile, the good bloke. Peacock would never become a conviction politician; he would never grasp the depth of the intellectual arguments against the Hawke government; he would not master economics. Peacock was polished but, unfortunately, he was just a performer.

Peacock's tragedy was that the public had known him for too long. They liked him as a politician but they had grasped his flaw as a leader. Doubts about Peacock as prime minister during a period of economic adversity were unleashed by the *Four Corners* program.

The idea of the prime ministership had no compulsion for Peacock since he had no will to power. Peacock loved the security of a political program, arriving at work at 9.30 am and being given a program with appointments, interviews and events. He had adjusted to the life of politics—overseas travel, contacts, media appearances. At that level of politics you set your own pace; Peacock now found himself proclaiming a national crisis but was unable to master the policies which he upheld as its cure. The irony is that in this final bid for the prime ministership Peacock was being promoted as a frontman for the hard right of Elliott and Hugh Morgan.

The party Peacock inherited had essentially resolved its philosophical dilemmas of the 1980s. The defeat of Macphee in the Deakin preselection symbolised the final eclipse of the wet–dry contest. Macphee, the most prominent wet, had been successfully deposed by the party rank and file despite Peacock's efforts to save him. Peacock's return as leader would not represent any swing back to policy influenced by the wets. The irony for Howard was that he lost the leadership at the precise time the internal divisions over his dry economic agenda were being resolved.

Peacock was happy to embrace the policy framework he had inherited: a tighter fiscal policy, more cuts in public spending, a lower two-tier personal income tax scale, a large-scale privatisation program, a higher priority for inflation control, deregulation of the labour market, reduction in union power, wage rises based on productivity, and support for the principles of smaller government, belief in the market and a winding back of government regulation.

But in Australian politics the onus falls upon the leader to explain and market his party's policies. This was Peacock's vulnerability and the media always sensed his policy fragility at press conferences. From his early weeks as Opposition leader Peacock invariably was caught in the 'second phase' of questions. He pledged to restore living standards but couldn't say when; he talked vaguely about Australia joining a Pacific trading bloc; he talked about solving the nation's problems but was weak on explaining how it would happen. Senior journalists in the first few weeks described Peacock as 'a puff of smoke' and likened his media conferences to 'wrestling with a greasy pig'.[4]

Eggleton, relying upon an enthusiastic report from Brian Sweeney and Associates, the party's qualitative researcher, argued that the switch of leaders had been a plus. Sweeney's conclusions were upbeat:

> Mr Peacock is seen as the best choice for the Liberal leadership and constitutes a breath of fresh air. Historical negatives associated with Mr Peacock have abated . . . Ultimately, Mr Peacock's pluses far outweigh any minuses. He is described as a match for Mr Hawke and Prime Minister material.[5]

This survey, undertaken by Sweeney's Ron Klein, who was responsible for the qualitative research, was extraordinarily optimistic. It also found, incredibly, that the *Four Corners* program had not damaged Peacock among swinging voters. By contrast an ANOP survey for the Labor Party said:

> Peacock was not seriously regarded as a leadership contender and [he] was seen as having 'run his race'. . . . He was still regarded as a

popular if jaded politician. The main doubts about Peacock were that he lacked substance and had had his chance. Peacock will initially be seen as more interesting than Howard, and he will be able to communicate better . . . any sign of falseness, weakness or lack of substance will, however, quickly be detected by cynical swinging voters.[6]

Three months after Peacock became leader the Morgan poll showed that he had made little impact. In the three months before Howard was deposed he had led Hawke 43.4 per cent to 42.9 per cent on average on primary votes. When preferences were distributed this meant a modest Hawke win. During the first three months of Peacock's leadership he led Hawke 43.7 per cent to 42.4 per cent which meant, after the preference distribution, a virtual dead heat. This insignificant gain came during a period when the Hawke government was being savaged in the media and interest rates had reached a new peak.

The most alarming measure for Peacock was the critical 'best prime minister' question, the most accurate guide to the relative standing of the leaders. Peacock's highest rating was on 12 May, three days after the coup, when Hawke beat him 51 to 35 per cent. But after Peacock's first week as leader he never scored above 30 per cent on this rating. By mid-August Hawke's dominance was 60 to 27 per cent, which was very similar to the lead Hawke would enjoy during the 1990 election campaign. In short, Peacock never had a honeymoon; the polls suggest that the Liberals derived almost no benefit from the leadership change in the post-coup period.[7] When parliament resumed for the 1989 budget session it was apparent that the leadership switch had failed to deliver any significant voting dividend to the coalition.

However Peacock still inherited an election-winning position because of the growing belief among voters that Labor's policies were not working. The nation had come to the brink of cancelling Labor's governing credentials. The people were ready to embrace an alternative model and Peacock was close to winning by default.

The coalition's performance over the next six months was characterised by two features—Peacock's personal failure to exploit Labor's policy vulnerability, and his supervision of the coalition's Economic Action Plan (EAP), a comprehensive policy of election-winning potential. The EAP, after Peacock's 1990 election loss, became the building block for John Hewson's 1991 *Fightback* manifesto.

During the formulation of the EAP Peacock's spirits revived somewhat—his moods and despondency abated. After a brief struggle between Kortlang and Eggleton over campaign strategy, Kortlang left Peacock's office. On Eggleton's advice his place was taken by Eggleton's deputy at the Federal Secretariat, Andrew Robb.

The coalition's fortunes peaked in October 1989 with the release of the

516

EAP. The package was produced by a small economic group chaired by Chaney and including Hewson, Carlton, Peacock's economic adviser Dr Peter Boxall, and only one National, John Stone. The policy thrust—fiscal restraint, lower tax, privatisation, contracting to the private sector, labour market deregulation, a firm monetary policy to fight inflation, and micro-economic reform—was the philosophy pioneered by the free market lobby during the 1980s.

The EAP proclaimed a national crisis facing Australia—the external debt servicing burden in the 1980s was matched only by that in the 1880s and 1920s. After both these periods the nation underwent depressions: 'Australia now faces the same dismal prospects if we fail to quickly recognise the magnitude of our problems and to respond to them.' The EAP ranked Australia third after Brazil and Mexico in terms of external debt owed to commercial banks. It now took 20 per cent of export earnings to service gross foreign debt compared with 5 per cent in 1980–81. Australia was facing a self-perpetuating debt trap and was dangerously exposed to even a small fall in commodity prices or an overseas downturn.

The solution was to boost Australia's competitive position. This required less consumption, more savings, higher productivity and sustained investment in the tradeable goods area. In a ringing declaration of ideological faith the coalition said: 'That liberalisation process must encompass almost all facets of our economic life: our market structures; our management; our work practices; our public sector enterprises; and our waterfront, transportation and other infrastructure.' The EAP in its rhetoric and goals represented the high tide, to this stage, of free market economics within the Liberal Party. Moreover, it was a coalition document; the Nationals had surrendered.

The EAP identified a better inflation performance and faster micro-economic reform as the keys to a more competitive economy, reflecting the new orthodoxy about Australia and the first influence of the new shadow treasurer, John Hewson.

The coalition pledged to cut Australia's inflation level to that of its trading partners over three years, to terminate Australia's record as a soft inflation nation. The method was to permit the central bank to assume a more independent stance in its relations with government and conduct monetary policy over the medium term with the aim of 'reducing and eventually eliminating inflation'. This rejected Keating's technique of using interest rates as a 'swing instrument' to control economic activity. The Liberals were influenced by international studies showing that the lowest inflation occurred in those OECD nations with strong central banks.

The coalition's comprehensive support for micro-reform involved terminating monopolies, promoting competition and preferring private to public ownership. While both parties were pledged to micro-economic reform the Liberals offered a faster pace of adjustment than Labor. The differences were significant. The Liberals wanted substantial wage-setting outside arbitration; foreign competition on the coastal shipping trade; full competition for Telecom and deregulation of the telecommunications industry; abolition of the industry-based employment system on the waterfront; privatisation of Qantas and Australian Airlines with the resulting capital injection both airlines badly needed. The risk for Labor was that it appeared to be falling behind in addressing the urgent economic reforms which Australia's debt situation demanded. There was little difference between government and Opposition on fiscal policy; the EAP increased Labor's existing surplus by only $140 million in the first year when asset sales were excluded.

Peacock needed an election bait and the economic committee created the opportunity by finding, from scratch, savings of $2.7 billion by cutting funds for the jobless, blacks, tertiary students, public servants and overseas aid recipients. The biggest savings of $815 million came from the termination of unemployment benefits after nine months when a special benefit subject to strict criteria would be available for the chronic jobless. This proposal came from Boxall with Peacock's strong support. The strands of coalition philosophy were distinct—the attack on welfare abuse, the user-pays principle with fees for tertiary students, the contracting to the private sector whenever possible of public services and programs. The cuts were cunning and hit Labor's constituency.

The savings were devoted to a family package which involved child rebates of $250 a year for the first child and $200 for subsequent children, to cost $1000 million a year. Direct coalition tax relief was entirely family based. This was supported by a child care rebate costing $820 million which had justifiably great appeal to working women. It tapped a constituency which Labor had spurned because of its ideologically blinkered approach to child care, where government funds were only given to public child care centres (despite the denunciation of this stance by Peter Walsh).

The coalition also pledged to abolish Labor's capital gains tax and replace it with a weaker speculative gains tax; a two-tier tax scale would be introduced during its first term. But the big battle—kept secret over the critical weeks—was over a broadly-based indirect tax, the forerunner to Hewson's goods and services tax.

Hewson spearheaded the campaign for the indirect tax, and made remarkable progress. Elliott, in an extraordinary move, addressed a shadow Cabinet meeting in Melbourne on the need to think audaciously and support the new tax. When Elliott met Peacock in Tokyo in September, he found the Opposition leader telling him: 'We'll force the consumption tax through.' But when Peacock saw Margaret Thatcher she advised: 'Don't introduce a new tax if you want to win an election.' Hewson and his staff ran a campaign for the tax and drafted the options—rates at 10, 12.5 and 15 per cent, which generated steep cuts in the personal rate scale. Peacock was aware of the opinion that such a tax was inevitable for Australia. Its appeal was as a sweeping reform; a dramatisation of the difference between government and Opposition.

The indirect tax issue went to the wire. It was backed by Hewson, Carlton and Fife, and its opponents were Chaney and the National Party—Blunt and Lloyd, with Stone being the most trenchant critic. Andrew Robb supported the tax but Eggleton insisted that it would be a mistake. The final meeting left the issue open and the casting vote was Peacock's—against. The clinching factors were the reluctance of the National Party since Stone's acquiescence could never be assured, and Peacock's own political doubts.

There is little debate that Peacock made the correct decision. The tax would have been hard to sell; it would have created acute coalition tensions; and it would have given Hawke and Keating a target. But it provided an insight into Peacock's approach, trapped as he was between his natural political caution and the ideological imperative to confront the Hawke government—Peacock chose the first option. By contrast, Hewson, the leader after the 1990 poll, would choose the second. This debate paved the way for Hewson to force rapid endorsement of the indirect tax through the coalition parties in 1990–91.

The EAP pledged a coalition government to six objectives over its first term—lower tax rates, lower interest rates, smaller government, lower inflation, higher productivity, and stabilisation of foreign debt. The question posed by commentators and the public was the same—did a Peacock-led team possess the will and the nous to implement its program?

This is the point where Peacock faltered, intellectually and psychologically. Too often Peacock was exposed for his inadequate grasp of his own program, thereby reinforcing doubts about his own commitment to such historic reforms. For the cognoscenti these doubts were exposed in two main areas, health and industrial relations. If there is a case study in Liberal policy failure during the 1980s—including privatisation, industrial relations, indirect taxation—then it is health.

It was an article of faith inside the coalition that it would disband Medicare, revive private insurance and offer 'freedom of choice'. It was a conventional wisdom among Liberals that Medicare wasted money and their reforms would produce savings to be spent elsewhere. The myth was exploded only under the successive periods of Tuckey and Shack as shadow health ministers—and the consequences were disastrous for Peacock.

The problem identified by Shack in a memo to Howard on 11 October 1988, was that the Medicare levy of 1.25 per cent funded only a third of the cost of health insurance and care. Any Liberal plan which abolished the levy and required people to take private health insurance inevitably meant that those who previously did not have private insurance (about 60 per cent) would be worse off. That is, there would be few winners and very many losers; nearly all singles and families paying only the Medicare levy would be losers.

Shack told Howard that such an arrangement 'is not politically saleable from where we stand at the moment'. He said that political reality demanded a more gradual implementation of the coalition health philosophy. Shack warned that any attempt 'to sell a policy which "rips the band-aid off quickly" leaves you open to bleeding to death politically'.

Shack wanted to reduce the number of people who were worse off in the switch from the levy to private insurance. This became the basis of the Shack scheme which was completed by June 1989 and was fully costed by the consultants Access Economics, and Bernie McKay. Tables showed the winners and losers across income groups. The scheme rested on the assumption of revenue neutrality—a major step for the Liberals which ended their delusions about great savings from a new health scheme.

Shack proposed a system of tax credits to encourage people to take out private insurance, which meant that now there were more winners than losers although the number of losers was still alarming. The consultants' report estimated that among uninsured singles there were 1.2 million losers, the bulk losing about $200 a year with the maximum loss being $365 a year; there were about 650 000 winners too. Among uninsured families there were about 600 000 losers, the majority losing an average of $400 a year with the maximum loss of $730 a year. Among families about 1.1 million with private insurance would be winners. In short, nearly everyone with existing private insurance would become a winner. But the total numbers of losers, an estimated 1.8 million, was enough to frighten many Liberals.

This fear was enough to stop the coalition leaders from including the health scheme in their EAP, a political decision inspired by the numbers, because the health scheme would destroy the income bonus from tax rebates which the EAP was delivering to middle income groups. In short, it would wreck the politics of the EAP. Shack always wanted his original scheme released with its winners and losers and the issue fought out honestly, but the coalition leaders rejected this as political folly.

For the time being—and only for the time being—the leaders took the correct decision. Their blunder was to turn a blind eye to health from this point. Peacock operated on the 'out of sight, out of mind' principle. But postponement of the health decision was no answer to the dilemmas in Shack's policy draft. Peacock cruised to Christmas fooling himself that the health issue would disappear.

In the interim Peacock had failed to exploit the protracted late 1989 pilots' dispute to nail Hawke on industrial relations, primarily because he seemed unable to articulate his own policy. Asked at one point how many workers would opt out of the centralised system under a coalition government Peacock defiantly replied, 'Who is to know?'

Unlike health, a final industrial relations policy did emerge, but not until 9 February 1991, a week before Hawke called the election. This was extraordinary given that industrial policy was probably the major difference between government and Opposition. For the first time the policy identified the three options available under coalition plans.

Option one, staying within the centralised system, would be the choice of most companies and industries. This proved that the coalition reform was evolutionary, not revolutionary. There would be new principles to govern the National Wage Case: explicit rejection of any wages–prices link; a target wage outcome that reduced unit labour cost growth and brought Australia's labour costs into line with its trading partners; and different wage results for different industries reflecting productivity performance. This repudiated the ACTU–ALP de facto policy of wages shadowing prices. There was only one way to interpret Chaney's policy—lower wages through the IRC in the early years of a Peacock government until better productivity was achieved.

The second option was a form of collective bargaining within the system for corporations anxious to begin productivity bargaining with receptive unions. The coalition would amend the Act to allow employers and unions to strike special deals based on productivity above the centralised industry benchmark. Such deals required approval from the Bench on a case-by-case basis to deny flow-ons.

Option three was the original formula secured by Howard and Henderson back in 1983—voluntary agreements which would apply essentially in the non-unionised and small business sector. Such agreements would be private, outside the Commission's ambit, and be struck on an employer–employee basis with minimum rate guarantees and the denial of flow-ons.

The policy overall was to satisfy two main economic policy objectives—cutting inflation and boosting productivity. The approach was sound but it was released far too late, after months of confusion and negative publicity.

The coalition's fiddling over health and industrial relations subsequently undermined the excellent reception accorded the EAP upon its release in October 1989, which marked a period of false optimism for the coalition. It was the start of a brief Peacock–Hewson collaboration which nearly took the coalition to victory. The EAP was well received, but the follow-up by the Liberals was poor.

The Liberal election-fighting machine constructed by Eggleton involved an expanded federal HQ under Eggleton himself and a new advertising agency for the federal party, George Patterson, led by a lion of the industry, Geoffrey Cousins, a political novice but an advertising giant. Patterson's success in winning the Liberal contract rested heavily upon Cousins. The Liberals were swayed by his pledge to be involved personally throughout the federal election campaign. But Cousins was alarmed by the leadership coup. The day it happened he told Eggleton: 'You've just lost the election.'

As early as August 1989 Andrew Robb wrote a briefing for the agency from which George Patterson began to develop the 'questions and answers' theme which became the basis of the 1990 Liberal campaign. Cousins wanted a positive theme to persuade the swinging voters on the Liberal program. He warned that the message had to be validated by hard Opposition policies. Robb assured Cousins that the Opposition would, in fact, produce the economic answers in its policies. So Patterson's went ahead and by late 1989 the Liberal marketing strategy for the next election was in place—Andrew Peacock was being sold as the leader with the answers.

The cruel irony is that Labor had discovered the truth. As early as mid-winter ANOP research for the ALP found a deadly deterioration in Peacock's standing. It was a devastating ANOP report:

> Peacock is not seen as the answer . . . the most damaging swinging voter judgement is that Peacock's return reveals that there is no-one else.
> Near the end of July 1989 he is a tarnished leader, not a new one. He is not exciting or inspiring the Australian electorate. Swinging voters' main criticisms and doubts about Peacock—apart from his not giving John Howard a 'fair go', are: (a) He is a 'has been', a 'recycled leader'. He has had his chance before and did not succeed then; (b) He is superficial. He has a show business image. He does not stand for anything. He will say and do what he thinks will look right and not what he necessarily believes in . . . (c) He cannot be trusted, because of Howard's demise but also because of his perceived superficiality; (d) The terms used to describe Peacock are now final judgements and not 'wait and see' temporary descriptions . . . Importantly, Peacock's image is not noticeably different anywhere in Australia.[8]

Labor's finding means that at the time when Peacock's credibility was fading, the Liberals were producing a campaign position which depended upon that credibility. The Liberals, in fact, were much slower than Labor to identify the decline of Peacock's credibility. This is revealed clearly in the contrast between the ANOP and Sweeney research.

The campaign position devised by Patterson's—which featured Peacock saying he had the answers—could only work if Peacock was seen as strong and credible. But he was not. The Liberals were creating an election campaign strategy which was flawed by this contradiction. The conclusion from the ANOP report is that the challenge of the Liberal campaign was to find a communications position which disguised the Peacock weakness. The Liberals, by trying to repair that weakness, were about to advertise it.

It was not necessary to read ANOP surveys to detect disenchantment with Peacock. In August the *Bulletin* produced a cover story on Peacock under the damning front cover title 'The Hollow Man—how can he ever make us trust him?' An advertising campaign for this issue featured Peacock under the label 'No meat, all feathers'.[9]

Hawke and Keating drew sustenance from the polls, anecdotal evidence, and the ANOP research on Peacock. The Liberal leadership coup had failed in its essential purpose—to strengthen the Opposition against the government. The 'first best' option for the Liberals was to unite behind Howard; if that was impossible they should have made a successful switch to Peacock; but they did neither.

Peacock was unpersuasive—but the Liberals could still win. Hostility was rife towards the Hawke government which had to revive its fortunes and image in order to prevail.

28
Green power

We won't win the election unless we save Kakadu.
Environment Minister Graham Richardson telling the Cabinet to defer
mining approvals and expand the Kakadu National Park,
5 October 1989

Although Australia struggled with its economic transition, the nation embraced the cause of environmental protection, which become an international fashion in the late 1980s. The universality of the environmental cause was revealed when the hard right's hero, Margaret Thatcher, adopted it in 1988. The next year the World Commission Report *Our Common Future*, chaired by Norway's prime minister Brundtland, aspired to serve upon the world 'an urgent notice . . . to take the decisions needed to secure the resources to sustain this and coming generations'.

The strength of the new environmentalism was its location in scientific research, its identification of a global crisis, and the link between 'thinking globally and acting locally'. The scientists gave the greens respectability. A biologist with the US Smithsonian Institute, Thomas Lovejoy, declared he was 'convinced that most of the great environmental struggles will either be won or lost in the 1990s and that by the next century it will be too late'.[1]

The global issues were the warming of the earth due to the greenhouse effect, damage to the earth's protective ozone layer, the depletion of forests and expansion of deserts, the pollution of rivers and oceans, the extinction of animals and plants, acid rain, and soil degradation. Above all was the fear that the combination of economic progress and population growth would bring famine, pollution and social collapse. Local environmental issues were seen in a global context as part of the so-called 'planet earth' awareness. This trend was pronounced in the Western industrial democracies and by the late 1980s it was an idea whose time had come.

The outstanding feature of the environment as a political issue was its capacity to cut across existing party allegiances. Genuine environmental concern was held by Liberal, Labor and National voters; it ranged from Balmain basketweavers to Mallee farmers. Advertising, packaging and product standards were affected. Recycling and effective waste disposal became watchwords; personal fitness was linked with environmental health. Political action was prompted by Sydney beach pollution, pulp mill discharge and forest logging.

The contentious issue before the 1990 federal election was the trade-off between economic growth and environmental protection. The leaders of the green movement were unrepentant in their claim that the techniques of wealth creation must be modified. The most influential environmental leader, Australian Conservation Foundation (ACF) director, Philip Toyne, said: 'The pendulum has swung too far towards the exploitation of our unrenewable resources and the use beyond capacity of our renewable resources. We have been liquidating our assets to produce quick income.' Toyne's solution was to 'settle for less material wealth in favour of an enhanced quality of life'.[2]

But this threatened the material living standards of Australians. The wealth creating industries saw Toyne's prescription as an attack upon themselves and Australia's national future.

The Labor Party stole a march over the coalition on the politics of the environment. Labor responded better and faster to the rising tide of opinion by developing stronger environmental policies. These policies were integral to Labor's 1990 reelection and became known, before the poll, as Labor's 'green strategy'. The strategy's chief proponent was the environment minister, Graham Richardson, who worked closely with the prime minister's office. In the winter of 1989, Richardson said the green strategy would become for Labor the difference between winning and losing the election. By the spring of 1989, environmental issues had provoked intense conflict inside the Hawke Cabinet. But these internal tensions were secondary to the polling lead which Labor had established over the coalition on the environment. The more the environment hardened as an election issue the more Labor was the political beneficiary.

By mid-1989 the fall in the primary votes for the major parties was well documented; this trend would shape the politics of 1990 and the nature of the election. Disillusioned ALP voters were switching to the Democrats, greens, independents and minor parties, but not to the coalition. The failure of the coalition to increase its primary vote despite defections from Labor revealed the public's lack of confidence in the alternative government. It meant that minor party preferences would determine the election result. As the total third party vote rose, so did the significance for Labor of its percentage lead over the coalition on the distribution of these third party preferences. It was because so much of the profile of the minor parties, notably the Democrats and independent greens, was shaped by the environmental issue that Labor saw a superior environmental performance over the coalition as central to maximising the flow of these preferences to it and winning the election on this basis.

Richardson was a contemporary man who still embodied the old Labor tribalism. He believed in the party, the faction and, above all, in power. Richardson was a practical politician with a killer instinct. Like Hawke and Keating he was driven by the thirst for victory. Richardson had helped to fashion the culture of the new Labor Party—the culture of winning. Labor in the 1980s was more ruthless, determined and clever than its opponents because it stayed more hungry. Richardson had been a machine man without peer in the late 1970s and early 1980s when he was John Ducker's protégé, Neville Wran's ally and Bob Hawke's promoter. He believed in the slogan that when NSW Labor was strong then Labor was strong; for Richardson the faction ran on loyalty, mateship and numbers.

Richardson's critics, most of whom never possessed a fraction of his political skills, denigrated him as a standover man with an empty head. But Richardson, who had risen from being Hawke's car driver to the party's most powerful faction chief, had other ambitions. He became a minister in 1987 and was given Cabinet standing in 1988. Richardson then aspired to transcend his image as a number cruncher and faction boss. He sought success where power properly resided, at the Cabinet table with portfolio responsibility. Richardson wanted political respectability but was loath to change his ways.

Richardson's conversion to the green cause was under way before the 1987 election; it was genuine but convenient. It coincided with his insight that the environment was the emerging political issue. Richardson decided before the 1987 election that he wanted to become environment minister. His conversion took place in 1986 when Tasmanian conservationist leader Dr Bob Brown invited him to see the green side of the Tasmanian forests issue after he had been feted by the timber industry. Richardson recalls:

> My helicopter landed at Lake Sydney up the mountains, a fantastic lake, mountains on one side, lake on the other. It was just brilliant. The day impressed me greatly. And I found Brown and these others much more impressive and their case better than the industry's.[3]

Before the 1987 election the environmental priorities of the Hawke government had been sharply elevated. This was reflected in three issues—Hawke's promise to Bob Brown that the government would preserve national estate values on the issue of logging in national estate areas; the decision to seek a World Heritage Listing to protect the North Queensland rainforests; and the decision to proclaim Stage III boundaries of Kakadu National Park. Richardson saw the rising electoral significance of the environment and became impatient with the existing environmental minister, Barry Cohen.

After Labor's 1987 election win, Richardson used the faction system to secure his own elevation to the ministry, at the expense of Cohen, and told Hawke he wanted the environment portfolio:

> I saw from the North Queensland rain forests issue that the environment was a political tidal wave only likely to get bigger. I knew it would also help to soften my image which could do with some softening. But I didn't realise then it would virtually win us the next election.[4]

In July 1987, on the Sunday after he became minister, Richardson met the ACF council and delivered a typical greeting: 'I believe in uranium mining and I won't change my mind. So we won't agree on that. But on just about everything else I'll be with you. I've got some clout so we ought to be able to help each other.'[5]

Richardson brought an overwhelming political focus to his ministry. His priority was to tie Australia's most influential green politicians and organisers into an informal network which became, in effect, a Labor–green alliance. This is the essential point to grasp about his administration. The alliance's depth was disguised because the greens could not afford to be seen as an extension of Labor political power and Labor could not afford to be seen to grant the greens such status. The alliance, latent but real, became fundamental to Labor's 1990 election victory.

Richardson targeted three green leaders—Bob Brown from Tasmania, the nation's most respected environmental leader; the rock star Peter Garratt, who had just failed to win a Senate place as a green candidate; and the ACF director, Philip Toyne, a moderate and shrewd political operator who had a strong organisational structure behind him in terms of people, research and finance. Richardson hired as his senior adviser Simon Balderstone, a close friend of Toyne, a consultant from the ACF and previously a Press Gallery journalist. This reinforced the Labor–ACF link at the working level.

Richardson succeeded in winning the confidence of these influential green politicians. They saw Richardson as genuine about their cause and bringing the clout of a political heavyweight to their interests. He took on the portfolio when the Wilderness Society had grown more radical, so Richardson's focus was directed towards the more moderate ACF and Toyne, a sectional politician with whom he could deal. The Labor government ran its environmental policy on the basis of virtual daily dialogue with the ACF. Toyne was its director and Garratt, at Toyne's instigation, became its chairman.

Fundamental to this ALP–green alliance was the radicalisation of the ACF over the previous fifteen years. It had been transformed from an establishment front to a body with a large grassroots membership, financial resources, extensive research capability and high political profile. The ACF had been influenced in turn by the anti-nuclear movement and now, the new environmental consciousness.

But the green movement was a grassroots force which lacked the discipline of an organised political party. Richardson eventually realised this meant that winning its leaders was not enough. He had to publicise Labor's environmental decisions and appeal directly to Democrat, green and minor candidate voters. Richardson, in effect, decided to launch a crusade to reach the grassroots.

He was assisted by Hawke's own reassessment before the 1987 election that the government must elevate its environmental priorities—a view only reinforced by that victory. So Hawke gave Richardson the portfolio and had one of his own aides, Craig Emerson, specialise on the environment. The overall result from Richardson's alliance with the green leaders, his determination to appeal to the grassroots, and the concord between Hawke and Richardson was a strong Labor–green alliance which the Liberals never had any hope of breaching.

After the 1987 election Howard called for a coalition rethink on the environment. He wanted a more national approach and a firmer pro-environment stance for the Liberals. He appointed the capable NSW Senator Puplick to the shadow environment post. It was a good choice since Puplick was energetic, environmentally aware and intelligent. But Puplick never had a chance against Richardson because of the advantages enjoyed by Labor— an interlocking net of personality, interest group and policy factors.

During the 1980s, environmental politics was tied to federalism, a dead weight which sank coalition credibility. Labor was willing to use the full ambit of Commonwealth powers to protect the environment and, if necessary, to override the states. The coalition, by contrast, fell victim to its states rights philosophy at a time when public opinion was behind the use of Commonwealth powers to protect the environment in the national interest. The coalition's dilemma was to reconcile its environmental concern with its refusal to use the properly tested powers of the Commonwealth. The greens drew the irresistible conclusion that the coalition's environmental priorities were not serious.

This had been revealed in the first environmental 'test' of the 1980s— Labor's use of the external affairs power to override the Tasmanian Liberal government and prevent the Gordon-below-Franklin dam. Hawke campaigned in 1983 on this pledge, won the election, fulfilled his promise and then fought the Tasmanian challenge in the High Court. The Court found for the Commonwealth, upholding a wide interpretation of the external affairs power, thereby setting the scene for Labor to repeat this technique throughout the decade.

So Labor was decisive while the coalition fell into a double trap—a constitutional defence of the states and an irresolute stance on the environment. Labor believed in the expansion of the Commonwealth's power which was consistent with its deeper roots in Australian nationalism. The ALP party structure and ethos, guided by the Whitlam and Hayden reforms over the previous 20 years, was more centrist than before, more so than the Liberals. Finally, the ALP found the major elements within its own constituency, the trade unions and its middle class backers, prepared to back its aggressive environmental positions.

The coalition, by contrast, found its own environmental policy a prisoner of its history. It had a distaste, expressed in its platform, and a difficulty reflected in its deregulatory rhetoric, of justifying the degree of public intervention which environmental protection usually demanded. In addition, the structure of the Liberal Party was heavily orientated towards autonomy for the states. This meant that non-Labor premiers such as Robin Gray were influential in environmental policy. Another problem was that the pro-greens within the Liberals had difficulty prevailing against the party's developmental pro-business ethos. Finally, the junior coalition partner, the Nationals, were resolutely pro-development.

The main environmental issue at the 1987 election was protection of the North Queensland rainforests after Hawke's pledge for their World Heritage listing underwritten by the external affairs power. The federal Liberals were trapped once more. Hawke would save the forests; Howard couldn't save them. Richardson's first task as minister post-election was to implement Hawke's rainforests pledge. This involved a bitter fight with the Queensland government; a physical assault upon Richardson in which he was punched and kicked during a visit to the timber town of Ravenshoe; and a vigorous Cabinet meeting at which he secured a $75 million compensation package for workers who lost their jobs. Queensland fought a doomed and costly resistance, sending delegations to Paris and Brazil to fight the World Heritage Committee listing.

The downside of Richardson's strategy soon became obvious—it would divide the Cabinet profoundly. This was first revealed in the protracted debate over the Tasmanian southern forests, the next big issue. It followed the Helsham inquiry, which recommended on a 2–1 majority that only 10 per cent of the forest was suitable for World Heritage listing—a result which enraged the Tasmanian greens who said that the towering mountain ash was unique; the tallest, if put against the Sydney harbour bridge, would begin to branch only at its road level. In a bitter battle Richardson managed to discredit the majority report, overwhelm resources minister Peter Cook, subvert an agreement Cook had reached with the Tasmanian government, secure protection for 70 per cent of the forest area, and obtain another compensation package, this time worth $50 million. In subsequent negotiations with the Tasmanian government, a truce was struck over a section for World Heritage listing and designated areas for logging.

Richardson declared that 'there weren't too many doubting me after that'. But the internal tension was severe—over both the technical aspects and the political value of the environmental vote to the ALP. The Cabinet debate, spread over several meetings lasting 14 hours—one of the longest examinations of any single issue in the Hawke government's history—saw a split on environment/economic lines which would deepen over the life of the government.

Four economic ministers—Kerin, Walsh, Button, Dawkins and foreign minister Evans—formed the nucleus of the anti-Richardson Cabinet camp. They believed the compromises were too pro-green; they feared that Labor's economic credentials were being damaged; and they disputed the electoral weight Richardson gave to the green vote.

This list of critics had two notable exceptions—Hawke and Keating. It was Keating who gave the decisive pro-Richardson speech in Cabinet on the Tasmanian forests issue, the first sign that Keating was prepared to be pro-green on major issues. Hawke had come down on Richardson's side only at the end of the meeting. Hawke and Keating had dual objectives— they wanted to retain economic credibility but also to win the green vote. They believed that Labor could not allow itself to fall into a mutually exclusive position in the environment/economic debate and, in the end, their judgement was vindicated.

Meanwhile Puplick had produced a detailed policy, the result of exhaustive consultation, which involved a 90-page discussion paper, 290 written responses and many seminars. But Puplick was unable to match Labor's position on Commonwealth powers. In a tortured compromise the coalition recognised the national responsibilities of the federal government and that Australia was 'a nation before we are a collection of States'. But it pledged to approach the environment in a 'co-operative and genuinely federalist fashion', avoid 'improper' use of the external affairs power and only allow World Heritage listings on the basis of federal–state agreement.

Puplick's comprehensive policy included support for the existing Antarctic Treaty and programs for soil conservation, land degradation and tree planting. In an effort to locate the environmental debate in a Liberal philosophical framework he identified 'personal responsibility' rather than government action as the key to a better environment. The ACF strongly disagreed with this analysis, another insight into the pro-interventionist convictions of the greens which favoured the ALP.

The next environmental 'test' triggered a sea change in Tasmanian politics and became the most misconstrued green decision of the Hawke era. This was the rejection of the $1.3 billion Wesley Vale pulp mill in north-west Tasmania. The partners, North Broken Hill and Noranda Canada, had proposed a 50/50 joint venture to produce pulp for sale to manufacturers of writing, printing and tissue papers. It would have been a major investment in domestic manufacturing, worth an estimated $300 million yearly in exports.

The project fitted exactly into the value-added processing investment strategy of the Hawke government in its efforts to address Australia's balance of payments problem. Button, who wanted a shift from woodchip production into pulp and paper production, was committed to the project. It typified the path for Australian industry which he had identified and striven to secure. It is extraordinary that at this point Australia had an annual forest products trade deficit of about $1 billion, proof of its failure to exploit its comparative advantage in forest industry based upon abundance of land and cheap natural wood supplies.

The incompetence of the Tasmanian government was a hurdle which the Wesley Vale project never surmounted. Robin Gray began by announcing very tough environmental guidelines to limit the discharge of deadly organic chlorine compounds into the sea in response to a campaign from farmers, fishermen and housewives led by a former school teacher, Christine Milne. But when the partners threatened to withdraw, Gray buckled; he softened the guidelines to meet the demands of the companies. Bob Brown called it 'an unparalleled display of company power over government'. Richardson came, saw and learnt: 'You had people from the Farmers' Federation, greenies and committed Liberals prepared to vote out Gray on this issue. I was amazed.'[6]

So Richardson, the court of last political appeal for the greens, attacked Gray for 'government by company'. In the biggest protest since the Vietnam war more than 6000 people marched in Hobart. The greens gained momentum for the coming state election and the dominance of development politics in Tasmania was broken.

The federal government's role fell under Keating's responsibility for foreign investment approval for Noranda. The Hawke government had been enthusiastic about the concept and had taken an earlier decision for a $80 million subsidy to support it. However, the ineptitude of the Gray government, its shoddy guidelines, and the campaign against the project had turned Richardson into a vocal public critic. This, in turn, bred resentment among senior ministers at his prejudgement of federal Cabinet's decision. Keating and Button recognised the obvious economic benefits of the plant. The upshot was that ministers sought a CSIRO environmental assessment; this report, along with another from the Bureau of Rural Resources (BRR), shaped the debate. It was these documents which killed the project.

The CSIRO recommended that the partners be obliged to modify their technology, if necessary, to ensure there was no increase in effluent discharge from their operations or until it was clear that their higher level discharge had no deleterious effect on the ecology. The BRR report which went to John Kerin was a clinical demolition of the environmental impact statement (EIS) prepared by the partners. It was even tougher than the CSIRO document and exposed the EIS as heavy with 'misinformation', unable to present accurate data and quite inadequate.

The Cabinet meeting began with an air of finality when John Kerin said: 'The EIS is ratshit and the guidelines are a joke.' Kerin was insisting that higher standards were necessary—and he was the most pro-development minister! From this point the result was ordained. Richardson was not required to fight because the pro-development ministers were insisting on greater environmental protections. Button was isolated, a lone voice; not even Peter Walsh backed the proposal. Hawke, Keating and Kerin wanted the mill to proceed, but not without regard to the environmental consequences. They were not prepared to assume that because Australia had a balance of payments problem it should adopt a 'third world' stance of seeking investment at any price.

The upshot was that Cabinet gave foreign investment approval to Noranda subject to enhanced environmental conditions—that is, it required the partners to make environmental concessions. Keating drafted the Cabinet decision at the table. Canberra was not going to be intimidated the same way the partners had intimidated Hobart.[7]

The next morning the partners abandoned the project and rejected the modifications required by Cabinet. The companies said the changes required were technically feasible but they refused to accept them. Keating felt that North Broken Hill would have proceeded but that Noranda had rejected the project. He believed that Noranda was worried about the implications for its existing mills back in Canada if it was seen to accept enhanced standards in Australia.

Bob Brown declared: 'It was only in 1983 that dioxins were known to come out of these pulp mills . . . now the alarm bells are ringing around the world on this score. A child drinking three glasses of milk is liable to get over the allowable limit of organochlorides.'[8] But Dr Robert Bain from the National Association of Forest Industries said there were three other pulp mill proposals and Australia would lose a total of $4 billion worth of investment unless it changed its ways.

The decision caused uproar but it was misunderstood. It was assumed wrongly that politics had prevailed. The irony is that science, not politics, had swung this decision. Button was terribly disappointed. Keating declared the conditions were 'in the national interest' and were 'reasonable and achievable'. Richardson was unpopular with senior ministers who believed he had worked for this outcome regardless of the project's merits, even though the pro-development ministers Kerin and Walsh had declined to endorse the project. The Cabinet saw the mill die with regret, not from any courting of the green vote. The reality is that the environmental gap was never going to be bridged with Noranda.

Within months the first green-sanctioned and supported government in Australian history was formed in Tasmania. For federal Labor the symbolism of this Labor–green Tasmanian alliance sent the perfect message but its significance was exaggerated. Richardson said: 'It is no longer the case that elections will be decided on pure economics—who will run the economy better. Environmental damage in Europe and the US is so bad that the cost of cleaning it up will dominate world politics for the next few decades.' He predicted, wrongly, that during the next decade the environment would replace the economy as Australia's most important electoral issue.[9]

In May 1989 the government, at Keating's instigation, decided to oppose the international treaty designed to permit but control mining in Antarctica. This was a debate about means, not ends. The overwhelming view at official level was that Australia should sign the treaty and foreign minister Evans and Richardson both approved signing. In September 1988 when Keating met French prime minister Rocard in Paris they canvassed the idea of turning Antarctica into a protected international park—a proposal Keating pushed as his own, not necessarily that of the government. But Hawke's office, like Keating, opposed the treaty, and this became Hawke's own view.

The upshot was that Cabinet overturned the long-established Australian position and adopted a more purist line, despite the risk that by sabotaging the treaty Antarctica might be exposed to uncontrolled exploration and mining. New Zealand attacked Australia for ditching an environmental advance for an 'unachievable Utopia'. Hawke said Australia wanted Antarctica saved as a wilderness park. This time the coalition avoided Labor's political trap—it had opposed the Treaty even before Labor. Subsequent international events pointed to the soundness of the new Cabinet position.

In mid-1989, as politics moved into the pre-campaign phase, Labor sought to maximise the differences between government and Opposition on the environment. This had always been Richardson's tactic. It was defined in an early 1989 memo to Hawke and Richardson from their advisers Craig Emerson and Simon Balderstone: 'We have to make sure the conservation electorate "knows its enemy and its friends", point out the difference in policy, point out what happened in NSW [the greens gave only lukewarm support for the NSW ALP and suddenly found that the alternative was far, far worse than they believed possible], point out what could happen federally, point out how relatively green we have been.'

The idea for a comprehensive environmental statement from Hawke had its origins in an early 1989 discussion between Hawke staffers (Geoff Walsh, Craig Emerson and Barrie Cassidy) and ANOP's Rod Cameron. The result was Labor's most planned environmental declaration, Hawke's July 1989 'Our Country, Our Future' speech at the junction of the Murray and Darling rivers. It was a tolerable balance between practical solutions and political extravagance. Hawke's aim was to sketch Labor's philosophy of environmental protection, summarise its results and pledge a new effort to tackle one of the nation's least publicised but worst environmental problems, the vast soil degradation in the Murray–Darling basin. Labor had won the active cooperation from both ACF director Philip Toyne and NFF director Rick Farley in this endeavour.

Hazel Hawke, celebrating her sixtieth birthday, planted the first of one billion trees, a program sold as the regreening of the nation. The former

Governor-General, Sir Ninian Stephen, was appointed Australian Ambassador for the Environment, an unusual post for a former head of state. The premiers of NSW, Victoria and South Australia attended, along with a vast media contingent flown from Canberra. In the afternoon a famous photograph was taken of Hawke, his arm around Richardson by the bank of the tortured Murray. Hawke's rhetoric was heavy: 'We have taken too much from the earth and given too little back.' Despite his involvement Toyne criticised the statement for a glaring omission—its failure to tackle one of the great issues of the green movement, the warming of the earth.

In the prelude to this statement, Richardson had been defeated in Cabinet when he sought a 20 per cent target reduction in the earth-warming greenhouse gases—carbon dioxide, methane, nitrous oxide and chlorofluorocarbons. Richardson publicly declared the greenhouse and ozone effects were 'threatening ordinary people' and he warned that reductions in living standards were essential to combat environmental decay. At this time (mid-1989), he sought to quantify the political significance of the environment by saying that at the next election it would determine the vote of 5 per cent of the people compared with 1–2 per cent at the 1987 election.[10] But Cabinet was not prepared to countenance greenhouse targets. Richardson's mistake was to seek the greenhouse target without qualifications and without a full admission of the economic costs. Most ministers were appalled by Richardson's hardline and Keating demolished him in the Cabinet—but Labor was adroit in disguising Richardson's defeat and nobody boasted about putting the greens in their place. In fact, the lesson was absorbed and 12 months later, after the 1990 election, the new minister, Ros Kelly, would win Cabinet approval for the 20 per cent reduction—but with the severe qualification that no action would be taken that hurt the national economic interest, a formula devised with Hawke and Keating.

Richardson went to the National Press Club on 25 July 1989 after Hawke's environmental statement, in an emotional mood, keen to attack the cynics who claimed that Labor was just vote-buying on the environment:

> If the first act of the Whitlam government was to abolish conscription, then the first act of the Hawke government was to stop the Franklin dam. From that first act we have continued to pile one good environmental decision on top of another for the whole term of government.
>
> My conversion to this cause had been labelled as cynical by many—though the numbers get less over time. But the government's track record on this is impeccable and the accusation that it was just a cynical vote-buying exercise just doesn't hold water. Sure, this is popular politics. But it's also right . . . If the government reacts to the obvious needs of the people, then we are cynically buying votes. If we ignore the obvious needs of people then we are arrogant and uncaring. Perhaps cynicism is in the eye of the beholder.

Green power

The Opposition recognised the pace at which green issues were moving and in mid-1989 the coalition released another series of documents which advanced further its environmental policies. They gave emphasis to land degradation and conservation, the use of the tax system to reward good environmental companies and punish the bad, protection of flora and fauna, the banning of mining in Antarctica and finally—where Puplick trumped Labor—a promise to cut greenhouse gas emissions by 20 per cent by the year 2000. When Puplick read Hawke's own mid-year statement he snorted, 'Our policy sets real goals and targets.' In 1989 politics was a virility contest over shades of green.

The criticism of Richardson's tactics of appeasing the greens was that they were insatiable. The economic ministers felt the electoral returns were increasingly marginal, yet the electoral cost was increasingly risky. The upshot was that Button, Walsh, Dawkins and Kerin became bitter towards Hawke and damning of Richardson. They said privately that Hawke was too soft with the greens and irresolute on the economy. They concluded that Labor was making a fundamental mistake in this environmental/economic trade-off. The issue split the Cabinet and had the potential to wreck the government.

Peter Walsh fluctuated between depression about the economy and rage about Hawke. He saw Hawke as incapable of taking hard decisions or following a consistent path. Walsh flirted with resignation and did, in fact, resign in early 1989 only to change his mind under persuasion from Dawkins and Keating. Walsh's disillusionment, which he vented in full when he left the ministry after the 1990 election and branded Hawke 'jellyback', became entrenched during the course of 1989. Dawkins, in fact, was even more critical of Hawke than Walsh and was pledged to a change of leader. Button was disenchanted with Hawke, worried about the economy, and alarmed at Cabinet's flirtation with the greens—but he disguised his feelings better than Walsh or Dawkins. John Kerin had always been remote from and suspicious of Hawke. As the minister responsible for mining and agricultural industries and exports, he was disgusted at the descent into green politics. Kerin was a low profile minister but in late 1989 he exploded in frustration.

These ministers saw Richardson as the villain; a Cabinet interloper and a corrupting influence who injected his own brand of politics in place of merit-based assessment.

However Keating's outlook was different. Keating had raged and gnashed his teeth about Hawke for years. But Keating in mid-1989 was driven by only one force—winning. He now had a strictly professional relationship with Hawke. He would work with Hawke; he would work with Richardson; he would work with the economic ministers. Keating saw a victory as the vindication of his policy framework and his career. He knew that the most explosive issue for Labor was any resurgence of Hawke–Keating leadership rivalry. If that was unleashed, then Labor would blow up.

Keating, like Hawke, wanted to maximise the Labor vote. That meant a strategy including both the economy and the environment.

Richardson dismissed the economic ministers as political amateurs:

> The more things went bad for us in 1989 the more I knew we had to run on the environment. I always thought Peacock was a dud. It meant that when voters left us, they wouldn't go back to Peacock. I always saw that the Democrats and the greens would get a much higher vote. It was obvious. We had to win by getting back those preferences. I kept telling Hawke this, but I didn't have to persuade Bob. He knew that already. That's why he made such access available to Brown, Toyne and Garratt. But not everyone understood. As for Keating, he supported me on every single environmental issue with two exceptions—the greenhouse gas emissions cut and Kakadu.[11]

Labor's fragile electoral position and its internal tensions came together in late 1989 in a convulsion over Kakadu. It was the biggest environmental decision by the Hawke government in its third term, the most overtly political and most bitterly contested. In a remarkable performance Hawke broke from his normal style and led his Cabinet in a reweighting of the environmental/economic balance towards the greens. The Kakadu decision was presented by Richardson as fundamental to a Labor win at the next election; post-election he claimed vindication.

There are three stages to Kakadu National Park. Stage I was proclaimed in 1979 and Stage II was proclaimed in 1984. Uranium deposits at Ranger, Koongarra and Jabiluka were exempted but vast mineral riches were locked away in these two Stages. Stage III was proclaimed in June 1987, on election eve. But an exploration zone was excluded from Stage III so mineral riches could be identified and excluded from subsequent incorporation into the park. It was also agreed in principle that BHP could proceed with its Coronation Hill gold and platinum mine, also in the exploration zone. These decisions embodied a delicate mining/environmental compromise.

On 9 October 1987 Hawke had reaffirmed by letter to BHP that 'there has been no change in government policy on the exploration zone concept or in relation to Coronation Hill.'[12]

But two years later, in September 1989, with the government facing a final decision on the boundaries, Richardson proposed a radical change. He wanted to delay approval for the Coronation Hill mine despite a favourable EIS from his own department, and, more significantly, lock away the bulk of the exploration zone into the park, leaving only a mineral-rich 20 kilometre strip from the zone's 2252 square kilometres. This meant that the bulk of the zone described by Gareth Evans in 1986 as 'clapped-out buffalo country' would go into the park without any detailed assessment of its mineral deposits. Richardson proposed a new EIS on the mineral-rich area to supersede the EIS on the Coronation Hill mine. While administrative services minister Stewart West had formal carriage of this issue, it was Richardson who called the shots.

Richardson's proposal was to extend the park and defer the Coronation Hill project until after the election pending another EIS. His private assessment was that eventually Coronation Hill would proceed but that the greens might be able to halt the development of the rich El Sherana deposit nearby, a focus of environmental concern.

The economic ministers were enraged. Walsh and Kerin saw Richardson's move as a national irresponsibility. From the start Richardson spoke to Hawke and secured his endorsement for the plan; he had no intention of buying this type of fight without Hawke's backing. The ALP Northern Territory Senator Bob Collins quipped, 'So you don't consider the mine on its merits. You consider instead the environmental impact of the first mine in the context of other mines even though you may never approve them.'[13]

BHP protested to Hawke:

BHP has painstakingly adhered to all government requirements . . . in total more than $10 million has been spent on the premise that there would be full evaluation of the mineral potential of these tenements . . . in the exploration zone. Further delays to the Coronation Hill project . . . is totally unacceptable to the Joint Venture given the time and effort we have put into the project in good faith and on the basis of assurances previously received.[14]

Richardson's justification was that public opinion had shifted significantly since 1986, therefore the Cabinet should change its policy—a philosophy which had the potential to destroy investor confidence in Australia. BHP and the economic ministers insisted that promises made by the Australian government should be honoured; that the government had an obligation to develop, not lock up, valuable minerals. Australia's balance of payments crisis could hardly afford such a luxury. The reversal of developmental ground rules at the time that Australia required massive overseas funds to fund its external deficit was a threat to the resources sector which was dependent upon long lead times for investment. Ultimately Richardson took his stand on the qualitative shift in public opinion on environmental issues—a remarkable but honest admission.

It was the ACF and the greens who were driving the push for a new Kakadu policy and they had a powerful bargaining position. Hawke and Richardson planned to win the election partly through a green-inspired preference distribution. At the time Richardson reopened the Kakadu issue, Balderstone, his adviser and confidant of Toyne, wrote Richardson a minute which gives an insight into the motivation. He said: 'Surveys show that Kakadu is an image, a symbol, a benchmark. Sacrosanct . . . Kakadu is a long-standing battle which Toyne firmly believes will make other issues

The end of certainty

look small if we make a decision to go ahead with Coronation Hill . . .
Toyne sees the key in shrinking the "exploration" zone.'
   The policy for which Richardson pushed was the policy which came
from Toyne and the ACF. Richardson accepted the argument that despite its
world heritage policy, Wesley Vale, Antarctica and Hawke's environmental
statement, the government had to do more to secure a successful preference
strategy. Richardson always knew that the two locations of overwhelming
environmental significance for the people were the Great Barrier Reef and
Kakadu. Kakadu was now the key; it was seen as 'sacred', the word the
ACF used in its assessment to government. The electoral logic flowed—the
wrong decision on Kakadu would threaten the very profile being created—
Labor as the environment protection party. It would threaten the significant
product differentiation Labor held over the coalition as the best party on
the environment; and Labor wanted to reinforce, not weaken, this perception.
A fortnight before the decision Hawke had a three hour meeting with Toyne
and Garratt; he never had similar consultations with BHP or the miners.
   Hawke saw the risk in backing Richardson—that Labor would appear
to put a short-term vote-buying exercise ahead of the national interest. This
interpretation was being promoted from the very heart of his own government by the economic ministers who were fighting Richardson. But the most
active opponent was Bob Collins, who slept in his office for five nights
while lobbying ministers and drafting submissions. Collins told his colleagues, 'The proper role of the government is to be an ally of the
conservation movement, not hostage to it.'
   The political argument underlying the Richardson proposition was put
into perspective by Beazley:

   We're watching a sea change in politics here and overseas. It's a
   reversal of what happened in the 1950s and 60s when the DLP and the
   Conservatives formed an electoral alliance which consigned Labor to a
   minority position . . . Now there is a real chance of a long-term
   alliance between the social democratic parties and green parties both in
   Australia and abroad . . . the greens can marginalise the conservatives
   in the 1990s the same way the DLP marginalised the Labor Party for
   so long.[15]

   Hawke did not finalise his position until the night before the Cabinet
debate, when he had a ninety-minute phone conversation with Toyne. The
ACF director said that the conservation movement saw Kakadu as the litmus
test which would shape the movement's attitude towards the government.
Hawke was left with the view that the Kakadu decision was needed to
validate Labor's preference strategy. That particular week, ANOP was in
the field testing attitudes towards the environment and other issues. Cameron
reached the same conclusion as Toyne and Richardson—Labor needed to
take environmental protection one step further to secure its strategy. Cam-

538

eron advised that Kakadu had the potential to become a 'stand or fall' question, like the Franklin. Labor then looked at its federal primary vote, likely to be about 40 per cent, the lowest ever. It looked at Tasmania where Labor now governed having polled only 34.7 per cent of the primary vote, the lowest since 1906. This was solely because of its superior links with the greens.

Hawke, believing that his decision could mean the difference between winning and losing the next election, went for the preference strategy and the greens. It is important to record, however, that Hawke believed the environmentally unique status of Kakadu meant that this decision could be legitimately defended in national interest terms.

When the Cabinet met Hawke took the rare step of speaking first in a forceful manner. This was unusual and signalled the importance Hawke placed on the question. He had lobbied ministers before the meeting. He ensured inside the Cabinet that every minister understood the importance he placed on the right decision. Hawke put his prime ministerial prestige on the line and ensured the outcome. Beazley told the Cabinet after Hawke's speech that it had no real option; it couldn't rebuff him. The opposition came from Walsh, Dawkins and Button who backed the counter-position put by resources minister Peter Cook. Keating suggested a compromise. But Keating was disengaged. He wasn't fighting and he wanted to eliminate any damaging perception that he disagreed with Hawke.

Richardson won decisively on the Cabinet alliance that sustained green decisions—the pragmatic right and the left. Hawke announced the decision at an 11.30 pm media conference on 5 October. The media reaction was bad and the business community was disillusioned. BHP chairman Sir Arvi Parbo was disgusted: 'I can't believe anything the government says anymore.' Richardson was elated. Peter Walsh retired beaten and sick, close to broken. Collins went to his office and played Schubert for his troubled soul. Keating, who said it was a straight prime ministerial decision, took his wife out for her birthday. Kerin, absent overseas from the Cabinet meeting, decided upon retaliation. Button retreated into his shell of despond; Dawkins maintained his rage against Hawke.

Collins was honest enough to say that while he opposed the decision on merit, 'I have to concede it's probably the best political decision for the party nationally. If I've failed as I have to convince my own 10 year old son that there should be mining, it's not surprising I've failed to convince the Cabinet.'[16]

Media commentators and business spokesmen savaged the government over the Kakadu decision. It was widely depicted as evidence that Labor was playing 'fix-it' politics—pandering to interest groups as Fraser did in his final months. This was an extremely damaging comparison, particularly since some ministers believed it. John Hyde attacked the decision, saying that only rich nations could afford real environmental protection and that

Australia needed the equivalent of a major resource project each year just to pay the interest on its record net $108 billion external debt. The Australian Mining Industry Council said the exploration zone had been reduced by 98 per cent and accused the government of 'total capitulation to the conservation movement'. A public row erupted between Hawke and Arvi Parbo. Hawke, stung by the criticism of the decision, declared that Parbo 'can't be trusted in terms of the relationship between the government and BHP'. It was a stupid exaggeration. The resentment within the Victorian business community for the Hawke government turned to loathing.

The Kakadu decision left the economic ministers unhappy about the electoral tactics and guilty that the national interest had been compromised. In a startling breach of Cabinet solidarity ten days later, Kerin criticised the decision, implied that the Cabinet had succumbed to 'environmental hype' and warned that Australia could not afford to 'keep on scaring off capital'. Kerin said that environmental decisions should be taken on evidence, not perceptions.[17]

Peacock said that Kerin's remarks demanded either his resignation or his dismissal by Hawke. At the Cabinet meeting which Kerin had missed, Hawke had instructed his ministers to keep a firm public front for the decision. Kerin was correct in his analysis of the motives behind the Kakadu decision but wrong in implying it was bad politics. Hawke quickly censured Kerin who apologised but never retracted his criticism.

In early November Kerin gave two powerful speeches on Labor's approach to the environment in which he called upon the government to embrace the notion of sustainable development in order to find the correct balance between environmental protection and economic growth. Kerin warned that 'it will be difficult for any government in Australia to remain in office for the long haul and to carry out its responsibilities to all constituents unless it adopts this approach'. The alternative was ad hoc deals and short-term political fixes.

Kerin said the environment was now firmly located in the thinking of middle Australia, yet the nation was also compelled to address its external debt and provide goods and services at affordable prices for its people. The only route was that of sustainable development. It meant a rejection of the 'sanctimonious behaviour by political parties as they clamour for the environmental vote'. He attacked the greens for 'lying to gain public support', criticised Richardson for 'wandering around the country bagging the miners and the farmers' and complained about a 'green network within the Labor Party'.[18]

This was a powerful critique of Richardson's approach as minister and an appeal for the Hawke government to recast the framework for its environmental policy. Richardson had won Hawke on the Kakadu decision, which helped Labor to win the 1990 election. But Kerin prevailed post-election on the methodology of sustainable development and the technique of science-based compromises. The reality is that Richardson's approach of meeting the demands of the green lobby had only a short-term life for any government. Hawke recognised that Kerin was prophetic in his warning that ultimately governments would have to embrace the sustainable development model.

Kerin attacked the class bias of green power, saying, 'The good old middle class who can live quite comfortably by using their brains and not their hands are quite happy to eat their lamb chops without ever seeing a cuddly lamb slaughtered, have beautiful timber in their houses without ever seeing a tree felled, and drive their cars and enjoy their goods without ever seeing an assembly line or an iron ore or coal mine. Other people can do that for them.'[19]

The economic ministers sympathised with Kerin. While Hawke finally procured Kerin's silence, the schism within his Cabinet ran deep. The economic ministers—Walsh, Dawkins, Kerin and Button—believed the basis for proper decision-making was being corrupted. But Richardson was unrepentant:

> The Kakadu decision, even after a month of bucketing by the journalists and editors in virtually every paper still had a 75 per cent approval rating. The lesson is, don't be afraid of doing what 75 per cent of the Australian people want. Kakadu's got a religious flavour to it.[20]

Hawke and Richardson were correct in thinking that Kakadu would tie the greens to Labor at the election. Some ALP critics said that Labor did not need to make the Kakadu decision to keep its electoral advantage over the coalition on the environment. This is true to a certain extent; the question is, to what extent? Richardson and the green leadership, notably Toyne, said that Kakadu was decisive for Labor in its environmental ascendancy over the coalition at the poll. The closeness of the 1990 election and the role of green preferences puts Richardson's critics on weak ground with their argument that Labor did not need this Kakadu decision to win the election.

Toyne rebutted Kerin, saying that 61 per cent of people were happy with the environmental/economic balance. He reaffirmed the ACF program for halting and stabilising population growth at a safe level, modifying resource use and controlling the emission of waste products.[21] Many intellectuals saw the triumph of the greens in epic terms. Dame Leonie Kramer said in *Quadrant*: 'The ideological challenges of the nineties, e.g. from the environmentalist movement, may be at least as difficult as the Marxist challenge of the fifties.'

WMC chief, Hugh Morgan, quoted the US sociologist, Robert Nisbet: 'I am obliged by the record of the Western past to see Environmentalism—of the kind espoused by Commoners and Ehrlichs—as the third great wave of redemptive struggle in Western history; the first being Christianity, the second, modern socialism.'

Such absolutism, which sought to deny the legitimacy of green policies, was the road to defeat for the non-Labor side. Morgan declared: 'The mining industry today is in the same position as the banking industry of the 1940s . . . over the last fifteen years we have been outspent and outwitted by our opponents in the environmental movement.'[22]

The coalition supported the development of the Coronation Hill mine providing the EIS was satisfactory. Its tactic on Kakadu was to attack Labor for compromising the national interest. But Puplick's challenge was how to prevent Labor from securing overwhelming electoral support as the pro-green party. Puplick needed a dramatic solution so he proposed in a policy revision in late 1989 that the coalition bury its states rights ideology and use full Commonwealth powers to protect the environment.

This was too much for the coalition leaders, who examined Puplick's submission and asked him in the name of unity to abandon his revision of the Commonwealth–state relations issue. Puplick's proposal had been to support cooperative federalism but provide that in the case of a federal-state deadlock the Commonwealth be able to use its constitutional power, including the external affairs power, to address the issue. Puplick recalls:

> Peacock had frequently made the comment that the question of State sovereignty was an absolute nonsense, a myth that had been perpetuated by Premiers and State Divisions of the Party. By the end of 1989 the Liberal Party was ready for a fundamental re-think of Commonwealth/State relations in the environment area. My proposal would have been acceptable to the majority of the Liberal Party through there would have been some opposition from Liberals in Tasmania and Western Australia. However the bottom line in this issue were the strains that were believed to be imposed upon the National Party. So the matter was not pursued further.[23]

Puplick exaggerates the extent to which the Liberals would have shifted. An irony is that the National Party misjudged the changing nature of its own seats. Its new leader, Charles Blunt, was resolute as shadow resources minister in pushing the cause of resource development, oblivious to the changing demography within the National Party strongholds in northern NSW where a new environmental consciousness was taking hold. This failure would prove fatal for Blunt, who lost his own seat on green preferences.

The Liberals tried to champion the middle course on the environment. Puplick sought to expose the green purists, attacking, in order, Malthus, the Club of Rome and Paul Ehrlich as doomsayers who had proved to be wrong. He said the solutions offered by the contemporary doomsayers were 'uniformly totalitarian' and called their collectivist answers 'economy-fascism'.[24] Puplick and Peacock promoted their green credentials by stressing the Liberal record which, in fact, was sound. It included many achievements of the Fraser era—banning sand mining exports from Fraser

Island, the ending of commercial whaling, the declaration of national parks at the Great Barrier Reef, Kakadu and Uluru. But Puplick admitted that the Fraser government's one failure—its inability to stop the Franklin dam—had overwhelmed its successes.[25]

It was the big symbolic issues which destroyed the coalition's credentials. In 1983 it was the Franklin; in 1987 it was the Queensland rainforests; in 1990 it was Kakadu. One story of the 1980s was Labor's political mastery of the coalition on environmental politics. Labor, unlike the Liberals, was able to marshal its tradition of central power and intervention in favour of the contemporary issue of environmental protection. It built successful bridges of support to the environmental lobby, notably the ACF, which by 1989 was one of the most powerful interest groups in Australia.

The upshot was the decision in early 1990 by the ACF and the Wilderness Society to recommend a vote in the House of Representatives for the Australian Democrats, green candidates and selected minor parties, with preferences to be directed towards the ALP. There was a strong 'put the Liberal/Nationals last' theme running throughout the greens' campaign. This was the result which Labor had striven to achieve. But the evidence suggests that the greens deceived the Liberals until the last moment.

On 15 January 1990, Peacock and Puplick met the ACF's Philip Toyne for lunch at an Italian restaurant in Melbourne. This discussion has passed into Liberal folklore as a great deception. Peacock and Puplick say that Toyne told them that the ACF would not be actively advocating a vote for either of the major parties in the House. It would be supporting the Democrats and minor parties in the Senate. Peacock and Puplick left with a misplaced optimism. The political truth is that there was no way that Labor's investment in the greens would be denied. The entire ALP was confident that it would have the green's backing. It is idle to think that Toyne was unaware of these realities.

Toyne said later that he told Peacock and Puplick that he personally believed the ACF should not support political parties but that he gave no promise on the ACF's behalf. Toyne's 'Pontius Pilate' defence is that the decision rested with the ACF council of which he was not even a member. So how could Toyne even know what side the ACF might support! Meanwhile ALP insiders would laugh at the way Toyne cut the political deals and kept himself publicly distant from the pay off—the ACF decision on preferences. Here was a politician they could admire.[26]

The Liberals were humiliated by the greens. After Hawke called the election the ACF council voted overwhelmingly to direct its preferences to the ALP. Peacock later told Hewson that Toyne had broken his word and that the Liberals had been misled and 'dudded'. The Liberals were left bitter and frustrated. The ALP–green alliance, crafted by Richardson, was firmly intact for the 1990 election.

29
The Labor revival

At the moment there is enough resentment and disillusionment with Labor to vote for a coalition despite Andrew Peacock.
ANOP's Rod Cameron in his December 1989 report to Bob Hawke

In November 1989 the fortunes of the Hawke government reached their nadir with a perception that Labor's economic policy was failing and that its environmental policy had compromised the government. This was also the view of senior ministers such as John Button, Peter Walsh and John Kerin. In late 1989 resentment towards the Hawke government ran deep, the accumulated impact of high interest rates, a grind in living standards and a recognition of national problems—high foreign debt, poor productivity and spectacular corporate failure.

The difficulty for Hawke was that after three terms his government was close to being seen as bereft of solutions. The nation was unhappy, sullen and restless. The 'time for a change' mood was growing. Peacock was still unable to persuade the people that he had a viable alternative, but Hawke's personal appeal, the most durable of any leader, was waning.

Bob Hawke was both a winner and loser from the 1989 pilots' dispute. With support from the ACTU, the domestic airlines and the Arbitration Commission, he had prevailed against the pilots, a victory necessary to halt a wages break-out which would have destroyed the government. But Hawke's confrontationalist style had alienated the community who saw him as lacking grace or generosity—qualities he had previously displayed. It was proof that Australians prefer strong but non-confrontationalist leaders. Hawke now had to re-establish his leadership image.

In late 1989 Paul Keating was a mixture of agitation, overkill and scheming. After winning the mid-year battle to prevail on economic policy, he was trying to defend his latest budget, spike the Opposition and persuade the cognoscenti that the ALP–ACTU Accord had enough flexibility to permit enterprise bargaining. Keating had failed to demolish the coalition's Economic Action Plan with a single shot but he was wearing it away. Keating was too supreme an egoist and too resolute a politician to concede that Labor's third term economic record was disappointing. He would make no concessions, either in public or private. Keating's political instincts were honed to one objective—victory.

Labor's problem was that Hawke and to a lesser extent Keating had made too many promises, particularly during 1988, of an early lift in living standards. Their mistake was to misjudge the severity of Australia's economic problems and the time required to restructure the economy. From April 1988, when Keating had begun to lift interest rates, the government had been stretching the political tolerance of voters. By late 1989 it was close to breaking point. High interest rates were a double political negative for the Hawke government—they hurt community living standards and left the impression that Labor's policies had failed.

In those circles where the economic debate was conducted—business, finance and the media—the Labor model had been under intense assault since late 1988. It was only a short step to the conclusion that Labor's time had expired, that its contribution was complete and that Australia's ongoing economic transition now required the tougher Liberal deregulatory model—with its faster pace of adjustment without the constraint of an Accord with the trade unions.

In November 1989 the Business Council of Australia (BCA) released an appraisal of the costs and benefits of the ALP–ACTU Accord. While finding that the Accord had played an important role in restraining wage costs, it concluded 'that on balance the price of the Accord is increasingly outweighing its benefits'. The industrial relations debate was changing from the need to restrain wage costs to the imperative to boost Australia's productivity performance.

Australia's net external debt had not stabilised: the nation had to finance the debt by selling assets, borrowing more or improving its economic performance. Australia, in fact, had entered a phase of the worst corporate crashes since World War II. Signs were manifest of a loss of national confidence, a growing pessimism and periodic xenophobia.

The high tide of Liberal fortunes was reached during the parliamentary sittings in November 1989. Peacock won a psychological victory when he restored John Howard to the front bench, exploiting a blunder by Wilson Tuckey whom Peacock was able to dump. For a few weeks the Liberals looked like winners—and then the coalition faltered. It made the classic Liberal mistake of the 1980s: going into holding pattern when its economic policy was received moderately well. It thought that Labor would defeat itself, a fatal misreading. Several senior ALP ministers were defeatists but Hawke and Keating had the killer instinct. They declared that the coalition would have to beat them; they would not defeat themselves.

In this climate of false optimism the Liberals settled upon the positive election advertising strategy recommended by George Patterson of a 'questions and answers' format carried by Peacock as alternative prime minister. The Liberals had an alternative communications position, but chose to ignore it. This was the South Australian election strategy for the 25 November state poll, one of the few excellent Liberal campaigns during the 1980s. The SA result saw the narrow reelection of ALP premier, John Bannon, but left Labor deeply worried because Bannon, the most popular political leader in the nation, had come to the brink of defeat.

Labor feared that if the Liberals ran a national campaign along the lines of their SA model then it would be hard to save the Hawke government. This was also the opinion of the architect of the SA campaign, the Liberal state director, Nick Minchin, who urged unsuccessfully that his federal colleagues should follow the SA model.

The SA Liberals had to address the same situation as the federal Liberals—popular Labor opponents (Bannon was more popular than Hawke); Liberal leaders with credibility problems (John Olsen, like Peacock, was unconvincing); and voter disaffection with high interest rates. Minchin's strategy was to attack Bannon on interest rates in a tough negative campaign with a 'send Canberra a message' line. He concealed Olsen's leadership weakness by virtually eliminating him from the advertising campaign.

The main Liberal themes were 'Enough is Enough' and 'Seven Years Hard Labor'. The Liberal polling day poster at all booths declared in bold black type: 'Say No To High Interest Rates—Enough Is Enough'. There was a 5 per cent two party preferred swing to the Opposition; Bannon only survived on independent Labor members. The most popular ALP premier had been taken to the brink of defeat, and Hawke was far more susceptible to this sort of attack than was Bannon.

The ALP strategists, national secretary Bob Hogg and Rod Cameron, assumed that the federal Liberals would wage a savage campaign along these lines—but they were wrong. Minchin found that nobody in the federal Liberal Party was interested in his advice. Eggleton and Cousins had closed the door on the federal strategy: it would be positive, not negative. Labor was being given a reprieve. Cousins explains: 'The research showed that it was not good enough for us to say that Labor had failed. People knew that. Their view was that "even so" they would not have Peacock as prime minister. We had to show new aspects of Peacock's political armoury if these attitudes were to change and he was to be elected.'[1]

Meanwhile the research from Labor's two main polling bodies, WAOP and ANOP, revealed a grim outlook for the ALP. In mid-October, a WAOP marginal seat study showed the swing against Labor was 5.5 per cent. During November ANOP conducted further qualitative research among swinging voters in Brisbane, North Queensland, Adelaide, Sydney and Melbourne. This provided the basis of Cameron's end year report to Hawke and Hogg, delivered at a series of meetings in Hawke's office on 4 December 1989.

The document Cameron gave Hawke is the best summary of ANOP's assessment. It said the mid-October anti-Labor swing in the marginals of 6 per cent had worsened. Cameron wrote:

> But it is not the poll numbers which concern us. The worrying aspect comes from the qualitative research among soft votes which indicates a serious decline in the government's standing . . . We cannot rely on the Liberals running an ineffective campaign . . . their South Australian strategy and execution was the best we have seen for a long time.
>
> The disturbing trend uncovered over November is that the electorate is starting to make near final judgements about the government's handling of the economy and its economic credibility.

Cameron documented five factors basic to Labor's decline:

(a) Interest rates . . . the overall effect of the interest rate issue is substantial and not improving.

(b) The growth of the 'it's not working' belief. The rash of bad economic indicators in October and November, the effect on 'suburban confidence' of the corporate crashes and the growing significance of the once esoteric term 'debt' have all helped swinging voters to come closer to the view that the Federal government 'has it all wrong'. The swinging voter impression is that the economy is not getting better, nor is it being well managed, and that the government is not doing anything to put it right. Worse—that the government, knowing that things are not improving, is standing still, denying that the economic approach is not working and is 'refusing to do anything about it' . . . This impression . . . will be very hard to turn around.

(c) Growing concern about the debt . . . Australia's economic problems are now perceived to be related to 'too many imports, not enough exports', balance of payments, debt, productivity—previously mystical concepts . . . high interest rates are not seen as a solution to these economic problems . . . The middle ground has been educated to the extent that they know that Bond and Skase have borrowed extensively. Their decline is not met with an 'it serves them right' response but rather—'if the big guys are in trouble, how much trouble are we [Australia] in?'

(d) Ripple effect of State election campaign impact. The extensive media coverage on State election campaigns over November has provided voters outside South Australia and Queensland with a 'focus of resentment': that is when they hear or read reports of voters sending messages to Canberra they feel renewed vigour in wanting to do this too—'If I thought Bob Hawke was going to take one ounce of satisfaction from my vote for Wayne Goss I'd shut my eyes, cross my fingers and vote for those crooked Nationals again'; 'I'm probably

The end of certainty

going to vote for John Bannon but I can't wait to send my own personal message to Hawke and Keating' (said through clenched teeth and with a grim determination that will not be easy to alter.)

(e) The Liberals seen to be 'getting their act together'. . . . The [economic] plan is eminently attackable but it has helped the definition of an alternative. And the profile and image of John Hewson is improving.

Cameron's report found that Hawke's abrasive style during the pilots' dispute had alienated the community; that a change in Hawke's personal demeanour was essential if the government were to recover. This December ANOP assessment was the most pessimistic Cameron had given the Hawke government. Labor had been rating badly before, notably in late 1986, but its excuses were now evaporating.

On 4 December Cameron spent an hour in a private session with Hawke advising that his behaviour during the pilots' dispute had endangered his leadership as an electoral plus; that Hawke must return to being measured, serious and credible. He said that Labor needed time to regain its lost ground which probably suggested a May 1990 poll.

A second meeting involving Hawke, Hogg, Cameron and Hawke's staff including his political adviser, Geoff Walsh, and press secretary Barrie Cassidy, exposed deep tensions between the national secretary and Hawke's office. Cameron said of the swingers: 'We've almost reached the stage where their views are so set in concrete that they'll never change. It's no good any longer trying to tell voters that we're on the right track. We have to change direction or find a form of words to say we are.' Hogg went further: 'We have to think about admitting that we haven't got it quite right.'

But Hawke's staff rejected this approach, Cassidy calling Hogg's idea 'madness'. The staff said that Hawke should keep his policy nerve. They were now converts to the Keating pre-budget electoral strategy. They said that high interest rates were slowing the economy and a new media strategy was being devised to revive Hawke's image. They said that Cameron's findings should represent the trough of Labor's position. When Cameron and Hogg left, the staff came to see Hawke in a delegation to advise that the government should stick by its present policies; Keating would have been proud.

The elements of Labor's reelection strategy were sketched at these meetings. First, Labor had to conceal its weakness on the economy. There was no point repeating Labor's 1987 'let's see it through' line because voters wouldn't accept it again. Labor had to argue credibly that interest rates had peaked.

Second, Labor had to stress its pluses—unity, leadership, and a better team. It had to exploit the problems of the non-Labor side and play on voter distrust of Peacock. Cameron reported: 'Peacock continues to be seen as

548

lacking substance—the words swinging voters use are "shallow", "superficial", "false", "spineless" and they still disapprove of the way he deposed Howard.' But Cameron warned: 'At the moment there is enough resentment and disillusionment with Labor to vote for the coalition, despite Andrew Peacock.'

Third, Labor had to combat the swinging voters' perception that there was little difference between the sides. It should seek to present a clearer choice to voters on Medicare, privatisation, wages, income distribution, economic management and industrial relations.

Fourth, Cameron recommended that Labor accentuate the environment to maximise its share of preferences. This meant the greatest possible product differentiation on green issues. Cameron warned that Labor might need to appeal direct to voters to secure their preferences where it lost the primary vote, a radical step.

Even as Cameron spoke, ANOP was in the field and its final report for 1989 conducted over the 5–14 December period was even worse for Labor. It was based on four seats, three in Victoria (Aston, Corinella and Isaacs) and the provincial seat of Eden–Monaro in NSW. The overall swing against Labor was now 7 per cent. Labor was just holding Eden–Monaro but in Melbourne the swing was in the 7.5 to 8.5 per cent range. The 'time-for-a-change' feeling was starting to take hold.

In mid-December Labor began to tackle its own advertising strategy at a meeting involving Cameron and Margaret Gibbs from ANOP, Hogg, and ALP advertising manager John Singleton. Cameron's view was that the optimum Liberal position was to use Peacock and Hewson as a duo; to travel, speak and hold media conferences together, with Peacock presenting Hewson as his economic guru and himself as 'board chairman'. This 'hiding' of Peacock would have been a variation on Cameron's Hayden–Hawke–Wran troika before the 1980 federal poll to assist Hayden. Labor felt the best slogans for the Liberals were 'Get Australia Back On the Track' or 'Enough is Enough. Seven Years Hard Labor', just like Minchin's SA campaign.

Margaret Gibbs prepared a preliminary brief for Singleton on 19 December 1989:

> Swinging voters are sick of empty statements, clichés, hollow promises, no substance, 'mudslinging', just attacking and criticising the opponent, personal attacks. They want: genuine direct straightforward messages; realistic achievable promises; positive constructive messages, some hope—they don't want too much gloom, doom and admission of mistakes . . . they are cynical and would really like a new fresh alternative. They are really concerned about Australia's and their own economic circumstances. And they are genuinely concerned about the environment.
>
> It will be harder for Labor to win this next election than it will be

for the Liberals. Success will depend on the state of the economy, the economic outlook and what Labor has to offer. 'Offer' means something new, not more of the same. They key is to convince swinging voters that Labor deserves more time.

What did this mean? John Singleton had no doubt—it meant 'we had no chance unless there was a miracle or the Liberals stuffed up entirely'. He packed up for Christmas. Cameron privately rated Labor's chance as not much above zero.

By this stage the curious nature of the looming 1990 poll had begun to emerge. Voter disenchantment with both government and Opposition was giving state factors great prominence—and Hawke had little control over state factors. The Cain and Dowding Labor governments in Melbourne and Perth were so discredited that Hawke faced the prospect of losing the election in these two states alone on the basis of voter disgust with these governments.

By January 1990 the fortunes of the Victorian Labor Party were burning in the streets of Melbourne. The Cain government was terminal, dying from a disease whose origins lay in the interventionist, pump-priming economic strategy devised by treasury head Peter Sheehan, overseen by treasurer Rob Jolly, and encouraged by the example of Massachusetts governor, Michael Dukakis.

The Victorian Economic Development Corporation (VEDC), the principal vehicle used by the government to provide loans and equity funds to companies and entrepreneurs, had collapsed two years earlier. The VEDC dispensed loans without proper assessment, squandered public funds and was caught by the October 1987 sharemarket crash. An independent report found the VEDC to be technically bankrupt and 'out of control'. Deputy premier and industry minister Rob Fordham had been forced to resign in January 1988. Now a more damaging revelation was imminent. The merchant arm, Tricontinental Corporation, of the State Bank of Victoria had collapsed from even worse financial mismanagement. The severe burden of State Bank losses would be borne by Victorian taxpayers. Bob Hogg, a former aide to Cain had been advising the premier for some time that both Jolly and Sheehan should resign. On Christmas Eve, Hogg told Cain: 'One can't defend your government in public. One can only be embarrassed by it.'

The New Year witnessed a farcical drama—an eerie four week silence in Melbourne streets, the result of a tram blockade which shut down the city's unique transport system. Marvellous Melbourne looked like downtown Bogota. Rebel tram drivers had hijacked 250 trams and blockaded the central business district. The people were disgusted; Cain defiantly stayed on holidays. The ALP's decade-long dominance of Victorian politics was collapsing. Victoria, the cradle of Liberalism, was coming home. Peacock's

550

research told him that a tidal wave was rolling across Victoria with anti-ALP swings in the 5–9 per cent range. Victoria was beyond salvation for Labor.

At the same time the WA government of Peter Dowding was sinking as the saga of WA Inc began to unravel and more data emerged on the government's bailout of Perth entrepreneur Laurie Connell's merchant bank Rothwells. The young WA Labor secretary Stephen Smith told Hogg at Christmas that he could only guarantee three of Labor's nine WA federal seats. One seat had become a Liberal seat in the redistribution so the objective was to hold eight seats. Smith's message was that five seats alone were in jeopardy in the West—enough virtually to doom Hawke.

Smith's research from ANOP and WAOP showed anti-Labor swings in the ALP held seats of Canning, Swan and Brand of 10–10.5 per cent which meant they would be lost. It showed that the swingers saw the Dowding government and WA Inc as vote-switching issues for the federal election. The threat to Hawke from WA Inc was an appropriate irony given Hawke's refusal over some years to criticise the morality or competence of the worst features of the WA state ALP government, and his friendship with former WA premier Brian Burke.

The exposure of the WA Inc deals was only just starting. Two former senior officials, Tony Lloyd and Kevin Edwards, who were closely associated with senior state ministers, had been charged. The Dowding government was paralysed, the state Liberals and Nationals were fighting over whether to block Supply. Labor faced collapse in the West at both state and federal levels.

It was amid this picture of unremitting gloom that the revival of Hawke's electoral fortunes began; to be precise, in December 1989, almost coinciding with his sixtieth birthday, celebrated at the Lodge on Saturday 9 December. This event was exploited with flair by his PR machine. Hazel said that Bob was more mature at sixty and that since he had abandoned infidelity and chosen temperance she had enjoyed the most relaxed period of her life! The birthday party included his ministers and his mates—Peter Abeles, Ted Haris, Greg Norman, Colin Hayes and Mick Young. Hawke put his arms around his extended family. It was a winner—the Hawkes as soap opera.

In late December Hawke tackled his summer ritual—the retreat to Kirribilli House for family, golf and relaxation; psychic repair after his toughest year. Lying on his sun chair Hawke deepened his tan beside the sail-splattered harbor. Life as prime minister was still wonderful, after seven years. Hawke was postponing prostate surgery until after the election; now he decided to give up cigars.

Hawke was tempted to defer the election until April or May, given the ground Labor needed to recover although he preferred to go earlier. He wanted to offer the voters some relief from high interest rates to enhance his economic credibility, but that would take time.

551

Meanwhile the factors which would produce Labor's remarkable political recovery were now emerging—an electoral revolution in Queensland; Keating's long awaited monetary policy easing which meant falling interest rates; a pathetic disarray within the Opposition over both health and monetary policy which confirmed the electorate's doubts about Peacock's grip; and the snap coup against WA premier, Peter Dowding, the circuit breaker to turn Labor's fortunes in the West. These events occurred largely independent of Hawke and their combined effect was to restore Labor as the election front-runner.

The epic event in the North was the smashing of the Bjelke-Petersen era when Labor won the 2 December poll to end 32 years of political exile. The new ALP premier, Wayne Goss, had closed the 13 year circle on the successive Labor wins across Australia in the post-Whitlam era under newer, attractive leaders selling moderate policies, which had started with Neville Wran's victory in NSW in 1976.

The ALP two party preferred vote in the Queensland election was around 54 per cent, with the primary vote at an extraordinary 50.7 per cent suggesting a swing on the primary vote of more than 9 per cent. The National Party primary vote dropped about two-fifths—from 24 per cent to 15.6 per cent.

The official report commissioned by the National Party from Queensland academic Margaret Cribb described the Nationals in these terms: 'Behind the brave public front, a thoroughly demoralised and destabilised Party, deeply divided within itself, not just over one issue, but over a considerable number . . . The Party's loss of office cannot be attributed solely to the revelations of the Fitzgerald Inquiry. The beginning of its electoral decline pre-dates Fitzgerald by several years.'

Cribb said that in the 1986–89 period the party's sources of strength and support were partly eroded from within and 'to that extent it can be said to have self-destructed'. She said:

> The ill-fated adventurism of the Joh-for-Canberra campaign and the divisions within the Party at all levels which this created gave the electorate its first clear view of the cracks appearing in the Party's facade of unity . . . Although he was almost 76 years of age when he won the 1986 election, Sir Joh's refusal to contemplate retirement until forced to set a date, or to name and groom a long-term successor, increased the internal conflict and did irreparable harm in the longer-term to his Party.

Cribb said the party should have faced up to the consequences of the Fitzgerald Inquiry. But Fitzgerald 'cannot be blamed for the disintegration of the party as a stable united force, for the absence of loyalty to leaders and leadership changes and for the party's less than acceptable record as government since the previous election. These things and more the party did to itself'.[2]

The change in Queensland politics represented the conjunction of three trends—the collapse of the National Party; the failure of the Liberal Party to occupy this political vacuum; and the revival of the Labor Party under an appealing leader. Labor's campaign director Wayne Swan said: 'Our greatest success was against the Liberal Party. They still don't know what hit them . . . The vacuum created by the decline of the Nationals could have always easily been filled by the Liberals, as it was ultimately filled by us . . . our attack on the Liberals was the major significant achievement of our campaign.'[3]

Labor's theme—a vote for the Liberals is a vote for the Nationals—painted Labor as the only alternative. It exploited the failure of the Liberals throughout the entire Bjelke-Petersen era and conspicuously during its demise to offer a sharp alternative. The upshot was that the Labor Party was the beneficiary of the moral and political collapse of the National Party, state and federal.

Andrew Peacock appeared on Christmas Day at church in the northern Sydney beach suburb of Avalon at the side of his former wife, Susan Renouf, part of a family holiday at Palm Beach with their grown-up daughters. But Peacock was suffering a political hangover. The coalition's Christmas prelude had involved a chaotic disarray over interest rates, the easiest issue on its plate.

From late November through early December, Stone and Howard warned that the coalition's economic policy would not mean rapid interest rate belief. They were the 'hard' men, preparing for power, putting down false hopes. Howard said: 'Interest rates are going to remain relatively high until we get on top of our overseas debt.'[4] Peacock's nerve cracked on 14 December when he took the opposite line and predicted 'massive' falls in interest rates.

The conflicting messages coming from the Opposition dominated page one of the newspapers for several days. It betrayed a lack of discipline within the Opposition front bench. At the next leadership meeting it took only five minutes to clear the air. Hewson complained, 'I'm the economic spokesman and I've said nothing. What are you guys doing?'

The basis for Hawke's 1990 election victory was laid in the eight weeks from mid-December to mid-February, particularly the latter month, at which point Hawke called the election. Hawke's technique was simple—masterly inactivity, a slow drift back to work, a three day New Zealand visit for talks and sharing the 'gold, gold, gold' Commonwealth Games syndrome. In an interview on 21 January 1990, Hawke said that parliament would be recalled, a pointer to an April or May election. But over the next month this April–May preference was abandoned as Peacock stumbled dramatically and offered Hawke an electoral gift.

The Opposition decided in late January that it would abandon its promise to provide a costed health scheme—the culmination of months of confusion and misjudgement for which Peacock has the final responsibility. Since the coalition's Economic Action Plan (EAP) the previous October, Peacock had tried to dodge the need for a detailed health policy. The fully costed scheme prepared by the shadow minister, Peter Shack, still lay on the table.

The dilemma with the scheme remained—Shack's revenue neutral model contained a number of losers and was risky politics. It is true that there were more winners than losers but the number of losers was substantial—an estimated 1.2 million uninsured singles and about 600 000 uninsured families. The maximum losses for these groups were $365 a year and $730 a year respectively. Peacock, aware of this political problem for six months, had failed to devise an alternative course of action. Shack assumed that Peacock wanted to delay the policy further or to ditch it.

The Opposition health policy was examined at a leader's meeting on 9 January in Melbourne attended by Peacock, Blunt, Fife, Shack, Eggleton and Robb. Shack realised at this meeting that his policy was doomed. Eggleton argued that health was not an issue in the research so there was no need for the coalition to take risks on health policy. Eggleton said there should be a 'holding of position' with Shack's policy quietly buried. This advice misjudged the politics of the issue and underestimated the damage to Peacock in such a debacle.

The leaders rejected Shack's health policy, but Peacock had no idea of how to manage the retreat and fell into inexplicable public confusion. A week after this meeting Peacock, interviewed by *The Australian* on 16 January, gave the opposite impression to the conclusion just reached, saying he was confident of producing a health scheme in which there were no losers.[5]

This remark was a fantasy. Indeed, it was because there were so many losers that Peacock wanted to bury the Shack model—and there was no substitute. When Eggleton read Peacock's interview on page one of *The Australian* he was astonished and Shack was baffled. Peacock told Shack later: 'I made a mistake. It's as much my fault as anything.' Peacock had set his own trap, the tyranny of expectations.

A week later health minister Neal Blewett made public a letter of reply to Peacock over health costings. Blewett taunted Peacock by pointing out that in May 1989 Shack had said the health policy was 'ready to go'; that 'costings have been finalised' (June); that 'we [the Opposition] have done the figures on it' and that 'the policy is finalised' (November). Blewett declared: 'Your four previous spokesmen have come up with six different health policies . . . Your aim to destroy Medicare and introduce new arrangements that are cost neutral but with no one worse off is obvious nonsense.'

The coalition leadership group met on 23 January and Shack presented a 24-page slightly amended but costed health policy. He was defeated on political, not policy grounds. Shack says: 'The majority view was that the least said the better, even if we did cop some flack.' The coalition decided on an inquiry and a set of health principles, but no policy. The advice from Eggleton endorsed by Peacock prevailed—retreat, absorb three days of criticism, rely on the Commonwealth Games to dissipate the damage. The final retreat betrayed a paralysis of will over six months and a refusal by the coalition to confront the policy dilemmas raised by its own philosophy.

After the leader's meeting, Shack wrote a six-page document which he described as 'devoid of policy detail and financial costings'. The principles governing the coalition policy were: the retention of Medicare for all pensioners and the poor; the revival of private health insurance; doctor of choice wherever practicable; competition between public and private hospital sectors; a pledge that no individual or family would be worse off; and a guarantee that state grants for public hospitals would be maintained.

On 25 January, the statement of principles was endorsed by shadow Cabinet and the joint party room. Senior coalition figures dashed off for the holiday weekend and left Shack with the wreckage. But Shack was too honest; he had no stomach for deception after his defeat by the leaders. His Canberra press conference was one of the most remarkable and damaging in years. He began with a confession: 'Now, I want to say to you, with all of the frankness that I can muster, the Liberal and National Parties do not have a particularly good track record in health and you don't need me to remind you of our last period in government.' He continued:

> You know the enormous problems we got into in 1987. Now, I've spoken about the track record in government, let alone the track record in Opposition. We have laboured under a misapprehension that there was a billion dollars to be got out of Medicare. There is not. And the parties now accept and understand it . . . we are going to be spending more money on health in this country and anybody who tells you different is wrong.

Shack admitted the leaders knew the previous October when drafting the EAP that 'it is not possible to have both a revenue neutral system and one where people are not worse off'. He promised to implement a coalition health policy in the first term. Asked what the abandoned coalition scheme would have cost, Shack said somewhere between zero and $2.6 billion, the latter being the extreme position if everyone opted out from the levy. Shack admitted that a new health scheme in current dollars would cost anywhere up to $2.6 billion—an invaluable weapon for Labor.

The coalition's health policy fiasco arose because the politics were too difficult. It was another example of its recurring failure during the 1980s— its inability to reconcile free market beliefs with practical politics. When the facts became obvious the coalition had neither the nerve nor the skill to confront them. The retreat followed repeated assurances by Peacock and Shack since May 1989 that the coalition would produce a detailed health alternative; it followed the failure of the Liberal health policy in the prelude to the 1987 election and the failure of the Fraser government over seven years to reach a consistent position.

However, the greatest electoral significance of this incident lay outside the health area. At election eve, when Peacock needed to convince the voters that he had the answers, he offered evidence to the contrary. The logic was inviting: if Peacock could not produce a health scheme, what prospect was there that he would tackle economic management?

This was the real turning point for Labor. Peacock was confirming the public's worst fears: he had no answer to Australia's problems. The Opposition leadership discussed but never grasped the psychological implications of its retreat. This is extraordinary since the finalised Liberal campaign rested on the theme 'The Answer is Liberal'. The health decision undermined this campaign at its core.

Media condemnation was universal. In *The Age*, Michelle Grattan wrote: 'If you were judging solely on its performance yesterday, you would conclude that the coalition, in one afternoon, forfeited its claim to office.' In the *Sydney Morning Herald*, Alan Ramsey said: 'On the Richter scale of man-made disasters, it was a Chernobyl . . . The Liberal Party will haemorrhage right up to polling day.' In *The Australian*, I said: 'It leaves the political impression of an Opposition unprepared to assume the administration of the nation . . . Peacock is the real loser from this exercise—his judgement, aspirations and priorities.'

The former editor of *The Australian*, Les Hollings, who had supported the coalition at the 1987 election, said: 'I would not advocate that an Andrew Peacock led coalition be given a chance to govern for the next three years.'

Hogg said in his post-election report that 'in a private discussion only a few days before Shack's press conference my position was that, on the balance of probabilities, we would not win. But the Shack/Peacock contribution a few days later gave us the key to the campaign—credibility or substance over style was back on the agenda.'

At this point Labor's campaign fell into place; it would use Hawke's leadership against Peacock's poor credibility.

Paul Keating had taken no summer holiday and stayed in Canberra with his family. True to his deepest instinct of aggression, Keating was crafting a political/economic strategy for early 1990 to spike the coalition. The previous year Keating had raised with Hawke the prospect of a September/October election and then a December 1989 election—proof of his aggression if not his judgement. But Keating did not want to wait for a May 1990 poll; he had settled on a 7 April election.

Keating had two big cards to play—the easing of monetary policy, and the announcement of a wage–tax deal for 1990–91. Keating sought vindication for the Hawke government and his own economic policies. The treasurer had long since convinced himself that neither Peacock nor the coalition was fit to govern the nation.

Keating moved to ease monetary policy and interest rates a fortnight earlier than the markets expected. He acted before, not after, the December quarter CPI and December balance of payments figures which were released at the end of January, both lagged indicators. The risk he took in a January easing of monetary policy was a run on the Australian dollar, which would have been fatal.

The timing of the turnaround in monetary policy was, according to the Reserve's deputy governor, John Phillips, 'very much an initiative of the bank's . . . we spent a lot of time debating when it should happen . . . it wasn't government imposed'.[6] Keating said later that the decision was made by himself and the governor, Bernie Fraser. Fraser had convened a special 22 January board meeting which honoured the formalities.

The Keating–Fraser objective was to validate a soft landing for the economy and ensure that the 18 months of tight monetary policy did not produce a recession. A recession would repudiate the central claim of the Hawke/Keating party: that its weapons of financial deregulation, the Accord and fiscal discipline could solve Australia's problems in a dynamic way without plunging the economy into recession, the type of 'scorched earth' policy which Keating had always pinned on the Liberals.

Keating's ability to avoid a recession would not be known until after the election. But falling interest rates before the poll was a long-awaited bonus. Keating never saw a fall in the sensitive home loan rate as necessary for Labor's reelection. If he had, he would have wanted the election deferred until May, the last option. He believed the major task was to secure a successful monetary policy easing which meant a fall in cash rates thereby creating the conditions for a subsequent fall in the home rates. Keating's aim was to show that the direction of rates was now downwards. He accepted that the 1990 poll would be a high interest rate election.

There were two dangers for Keating. First, an interest rate overkill leading to a post-election recession and second, a premature policy easing which the markets would repudiate at severe cost to Keating and the government. The latter would finish Labor before the election; the former would ruin it post-election.

On 23 January the Reserve operated in the domestic market to secure a cut in official cash rates of between one half and one percentage point. The governor said a reduction of this order 'is judged to be appropriate' given 'the slowing in the economy which has occurred and is in prospect'. But Fraser stressed the need for ongoing action to combat both inflation and the current account deficit.

At his press conference the same day Keating's message was that after

18 months of rising interest rates, the hump was over. Keating had one eye on the slowing economy, the other on a 7 April poll. He said it was a 'correct decision, properly taken', pointed to the concurrence of the Reserve's Board, and predicted it would impact on home rates—but not 'today or tomorrow'. The decision was neither an interest rate 'fix' to save the government nor devoid of politics in its timing.

For the election Keating had his own strategic timetable: this late January easing in monetary policy; a mid-February wage/tax announcement negotiated with the ACTU to hold the economic line and maintain living standards; and, if possible, a second monetary policy easing before Hawke's election announcement. That afternoon Keating told Hawke; 'I think our best date is 7 April but it's for you to decide.'

Hawke and Keating then laughed at the Liberals. The press had reported that morning that a 'central theme' of the Liberal campaign would be the line that 'a vote for Bob Hawke is a vote for Paul Keating'. It was a sound tactic to tap the community antagonism towards Keating and the doubts over whether Hawke would serve another full term—Eggleton was keen to exploit the line. But Keating had borrowed a counter from Hawke's press secretary, Barrie Cassidy, and, when asked at his press conference how Labor would respond to the Liberal campaign, he fired: 'It's obvious . . . a vote for Andrew Peacock is a vote for Andrew Peacock. What you see is what you get . . . not much.'

His delivery was perfect and his line hit the television news. The Liberals, unsure about Peacock, were unnerved. Their campaign thrust on the Hawke–Keating issue collapsed. The Liberals, worried about their own leader, lost their will to exploit Labor's leadership vulnerability.

The markets accepted the monetary policy easing but shadow treasurer Hewson was critical. He warned that Labor's wage and fiscal settings were too weak to sustain lower rates and that Keating had intimidated the Reserve—and he was wrong on both counts. In hindsight it is clear that Keating should have cut interest rates sooner and faster—a course which would have helped Labor's reelection and limited the impact on the subsequent recession. Keating, in fact, erred on the side of caution.

Keating's monetary policy easing and Peacock's health policy fiasco swung the climate Labor's way. They triggered a surge of Labor confidence and took Hawke on to the offensive. He began to harden on a pre-Easter election. Then in early February Hawke was given two pieces of information which settled his mind on a 24 March poll.

The first was the latest ANOP research showing that Queensland was falling towards Labor after the collapse of National Party rule. Hogg received a WAOP report dated 5 February on four Queensland marginals—Brisbane, Fisher, Leichhardt and Dawson—showing that Labor would hold the first three and almost win Dawson from the Nationals. This meant that Labor could actually win seats in Queensland! The next day, 6 February,

Cameron advised that from ANOP research Labor would win the Queensland seat of Moreton from the Liberals. Wayne Goss momentum was having a spillover effect into federal politics.

The second news came from Western Australia, one of Labor's two worst states, and it was sensational. The WA Labor Party was about to execute its premier, Peter Dowding, in an effort to save itself from the WA Inc debacle. This message came from the party's WA secretary, Stephen Smith, destined to become the principal architect of Peter Dowding's demise as premier.

Dowding had inherited the problem of WA Inc from his predecessor, Brian Burke, and he chose the fatal course of making fresh fixes to resolve old fixes. Within a year of his reelection the legacy of WA Inc was destroying Dowding and threatened to destroy Hawke's position in the West. If WA Labor had shown the same paralysis as Victorian Labor then Hawke would not have won the 1990 election. His victory owes a special debt to the fighting instinct of the WA party.

The state where Peacock hoped to make an election killing would deliver its full contingent of reelected Labor MPs. The West returned from the brink—all the way. The reason lies in the Dowding execution.

By December 1989 Stephen Smith had concluded that Dowding was no longer capable of taking advice and that he could not work with the premier. During the Christmas–New Year period Smith told Hogg and the other party intimates that he feared a 'falling dominoes' scenario in which WA Labor lost many of its seats at a federal election, which would encourage a blocking of Supply and annihilation of the state government. Smith knew that sentiment was turning against Dowding in the caucus, but he believed that any snap coup would be too divisive and hurt Labor's federal election prospects.

Smith told Dowding on 17 January: 'You can't lead us to another election and you need to set the scene for your departure in mid 1990.' This advice rocked Dowding. 'I reject your position,' he replied. 'If I go then Supply is certain to be blocked.' But Dowding made too many mistakes. He betrayed his insecurity to his colleagues by indicating that he would be prepared to resign later in the year. He also told the party room that Tony Lloyd, one of two former officials on trial, would not be convicted. Then he left on an extended overseas trip to Davos, Switzerland, and other places.

Smith knew that a trigger was needed to finish Dowding; it came on 31 January with the conviction of Tony Lloyd, the first conviction in the WA Inc saga. Lloyd was a former Rothwell's Merchant Bank managing director; he had taken the post reluctantly at the insistence of the government after the first Rothwells rescue in October 1987. He was convicted on a fraud charge involving $15 million but the trial was seen as a test for the state government. The jury found that Lloyd had breached his duties as a director of the then Rothwells subsidiary, Western Collieries Ltd, over his handling of a $15 million cheque from the State Energy Commission. The trial was told that Dowding had ordered the payment to Western Collieries at a meeting on 21 October 1988 to discuss Rothwell's cash crisis and that Lloyd had acted on Dowding's instructions. During the trial, Lloyd's counsel said, 'It is not up to him to carry the can for WA Inc, carry the can for politicians who made the decisions.'

Inside the Labor Party the feeling was that the jury had convicted Dowding. A number of ministers and backbenchers approached Smith on 1 February, saying that action would be taken against Dowding. Smith called a meeting for Saturday 3 February of eight prominent party figures—deputy premier David Parker, senior caucus figures Ian Taylor, Carmen Lawrence, Pam Beggs, Keith Wilson and Kay Hallahan, and union chief Jim McGinty. Before the meeting Smith decided that Dowding should be removed as soon as possible.

When the group assembled at Pam Beggs' home, Smith opened the discussion with reference to the Lloyd conviction and declared: 'I have reluctantly come to the view that we have to secure his [Dowding's] removal as quickly as possible.'

Agreement to remove Dowding was unanimous. A plan was drafted with Smith as coordinator. Dowding would be told on his return and given the chance to resign. The story broke in the Perth papers on Monday morning and by that evening Smith had 24 votes out of the 47 to finish Dowding. By Wednesday there were 30 votes.

At this point Smith moved to promote the claim of Carmen Lawrence as successor, a personal view which was confirmed by Cameron's ANOP research. Smith told deputy premier David Parker that he was an unacceptable successor because of his association with WA Inc. Smith saw Lawrence as the best candidate because she was both capable and represented the sharpest possible break with the Dowding style. Lawrence was a woman, untainted by WA Inc, and opposed to sleazy deals and the business buddies system.

Hawke, visiting the West for three days, was told before he left Canberra that Dowding was virtually finished. He was briefed by Smith in Perth on the evening of 6 February that Dowding was terminal, that Lawrence would be the new premier within days and the only issue was whether Dowding resigned or forced the caucus to depose him. The WA party was about to make history—the election of Australia's first woman premier in dramatic circumstances. Smith wanted Hawke to endorse Lawrence publicly.

The next day Hawke pulled the political plug on Dowding and sanctioned an execution which would save his own political neck.

Though Dowding's demise was driven by the state party, state and federal interests were in harmony. Dowding's removal was necessary to revive Hawke's position in WA. It was proof again of Labor's political sophistication. Smith was the latest example of the effective machine politician which characterised the ALP during the decade. More important, though, is that Labor, unlike the Liberals in the 1980s, had alternative leaders available. In WA alone, despite WA Inc, the ALP had produced Burke, Dowding and Lawrence—all capable of winning elections.

Hawke's aide, Geoff Walsh, now rang the prime minister's department to investigate all aspects of calling a 24 March election on 16 February. There was universal support in Hawke's office for a 24 March election, led by Hawke himself. A window of opportunity was opening for Labor.

The extent of Liberal Party deterioration was revealed when Eggleton convened a meeting of all state Liberal directors in Melbourne on 8 February. Eggleton and Robb briefed the meeting on the campaign and the communications theme 'The Answer is Liberal'. A majority of state directors now argued for a tougher, more negative campaign of varying degrees. The SA director, Nick Minchin, and the Victorian director, Petro Georgiou, led this movement, a direct assault upon the agreed strategy, with support from the NSW director, Peter Kidman. Minchin said it would be unwise to focus a campaign around Peacock; that Labor had to win if leadership became the issue; that the coalition needed a negative campaign to expose Labor. Georgiou wanted a strong negative campaign but was less critical of Peacock. All directors were sceptical about Eggleton's strategy and pessimistic about the prospects. Robb, shocked at the pessimism, retreated that night to an escapist movie.

The next day, 9 February, at the Federal Executive meeting the Victorian and South Australian presidents, Michael Kroger and Bruce McDonald, argued for a reweighting towards a negative campaign. They were backed by federal president John Elliott. Minchin had already told Eggleton that the 'Q and A' theme could not sustain an entire campaign. But this was precisely the intention, as Geoffrey Cousins revealed in a forceful presentation to the executive. 'With Coca Cola we run these campaigns for three months,' he said. 'You want negative, then I'll give you negative,' Cousins told the meeting. He said the format was flexible and could be weighted more positive or negative at will. Cousins carried the meeting and the executive took heart at the overall communications message. It was the final chance for the Liberals to change their strategy. The state directors knew the politics had changed since their marketing position had been devised the previous year—Peacock's credibility was now shot—yet the campaign was pitched to his credibility.

The Liberal Secretariat had a Sweeney research report done in January which verified its strategy:

> If the Opposition can establish itself as the viable alternative
> government, the election will be a favourable foregone conclusion . . .
> Negatives regarding the government are firmly in place. Whilst there

might be a need to continually remind the electorate of the negatives, we are of the view that the campaign thrust and Mr Peacock must be positive.

However, the same Sweeney report revealed that the community was unpersuaded about the Peacock Opposition. It said:

Most uncommitted voters . . . were not at all keen on the prospect of another three years under Labor but consistently came to the same conclusion . . . namely, the Liberals are not a voting alternative . . . Attitudes to the Liberals were consistently unfavourable throughout this study . . . the Liberals seemed unsure of themselves; the Liberals are weak; the Liberals are wanting in the policy department.

The good news concerned John Hewson, who 'emerged as a real Liberal asset . . . He knows what he's talking about . . . and is identified as a potentially excellent Treasurer'.

The contradiction in this Sweeney report is obvious: it found the Opposition unconvincing but recommended a campaign based on its 'positives'. It was playing to coalition weakness. Labor, by contrast, had been advised by Cameron that the electorate's view of Peacock was final and damning. Liberal advisers like Minchin said his colleagues were making a mistake—they hoped that the campaign advertising could turn around the community's perception, but that was asking too much of advertising.

Peter Dowding surrendered his career on 11 February, when he resigned along with deputy premier Parker. When Dowding tested opinion in his Cabinet it was 10–8 against him; it was a case of resignation or execution. Parker decided to resign as deputy to give Carmen Lawrence a clean slate. On 12 February Lawrence was elected unopposed and committed herself to a sharp break with the policies and style that had led to WA Inc. Lawrence's honeymoon would coincide with Hawke's campaign.

Hawke's secret fear was that Peacock might be deposed before the election. Hawke studied the Liberals through the prism of his own history as the victor of a 1983 election eve leadership switch. Before the 1987 and 1990 elections, Hawke weighed the prospects of the Liberals playing the same card against him. He thought there was a chance, just a chance, of a return to Howard if the government recalled the parliament. It was remote, Hawke reasoned, but why take the chance? It was another argument for 24 March.

On Wednesday, 14 February, the Morgan poll showed Peacock's leadership rating plummet to 18 per cent compared with Hawke's at 55 per cent and Howard's at 28 per cent. The poll showed Hawke would be returned with about the same majority. Hawke had a busy day as host to visiting Soviet prime minister Ryzhkov, and talking to ministers Keating, Beazley, Evans and Richardson about the decision. The choice was simple—an election on 24 March or 7 April. The issue was whether to recall the parliament for a few days to allow for Keating's economic statement and further exploitation of Liberal blunders. Hawke's staff all supported a snap 24 March election.

In the early afternoon the news filtered through Parliament House that the ABC's *7.30 Report* correspondent, Paul Lyneham, would put to air that night a damaging interview with Liberal Senate deputy Austin Lewis. Labor was well briefed: the story would seal the election decision.

Just before 7.30 Hawke left his office to attend the dinner he was hosting for Ryzhkov. In the interview Lewis predicted Peacock's demise if he lost the election, criticised Howard and said the party would never return him. With hindsight the dumping of Howard was 'the right thing to do; John had had his chance and I think that if he had remained in office we would have had an election by now and we would be facing another term of the Hawke government'. Lewis criticised the Opposition's performance, saying it had not convinced the voters.

These remarks reopened personal and factional wounds which the Liberals had been nursing since the Peacock coup and the *Four Corners* program. The Lewis comments invited a reply from Howard and fanned demands for his head.

While Peacock was in the air en route to Perth, Fife as House deputy advised Lewis to offer his resignation, but Lewis was as stubborn as he was foolish. Peacock sacked Lewis by phone from Perth after he was briefed, and announced the dismissal on the *7.30 Report* in Perth. It was after 10.30 pm in Canberra and the Ryzkhov dinner was just breaking up.

The news spread amongst the ministers leaving the dinner—they smelled Liberal decay. Hawke saw the *7.30 Report* video of the Lewis meltdown at 12.15 am in his office. When the program finished, Hawke said: 'I want to go to Government House first thing Friday morning.' Later that day Hawke gave a newspaper interview:

I will be going harder in this election than in any election I have ever fought because this is the most important election in Australia since 1949 . . . The government that is elected here will determine, I believe, the sort of Australia that will go into the 21st century.
I do have a profound belief in the good sense of the electorate. They rarely get it wrong. I can't believe that in 1990 they would make that mistake . . . It would be a profound misjudgement to put the future of this country in the hands of people who can't run themselves. They are profoundly unable to run this country.

Meanwhile Peacock, sensing an election, jumped a plane back to Melbourne to be on home turf.

Hawke met Hogg, Cameron and Walsh in the afternoon for a final assessment. They considered three sets of research: the WAOP Queensland surveys of 5 February; a new WAOP survey of three seats, Melbourne Ports,

La Trobe and Denison; and an ANOP six-seat study of Ballarat, Hawker, Petrie, Phillip, Aston and Corinella. The key to Labor's election strategy was to win seats.

The first WAOP survey pointed towards wins in three Queensland seats—Kennedy, Moreton and Dawson. Cameron said in Queensland there was a slight overall swing to Labor. In Tasmania prospects were held for winning Franklin, perhaps Lyons. Victoria was Labor's problem. Cameron advised the anti-Labor swing in Victorian marginals had fallen from 7–8 per cent to 5–6 per cent. A loss of five to seven seats seemed likely in Victoria, with nine seats being the worst possibility. Cameron said the campaign in Western Australia should become a launch of Lawrence as the new leader. He believed the anti-Labor swing in the West had fallen from 9–10 per cent to around 7 per cent. It would be difficult but not impossible to hold all the WA seats. If Labor could hold the West and win in Queensland then it would probably win the election.

In South Australia Labor expected to win back Adelaide, but it was battling to hold Hawker and struggling in Kingston to defeat Janine Haines, the Democrat leader. NSW was the hardest state to analyse because of its diversity. Labor knew that Phillip was safe and felt confident about its Sydney marginals. It expected the Liberals to lose North Sydney to an independent, Ted Mack. But it had to watch four seats outside Sydney—Hunter, Calare, Eden–Monaro and Robertson. The north coast seat of Page was a possible win from the coalition.

Overall Labor had to improve an extra 1–2 per cent nationally and more in the West during the campaign to win the election. There were three possible election outcomes: a narrow Liberal victory if Labor failed to hold the West; a hung parliament with independents Haines and Mack in control; a narrow ALP win if the West was held and seats won in Queensland.[7]

Cameron and Walsh supported Hawke's 24 March date; Hogg preferred a later date, saying there was an argument for waiting in both Victoria and the West. He was worried about the imminent report on the Victorian State Bank. 'We'll have to sell the bank to save it,' he said. But Hogg knew that Hawke's mind was set.

Hawke arrived at Yarralumla at 8.30 am on 16 February to procure his election from Hayden. In 1983 Hayden had said that a drover's dog could beat Fraser. But this was no drover's dog election. Hawke was the favourite to win a fourth election in an economic climate which dictated a change of power. Labor's position had returned from the brink of despair ten weeks earlier. It had been one of the most remarkable turnarounds in Australian political history. But the result still hung on the campaign.

30
The 1990 campaign

What was an unlosable election appears to be lost.

John Howard's summary of the 1990 poll

The 1990 election again undermined the theory that governments lose elections. At every post-war election which has seen a change of power in Australia—1949, 1972, 1975 and 1983—the Opposition succeeded because it took control of the political agenda. The Opposition failed in 1990 because it was unable to satisfy this requirement.

A quick historical analysis proves the point: R. G. Menzies offered to restore the free enterprise system in 1949; E. G. Whitlam rode the 'It's Time' chariot in 1972; Malcolm Fraser promised in 1975 to 'Turn on the Lights'; and Bob Hawke in 1983 offered recovery, reconstruction and reconciliation. By comparison Andrew Peacock's 'The Answer is Liberal' was a hollow incantation.

In each of these four transitions the leader's role was paramount and the leader was true to his role—he led. Reformers do not sweep aside an old order without becoming propagandists for a new order. Australians are a cautious and conservative people; they will change but they want evidence that change means improvement.

Tony Eggleton's research was the same as Labor's—it showed the community was hostile to Hawke but unpersuaded by Peacock; that a vote against Hawke did not mean a vote for Peacock. The 1990 election was a poll that the Opposition had to win by offering evidence as a credible alternative.[1]

Labor was weaker than at the 1987 election, but the Hawke–Keating government was different from previous Labor governments facing elections—Whitlam, Chifley and Scullin. Hawke and Keating would not surren-

565

der power; they were publicly united, strong and stable, disguising their negatives, highlighting their positives.

Labor's 1990 victory reflected its three basic strengths. First, Hawke's popularity and superiority over all rivals, qualities which he continued to revive, so that Hawke outpolled Peacock 59 to 29 per cent on the 'best prime minister' question after seven years in office. Second, the grudging respect for Keating as economic manager despite his unpopularity, high interest rates and the fear of recession. Third, the continued image of Labor as a more united force than the Opposition. This image of stability owed much to the secret Kirribilli pact between Hawke and Keating which kept repressed one of the great power struggles in Australian history.

In this climate Eggleton's strategy was to improve perceptions of the Opposition rather than reinforce hostility towards the government. Eggleton says:

> Fundamental to the strategic judgement was the conclusion that the coalition could not win the election by default. Labor's vulnerability did not translate into support for the Liberals . . . Attacking Labor (ie: 'enough is enough') would not be enough . . . negative campaigning would simply consolidate support for the Democrats and minor parties . . . The Liberals would have to convince the electorate that they had the credentials to deserve support.[2]

Peacock needed an overall ten seats to win and a 2.6 per cent national uniform swing. On the new boundaries Labor's notional majority was 18 seats. For Peacock a victory would be difficult but was still within reach. Peacock hoped to best Hawke in the Great Debate; this would be the antidote to his loss of credibility.

The 1990 campaign was Peacock's second shot at the prime ministership. He understood the discipline, demands and dialects of the election trail. In 1984 Peacock beat Hawke in the campaign, but he still lost the election. But the differences between 1984 and 1990 far outweighed any similarities.

In 1984 Peacock had merely turned a pro-Labor swing into a slight pro-Liberal swing. The task in 1990 was different—Peacock had to win. But in psychological terms there was another difference. In 1984 Peacock ran a cynical negative campaign and never had to present himself as an alternative prime minister because he had no hope of winning. In 1990 his prospects of victory depended totally on his ability to offer a convincing account of himself as the alternative prime minister.

The economic climate pointed towards a change of government since Australia had undergone a protracted period of high interest rates—business rates at 20 per cent, the floating home rate at 17 per cent and cash rates at 18 per cent. Labor's economic credentials, which had been basic to its electoral success in the 1980s, were in severe jeopardy.

The 1990 campaign

The Liberals had a sound technical and organisational preparation for this campaign. The defect lay in Eggleton's election strategy: how could a campaign revive confidence in Peacock when his credibility weakness had become entrenched over the preceding month?

When Hawke called the election there was a whiff of demoralisation within the coalition. But the Liberals ran their first radio advertisement at 10.30 am, just over an hour after Hawke had left Government House. That night their television campaign began; the next morning the newspaper spreads. It was a propaganda win. Eggleton declared that the ALP organisation 'wasn't really ready for this election'.[3]

The 1990 election saw a Bob Hawke more realistic than before, introspective enough to confront the truth—there was a palpable prospect of defeat. Hawke's performance was driven by a greater sense of discipline than in either the 1984 or 1987 elections. 'He was frightened and he responded to fear,' Richard Farmer said.[4] Hawke knew that Labor's fate would depend essentially upon himself.

When Rod Cameron saw Hawke on 15 February at the meeting which confirmed the election decision, he gave Hawke ANOP's final brief on Labor's position. It summarised Hawke's campaign message:

> We know it's been hard but if there was an easy way we'd have done it long ago. Our economic policies are starting to work. It is better for Australia to keep Bob Hawke and Labor—a strong Prime Minister and a united government with a clear direction. Andrew Peacock lacks substance and is a weak leader, and the Liberal policies are confused and will not work. We have a positive plan for the future. It will take time, but it will work.[5]

In his elaboration of this position Cameron advised:

> The swinging voter mood is disillusioned, despondent and cynical. Many would genuinely like a change of government but some are not changing their vote because they lack confidence in the Opposition. To potential swingers not changing from Labor to Liberals, Labor is the 'lesser of two evils'.
>
> The basic problem with Labor is that its economic policies have hurt middle ground voters . . . we are not much better than late 1989 but the Opposition is a whole lot worse . . . Labor's task will be to continue to prove the Liberals are not offering a viable alternative . . . and most important, to indicate Labor does have direction and solutions and has not yet run its race.

Cameron said that Labor should focus on its economic credentials, the environment and its leadership, including strength and stability. Labor was most vulnerable over Liberal promises to lower interest rates and abolish the dole after nine months.[6]

Interest rates had the potential to make or break the election outcome.

The end of certainty

But the Opposition had another weapon—the threat of recession. That meant rising unemployment and a collapse of business confidence. The most spectacular corporate crashes in Australia's history had just occured or were about to occur—George Herscu's Hooker Corporation, Christopher Skase's Seven Network, Abe Goldberg's textile empire, Alan Bond, Warwick Fairfax and Tricontinental. It was a weapon the Liberals never deployed.

The structure of the ALP campaign had been discussed for some time by Hogg, Walsh and Hawke's media aide, Barrie Cassidy. The idea was to convey just one message each day, reinforced by pictures for the television news; a disciplined campaign with a tight focus. There would be almost no evening activity. Hawke faced little pressure from the party for morale-raising dinners. The staff wanted him to rest at night, sleep well and stay fresh for the days. Cassidy planned plenty of press conferences to put Peacock under matching pressure.

The Hawke camp had devised a 'rose garden' tactic—the selling of Hawke during the campaign as a governing prime minister. Hawke would announce a series of government decisions in an effort to maximise the advantage of incumbency—on science, the environment, export assistance, and a US agreement to allow Australia to assume full control of the North-West Cape base. The aim was to market Hawke as the natural prime minister.

Labor made only modest election promises which it funded fully from cuts identified by the Expenditure Review Committee. Labor wanted to nail down its own financial credibility to prepare for the assault upon Peacock. These savings of $348 million in 1990–91 were announced in Keating's Economic Statement, the major policy event of the election and the serious business of the first week.

Keating's Statement fell between the two competing tests—economic responsibility and 'cash-in-hand' for people. In announcing the Accord Mark VI, the product of Keating–Kelty collaboration, the treasurer offered a 7 per cent wage rise for 1990–91, predicted inflation at 6 per cent, and a gradual rise in living standards through a slight real wage gain plus tax cuts through a new rate scale from 1 January 1991. Keating trumpeted that the new rate scale meant taxpayers would be better off than if the 1983–84 scales had been indexed for inflation. The greatest proportional benefit went to income earners under $10 000 a year and in the $19 000–$38 000 range. But Keating's selling point was a $50 a week 'wage equivalent' package for average income earners through wage rises and tax cuts—a figure which was deceptively attractive but which, when analysed, revealed ongoing wage restraint.[7]

Keating was unashamed in his selling and ridiculed the complaint of a journalist who called his statement 'a very political document'. Keating mocked, 'What a shocking thing! This is an election campaign but don't be political.' The Statement stands in retrospect as testimony to Labor's self-delusion about its ability to avert a recession.

The long-term reform was the boost to national savings through the Labor–ACTU decision that the IRC be asked to ratify a further 3 per cent round of superannuation payments to workers by employers. Keating depicted this as a boost to retirement incomes and an impetus to national savings. It was the next step in Labor's attempt to construct an award-based superannuation edifice in the 1990s, a campaign that foundered post-election.

Two other features of the Keating package were research-driven—a $100 million extra tax on luxury cars and a new unemployment benefit system which abolished the dole and substituted in its place two new payments, a short-term job search allowance and a long-term retraining allowance. The car tax was the remnant of Cameron's advice in December to produce new policies. It was included on urging from Hawke's office, not the treasury. It was a straight political decision to appeal to the prejudices of ANOP's swinging voters by hitting luxury imports and the mega-rich; the worst type of corruption of the policy process by market research. It was abandoned post-election. The unemployment benefit change followed Cameron's advice in his election eve memo to Hawke about the electoral potency of the Liberal dole abolition pledge. Labor was trying to be tough but constructive with its retraining schemes.

There was a sharp note of cynicism in media reaction to Keating's Statement and the business community was disenchanted. Its critique was that Keating's progress in tackling the fundamental economic problems was too slow. The document rested upon the ALP–ACTU Accord—but the Accord's utility was now severely limited.

The Liberals won the first week of the campaign and sent a scare through the ALP camp. Hawke's first campaign day, Monday 19 February, was a disaster but an insight into modern election techniques. In the morning Hawke arrived at the Opera House to a pilots' demonstration and once inside he angrily pushed away a cluster of microphones. His short fuse on opening day became a massive television event; the microphone incident was played and replayed. Swinging voters had no truck with leaders who showed abrupt anger. Hawke could perform superbly all day but if, in the space of thirty seconds, he was guilty of the wrong gesture or misplaced remark, devoid of import but captured on celluloid, then the day was lost. Politics, like football, had become dominated by defence.

Peacock opened with a visit to an export cheese factory that had gone into liquidation blaming the interest rates which the opposition pledged to cut. It gave ALP tacticians the chills that night—a glimpse of the 'human drama' of high interest rates which Peacock might produce for every television evening news.

But Labor was plagued by three bigger events. First, the release of the

Victorian auditor's report showing a potential loss for the State Bank of $1.3 billion—the incident which Hogg had been dreading. Victorian taxpayers would bear the brunt of the loss, as the media emphasised. The Cain government agreed to inject $795 million to cover the expected losses by the bank's merchant arm, Tricontinental, which would hurt future state budgets. The Bank board resigned en masse, some reluctantly. Cain, with typical self-righteousness, defended his treasurer, Rob Jolly, and said there was no need for him to resign—a sentiment few Victorians shared. At no stage did Cain or Jolly admit their policy or philosophy was to blame, a defiance which fed electoral retribution. Honest people were forced to the logic of the ballot box to deal with such a government. A stench rose from the Victorian Labor government as it sank into a political abyss beyond salvation.

Second, Hawke, the figure of consensus in the 1983 campaign, was being hounded by symbols of division and demonstrators full of hate. The pilots were tormenting him and his staff feared an over-reaction. They knew Cameron's warning from December: if Hawke reverted to his 1989 aggressive rhetoric against the pilots then Labor's position would collapse. The pilots sensed Hawke was uneasy but they were politically inept, unable to provoke the response which could turn the election. Late in the first week the television pictures showed Hazel as well as Hawke being hounded by angry pilots. From this point the pilots were finished.

Third, Labor was rocked by the sensational revelation that the National Crime Authority (NCA) was investigating John Elliott over dealings involving Harlin and Elders–IXL. The ABC's *7.30 Report* broke this story on 20 February, which was damaging for Labor because it appeared to be an ALP 'dirty trick' against Elliott for political reasons. Elliott went public with fanfare, declared that nobody from the NCA had approached him or Elders, announced his innocence and pointed to a political witch-hunt.

Hawke was bound by secrecy which meant he could neither confirm nor deny any NCA inquiry; to defuse the issue he offered Peacock access to any NCA references relating to any Elliott inquiry. But the two men subsequently fell out over the degree of access and the conditions. Meanwhile Elliott unveiled at a huge Melbourne business lunch his plan to restructure Elders. It would be a brewing company called Fosters, quite different from the conglomerate Elliott had spent years building. Elliott would resign as its chief executive but remain as chairman. It was an exquisite irony: Elliott had become a campaign issue at the very time his business situation was growing desperate.

At the end of the first week Hawke's media boss, Barrie Cassidy, declared it a substantial win to Peacock. Morale inside the Liberal camp was rising. Peacock had regained momentum after Hawke's election strike just eight days earlier.

The result was a sharper focus on the Great Debate on television on

The 1990 campaign

Sunday 25 February. Labor had put the debate at the start of the campaign to reduce its importance, but events had conspired against it. If Peacock outdebated Hawke then Labor's campaign ace—Peacock's poor credibility—would be demolished. Eggleton said: 'Andrew only has to draw to be in a good position and I'll be surprised if he can't get a draw.'[8] Hawke faced a moment of destiny; it was the decisive point of the 1990 election.

From late Saturday Hawke was at Kirribilli where he wrote out and memorised his pitch using the egg-timer from the kitchen to get his timing exact. On Saturday morning he spoke to his mate, horsetrainer Colin Hayes, about the form and the debate. Hawke believed he was better than Peacock—on detail, policy and debate. The orthodoxy was that Peacock had won the 1984 debate, a point Peacock hammered when he had demanded another debate. There was only one way for Hawke to spike Peacock's claim—debate him again. It was a risky decision for Hawke which could be fatal if he lost.

In 1989 both Graham Richardson and Geoff Walsh had agreed that Hawke should debate Peacock. Yet most ALP machine chiefs were horrified. Hawke's office had tried to ensure a sterile encounter, without journalists, just a moderator with set piece presentations from the leaders. Hogg and Hawke's office fought over the format until Hogg finally prevailed and a more lively format involving media questions and giving the leaders the right to question each other was agreed upon.

Hawke's preparation had been for a debate without notes, but this guideline was not watertight. The day of the debate Geoff Walsh had to tell Hawke that Peacock would be using notes; he had seen the lectern being erected at the studio. It was the toughest message Walsh ever gave Hawke, who was shocked and demanded that the rules be checked. Hogg faxed them to Hawke—a debate without notes was preferred but notes were not banned. Hawke was angry, blaming Hogg for the blunder. Still, he went without notes—and he was right. In the afternoon Cameron and Gibbs briefed Hawke with Cameron advising that the voters wanted substance, substance, substance. They would be repelled by personal criticism or smart remarks.

Peacock's office had briefs from shadow ministers in the three areas for debate—the economy, social policy and environment. Peacock had plenty of notes. But his organisers had blundered on the rules which allowed the leaders to question each other and then ask a supplementary question. Peacock was unprepared for supplementary questions.

Hawke won the toss and spoke last, an advantage. At 7.20 pm leaders and journalists, wired up, made up, tensed up, were ready in the ABC studios. They stayed stock still in their places for a long ten minutes before opening to a television audience which totalled on average eight million viewers through the ABC and Nine National Network.

Peacock began with confidence and flourish; Hawke was nervous, subdued and looked old. Peacock called for 'a new era, a new epoch and a new spirit . . . you know and I know that the economy is on the brink of collapse'. Hawke relied on relativity: 'Next month you must make the decision as to who is the best equipped to run the Australian economy.' Peacock started better but Hawke was more consistent. Peacock appeared to grow over-confident. He sensed he was on top of a nervous Hawke and he lost concentration. When the debate hit the environment segment Hawke moved into the ascendancy. Three times Peacock declined to ask Hawke questions while Hawke's questions were pertinent. Hawke finished stronger in the final summaries. Peacock left the ABC studios immediately, saying that he had won. Hawke and Hazel stayed and mingled with the media and ABC staff. Hawke said he felt comfortable.

Hawke and his entourage returned to the Ramada Hotel, their Sydney HQ, where Hawke stepped out of the lift to spontaneous applause from ALP staff and workers. Then the calls came—Keating, Singleton, Richardson, declaring Hawke the winner. In his post-election report Eggleton dismissed the debate as a 'non-event' and the result 'probably close to a draw'.

But the only poll showing Peacock doing well came from the Liberal perception analysers on the night—an audience of 100 in a theatre twirling knobs showing how they felt. Every other published poll pointed to a Hawke win. Newspoll scored a 46 to 36 per cent Hawke win and 13 per cent said they were likely to change their vote as a result of the debate. It found that seven out of ten adults watched at least part of the debate. The Nine Network phone-in, a dubious method, had 736 000 respondents breaking 55 to 47 per cent for Hawke. Labor's ANOP surveys found Hawke won the 'most impressive' test 42 to 26 per cent and the 'most believable' 51 to 26 per cent.

Peacock says: 'I still think I beat Hawke. But I made a mistake—I got too cocky during the debate. Half way through I was so confident that I let him get back into it. I didn't fight to the end.'[9]

In retrospect Labor advisers saw the debate as central to Hawke's reelection. Margaret Gibbs, ANOP's qualitative research director, who spent the entire campaign with swinging voters, said she believed the debate was crucial. Peacock had failed to use the debate to break his central problem, credibility.

It was clearly the turning point of the campaign for Hawke. From this point he was a model of disciplined confidence. Hawke's judgement of himself and Peacock had been confirmed.

Post-debate the Liberals adjusted their advertising strategy to present Peacock as merely the leader of a team. Eggleton began to run advertisements featuring Hewson, Howard and Chaney. 'I want to present Andrew as chairman of the board,' he said. 'It makes sense for the Opposition to present itself as an alternative government with a team of people. I'm not embarrassed talking about Andrew Peacock as chairman of the board.'

By contrast Labor's advertising campaign began with four television commercials featuring Hawke sitting at a shiny desk in brown suit, light tie, crisp white shirt, crowned with silver hair, looking confident and confiding, the most natural PM since Menzies. When John Singleton made the commercials he was amazed at Hawke. 'A professional actor couldn't have done it any better,' Singleton said.

The themes were Labor's superiority on leadership, unity and affordable policies, recognition that 'nothing worthwhile comes easy', and that the nation was now in a position to benefit from its sacrifices, and finally the contrast between Labor competence and Liberal division. Hawke's script read: 'The office of Prime Minister is a great responsibility and privilege, but it's not an easy job. I know just how hard it is and I know you just couldn't do it without loyal support of your family, your colleagues and your party . . . if you can't govern your party in Opposition then there's no way you can govern the country.' The pictures showed Hawke, then Hawke and his ministers, then Hawke, Hazel and family. From the start to the end Labor's advertising campaign focused on Hawke. Labor played Hawke while the Liberals were apologetic about Peacock.

The National Party launched its campaign on 28 February, a low key affair in Bathurst since Peacock had persuaded Blunt that most of the main pledges should be left for the Liberal launch. Former leader Ian Sinclair was not present. Blunt's support for a uranium enrichment industry for which there had been no public demand got most media attention, although the Nationals had not planned this. Blunt promised that the Coronation Hill mine would proceed, pledged that Labor's 'three mine' uranium policy would be abolished and rejected the use of the external affairs power to protect the environment. His speech betrayed the Nationals' grim attachment to development at a time when some of their own seats were turning 'green'. The Australian Conservation Foundation and the Wilderness Society attacked the speech.

The Nationals aspired to protect their own turf and let the Liberals win the election, and failed on both counts. Blunt and Peacock spoke each morning of the campaign to coordinate their positions. Blunt's campaign was too defensive. He was a new federal leader, unknown even within traditional National areas, unable or unwilling to project himself in the campaign. He failed completely to counter the adverse National Party image in NSW and Queensland which was the product of state political factors. He dreamt about becoming deputy prime minister but lacked the will to power of his predecessors.

The Liberal launch on 5 March, ironically the seventh anniversary of Hawke's election, was a slick television 'documentary' featuring Peacock and Hewson, families discussing their plight and the Liberals pledging to 'stop the hurt'. The lunchtime 'live' meeting in Melbourne was strictly for the faithful, who heard Fred Chaney introduce Peacock with a gushing: 'Isn't it marvellous to have the smell of victory.' But the public only saw the professional television package where Peacock promised to cut interest rates, cut taxes 20 per cent for an average family, protect the aged and give higher pay for harder work. There were three themes in the Peacock pitch—the failure of the Hawke era, the promise of a better deal for families and Middle Australia, and a coming new era of productivity.

Peacock's claims were immense—lower taxes, interest rates that will 'come down and stay down', lower inflation, spending cuts, higher real wages and foreign debt stabilisation. His speech was a relaunch of the EAP from the previous October. He offered few specifics that were new—a $1000 million road program, a special environmental deal for NSW, and a claimed $550 million instant gain from the licence sale for a second mobile phone service. The conflict in Peacock was between the national crisis he proclaimed and the relatively painless solution he offered.

Peacock's pitch was weighted more to family compassion than economic management. It is true that the EAP was radical in its micro-economic reforms—labour market deregulation, privatisation, and reforms on the waterfront, to coastal shipping and telecommunications. Yet Peacock never put these 'hard' policies into the campaign foreground. The bias in Peacock's launch and rhetoric was to family relief. lower interest rates and better living standards. Peacock never really tried to win the election on superior economic management credentials.

The Peacock launch was a marketing success, slick, smooth, professional. Eggleton called it 'our single most important communication of the campaign'. But the real story of the television package was the projection of John Hewson. In retrospect, the significance of Peacock's launch is that it launched Hewson on the national stage for the first time. Hewson was given almost equal billing to Peacock. He spoke quietly, sensibly, naturally about the economy.

However the momentum from Peacock's launch was squandered the next day when he refused to hold a media conference and sent Hewson in his place. At the 6 am strategy meeting the day after the launch, Peacock's press aide, John Wells, pushed for a Peacock media conference the same day. But the senior advisers Eggleton and Robb disagreed, preferring to use Hewson—a decision which betrayed their sensitivity about Peacock. They sought to protect Peacock at the precise time that he should have been aggressive. The 'protection' of the leader for nearly two full days after the launch was a mistake, as Eggleton later admitted.

These events highlighted a feature of the 1990 campaign—the roles of Keating and Hewson as economic spokesmen to Hawke and Peacock. Given Keating's unpopularity Labor strategists were keen to keep him off the television news and he did not appear in the paid advertising campaign. Keating declared that he wanted to remain in politics to preside over Australia's economic restructuring. After that he said: 'I become the good

574

time person that Andrew Peacock wants to become without the hard work . . . I become the nice guy.'

The Hawke–Keating team, despite their repressed power struggle, was a vital plus for Labor. By contrast, the coalition was unable to strike a matching complementarity between Peacock and Hewson. ANOP's Margaret Gibbs said of the research groups: 'I would hold up a photograph of Peacock and the group would be unimpressed. When I put a photograph of Hewson with Peacock they'd like it. Then they'd ask if I could remove the Peacock photograph altogether.'[10]

Hewson's credibility was a function of Peacock's credibility problem. The better Hewson looked the worse Peacock looked. This process offered no net gain to the coalition. Hogg, convinced by the ANOP research on Peacock, said: 'His rating is about as low as you can get. Peacock is seen to be without substance and there's no way this will change over the course of the campaign.'[11]

A Newspoll published two days after Peacock's launch showed that Labor headed the coalition on every single 'issues' test. Labor was seen as the best party to manage the economy by 38 to 31 per cent; the environment by 38 to 17 per cent; welfare by 43 to 27 per cent. On leadership Labor's lead was 52 to 17 per cent.

In Bob Hawke's launch, three days after Peacock's, the tone was muted, the style was straight, and the tactic was to stage a diversion. The television presentation, unlike the Liberals', was merely a film of the lunchtime launch. The site was perfect—Brisbane, where Labor was the flavour after decades in the wilderness. The Hawke launch was a masterpiece of research-driven politics where Hawke was positioned to convey images of substance, realism and compassion.

The key to the Hawke launch lay in Cameron's strategic appreciation: 'We must create diversions and camouflage the situation because we're naked.' Cameron told Labor to conceal its weakness—the state of the economy; exaggerate its plus—the environment as an issue; offer hope through themes with a futuristic flavour suggesting Labor still had answers. Hawke's real policy position was 'more of the same' since Keating had imposed this stance on the government. Labor's aim in the campaign was to disguise this position because the voters would not accept 'more of the same'.

Hawke appeared in dark grey suit against a brown backdrop, his hair whiter than ever. 'It's Uncle Bob,' quipped Bill Kelty. The television presentation was simple—Hawke reading his speech, no graphics, no film. Labor did not mind being boring. The marketing had one message above all—Hawke is a leader of substance. The prelude to Hawke's arrival was speeches from John Bannon and Wayne Goss, the oldest serving and latest elected Labor premiers—the two most popular politicians in Australia.

Hawke began with an admission of the pain caused by his high interest rate policies. He was understanding but not apologetic. He said that 'anybody who tells the people of Australia that the future lies at the end of an easy road is not fit to be your Prime Minister'—an obvious dig at Peacock. The tactic was to paint Peacock as the pedlar of easy promises and Labor as the upholder of responsibility. Hawke's speech was strictly political; it was sterile as an economic or policy blueprint. He had a grab-bag of ideas and some policy changes, packaged as vision, heavy with rhetoric about an 'historic step' and 'great national goals' but much oversold.

Hawke marketed the idea of the 'clever country' through a $100 million annual initiative over five years for fifty new world class research centres—an idea invited by the research. Hawke announced a lifting of child care places to 250 000 by spending an extra $398 million, but sensibly modified policy by funding private as well as public places. He defended the capital gains tax on fairness grounds, put more funds into urban transport, got his biggest cheer for his 'Medicare stays' declaration and attacked the coalition with the best slogan of the campaign: 'A party that cannot govern itself cannot govern Australia.'

Hawke, unlike Peacock, gave a full media conference the day after his launch and kept it mistake-free. Newspoll and the Morgan poll taken the weekend before the launches had both shown Labor leading 42 to 39 per cent on the primary vote. Labor was sure the policy launch week was a further plus. In the highbrow press the economic commentators attacked Labor's failure to address the issues of foreign debt, the current account and national productivity—but Hawke and Keating were not chasing this constituency.

It became apparent that Peacock, unlike Howard in 1987, was not lifting his approval rating, which was normal for an Opposition leader during a campaign. This left the conclusion that Howard had been a better campaigner for the Liberals in 1987 than was Peacock in 1990. During the 1987 campaign Howard's approval rating had risen to from 34 to 44 per cent while Peacock's rating in the 1990 campaign went from only 25 to 30 per cent on the Morgan figures.

During the campaign Labor received quantitative research (the numbers) in thirty marginal seats from ANOP and WAOP. Its qualitative work (the mood based on group discussions) came from ANOP under Gibbs' supervision. This drew on a total of 150 individual groups and provided valuable input for Cameron's campaign update each second day to Hogg at HQ, Singleton at the agency, Walsh in Hawke's office and all state secretaries. This featured 'lines and themes' showing what the swingers felt. Virtually every major line used by Hawke during the campaign was drawn from these research briefs.

For instance, Gibbs found the swingers could not accept 'the economy is starting to improve', but they were a touch receptive to 'our economic policies are starting to work'. So Hawke used one, not the other. Once a week Cameron provided a bigger overview of the campaign's progress, dealing with trends state by state.

Gibbs reported from the groups that the Liberal 'questions and answers' campaign was not working. Her groups would watch the Peacock pledge to cut interest rates and say, 'But how will he do it?' She found the swingers aware of conflicting Liberal remarks on interest rates. She advised the use of the line: 'The Liberals can't reduce interest rates and John Howard has been honest enough to admit this.' Paul Keating just satirised the Liberal theme: 'If the answer's Liberal then it must have been one helluva question.'

The greatest campaign shock for Labor was delivered not by the Opposition but by the Australian Democrats in Perth on 12 March. The WA Democrats decided to direct their preferences against sitting members, which was the contrary to the Democrat split ticket approach in other states. Its consequences in the West would be disastrous for Labor, which was fighting to hold as many as six marginal seats. If this Democrat decision were implemented then Labor's preference strategy as far as WA was concerned would collapse.

The decision, typical of the Democrats, was made without any appreciation of what it meant. The rationale—a plague on both their houses—was aimed at securing the defeat of all sitting members since both major parties had failed. In practice it was a body blow to Labor and a boost to the Liberals. The Democrats were angered by Labor's earlier decision to give its preferences to the strong WA Green party ahead of the Democrats, a move which had an outside chance of costing the Democrats a WA Senate seat. The Labor camp was outraged and ALP WA secretary Steve Smith declared, 'If the position is maintained what it means is that a vote for the Democrats in Western Australia is a vote for Andrew Peacock.' He said the decision had the potential to lose Hawke the election. Malcolm Mackerras declared, 'In every WA seat that matters, Labor is now in danger.'

As soon as the WA Democrat decision was announced the ALP launched a counter-offensive. Graham Richardson called upon Janine Haines to show some leadership and get the decision reversed. Smith spoke to the WA Democrats, warning that this decision alone could make Peacock prime minister. Hawke said that the coalition, which would benefit from the WA Democrats' decision, stood for more uranium mining, a uranium enrichment plant, mining in Kakadu and abolition of the capital gains tax—all abhorrent to the Democrats. The upshot was probably inevitable—the WA Democrats agreed to reconsider and switched to a split ticket, a decision that was fundamental for ALP fortunes.

As the campaign neared its final week it was dominated by two trends—Labor's historic decision to appeal directly for minor party preferences, and the Liberal search for a circuit-breaker to turn sentiment in its favour.

The entire weight of Labor's preference strategy, pursued by Hawke and Richardson over the preceding 18 months, was now brought to bear. It was Rod Cameron who persuaded Hogg to launch an advertising campaign to win the preferences of third party voters. This was a new step for Labor; it had never made such a campaign appeal before. It implicitly conceded the loss of the primary vote in a bid to win the preference vote, which is why it was contentious.

Hogg had to coax some state branches to secure their agreement. Queensland secretary Wayne Swan asked Hogg to speak on a phone hook-up to persuade his people. When asked whether the advertisement he proposed would only reinforce Labor's loss of the primary vote Hogg replied: 'Yes, it does. We don't pretend otherwise. But you must understand these votes are lost and they're not coming back. These people have decided against us. So our aim must be to win their preferences.'

These words captured the entire Hawke–Richardson preference strategy. The advertising campaign during the last week was the logical extension of this strategy. Labor stuck by this line until voting day. It was a policy and electoral strategy which finance minister Peter Walsh had criticised before the election and would savage after the election from the backbench.

Hogg and Cameron wrote the script for the famous advertisement; it was rewritten by Gibbs and given to Singleton on 10 March. Gibbs pitched the script to the thinking of the undecided voters:

> The decision to be made by Democrat, Green and Independent voters is: who will govern the country? Labor or the Liberal–Nationals? That's why preferences will count in the House of Representatives. The choice for Democrats and Greens is crystal clear. A Liberal–National government would mine Kakadu, build uranium enrichment plants and dismantle Medicare. The Liberal–Nationals stand for just about everything the Democrats and Greens oppose. But the real choice for Democrat and Green voters is who you want to be Prime Minister of Australia—Bob Hawke or Andrew Peacock? If you care about the environment, if you care about the future of Australia, your preference choice must be Labor. Put the Liberals and Nationals last.

During the final week both Liberal and Labor research showed an alarmingly high number of 'undecideds'. Preferences would decide the result, as Labor had known for eighteen months. Hogg as campaign director took the responsibility for this advertising strategy. He did not seek Hawke's approval although Hawke was aware of the plan. Hogg regarded this advertisement as the most successful of Labor's campaign.

ANOP found during the campaign a steady rise in the percentage of Democrat preferences towards Labor, from 50 per cent at the start to 60 per cent at the end. If this was accurate and this lift was secured during the campaign then it would have been decisive. It meant a switch of one in ten Democrat preferences to Labor. Given that the Democrats polled just over 10 per cent of the primary vote, this represented a shift in the national two party preferred vote of one per cent—potentially the difference between winning and losing the election.

A fortnight from home the Liberals knew they were losing. Their intelligence came from their quantitative research program organised by Federal Secretariat research director Ed Lockhart, and conducted by Morgan in a total of 16 marginal seats. These results were similar to those of the Morgan published polls during the campaign.

At Liberal campaign headquarters in Melbourne there was a revolt under way. The professionals—Jon Gaul, Alistair Drysdale, Graham Morris, along with Lockhart—wanted drastic changes to the strategy. Their instinct and their research told them the Liberal campaign was not impacting. Lockhart's results and the published polls were now supported by the Sweeney qualitative research.

Ron Klein, who conducted the Sweeney groups for the Liberals, had begun the campaign with confidence. By mid-campaign Klein's group sessions had convinced him otherwise. He told one staffer, 'Our advertising is passing the voters like a ship in the night.' Klein found that Peacock's standing was not improving, that interest rates were not biting for the Liberals and that their campaign was going nowhere. The swingers saw little difference between the sides.

The story of the last fortnight of the 1990 campaign for the Liberals was their futile but timid search for a new twist—a scare on capital gains tax and superannuation, Peacock's effort to generate enthusiasm by moving into public rallies and finally, the surprise issue of the election, the Multi-Function Polis (MFP) uproar. At the strategic level it saw a battle within the campaign headquarters over the advertising campaign which was won comprehensively by George Patterson's chief, Geoffrey Cousins, who quashed the revolt of the advisers.

Peacock and Hewson began the second last week with the claim that Labor's capital gains tax would hit superannuation payouts, a research-inspired ploy. Eggleton declared the aim was 'to spell out more the differences and the choices'. The effort began when the Association of Superannuation Funds said payouts could be cut by about 2 per cent, or $2550 off a $150 000 benefit.

Labor, familiar with the pattern of Liberal campaigns, was ready. Keating, playing the role of defensive sweeper in this election, hit back hard at the Liberals with an effective reply—the coalition was promising to abolish Labor's system of award-based superannuation. In short, the coalition was hardly in a strong position to win a debate on superannuation when it opposed Labor's policy of another 3 per cent employer contribution to employee superannuation for seven million workers as part of the next national wage case. Keating and the Opposition fell into an arcane squabble about the impact of capital gains tax on such retirement benefits.

As the final week approached Peacock's frustration finally exploded.

He reflects: 'Being honest, I don't think that I have ever campaigned so badly. I was prepared to tolerate a sterile campaign which was wrong. It was largely geared to photo and television opportunities. I realised as the campaign progressed that this wasn't my style, it wasn't me. I refused to continue and demanded a switch to public rallies which meant my last week was my best.'[12]

The rallies began in Perth on Friday 16 March and followed in Melbourne, then Sydney. Perth was the best, with more than 5000 people including many shoppers crammed into Forrest Place, 16 years after Gough Whitlam was pelted with eggs and tomatoes at the same site. The rally was a tonic for Peacock; the Liberals had brought spontaneity into an artificial campaign.

However, the same day at the Liberal campaign headquarters, the final push to revamp the Liberal advertising campaign was broken. The professionals wanted a change in advertising. At this meeting Klein warned, 'We're going to lose unless we change advertising strategy.' Klein wrote a 15-point summary for himself from the group discussions, concluding: 'Nobody believed the answer was Liberal.' It was a deadly conclusion by the party's commissioned researcher. Klein's appreciation was shared by Gaul, Drysdale and Graham Morris, who had been pressing for changes—but their demands were thwarted.

The dominant figure at the Liberal headquarters was Geoffrey Cousins, who says: 'The research clearly showed that the Australian people thought they knew every wrinkle on Andrew Peacock's face. They knew him well and they did not want to elect him. According to that research a negative campaign would not have produced a win for the Liberals. Unless we could convince voters that Andrew Peacock had some answers then his chances of being elected were slim.'[13]

While Labor had a preference strategy, the Liberals strove to win on the primary vote. Eggleton said: 'From our research I think we started the last week with 15 to 20 per cent of voters undecided.' His research showed that the voters were stubborn—they wanted a change, they didn't trust the coalition, and they had trouble differentiating between the sides.

The final week saw the bizarre eruption of a 'sleeping issue'—the Multi-Function Polis (MFP), the hi-tech futuristic city which was the subject of a joint Japan–Australia feasibility study. The lack of definition of the MFP had allowed a climate of mistrust to ferment, reinforced since nobody knew if the MFP concept was viable. An alliance from the far-right League of Rights to the far-left Rainbow Alliance was campaigning against the MFP.

Several coalition figures—Charles Blunt, Wal Fife and Andrew Robb—detected a strong grassroots hostility towards the MFP. Robb obtained a copy of a recent consultant's report on the MFP by Arthur Anderson and Company and decided the proposal was a nonsense. Fife had requested a position on the MFP from Peacock's office. The existing coalition policy had been restated during the campaign: 'The proposal is unique for Australia and deserves extensive consideration.' The relevant shadow minister, John Howard, declared in mid-campaign: 'I don't think we should bury the concept in a sea of hostility before we know anything about it.' The coalition over three years had thought little about the MFP; but it now had an incentive to bury it.

Robb encouraged Peacock to oppose the concept; Peacock raised the MFP issue on 15 March in his phone hook-up with the other leaders, put the policy change to the meeting and secured their backing. Public opinion, to the extent it knew about the MFP, was adverse, driven by hostility towards Japanese investment. Peacock did not see the MFP as a major national issue nor did he aspire to make it one; he merely aimed to win votes in certain areas by reversing the coalition position eight days before the poll. In a tight contest any edge might make the difference. The Opposition never planned any high-profile announcement of this policy change. But there was a blunder in Peacock's office.

On Friday 16 March a telex was drafted in Peacock's office under Robb's direction, saying a coalition government would not proceed with the MFP. In explaining the reason the statement said: 'Our policy on immigration is well understood. We reject the notion of any development which would establish an enclave.' The statement said the MFP would achieve nothing that could not flow from direct investment, scientific exchanges and joint ventures.

This gave coalition candidates the clearance from Peacock to condemn the MFP on immigration grounds as threatening an enclave in Australia. This message was intended for transmission to Fife, who had requested a clarification, and to all Liberal candidates. But in a misunderstanding the statement was also issued as a Peacock press release. It was put into the press boxes of a deserted Canberra Press Gallery at 7.30 pm Friday evening, with most bureaus empty. The formula which Peacock had only intended his candidates to use at their discretion was promulgated, by mistake, formally under his own name.

The policy change was important and Robb was aware of the criticism which the coalition might incur. He let Peacock make his own judgement. The symbolism of the decision was powerful. Peacock was telling Japan that Australia was not interested in a decision on the MFP on the merits. The MFP might or might not prove feasible—but the Opposition rejected it on 'enclave' grounds.

In fact, the 1987 principles which governed the Australia–Japan feasibility study explicitly rejected the enclave concept. The idea of any Australian government planning a Japanese enclave in Australia was absurd. The Japanese involved in the MFP study included, among others, the head of Nippon Steel, whose company alone took more Australian exports each year than the entire United Kingdom.

The substance in this issue transcended the MFP itself. The real point was best made by ANZ chief executive Will Bailey:

> Asia in the 1990s will have a surplus of funds and a growing and wealthy class of entrepreneurs looking for a place to invest. If Australia does not accept and accommodate Asian investment it will go elsewhere and we will be locked out of Asian markets . . . we will merely become white servants to Asian tourists.

On 19 March *The Australian* published a page one commentary in which I said:

> Mr Peacock has stooped to exploit immigration fears and anti-Japanese sentiment in a way which suggests that Australia's national interests are best preserved by keeping Mr Peacock in opposition. Contrary to Mr Peacock's claims in his latest election ploy, there has never been any prospect that a Japanese 'enclave' would be established in Australia under the 'future city' MFP concept . . . This is accepted by both the Australian and Japanese governments.[14]

During his morning conference call, Peacock reached his lowest point. 'We've lost,' he told Eggleton, 'It's the Kelly article about not being suitable to be Prime Minister.' Eggleton delivered a strong pep talk. He told Peacock not to worry, that the MFP issue had been a blunder, not a strategic mistake. But Peacock and Hawke were now emotionally involved in the issue.

Hawke was emotional because he believed that Peacock had damaged the national interest by trying to win votes on a racial theme. Hawke said that Peacock's enclave claim was a 'lie'. Hawke asked: 'What sort of vein in Australian politics is he trying to tap with that lie?' Peacock was rebuffed by the NSW Liberal premier, Nick Greiner, who wanted Sydney to become the MFP site. Greiner said that Peacock's description of the MFP as an 'enclave' had already been unanimously rejected by all involved in the project—a repudiation of his federal leader.

The issue dominated Peacock's National Press Club appearance on 20 March where he was passionate in denying any exploitation of racial sentiment. But he still launched an emotional attack upon the MFP, claiming that Australians would either be denied access to the MFP or employed there on a subservient basis: 'I don't like enclaves. I don't think most Australians do . . . Doesn't have to be an enclave based on race. This is a very elitist concept . . . I mean you try and get a job in there, give it a try, I'll have a few bob on now that you won't be able to get in there unless you're tackling one of the lesser tasks within the city.'[15] The lunch finished with a nasty exchange on the floor between Peacock and myself which was filmed and run on the television news that night. Eggleton's post-election opinion was that the MFP issue was a net gain for the coalition and the Sweeney post-election research said that 'there were some Liberal votes won on the MFP'.[16] Robb believed the MFP provoked Peacock's fighting instincts at the right time.

However, the greatest potential gain for the Opposition towards the campaign's end was the evidence that Keating's policy was being derailed. In the second last week the February jobless figures showed a sharp lift in unemployment from 6.1 to 6.5 per cent. Keating attributed the rise to an increase in those who were actively seeking work. He pledged that Labor would deliver a managed slowdown. The alternative from the Opposition was 'the same solution they inflicted upon Australia last time—a very deep recession . . . the early 1980s revisited, but revisited with such severity that Australia may never recover. We will avoid that outcome because the government has applied policy in a properly structured way'.[17]

The national accounts figures on 21 March, three days before the poll, showed the economy contracting 0.2 per cent during the December quarter, which went halfway to meeting the textbook definition of a recession as two successive negative quarters. Hewson said the figures confirmed the Opposition's warning about a recession. But Keating called the figures a 'beautiful set of numbers', because national spending had fallen below production which was leading to an increase in exports.

Keating denied that the figures suggested that Australia was on the brink of a recession. In typical fashion he argued that 'the switch the government wanted from the domestic to the external sector is actually occurring'.[18] Keating was correct in his prediction that this quarter would later be revised to show positive growth—but the June and September quarters 1990 would confirm a recession nine months later. The newspaper headlines the next day were lethal for the government, with the threat of recession receiving vast publicity. It was at this point that Keating began to reveal his nerves. Hawke and Keating feared a defeat.

The next day Keating declared that if reelected he would tell the Reserve Bank to lower interest rates by as much as one percentage point. This would quickly flow through into housing to take rates below 17 per cent. This was a 'last resort' declaration by a treasurer who always refused to nominate either the time or size of future interest rate changes. Keating was alarmed both about the economy and the apparent swing back to the Liberals in the final week.

Labor, having begun the campaign by ridiculing Peacock for offering 'massive' interest rate cuts, finished by doing exactly the same. It was frightened about the Liberals's final throw—their 'poll-induced' late swing.

The Morgan poll, which had shown a strong ALP win throughout the campaign, registered a sharp pro-Liberal swing in the final week. Morgan produced a poll taken on 20 March and another from 21–22 March, on the eve of the 24 March election. The first poll showed a coalition primary vote lead of 40.5 to 39.5 per cent. The second showed an even greater coalition lead of 42 to 39.5 per cent. The ALP was furious with the impression of a poll-induced 'Liberal bandwagon'. The Morgan trend, however, was contrary to Newspoll's, which still showed a clear Labor win.

As the campaign closed Peacock and Eggleton were hopeful but not confident. Hewson, though, believed he was about to become treasurer. Hawke was still optimistic. In their final phone hook-up the ALP secretaries estimated a very narrow ALP win with big losses in Victoria, gains in Queensland and the election being decided in the West.

31
Why Labor won

For much of the campaign voters perceived that, if elected, the coalition would do a worse job than Labor.
Tony Eggleton's post-election report as Liberal director

The 1990 election mirrored the tribulations facing Australia in its transition from a closed to an open economy. The issues in 1990 were different from those which had shaped campaigns since 1949—bank nationalisation, Communist Party dissolution, the United States alliance, State Aid, the Vietnam commitment, the Whitlam dismissal or the hip pocket nerve. The voters knew that Australia faced a protracted challenge and they were dismayed by the choice between a fourth term government and an uncertain Opposition.

But the Hawke and Peacock platforms, contrary to their rhetoric, revealed the convergence of Australian politics in the 1980s around the orthodoxies of smaller government, deregulation, belief in the market and the move towards an open economy. The differences between the sides would grow rapidly after the election when the 1990s recession would see Labor attempt to revive its traditional support for a government inspired economic and employment recovery. However before the recession, still in the twilight of the 1980s expansion, the community struggled with the dialogue over productivity, national savings and export performance, and had trouble drawing sharp distinctions between the parties.

The main difference, in fact, was over the ALP–ACTU Accord. Labor promised to make the economic adjustment within an Accord framework, negotiating trade-offs with the unions. The Liberals pledged to deregulate Australia's centralised wages system, reduce union power and allow more direct employer–employee bargaining. The Liberals offered a faster pace of economic reform, but they failed to capture the community's mind or heart with their appeal.

585

The impact of fiscal discipline was apparent, neither side issuing grossly irresponsible promises—they left this to the Democrats. Hawke's three year $1484 million program was fully funded; so was Peacock's first-year $2568 million program. Most Opposition policies were detailed and released a fair time before the campaign. There was an abundance of detailed published data about the Hawke government performance.

The central message from the election cannot be ignored as an insight into Australian democracy. It defied the axiom 'governments lose elections'. The 1990 poll showed that voters will only change the government if they have a degree of confidence in the alternative.

The election revealed the high costs of the modern campaign. The Liberal campaign cost $9.5 million plus extras—about $10 million in total. For the ALP Bob Hogg had planned an $8.5 million paid media campaign over a 28-day period. Hogg stuck by his program though Labor did not have the funds. The ALP sank into a $6 million debt post-election, inspiring its move to ban television advertisements.

The 1990 election saw a national two party preferred swing to the coalition from Labor of only 0.9 per cent. The bias in electoral boundaries and wasted coalition votes in safe seats saw the coalition lose the election, despite beating Labor on the national two party preferred vote 50.1 to 49.9 per cent. The swing to the coalition was substantial in two states: 4.8 per cent in Victoria and 3.8 per cent in Western Australia; it was slight in another two: 0.9 per cent in Tasmania and 0.7 per cent in South Australia. But Labor won in NSW with a 1.8 per cent swing and in Queensland with 0.9 per cent. The largest two party preferred swing to the Liberals occurred in Victoria with 9.2 per cent in Lalor and, for Labor, in NSW with 7.1 per cent in Richmond.

Labor was returned with its notional majority of 18 seats on the new boundaries reduced to eight. Labor lost ten seats to the Liberals, nine in Victoria and one, Hawker, in South Australia. This means that outside Victoria the Liberals won only one seat from the Hawke government plus one Queensland seat from the Nationals—proof of Peacock's failure outside Victoria to inspire any voter confidence.

Labor held all its Western Australian seats on the new boundaries. The ALP won three seats from the Nationals—Page and Richmond in NSW and Kennedy in Queensland. Labor won two seats from the Liberals—Moreton in Queensland and Adelaide in South Australia, which it had lost to the Liberals at a by-election. The Liberals lost a total of three seats—the third to an independent in North Sydney.

The state of the sides in the new parliament was Labor 78, coalition 69, and one independent. The composition of the new Senate was Labor 32, Liberal 29, National five, Democrat eight and two independents.

The 1990 campaign was Hawke's best, better even than 1983, given the difficulties. This was Labor's tightest election and it had to win by maximising the leadership issue. Hawke learnt from his mistakes in the pilots' dispute and performed with moderation, discipline and strength. Hogg, not a fan of Hawke's campaign abilities, said of Hawke's 1990 campaign: 'It was his finest—a bit grumpy at the start—but his finest to date.'[1]

Keating played second fiddle to Hawke and was too aggressive. His message was that only Labor could deliver jobs, real wage rises and social justice. He declared: 'Before 1983 Australia was run by the bureaucracy. This government runs the whole outfit. I run economic policy—and the government.' Keating signalled he would quit politics if the Liberals won. He had spent seven years 'cleaning up' after the last recession: 'I don't want to be around cleaning up after the next one.' Keating's personal ambition was tied to his conviction that the economy would have a soft landing. This was his pledge, Labor's pledge; it was vindication. Keating was not lying— his judgement was just wrong.

Labor sneaked back into office before the recession arrived. Strategists Hogg and Cameron believed the Liberals blundered in May 1989 by switching from Howard to Peacock, although this was not Hawke's considered view. Hogg says: 'It is not possible to be categorical and say if John Howard had been leader they would have won . . . it is my view their position would have been enhanced had Howard remained leader.'[2]

The optimum position for the Liberals was to have united behind Howard as their best prospect, given his performance in the 1987 campaign. If the party had supported Howard then Howard may have served the party better. But the Liberal Party lost its confidence in Howard in the 1987–89 period and Howard, in turn, lost his confidence in his colleagues.

The Liberals, having destroyed their optimum position, threw their fate into a leadership switch to Peacock. The success of the Peacock coup had the potential to change the political landscape but these hopes were dashed within days because of the *Four Corners* program. Peacock's legitimacy as leader was compromised just after his destruction of Howard's leadership. So the Liberals had a double failure, being unable to make either Howard or Peacock work as a successful leader. This was a defect not just within these men but within the Liberal Party as an institution.

The 1990 result reveals that most voters unhappy with the Hawke government switched to minor parties, not to the Liberals. The Liberal post-election report said: 'Voters wanted a change of government but for much of the campaign perceived that if elected the coalition would do a worse job than Labor thus reinforcing the notion that the coalition was not a viable voting alternative.' Liberal research showed that at the end of the campaign, 33 per cent believed the coalition would do a better job, 34 per cent believed it would do a worse job, and 33 per cent were indifferent.

The Liberal failure is measured by the slight lift in its share of the primary vote from 34.6 to 35 per cent. This 0.4 per cent rise in the Liberal vote contrasts with the fall in Labor's primary vote from 45.8 to 39.4 per cent. The Liberals were unable to benefit from the desertions from the ALP.

The poll left the National Party in a weak position. It lost its leader, Charles Blunt, and its shadow finance minister, John Stone. The Nationals polled only 8.4 per cent, behind the Democrats—the worst National primary vote since the 1955 poll and second worst since the party's inception. This was ironic, given the pretensions of the Joh-for-Canberra push three years earlier to make the Nationals into the senior non-Labor party.

After the election many Liberals blamed the Nationals for the coalition's loss. They argued that Labor's majority of eight seats would have been reduced to zero if the Nationals had retained Richmond, Page and Kennedy, and if their vote had held up in Moreton sufficiently to allow the Liberals to hold this seat on National preferences. The Liberals were right in their accusation that National Party weakness had denied them victory, but it was the poor Liberal results outside Victoria which made this National Party weakness fatal. Liberal criticism of the Nationals obscures their own failure to make gains from Labor outside Victoria, an exceptional failure given the economic situation.

The 1990 election is remarkable in that Labor won despite recording its worst primary vote in the post-war period. Labor's 39.4 per cent of the primary vote was just less than its 39.6 in 1977 when it suffered its most humiliating defeat against Malcolm Fraser. In 1990 the coalition outpolled Labor 43.4 to 39.4 per cent on primary votes. But the coalition failed to win the election — first because its own primary vote was still too low, and secondly because it won too small a share of the minor party preferences.

Labor's victory was built on minor party preferences. The total vote for the Australian Democrats, minor parties and independents was 17.2 per cent compared with 8.1 per cent in the 1987 election. The Democrats lifted their primary vote between the two elections from 6 per cent to 11.3 per cent, a result achieved more through major party negatives than through Democrat positives. It interrupted briefly the pattern of decline for the Democrats since their previous best vote of 9.4 per cent at their first election in 1977.

The distribution of Democrat preferences saw a record pro-Labor split. In 1987 Labor won 56.7 per cent of these preferences but this rose in 1990 to 63.3 per cent. Since the Democrat vote rose, Labor, in fact, won a bigger share of a bigger vote. The share of Democrat preferences directed towards the Liberal–National parties fell between these elections from 43.3 to 36.7 per cent. In the 1990 election, therefore, Democrat preferences split almost two-thirds to Labor, one-third to the coalition.[3]

The estimates from election analyst Malcolm Mackerras show that the flow of green preferences to Labor was even better, the distribution being: Labor 44.4 per cent, Democrats 35.5 per cent and coalition 20.1 per cent. Mackerras concluded that when these Democrat preferences were divided further between the major parties the split was 69 to 31 per cent in Labor's favour—better than a two-thirds, one-third division for the ALP.[4] This appears a conservative estimate, with the Liberal post-election report suggesting the split could have been 80 to 20 per cent. There were ten seats won by Labor after being behind on the primary vote—Cowan, Canning and Stirling in WA; Page and Richmond in NSW; Moreton, Fisher and Kennedy in Queensland; Melbourne Ports and Jaga Jaga in Victoria.[5]

The primary vote for the 'other' category rose from 2.06 per cent in 1987 to 4.88 per cent in 1990; much of this was a green vote. In WA where the greens were most organised and ran as a separate party, they polled 7.5 per cent of the vote compared with 8.4 per cent for the Democrats. This reinforced the benefit to Labor from its preference strategy.

The belief that Labor would have done better without its environment/preference strategy—the argument from Peter Walsh, among others—demands heroic assumptions. Walsh said that the campaign for second preferences only legitimated primary vote defections from Labor. It seems that the net gain from higher preferences for Labor in 1990 compared with 1987 is at least 3 per cent, a remarkable figure which suggests that Labor followed the correct strategy (rather than concentrating on the primary vote). This was the assessment of Hawke, Hogg, Cameron and most ALP marginal seat members. While several factors influenced these preferences, the environment was clearly an important one.

Morgan research showed that Labor's lead over the coalition as the best party on the environment rose from a hefty 24 per cent in late 1989 to a mammoth 32 per cent in the campaign. Peacock lacked the policy weapons to combat this.

Contrary to immediate post-election claims for a 'green era', there are several reasons why green power will not transform party politics. First, the environmentalists were unable to organise their own national green party because they could not agree to cooperate. History suggests that single issue movements have difficulty in making the transition to party status, with the Nuclear Disarmament Party offering evidence of this in the early 1980s. Secondly, the Australian Democrats, as an existing party, were the direct beneficiary of the environment as a voting issue. The Democrats reoriented their platform and campaigned as the party best equipped to champion environmental protection. Third, the platforms of both government and Opposition revealed a sensitivity towards the growing environmental consciousness of the community. The major parties were adapting, as they have adapted before, to incorporate environmental concerns into their own platforms.

Finally, it became apparent in 1991 that public opinion wanted a balance between environmental protection and economic growth. Green absolutists will never win more than a small minority of the Australian vote because of the electorate's conservatism—its rejection of greens preaching lower

589

living standards, population reduction and agrarian collectivism. The 1990s recession only reinforced this view.

The variation in swing across states points to the startling strength of state factors at the 1990 election. In Victoria resentment towards the Cain government assisted Peacock; in WA Labor succeeded in limiting the swing by changing the premier; in NSW the Liberals suffered because of resentment against Greiner's government and because of disaffection over Howard's removal; in Queensland and northern NSW the coalition suffered because of hostility towards the National Party generated within the state arena.

While Labor won on preferences, this technique has left the ALP vulnerable at the next election. Labor started its fourth term with its primary vote at a perilous 39.4 per cent. The extent of ALP vulnerability is best revealed in Victoria and Western Australia where its primary vote was 37.1 per cent and 35.3 per cent respectively. Labor will enter the next campaign in the West in an extremely fragile position. In his post-election report Bob Hogg said: 'The decline in our primary vote is a major concern . . . We must broaden the "umbrella" of the Party and do whatever is possible to incorporate rather than encourage or observe the growth of the Greens or Democrats.'

In relation to the Senate Hogg warned: 'The Senate result is of considerable concern. A repeated result by the coalition plus a 400 odd vote gain in NSW next time would give the coalition a tied Senate with Harradine's support . . . The Democrat, independent representation in the Senate is at our expense, not the coalition parties.'

The election further reversed the pattern of the 1950s and 1960s, when the minor parties were breakaways to the right. In 1990 the minor parties, Democrats and greens, were aligned on the left. The Democrats aspired to a synthesis of radicals, lefties, greens, the disenchanted and the caring nice people. Their leader, Janine Haines, was young, female and unaffected— unlike Hawke and Peacock. The Democrats campaigned for old fashioned economics—the reinstitution of tax rorts, reregulation of the financial system, and use of government power to deliver economic equity. They threatened to oppose in the Senate the far-reaching Liberal reforms of labour market deregulation and privatisation.

The gulf between Labor's economic rationalists and the Democrats was deep, yet the Democrats and the Liberals were divided by an ideological chasm. The entrenchment of the Democrats on the political left only made Labor more likely to receive a higher share of Democratic preferences.

Peacock failed to run a hard election campaign geared to the national crisis which the coalition proclaimed. He sent mixed signals—better living standards, a family package, lower interest rates. If the coalition was serious about its warning in the EAP that Australia's predicament was similar to that before the depressions of the 1890s and 1930s, then it would have run a campaign which reflected the gravity of the situation.

An alternative Liberal campaign could have been hung on the framework of record national debt and threatened recession. This was the campaign which Labor had feared. Using these concerns, which research showed the voters understood, the Opposition could have spent the campaign selling its economic policies as the answer to Australia's problems. ANOP research showed the voters had grasped the sense of national crisis through Australia's debt burden—but the Liberals never exploited it.

The Peacock campaign betrayed a defect within non-Labor politics in the 1980s which has remained unresolved: how to win elections on a platform of free market economics. The political reality is that free market economics can only be sold one way—as a national benefit. It threatens interest group after interest group. It defies the traditional approach to vote gathering and in orthodox terms it is an electoral negative. It is a doctrine which offends too many people for benefits that are national, not sectional. John Hewson's problem post-election was that free market economics became even more unpopular during a recession.

Peacock's instinct was to campaign by offering a better deal for the hip-pocket, an unsophisticated pitch in 1990. Peacock lacked confidence in his own grasp of economics—the area where he had to be convincing. He didn't know how to market his major policies—micro-economic reform, labour market deregulation, lower inflation and the new health scheme which he actually ditched.

The 1990 campaign is a case study of Labor's superior professionalism. The primary credit for Labor's election triumphs lies with its political leaders, notably Hawke, then Keating. But an associated element was the professionalism of the ALP campaign team which had been applied in federal and state campaigns throughout the decade.

In the ten years from 1981 to 1990 there were 22 state and federal elections, with Labor winning 17 and the non-Labor side only five. But of these five successes two were victories for the National Party in Queensland under Bjelke-Petersen, which means that the major non-Labor party, the Liberal Party, won only three out of 22 elections in this decade. Two of these wins were in the smallest and most isolated state, Tasmania. On the Australian mainland the Liberals won only one election, Nick Greiner's victory in NSW in 1988. The Labor Party won the four federal elections in this period, the three elections in Victoria, three in Western Australia, three in South Australia, while Neville Wran won his final two elections in 1981 and 1984. Labor lost in NSW in 1988 but regained both Queensland and Tasmania in 1989. The record overall is Labor's most successful decade and non-Labor's most dismal.

The 1990 federal election betrayed the technical differences between

Labor and Liberal involving leaders, research, advertising and organisation which made Labor a more sophisticated operation during the decade.

Labor waged an integrated campaign selling through Hawke and its paid advertising a consistent message. The Liberals were unable to achieve this. George Patterson chief, Geoffrey Cousins says: 'The point I constantly made to the Liberal Party is that advertising is the weakest form of campaign communications. Radio, press and television news and interviews are much more powerful. Advertising acts like a turbo charger on a motor. Our problem was that the advertising message was contradicted by the events of the campaign, people not being able to answer questions and so on.'[6]

Labor's team in the preparation of its 1990 campaign position was Hogg, Cameron, Gibbs, Singleton and Geoff Walsh from Hawke's office—an integration of party, research, agency and leader. By contrast, the Liberal 'Question and Answer' message was devised within George Patterson's, based upon the party brief, sold to Eggleton and in turn to Peacock. The researchers had little direct input into this message—a distinct contrast with Labor's integrated campaign team. For instance the Liberal's main researcher, Ron Klein, only discovered the party's 'Question and Answer' message—its communications device for the campaign—when he heard the advertisements on his car radio. Under Labor this would have been inconceivable; it would not have allowed a communications strategy to go to air without being research tested.

Within the campaigns the advertising agency had much greater influence in the Liberal structure than in Labor's operation. The reports from Liberal headquarters suggest that Geoffrey Cousins from George Patterson was dominant and that during the campaign the Liberal strategists were defeated by Cousins in their efforts to swing the advertising message onto a stronger negative path.

Cousins, in effect, was defending the communications message devised by his own agency against the Liberal professionals, Jon Gaul, Alistair Drysdale and Graham Morris, who wanted a tougher negative line. This was a case of the agency telling the Liberals what campaign position they needed, not the Liberals telling the agency, a situation that was the fault of the Liberals. By mid-campaign when the Liberal researcher, Ron Klein, reported that the campaign was making no impact, he lacked the clout or seniority to persuade the Liberals to rethink. Indeed, Klein had little role in the campaign and attended meetings at the campaign HQ only twice a week.

Cousins asserts that the accusations about his dominance are untrue pointing out that 'Tony Eggleton was the campaign director and he set the strategy'. In practice, Eggleton supported Cousins in the arguments about the Liberal advertising which Cousins describes as 'intense but not to the point of violent'. Cousins says that, 'in retrospect I wouldn't change anything and nothing went wrong. The advertising at this late stage was not going to swing the result. As for those who wanted to be more negative, all I can say is that they should have read the research.'[7]

The best commentary on this comes from ANOP's Margaret Gibbs: 'Of course the research said the voters don't like negative campaigns. They rarely do. The question is not whether they will like a negative campaign but whether a negative campaign will work.'[8] The Liberals, as ANOP realised, should have run a negative campaign demolishing the Hawke government.

In his post-election report the Liberal research director, Ed Lockhart, agreed with the ALP that many voters delayed their decision until the last possible moment. He estimated this figure was as high as 20 per cent— another reason why the Liberals should have turned the heat on Labor in the last week.

Eggleton was a cautious federal director, prepared to make some modifications, such as greater use of Hewson, but he dismissed any radical departure. Labor was more audacious—it was during the last week that Labor made its explicit appeal for minor party preferences. Labor was also relentless in repeating its own negative message, the best of the election: 'if you can't govern yourself then you can't govern the country.'

Labor's own advertising chief, John Singleton, worked within tight guidelines laid down by Labor's campaign team, led by Hogg and Cameron. Singleton joked later about the rigidity of his 'riding orders' and called ANOP the 'Seeing Eye Dog' research company because 'they believed in keeping me in the dark until there's about one hour to come up with an answer'.[9] Hogg and Cameron asked Singleton to implement their strategy, not to create his own.

The sharpest difference between Labor and Liberal was in their approach to research. The Liberals relied upon Brian Sweeney and Associates for their qualitative work, and the Roy Morgan company, whose chief was Gary Morgan, for their quantitative surveys. At Sweeney's the consultant was Ron Klein. The ALP used ANOP as its main source of advice although most of ANOP's work was qualitative and it relied upon WAOP for the quantitative work. The ANOP work was jointly managed by its principals, Cameron and Gibbs.

One Liberal strategist declared: 'The Liberals do the research, but Labor acts on the research.' Yet this is too simplistic. The real difference was that the ALP, unlike the Liberals, used its researchers to formulate a total campaign and communications strategy. The Liberals never expected Sweeney or Klein to perform this function and would have said it was inadvisable. This is where personal chemistry becomes important. Cameron and Gibbs had been working for Labor on federal and state campaigns for more than 15 years.

Their approach was to distil from the research a comprehensive campaign strategy, a position which would win Labor the election. ANOP didn't just tell Labor what the voters felt. The agency built upon this data to recommend an election strategy; this often involved recommendations on policy, personnel and leadership as well as style, presentation and tactics. Cameron had enough standing with the ALP—party secretaries and its leaders—to offer frank advice on the requirements for a winning Labor campaign. The Liberals had no equivalent. The upshot was that throughout the 1980s there was a distinct difference between the two sides in the role of researchers.

Richard Farmer says: 'The Liberals were better organised than us. Tony Eggleton was right saying we weren't quite ready for the election. But our side was smarter and more flexible. We didn't need all our advertisements to be ready. Our job, above all, was to find the right message.'[10]

In his debriefing to the ALP, Rod Cameron identified five elements in the election victory: research targeting to find the vulnerable seats to focus Labor's effort; a better national election campaign; a weak Opposition election campaign; the environment/second preference strategy; and the local campaigns.

Tony Eggleton's post-election report summarised why the Liberals lost in 1990:

> For much of the campaign voters perceived that, if elected, the coalition would do a worse job than Labor . . . The quantitative election day survey by Morgan takes us back to the nub of the credibility issue. When asked what one thing more than anything else influenced their votes, all the economic issues were surpassed by one pre-eminent factor—credibility. When asked what improvements they would like to see in the Liberal and National Parties, the respondents listed (1) leadership; (2) party unity; (3) quality of the team.

Eggleton's research showed that 'Labor voters were dissatisfied with the incumbent, but not sufficiently for "the devil you know" principle to be over-ruled'. The Liberal campaign failed—perhaps it was doomed by the Liberal divisions and mistakes over the previous year. The result was Hawke's finest victory and a personal triumph.

Hawke, a four times winner, would face a cruel fate—a recession and a coup. But not before he put the final seal on his prime ministership—the plan to bury Protection, the central pillar of the Australian Settlement.

EPILOGUE

INTO THE 1990S

32
Hewson—the free market purist

I don't regard myself as a born-to-rule Liberal and I believe the
Liberal Party has got to earn the right to rule.

John Hewson, August 1991

The election of John Hewson as leader after its 1990 defeat completed the transformation of the Liberal Party during the 1980s. Hewson was a unique commodity in terms of ideology, strategy and allegiance. Hewson had a contempt for the old Liberal Party, the party that managed the Australian Settlement. He was a working class boy devoid of roots or powerbase within the Liberal establishment. Hewson repudiated the born-to-rule ethos of the old Liberal Party along with its economic philosophy. He was a careerist and a free market purist, a product of the economic orthodoxy of the 1980s.

The Liberals, after a decade of economic debate, elected the first professional economist ever to lead their party. Hewson's principal article of faith was the efficiency of the market. His life and career—from working class Sydney boy to international banker—was that of a man who believed absolutely in the capacity of the individual to advance without the assistance of the state.

In ten years the Liberals had travelled from Fraser to Hewson, a journey from Tory paternalism to laissez-faire individualism. The two leaders symbolised the transformation of the Liberal Party. Both Fraser and Hewson were products of their time and symbols of changing times.

Hewson's election signalled the demise of the old Liberal Party. It is a testimony more to Liberal weakness than to Hewson's appeal that a politician elected only in 1987 could become party leader less than three years later. This was a rate of progress faster than Menzies' and virtually as fast as Hawke's. It was remarkable given Hewson's political inexperience.

Hewson assumed the Liberal leadership with a narrow but determined view of his destiny reflected in three beliefs. First, that Australia was in an economic crisis and that its future depended upon the imposition of a radical free market agenda to replace the old policy framework pursued by both parties. Secondly, that the strategy for the Liberals was to nail their new ideological colours to the masthead, that they must win an election not by default but on their policy credibility, despite the electoral 'nasties' in the free market agenda. This meant, in effect, that the Liberals had to generate a new faith in themselves. Finally, Hewson said that the Liberals had to become as tough and as professional in their approach to politics as the Labor Party of the 1980s.

The election of Hewson was an insight into the revolution within Liberal politics over the previous decade. Hewson's beliefs were anathema to the Fraser government which Hewson himself had advised and from which he had departed with a sense of disgust. This experience left Hewson with the conviction that the next Liberal government must display policy courage as its primary quality. He believed that the next Liberal government had an obligation to redeem the party from the Fraser debacle. It was this very sentiment that provoked Hewson's entry into politics. A public critic of the Fraser era post-1983, Hewson felt, to use his own words, that he eventually had no choice but to 'put up or shut up'. He entered parliament with a declared mission of confronting the Liberals with the courage of free market beliefs.

Once in politics Hewson's seminal experience was as shadow treasurer to Peacock before the 1990 election, a period which reinforced all his existing convictions. Explaining the defeat of the Liberals at that election Hewson says: 'We were our own worst enemies. We always had a credibility problem. People wanted a reason to vote for us in 1989 and 1990 but we failed to provide it enough, we stopped short of a fully credible policy package. Our divisions confirmed that argument that if you can't govern yourself then you can't govern the country.'[1]

After the 1990 election there was an irresistible logic to Hewson's election as Liberal leader. He was a symbol of generational change at a time when the Liberals had to consign the Peacock–Howard–Chaney era to history. He was a figure of economic credibility who could provide the Liberals with the quality which they had lacked at the election. He was a fresh face offering the Liberals a prolonged electoral honeymoon under a 'new order' landlord. His election meant that the Liberals were reconciled, if not converted, to the free market ideology after a decade of internal disputes.

'I regard John Hewson as the luckiest politician I've encountered,' outgoing Liberal director Tony Eggleton told his colleagues. Hewson was exactly the right man at exactly right time. But astute judges put two queries against Hewson: was he a leader and was he a politician?

Hewson was skilled at using networks but was the quintessential loner, a self-made man who had created a career with determination and self promotion. Hewson rose from his working class background with a workaholism that carried him to a doctorate in economics at John Hopkins, a consultancy at the IMF, and an economic research post at the Reserve Bank. Frustrated with the bank's distance from the decisions, Hewson went to work for Lynch, then Howard, the Liberal treasurers, and plunged into the political melting pot. He developed the technique of the multiple job: consultant to the treasurer, economics professor at the University of NSW, a financial market consultant, pioneering through the university a program of Asian financial market tours, and then Macquarie Bank director.

His career revealed a dedication to personal advancement. Hewson found that he could survive comfortably on three hours sleep which provided almost enough waking hours for his ambitions. In the process he became rich: a Bowral property, a home in Bellevue Hill, champagne at the Regent, and a mini fleet of classic cars including the famous Ferrari. Hewson's success made the next step almost inevitable—he crashed through Liberal preselection into Wentworth, based upon some of the poshest suburbs in Sydney's east.

In parliament Hewson exploited his econocrat credentials and, with patronage from Howard, then Peacock, became shadow treasurer, partly because of the dearth of talent within the party. Hewson was a unique and risky prospect for the Liberals: an academic economist who believed in free markets, a politician who repudiated the deal-making techniques by which the Liberals had delivered for the business community, and a product of financial deregulation which had made his fortune and which was basic to his outlook and values.

It is no surprise that Hewson only joined the Liberal Party in the mid-1980s when he was in his mid-thirties and about to assess a parliamentary career. This contrasts with his counterparts in the ALP, nearly all of whom established their party ties during adolescence. Hewson was a fast-tracking careerist who advanced quickly within a Liberal Party that faced both an identity transition and dearth of talent.

In 1990 Hewson and Nick Greiner, at the time the only Liberal premier in the nation, were the symbols of a strange new Liberal Party. They represented the party's new strengths and flaws after its absorption of economic rationalism. Hewson and Greiner were distinguished by their commitment to dry economics, management efficiency, a lack of orthodox political skills, and their emergence from outside the Liberal mainstream.

Greiner was a Catholic Hungarian immigrant, a loner, devoid of a party powerbase, a social progressive who was hostile to Liberal traditions such as states rights and to Liberal tactics such as the great socialist scare. Hewson had come to the Liberal Party not through family, class or society, but as the result of his intellectual belief in free market economics and his search for self-advancement.

Hewson and Greiner were symbols of a revolution in Australia's political culture: the collapse of the ideas and the political techniques which had guided Australian conservatism since its inception. The old Liberal Party, the born-to-rule generation, had failed. It had failed the test of economic management under Fraser and it had failed as professional politicians to beat the Labor Party during the 1980s. The demise of the old order, intellectually and politically, turned Liberal politics into an open market. Hewson and Greiner were products of the new system in which managerial efficiency and competent presentation could deliver the leadership to young politicians who had no powerbase within the party and no natural affinity for politics.

Hewson and Greiner both had many critics—but the Liberals were lucky to have them. The absence of depth in leadership talent which had plagued the party during the 1980s was likely to continue during the 1990s. Greiner was the first 'new generation' Liberal to form a government and Hewson aspired to become the second. Greiner and Hewson, despite their mutual antipathy, would determine not just the immediate fate of the Liberals in the early 1990s, but the ability of the Liberals to implement successfully from office their new agenda of economic rationalism. They would determine, in fact, whether the free market revolution within non-Labor politics would succeed.

The reconstruction of the federal Liberal Party after the 1990 election was fast and relatively painless. The decision was for a generational change. Peacock knew that his second election defeat had cancelled his leadership credentials. Howard aspired to return to the leadership but conceded reluctantly that the party's mood was to look forward not backwards. Chaney was briefly deluded about his leadership prospects before discovering that he would not survive as deputy. Hewson was the success of the 1990 Liberal campaign and his elevation was natural. The symbol of party consensus was the support for Hewson from the veteran and House deputy, Wal Fife.

Hewson and his wife Carolyn, a Sydney merchant banker, agreed that Hewson would make a leadership commitment. They even discussed a period—a full two terms as prime minister, if Hewson made it.

Peacock supported Hewson, and Howard, with natural reluctance, also supported his former staffer for the job which the party was denying him. The only hiccough was Hewson's endorsement of Peacock as his deputy, a mistake which drove the Howard forces into a fury. Howard told Hewson that he would never accept this move. The result was that some of the Howard camp began to support Peter Reith as leader, with the real intent of eliminating Peacock from any position of influence. Peacock who was not interested in being deputy happily withdrew. The Peacock–Elliott forces who had masterminded Howard's May 1989 overthrow backed Hewson to ensure that Howard would never return to the leadership.

Hewson defeated Reith 62 to 13 to become leader, a margin close to a consensus. The ballot did not entrench a leadership rival, as had been the pattern in many previous Liberal leadership ballots. Reith defeated David Jull, a prominent Peacock supporter, 44 to 35 to become deputy leader. The Peacock camp voted solidly against Reith, and Hewson also voted for Jull. The old Howard–Peacock rivalry was reflected in the deputy's but not the leader's ballot.

As Liberal leader Hewson was true to the spirit of his election—he cut adrift the old politics. Hewson pledged 'changes across the board', and in one briefing declared, 'I'm not committed to Menzies' policies'—an obvious statement but significant since Hewson was the first post-Menzies leader prepared to shatter the myth by which the party had lived.[2]

The Hewson era symbolised four fundamental changes for the Liberal Party after the upheavals of the 1980s, each with its own special consequence.

The first was the formal triumph of the free market economic agenda and reestablishment of policy unity on the basis of dry economics. It meant that the Liberals and the coalition were, in policy and philosophical terms, parties of the radical free market right. For the first time in its history, Australian conservatism had been recast as Australian radicalism. A Hewson government would mean that for the first time a coalition government would be pledged to massive changes in the status quo, in particular, a transformation of national attitudes and the business culture.

Hewson's program for the 1990s was an aggressive deregulatory agenda; a completion of the directions which the Hawke–Keating government had initiated in the 1980s.

The problem within both Hewson and the coalition was whether a new party ethos would match the new party ideology. For instance, few people seriously saw the Liberals as political reformers—and there was little sign that the Liberals regarded themselves as political reformers. They neither acted like reformers nor sounded like reformers. They made little effort to sell, persuade or propagandise for their policies. They paid little heed to the requirement of grassroots support for their declared positions. There was neither passion in their commitment nor much skill in their political appreciation. The Liberal Party had become a schizoid beast: pledged to a remaking of Australian institutions and culture through its formal support of free market policies, yet retaining in style, emotions and disposition the mentality of the status quo. The issue was whether the Liberal Party had made itself into a party with a reforming ethos and almost noone seriously believed that it had done so.

Given that Hewson's program would provoke divisions and upheaval—the usual consequences of radicalism—there were severe doubts whether the Liberals possessed the belief, skills and courage to implement successfully their own program. There was little sign that they grasped the social and cultural dimensions of their economic reforms such as labour market deregulation and the abolition of protection.

The second change was the termination of the internal leadership rivalry within the federal party which had destroyed the 1980s Liberal generation. Hewson prospered because of the failure of his predecessors. Peacock and Howard had lost elections and had been unable to establish internal authority. John Elliott had never made the transition to politics. Chaney was too compromised to become a leadership candidate. Ian McLachlan had been preoccupied by the New Right instead of the formal Liberal Party process. Fraserism was as discredited in 1990 as it had been in 1985—there was no politician of substance within the party who tried to uphold Fraserism as a philosophy. Yet the economic dries had failed during the 1980s to produce an outstanding leader.

All these trends intersected in 1990 to make John Hewson the overwhelming choice, the only real choice, as leader, and to unite the federal party behind him (federal, not necessarily state). The decentralised nature of the Liberal Party remained a potent threat to Hewson's program. The state Liberal parties were sceptical, often antagonistic, towards Hewson's program. In Victoria the Liberal leader, Jeff Kennett, was openly critical and grave doubts existed about the support of future Liberal state governments. The authority of the federal party over the states remained as ineffectual as ever; the 1990 Federal Council threw out a modest proposal pushed by Victorian president, Michael Kroger, to give the Liberal Federal Executive 'a residual power' to intervene in state divisions. Kroger knew that the Liberals would never become a truly national party until its Federal Executive had such powers—but the party could not grasp this obvious point.

The third change was the reconstruction of the federal coalition with a significantly reduced position for the National Party and an acceptance by the Nationals of their subservience. This represented a return to realism within the federal National Party, following the delusions of the 1980s when the Nationals fell into crazy speculation about becoming the major non-Labor party, and their folk hero, Joh Bjelke-Petersen, indulged his prime ministerial fantasy. The new National leader was Tim Fischer, who had an old-fashioned style but possessed the redeeming virtue of commonsense.

Hewson and Fischer exchanged letters as the basis of a new coalition agreement. The Nationals were reduced from eight to six shadow ministries which included initially a reduction from five to three shadow Cabinet places. The Nationals initially lost portfolio responsibility for trade, finance, land transport, veterans' affairs and child care—a massive reduction in power.

Hewson and Fischer agreed that they would work as coalitionists—but this put great pressure on Fischer. He had to carry the Nationals to support tough free market policies, and he only achieved this with the traditional argument that the Nationals had no future outside the coalition. Fischer was a traditionalist and a hard worker who preached the gospel of 'back to basics' in the bush. But in Canberra Fischer buried his pride and bowed to the free market dogma demanded by Hewson.

The issue which this raised and which Fischer tried to suppress was whether the National Party had any future. The triumph of free market economics within the Liberal Party made this an unavoidable issue. Political parties exist only to deliver for their supporters; once they cease to perform this function they must cease to exist. Fischer faced a terrible dilemma: if he accepted the new free market agenda of the Liberals then the National Party was rendered obsolete. On the other hand, if he rejected parts of this agenda he would undermine the coalition and its prospects of winning an election. His choice was between the loss of National Party identity and the denial of coalition unity.

The great coalition partnerships—Bruce and Page, Menzies and McEwen, Fraser and Anthony—were rooted in personal respect and policy trade-offs. These Liberal leaders had always given these National leaders substantial policy concessions ranging from protection policy to control of the apparatus of rural subsidies and statutory marketing and trade policy.

But Hewson would not surrender such economic policies to the Nationals, except to implement his new deregulatory agenda. The upshot was that Fischer was left with rhetoric but no substance to deliver to his own constituency. The National Party remained tied to the past. It was hostile towards Labor's taxes and trade union power as always, but it was suspicious about the new Liberal agenda: the GST, deregulation and free market economics. The National Party was far more reluctant than either the Liberal or Labor parties to change its policy habits, and it was undergoing a crisis of identity: if the Nationals existed only to support Liberal policies then it made sense for them to amalgamate with the Liberals.

Doug Anthony had supported such a merger after his retirement. The 1988 review of the party's future, chaired by Peter Nixon, had canvassed amalgamation in positive terms. Ian Sinclair had also spoken in favour of a merger, although he said later: 'The party had been weakened by being in opposition because you can't deliver to your constituency, by the more national orientation of the media and the troubles of the rural sector. But I don't believe the party will either amalgamate or die on a limb.'[3]

The Liberals were arrogant enough to conclude that the Nationals would succumb to a merger. In his final address as federal president, John Elliott predicted that 'within a few years John Hewson will be leading a government of one party—a single united conservative anti-Labor party'.[4]

In fact, while the preferential voting system remains, the non-Labor side should benefit from having two parties to maximise its vote. But this depends upon the coalition having sufficient unity to remain a plus rather than having its disunity become a negative. The key to the unity requirement is whether the Nationals can both reconcile themselves to the free market philosophy of the Liberals and find a place for themselves in this new world.

The fourth change lay in the political strategy articulated by Hewson—the embrace of conviction politics. Its origins lay in the belief that Australia was in economic crisis and that national governments had been too weak for too long, a diagnosis based upon the free market understanding of Australia's problems. Hewson openly declared that he was not a career politician; he had come to do a job. His entire rationale as leader was to commit the coalition to the free market philosophy and then win an election on this mandate as a prelude to imposing it upon the nation. Hewson's political strategy was based upon strength—winning power on his terms—and it fitted the cycle of post-1990 politics which saw a recession-weakened Labor government.

The historic significance of Hewson is that he promises to be the Liberal leader who will implement the new Liberal philosophy from office. His success or failure will determine whether the Liberal Party's transformation of the 1980s can be successfully carried through into a Liberal administration.

Hewson, unlike Howard, never sought a marriage between free market economics and social conservatism. As a student Hewson had participated in anti-Vietnam marches. He believed that abortion was a matter of conscience which politicians should not decide. He supported a multicultural Australia while insisting that migrants accept an obligation to make a commitment to being Australian. He was not interested in running an agenda of social conservatism because he saw this as peripheral to the economic priorities.

While Hewson accepted the Liberal foreign policy orthodoxy he added a new dimension—a dynamic Australian role in the Asia/Pacific. Hewson had done business in Japan and was interested in the Asian economic models. He was the first Liberal leader to approach the Asia/Pacific not with a traditional security mindset but viewing it primarily in economic terms as a region of challenge and opportunity for Australia.

In his shadow ministry appointments Hewson put economic dries in control of every major policy area. His inner circle was obvious—Reith as shadow treasurer, Howard in industrial relations, Ian McLachlan in industry and commerce and Jim Carlton in social security and health. There were prominent roles for David Kemp, Peter Costello, Alexander Downer, Bob Woods and Warwick Smith. Peacock was both a political adviser and the next Liberal foreign minister.

Within the Liberal organisation that great professional, Tony Eggleton, departed with swansongs and some wonderful anecdotes. Eggleton told the testimonial dinner to celebrate his thirty year's party service that the 'key tasks for the Menzies press secretary were to guard him from chatty passengers on commercial flights and to hose him down with fly spray before public events'. Eggleton related that Harold Holt beat Gareth Evans with the phrase, 'It seemed like a good idea at the time.' Holt had ad-libbed the final line of his White House speech, 'All the way with LBJ.' When Eggleton asked why, Holt said that it seemed like a good idea . . . at the time! Referring to his closest relationship, Eggleton told the dinner that 'life wasn't always easy working for Malcolm Fraser . . . they were seven years of government in which no leader could have given more of himself to his job . . . Malcolm was inclined to be a bit determined and we lost him in a broom cupboard at the Savoy Hotel in London when, better than me, he knew which was the right door'.[5]

Eggleton was replaced as federal director by Andrew Robb, who had come from the NFF to the Liberal Secretariat. Robb, whose background was agriculture and economics, was a protégé of McLachlan and Elliott. Where Eggleton was pragmatic, Robb was a policy man. Where Eggleton was the supreme party bureaucrat, Robb was blunt about the need to revamp campaign techniques.

From the start of Hewson's leadership, the Opposition revealed its new policy toughness with a trio of decisions which would shape the politics of Labor's fourth term. They were: in-principle acceptance of a goods and services tax (GST), the most sweeping reform to Australia's tax system; the virtual elimination of industry protection by the year 2000; and the sale of the three main government telecommunication bodies, Telecom, OTC and Aussat, an operation that would see the biggest floats in Australian history worth an estimated $20 billion.

Each area, taxation, protection and privatisation, had been the source of internal strife during the previous decade. Hewson wanted to settle these debates decisively on a radical free market basis. He wanted the Opposition to commit to these policies at the start of the parliamentary term, not panic over them at the end of the term. None of these three policies—the GST, negligible protection and telecommunications privatisation—had been Liberal policy at the 1990 election. They were evidence that Hewson was pushing the agenda hard and early. He believed that these policies were election winners and rejected the orthodoxy that they were election losers. This was the essence of Hewson's trying to win on his own program, not just on Labor's recession.

But the recession underwrote Hewson's aggression. It was because Hewson believed that Labor was finished, that government was waiting to be taken, that he could act from strength. It is why Labor was correct to switch from Hawke to Keating in an effort to break the mould.

For Hewson the supreme test of credibility was support for a GST. It was a threshold issue to herald the coalition's passage from old to new politics. Hewson was aware of history's curse on the indirect tax. It had been considered and rejected by the Liberals in the early 1970s, the late 1970s and, more recently, before the 1983, 1987 and 1990 elections. It had been considered and rejected by the Labor government in 1985. Yet such a tax existed in most OECD nations. It had become a symbol of Australian policy paralysis.

Hewson had been involved in some of these battles, notably the finalisation of the Economic Action Plan (EAP) in late 1989 when he had fought unsuccessfully for an indirect tax on both economic and political grounds. 'I have no doubt that the tax would have been a political plus for us,' Hewson says of the 1990 election. 'We had to prove to people that we should govern and it [the tax] would have been fundamental to that credibility.'[6]

When Hewson won in-principle acceptance of the GST, the issue was debated for nine hours in the shadow Cabinet and with some tension inside the party room. Hewson followed a two-step approach; first, the agreement that the policy was correct, next, the coalition's formal embrace of a correct policy. When members complained about the electoral risk it posed for them, Hewson replied: 'It's really my job that's on the line.' He elevated the GST to an unprecedented status saying: 'If we can't win with the GST then we don't deserve to govern.'

The second commitment, the reduction of protection to negligible levels by the year 2000, was designed to quicken structural change in the economy and assist exporters. The target applied to the most protected industries including cars, textiles, clothing and footwear. The IAC had estimated that the abolition of protection would increase real GDP by about $4 billion a year. The Garnaut report in late 1989 enshrined as its central recommendation the abolition of protection by the new century. The Opposition, under its industry spokesman Ian McLachlan, was accepting the Garnaut target which, at this stage, Labor was still rejecting. This decision had two important consequences.

First, it affirmed the bipartisan nature of low protection. This was a decisive break from the destructive protection politics of the 1970s. The Opposition gave Hawke an incentive to introduce his own bolder low protection program in his March 1991 industry policy statement. The economic rationalists in both parties were reinforcing their cause after the 1990 election—an important event before the full impact of the recession which provoked a revival of high protection sentiment.

Secondly, the Opposition saw low protection not in isolation but as an integral part of two other great reforms—deregulation of the labour market and comprehensive micro-economic reform throughout the transport sector. It accepted that the competitive pressures released by the abolition of protection would demand a more efficient economy, higher workplace productivity and an end to the rigidities in the waterfront, coastal shipping and land transport areas.

Finally, telecommunications reform underlined the Opposition's principles on privatisation. Committed to competition first and privatisation second, the Opposition put the benefits of a deregulated telecommunications market before the benefits of privatisation. It promised to maintain its 'community service obligations', which meant concessional rates for country people, but to pay these concessions from the budget, not as a hidden subsidy. The Opposition rejected Labor's telecommunications duopoly as 'a policy for wimps'.

As Opposition leader Hewson enjoyed an extended honeymoon watching a fourth term Labor government, tired and dispirited, descend into a leadership struggle and a recession—an Opposition's dream. The Liberals, having endured a decade of their own disunity and leadership strife, saw this affliction bedevil the Labor Party. Howard shook his head in amazement at Hewson's luck. The powerful political position in which Hewson found himself post-1990 was due to far deeper political forces than his own achievements. Hewson remained an untested leader and, amazingly, an untested politician.

It was the Opposition's opinion poll dominance which guaranteed Hewson's authority. With Labor sitting on a primary vote around 35 per cent, the Opposition was staring victory in the face. This was a powerful incentive to maintain unity and support Hewson. There was some speculation that McLachlan was the preferred candidate for powerful Liberal supporters beyond the parliament, but the issue would never arise while Hewson appeared a certain winner.

There was, however, much private speculation over whether Hewson possessed the range of personal qualities necessary to meet the task he had defined. Hewson remained a stranger to the party he led. He had trouble inspiring friendship or enthusiasm within the Liberal Party. At the 1990 Federal Council, Hewson was never seen working the delegates, cup of tea in hand, chatting here, dealing there. Hewson was always busy, often so busy that he forgot the 'people' dimension of politics. In 1992 Hewson failed to support a loyal colleague, Wal Fife in a redistribution dispute with the Nationals which provoked Fife's decision to leave politics. It typified the criticism made of Hewson—that he lacked loyalty, that he had weak political touch and, above all, that he was a poor judge of people.

Labor's pollster, ANOP's Rod Cameron, described Hewson as 'an apparently honest man, devoid of charisma, wooden before a crowd or television camera and relying for appeal upon a narrow intellectualism built around economic rationalism'.[7]

Hewson's appeal was due to two factors—perceived economic credibility and a fresh image. But the voters felt no warmth for him and Hewson was often seen as cold and remote. He didn't generate an emotional response and during 1992 his lead over Keating on the 'better PM' question was rarely about 5 per cent and sometimes he fell below Keating. Labor tried to depict him as brutal and uncaring, a mechanistic theoretician.

Another dimension of this problem was the narrowness of Hewson's ideological wellsprings: 'The basics of my beliefs are in economics. They stem originally from a lot of theoretical work that I did myself, building multi-country [computer] models of regulated financial systems, for example, then breaking down the regulations in the models. And then cranking out all the properties to see what effect it has on interest rates and exchange rates, growth and employment and things like that.'[8]

Hewson displayed more than a touch of paranoia and was prone to conspiratorial interpretations of events and motivations. He was distrustful of and kept his distance from the media whom he tended to regard as part of the grand ALP coalition. Among the professionals in newspapers, television and radio, Hewson became known for his reluctance to use the media to persuade the people to his side. It almost appeared that Hewson was trying to win without the media, again to maximise his strength from office. Hewson probably did not need the media to win the election. But he could not implement his program from office without carrying the nation and that would require exploiting the media to market his message.

While Hewson lectured the nation about the necessity for painful solutions he was rarely persuasive. The new Liberal leader seemed to underestimate the obligation upon him to explain and persuade whether he was dealing with business, unions or sectional interest groups. While Hewson announced that the 1990s would see a new brand of politics he failed to inspire the nation or project a vision of the Australia that would emerge from the application of his policies.

But Hewson's emotions were provoked in his repudiation of the personal attacks upon his character. For instance, in his revealing personal speech to the 1990 Federal Council Hewson confronted the Keating accusations that he was a 'class traitor' and 'out of touch' with ordinary people. 'I make no apology for my success,' Hewson said, 'It was totally devoid of privilege.' Hewson said that Labor 'fear me' because 'I come from what they have taken for granted—working class Australia'.

It was difficult to assess Hewson because he was climbing a steep learning curve. Mistakes were inevitable; the only surprise is that he didn't make more. But some adverse points kept reappearing: Hewson was deeply sensitive to personal criticism; he was often weak on policy detail; and he was deficient in packaging and selling his policies to the voters. Too often Hewson seemed to assume that the mere statement of his policies was evidence of their truth.

Liberal intimates confirmed that Hewson was obsessed by Keating as a politician and economic manager. On the wall behind his desk there was even a painting of Keating! The indelible impression from late 1980s and early 1990s politics is that Hewson's battle with Keating was shaping Hewson's political character. When Hewson attacked Keating there was a passion in his thrust. Keating, in turn, dismissed Hewson as 'a financial markets yuppie shoehorned into politics' and a 'feral abacus'.

Hewson realised that Keating, more than any other politician, had shaped the contemporary view of the 1980s. Keating had pushed consistently three ideas: Labor's superiority as economic managers; the intellectual bankruptcy of the non-Labor tradition from Menzies to the present; and finally, the unfitness of the non-Labor side to return to office. In the process Keating had been responsible for creating divisions and generating low esteem within the non-Labor camp. Hewson understood that Keating was Labor's internal dynamic; that if Keating were destroyed then Labor would fall apart.

Hewson decided that Keating had to be fought relentlessly at his own game at every stage, a correct assessment. When Labor attacked Hewson in 1990 over his so-called brutal social theories Hewson threw the lot back at Hawke and Keating:

> I knew they'd [Labor] slam me whatever I did. I don't care what they
> say . . . they can scaremonger all they like but they won't be in
> government next time . . . If I can't win the next election by having
> tried to do this job properly, then I don't win. I'm not going to get
> there by trying to buy my way, by taking positions which are
> half-truths or by doing what was suggested in relation to the
> consumption tax—doing all the detail, leaving it in the drawer and then
> dropping it on day one.[9]

By 1991 Hewson had grown more dogmatic or resolute under attack: 'I don't care about my popularity. I'm not going to be poll driven. I didn't come into this business to be popular. I came . . . to make a change in this country . . . I'm embarrassed when I travel internationally and people talk about how we failed to get our house in order, how we failed to keep up with the rest of the world.'[10]

Hewson scarcely realised that by exaggerating his commitment to good policy he was creating an expectation that would be impossible to honour. But Hewson, like Keating, possessed the arrogance required of leadership:

> Go back over any of our governments and you'll find that they weren't
> ready to govern. You can do that with Gorton and McMahon. Even
> with Whitlam who had years as Opposition leader. He didn't have
> proper plans. And then Malcolm [Fraser] won. He wasn't ready to
> govern and when he did get the chance to govern he lost the
> confidence to govern. After a few weeks in the job Hawke said 'we'll
> have a summit' and try to pull the country together. But he wasn't
> ready. We can't afford this anymore. With a three year time limit and
> the electorate shell shocked and cynical. We've got to lift our game.[11]

In November 1991 Hewson produced *Fightback*, the decisive event of the parliamentary term for the coalition. The key to its favourable reception was that Hewson turned the GST into a comprehensive blueprint for reform through a synthesis of coalition policies. Labor, which had long deluded itself that the package would be an electoral negative, was stunned by its sweeping nature. The media response was positive not because of *Fightback*'s substance but because of its psychology. At a time of national crisis and pessimism engendered by recession, Hewson unveiled a grand plan for the nation; it was precisely the tonic required when the Hawke government appeared arthritic.

Fightback had three dimensions—tax reform, spending cuts, and a micro-reform program. Its economics reflected the international orthodoxy of the free market school.

The coalition proposed a 15 per cent goods and services tax effective from 1 October 1994, with the main exemptions being for health, education, financial services, building and exports. It was a version of the value added tax which was the preferred indirect tax used by OECD nations. The GST would be levied at all stages of production and distribution with credits available for the tax paid on business inputs to avoid double taxation. The coalition would apply the new tax across as broad a base as possible, including food, and then target the disadvantaged for compensation. The GST was not a tax on business or profits but a tax on consumption, since the tax burden would fall on the final consumer.

With the introduction of the GST a vast array of other taxes would be abolished: the wholesale sales tax, payroll tax, excise on petroleum products, customs duties, coal export duty, training guarantee levy and other business imposts. The intention was to ease the tax burden on business, in particular on the export sector.

For individuals the trade-off for higher consumption costs through the GST would be a lower personal income tax burden and targeted compensation from higher welfare payments. About 95 per cent of taxpayers would face a marginal rate of 30 cents or less with a top rate of 42 cents. The corporate rate would be lifted to 42 cents to align it with the personal rate. The coalition pledged the return of 'bracket creep' to taxpayers. A series of across-the-board cash payments would also be made, notably an 8 per cent increase in all pensions, a 6 per cent increase in all other welfare payments, and a 4.8 per cent lift in tax related benefits like sole parent rebates.

The Opposition said that the total impact of these measures was to 'over-compensate' for the impact of the GST, which it estimated would add 4.4 percentage points to the CPI. This enabled the coalition to argue that there would be only winners from the *Fightback* package across all income levels. On average the increase in household income from *Fightback* was estimated at a hefty $33.54 a week or about 4.6 per cent, after allowing for the net price effect of the package. The *Fightback* tables showed that the greatest percentage gains went to the lowest income earners.

The tax objectives were similar to those of Keating at the 1985 Tax Summit—a simpler, fairer system which encouraged business investment and raised revenue efficiently by eliminating avoidance and evasion. Overall the tax burden would be shifted from income to consumption which meant that the level of national savings should be increased—although this effect might be marginal.

Since the GST went nowhere near raising the revenue required to fund the personal tax cuts, the higher welfare payments, and the abolition of the wholesale sales tax, payroll tax and other taxes also being abolished, the shortfall had to come from massive spending cuts. *Fightback* envisaged a major reduction in the size and cost of government, despite its contraction during the Hawke era and the fact that Australia's public sector rated around the mid-point among OECD nations.

The total savings were estimated at $10 billion, a figure which the Labor government greeted with open disbelief. Given the welfare and family benefits in *Fightback* the net saving was reduced to $4 billion, which meant a crunch for the programs of many departments. The spending cuts were the absolute key to *Fightback*—the factor which enabled the coalition to present an overall tax package with wall-to-wall winners. The coalition had decided the only way to sell a package containing a 15 per cent GST was to produce a net outcome where everybody was a winner. But Keating was always determined to attack the funding of Hewson's tax cuts arguing that the massive spending cuts required were unavailable without destroying the social fabric.

The third element of *Fightback* was an attack on inflation and the current account deficit. This would be delivered through running monetary policy to achieve price stability, the promotion of deregulation of the labour market, and a faster pace of micro-reforms.

Fightback pledged a coalition government to achieve an inflation rate of 0–2 per cent, an objective to which Hewson was personally committed. This smashing of inflationary expectations was described as 'reasonable and sensible', and an 'almost impossible' task for Labor because it was hamstrung by the ALP–ACTU Accord. The Opposition said it was essential to ensure that inflation was kept low, not just during recession, but when the recovery came.

To achieve these objectives the Reserve Bank Act would be amended to terminate its 1980s 'sorry saga of compromise and influence'. It would be required to run monetary policy to achieve the target objective, which would mean greater visibility, clarity of purpose and accountability in interest rate policy. Hewson insisted that the real effect would be less emphasis on monetary policy in controlling inflation because of the anti-inflationary impact of fiscal and micro-economic policy.

The commitment to labour market deregulation was deepened with a declaration that under the coalition there would be no further national wage cases. The coalition would proceed to implement its policy of 'workplace productivity-based wage settlements'. This approach would be designed to devolve wage fixation to an enterprise level to secure better national productivity. This reform would be supplemented with a faster pace of protection reduction and faster efficiencies in transport, on the waterfront and in communications.

Hewson raised expectations, contrary to his usual approach, by promising that the program overall would create 2 million jobs and take Australian productivity to new levels. *Fightback* was marketed as 'a generational change in politics and attitudes'. Its content and rhetoric positioned it as a manifesto for a new decade. In reality it was a call for a renewed national effort to maintain the directions in which Australia had been moving during the 1980s Hawke–Keating era—although Hewson would never concede this.

Three problems in Hewson's strategy became obvious in the six months after its publication. They concerned its implementation, its marketing and its acceptance by the investment community.

As a leader Hewson was strong on objectives and weak on means and this may be his chief defect as a politician. He talked a lot about goals but usually looked vulnerable when quizzed about details, tactics and practicalities. The flaw in Hewson's program was the transition phase. The commentator Alan Wood warned: 'The precise outcomes of these policies [*Fightback*] are unpredictable, depending upon cultural as well as a host of economic factors. The one thing we do know with reasonable certainty is that the transition phase is going to be painful.'[12]

After a study of the New Zealand experience, Alan Wood advised the Opposition to defer the GST until its second term and concentrate on inflation control, labour market deregulation and micro-economic reform during its first term. A harsher version of this advice came from John Stone: 'The Opposition seems to be in danger of sacrificing reforms [that is, of the labour market] which are fundamental to Australia's future, for the sake of a third-order reform [tax] which is not.'[13]

Hewson was mounting from Opposition some of the most radical reforms put before the voters. His 'big five'—the GST, labour market deregulation, zero inflation, faster protection cuts and faster micro-economic reforms, including massive privatisation—would require an astute timetable, clever execution and genuine leadership. But there was little evidence that the Opposition had grasped these points.

The risk was that Hewson's reform agenda did not have its priorities properly defined and that its objectives would conflict with each other: for example, the achievement of low inflation with the introduction of the GST. It was important that the low inflation objective be installed first so that the tax and labour market changes occurred within this framework. The risk before the election was that the priority given the GST was too great and would give Keating a chance to win the poll. Keating was planning to make the GST the centrepiece of his campaign and the chief difference between the sides. The risk post-election was that the GST would prejudice more critical reforms.

In 1991–92 Hewson came under media pressure to abandon the GST, an option he recognised as politically counter-productive. Hewson and the Liberals would be ruined if, having embraced such a fundamental reform, they abandoned it because they lacked either the courage or the skill to market the GST. That would crucify Hewson and discredit his leadership at its central point—his claim to put policy conviction before popularity.

Ultimately Hewson's success will depend upon his capacity to carry a national argument—an essential requirement for a reformist prime minister. Yet Hewson seemed to lack the discipline or the strategy to sell *Fightback* after its initial reception. If Hewson could not market his program from the Opposition benches what was the prospect that he could successfully implement the program from office?

In office he would face another array of obstacles: a possibly hostile Senate, several Labor states, the trade unions and the ALP. Australia under Hewson might witness a repeat of Whitlam era politics. The entire range of Hewson reforms depends upon the passage of legislation. Hewson, following advice from Howard, declared in mid-1992 that his government, if its programs were thwarted in the Senate would establish the grounds for a double dissolution, conduct a second election and then pass the bills through a Joint Sitting. This is an audacious task which required, above all, political skills of a very high order. Hewson's real aim, in invoking this threat, is to put pressure on the Senate to recognise his mandate and give passage to his bills.

The irony for Hewson is that the recession did not just undermine Labor; it also made the selling of *Fightback* more difficult. Hewson's economic program was not devised to solve a recession. Indeed the pledge of zero inflation, faster protection cuts, a GST and labour market deregulation was an onerous package to apply to a deeply recessed economy. The Liberal economic program had evolved during the 1980s which had been a prosperous decade and it was geared to the long-term issues of securing a more productive, high saving, export orientated economy. It was not designed to remedy a recession and a recession would only make this program more daunting, even frightening, to many voters. The recession, in effect, was a new threat to the selling of Hewson's policies. Another threat was Hewson's tactic of assaulting interest groups—the car industry, the welfare lobby and home renters—in a fashion that only generated hostility towards himself and his policies.

In a wider sense the coalition, with the exception of John Howard, failed to respond to the 'age of greed' legacy of the 1980s. The excesses of the 1980s undermined community support for free market economics and economic rationalism. This is because these policies were seen by the community, by and large, to be devoid of a moral base and to have allowed an immorality in business and finance that was unacceptable to the public. Hewson's great task was to rehabilitate free market economics, to instil his philosophy with a moral dimension, to overcome the distrust of so many ordinary Australians who felt that the ideas Hewson championed had been applied to a fair extent in the 1980s and had failed both in economic and moral terms. Yet Hewson rarely showed any understanding of this challenge.

Hewson's style represented a dramatic break with Hawke's consensus. On the basis of his speeches, Hewson was a consensus buster: his message was that reform must be advanced and Labor's political log-jam blown apart. At the National Press Club Hewson declared that, if necessary, he would put troops onto the waterfront to secure the changes needed. It was a provocative remark, significant more for its symbolism than its intent. Hewson projected himself as a leader who would smash, if required, the obstacles denying Australia an internationally competitive position.

There were two great challenges for Hewson in office: could he carry the nation on his program and could he maintain the confidence of the investment community while implementing his reforms? The difficulties Nick Greiner faced in NSW carrying far more modest reforms revealed the magnitude of the task. If Hewson can't carry the nation or if he frightens the business community his program will be jeopardised. Hewson seemed unable to explain simply to the people the practical and social aspects of his economic program so they understood the sort of Australia that he wanted.

History suggests that Hewson would win the next election. No government has been reelected after a recession like 1991–92. No Opposition has failed to win after holding such a sustained lead in the polls. Coalition unity and the recession legacy make Hewson the favourite to become the first non-Labor prime minister since Malcolm Fraser—ironically, Hewson, a leader without Fraser's political skill, is pledged to repudiate the Fraser record.

In this situation Hewson would become the first free market reformer to form a government on behalf of the Liberal Party; the first Liberal prime minister elected to transform the status quo which his predecessors expended their energies building; the Liberal leader constructing new ideas and institutions to replace the Australian Settlement. But a close study of Hewson suggests that he cannot succeed as a reforming prime minister without a change in tactics, style and policy marketing.

33
The Keating coup

The recession and the GST got Hawke.

Paul Keating, January 1992

I

Support for the Hawke government collapsed after its 1990 election victory, due to public disenchantment, a protracted recession and a leadership struggle. The recession demoralised Labor. It meant that Labor's economic policy, judged by its own criterion, had failed. The paradox of Labor's fourth term is that Hawke, a four times election winner, fell victim to the recession and that Keating, despite his unpopularity, finally deposed Hawke.

The leadership crisis in Labor's fourth term was triggered by Hawke's decision to repudiate the 1988 Kirribilli agreement and remain as prime minister and Keating's refusal to accept this and his resort to a challenge. Once Hawke told Keating on 31 January 1991 that he was breaking their agreement, a leadership challenge was inevitable. Keating, denied a managed transition, sought the mantle by force.

A few months after the election Kim Beazley, a Hawke loyalist, rated a Hawke retirement during the term at a 90 per cent probability—a misplaced judgement. Hawke had never completely closed the door on this option in talks with Keating before the 1991 challenge. But ALP national secretary Bob Hogg had a different view: 'I don't think that Hawke had any intention of delivering on the Kirribilli Agreement and leaving.'[1] Keating had a choice: he could submit to Hawke or put the issue before the party through a challenge.

The Labor leadership was a likely poisoned chalice with the collapse of Labor's fourth term position creating the basis for a coalition win at the next election. But Hawke and Keating, like figures in a Shakespearian tragedy, were compelled by their history and their natures to their battle. Each man had a dual identity—Hawke the successful prime minister who refused to recognise the exhaustion of his tenure, and Keating the legitimate successor whose optimum time to become a successful prime minister had passed.

Keating's mistake was to belittle Hawke, thereby turning Hawke against his 'retirement with dignity' option. Hawke convinced himself that Keating's claim was illegitimate; that he was entitled to defy Keating and dishonour his pledge. As their mutual obsession intensified, Keating decided to challenge Hawke rather than leave politics; and Hawke, in turn, decided his responsibility was not to manage a smooth transition but to stay in office.

After the 1990 election the Hawke government was changed in power and personality dimensions. Keating became deputy unopposed after Lionel Bowen's retirement. The left won three Cabinet posts, for Howe, Hand and Bolkus, and was fully integrated, ready for the strangest political alliance of the Hawke era: Hawke and the left against Keating.

The right wing emerged stronger but divided. Beazley took the main micro-reform portfolio, transport and communications; Kerin remained in resources and primary industry; Crean became a junior minister; and Ray and Richardson had senior Cabinet posts. Evans stayed foreign minister and Willis became finance minister. This was a diverse group but in policy terms it was more sympathetic to Hawke's gradualism than to Keating's firmer economic line. Hawke was positioning Crean and Beazley against Keating.

At the same time the 1980s era economic ministers—the 'engine room' of that government—were outflanked: Walsh went to the backbench, Button survived on borrowed time, Dawkins was unpopular within the party. This group, which had been Keating's Cabinet base, was no longer the anchor of the Hawke Cabinet. Keating's grip on the Cabinet was slipping and Hawke's was tightening.

Hawke, in fact, had wanted a bigger restructuring, and had spoken to Button, Willis and Richardson about their leaving politics. Richardson was shocked when Hawke had sounded him out on a possible retirement and overseas posting; he rang Keating at once: 'You won't believe what the bastard's just suggested.' Yet Richardson himself had told Hawke to dump Button and Willis! Hawke wrote a letter to Beazley in April 1990 declaring that Labor's fourth term would be judged by its micro-reforms, and instructing Beazley to pursue this agenda with determination. This went to the core of the case against Hawke—that since its May 1988 Economic Statement the government had been drifting and Hawke's shelf-life as prime minister had virtually expired. The malaise continued from Labor's third term into its fourth; by 1990 the government was adrift, devoid of any strategic leadership. Hawke remained a relatively popular leader with an approval rating in the 40–45 per cent range, but leadership had ceased largely to be an electoral asset for the Labor Party. Labor's support fell to below 35 per cent of the primary vote.

After the 1990 election Keating moved to stake his claim to the leadership on policy grounds: he threw himself at the micro-reform agenda and ridiculed Hawke's technique of 'reform by consensus'. The battlefield was telecommunications reform, where Hawke was aligned with Beazley to introduce a competitive duopoly in the local industry while Keating sought to replace Telecom's monopoly with a fully competitive model. It was a bitter, emotional, and symbolic struggle. Keating assumed for himself the 'crash through or crash' mantle of policy leadership. By his actions Keating claimed to be the real leader, replacing Hawke. The irony is that Keating's fury only accentuated the growing Cabinet majority for Hawke.

The dramatic moment in the communications battle came when Keating, frustrated beyond endurance, threw his pen on the table and walked out of the Cabinet room complaining, 'This is a fucking second-rate decision from a second-rate government.' Keating's nemesis, Robert Ray, taunted, 'Go on, spit the dummy.' But Keating was being driven by power, not just ideology, in this dispute.

Hawke asked himself one question: why was Keating trying to become a hero on micro-reform now? Why was Keating calling for airline sales and telecommunication competition now? Hawke recalled with bitterness the events of 1988, when Keating had not raised his voice to support Hawke when Hawke himself was under internal assault for his pursuit of airline privatisation.

Keating's dilemma during 1990–91 was to sustain his claim to the prime ministership while explaining away the recession, an immensely difficult task. Keating became agitated, frustrated and prone to self-destructive actions—during 1990 he committed a series of blunders which reinforced the hostility which sections of the public held towards him.

In May 1990 Keating made a devastating public assault on Button, breaking Cabinet solidarity to declare a virtual 'no confidence' in his colleague, provoked by Button's penchant for soliloquy. Then he used a VIP jet to fly to Melbourne with journalists to attend a Collingwood football game, his latest loyalty in the cause of a more knockabout image. This fanned public concern about Keating's elitism and double standards. In September 1990 he attacked the National Australia Bank's outgoing chief, Nobby Clark, claiming the bank had been 'technically insolvent' a few years earlier, an extraordinary claim by a treasurer. Keating retreated but Howard hurt him: he accused Keating of playing 'fast and loose with the confidence of ordinary Australians in the stability of the financial system'.

But Keating's most memorable mistake came on 29 November 1990 with the release of statistics showing that Australia was in a second quarter of negative growth, the technical definition of a recession. Keating had a press statement prepared by his advisers which he read to the media—it contained the infamous line, '... this is a recession that Australia had to have'.

In one blow Keating destroyed two years of promises that Australia could avoid a recession—the pledge made by Hawke and Keating at the 1990 election. Keating's comments were a terrible political blunder, a mistake he later conceded. But he was also wrong when he suggested that 'the worst impact of the recession' might have passed. The contrast between Hawke and Keating was sharp: Keating was brazen in his reluctance to admit his mistake while Hawke flashed humility and a caring countenance. Within the party there was talk about eliminating Keating as a recession scapegoat—but this was too dangerous for Hawke.

The key to Labor's political crisis during its fourth term was that Hawke's leadership malaise transcended Keating's unpopularity, a considerable achievement. This was because Keating, popular or unpopular, was perceived to be the dominant figure in the government. Most people believed that Keating would replace Hawke as prime minister during the fourth term. Hawke's problem was summarised by NSW Liberal advertising adviser, Greg Daniel, chief of Clemenger Sydney: 'It would seem to me that Australia is in the peculiar position, almost, of having two Governors-General [Hawke and Hayden] and a Prime Minister [Keating] who is called the Deputy Prime Minister.'[2]

This perception had been revealed in ANOP's research before the 1990 election, and Rod Cameron said in late 1990 that Keating had as much chance of being an 'electable Prime Minister' as Hawke. Another study by Mackay Research in mid-1990 concluded: 'Consistently participants spoke as though it was beyond question that the Prime Minister would retire during his present term.' The study found that Keating 'is consistently described as arrogant, cold, aloof and gratuitously insulting yet there is continuing grudging respect for his performance as Treasurer'.[3]

Hawke and Keating were a study in contrasts. Hawke played more golf, travelled overseas, including a memorable trip to Gallipoli for the 75th anniversary commemoration of the ANZAC landing, and thrived at the Lodge. Keating was burning with frustration, fearful that Hawke would repudiate his Kirribilli pact, yet resentful that if he became prime minister he might inherit only the ashes of an era.

It is extraordinary that the two men discussed their agreement again only on 9 October 1990, six months after the election. Hawke told Keating that he wanted 'to be around' for a settlement in South Africa and said he was likely to be honoured with the keys to the city of London for his contribution to the Commonwealth. He said, 'I want to stay until CHOGM [the Commonwealth Heads of Government Meeting] in Zimbabwe next year.' That meeting would be in October 1991, late in the term for a leadership transition. Keating appealed to Hawke: he would need time as prime minister to change his image before an election. Keating reminded Hawke that he had given an unconditional pledge to retire in front of witnesses. But Hawke deferred further discussion and Keating left an unhappy man.[4]

The upshot was that Keating encouraged the two witnesses, Kelty and Abeles, to approach Hawke to seek a reconvening of the Kirribilli meeting. But Hawke was not interested. The equation was set: Hawke's resentment of Keating's pressure and Keating's hostility to Hawke's obstinacy.

Keating had two powerbases against Hawke—the NSW right and the centre left. This time, unlike 1988, the NSW right wanted a leadership change. Its powerbroker, Graham Richardson, had taken this decision before the 1990 election—a point few ALP figures had grasped. But Richardson's resentment towards Hawke hardened post-election when Hawke 'tested' if he wanted to quit politics and then gave him social security, a job Richardson disliked. Keating had fought with the NSW right at various stages of his treasurership, but Keating and his base were reuniting; the challenge would be rooted in NSW tribal loyalty.

Richardson had always known that eventually he would move from Hawke to Keating. Keating's ultimate aspirations were part of NSW Labor's tribal culture over the previous twenty years. Richardson knew that Keating would be a great gamble but he also felt that Hawke's leadership was dying—that with Labor's primary vote sinking below 35 per cent, only a new leader could break the cycle.

However, the right wing was divided on the leadership between NSW and Victoria. Victorian right powerbroker, Robert Ray, was Keating's chief critic within the party. The Keating–Ray relationship was rooted in a deep and mutual antagonism. Keating had vetoed Hawke's earlier plan to make Ray the finance minister. He called Ray 'the fat Indian' and never concealed his contempt for Ray's political judgement. Ray felt that Keating was electoral poison, a man who put his self-interest before the party's interest and that his unpopularity with the party and the public made absurd the talk about his leadership. Ray and Keating fell out badly before the 1990 election over proposals to give permanent residence to Sheikh Tajeddin al Hilaly, the controversial leader of the Lakemba Mosque in Sydney.

Ray was determined to stop Keating; even further, to destroy Keating if he mounted a challenge. Ray was the arch defender of Hawke's leadership. The Richardson–Ray right-wing faction faced a potentially fatal schism over the leadership. This danger was the origin of the Richardson–Ray pact; to ensure that their leadership dispute did not destroy the faction.

Most of the centre-left faction was passionately pro-Keating. The faction's origins lay in the old Hayden caucus group, the last people who came to Hawke in 1982–83. Button had been the final defector and Dawkins, Walsh and Blewett the final Hayden loyalists. The 1980s had seen the growth of an unusual political alliance, Keating and the centre left, whose organiser, Chris Schacht, had wanted to see Keating replace Hawke in 1988. The alliance was symbolised in the Keating–Dawkins connection as prime minister and treasurer in an alternative ALP government.

During the late 1980s and early 1990s the senior centre-left figures had settled for Keating against Hawke—Hayden, Dawkins, Button, Walsh, Peter Cook, Neal Blewett and the faction leaders, Chris Schacht and Michael Beahan.

The problem for Keating was that the NSW right and the centre-left did not constitute a caucus majority. So Keating briefly courted the left, an exercise doomed to disappointment.

Keating had been cultivating Howe as his future deputy since 1987. He knew that Howe had favoured a leadership change both from his own talks and from a remarkable Howe–Hogg exchange in the street in late 1990. Hogg recalls: 'Brian [Howe] bailed me up at the shops. His message was the need for a leadership change; that Cabinet was hopeless, the government was stagnant. It was beyond Hawke and we had to have Keating. Now I had some reservations. But Brian helped to persuade me that he was right.'⁵

In 1990 Keating tried to win Nick Bolkus to his side, giving Bolkus three hours at his home, including the 'treatment'—music, art and politics. But Keating misjudged the left: it was not going to ditch Hawke for a recession treasurer.

Following a report by Alan Ramsey in the *Sydney Morning Herald* on 24 November 1990 that Cabinet ministers were moving towards Keating, the left leaders, Gerry Hand and Nick Bolkus went to see Hawke. When Hawke told them that he was staying the left was unequivocal: 'The firm feeling within the left is to support you.' Hawke's office leaked the assurance to the media.

The upshot was that Keating spoke to Bolkus and Hand the next day. 'You blokes are mad,' he began, 'latching onto the fella around the corner.' They had a good talk—but Keating's fatalism was manifest. He didn't make a direct bid for their support, instead asking them to 'keep your minds open on the leadership'. Hand and Bolkus issued a warning to Keating—the caucus would not tolerate any leadership change through confrontation. Bolkus said that Keating's three major left-wing backers, Stewart West, Peter Duncan and Frank Walker, were only a minority inspired by vindictiveness.

Keating shocked Hand and Bolkus by revealing his timetable: if he was not prime minister by June 1991 then he would have resigned as treasurer and if he was not prime minister by the end of 1991 then he would have left politics. Keating wanted the party to grasp that its preferred position, the Hawke–Keating partnership, was no longer available. They party had to choose—and he was serious.

Hawke's links with the left had over the years moved from hostility to a respect founded in self-interest. The old left, which Hawke in 1979 had abused as 'an eating, spreading sore, an ulcer, a gangrene', was dying. Hawke's hate-figure, Bill Hartley, had been expelled from the party. Hawke had integrated the parliamentary left into his government and had an effective relationship with its key ministers, Howe, Hand and Bolkus, people he had previously criticised. Now Hawke said he was proud of the 'new generation' left ministers, firmly installed post-1990, which included Peter Baldwin, Robert Tickner, Peter Staples and Wendy Fatin.

Hawke paid respect to the left and the left wanted respect; it was developing a taste for power and flattery. But the growing bond between Hawke and the left was rooted in Hawke's survival. The left had known that, finally, it would have to choose between Hawke and Keating. As early as its mid-1982 meetings, when the left was rejecting Hawke for Hayden, the point had been made. 'We're opposed to Hawke now,' Gerry Hand told a national left meeting in 1982. 'But one day I think we'll have to choose between Hawke and Keating and I'm sure we'll be on Hawke's side then.'

Part of Keating's trouble with the left was his elitism. The caucus loved Keating's arrogant parliamentary attacks upon the Opposition, but it was a private victim of the same arrogance. As the economy slid into recession Keating became an isolated figure—from business, the media and the ALP. 'The Berlin Wall is alive in Parliament House,' the left joked about Keating's office.

The trigger for the intensification of the battle was Keating's appearance at the annual Press Gallery dinner on 7 December 1990, where as guest speaker he delivered a long homily on leadership. It was an annual off-the-record function, valuable for its insights but not normally for its news. Keating arrived at the Press Club at 8.15 pm in an unsettled condition. The previous evening his departmental head, Chris Higgins, 47, seven months older than Keating, had died. Keating had been with Higgins two hours before his death after a footrace.

Keating's speech started with a saga about a farting horse, Idi Amin and the Queen, and jokes about Michelle Grattan and Laurie Oakes. He praised Chris Higgins as a 'great participator' in national affairs and told the Gallery it had to choose 'between being participators or merely voyeurs'. Then he launched his theme—Australia's ability to become a great nation.

Keating said that Australia had much of which to be proud—its standards, decency and compassion. It occupied a continent; it had absorbed people from many other nations. He said most Japanese still lived in 'dogboxes'; Germany's environment was being destroyed by acid rain. The public was hostile towards politicians but it was politicians who changed things. Politics, above all, was about leadership and leadership changed the future of nations. 'Leadership is not about being popular, it's about being right,' Keating said. He pointed to the great difference between America and Australia. The US had had three great leaders—Washington, Lincoln and Franklin Roosevelt. 'The trouble with Australia is that we've never had such a leader. We've never had one leader, not one, and it shows.' The Labor heroes weren't great leaders; Curtin was a 'trier' and Chifley was a 'plodder'. Australia was 'teetering on the brink' of becoming a great nation. But it needed a leader who could communicate a vision, and not by 'tripping over television cables in shopping centres'.

Winning elections was about leadership. Keating said: 'I got the election date right this year and I got it right in 1987.' (So much for Hawke!) Keating said that he had the right blend of politics and economics. He called himself the 'Placido Domingo of Australian politics' while Hewson was 'the hall attendant at the back of the theatre'. Running Australia was no easy task and the media should grasp the unique position he had established as treasurer. 'I've got the confidence of the financial markets, I've got the central bank, I've got the support of organised labour and I've got the confidence of the Treasury and the policy-making centres in Canberra.' Keating went on: 'If you can't manage these, then things will fall apart quickly.' He ridiculed the shadow treasurer, Peter Reith. 'Now, I'm not interested in Reithy,' Keating said. 'I'll leave Reithy to you. I'm interested in Hewson but I can't get a run at him because he won't debate me.' Keating said he had already established a 'psychological ascendancy' over Hewson who, he said, had no capacity to lead the nation or to inspire. Hewson was a 'Waverley cemetery headstone'.

Keating hammered the idea that Australia had the chance to establish itself as a low-inflation nation—an historic breakthrough. But its consolidation would need leadership and the government was ten years old (in fact, it would be ten years at the next election). Labor would have to win the next election on leadership. He praised the Gallery for playing a constructive role in advancing the economic debate during the 1980s, and appealed to it to maintain these standards—but this appeal carried another message. At the end of his 45-minute speech Keating said: 'I know that some of you are with me. Others of you are not with me. But you need to get involved. You've got to address the questions that we face.'

Hawke's name was not mentioned but the speech was an appeal to the Gallery to support Keating's credentials as leader against Hawke. The truth is that Keating had miscalculated. He had intended to stimulate the Gallery and to provoke it, but not to launch a showdown with Hawke. This was established by a number of reporters in their chats with Keating after his speech in the several hours before he left the Press Club. Although the Gallery dinner was an 'off-the-record' function, such remarks to about 120 journalists could not stay secret.

The next day Keating flew to Blackall in central Queensland for ALP 100th anniversary celebrations. Hawke was given a detailed account of Keating's speech on Saturday morning. He was angry and hurt; one confidant said he was 'enraged'. Here was confirmation of Hawke's fears about the destructive potential of Keating's ego; he was brilliant but flawed. Hawke felt that Keating had insulted his leadership before the entire media corps. But his offence was worse than that—Keating had insulted the party, its history and its past leaders, including Curtin, the leader Hawke upheld in self-reflection. The situation grew more serious with the Sunday newspapers' reports of the speech, despite their brevity.[6]

The Keating coup

The psychological impact of the speech was devastating. Hawke felt that Keating wanted to destroy his place in history as a prelude to stealing his job. How could Hawke retain his honour against this dual threat to his position and his reputation? Hawke hardened against resignation and against Keating.

The paradox, of course, is that it was in Hawke's interest to depart, to retire undefeated. But Hawke's passions had been aroused by Keating, and passions disturb judgement. The Press Gallery speech was a turning point in Hawke's relationship with Keating; the culmination of a long developing sentiment. Hawke believed that Keating had engaged in 'an act of treachery'. Hawke took a far-reaching decision—to oppose Keating as his successor. He concluded that such disloyalty from a deputy to himself and the party meant that the party should look beyond Keating for its next leader.

For months, whenever Hawke had been on the racetrack or at the ALP branches, he had faced a 'Keating has got to go' chorus. Hawke was not prepared to act on this, since he knew it would precipitate the crisis. But Hawke felt exasperation that Keating—whom he was under pressure to dump—was claiming to be the real leader. From this point Hawke assumed that a challenge was almost certain and began his defence.

Keating's speech had two results—it alienated the caucus and it destabilised Hawke's leadership. Keating went on radio on Monday morning and performed a *mea culpa*. But Hawke called Keating to a meeting that afternoon, 10 December, in his office. If Hawke was ever going to confront Keating and remove him as treasurer this was the moment—but Hawke wanted a public relations solution, not a power solution.

Richardson saw both men before their meeting. His interests were the transition to Keating, the unity of the right wing and his reputation as a powerbroker. He told Keating to apologise, admit his blunder and be humble before Hawke. He told Hawke to avoid any showdown with Keating and settle for a compromise.

It was a rambling three-hour discussion which traversed leadership, Curtin's record and Keating's speech. Keating told Hawke he had not attacked him and did not undermine him. Hawke retorted that there was no need for Keating to insult his intelligence; Keating, of all politicians, knew the effect of such comments on the media. It was 'bullshit' for Keating to pretend his remarks were made without intent. Keating said there was no point in Hawke getting angry now, more than two years after their leadership agreement which Hawke didn't even want to discuss.

Hawke said he was deeply hurt by Keating's speech; he was upset about Keating's line that Australia had never had a great leader, and wanted to pursue it. But Keating dodged, saying that he had been referring to the pre-1983 period. This was fudging the truth. Keating knew and the media knew that he had not put such a limit on his judgements of Australian leaders.

'The worst I've done is to exclude you from the pantheon of great American leaders,' Keating said. But what about Hawke's cult hero Curtin? Hawke went to his hero's defence. He gave Keating a long lecture on Curtin's greatness, both as wartime leader and economic manager, saying that at the very time Curtin was saving his country he was establishing the apparatus for post-war reconstruction. Keating should read the Hansard from the 1930s, years before Keynes published the General Theory, which showed that Curtin was 'light years ahead of his contemporaries in understanding the nature of the economic challenge'. Curtin had also forged a remarkable relationship with Douglas Macarthur, basic to Australia's wartime success. Curtin, in fact, became a surrogate, allowing Hawke to triumph over Keating. 'I persuaded him,' Hawke said later. Hawke couldn't argue with Keating on Hawke's own greatness, so he argued on Curtin's greatness. And Hawke won—he beat Keating on Curtin.

The Kirribilli pact was neither reaffirmed nor repudiated. Hawke told Keating that he would think about the leadership and they would talk again before the end of January. But Hawke wanted a public statement and produced a draft in which Keating would say that he had not 'implied any challenge' to Hawke nor 'intended any offence' in his Gallery speech. It said that Hawke intended to remain as prime minister for the term and that he wished Keating to remain as his deputy and treasurer, a course with which Keating had 'totally concurred'. The statement was a nonsense; the entire media corps knew it was a public relations fantasy. When a draft was phoned through to Richardson at a Canberra restaurant he snorted: 'No journalist is going to be stupid enough to believe this.'

After the meeting Hawke sought a solution to the argument being put against him inside and outside the party—that he was now a 'lame duck' leader. The pro-Keating forces said that since the Liberals would campaign at the next election against Keating as the 'real' prime minister, Labor should accept this logic and install Keating now.

Hogg and Richardson had explained this problem to Hawke. Acting on advice from Richardson and his own staff, Hawke tried to kill the 'lame duck' argument at his 11 December press conference. He announced revised plans for his political future: 'I now make it clear that I will lead the party to the next election with the intention of going through that term . . . I'm giving you my commitment, you see, for some five years.' Hawke said that his new five-year pledge was given in response to party requests, and enunciated his bedrock position on the leadership: 'I believe I can win but I always listen to the party's will.' Hawke said he was Labor's best vote winner. If he believed that Keating had a better chance then he would defer to Keating.

The reaction to Hawke's five-year pledge from the party and the media was adverse. A group of centre-left members in the dining room set up a mocking chant: 'Five more years, five more years.' One of the centre-left conveners, Chris Schacht, was filmed making the quip, 'It's peace in our time.' Hawke's pledge only betrayed his vulnerability. Nobody believed that Hawke would stay another five years.

These events in December 1990 were a milestone for the Labor Party. At this point it became clear that the Hawke–Keating partnership was destroyed. It had moved decisively from being an asset to being a liability. The partnership, with its unique mixture of popularity and steel, had been broken irretrievably, leaving the leadership situation unstable and unpredictable as the conflict continued unabated, unresolved and intensified. Senior Gallery commentators now asserted as a fact that the Hawke–Keating partnership was finished.[7]

Meanwhile the polls showed the Opposition leading the government 49 to 32 on the primary vote, with unemployment heading towards 10 per cent.

Richardson, sensing that Hawke's 'five more years' pledge had inspired ridicule, exploited the fallout. He had an ambivalent role, being both Hawke's adviser and Keating's ally, a conflict he tried to reconcile by persuading Hawke to leave. That required the correct mixture of scare and incentive. Richardson's experience told him that in such situations the challenger usually prevailed. He visited Hawke at 8.30 pm on 20 December 1990.

'You should know that a majority of the party want to see you leave,' Richardson told Hawke. He said if there was a party room test now, Hawke's survival would depend on Richardson. That was a situation, said Richardson, he didn't like. Hawke had the numbers in the party room now but Richardson could not be sure that Hawke would have the numbers for much longer.

Hawke gave Richardson a lecture, but he knew that Richardson had put him on notice. Hawke took out some political insurance during the Christmas break when Richardson went overseas. Summer was usually a lucky season for Hawke and 1990–91 just proved the rule. Ray made a number of soundings to satisfy himself that Hawke was still secure. Hawke was advised by some of his staff to ditch Keating as treasurer but he declined. Meanwhile US President George Bush, backed by the greatest alliance since World War II, initiated a strike against Iraq's Saddam Hussein to force the liberation of Kuwait. The war, to which Australia contributed three ships, began in mid-January 1991; it was a decisive boost to Hawke's leadership.

Hawke was consumed by the war, involved in extensive daily briefings, contact with overseas leaders and debate within the government and the party. His judgement was vindicated on the extent of Australia's contribution, which was commensurate with its size but proof of its commitment. It revealed Hawke's penchant for diplomacy and his search for a great uniting issue—he handled Australia's involvement with just the right mixture of balance and determination.

On 31 January 1991 Hawke called Keating to their second meeting on the leadership. The Gulf War was a fortnight old and Hawke had completed the special two day sitting of federal parliament to endorse Australia's commitment. The war had two domestic political effects: it boosted Hawke's standing as prime minister; and it terminated any leadership lobbying within the party, thereby stalling Keating's campaign.

Hawke now told Keating that after consideration he had decided to remain as prime minister for the full fourth term. Keating hit back: 'That's a total breach of your Kirribilli undertaking and the arrangements on which I've relied for the past two and a half years.' Hawke said: 'I recognise this. I'm not trying to pretend that this is not in breach of our agreement. I'm not trying to hide that. But I believe that I've clearly got the best chance to lead the party to victory at the next election and I'm staying on this basis.' Keating replied: 'Bob, you'll never win another election. You're dead meat. You'll just hang around for a punch on the nose.'

Hawke put a question to Keating: you're surely not suggesting that if you think I can win better than you, that I should still stand down in your favour? Keating denied that Hawke had a better chance of winning than him. But this wasn't the point. Keating said that the 'agreement is unconditional'. It didn't matter whether Hawke thought he had a better chance of winning than Keating.

But Hawke felt differently: he believed that Keating was a victim of his dogmatic belief that 'it was his turn' to be prime minister.

Keating said, 'A short war is good for you,' and Hawke admitted that the war had helped him. Hawke said: 'Even if I wanted to go, I would never tolerate being seen to be pushed out by the likes of Gary Punch.' Keating then put a proposition to Hawke: 'I claim, and nobody can refute, that even today, if you left, you wouldn't be seen to be pushed out of the leadership. That will be even more true after the war.' Hawke paused and replied, 'Yes, that's valid.' Keating then put another proposition: 'Are you prepared to think about departing when the war is over when nobody can believe that you are being pushed?' Hawke considered his answer: 'Yes I'm prepared to think about that.' But the key was his tone—Hawke was not encouraging Keating, just offering a crack of hope.

Keating asked, 'How can you have your ear to the ground and not hear it?' 'Hear what?' asked Hawke. 'Hear that you're finished,' said Keating. 'Our primary vote was 39 per cent at the last election. It's got lower at every election. We can't win any more on a falling primary vote and a high share of preferences. We've got to reverse the trend and that means getting the primary vote up. You say you can turn it around but how, how are you going to do it?' Hawke found these questions extraordinary. He shot back: 'You mean I can't, but you can?' Keating answered: 'Maybe I can. Maybe. I say to other people that maybe I can. But for you, I say that you can't. I just want you to honour your agreement.'

Hawke rejected Keating's assessment as a fantastic delusion. He was breaking his word, this time using as justification the party's interest, not

Keating's Gallery speech. He couldn't leave because that would damage Labor's reelection hopes. Keating said that he would probably remain in politics but this was not necessarily the case if Hawke continued as prime minister. With the Middle East ablaze and Hawke's authority enhanced, Keating had no immediate option but acquiescence. The battle was deferred, not cancelled.

From this moment a Keating challenge was inevitable. Keating, given his character, was compelled to challenge. In the interim, Keating was too weak, a victim of war and recession. The war gave Hawke a false security and the recession gave Keating an accumulated burden.

Keating, irritated by Hawke's conduct over the war, had stopped going to the morning briefings. He compared Hawke to a 'Napoleon without the hat' as Hawke sat grim-faced and cigar smoking through briefings by military and civilian advisers. In one sense Keating never recovered from the war. He complained later that his support had peaked before Christmas 1990 and never returned to this level before the challenge. 'The war changed the thinking about my leadership from being an expectation to an act of sedition,' Keating bemoaned.

As 1991 advanced Richardson tested Keating's intent by putting to him the arguments against a challenge—that the leadership was a poisoned chalice; that Keating was unlikely to have the numbers; that they would be depicted as wrecking the government; that Keating's chances of beating Hewson were not good. Keating was moody, caught between fatalism and realism. But Richardson knew that Keating was a crazy brave. He grasped the political and emotional logic of the broken Kirribilli pact—that Keating would challenge for the mantle which Hawke had promised and then denied.

As 1991 advanced Keating drew his own deadline—a challenge before the winter recess. It became a career imperative which transcended tactics or arithmetic. Keating was hellbent upon a showdown in the current term. He could not wait until the budget session; the term would be too advanced, he would be conscripted to the selling of the budget. Keating recognised that he would need two 'hits', as he was unlikely to have the numbers the first time. Finally, if Keating had any hope against Hewson, he had to replace Hawke sooner, not later.

The opening came with Hawke's debacle over the WA Inc issue during the Royal Commission hearings in Perth. Hawke was under attack over revelations that he had attended a Perth lunch on 15 June 1987 organised by premier Brian Burke at which nearly $1 million was pledged to Labor's federal campaign by businessmen including 'last resort' Laurie Connell. The lunch and pledges were a fact. But the implication—that Hawke took the funds in return for a promise not to tax gold—was false. Yet Hawke stumbled in parliament, unable to defend himself, and it was Keating who, in a memorable sitting week in April 1991, salvaged Hawke and turned the issue back to Hewson.

Hawke's worst mistake was his passionate refusal to stand down his mate Brian Burke as Ambassador to Ireland, despite the evidence of impropriety against Burke. Even after admitting that Burke had acted unwisely and improperly Hawke refused to seek his immediate resignation, much to the horror of his staff, foreign minister Evans, and the party. Hawke's stand was backed by Beazley and Richardson, Burke's other mates. The upshot was humiliation for Hawke in the parliament and the media. It was confirmation of a truth about Hawke's leadership: that each six months he would fall into a self-created hole. The significance of the WA Inc issue is that it gave Keating the confidence to stick by his deadline for a challenge before the winter recess.

But the key to this mid-year challenge was that Hawke had out-manoeuvred Keating. Hawke's defensive preparations were so thorough that Keating never had a hope. Hawke had three pluses which made Keating's task impossible: his proven record as Labor's greatest election winner; Keating's recession-induced unpopularity; and a determined factional alliance supporting Hawke as prime minister.

The Hawke alliance was better prepared for the challenge than was Keating. It constituted the Victorian right led by Ray; the left caucus led by Hand and Bolkus; the Queenslanders, where the AWU powerbroker, Bill Ludwig, who influenced or controlled six Queensland members, gave a personal pledge to Hawke in May; the Tasmanian caucus; senior right-wing ministers Beazley, Evans and Kerin; and Hawke's superior appeal to non-aligned caucus members, symbolised by the attorney-general, Michael Duffy. Hawke's alliance was far too broad for Keating.

Hawke sent the message to the party that he would never buckle and resign under pressure. He would only leave in one of two ways—if he decided, miraculously, that Keating was a better vote winner, or if the caucus had the guts to depose him. Hawke would deny Labor any easy option. In mid-May Hawke was interviewed by Jana Wendt and announced that he would refuse any 'tap on the shoulder'. He said that he was 'the best' for the party and (if a delegation of colleagues asked for his resignation), 'I'd say, "That's very interesting, but I'm not going".'[8]

In the fortnight before the challenge the Hawke camp accurately briefed the media that the margin was 70–40 Hawke's way. Ray and Bolkus kept an up-to-date check list. Hawke went public, complaining about destabilisation. The media was consumed with speculation about a leadership showdown. But Keating's strike was delayed by the NSW election on 25 May—he could not provoke a federal leadership crisis that hurt Labor's chances in his home state, where he hoped to win most of his support.

On 24 May, the day before the state election, ALP national secretary Bob Hogg, the party's campaign director, met Hawke and advised him to organise a transition to Keating. Hogg embodied the puzzling paradox of the Keating push: why would Labor dump Australia's most popular leader for its most unpopular treasurer? Hogg explains:

> The critical factor was the internal dynamics. You can't win if the party's divided. The challenge, obviously, wasn't going away and would only get worse. The core problem was that Hawke had been deserted by his own base, the NSW people who backed him against Hayden. His position was inherently unstable. The party was more likely to unite behind Keating than Hawke. Of course, Keating was going to be a problem electorally. But I think Hawke was beyond the point of electability. In terms of getting energy, drive and unity in government I just don't think it was possible under Hawke.[9]

Hogg told Hawke that if the Keating camp didn't get him the first time they would succeed the second time. He predicted a challenge 'at least within the month', and gave Hawke a letter setting out his advice, a move heavy with symbolism given Button's letter to Hayden nine years earlier asking him to resign. Hogg warned that the Kirribilli agreement would be used against Hawke.

Hawke told Hogg that his assessment was wrong and his judgement faulty. Hogg left with a strong impression of Hawke's deep hostility towards Keating. He told a friend: 'Hawke once said to me that guilt, hate and envy are the corrosive elements of the human character and that he had guilt but not the others. I think to be fair to him, he's got the full range.' Hostility towards Hogg deepened within the Hawke camp. Hogg, in turn, told Richardson that Hawke's hostility towards Keating was profound; it would be a nasty, bitter and brutal contest.

As Keating's deadline for the challenge approached Richardson had a duel nightmare: if Keating won then history might cast him as the executioner of Labor's most successful leader for its most unsuccessful; if Keating lost badly then both himself and Keating might be ruined forever.

In mid-May Richardson told Hawke's political aide, Colin Parkes, 'I'm not playing a role in this.' On 24 May, the day Hogg saw Hawke, Richardson declared there was no challenge and that the Hawke–Keating team 'is the one we ought to keep . . . the one that gives us the best chance of winning'.[10] Richardson was apprehensive about a challenge.

The following week the parliament gathered for the final fortnight before the winter recess. In parliament on Tuesday 28 May Keating inexplicably declared that the leadership 'will only be an issue of relevance on our side of politics when the Prime Minister deigns it to be'. The same evening, however, Keating, Richardson and Laurie Brereton ate a takeaway curry at Brereton's Canberra apartment at a meeting in which they decided upon the challenge. Keating gave them a long pep talk in which he said that Hawke deserved to be challenged. The Kirribilli pact would be used as a hook of legitimacy. Richardson would raise the agreement with Hawke and if Hawke, as expected, refused to back off then Richardson would threaten a challenge. Richardson wanted to use Channel Nine's Laurie Oakes to break the Kirribilli story to a startled party and public. The target was a party room challenge the following Tuesday—a week away.

The Keating camp hoped to get fifty votes and didn't expect to get below forty votes in the 110-strong caucus. The tactic was to document Keating's strength in the party room, thereby creating the momentum for a majority a few months later. Richardson's inclination was to wait another ten days until Hawke went overseas, and mobilise with the Emperor abroad. But Keating refused to wait.

Keating was a strange mixture of propriety and impropriety, a description Button later used. He had still done no lobbying of swinging members himself. His lieutenants had stirred the pot for months but to little effect. Keating had willed himself to this challenge; he was heavy with Shakespearian inevitability.

Ultimately, Keating's position was simple: he refused to accept Hawke's legitimacy any more. He wanted the party to make a judgement on his own leadership claim. Keating rationalised that he owed it to the party; he believed he owed it to himself. He hoped for an honourable result but never believed he would win. He would retire to the backbench afterwards and let Hawke govern without him. Keating was a sublime contradiction, overflowing with nerves and relish.

Richardson went to Hawke's office about 10 pm on 29 May. Asked if he intended to honour the pact, Hawke said he had told Keating on 31 January that he would remain because he was Labor's best vote winner—win, lose or draw, he was the best hope. He said that Keating's Press Gallery speech was 'an act of treachery' and that Keating had forfeited any claim to the agreement at that point.

Richardson warned Hawke that the story of the broken agreement would be revealed and his integrity would be damaged. Hawke responded that the broken agreement was 'manageable'. He began to tell Richardson about his special relationship with the Australian people. But Richardson interrupted, 'It's me you're talking to, for God's sake, it's me, don't peddle this bullshit to me.' Richardson said that if Hawke dishonoured the agreement a challenge was inevitable: 'I don't know if Keating will challenge tomorrow, next week or next year but the challenge will come.'

Richardson and Hawke had an exchange of excuses for the severance of their alliance. 'My door is there,' Hawke said; 'It hasn't gone anywhere and it's always open.' Richardson replied, 'And my phone still sits on my desk and it doesn't ring.'

These veterans of past battles were honest. 'We'll get more than forty votes but you'll win,' Richardson said. The discussion dragged on for three hours. It had been a long journey, many years since Richardson as Hawke's car driver had carried a drunken Hawke to his bed. Nine years since

Richardson had helped to knife Hayden for Hawke. Now Richardson carried Keating's knife against Hawke.

Both men knew that ultimately anything could be negotiated. Before Richardson left, Hawke said: 'What exactly are you putting to me?' Richardson replied, 'I'm not in a position to put anything exactly to you.' Richardson knew that only one person ever decided what Keating did—Keating himself. Hawke said he'd think about things overnight and talk to Richardson tomorrow. Richardson left at 12.45 am after a complex discussion. He forgot that Keating was waiting in his office for a report and went home to bed.

The next day at lunchtime Hawke told Richardson: 'I'm prepared to consider this question on my overseas trip but you should know that I don't think I'll be changing my mind.' It was typical Hawke: saying 'no' but leaving a crack of hope. 'You know what Keating says about you,' Richardson told Hawke. 'He says you live your life asking for another three months at a time. Now you're telling me you'll think about it for another three weeks.' The showdown was coming.

Meanwhile Hawke was keeping a secret from the party—the purchase of a $1.2 million steep waterfront property at Sydney's Northbridge, backing onto Middle Harbour. If the caucus discovered that Hawke was buying a Sydney property it could easily be read as a departing gesture. Hawke's advisers were terrified the story might leak.

That afternoon Richardson reported to Keating, who snorted with contempt at Hawke's 'three more weeks' reply. Keating was ready to strike. But Richardson, worried about the numbers, still hoped to cut a deal. Late that afternoon Richardson went to see Beazley in an effort to secure a compromise and persuade Hawke to an arrangement. 'Go and see Hawke and talk some sense into him,' he told Beazley. Beazley was dubious but, like Richardson, he did not rule out a settlement. But Richardson had misjudged Hawke. After all, Hawke had the numbers and knew that he would win any contest.

Keating went to see Hawke about 4 pm but he was busy with three Queenslanders—premier Wayne Goss, ALP state secretary Wayne Swan, and AWU chief Bill Ludwig—a trio who would be vital to Hawke's survival. They had met to discuss compensation arrangements in relation to Fraser Island. So Keating returned at 5 pm, pacing up and down outside Hawke's office.

Finally Keating stuck his head in the door and Hawke adjourned his meeting. 'I know you've told Graham that you're staying in breach of our agreement,' Keating said. 'I told you a long time ago that if I ever organised against you that you'd be the first to know. I'm telling you I will now organise against you.' Hawke said, 'Okay, but sit down. You know I said to Graham that I'd think about it.' But Keating was finished with delays. He warned: 'I wouldn't be going overseas if I was you, Bob'—a reference to Hawke's planned European trip the next week. Hawke said, 'I have a different idea of my responsibilities than you think I have.'

Beazley came to Hawke's office during this exchange to pursue Richardson's compromise efforts, but it was too late. When Keating left, Hawke resumed the Fraser Island meeting, showing nerves of ice. Then he informed his staff of Keating's declaration and called a meeting of his main supporters including Ray, Bolkus and Hand. Ray had detailed lists dividing the caucus into rival camps and waverers.

Oakes was unable to get the Richardson-inspired Kirribilli story to air until well into the 6 pm television news bulletin. Within thirty minutes Keating's press secretary had confirmed the story to a torrent of media enquiries. It was only at this time, on Thursday 30 May 1991, that the ALP, the media and the public became aware of the secret Hawke–Keating agreement made at Kirribilli in November 1988. It was one of the biggest stories in Australian political history. Keating hoped its revelation would legitimise his challenge and win more support.

But Keating and Richardson had made a terrible tactical mistake. By releasing the Kirribilli story simultaneously with the declaration of the challenge they failed to exploit its value or condition the caucus to its magnitude. Keating lost ground because caucus waverers resented the manner of his challenge—just two days after he had denied any challenge in parliament!

Keating's interests would have been better served by releasing the Kirribilli story and then speaking privately to the swell of Labor MPs coming to his door. By moving so quickly and trying to 'snatch' the leadership he shocked much of the party.

Cabinet reconvened briefly to discuss proposed mining at Coronation Hill. A hostile Gareth Evans asked Keating, 'Why are you doing this? Why didn't you talk to us?' Keating resented Evans—he knew that in 1990 Evans had favoured a change. Bob Collins, whom Keating hoped to win, was solid for Hawke. Cabinet, once Keating's powerbase, was behind Hawke. Keating only had Dawkins, Button, Richardson, Peter Cook, Ros Kelly and Neal Blewett. The meeting dissolved in deference to the rituals of power.

Parliament House descended into chaos for the night, with some members sleeping in their offices. The Hawke camp held a series of floating meetings in his office until 3.30 am, when Hawke went to the Lodge. Chief organiser was Robert Ray, supported by Hand, Bolkus and Staples from the left, Neil O'Keefe from the non-aligned group, and Beazley, Evans, Crean and Duffy. Ray was the chief coordinator and gave Hawke a list of waverers to contact.

The keys to Hawke's victory were the delivery of the left, virtually en masse; the split in the right where Hawke lost NSW but kept Victoria and Queensland; the non-aligned caucus members, who voted strongly for Hawke; and a complete Tasmanian sweep.

The Keating coup

The Hawke camp, acting from strength, decided to call a special caucus meeting for 8 am the next day to force the vote. This was announced just after 10.30 pm. The aim was to catch Keating with his pants down. Hawke's organisers were shooting for a 70–40 win, a Keating humiliation. They would deny Keating four days to organise before the Tuesday meeting.

The factions broke to hold their own meetings. The left caucus went until 1 am with only three members, West, Walker and Duncan, declaring for Keating and three others uncertain. Bolkus and Hand decided to give the 'Keating three' the discretion to vote according to their will. The left formally endorsed a Hawke–Howe ticket as a first preference. The left had cut a deal with Hawke—Howe would be deputy leader—although the left's support was not conditional upon a deal.

The centre-left was overwhelmingly for Keating but there were waverers. Hawke saw a number of centre-left and non-aligned members during the night. The Queensland power structure reinforced the instinct of most Queenslanders to vote for Hawke. Keating only had two votes in Victoria—Button and Alan Griffiths.

The Hawke camp had the numbers but they botched their tactics. They assumed that Keating would move in the caucus to declare the leadership vacant—a vote taken on a show of hands. But Keating wanted Hawke to vacate his office and allow both men to nominate for the leadership and run on an equal basis—a vote taken in a secret ballot.

The Keating forces struggled most of the night. In the early hours of the morning an announcement on the building's paging system requested all caucus members who had not spoken to Keating's office to contact it. The Keating lobbyists were pleading for votes to avoid humiliation. The dawn saw gloom breaking in the Keating bunker. Hawke was grim, but ready for the kill.

The party meeting began at 8 am with a short address from Hawke: 'I've called this meeting because the deputy and Treasurer said he wanted to challenge for my job. I think the best way to facilitate this is to have this meeting to enable the challenger to move that my position be declared vacant.' Hawke was putting the words into Keating's mouth. But Peter Walsh, a Hawke hater, interjected from the back: 'That's not what Hayden did in '82'—a reference to Hayden's decision to resign and allow a direct Hayden–Hawke contest in a secret ballot.

Keating seized Walsh's line and said: 'Bob, in a similar situation in '82 Bill Hayden stood down to allow a proper contest. I should have thought that you would have the courage to do as much now. There should be a secret ballot. We know members have been threatened with loss of pre-selection and we should avoid a show of hands. I invite you to do the honourable thing and surrender your position for a ballot.' At this point an angry Kim Beazley rose, pointing at Keating: 'You brought this situation on. You move for the leadership to be vacated.'

Hawke was frozen, for three, four, five seconds. It was an exquisite silence for the Hawke haters. Peter Walsh said later: 'Hawke sat there as mute as Gough Whitlam when the Iraqi loans affairs broke over his head in 1976.' Loosley said: 'It was worthy of Evatt at his worst.' Hawke then replied, 'I reject that course of action and that comparison [with Hayden].'

Hawke had his gun, loaded and ready, but couldn't pull the trigger.

There were several more interjections from the floor. Then Keating spoke again: 'If that's what I have to do then I'll do it at a time of my choosing. Not now. It will be at the next regular caucus meeting [the next Tuesday].' Some members called out, 'Where do we go from here?' The caucus chairman, Carolyn Jakobsen, said there was no further business. Richardson responded, 'Let's get out of here.' The Keating forces streamed out of the party room as fast as possible, knowing that Hawke had a majority close to 70–40 even in a secret ballot. They wanted to fight another day. Hawke's blunder was to adjourn this meeting; it was over within 15 minutes. He lost his chance to humiliate Keating.

Hawke returned to his office with his main advisers, Ray, Bolkus, Beazley, Hand and Evans. Ray admitted the mistake, his mistake as chief organiser. Late he concluded, 'I fucked up in the party room.' Hawke had the numbers but failed to force a vote; Keating had escaped. The Hawke camp reassessed—if Keating wanted a secret ballot then he could have it. Hawke ordered a second caucus meeting for 10 am. But it was too late.

When Keating rang Hawke a few minutes later to discuss plans for that day's Premiers' Conference he got a nasty shock: Hawke said that Keating could have his secret ballot at the 10 am meeting. Now Keating retreated. Members had left the building, he said. Ah no, replied Hawke, we're calling them back, in the cars, at the airport, in the transport pool. Keating, the challenger, said he wanted more time. Hawke was incredulous. Whose challenge is this? But Keating refused to give Hawke another chance that day. Keating and Richardson quickly sent the message—their troops disappeared into the thick fog around Parliament House. They staged a boycott. The Hawke camp chanted 'cowards'. Ray boiled in the lobbies about 'the gutless challenger'. Beazley said the boycotting of a properly called caucus meeting was a serious moment in Labor's history.

About 70 caucus members attended the 10 am party meeting, but not Keating, not his supporters. Hawke explained that this situation was different from that in 1982 when Hayden, the leader, had precipitated the contest against Hawke, the challenger. This time Keating, the challenger, was forcing the contest. This is why, Hawke told the caucus, the onus lay with Keating to move a motion to vacate the leadership. Having made this point, Hawke explained that he was still prepared to accept Keating's request for a secret ballot. But Keating had refused to attend this 10 am meeting. Hawke proposed a special meeting at 10 am on Monday 3 June to allow a secret ballot and a final resolution.

It is agreed by both sides—then and later—that the three days delay helped Keating by as many as four votes. This suggests that if the Friday ballot had been held, history might have been different. Hawke's margin would have been about thirty votes.

Hawke and Keating had to spend the rest of Friday together at a Premiers' Conference and on Saturday attend an ALP National Executive meeting. After the Executive broke Bob Hogg held an extraordinary press conference.

The national secretary said the challenge was likely to damage Hawke more than Keating; he warned about the risk of months of instability with Keating on the backbench; he denied that it was impossible for Keating to win an election as leader; he refused to confirm or deny newspapers reports that he had recently asked Hawke to resign; and he warned against intimidation of MPs in the ballot—a reference to the pro-Hawke Queensland push.[11]

Hawke was furious.

The public symbol of Keating's progress was the weekend television appearance of Bundaberg backbencher Brian Courtice, wearing a red T-shirt, declaring that he would defy standover tactics and vote for Keating.

The challenger went public on Sunday morning with an appearance on Channel Nine's *Sunday* show—an opportunity which Hawke had been offered and had declined. Keating outlined a policy agenda including a national retirement income scheme, a revival program for the cities, a more independent foreign policy.

Asked about being a wrecker, Keating replied that arrangements had been made for a transition but Hawke had broken them. Keating put the essence of his position: that after more than eight years of office it was 'time for a generational change in leadership'. Keating said that the party should not vote upon popularity but for 'whoever provides the best government in the next two years' since that would maximise Labor's reelection hopes. He finished with a promise to provide 'direction, strategy, esprit de corps, enthusiasm and, dare I say it, where necessary, a touch of excitement'.[12]

The Hawke forces spent all Sunday at The Lodge—and the ministers wanted Hawke to reply to Keating in the media. But Hawke's aide, Colin Parkes, resisted, fearing a bloodbath. He said the first question to Hawke would be, 'Why did you tell a lie?', referring to the Kirribilli agreement. Hawke's job was to persuade the caucus, not the public.

Hawke's most fateful decision was to ring John Kerin and offer him the treasury portfolio. This was a choice Hawke made on merit, not to win votes. He was influenced by Kerin's political success in handling the farmers and miners, but he misjudged Kerin's ability to succeed as treasurer—and the consequences would be severe. Ray believed that Hawke had made a mistake. Hawke then sent Ray and Kerin onto Sunday night television to defend his position.

Over the weekend Kerin had told Keating: 'I'm torn. I can see the arguments for both sides. I'm prepared to talk to some people for you if you like.' Keating thanked Kerin, then a few hours later heard that Kerin was appearing on television representing Hawke. Keating rang Kerin back. 'I won't be criticising you,' Kerin said. 'I've made a commitment to Hawke to do this.' The next morning Keating rang Kerin just before the party room meeting: 'Did you ask those people for a vote for me?' Keating asked. Kerin said that he hadn't, 'How are you voting, John?' Keating asked. 'Oh, I'm voting for Hawke but I wish you the best in the ballot,' Kerin replied.

Before the ballot Keating rang Willis and Evans. Willis told him, 'I'll be voting for Bob.' 'That's okay, Ralph,' Keating replied. He felt that Willis expected to be Hawke's new treasurer but Keating doubted that this would happen. When Evans said he would be voting for Hawke, Keating remembered Evans' jokes about being Gary Glitter's foreign minister. He replied: 'Gareth, you've left your intellect in the bottom drawer.'

Robert Ray told the ABC that a 20-vote margin for Hawke should be recognised by the party as sufficient to neutralise an ongoing Keating push. The Hawke camp said that Keating must abide by the result. When centre-left organiser Michael Beahan said that Keating would launch a second challenge if the first failed, he was unwisely articulating the 'second agenda' of the challenge.

Hawke was vindicated with 66–44 victory. It meant that the caucus was divided exactly 60 to 40 per cent, and that a shift of one vote in ten would change the leadership. Hawke declared the challenge dead. But Keating was happy, since 44 votes was respectable and kept him 'alive'. Keating promised there would be no 'second round'; and the media, with justification, promptly declared the start of 'round two'.

Hawke was in a fury at the media—the senior Gallery correspondents in their columns and the newspaper editors in their editorials had backed Keating. They offered two reasons: that Keating would govern better and that the party split could only be resolved by a change.

When the divided right wing faction met after the ballot the Keating forces encouraged Kerin to nominate as deputy. Why shouldn't the right wing keep the deputy's post, they asked mockingly. Kerin thought it a good idea. Then Ray came clean: the right couldn't take the deputy's post because Hawke had dealt it to Howe. About 29 out of Hawke's 66 votes were from the left wing.

After his victory Hawke faltered under pressure when quizzed for the first time about the Kirribilli pact, which John Hewson likened to 'trading the Prime Ministership like a sack of potatoes'. Hewson said that Hawke's integrity was fatally undermined. Hawke said he entered the agreement with 'reluctance' and that 'political realities' had 'forced' him to keep the deal secret—otherwise Labor would have lost the 1990 election. This was the justification for misleading the people. Andrew Peacock interjected: 'I copped the consequences of your lying.' At one stage Hawke left the fantastic implication that his misrepresentation was justified because 'it would be bad for this country' if the coalition had won the election. Hawke said he had hoped Keating would come to realise that Hawke was Labor's best hope.[13] Hawke and Keating had made a pledge, both lied about it, and then Hawke dishonoured the pledge by refusing to quit.

Keating at his press conference carried the relief of the loser. He charmed his way through a 45-minute conference with all the panache of the golden days. 'I had only one shot in the locker and I fired it,' Keating said. He pledged no new challenge and no destabilisation.

The vote was a diabolical result for the Labor Party, since both sides could claim that their aims had been achieved. Hawke won by more than twenty votes; Keating had taken 40 per cent of the caucus. Hawke survived but was wounded. Keating had hurt him but there was no certainty of finishing him off. The leadership issue remained unresolved. Hawke's margin was not enough to destroy the challenge; Keating's defeat was too great for him to follow up with a quick kill. After a brief stand-off the battle would resume. This was understood by the party, the media and the Opposition.

The Labor Party was a house divided against itself. The issues between Hawke and Keating were power, history and legitimacy. Hawke said he was the legitimate leader, sanctioned by the people, the party and his performance. Keating's message was that of generational change, that no peace existed until power changed hands. Keating was breaking new ground—trying to defeat a Labor prime minister from within.

Hawke now faced a dilemma and a chance—to govern without Keating; to prove he was a winner without Keating; to destroy the Keating view of history. If Hawke could govern without Keating he would also destroy Keating. Such a success would drive Keating from politics. But if Hawke failed Keating would destroy him. The onus now rested with Hawke as he sought to reconstruct his government and redirect himself to the recession.

II

The tragedy of Bob Hawke's career was that Labor's most successful leader squandered the opportunity to leave the political stage voluntarily. Hawke declined his chance to become the first prime minister since Menzies to achieve this feat. Unable to imagine a Labor government without his prime ministership, Hawke willed himself to the office and provoked his own removal. His departure marked another record in Hawke's record-breaking career—the first Labor prime minister to be dumped by his own party. Hawke succumbed to Keating, ultimately not because of Keating's strength but because of his own failure to govern effectively without Keating in his Cabinet. Hawke's reconstruction of his government in June 1991 when Keating went to the back bench and Kerin became treasurer was not a success. Keating became prime minister only on the back of Hawke's failure.

The balance between victory and defeat is often fine—rarely more so than in the Hawke–Keating contest. By mid-November 1991 Keating had played most of his shots. He had sweated to bring his caucus support from the 44 votes of the June challenge to fifty votes. But here he had apparently stalled and Graham Richardson was dubious about Keating's capacity to secure a majority, especially as the factional alliance for Hawke was still intact. Keating had concluded that he was unlikely to prevail and was preparing for his departure from politics.

For Keating Christmas 1991 was his deadline. A change of leadership could occur at the latest in early 1992. A pessimistic Keating had decided to remain for the opening parliamentary sitting weeks in February 1992. Unless there was a shift in support at this time he would announce his retirement from parliament and seek an alternative career. Keating was on the brink of conceding defeat and leaving politics.

Hawke, in turn, was close to victory in one of the most intense power struggles in the history of federal politics. But at this point, with victory in his grasp, Hawke stumbled; he fell victim to Hewson's GST package and the recession.

The markers of Hawke's failure on both counts can be identified precisely. On 26 November 1991 Hawke sat mute in the parliament while the government used its numbers to gag a series of Opposition motions seeking leave to debate its GST package, released the previous week. Here was the final ignominy: Hawke, after boasting for 12 months that Labor would destroy the Opposition package, was too frightened to debate the issue in parliament. The ALP back bench saw its leaders devoid of the confidence or skill to puncture the GST package, which was apparently taking the Opposition into a 'blue skies' future. The government, for the first time in its history, was reduced to political impotence.

The symbol of Hawke's failure to address the recession was his 6 December decision to dump John Kerin—his own choice as treasurer six months earlier—in favour of Ralph Willis. This was a prime ministerial judgement that the political management of economic policy during the recession had been a failure. Hawke did not realise that his condemnation of Kerin would be interpreted by others as a condemnation of himself. He forgot Harry Truman's axiom: 'The buck stops here.' Hawke's December 1991 reshuffle was born of desperation; its urgent and piecemeal nature betrayed a panic within its architect. Hawke fed Kerin to the sharks, but this started a crazy feeding frenzy which saw himself devoured 13 days later.

Keating's adviser, Don Russell, had long ago asserted: 'The caucus will only turn to Keating when it feels the government is completely demoralised.' This condition, finally, was met.

The irony of Hawke's demise is that he fell victim to the recession. It is an equal irony that the recession delivered Keating to The Lodge. The man disliked by most and detested by many as the engineer of Australia's longest recession since the Great Depression became the surprise beneficiary of that recession in one of the strangest twists of politics. It was a cruel end for Hawke who had lived for two years on the belief that Keating's recession-induced unpopularity made him ineligible for the highest office. In Canberra it was often said that Keating was 'as popular as rat poison'— that Keating overcame this legacy was a commentary upon Hawke's defects.

In 1991 Hawke had forgotten the technique which he had marketed to become prime minister in 1983—hope to break the recession. Hawke's tenure in office from the 1980s to the 1990s spanned recession to recession. But Hawke was a contrast in these recessions: his image changed from a symbol of hope to a monument to inertia.

However, Hawke was both determined and confident in June 1991 when he reconstructed his government without Keating. He publicly identified Kerin, Howe, Beazley and Crean as potential leaders. He told his colleagues that Keating should leave politics. Many within the Hawke camp now envisaged an ALP caucus without Keating; he had lost; it was departure time.

Hawke was confident about his new Cabinet, which he called 'a fully manned Cabinet and a very well manned Cabinet'. Asked if he now felt under greater pressure Hawke replied: 'No greater in a sense than I've been under for eight years.' This answer was not just public relations; it was mirrored in the way Hawke now governed. It is the key to his failure.[14]

In fact, the Cabinet was much weaker than before and the pressure on Hawke was much greater. Kerin was an inexperienced treasurer and Howe was an inexperienced deputy. The party was split; Hawke was under Keating's threat; the nation was in recession. Hawke was facing a unique series of difficulties, but he changed neither his approach nor his style as leader. He just left his ministers with plenty of rein and assumed that the wheels of power would click over as before—but the engine was stalled.

Hawke, Howe, and Kerin, the new 'engine-room' of the government, sealed their own fate. When Hawke fell Keating had not uttered a word in public for a month. From mid-year it was obvious that Keating could only prevail if the budget flopped, the opinion polls plummeted, the Cabinet imploded, and the new team failed—and each condition was met in succession.

The proof that the Keating camp would continue its campaign was

Hawke's 2 July meeting with John Dawkins to censure him for his remarks after the National Conference that 'the only attempt at inspirational leadership was in bagging the Opposition'. Hawke asked Howe to attend the meeting also as deputy leader. Hawke told Dawkins that his remarks were damaging and inspired by Keating's failed leadership bid. Dawkins said his comments were not aimed at Hawke personally; if Hawke didn't believe him, then there was no basis of trust between them. If so, Dawkins said, his only option was to resign—a threat that alarmed Hawke.

Dawkins implied that Hawke was putting his personal interests before those of the party. Hawke said that his campaigning skills had won the 1987 and 1990 elections, a point which Dawkins disputed. When Howe tried to support Hawke, Dawkins cut him dead, saying he might care to discuss his own previous position on the leadership—a reference to Howe's comments a year before that Hawke should stand down for Keating. The meeting settled nothing; it just left Hawke impotent before a destabilisation campaign that was just starting.[15]

From the back bench Keating promoted himself in two ways—as a human face and as a policy man. After eight years of office Keating now had the time and the inclination to attend a range of party functions across the nation. As the rituals unfolded Keating offered a synthesis between politics and showbusiness. When he was not being sullen about his future he was polishing his actor's skills. On policy, Keating went into reflection mode, promising 'more reflections than the Versailles Hall of Mirrors'. Parliament, once his domain, was now irrelevant since Keating's backbench status afforded few opportunities.

The Keating forces were relentless in their drive against Hawke from July 1991. Hawke's backers later charged: 'The failure of the government can't be divorced from the terror campaign.' Keating had his zealots within each faction, Duncan from the left, Schacht from the centre-left, Brereton and Punch from the right. His former advisers kept their dialogue with the Press Gallery. Hawke and Kerin couldn't afford too many mistakes.

The 'Keating-as-statesman' program was launched on 10 July with a much touted but disappointing address on urban policy and the cities. 'An elegant re-entry into politics,' was the description of the Keating camp. On 17 July Keating appeared on Ray Martin's *Midday Show* to announce—surprise—that he still wanted to be prime minister. The same day Bill Kelty, Keating's mate, in a long interview with John Laws, another Keating mate, said the challenger was 'one of the great political figures of the generation'. Hawke retaliated, telling Kelty that 'I run the government' and Kelty should look after the unions.

On 25 July, in a revealing speech, Keating called upon the government to respond to the Full Bench's refusal to ratify the next stage in award superannuation by providing for legislated superannuation in the budget. Keating endorsed the ACTU target of 12 per cent of income as superannuation over the decade, selling the need to raise national savings to address both the foreign debt and provide for the post-war baby boomers in retirement. He endorsed the ACTU model of a national superannuation scheme achieved through tax cuts paid by the Commonwealth into 'super' funds plus legally imposed employer contributions. This speech brought to a zenith the Keating–Kelty 'super' program on which they had embarked in 1983 and which was basic to their relationship.[16]

The Keating–Kelty pressure left Kerin with little option but to introduce the superannuation reforms in his budget. But this did not avert a dispute between Kerin and Kelty over the wages growth target for the budget—a dispute in which Kelty threatened to dump on the government. Meanwhile Richardson, more brazen than ever, insisted that on the leadership, 'there is no campaign'.

Keating took two policy decisions during his period on the back bench which were instrumental in his triumph. They are a classic study of Keating as a policy strategist combating Hawke as a political populist. First, Keating decided to destroy Hawke's 'New Federalism' initiative to the extent it undermined the revenue powers of the Commonwealth. Hawke had given no pledges but the agenda involved some devolution of revenue powers to the states or, at best, some guarantee of a fixed share of federal revenues. Keating's attack on 'New Federalism' was driven by two factors—personal conviction and the accurate assessment that the ALP caucus, forced to choose, would back Keating's centralism against Hawke's devolution option.

However, the decisive backbench experience for Keating was his reassessment of the economy and his campaign for a recovery strategy. This had enduring consequences for the leadership, the ALP and the nature of the subsequent Keating government.

As treasurer Keating had first denied that there would be a recession and then misjudged its severity. The government which he left and the treasurer who followed him inherited his policies and his outlook. But Keating quickly abandoned his own legacy. He became a critic of the treasury and the policy framework which he had left. Kerin and Hawke were shocked at the audacity of Keating's backflip. Hawke claimed that Keating was just trying to win more caucus votes but this was only part of the story.

Keating's assessment that the recession was worse than the treasury and the government predicted proved to be correct. Keating believed that policy had to become pro-active: that strong measures were needed to promote recovery. He called for faster and deeper interest rates cuts, tax incentives to generate new production, encouragement of new resource projects, a program to boost public infrastructure and better assistance to the long-term unemployed.[17] He had a motley collection of partial allies—the Reserve Bank, business, the Victorian ALP government and the ACTU.

The motives driving Keating were a mixture of convenience and conviction. He was scoring points off Hawke and Kerin, yet he wanted policy modified, realising that if he became prime minister he would inherit an even deeper recession. The more Hawke and Kerin refused to budge, the more incredulous Keating became. Keating told his advisers: 'Hawke can't be this stupid. If he sees the light and shifts economic policy then I'm finished.' Hawke did change—but too late. He was planning a January 1992 economic statement when he was deposed; a statement designed to address the severity of the recession and follow Keating's lead.

Keating believed the 1991–92 budget should be built around a strategy for recovery and interest rate cuts—but Hawke and Kerin, listening to treasury advice, refused to move.

It is at this point that the most significant split between the treasury and the Reserve Bank occurred since the float in 1983. The treasury misread completely the severity of the downturn; the Reserve, closer to the financial community, grasped its depth. This meant the Reserve was pushing for lower interest rates while the treasury was reluctant to move. Kerin listened to the treasury; Keating was ahead of the Reserve. The treasury recorded another forecasting failure. It predicted in 1990–91 a mild slowdown with GDP rising only 2 per cent; in fact, it fell 2.4 per cent, producing a severe recession.

The June quarter national accounts released the week before Kerin's 1991–92 budget showed that GDP had fallen 1 per cent and that over four of the last five quarters activity had also fallen. A confused Kerin, asked about the outlook, replied: 'Your guess is as good as mine'—the first of his gaffes.

From this point Keating closed in on Kerin. Keating, on the back bench, became a critic of the Keating legacy. This had a great significance: it meant if Keating became prime minister he would have to synthesise a new policy direction.

The course of politics was now shaped by Kerin's performance as treasurer. His job was immense: to pilot the economy during a severe recession serving a split government. Kerin was a likeable bloke, a competent minister and a success story of the Hawke years. Hawke liked the honest-broker image with which Kerin managed his farming and mining constituencies. But Hawke had promoted Kerin into a political inferno.

It is possible that with a better treasurer Hawke might have survived. Kerin was not the obvious candidate for the job. He had not been part of the ERC process during the 1980s. His reputation had been made in the specialised field of rural policy. He had not been subjected to the sustained political and media pressure which would become the daily diet of a treasurer. His distaste for the treasury was legion, along with his anti-treasury jokes. But Kerin's obsessive jokes were a defence mechanism; he was a very cautious minister.

Apart from Keating's recession, Kerin was responsible for one of the worst mistakes of the Hawke era—the failed reserve price scheme for wool which produced a $3 billion debt and a crippled industry. An analysis of Kerin's career suggested that his appointment was a gamble. Willis had superior economic claims; Beazley greater political claims; Dawkins had long been Keating's understudy; Evans, though in the Senate, had a capacity and work rate without peer in the Cabinet.

As treasurer Kerin was a diligent administrator of the treasury line. But Kerin lacked touch, dexterity and clout. Kerin could not carry the Cabinet on an argument, let alone the country. His comments unnerved financial markets; he failed, probably not through his own fault, to establish trust with Kelty; he was inept with the media and unsure in the House. Kerin had never been a hot politician. He possessed neither killer instinct nor factional allies. Though promoted by Hawke, he was never a Hawke man, never a mate. But Hawke expected him to perform.

Kerin accepted the treasury line, which he advanced in his 12 July EPAC speech, that the economy 'is now either at or approaching a turning point' in the trough. Kerin predicted a moderate recovery over 1991–92 and said his stance would involve 'firm monetary policy settings, maintaining the structural integrity of the budget and further progress on industry reforms'.

In his August budget speech Kerin was honest; he said that Labor's aim of achieving 'lower growth but stopping short of recession was not achieved'. He noted that the recessionary experience was being shared by America, Canada and Britain. His solution—'to ensure that the recovery proceeds at a sustainable pace [slowly] and that we lock in the economic gains of the past year', notably low inflation and a low current account deficit. It was a classic medium-term strategy as advocated by the treasury. The forecasts predicted GDP average growth at 1.5 per cent for 1991–92 (the outcome was only 0.2 per cent), inflation to average 3 per cent and unemployment at 10.5 per cent.

The budget initiatives were modest, the main ones being a Medicare 'up-front' payment to reduce overservicing; an $800 million 'better cities' program over five years; and a superannuation levy with a target by the year 2000 for prescribed employer support to be 9 per cent of earnings. Kerin's message was an economic structure based upon 'sustainable longer-term policies' and a slow recovery in 1992.

Kerin's economics were praised by the financial press—since he had not lost his nerve—but his salesmanship and his politics were deficient. He was unable to cope with the internal backlash. The caucus revolted over the Medicare decision; the Victorian government, where the recession was deepest, dismissed the budget with contempt; and Keating led the charge for a two percentage points cut in lower interest rates, a demand Kerin rejected. The upshot was that when Kerin announced a one percentage point cut on 3 September it was interpreted by the markets as a sign of political weakness.

After this post-budget political debacle Hawke tried to limit the leadership damage by admitting the gravity of the destabilisation campaign. 'It can't go on like this,' he said, conceding his government looked 'tatty at the edges'. But self-pity is a weak defence. Hawke failed to offer any solution. He ruled out another leadership vote; he dismissed action against the plotters. Hawke was offering his impotence as an incitement to discipline—a ploy that was doomed.[18]

However, Keating's challenge was still far from irresistible and Hawke's factional alliance was holding. It was, in fact, a sobering event for the Keating camp. The budget had flopped, Kerin had bungled, the recession continued, but nobody rushed to Keating. A severe attack of nerves afflicted the Keating supporters. Any understanding of the Hawke–Keating struggle must be rooted in an appreciation of the uncertainty that plagued both sides.

This ambiguity was reflected, above all, in Graham Richardson, whose subsequent elevation as 'the man who kingmade Keating' is a media myth. Richardson was adviser to both Hawke and Keating and, like everyone, was unsure of the outcome. So he took out insurance—and neither Hawke nor Keating fully trusted him.

Ten days after the budget Hawke and Richardson at a late night Lodge meeting agreed that the destabilisation of Hawke could not be maintained without destroying the government. Richardson told Hawke that provided he didn't fall over, the destabilisation would be curbed. A fortnight later, on 16 September, Richardson interviewed Hawke on Sydney's 2KY in what the Keating camp later dubbed a 'love-in'. Richardson said: 'We've got no challenge planned. It's pretty hard to challenge—it's been proved in the polls that Hawke's doing well . . . Keating himself knows that there's no hope for challenging in these circumstances.'[19] Two days later Richardson said on the ABC's *7.30 Report*, 'At some point you've got to say to yourself, you just can't bat on with this. And I think we've reached this point.' Keating's other lieutenant, Laurie Brereton, was furious.

Richardson had told both sides that unless Keating had the numbers by the end of October he would be 'tapping him on the shoulder' to announce the end of the campaign. Keating felt that Richardson was seeking a hero's role on two levels, depending upon who won: as the man who ended the destabilisation of Hawke or as the organiser of Keating's brilliant tactical retreat as a prelude to victory.[20]

Richardson described himself as 'a campaign director not directed by the candidate'. Richardson, in fact, had always been ambivalent about how successful a leader Keating might be. While Richardson was pledged to Keating he told intimates that he was under an obligation to ensure that neither the party nor the government was destroyed if Keating did not have the numbers.

But Keating didn't wait upon Richardson.

On 28 September Keating called for an economic policy change; he

644

appealed for Labor to return to its 'great charter of creating jobs'. He said it was 'pointless to try and get a bigger return on inflation with levels of 2 and 3 per cent and to puncture the current account deficit more stridently by doing so with a more pronounced recession'. A few days later at Tweed Heads Keating declared: 'Inflation is cracked, not cracking . . . We've heard the crack in every factory in the country.' He wanted the government to 'traffic in the basic creed of Labor—looking after working Australians'.[21]

Keating said the balance in policy should now favour lower interest rates to boost growth. But Kerin rejected Keating's argument: 'You can't snap the inflation stick just once and think it's beaten . . . the inflation bear has to be kept in its cage.' Kerin refused to follow Keating on interest rates; he gave more weight to fighting inflation and the current account deficit than kindling growth. Here was a great paradox: Kerin was the champion of the treasury line which Keating now rejected.

Keating was striking not just at Kerin but at the treasury. It was a disenchantment born in the recession and it reflected a philosophical split between Keating and his old department. Within the economics profession— in the treasury, the Reserve Bank and the media—a lesson from the 1990s recession was that monetary policy had been mishandled and that its true role should be to achieve price stability over the medium term. That is, it should not be used as Keating's so-called 'swing instrument'. Hewson had embraced this position as a dogma. Kerin had also adopted the orthodoxy; he talked of monetary policy settings for the medium term.

It was this outlook which Keating still rejected. He said it had been 'pushed by officials' in his last year as treasurer. Keating believed that it was contrary to Labor's basic interests, and declared that 'interest rates should not be set simply with inflation in mind' but rather 'to achieve a recovery which is consistent with the locking-in of the gains on inflation'. Keating, whose monetary policy judgement had been fatally wrong, still insisted that treasurers had to exercise this judgement—not surrender to the central bank. He warned that the 'medium-term rumble is an echo of an old conservative incantation that did not work in the past and should be dismissed by any government worth its salt—especially a Labor government'.[22]

The Keating–Kerin conflict grew intense.

By late October treasury officials conceded that the recent budget forecasts, only two months old, might have been too optimistic. It was the omen of another forecasting failure by treasury. Meanwhile Kerin said in an overseas speech that Australia had suffered its most severe recession in sixty years—the exact propaganda line from John Hewson. A frustrated Hawke chided Kerin openly. Even worse, Kerin was wrong—the recession at this point was longer but not deeper than that of 1982.

On 2 November Keating spoke at the Collingwood Football Club to advance his new agenda—the push to reposition himself from Mr Recession to Mr Recovery. While stressing that the gains on inflation must be held Keating turned the focus to recovery. He called for another one percentage point cut in interest rates, bringing the total cut since the budget to two percentage points. He wanted a $300 million one year stock allowance to encourage companies to boost production and generate 40 000 jobs, more assistance to the long-term jobless, a boost to public infrastructure, possibly through the use of the $850 million earmarked for the 'better cities' program which meant an easing in fiscal policy, and cutting red tape to get major resource projects moving. The Keating plan drew heavily upon the ACTU jobs charter.[23]

Keating claimed that the Hawke–Kerin policies would keep unemployment above 10 per cent for a considerable time and delay the recovery until well into 1992. Former colleagues called Keating a betrayer but Keating was forging some new and strange friendships.

This Collingwood speech brought to a high point the alliance between Keating and the doomed Kirner government in Victoria. Victoria, the pit of the recession, had a direct interest in politicians preaching recovery strategies. Keating, in turn, was infiltrating the Victorian ALP, a beast he had never mastered. The premier, Joan Kirner, had been a Keating supporter since the 1990 State Bank crisis and rolled out a welcome mat. Keating became friendly with Victorian industry minister David White, from the pro-Hawke Victorian right, who introduced him to the Victorian left— finance minister Tony Sheehan; and left-wing meatworkers' union chief Wally Curran.[24]

The Victorian left's main interest was in saving Kirner, not the federal leadership struggle. But Kirner's survival depended upon a comprehensive recovery strategy and that involved Canberra. It was Keating, not Hawke, who listened. Political sophisticates were agog as Keating plunged into this amazing new alliance.

The Hawke camp attacked Keating for hypocrisy—the architect of the recession re-dressed as the saviour. This was Keating's flaw—his lack of credibility and his effrontery. But Keating's entire career had revealed him as a political animal and his skill had been the blending of economics and politics. Keating said the ideas he was marketing—growth, the Accord, a flexible monetary stance, combating the current account while encouraging job creation—had been his consistent themes during the 1980s.

But courting the Victorian socialist left was not a value-free exercise. Victoria was the heartland of the 1990s reactionary politics—pushing for protection, intervention, more spending and special tax deals. Victoria refused to admit that its peculiar problems were the legacy of its own mistakes. Keating pandered to this sentiment at the risk of releasing Labor's old demons.

Meanwhile he had opened up a second front.

On 22 October in his National Press Club speech Keating launched his assault upon Hawke's New Federalism. Within five weeks the mooted revenue reforms of the New Federalism were buried. Keating exploited Labor's traditional centralist sentiment and argued against surrendering any Commonwealth revenue powers. He made the correct judgement that the caucus would ultimately reject the New Federalism.

The battle was lost by the terrible tactics used by Hawke and Kerin. They told a caucus seminar that no tax powers would be surrendered to the states, although Kerin had circulated a Cabinet submission leaving this option open. Keating then obtained a copy of the premiers' submission to Hawke seeking a massive reform—a tax sharing arrangement that would see $10 billion or 6 per cent of national revenue handed to the states. He wrote his own rebuttal and sent it to caucus and Cabinet ministers.

Hawke's first mistake was to allow these revenue reform deliberations to reach this advanced stage without preparing the political ground within the ALP. Secondly, he had raised the expectations of the premiers on access to tax powers or revenue. When he was unable to deliver, the states abandoned the New Federalism process. The upshot was that Hawke's New Federalism, which he had launched in 1990 as a keystone of his fourth term, was ruined. It was a policy humiliation for Hawke—having his vanquished former treasurer reach out from the back bench to strangle his initiative. Keating was a saboteur, pure and simple, but Hawke was inept.

The Keating camp now set up the inevitable chant: 'The emperor has no clothes.' On each issue—superannuation, the economy, New Federalism—Keating, not Hawke, had called the play—but Keating was on the back bench.

The real point was that Hawke had failed to take firm control of the government after Keating had left. The economy was in recession, he had an inexperienced treasurer and faced a leadership challenge. Yet Hawke didn't change his leadership style; he thought he could continue as before. This was a fatal mistake which cost him the prime ministership.

The tensions Keating had generated burst into ugly prominence in early November when the Queensland deputy premier, Tom Burns, savaged Keating for 'gross disloyalty', claimed that the NSW right was bent upon 'destroying the government' and called upon the National Executive to silence Keating. National secretary Bob Hogg dismissed the call and criticised Burns. Richardson used the occasion to reestablish his Keating credentials with a personal attack upon Burns. Burns in turn called Richardson 'a low slimy mongrel'. Labor veterans felt a thrill of nostalgia.

But the immediate loser was Keating, as the ALP descended into the self-destructive pattern of the Whitlam era. Keating, Richardson, Brereton, Gary Punch and Leo McLeay caucused on 7 November and decided on a retreat. The estimate was that they had only 50 to 52 votes when they needed 56. Keating said that he needed 56, plus an extra 7 or 8 votes, for a guaranteed win. In Richardson's words, the campaign 'must be abandoned unless and until we have the numbers'. The Hewson *Fightback* package was being released the following week and Keating could not be seen to prejudice Labor's attack on it. Richardson told Keating to make the retreat public.

Keating's personal advisers rejected this step, but Richardson insisted. Keating felt that he had to respect the wishes of the people who backed him, and on 8 November told the ABC's *PM* program: 'I will not be challenging the Prime Minister'. The irony is that such words had now lost much meaning and the media took little notice. Richardson rang Hawke's aide, Colin Parkes, and said this was a genuine position—the fight was off. An agitated Richardson then launched a massive media offensive. He rang the three correspondents for the major papers—Michelle Grattan from *The Age*, Peter Hartcher from *The Sydney Morning Herald*, and Glenn Milne from *The Australian*—on Friday night and told them the Keating push was finished.

The withdrawal was an admission of Keating's inability to nail Hawke after a three-month effort. But Keating was furious with Richardson's solo media effort. Brereton attacked Richardson, 'This is the 2KY show repeated.' Keating said he had agreed to back off, but complained that Richardson had announced a surrender. The Keating loyalists believed that Richardson had sold out. It was the weekend of 9–10 November, seven weeks before Christmas. Hawke began to feel that he had prevailed; that he had Keating beaten, a judgement Keating could not dispute.

Keating now sank into reflection: if the caucus refused to move he would end the contest. Keating's mind turned to his Sydney house and his departure from politics in early 1992. 'If I'm not leader when Parliament resumes in February then the opportunity will have closed,' Keating conceded privately. That meant a change before Christmas—which now seemed remote. Keating began to reconcile himself to defeat, a new life and the bitter admission that Hawke, despite his weakness, had won.

On 14 November Hawke unveiled his economic package to foil Keating further—an extra $300 million for 1991–92—a classic compromise betraying weakness. Hawke was stranded between Keating and the recession. The Keating campaign compelled Hawke to action, but his advisers told him to sit out the worst of the recession. It was in this political vacuum that John Hewson released his *Fightback* package on 21 November. It was the perfect environment for a policy release, since *Fightback* represented change while Labor was becalmed.

Hewson's *Fightback* was the most sweeping program ever released by an Opposition party, with a series of trade-offs around its centrepiece—the 15 per cent goods and services tax. Labor was shocked by the favourable media reaction Hewson received. Richardson had wanted Keating to attack the GST but Keating felt that it was best to stay silent. It was his silence which gave him the prime ministership.

The final proof that the Hawke government was paralysed was its failure to mount any effective reply to Hewson's *Fightback*. The package was, above all, a political statement, but Labor was mesmerised by statistics. It had lost its commonsense and its political touch. The Labor attack was led initially by deputy Brian Howe who, in an inexplicable disaster, named Hewson's first wife, got his figures wrong, and eventually walked into a cupboard after a media conference. Labor's performance invited ridicule and was redolent of Billy McMahon.

Kerin made the extraordinary claim that Labor needed neither its own package nor a policy change to counter the *Fightback* strategy. Kerin was immobilised, utterly unable to grasp that the entire nation—business, unions, consumers—demanded leadership and a government that had the will to restore national confidence. When asked how the government would re-establish its own policy position Kerin's response was: 'Watch this space.' In a black mood Bob Hogg joked that 'Howe and Kerin are suffering from guilt'.

The Hewson *Fightback* package meant that the Opposition, for the first time since the inception of the Hawke era in 1983, was in command. Labor acted like a divided, demoralised and beaten unit. Further humiliation came on 26 November when Beazley repeatedly moved the gag motion in parliament to prevent the Opposition debating its *Fightback* package—this from a government which had made its reputation demolishing coalition policies! Sitting on the back bench Keating sensed that the hand of fate had reached out to resurrect his career, just when he had began to bury it.

So complete was the transformation generated by the GST that Keating told his wife Annita: 'It's Hawke's luck again. If this was a fortnight sitting then he'd be gone at the end.' The GST was the turning point.

Hawke knew that he had to act and it was Labor's disastrous response to the GST which provoked Hawke's reshuffle—but he botched the move.

In the week starting 2 December, Richardson and Ray had told Hawke that he needed a major reshuffle, the centrepiece being a new treasurer. Given the leadership struggle, such joint advice from the right wing powerbrokers was potent. Hawke accepted this view; he knew that Kerin's confidence was shot. Hawke had lost faith in Kerin a short time before when his treasurer had announced a 1 per cent interest rate cut but refused to be interviewed by the media about the good news. Given that Hawke wanted Kerin to send a message of national confidence such behaviour was incomprehensible. Now, almost on cue, Kerin blundered again.

It was during his 5 December press conference on the September national accounts which revealed that Australia was in its most prolonged—but not its deepest—slump since the Great Depression. Kerin, in the words of one reporter, 'exuded uncertainty, tremulousness, even a touch of fear'.[25] The following exchange was shown on television that night:

Kerin: The gross operating, sorry, the gross, aah . . . (pause) share rose, gross, aah . . . (pause) what's 'GOS'?
Reporters: Profit share.

Kerin: The gross profit share rose by 4.1 per cent in the quarter . . .

It was a small slip but revealed the collapse of Kerin's confidence. Reporters were explaining his own notes! Kerin's job was to restore confidence in the national economy but he had no confidence in himself.[26]

The media liked Kerin and felt sorry for him. It was frustrated by the utter inability of Kerin and his office to help himself. Kerin was a classic victim—unable to meet Hawke's desire for smart politics; unable to grasp that his statements would swing financial markets; unsure of how to deal with the ACTU; lacking confidence with the media through whom he had to communicate; resentful of Keating behind his back; the former treasury critic now totally dependent upon reading treasury speeches line-by-line.[27]

The trigger for the reshuffle was the page one story by Peter Hartcher in the *Sydney Morning Herald* of 6 December which revealed the Richardson–Ray advice to Hawke. When Hawke's political aide, Colin Parkes, read the papers at 6.30 that morning he decided that time was the essence. 'Kerin's gotta go and it's got to be done today,' Parkes told Hawke at 7 am. 'Otherwise the media will go into complete crisis mode over a reshuffle.' Hawke reluctantly agreed—he had a golf game scheduled that day. But he decided to postpone it; he had to sack Kerin.

Hawke settled upon his reshuffle: Kerin to transport, Willis to treasury, Beazley to finance. But this was a panic reshuffle, its timing determined by the *Herald* story. It was a mistake which sealed Hawke's fate.

If there had been no reshuffle Hawke might have survived until January and might even have survived permanently. The contest was always very fine. It was Labor's failed GST attack which forced the reshuffle and it was the reshuffle which destroyed Hawke. The party was shocked by the move, made aware for the first time of the depth of Hawke's survival fears. The Richardson–Ray advice was for a more extensive reshuffle. Hawke, however, acted prematurely and without effect, the reshuffle rushed, partly because Hawke had to fly to Canberra for Kerin's execution and hoped to return to Sydney for golf.

Richardson later told colleagues that he had always believed that Hawke would stumble at the reshuffle; that Hawke lacked the courage for a major reshuffle because he would never touch Howe or Button and did not understand that a minor reshuffle would be a disaster. Richardson created the climate for a major reshuffle that was beyond Hawke's willpower.

Hawke and Kerin met twice just after 11.15 am. Kerin had no prior warning that he would be demoted—he thought he was talking to Hawke about foreign investment decisions for the Fairfax group purchase. Instead his treasurership was terminated by an unusually determined Hawke.

The Keating coup

When Hawke saw the media to announce the reshuffle he bore a worried, almost agonised countenance. He revealed that he had been contemplating the move for some time but the final decision had been his alone. He did not reveal that the timing had been forced by the *Herald* story.

The reason Hawke gave revealed the bankruptcy of his prime ministership—Kerin was being removed because of his failure to communicate, not for policy reasons. Having stabbed Kerin before golf, Hawke then praised him as a 'big man in every way'. Even for Hawke loyalists this was too much to stomach.

Where had Kerin failed to communicate? In his efforts to attack Hewson's GST. Yet this charge applied with equal force to Hawke himself.

Hawke's record had been to defend ministers in trouble. Now he was expending Kerin. It was one thing to decide that Kerin had failed; it was another to orchestrate such a humiliating execution. Hawke's action exposed his weakness—and that only made him weaker still. Some ministers drew the obvious conclusion: that Hawke had been disloyal to Kerin to save his own neck. Hawke had had eight years in the Cabinet room to decide if Kerin would make a good treasurer. He had passed a harsh judgement on Kerin without grasping that this would only encourage others to apply a harsh judgement to him. From this moment the Keating camp had a single question: 'When will Hawke apply the Kerin test to himself?' The instinct behind Hawke's strike was political fear; it was seen with a clarity that made it self-fulfilling.

The reshuffle was a political earthquake whose impact was deadly within the media and the ALP—its haste and its scope proof of Hawke's extreme vulnerability. It sent new hope racing through the Keating camp. It meant that Hawke had wasted the chance for a proper restructuring of his government which was the real need.

The afternoon of the reshuffle there was talk within the caucus that a delegation might approach Hawke asking him to stand down. The Hawke loyalists, particularly Kim Beazley, were now pessimistic. It was obvious that the reshuffle had given the party a licence to reassess its leader, just as Hawke had reassessed Kerin.

The newspaper coverage of the reshuffle on Saturday 7 December was completely devastating for Hawke. He was depicted, almost universally, as a desperate leader; his caucus backing began to disintegrate. An embattled Hawke was heard in stony silence the same day when he addressed the NSW ALP state conference. The shadow of death followed Hawke into Keating's base: the NSW party president, Terry Sheahan, demanded that Keating, 'our most potent batsman', be recalled from the pavilion; the shadow attorney, Paul Whelan, told Hawke to resign. On the floor delegates declared that Hawke's departure was a matter of when, not whether. The next day in Melbourne, the day before his sixty-second birthday, Hawke defiantly declared that he wouldn't step down.

But this weekend of 7–8 December proved to be decisive, because now there was movement within the caucus and Cabinet against Hawke from his own loyalists. Richardson was told over the weekend by some members that they were shifting from Hawke to Keating. Within the Cabinet, Duffy, Beazley and Evans felt that Hawke was terminal. But they were agonising over the ultimate delicacy: who would tell the messiah? It was obvious that a resolution was required—and that meant removing Hawke. On 9 December Michelle Grattan reported: 'A change of leadership is becoming inevitable in the minds of even many Hawke supporters . . . if a vote were pulled on next week I suspect Paul Keating probably would win the required 56 votes to make him leader.'[28]

Richardson asked Ray and Beazley to persuade Hawke to resign and permit a smooth transition. Then he asked the defectors to signal their switch to the media. By 10 December at least half a dozen backbenchers had confirmed to journalists their switch from Hawke to Keating. But Hawke's worst blow came that evening when the left caucus decided that it would not attempt to hold the faction as a bloc in any future leadership vote. This was a body blow; it signalled the break-up of the Hawke alliance. Hawke's response was a touch hysterical:

> I've been in public life now since 1958. I assert that I understand the politics of this country better than anyone else in it. I assert that my judgement on major political events has been impeccable. I've been right against the overwhelming majority of my colleagues. I've certainly been right against the overwhelming majority of the media. I've lost count of the number of times that they have written either me or the government off. I have been right and I will be proved right again on this occasion because I know the people of Australia. After all, I've worked with and for the people of Australia since 1958 . . . I have been right on every occasion in my major political judgements. I will be proved right again. I am only staying because I know that to be true and that the future of Australia demands that these Tories be defeated.[29]

Meanwhile Keating went to ground.

The next day, 11 December, the Morgan poll in the *Bulletin*, by which Hawke had lived for years, showed the coalition leading Labor 51 to 33 per cent and Hawke's approval rating at 33 per cent, its lowest yet. In fact, Hewson headed Hawke on the 'best PM' question only 46 to 39 per cent, a good result for Hawke given the situation. Nobody had any delusions about Keating's unpopularity but the evidence was overwhelming that the Hawke era was finished.

The same day senior ministers from the Hawke camp began to canvass the prospect of an approach to Hawke to resign. Late on the night of 11 December, Beazley, Duffy, Evans, Ray, Hand and Bolkus met away from Parliament House, the venue changed from Evans' to Ray's place to fool the media. One catalyst for the meeting was Duffy who, when asked what he did during the day replied, 'I just sat around and bled.'[30]

The group reviewed all possible options—that Hawke leave now, leave in January, or that a 'third man' emerge as leader. Beazley was the obvious 'third man' but he wouldn't entertain the idea. Nobody wanted a ballot; the opinion was that any transition should be as bloodless as possible. Hawke's chief numbers man, Robert Ray, admitted that Hawke's position was probably untenable. Ray felt the situation was uncertain but that it would be hard for Hawke to win a ballot.

Hawke's chief aide, Colin Parkes, advised him that he had lost majority support within the caucus. Hawke was a sad but determined figure, unable to accept, above all, that Labor could dispose of him just as it had disposed of other unwanted leaders. Meanwhile *The Age* named ten defectors from Hawke to Keating, six from the right and four from the left.[31]

The meeting of ministers broke at 1 am, having reached a necessary conclusion. They would approach Hawke in a delegation, inform him that they believed he had lost majority support, and ask him to resign. The aim was to protect Hawke's dignity and to permit a smooth transition. These were Hawke's friends, coming as colleagues, not enemies. They had decided that if Hawke stayed to fight they would not condemn him. But their collective decision was Hawke's death warrant. It meant that Hawke had lost his own Cabinet loyalists.

The press had the story and the morning newspapers of 12 December predicted Hawke's demise to the nation. Hawke had two meetings with the delegation, at 8 am and again at 3.45 pm and he stared down his six-man execution squad—Beazley, Ray, Evans, Duffy, Bolkus and Hand. At the first meeting they put the main options—immediate resignation or a January transition after George Bush's visit. The delegation was agreed that the best option was an immediate transition. They talked about the implications of Hawke's staying until January. It was obvious that Hawke was not likely to accept their advice but he agreed to consider the issue and speak with Hazel.

Hawke's bottom line was his refusal to accept Keating's legitimacy. He determined that if the party were to install Keating then it must be the party's decision by a vote. He would not depart voluntarily thereby absolving the party from the obligation to make its own decision and to accept the responsibility for that decision. Hawke felt that the true course of dignity was to stand on his honour.

At the second meeting Hawke told the delegation that he had considered their submission, discussed it with Hazel and had decided to fight any challenge that might take place. His will to power remained intact. He was concerned about his wife's health, his family and the party. The delegation accepted Hawke's position and said that they would help him!

During 150 minutes of talks spread over two meetings Hawke had called the bluff of the 'gang of six'. Hawke told them what he had told the world—that he was not resigning because he was convinced that he was Labor's best election hope and that he would only be removed by a vote of the caucus. Hawke had been a mixture of steel and cunning during these talks. He conned the delegation; but the delegation came to be conned.

Hawke forced the delegation to a bedrock position—it had to support him or Keating in a ballot. He was talking to his loyalists—men who wanted him to resign for his own good, not for Keating's. The delegation forgot the law of ALP politics—don't ask people to resign unless you can enforce the offer. The ministers buckled; even worse, they agreed that if Hawke was determined to fight then they would back him, not Keating. The execution squad didn't have the courage to pull the trigger. It started from the premise that Hawke was finished and concluded with a declaration of support. The media, watching this agony outside, was agog at the upshot.

The Age's Michelle Grattan summed up: 'We now have not only a crippled Prime Minister but also a collection of Ministerial mice . . . their lack of guts is amazing.' The fiasco provided another insight: despite their battle, Hawke and Keating were in a class of their own compared with their much overrated colleagues.[32]

The ministers did a disservice to everyone. Their mission could not be kept a secret and they knew it. The delegation weakened Hawke, dishonoured their own reputations, and left the Cabinet corrupted. A Keating supporter said: 'Hawke now presides over a Cabinet in which nobody wants him.'

Kim Beazley became the bunny to announce that the delegation 'unanimously' supported Hawke's decision to remain. But Beazley did not dismiss a challenge. Indeed, he seemed to think one likely. Glenn Milne of *The Australian* commented that Hawke had embarked upon a 'futile strategy of personal survival that will damage the country, divide the Labor Party and ultimately destroy him'.[33]

Later that day Richardson visited Hawke in another unsuccessful attempt to persuade him to resign. His message was that the onus rested with Hawke. That night Hawke hosted his annual drinks for the Press Gallery at The Lodge—and performed with grace despite the media onslaught against him.

Hawke's refusal to imagine a future for the ALP beyond his own leadership was shaking the government to its core. It was obvious that Hawke could not survive when the nation knew that his six closest supporters had asked him to resign. His prime ministership was crippled. The delegation had destroyed him—incredibly the ministers did not grasp the magnitude of their folly nor the absurdity of their position.

Labor's crisis had almost obscured the release of the November jobless figures which showed that unemployment was now 10.5 per cent—the highest since the Great Depression. Hopes of the imminent recovery mooted by the government were now lost. Unemployment was 11.5 per cent for those looking for full-time work, 31 per cent among youths and 10 per cent among females. The collapse in national confidence only made imperative the restoration of effective government, but Hawke could not grasp that his departure was the necessary condition.

The contrast between Hawke in 1991 and Hayden in 1983—as leaders under challenge—was sharp. Hayden eventually put the party's interest before his own. Although convinced that a 'drover's dog' could win the 1983 election Hayden resigned rather than force a ballot and thus gave Hawke a smooth transition into power. But Hawke, convinced that his view of the party's best interest was paramount, refused to resign or to allow Keating a smooth transition. Hawke insisted upon a ballot. That was his right, just as it had been Hayden's right. But it did Labor a disservice, where Hayden did Labor a service. Hawke refused to give Keating the transition which Hayden had given him. It is no wonder that Hayden's sympathies were with Keating.

The weekend of 14–15 December saw Labor locked in an impasse with much speculation within the party about Hawke's motives. The Keating camp claimed that Hawke was having emotional difficulties surrendering his lifetime's goal.

The following week the parliament was returning for a special one day sitting and the caucus was meeting on Thursday 19 December. It was a deadline for the party. If Hawke refused to budge and Keating refused to challenge then the impasse would remain until the New Year. The three major national broadsheets, the *Sydney Morning Herald*, *The Age* and *The Australian* in their editorials had each called for Hawke to resign.

Hawke had won the 1990 election on the slogan that a party that cannot govern itself cannot govern the nation. Those words now mocked him. In 1991 it was the Labor Party which could not govern itself and therefore could not govern the nation. Unless Labor killed the leadership crisis, then the crisis would kill Labor.

As the decisive week began Keating's strategy was to persuade Hawke to resign without a ballot; if a ballot were needed he wanted to wait until the majority was overwhelming. The caucus numbers were tight but favoured Keating.

At the start of the Cabinet meeting on Monday 16 December John Button, who had been overseas the previous week, requested a meeting with Hawke on the leadership. This followed a lunchtime meeting between another five Cabinet ministers—Keating backers from the June challenge—who decided that Hawke should be asked to resign. (The ministers were Button, Dawkins, Blewett, Cook and Kelly.) This would take to 12 (including Richardson) the number of Cabinet ministers who had asked Hawke to resign—although the first delegation had changed its mind. Button was serving as spokesman for this second group. The story was leaked promptly to the media. Meanwhile at a press conference Ralph Willis refused to endorse Hawke.

Hawke spent the next day, 17 December, at one of the functions he loved most—the annual Prime Minister's XI cricket match—while the Morgan poll had his approval falling to 26 per cent—strictly Keating territory! The coalition lead was 52.5 to 31.5 per cent, probably the worst Labor figure for half a century. Hawke, the greatest poll-driven politician in Australia's history, was crushed by the polls. The poll that counted—state of the parties—revealed the Hawke government was bankrupt; worse than Whitlam. Hawke declared that he wanted a new economic statement for early 1992 but what he got that night was Button, urging his resignation.

En route to Canberra the shipping minister, Bob Collins, announced that the leadership had to be settled and it was 'unthinkable' that it drag into New Year. Collins had defected from Hawke to Keating. On the *AM* program another junior minister, Alan Griffiths, called upon Hawke to leave. Colin Parkes advised Hawke it was his last chance to leave without a caucus defeat.

Keating didn't want to challenge for many reasons—he wanted Hawke to resign; he was unsure of the numbers and he had pledged against a second challenge. Keating felt he had 56 solid votes by the Monday and more by Tuesday. Everyone said to Keating, 'It's got to be resolved.' He replied: 'Tell Hawke to apply the John Kerin test.' But Keating reluctantly accepted that if Hawke refused to budge then he would have to strike.

Only on Wednesday evening did the Keating camp become convinced that it would prevail. Richardson, for the first time, was confident.

As the prospect of a ballot on Thursday 19 December grew more likely the left faction met the night before to agree formally to allow a free vote on the leadership. The faction felt that Hawke would be discredited if he won on an instructed vote from the left. Howe and Hand spoke in favour of this position, proof that the left could no longer hold its members behind Hawke. Keating was amazed that Hawke had not cancelled the special one-day sitting which had brought Labor MPs to Canberra, giving them a chance to change leaders.

Beazley had spoken to Hawke at length on 18 December to urge him to retire with dignity but Hawke was unmovable. The Keating forces were considering a petition of caucus members for a change, confident of having 60-plus votes. That evening Hawke entertained the caucus at its annual Christmas dinner at The Lodge. Keating was absent on another engagement.

Late that night Hawke met his close supporters who warned him to expect an approach for a ballot. Richardson had told the Hawke forces there would be a challenge, an effort to force Hawke's resignation or, at least, a Hawke-initiated contest. Some of Hawke's 'gang of six' loyalists tried again to persuade him to resign, but Hawke was staying. So they advised him to bring on the battle, to have 'an honest fight'. Hawke accepted this view; he felt this was the dignified way.

Hawke drafted a letter for the caucus chair, saying that because of the imminent challenge he would initiate a leadership ballot. He and his loyal press secretary, Grant Nihill, repaired to The Lodge at 3.30 am, woke Hazel and told her the plan. Hawke went to bed at 4.10 am for three hours. He distributed copies of his letter at the 9 am caucus meeting; another meeting was set for 6.30 pm where Hawke would resign the leadership and face Keating in a head-to-head contest. It was sudden death.

In parliament Hewson taunted Hawke: 'Is it a fact that no Labor Prime Minister had ever been rejected by his own party in a caucus ballot?' Hawke showed courage and humour to reply: 'I hope history repeats itself.'

The contest was intense throughout the day. Ray and Bolkus pulled every string to maximise Hawke's vote with the right and left. At 4 pm Bolkus put down his phone and said, 'We're within two votes.' Crean was working furiously for Hawke. At 5 pm Brereton was worried. 'They're tearing votes off us everywhere,' he told Keating. There was a distinct swing back towards Hawke. Richardson had told Parkes that when he was satisfied that Keating had sixty votes he would offer a pair for the absence overseas of Gareth Evans—but Richardson was never satisfied. The hope of a Keating 'bandwagon' effect was destroyed. Ray said later: 'Honour was served and we got every vote we could.' Keating told his supporters, 'If we can't win now then pity help the Labor Party.'

Keating won 56 to 51, a narrow margin, but an increase of 12 votes on his June performance. Hawke had achieved his purpose—he made the party force him from office and would hold the party responsible for what he believed was an historic blunder.

In defeat Hawke gave a superb nationally televised press conference with Hazel sitting at one side. He called for unity and paraded a mixture of compassion, pride and emotion. 'If this was 11 years ago I'd be getting pretty thoroughly drunk . . .' Hawke hoped he would be remembered 'as a bloke who loved his country, still does, and loves Australians . . . I hope they still think of me as the Bob Hawke they got to know, the larrikin trade union leader who perhaps had sufficient common sense and sufficient intelligence to tone down his larrikinism and behave in a way that a Prime Minister should . . .'

Keating, by contrast, was nervous, tentative, immediately conscious of the burden of power. His first words were that it was 'a very humbling experience'. He apologised for his 'recession we had to have' statement, saying his policy had been to slow the economy, not to provoke a recession. He made three pledges—dedication to the office, telling people the truth, and fighting the battle against unemployment. Keating said he wanted 'to get confidence in Australia going again'.

The best assessment of Hawke came from Peter Walsh:

The British historian Lord Bullock said a few weeks ago that if Hitler had died in 1938 history would have recorded him to be Germany's greatest statesman. Ditto for Hawke 50 years later. Well, almost ditto . . . the best advice he ever got came from John Dawkins in the spring of 1988 when Dawkins told Hawke it was time to quit. Had he taken that advice Hawke would have left office almost unsullied and unblemished—or at least would have been seen and judged to be so. Hawke certainly did not think so at the time. Neither does he now, and I doubt that he ever will. Political leaders, especially Labor leaders, tend to hang on for too long. With the exception of Hayden, every federal Labor leader since Chifley has, with the compliance of caucus, done that.[34]

After his defeat Hawke said the caucus decision to dump him was 'a decision my colleagues will have to live with'. He offered Keating some advice which provided the best insight into Hawke's conception of leadership. He said there were two leadership requirements: giving a free leash to your ministers while operating as a safety net; and getting close to the electorate. 'I had those characteristics,' Hawke said. 'Paul will have to learn to acquire them.'[35]

But Hawke lost the prime ministership because he failed to display leadership; if Hawke had been good enough then Keating would have stayed a prisoner in his back bench room 101. The caucus only elected Keating when it felt that Hawke's government had reached its last gasp. Hawke's relaxed leadership style worked when Keating was his treasurer but it failed when Hawke had to govern without Keating. The release of the Opposition's *Fightback* package revealed that the people wanted stronger leadership but Hawke had failed to respond.

Keating's conception of leadership was more dramatic and dangerous: to strike from the front, or to use his own words, 'to kick through the big reforms'. He had a dose of Gough Whitlam's 'crash through or crash' style and a streak of Jack Lang's deep hatred of his opponents.

The victory Keating had won was proof of his immense political skill and testimony of his central claim as the politician who had driven the policy changes of the 1980s. The conundrum of the Keating prime ministership was put by Keating himself on this first evening—he pledged both to promote recovery and not to abandon the policy gains of the 1980s. A difficult mixture.

Keating's campaign had raised expectations, notably in Victoria, about urgent job creation measures. But there was little he could do immediately without prejudicing the longer term basis for a sustained recovery. There was no 'quick fix' for the economy—a 'quick fix' for an election in 18 months would corrupt the national interest for misguided self-interest.

The paradox of Keating's victory is that when the prime ministership came he was almost surprised. Sitting in The Lodge, eerie with the echo of an absent Hawke, Keating was filled with an overwhelming sense that he had little time; so much ground to recover and so few months. Keating, however, would improvise as usual and govern by instinct.

He faced two great questions: what policy strategy would Keating follow in his effort to snatch back the election from Hewson? And how would the recession influence Keating to modify his 1980s policy framework for the 1990s? In short, what did a Keating prime ministership represent?

34
The end of certainty

Booms and recessions are similar in one respect—they all fade away. The challenge posed by the 1980s is to separate the structural trends from the cyclical changes. The story of the decade is the embrace by both sides of politics (although to different degrees) of the free market agenda and its gradual application as the solution to Australia's underlying problems. Despite the significant differences between them, the major proponents of the new philosophy—Hawke, Keating, Howard, Hewson and McLachlan—believed that their remedies were an historic break from the past. They were involved in the demolition of the Australian Settlement ideas and their replacement with an alternative philosophy.

In the 1980s both Labor and non-Labor underwent internal philosophical revolutions to support a new set of ideas—faith in markets, deregulation, a reduced role for government, low protection and the creation of a new cooperative enterprise culture.

The magnitude of this attempted transition should not be underestimated: it is an effort to take Australia into the third phase of its European history. The first phase from white occupation to the late nineteenth century was the foundation period; the second, from the late nineteenth century throughout most of the twentieth century was the experiment in nation-building guided by the post-Federation Australian Settlement ideas. The issue for the 1990s is whether the market philosophy of the 1980s eventually becomes this third phase, as Australia adapts to international revolutions in communications and global markets and is integrated into the Asia/Pacific region.

However, a shadow has fallen across this transition—the early 1990s recession which has plunged Australia into a malaise that has weakened its confidence, its institutions and its belief in the free market philosophy. The 1990s have begun amid national pessimism with damage to many institutions—state and federal governments and their treasuries, the corporate sector, manufacturing and rural industry, banks and credit institutions and the media. The shocks from the early 1990s recession are deeper than from its predecessors in the 1970s and 1980s. There is a disenchantment with leadership, hostility towards the excesses of the 1980s, and a confusion about the national direction.

But one conclusion is manifest from the 1980s—the old order is finished. There is no returning to past certitudes. By 1991 it was beyond question that the five ideas of the Australian Settlement were in irreversible stages of collapse or exhaustion—White Australia, Trade Protection, Wage Arbitration, State Paternalism and Imperial Benevolence. Neither disenchantment nor nostalgia had any hope of reviving these beliefs, although there was a bitter dispute about the rate of change. It followed, therefore, that the 1990s would witness an intensification of the battle over a new set of ideas to shape a new Australia.

In this struggle there were three positions in the prelude to the 1992–93 federal election—the sentimental traditionalists who wanted a future based largely upon a re-shaping of the ideas of the past and whose most eloquent spokesman was Malcolm Fraser; the free market purists represented by John Hewson's coalition who aspired to apply market ideas further and faster; and a re-fashioned ALP position spearheaded by Paul Keating who sought, as a recession prime minister, a new political synthesis between market orientated reforms and a revived role for government intervention.

There were many spokespeople and forces representing the sentimental traditionalists—Phil Clearly the independent who won the Wills by-election when Hawke retired, the academic Hugh Stretton, the commentator B. A. Santamaria, *The Age*'s economic editor, Ken Davidson, the Australian Democrats, the Kerry Packer-owned magazine *Australian Business*, virtually the entire ALP left and sections of the ALP right, most of the National Party's formal membership, sections of manufacturing industry, a number of powerful trade unions, the Melbournian conservative intellectuals based upon *Quadrant* magazine, the 'new class' teachers and public sector professionals, most of the literary establishment, the Fraser era Liberals, and the opponents of the 1980s dry revolution within the Liberal Party.

This was an alliance which defied the established pattern of Australian political conflict. It revealed the real, as opposed to the nominal, division in Australian politics at the start of the 1990s. It was a division which cut completely across the existing party system. This split was between the market-orientated reformers and the Australian Settlement traditionalists. Both groups existed in the two major parties. The reason these divisions had not occurred before was because such a fundamental debate had not been conducted since the immediate post-federation period.

661

It should be no surprise that the most aggressive and sustained champion of the traditionalist position was Malcolm Fraser. At the decade's end Fraser emerged with pent-up intellectual and personal scores to settle. As usual, Fraser went for the jugular; it was a reminder of his clout as a political figure. Fraser blamed Keating, the treasury, the free market economic rationalist philosophy, the Liberals (for backing Keating), and the banks who exploited financial deregulation for their own ends. In an assault which reflected the force of the traditional ideas Fraser declared:

> Without Paul Keating the Labor government would never have fallen for the three card trick. We would have been better-off with no government at all because this government has denied its responsibility to maintain a balanced and strong economy . . . Under this government the rich and powerful have prospered greatly, players in the financial markets have absorbed massive wealth at the expense of Australian workers, manufacturers, farmers and miners . . . Keating was the strongest advocate of the treasury view. He blithely accepted denial of government responsibility as a virtue, the renunciation of equity as a political concept and the abolition of competitive fairness in the marketplace. His political skills were great because he persuaded the Opposition that most of what he did was right . . . is there a body in the ALP caucus that realises that the wasteland of 1991 is caused not by all the decades that preceded 1983 but by the years that immediately followed? Is the Labor Party capable of recognising the hypocrisy and cant of the eighties and recapturing not an outdated socialism but the essential core of Liberal Democracy . . . We desperately need a re-examination of the idols of the 1980s. Unfortunately that is the one thing we are unlikely to get from the Government or Opposition.[1]

Fraser had waited a decade; now he pointed to the 1990s recession to attack those who had ridiculed him. Fraser's charge was that Australia had gone wrong in the 1980s and that both Labor and non-Labor were accomplices to the crime. He bemoaned that during the 1980s the Liberal Party had 'believed it necessary to dramatically change its philosophy'.

With support from Doug Anthony, the man from Nareen declared:

> I know of no other country that has so blatantly and deliberately deserted its wealth-producing base in favour of a milk bar, froth and bubble economy . . . It is not just the Government, it is the entire political process, Government and Opposition, which has embraced this extraordinary abdication . . . a political process that believes that government had no duty to defend its own. For the great, the powerful, the wealthy, the organised, the unions, such a philosophy may be of no great moment. They survive, even thrive, in the jungle. For ordinary Australians it spells disaster.[2]

The irony for the traditionalists was their lack of a leader since Fraser

662

could never stage a comeback. It is fascinating that there was no left wing party (Democrats excepted) to champion the re-regulation of the economy and the return to the Australian Settlement beliefs. It is axiomatic that if public sentiment for this idea remains strong then either new parties will emerge to give it expression or existing parties (such as Labor) will eventually embrace it.

There was much truth in Fraser's protest. The great truth was his assertion that people had no faith in the free market reforms as a result of the recession. This is John Hewson's greatest challenge if he becomes prime minister—implementing an agenda which the people appear to dislike and distrust. Hewson stands as the extreme opponent of the traditionalist push. His ideology is free market radicalism and his complaint is that Labor was too hesitant in pursuit of free market economics during the 1980s. Hewson acts from a belief in Irving Kristol's famous line that 'a neo-conservative is a liberal who has been mugged by reality'. Hewson's philosophy is a faster and purer brand of free market economics to destroy the old rigidities and establish a contemporary economy.

Within the Hewson Liberal Party there is the belief, articulated by David Kemp, that 'the 1990s will be the most important decade for Australian politics since the first decade of this century'. The message could not be more explicit—during this decade the Hewson Liberals intend to erect their philosophy of market economics and individual freedom in place of the Australian Settlement. This involves a revolution within capital as well as labour; a cultural change for business as much as for unions.

Hewson was uncompromising because of his conviction that time was fast running out for Australia. The history of the past 30 years revealed that the trough of each recession was deeper than its predecessor. There were four landmarks of growing severity—the 1960s credit squeeze downturn, and the recessions of the 1970s, 1980s and 1990s. Hewson had plenty of evidence to conclude that Australia's underlying problems were deteriorating and that a decisive break point was required.

In the prelude to the 1992–93 election Hewson, to the date of writing, has refused to make concessions from any of his main policies—low inflation, labour market deregulation, the reduction of protection to negligible levels by the year 2000, the GST, a reduction in the size and reach of the public sector, and faster micro-economic reform including large-scale privatisations. But the ultimate sanction for free market reforms lies in the people's mandate; without sustained electoral backing during the 1990s there cannot be a new national ideology. And electoral backing throughout the 1990s will be delivered only upon one condition: the proof that the new policies are making Australia a more prosperous nation.

Keating's prime ministership was a story of desperation driving creativity. Keating sought to create a new Labor position to sustain the party both in recession and beyond. He approached the election with a remarkable synthesis—Labor as the party of consensus-based market reforms but still relying upon government as a force for job creation and enlightened intervention to secure better economic and social progress. This attempted synthesis was a result of the two forces that drove Keating—a belief in the 1980s policy direction of which he was the principal architect and the need to pull Australia out of the 1990s recession as fast as possible.

Keating used Hewson as a symbol of primitive and heartless capitalism in an effort to maximise the differences between Labor and the coalition. His political objective was twofold—to depict Hewson's ideology as falling outside the limits of acceptable social change within Australia and eventually to force a split within the non-Labor side over its new philosophy. Keating attempted to orchestrate a grassroots ALP revival using the Hewson bogy—the GST, abolition of protection and public sector cuts—and was remarkably successful in uniting the party behind him after the convulsions of the Hawke–Keating struggle. The old 1980s echo about Keating betraying traditional Labor values was virtually dead—except among the middle class intellectuals campaigning against economic rationalism. Whitlam was almost reconciled with the new Labor direction, in particular, the public sector inspired effort to restore the national infrastructure; he praised Keating in private and dismissed Hawke with the snort that 'he reigned but never ruled'.

The message Keating delivered to capital was that a competitive internationalised economy would best be achieved through Labor's consensus based economic reforms, not the shock therapy promised by Hewson. Keating played on Hewson's absolutism and tried to exploit the alarm within sections of the business community about Hewson's plunge towards faster industrial deregulation and protection cuts. Keating assumed a new political persona—the leader pioneering the demolition of the Australian Settlement but promising to retain the values of egalitarianism, income justice and social stability which had always been hallmarks of Australian democracy. At the time of the 1992 budget Keating declared:

> The successful models are the social democracies where government is involved in making the societies tick, where there is a happy mix between efficient economics and a comprehensive social policy in this post-monetarist, post-communist era. Ideology today is a luxury . . . the notion that some ideology whether it be Adam Smith, or survival of the fittest, or the market knows best . . . can't work. What's the key ingredient in competitiveness? Basically the inflation rate. How do you keep it? Basically by co-operation, consensus and agreement. You can't keep it by a draconian policy with a flame-thrower burning business off the pavement. You can't do it by regarding the workforce as enemies of the management . . . Medicare, aged care, child care, occupational superannuation, access to education, are all part of the fabric of Australia. And to get that fabric and tear it, rip it, will produce a social reaction the likes of which we have not experienced.

This was Keating taking command of the middle ground, a stance that might not save his government but would offer Labor a charter for the 1990s if it lost office.

The philosophical question for the 1990s is whether Australia will renew or lose its mid-1980s momentum to create an open, internationally competitive, more productive economy. While public opinion is tentative and often hostile to free market reforms, the continued pressure for these reforms will be strong, probably irresistible, and intellectual backing for economic liberalisation remains powerful both at home and abroad. The judgement, on balance, favours the continued implementation of the free market agenda—despite intense disputes about the agenda's timing, its social and income equity, and the methods by which it is applied.

One myth can be dispatched: that the market agenda was responsible for the 1990s recession and that therefore it has already failed. Such claims are intellectually dishonest: the market agenda cannot have failed because it had not been implemented. This is an elementary but fundamental point. The 1990s recession was largely a result of the difficulties in the transition from a closed to an open economy and, in particular, the adjustment to financial deregulation. But it is only during the course of the 1990s that Australia will have the chance to deregulate its labour market, eliminate protection, break its high inflation psychology and reduce government intervention in a series of enterprises and industries. It is realistic to think of the new order being established by 2000 with the early 1990s being a half-way house for agonised reappraisal.

A survey of Australia's situation in Labor's fourth term points decisively towards the demolition of the Australian Settlement ideas. The major achievement of the Hawke government in its fourth term was Bob Hawke's March 1991 Industry Statement which stands as an historic milestone. At this point Hawke, unaware of the depth of the looming recession, consigned his destiny as a politician and Australia's fate as a nation to the belief in free trade. In his final act Hawke demolished the edifice of Protection, the cornerstone of the post-federation Settlement. It is this decision, providing it sticks, which will guarantee that the direction of the 1990s maintains the course launched in the 1980s.

Hawke announced the general level of tariff assistance would be reduced from 10 and 15 per cent in 1992 to 5 per cent by 1996; that tariffs on cars would be reduced from 35 per cent in 1992 to 15 per cent in 2000; and that tariff cuts on footwear, clothing and textiles would be accelerated, in breach of the existing plan, so that quotas would be eliminated in 1993 and the maximum tariff by 2000 would be 25 per cent. This would reduce the average nominal rate of industry assistance to 3 per cent overall.

Hawke declared that these phased reductions would help to keep inflation low, make Australia internationally competitive and generate a net increase in the number of jobs. Ross Garnaut, who influenced Hawke to the

665

plunge, said the changes were 'bigger than the end of the British Corn Laws that earned Peel and Cobden a dozen pages in our high school history books.' Hawke's announcement effectively terminated Australia's century of Protection.

Confidence that the timetable will stick depends entirely upon the bipartisan embrace of low protection. The Hewson-led coalition is pledged to a similar though more rigorous program, and the reduction of protection to 'negligible' levels by 2000. Such bipartisanship at the federal level is the essential condition for the decade-long delivery of the reductions. Within each of the three parties, Labor, Liberal and National, the opponents of low protection were staging, in the early 1990s, an aggressive counter-offensive on the back of the recession. It was proof that the real division in Australian politics was horizontal, a split running through all parties that separated market-orientated reformers from state power traditionalists.

However a new danger emerged in 1992—an alliance between Keating, the motor industry and the unions—attacking the opposition for its 'negligible' protection pledge. This saw a split between the parties over the rate of tariff reduction. Keating sought to revive protection as a political issue but the risk was that he might lose control of the debate and help to revive protection itself.

This counter-offensive was assisted by those states, notably Victoria, which face the most severe adjustment. Victoria, in fact, confronting not just an economic crisis but a crisis of identity, became the heartland for the counter-reaction. This was no surprise since the demise of the Australian Settlement would have the maximum impact in the state which created Deakinite Liberalism and whose commercial, intellectual and political influence shaped the early post-federation beliefs in Protection, Arbitration and State Power. Victoria was undergoing a worse recession because of the crisis in its financial institutions; Victoria would also be the state most affected by the 1990s protection reduction timetable.

This combination of recession today and low protection tomorrow demanded, in effect, that Victoria reinvent itself. This was the challenge— but the response testified to the stubborn survival instincts of the decaying Victorian establishment and to the endurance of the old Deakinite employer– union alliance on behalf of 'New Protection'. The age of Deakin had seen Victoria's vision accepted as Australia's vision; now at the century's end the rest of the nation was imposing a new vision upon a reluctant Victoria. As protection fell, the shift in jobs and investment would favour NSW, Queensland and Western Australia against Victoria, South Australia and Tasmania. Greater regional and state disparities would become a feature of the emerging protection-free Australia.

Hawke's Statement was a logical but courageous step for the government. It was made possible only because of financial deregulation in 1983, the May 1988 Statement unveiling substantial protection cuts to 1992, and the committed rhetoric of the government throughout its life.

There had been smaller steps along the way—the removal of import quotas on steel in 1983; the 1984 car plan; the removal of quotas on white goods and other durables; the easing of mineral export controls; the abolition of the crude oil allocation scheme; the eventual suspension of the wool reserve price scheme; the entry of new banks and more liberal foreign investment rules; Australia's aggressive diplomacy in the GATT round and its commitment to an open trading system, an international stance which required validity at home.[3]

After the announcement Ross Garnaut predicted that 'Australian industrial transformation can be expected to proceed rapidly over this decade—at a pace that surprises most Australians . . . I expect the emergence of an internationally-orientated Australian economy over the 1990s with strong specialisation in a range of services and manufactured exports'. He said that the evidence of structural change was manifest in the growth of manufactured exports—chemical, electrical, transport, telecommunications and processed metals.[4] In a series of speeches Garnaut showed that Australia's manufactured exports were rising, contrary to prevailing myth.

Responding to Hawke's Statement the former Reserve governor, Bob Johnston, was passionate:

> We humble citizens who read about this jellyback government can only be surprised when we find that they have some guts! I can't claim to have been a lifetime Labor voter—and I was appointed by the Fraser government—but I admire these blokes. The reason I stuck with them was because they did things instead of just talking about them. The tariff changes are an act of real courage.[5]

The attack on protection has been protracted; it represents the triumph of an intellectual movement with deep roots in Australian history that was overwhelmed at the time of the Australian Settlement. Despite the 1980s rhetoric about the Reagan and Thatcher Revolutions the real triumph of low protection in Australia owes nothing to such overseas phenomena. Ronald Reagan was the most protectionist US president for half a century, a fact of which his local free market backers remained in sublime ignorance.

It is over twenty years since Alf Rattigan as chairman of the Tariff Board declared that Australia had to reverse its course. This position has been championed since by an influential alliance of economic opinion makers, Canberra policy advisers, farm groups, exporters, selected business figures and political leaders. It is to the lasting credit of the Labor Party that the reductions in protection have been achieved entirely as a result of decisions by the Whitlam and Hawke governments.

Protection fell because of growing acceptance of the idea in Australia that protection stifled growth and employment; that low protection was the better path to prosperity and growth; and that the costs of protection could no longer be carried by the trading sector and the consumers. This was accentuated by a recognition that commodity prices were deteriorating relative to other prices; that Australia had to diversify its export base while exploiting natural comparative advantage; and that low protection was the route to integration with the high growth economies of the Asia/Pacific.

The early 1990s backlash resurrected the old argument that Australia needed tariffs because other nations persisted with various forms of protection. This missed the main point—that lower protection would help Australian producers anyway. It would guarantee an internationally competitive economy. As protection is reduced the 1990s will witness more structural change at a faster rate than occurred in the 1980s. In the new system the imperative for productivity will be paramount.

Hawke's Statement confirms the transformation in politics and economics which his government launched in the 1980s. This is because in Australia protection had had a more pervasive impact than in probably any other Western nation.[6] Protection's abolition will internationalise the industrial base, just as the float internationalised the financial system from 1983. It will change Australia's corporate culture, since individual companies, without a protected economy to sustain their profits, must look to better management, marketing, industrial relations and productivity. It will bring a new intensity to the demand for micro-economic reform, since without protection to guarantee profits, companies must have a more efficient infrastructure— ports, wharves, aviation, road, rail, communication and energy. It will terminate the division between anti-protectionist exporters and protectionist manufacturers. It will unite industry—farmers, miners, manufacturers, the service sector—in favour of more efficient supply lines and enterprise practices. Finally, it will smash the reliance upon a centralised wages system embodied in the Industrial Relations Commission; a free market for goods and services must be linked with a relatively free market for labour.

This is the starting point for the second phase of the debate—what are the policies necessary to deliver the efficiencies which the open economy of the 1990s demands? This is where differences between Liberal and Labor are sharper. The Liberal Party under Hewson and the free market lobby (sometimes tagged 'economic rationalists') argues for the market philosophy to be applied throughout the economy to induce changes in individual and corporate culture. On the other hand Labor under Keating tries to find an accommodation between market ideas and government intervention. It concedes that the old system is dying but wants government to limit, contain or cushion the market adjustment. The immediate battleground after protection is the labour market.

The ALP–ACTU Accord underwent a remarkable transition from 1983 to 1991. It was conceived as a revival of Arbitration and centralised wage fixation but by the decade's end it had become a mechanism to implement

Labor's vision of enterprise bargaining. That is a measure of the 1980s shake-out.

The Accord was a success for much of the decade. In the seven years to mid-1990 a total of 1.6 million jobs were created, overwhelmingly in the private sector; the school retention rate to Year 12 rose from one in three to two in three; per capita real disposable income rose an average of 1 per cent a year and real unit labour costs fell by 9 per cent overall, thereby delivering a profits surge.[7]

Bob Hawke is correct in describing the Accord as the most successful national wages policy implemented in Australia; an appreciation of the previous confusion is required to grasp the validity of this claim. But Hawke, the architect of 1983 Accord consensus, admitted in 1992 after he left office that a different approach is now required, in a speech which was further testimony to Labor's pragamatic tradition. Hawke, in effect, supported an entirely new approach to that of the original 1983 Accord. He declared that the way to higher living standards was that 'workers, their representatives and the managements be engaged directly in determining wage outcomes in their own workplaces . . . with an increasing emphasis on workplace bargains based on productivity'.[8]

The Accord's defect is that its success derived from employment growth, not productivity. The Hawke–Keating years delivered on jobs, and to a lesser extent, living standards, until the recession. But living standards were improved through a combination of falling real wages and employment growth—an unsustainable mix. Lasting prosperity derives from the combination of rising real wages and employment growth. The missing link is productivity and micro-economic reform. Economics commentator Alan Wood remarks: 'This is a devastating conclusion for the Accord partners because the two areas where the Accord has been a notable failure are productivity and micro-reform. It is hard to avoid the conclusion that the policies required to keep living standards rising in the 1990s can be implemented only by a change of government.'[9]

However the Accord partners, aware from the late 1980s that change was required, had adapted the two-tier wages system of Accord Mark III into an emerging model of enterprise bargaining under the Accord Mark VI, only to find the Industrial Relations Commission, for the first time, refusing to ratify an Accord deal. The IRC in its April 1991 decision, by declining to authorise a shift to cooperative decentralisation, signed the death warrant for its influence. Bill Kelty and Paul Keating turned against the centralised tribunal with venom; they began to undermine the legitimacy of the IRC with a degree of potency that could only come from such prestigious figures within the labour movement.

Kelty's strategy was a recognition of the inevitable—that enterprise negotiations were the route to more productivity. He decided to train the union movement on the terrain where it would have to battle the deregulatory purists of the Hewson–Howard–McLachlan Liberal Party—at the level of each individual enterprise. In effect Keating and Kelty devised their own system of enterprise bargaining.

Kelty pontificates with the wisdom of hindsight on the Accord's evolution:

> We had a long term strategy: first step, wage restraint; second step award restructuring; third step, implementing it on an enterprise basis. We were always going to do it. I think the government understood the wage system had to evolve. We wanted, ultimately, to devolve authority from the ACTU to unions; give unions more independence. We adopted this philosophical approach from 1986. The ACTU used its authority for a series of objectives—employment, superannuation, rationalisation of the union structure, change in the wages system. We say that the future of the union movement lies, not with the ACTU, but with the individual unions.[10]

In fact, genuine enterprise bargaining depends upon the freedom to create enterprise unions and to negotiate voluntary contracts absolutely outside any award system or centralised structure. This is the essence of the coalition policy. It is this deregulatory purity which the unions are prepared to fight and it is the battle which organised labour eventually is unlikely to win. The coalition strategy is to make unions less relevant and to undermine their power within the workplaces.

Post-protectionist Australia will be subject to powerful international forces—the world economy is becoming more global; financial markets are global; product markets are relatively open despite the influence of protection; huge deregulated labour markets operate in America and the Asia/Pacific; the European Community will become one vast labour market; the 'trade-in-services' provisions of the GATT round recognise the greater freedom of international movement; technology and communications are destroying national borders. In this climate the task of national economic policy will be to create a setting for efficiency and productivity; to make Australia a proposition for overseas investment for competitive industry. This means that workforces which are overpaid by world standards will not maintain their jobs.[11]

It is a culture alien to that of the early twentieth century when the Deakinite–Labor alliance created the Arbitration system on the back of Protection in a bold effort to realise the ideal of wage justice and equity.

The wages issue, as John Stone said after Hawke's 1991 protection announcement, is whether the consequences for the labour market are acknowledged quickly or 'whether it will take a decade of stagflationary malaise before that inevitability is grudgingly accepted'.[12] That depends partly upon who governs.

Before the 1992 budget the Keating–Kelty model was further advanced with a proposed alternative to the National Wage Case in which minimum award rates were adjusted but the rest of the workforce would rely upon enterprise bargaining based upon productivity. It was obvious that the Accord was moving beyond and outside the IRC. The cynics said this was merely tilling the field for Hewson. In fact, Labor was moving to deregulate on its terms—retaining the award system, creating a series of large and powerful unions and trying to limit the growth of a poorly paid underclass. Hawke's historic move on protection, followed by the Keating–Kelty move towards an enterprise bargaining system, establishes the conditions for the decisive initiative of a Hewson government—full labour market deregulation.

In a similar fashion Labor's embrace since 1987 of an ambitious micro-economic reform agenda has only created the conditions for a more assertive push by a coalition government. A clarion call for comprehensive micro-reform came in the 1989 IAC annual report, appropriately the body which had spearheaded the assault upon protection: 'The search for better ways of doing things must extend to all aspects of economic life. A start has been made in a number of areas, but there is much to be done.' The report pointed out that micro-economic reform was proceeding apace in other nations:

> If we do not act now our competitive position and our standard of living are in danger of decline. Significant domestic reform can prevent this. The removal of major inefficiencies in domestic water transport, international liner shipping, the transport and handling of bulk commodities, domestic and international aviation, road and rail transport could collectively increase GDP by around $9 billion annually. Improved efficiencies in the postal, telecommunications and electricity sectors could provide a further stimulus to GDP of around $3 billion annually.[13]

The IAC said that while some reforms had promoted efficiencies they fell short of creating a competitive climate: the real guarantor of 'first-best' international practice. This was a plea for a faster pace of reform; it was also the exact coalition criticism of Labor's micro-reforms.

The criticism of Labor's pace of micro-reform reached its peak following Hawke's protection announcement in March 1991. Hewson went for Labor's jugular with deadly accuracy: 'You can't cut protection without delivering widespread and fundamental micro-economic reform—in the labour market, transportation, aviation and coastal shipping, on the waterfront, in telecommunications . . . To cut tariffs alone will simply send more companies broke and increase the dole queues.'[14] This was the precise message from the Business Council of Australia (BCA), which reflected the outlook of Australia's major companies. The message was obvious: if Labor was ruthless in cutting protection it must be equally ruthless in pushing through micro-reforms which would help to give the country an internationally competitive infrastructure.

Labor, in fact, was guilty of a double standard born within politics. Hawke believed in consensus when dealing with trade union and public sector sensitivities, which is why micro-reform was so protracted. But he was prepared to impose ruthless change upon capital—financial deregulation, protection cuts and environmental vetoes such as Kakadu. Hewson was merely pledged to apply the same standards to micro-reform which Hawke had applied to cutting protection.

Labor's fourth term did see decisive micro-reforms in two industries—telecommunications and aviation. A special ALP National Conference post-election changed Labor's platform to break Telecom's monopoly and allow competition into telecommunications along with selling equity in Australian Airlines and Qantas. This smashing of Labor icons was a delayed recognition that Telecom's monopoly and government owned airlines were obstacles to, not bulwarks of, a more efficient economy.

Keating, in fact, had pushed out the borders of both reforms. He failed to secure true deregulation of telecommunications although this was the next step. As prime minister he won the merger of Australian Airlines and Qantas in 1992 and Cabinet agreement to a 100 per cent sale of the new airline—a humiliating defeat for the ALP traditionalists who had resisted such moves for a decade. However, Labor had to pay the penalty for refusing to sell the airlines in the late 1980s when the market was high.

Keating's most dramatic coup was his 1990 exploitation of the Victorian State Bank crisis when, with the backing of the left-wing Kirner government, he cut a deal for the Commonwealth Bank to acquire the State Bank of Victoria through a float of 30 per cent of the Commonwealth's equity, thereby partially privatising the most sacred of ALP icons. It was only five years since Hawke and Keating had savaged the Liberals for suggesting the sale of the Commonwealth Bank. Now it had become their own policy. It symbolised the collapse of Labor's traditional position and the end of ideological struggle over government ownership. The float was a success with the public.

Overall, these changes mocked Keating's arrogant late 1988 remark that 'we've got almost nothing left to reform'. The free market reform process had its own momentum for a nation with Australia's external debt. Once launched it was very difficult to quarantine sections of the economy from its impact.

The most dramatic tactical analysis of micro-economic reform came from Roger Douglas, the former New Zealand Finance minister and free market reform spearhead. Douglas offered several revealing axioms:

> The abolition of privilege is the essence of structural reform . . . use
> your program to give power back to the people . . . speed is essential,

it is impossible to go too fast . . . there are serious dangers in seeking to hold down the pace of change in order to satisfy groups that claim a slower pace would give the community more time to adjust with less pain . . . once you start the momentum rolling, never let it stop . . . continuous credibility is essential to maintain public confidence.[15]

Keating had used this approach selectively; Hewson was pledged to apply it systematically. But it demanded political skills of the highest order—as the career of the departed Douglas demonstrated.

The most comprehensive statement during the late 1980s of the dimensions of the national challenge was the 1989 report on 'Australia and the Northeast Asian Ascendancy' by Hawke's former economic adviser, Ross Garnaut. The report was optimistic about the future but urgent about the need for rapid reform. Above all, the report was founded on the idea of an integrated approach to change, namely, that the economic and social changes required were tantamount to a new Australian identity—the type of Australia which would be needed to meet the opportunities involved in genuine partnership within the Asia/Pacific.

This required a conscious effort to reject Australia's protectionist, isolationist, introverted past and many of its recent by-products—inflation, poor growth, low productivity, declining relative living standards. Garnaut called for an increase in the rate at which the Australian economy was internationalised. He wanted faster economic liberalisation to lock Australia into the Asia/Pacific. His report grasped the real danger of the 1980s—that Australia had only a narrow window of opportunity which would close unless it moved fast.

This necessitated faster cuts in protection, a lower inflation policy, more Asian investment, new foreign-financed port facilities, foreign competition on shipping routes, complete aviation deregulation, more emphasis on age, skill and education in the immigration program, compulsory Asian history and language courses at schools, and new links between Australian and regional tertiary institutions. Garnaut set a medium-term objective—the elimination of protection at Australia's borders by the years 2000, which would be a test of the government's commitment. His report was a catalyst for Hawke's March 1991 Statement, probably its driving force, and Garnaut's protection prescription was accepted by Hewson.

The Garnaut thesis was that closer economic integration between Australia and the region would produce significant export dividends in the three areas of primary products, secondary processing and services. Garnaut said that if the Australian economy were normally efficient it should be exporting an extra $20 billion a year in goods and services for its current size. That goal depended upon the removal of policies which penalised exporters and upon raised productivity. Garnaut saw great potential in trade in tourism and education services, providing Australia was prepared to reform its transport and aviation industries. He predicted that by 2000 Northeast Asia alone would provide the equivalent of 150 per cent of the total tourist market in 1989.

The report argued that by integrating with the fastest growing region in the world the benefits to Australia would be considerable. The prospects for semi-processed raw material exports to Northeast Asia—notably aluminium, wool and steel—could alone make up half of Australia's export deficiency. Australia had built a new export industry in aluminium in the 1980s but the greater task in the 1990s was the relocation of steel processing to make Australia a major steel exporter to the region. Ultimately Garnaut's message was that Australia must decide upon the place it wanted in the emerging western Pacific division of labour—a worthwhile role aspiring to excellence, or mediocrity beginning a couple of rungs below Japan, Korea, Taiwan and Hong Kong, then falling further.

The Garnaut Report was written on the basic premise that Australia had matured enough to have an intimate people-to-people relationship with Asia/Pacific nations. This meant an immigration policy active in the region and a foreign investment policy which recognised that Northeast Asia was the chief source of surplus savings for world investment. It assumed that the dynamic of regional integration and multiculturalism had replaced White Australia as the national objective.

Within Australia the notion of Asia/Pacific integration was an idea whose time had almost come. The dramatic economic performance of Asia/Pacific nations gave Australia little choice. The 'middle-classing' of Asia, the thousands of tourists arriving from the region and the purchase by Asian interests of prime local real estate was enough warning: unless Australia reformed its economy it might become the 'poor white trash of Asia', a pointed phrase to push the country to choose its own destiny in Asia.

Yet Australia's leaders were still hesitant in addressing the changes to Australia's social norms, imperative for a debtor nation being compelled to finance an annual $15 billion current account deficit, much of which would be funded from Asia. This meant not just a more efficient society as the Liberals kept preaching; it also meant a greater Asian presence in Australia in various ways—as migrants, investors, tourists, students, property owners, employers, professionals, businessmen and joint venturers.

The Multi-Function Polis diversion in the 1990 campaign was the third occasion during the decade that coalition leaders had flirted with anti-Asian sentiment. It revealed a periodic theme of politics in the 1980s—that Labor, once the bedrock party of the old White Australia, had undergone a more complete transformation on the issues of race and non-discriminatory immigration than had its conservative opponents. The Liberals who paraded their belief in dry economics were weak on the social and cultural changes without which free market economics and Asia/Pacific integration could not be achieved.

It is true that Labor pandered too much to the ethnic lobby; its enthusiasm for multiculturalism detracted from the promotion of an Australian identity and declaration of Australian allegiance from new arrivals. But Labor had not countenanced the type of anti-Asian electoral sentiment with which the Liberals and Nationals had flirted under pressure. The new Labor generation, starting with Whitlam and ending with Hawke, had closed this door, probably forever, inside the ALP. The signs suggested that the 1990s Liberals had reached, finally, the same conclusion. This meant bipartisan political acceptance of the racial and ethnic pluralism of the new Australia. It heralded not just the demise of White Australia but the creation of a diverse tolerant Australia as a powerful new political idea.

The fourth pillar of the Australian Settlement—State Paternalism—was still crumbling despite Keating's recession-induced public sector stimulus to create more jobs. As prime minister Keating moved towards a policy mixture of recovery via government stimulus while holding the gains on inflation and the market economy from the 1980s and early 1990s.

Keating's actions signalled his belief in the traditional Labor faith that government had a role in creating jobs and facilitating the return towards a growth economy. While declaring job creation to be his priority, Keating and his treasurer Dawkins also tried to dispel the fears that they would re-regulate the economy and restore the old faith in state power. But the exact nature of this trade-off remained in the balance during 1992. Labor, in fact, had no option but a 10 per cent plus unemployment election, though the risk remained that it might lose its nerve and sink the public sector into a massive structural deficit.

Keating's *One Nation* reply to Hewson's *Fightback* contained a fiscal stimulus for infrastructure projects and hefty income tax cuts for the next term. But it pledged to return the federal budget to surplus in 1995–96, a recognition that the ultimate fiscal objective after the recession was a public sector surplus in order to maximise the level of national savings. In fact Keating was too optimistic and had to concede in the August 1992 budget that the return to surplus could not be met by 1995–96. His priority was to put the fiscal stimulus and the tax cuts before the surplus. The *One Nation* statement also repudiated ALP and ACTU demands to slow the timetable for protection cuts and dismissed the push for a more interventionist industry policy.

Keating's overall position amounted to a rejection of the left traditionalist case, put by the academic Hugh Stretton, that Labor had come close during the 1980s to denying the role of the state in building the nation. Keating, in fact, was now the champion of a strong government role to bring the nation out of recession and uphold Australia's egalitarian ethos and he attacked the laissez-faire policies of the Liberals. Yet Keating could also pivot to face a new audience and assert the ongoing need for a disciplined public sector post-recession, a timetable for a return to a budget surplus and reject any notion of a re-regulation of the economy.

The 1990s loomed, on balance, as a decade that would be dominated by a winding back of the early 1990s public sector deficit. The 1990s are not likely to see a large-scale reversion to faith in state power to solve problems, a conclusion manifest from the debate over both industry policy and inflation.

Industry minister John Button was a critic of the treasury's free market economics but his critique was never rooted in old-fashioned protectionism. Button wanted a greater acceptance that export success would be a function of efficient firms, not just of an efficient economy. He argued that Australia required a 'smart' approach to industry intervention based upon better strategies for firms and industries.

The early 1990s saw two benchmarks in the industry policy debate: the purist non-intervention position of the Garnaut Report and the sophisticated case for greater intervention made in the Pappas Carter Evans consultants' report for the Australian Manufacturing Council (AMC). These reports shared much common ground, their chief difference being Garnaut's emphasis on national economic policy against the AMC's advocacy of government intervention at a firm or industry level—through tax breaks, incentives, research and development, trade deals, partnerships—to help build a series of major export-orientated firms. (In 1990 nearly half Australia's export revenue was produced by only ten firms!)

During the 1990s policy will draw upon both approaches, since Australia will require not just an internationally competitive economy but a strategic effort to build a number of multinational firms without which a better export performance will be elusive.

However, the significant commitment heralding a new economic discipline for the 1990s was the bipartisan pledge to purge the excesses of the 1980s with a low inflation culture—a daunting task. This pledge is the chief gain from the early 1990s recession, though its longevity and success is largely guesswork.

During the early 1990s unemployment moved above 11 per cent and the underlying inflation rate fell to below 3 per cent. Keating looked for the silver lining. He elevated low inflation as an economic and political bonus for Australia. The treasury and the Reserve reincorporated low inflation as an article of faith. The coalition insisted that its long-standing emphasis on inflation control had been the correct national course.

The Reserve's deputy governor, Ian Macfarlane, admitted that during the Reserve's application of a high interest rate policy to slow the economy it had also pursued another objective: 'The central point is that on this occasion we had to run monetary policy somewhat tighter than in earlier recessions and take the risk that the fall in output would be greater than forecast. To do less than this would be to throw away the once-in-a-decade opportunity for Australia to regain an internationally respectable inflation rate.'[16]

That is, the Reserve sought not just to slow the economy; it decided, after the mid-1980s confusion over policy objectives, that monetary policy must be conducted to keep inflation low over the medium term.

Macfarlane predicted a sea-change in inflationary expectations during the 1990s, saying that the 10 year bond rate showed that 'the market has factored in 3.5 to 4 per cent a year for inflation over the next 10 years. I think we will do better than that . . . I imagine that we [the Reserve] would act if we thought it was seriously going to go above that'.[17]

The governor, Bernie Fraser, made it clear that the Reserve would conduct monetary policy in the 1990s to secure a low inflation economy—a change to the philosophy of monetary policy during the post-financial deregulation period of the 1980s. But Fraser still refused to repudiate the employment objective in the conduct of monetary policy which suggests his relations with a Hewson government will be difficult.

The outgoing deputy governor, John Phillips, summarised the merits of lower inflation in a fashion that must have left Labor ruminating its misplaced priorities in the 1980s:

> Low inflation helps the poor and the underprivileged; it helps long-term investors; it helps exporters and those seeking to compete with imports; it helps families seeking to own their own home, in other words, it helps ordinary Australians . . . it won't necessarily help real asset speculators or those committed to various tax minimisation schemes. But . . . I can't get too upset about them. There is nothing in the laws of God that requires Australia to be a high inflation, high interest rate country. We achieved that state in the seventies and eighties all on our own . . .[18]

In the 1990 budget the treasury said: 'Most of the major industrialised countries disinflated their economies to combat the strong cost pressures of the early 1980s—at the cost of reductions in output and employment for a time—but the resulting fall in inflationary expectations has served them well since.'

This was an adverse reflection on Australia and on the Hawke–Keating model, which had chosen a growth path without the micro-economic flexibility to sustain such growth. Under Labor the Accord had set inflationary expectations and monetary policy had to adjust to those expectations, which is why interest rates were high during the decade.

The problem the politicians had faced was the weakness of the anti-inflationary constituency. How many votes did low inflation deliver? Bernie Fraser said: 'People generally feel that inflation is bad but for the most part, not so bad that they want the authorities to get too serious about eliminating it.' John Phillips reflected in similar vein: 'In the battle for national advancement, inflation ranks as one of the three or four great scourges. It probably ranks behind greed and apathy although it is closely related to both. And yet, there appears to be no organised group in the community spearheading a campaign against inflation.'[19]

The best political sell for low inflation came from the former New Zealand finance minister, Roger Douglas: 'Interest rates will always be inflation plus a margin. If inflation is 15 per cent, interest rates will be 15 per cent plus a margin. If inflation is 2 per cent, interest rates will be 2 per cent plus a margin.'[20]

Australia finished the 1980s with a renewed appreciation of the benefits of low inflation—that it encourages national savings, international competitiveness, better living standards and, in its own right, better equity. But the immediate cost of low inflation is less production and higher unemployment.

While Keating referred to 'snapping the inflation stick', sharp differences remained between Labor and Liberal over the low inflation policy. The recession had given greater impetus to the intellectual movement, which claimed that the overriding objective of monetary policy should be to achieve price stability (beat inflation) over the medium term, and that monetary policy had been asked to perform heroic tasks in the late 1980s which were beyond its capacity as an economic instrument.

The best critique came from John Phillips: 'Monetary policy is not primarily about resolving, in any structural sense, Australia's balance of payments problems . . . While monetary policy does have a counter-cyclical role [Keating's swing instrument], that role needs to be seen within a medium-term framework. And the appropriate medium-term objective for monetary policy is low and stable inflation.' Phillips said it was 'blindingly obvious' that monetary policy was 'not an effective weapon to fight a balance of payments problem' since this problem was about savings, consumption, investment and debt.[21]

The Reserve knew that tight monetary policy had kept the Australian dollar high. This, in turn, had frustrated the manufacturing and export sectors during the 1980s and had inhibited the growth of an export orientated industry structure.

Keating championed low inflation but he attacked the proposals for greater central bank independence and changing the Reserve's charter to give explicit priority to low inflation—hallmarks of the Hewson policy. In 1990 Keating slammed Hewson, declaring that 'this fight-inflation-first policy amounts to no more than a strategy to keep the economy comatose over a long period'.

It will take more than a recession to kill Australia's high inflation culture. It will require a change of priorities on the part of politicians, the Reserve and the investment community. The prospects are encouraging—but no more.

Overall there are two conflicting judgements on the 1980s—optimistic

The end of certainty

and pessimistic. The optimistic is rooted in an appreciation of the progress towards a new national compact. The decade witnessed an internationalisation of the economy unlikely to be reversed, which meant that the old ideas of the Australian Settlement were being decisively replaced.

White Australia had surrendered to the belief in regional integration and multiculturalism; Protection was slated for demolition; Arbitration was crumbling at its foundations; the belief in State Paternalism was unlikely to be revived, even by the recession. The imperative for micro-economic reform and higher national savings dictated a less interventionist and smaller public sector.

Despite the length and pain of the recession, the financial system was not being re-regulated, the protection cuts had not been cancelled, the backlash against a pluralistic multicultural nation had been limited; there was little sign of a revived belief that the solutions lay with government and that the economy could be re-regulated to health. This suggests that the recession would not save the decaying ideas and institutions of the Australian Settlement.

The ascension of Paul Keating as prime minister had also seen a naked assault upon the final Settlement belief—Imperial Benevolence. Keating became the first prime minister to launch a campaign for a Republic and a new flag. His tactics may have been faulty but his stance was a milestone. He put the Republic on the agenda in a way that invested its arrival with a sense of inevitability. Although Keating was also trying to revive his own political fortunes, that was not the point. He was the first prime minister to identify his electoral self-interest with the idea of abandoning the constitutional monarchy and accepting a republican system.

Keating used the republican symbol to try to discredit the legitimacy of the non-Labor tradition; to assert that over the decades the conservatives had confused Australia's national interests with those of the imperial benefactors. But Keating had another motive: to dramatise the cultural divorce from the past in order to facilitate Australia's integration with the Asia/Pacific. Keating, in fact, was following Hawke's 'enmesh with the region' strategy but promoting it with the zeal of a prime minister trying to extend his honeymoon. His strategic message for Australians was that for the first time in their history they had no imperial overlord—no Britian, no America—to deliver trade, defence or financial guarantees. The age of the imperial protector was finished.

The Keating campaign for a republic stunned the Liberals who were utterly unprepared for this issue. He tapped a deep sentiment within the community and a wellspring of support which suggests that the centenary of Federation in 2001 will bring a focus for a shift from constitutional monarchy to republicanism that may well succeed.

The essence of the new Australian compact was national maturity, more emphasis on individual responsibility and less on state power, a more open

679

and tolerant society, an economy geared to a new test of international competition, a greater reliance upon markets to set prices, an emphasis on welfare as a need, not a right, a growing stress on individual skills and enterprise productivity and a belief in Australian achievement, history and national destiny.

The pessimistic assessment of the 1980s came from two competing and hostile schools—the unsentimental free market right and the sentimental traditionalists—both of whom were critics of the 1980s legacy but from opposite ideologies.

The free market right was represented by figures and forces such as John Hewson, John Stone, Ian McLachlan, the Business Council of Australia, the NFF, commentators Max Walsh and P. P. McGuinness, the shadow Cabinet and a wide body of influential business and economic opinion makers. The thrust of their attack was that Labor lacked the political will to prosecute its agenda of free market reform to its logical end.

Their focus was the need for Australia to change its ways to address the mounting net foreign debt which had grown throughout the decade—from $7 billion in June 1980 to $150 billion by late 1992, or from about 5 per cent to 32 per cent of GDP. Their argument was that Paul Keating had not delivered on his 1986 banana republic warning; that he had raised the alarm but failed to extinguish the fire.

Foreign debt had been used in different ways—to finance the current account deficit and to fund through the banking system the great leap in Australian equity investment abroad from companies as different as BHP and Alan Bond's group. Had this overseas expansion not occurred then net foreign debt would have been about $60 billion lower. This situation reflected the impact of the abolition of exchange controls—the most potent aspect of financial deregulation. It meant that unless Australia performed then its investment funds would be sent offshore.

Reserve Bank figures show that about 65 per cent of total net foreign debt is incurred by the private sector[22]—but the economy must service the debt whoever borrowed it. In February 1990 Bernie Fraser said that the question was whether the borrowed funds had been employed profitably. If so, the debt could be seen as 'good'; if not, and used for consumption, then it was 'bad'. He concluded that Australia's debt had its 'good' and 'bad' aspects—but he sounded a warning that the extent of investment in the tradeable goods sector was 'disappointing'.[23]

Australia's problem is the debt servicing ratio, that is, the capacity to service the debt incurred. An EPAC study published in 1992 shows that the servicing cost of Australia's debt as a proportion of its export revenue is 22 per cent, the highest of any OECD nation. This study argued that Australia's problem during the 1980s was not excessive growth in its own right, but growth that was too strong for the largely regulated Australian economy to handle. Foreign borrowings are now being used to repay the interest on past borrowing. The debt constraint will dominate economic policy during the 1990s and it requires an optimistic scenario to see Australia stabilise its foreign debt at just under 40 per cent of GDP by the mid-1990s.[24]

This means that in the 1990s Australia can't grow faster than the rest of the world. Australia will follow world growth, not lead it. Australia will shift resources into the trading sector of its economy. It will export more and import less in relative terms. It will save more and consume less in relative terms. It will produce more and spend less in relative terms. A greater share of production will be pushed into the trading sector. These trends will occur because economic necessity and foreign debt stabilisation will require them. Ultimately, markets will insist upon them.

Until Australia becomes more efficient and productive, thereby addressing its balance of payments problem, the economy will grow relatively slowly. This is where the argument of the free market right becomes compelling. Its proposition is simple—the faster Australia hastens its reforms and becomes more productive, the sooner it can return to the path of sustained growth and employment creation; the slower Australia makes the reforms, the longer it will linger in a low-growth low-confidence limbo.

The cultural test for Australian society is whether the business and investment community grasps these changed rules—that future growth must come not from the domestic market but from the trading goods market; that economic policy will be run to keep growth modest until enough resources are shifted into the trading sector to improve Australia's current account deficit. This is the leap in corporate strategy without which Australia's transition cannot succeed. This is the real reason a better strategic cooperation is required between government and the investment community. Until both work in tandem to secure a better trade performance then Australia's progress must be retarded.

The foreign debt burden is a legacy of the 1980s, a function of Australia's inept handling of its transition from a closed to an open economy. The lesson is to perfect the transition; the mistake is to retreat. These are two options now facing Australia.

The second group of 1980s critics, the sentimental traditionalists, are those who fight to turn back the tide, with their most effective (as distinct from popular), spokesman being Malcolm Fraser.

These critics point to the 1990s recession to demand a change of policy direction. Their influence will grow while the downturn is prolonged and two factors work in their favour. These are the time lag before the benefit of new policies is fully transmitted, and the 1990s national psyche which sought stability, not more rapid change. The 'time lag' problem undermined Hawke and Keating and it will undermine whoever governs in the 1990s. This risk was grasped very early by Ross Garnaut, who warned at the close of the 1980s against national disillusionment because the free market philosophy had not yet brought rapid returns: 'The prevailing mood in the Australian spring of 1989 is of disappointment that internationalisation has not generated strong export and productivity performance . . . there is a danger that disappointment will turn into disillusionment.' This is exactly what happened when the recession arrived.

Garnaut warned that 'the path ahead is long', the danger 'that Australians will think too soon that they have changed enough, that it is enough to weaken the pillars of our protectionist minds and policies without bringing the great monuments to past mistakes crashing to the ground'. Garnaut felt that the internationalisation of the economy sought by Hawke and Keating was at best only half achieved. He had one message—go faster. Then came the recession to squander resources and smash national confidence.

The defect in Malcolm Fraser's analysis is his failure to separate the causes of the recession from Australia's long-term reform requirements. The recession was home-grown, a theoretical and practical failure to handle financial deregulation. It was the result of Labor's deregulation of finance before its deregulation of the real economy. It was a function of putting employment growth before inflation control, thereby running the economy at too high a temperature. In its widest sense it was a miscalculation made in the transition from a closed to an open economy—the greatest national challenge since the post-federation Australian Settlement.

The responsibility rests with a wide range of individuals and institutions—Hawke, Keating, the treasury, the Reserve Bank, state ALP governments, banks and other lending bodies, the borrowers large and small, the accountants, auditors and many others. It is tempting to believe that more vigilant official action could have averted the recession. But former Hawke and Fraser economic adviser Ed Visbord notes: 'If the banks had been able to anticipate the financial difficulties they would get into in the late 1980s, they would not have needed government assistance to avoid them. If they did not anticipate these problems, neither could the government.'[25]

The lesson from the ineptitude of the banks and lending institutions during the 1980s was that markets will fail. This was not the first time that banks have behaved irresponsibly and it will not be the last. In this case the government deliberately cut its own borrowing in the 1980s to maximise the scope for private lending and investment. But the market failed to perform; it let the government down. Most funds were directed into unproductive paper, property or speculative investments—contrary to the national interest. The moral is clear: markets are not perfect and do not necessarily advance the national interest. The realistic free market reformers never pretended that markets were perfect; they just said that markets, on balance, would deliver a better result than governments.

Keating was correct in saying that his economic advisers had missed too many major trends—the 1980s boom, the asset price surge, then the fall in inflation, the asset price collapse, the extent of the downturn. They missed the magnitude of both the boom and the bust—but they were advising on unmapped terrain.

The recession alone is not an argument against the philosophical direction of the 1980s. That argument must be won or lost on merit: how best to make Australia a competitive, productive, high saving society integrated into the overseas marketplace and delivering both prosperity and satisfaction for its people. Returning to tradition is unlikely to provide the solution, an assessment based upon both economic theory and political instinct.

The overseas observer David Hale, after making a critical appraisal of Australia's 1980s economic reforms, warned that there was no choice, that Australia must press ahead. Hale painted a grim picture of the alternative: 'An Australia with the siege mentality of New Zealand in the final months of Robert Muldoon's premiership, an economy with a nominal per capita income one third of Japan's and one half of Singapore's and a society with such a profound sense of inferiority about its low level of achievement that many talented young people would probably emigrate.'[26]

The traditionalists who predict that the decade of the 1990s will witness a counter-revolution, a decisive swing of the pendulum towards state power, may have misjudged the historical cycle. The embrace of free market belief and deregulation is a recent phenomenon driven by politics, technology and intellectual force. It is a movement which is likely to sustain setbacks flowing from the excessive credit expansion of the 1980s and the possible shift towards regional trading blocs, but it also draws sustenance from the central event of the 1980s, the collapse of communism. Deregulation is fed by the integration of world financial, product and communications markets. Some aspects of deregulation will fade and others will rise. But deregulation is a little like communism; once established it tends to be pervasive.

The traditionalists have misread the international trends. They have failed to understand 'the magnitude of the intellectual upheaval now occurring in third world political centres such as Mexico City, New Delhi, Jakarta and Buenos Aires. The movement towards the market orientated economic rationalism is global, not a phenomena unique to Australia or New Zealand'.[27] This movement is likely, in global terms, to become stronger, not weaker, in the 1990s.

But the problem for the market reformers of the 1990s is that the Australian people are resistant to more deregulatory experiments. This should be a particular worry for the Hewson Liberals who seem unaware of this aspect of the national mood. Individuals, families and companies are motivated in the 1990s by a desire to regain control of their lives. This mood transcends economic issues; it extends into the social arena. It might underwrite support for a greater role for government along the lines pushed by Keating.

The recession has helped to generate this uncertainty in three respects—

households and businesses have been left with high debt levels which they want to discharge; falling asset and real estate values have diminished the asset wealth of people and made them very cautious; and while unemployment is so high the fear of becoming unemployed is far more widespread and runs into the middle class. These worries are reinforced by several others—a crisis in family values, a loss of faith in institutions and a fear about personal safety. The combined impact of these sentiments is that people want more control of their lives and will reject Hewson's free market ideology unless it is implemented with sensitivity and skill.

The Hawke–Keating government will occupy a unique place in Australian history because it launched in this country the great transition which sought to recognise the arrival of the global free market economy. Labor can hardly be criticised for failing to complete the journey. Its course was marked by audacity, improvisation, deals, consensus, political skill, miscalculation and recession. It was led by a remarkable team, Hawke and Keating, masters of popularity and power respectively.

They grasped the need to escape the past but to build upon history; to impose reforms but to win a popular mandate. They were significant because they recognised that ends were greater than means; that the ALP had to find new policies to realise its old objectives of growth, jobs and security. The 1990s is likely to see those policies extended, not repudiated.

For the Liberal and National parties this poses their greatest challenge. Australian conservatism underwent its decisive transition in the 1980s—from champions of the status quo to zealots for a new order. The coalition failed in the 1980s because it faced a more formidable Labor Party; it was preoccupied with the transformation of its own identity; and it lacked the necessary leadership, unity and professional skills. History suggests that the coalition will govern for part of the 1990s. That will provide the test of its new mettle since political character is revealed only by power.

The coalition professes its belief in free market globalisation—but the application of these radical policies will require a courage, a reforming zeal and a political ethos that has been foreign to the conservative tradition in Australia. Hewson looms as the leader who will either confirm the remaking of the non-Labor side from office or preside over another of the periodic convulsions that has bedevilled Australian conservatism.

The excess of the 1980s has done great harm to the economic rationalist or market based reform agenda. This is because these policies were seen by the community to be devoid of any moral base and to have produced immoral results. In one sense a recession was required to restore value and punish the offenders. Hewson's problem is that the voters grasp that his policies are a purist application of Keating's program from the previous decade. For many people this program is already discredited.

This does not mean that Hewson will not win an election; but it casts serious doubt upon whether the people will accept his program. Hewson's challenge is to be persuasive and to rehabilitate free market economics from the grave of the 1990s recession. That means, above all, he must dress his philosophy with a moral cause. It is a task which he has failed to tackle as Opposition leader. It goes to the question of Hewson's social vision of the nation and the social costs which he will expect Australia to bear in the cause of his economic reforms.

The associated difficulty for Hewson is the response of the investment community to his shock therapy. The Hewson package involves a shakeout not just for labour but also for capital. Hewson must both implement his reforms and maintain a favourable investment climate to bring Australia out of the downturn: a daunting task.

The sustained recovery Australia needs cannot occur until the underlying problem Keating addressed with his 1986 'banana republic' statement is solved. Australia in the early 1990s does not have a level of competitiveness and savings which will produce a growth economy without another balance of payments crisis. The fundamental problem of the 1980s remains unsolved. The price of its solution will be high in terms of depressed living standards which will put governments during the 1990s under intense pressure.

The question for Labor's future is whether it launched in the 1980s a revolution that is tantamount to its own death warrant. This is a dangerous question to ask since history is littered with so-called terminal crises which Labor overcame. Indeed, the greatest quality of the ALP seems to be its capacity for self-renewal. But the 1980s has left two great legacies for the ALP—crises of both structure and ideology.

The dilemma arises from Labor's campaign to internationalise the economy, which will hasten the decline of trade union power and the demise of the old Labor ideal. The Labor Party rose in tandem with the unions, White Australia, Protection, Arbitration and State Paternalism, riding to success on the back of popular democracy and the industrial state. Labor never won elections because of Socialism, let alone Marxism, neither of which has been popular in Australia. Labor won elections because its appeal was implanted deep within Australia's institutions and ethos. But these foundations are being destroyed. The new Australia will rest upon free trade, greater individual skills and responsibility, and a new enterprise culture with a distinctly weaker role for the trade unions.[28] As the structural edifice which sustained ALP power is dismantled, the ALP will be required to modify its political structure and reassess its links with the wider community.

The crisis of ideology arises from the ascendancy of free market economics. These ideas are rooted in the abolition of sectional interests and the denial of class politics. They celebrate the spirit of individualism, faith in improvement through competition and the pursuit of excellence. This is a political culture utterly divorced from Labor's traditional belief in class politics, government intervention, solidarity and egalitarianism. The ques-

685

tions haunting Labor are manifest. Does it sell out and join the Liberal free market purists? Does it revert to old fashioned traditionalism and turn its face against the future? Or does it try to strike a reconciliation between market efficiencies and government intervention?

The third option is the only real choice and it is fitting that as ALP leader and principal architect of Labor's 1980s policy revolution, Paul Keating has the chance to attempt a new synthesis between the ALP ethos and the Hawke–Keating legacy of market economics. It is a new challenge for the ALP—the identification of a position for a social democratic party in a new world order of growing and international market competition. But there is such a position. Labor can still attempt to offer social and economic justice—but through a new array of policy tools, not protection, not government ownership, not an absolutist belief in arbitration, not through policies that distort prices and hurt efficient resource allocation. Nations in Europe and Asia have shown the benefits from intelligent government actions via the tax system and the investment in human capital. The alternative for Australia is not and never will be the American model whose inequalities and inhumanity would be rejected at the ballot box.

The challenge for Australian leadership is to internationalise the economy within a framework of social justice and equity thereby retaining the deepest and oldest Australian values. This is what the public expects and demands. But the first step in delivering justice is to secure the new path to national prosperity.

Australians knew during the late 1980s and early 1990s that the nation was undergoing a decisive transformation, that it had reached the end of certainty. The task of leadership now is to create a synthesis between the free market rationalism needed for a stronger economy and the social democracy which inspired the original Australian Settlement ideals of justice and egalitarianism. The end of certainty is not the end of history; it heralds the challenge to create a new history.

Endnotes

Introduction

1 Commonwealth Parliamentary Debates, House of Representatives, 12 September 1901, pp4804–17
2 Humphrey McQueen *A New Brittania* Ringwood: Penguin, 1970, revised edition 1986, pp253–72
3 Commonwealth Parliamentary Debates, House of Representatives, 9 March 1996, pp68–70
4 W.K. Hancock *Australia* London: Ernest Benn Limited, 1930, pp89–102
5 J.A. La Nauze *Alfred Deakin* Melbourne: Melbourne University Press, 1965, pp37
6 W.G. McMinn *George Reid* Melbourne: Melbourne University Press, 1989, pp9–11
7 Edward Shann *An Economic History Of Australia* London: Cambridge University Press, 1930, pp427–47
8 Leon Glezer *Tariff Politics* Melbourne: Melbourne University Press, 1982, p6
9 ibid, Leon Glezer *Tariff Politics*, p11
10 Paul Kelly, *The Weekend Australian*, July 26–27 1986; *John McEwen, His Story*, unpublished transcript of National Library taped autobiography; Kym Anderson and Ross Garnaut *Australian Protectionism* Sydney: Allen and Unwin, 1987, p6
11 Commonwealth Parliamentary Debates, House of Representatives, 30 July 1903, p2864
12 Hilmer and McLaughlin *Avoiding Industrial Action: A Better Way of Working* Melbourne: Allen & Unwin in association with the Business Council of Australia, 1991, p21
13 Stuart McIntyre and Richard Mitchell (eds) *Foundations of Arbitration* Melbourne: Oxford University Press, 1989, p182

14 John Rickard *H.B. Higgins* Sydney: George Allen and Unwin, 1984, p141
15 ibid, John Rickard *Higgins* pp172–3
16 ibid, John Rickard *Higgins* pp173–5
17 ibid, John Rickard *Higgins* pp175–85
18 La Nauze *Deakin* op cit, p144
19 Hancock *Australia* op cit, pp72–3
20 F.W. Eggleston *State Socialism in Australia* London: P.S. King & Son, 1932, pp1–21 and pp282–306
21 Dean Jaensch *The Hawke–Keating Hijack* Sydney: Allen and Unwin, 1989, p26
22 La Nauze *Deakin* op cit, p573
23 F.H. Gruen, 'How Bad is Australia's Economic Performance and Why?' Paper No 127, Centre for Economic Policy Research, Australian National University, 1985
24 Andersen and Garnaut, *Australian Protectionism* op cit, pp15–17
25 *The Economist*, 17 March 1984, p16
26 Report of the Committee for Review of Export Market Development Assistance, Canberra, Australian Government Printing Service (AGPS), July 1989, pp5–16

Chapter 1   The new Labor Party

1 Paul Kelly *The Hawke Ascendancy Sydney*: Angus and Robertson, 1984, pp1–4
2 Bob Hawke, personal interview, March 1991
3 Kelly *The Hawke Ascendancy* op cit, p115
4 Kelly *The Hawke Ascendancy* op cit, p351
5 B.A. Santamaria *Australia At the Crossroads* Victoria: Melbourne University press, 1987m p70
6 *The Australian*, 15 April 1986

Chapter 2   The revolt against the Liberal tradition

1 John Carroll 'The Tragedy of 5 March 1983—A Personal Tribute to Malcolm Fraser' *Quadrant*, May 1983
2 See Paul Kelly *The Unmaking of Gough* Sydney: Angus and Robertson, 1976, p153.
3 Philip Ayres *Malcolm Fraser, A Biography* Melbourne: William Heinemann Australia, 1987, p308
4 Malcolm Fraser, Liberal Party Policy Speech, 1980
5 Patrick Weller *Malcolm Fraser PM* Melbourne: Penguin, 1989, pp214–34
6 The *West Australian* 29 October 1980; and Commonwealth Parliamentary Debates, Hansard, House of Representatives, 26 November 1980, pp107–9
7 John Hyde, personal interview, 1987
8 *Australia At The Crossroads* Sydney: Brace Jovanovich Group, 1980
9 ibid, pp85–7
10 ibid, pp85–93
11 ibid, pp182–213
12 ibid, pp211–12
13 John Hyde *Deregulate Or Decay* AIPP Policy Paper No 14, 1988
14 Jim Carlton, personal interview, 1989
15 John Hyde, personal interview, 1987

16 Paul Kelly 'Black Jack: The Godfather of the Banana Republic' *The Weekend Australian* 26–27 July 1986
17 A. Rattigan *Industry Assistance: The Inside Story* Victoria: Melbourne University Press, 1986
18 ibid, p190
19 David Trebeck, personal interview, 1989
20 Refer to David Trebeck 'Farmer Organisations' in Don Williams (ed.) *Agriculture in the Australian Economy* Oxford: Oxford University Press, March 1990.
21 John Hyde, personal interview, 1987
22 David Kemp 'Liberalism and Conservatism in Australia' in Brian Head and James Walter (eds) *Intellectual Movements in Australian Society* Brisbane: Queensland University Press, 1988, pp344–55
23 John Howard, personal interview, January 1989
24 Paul Kelly *The Hawke Ascendancy* Sydney: Angus and Robertson, 1984, pp157–70
25 Ian Macphee, personal interview, 1989
26 Statement No 2, 1982–83 Budget Papers, p51
27 Max Corden 'The Lessons Australia Must Learn' in John Hyde and John Nurick (eds) *Wages Wasteland* Sydney: Hale and Iremonger in association with AIPP, 1985, p18
28 Kelly *The Hawke Ascendancy* op cit, Chapter 14, pp245–66; the *Independent Monthly* October 1989
29 John Hyde, personal interview, 1987

Chapter 3   The Hawke–Keating model: the Accord

1 28 January 1983; for full text, see Paul Kelly *The Hawke Ascendancy* Sydney: Angus and Robertson, 1984, pp1–4.
2 John Stone memorandum to John Howard, Treasurer, 28 February 1983
3 Hawke, personal interview, April 1991
4 Edna Carew *Keating* Sydney: Allen and Unwin, 1988, p86
5 The *Sydney Morning Herald*, 4 April 1983
6 Bruce J. Chapman and Fred Gruen, 'An Analysis of the Australian Consensual Incomes Policy: The Prices and Incomes Accord', Australian National University (ANU), January 1990
7 See Statement of Accord by the ALP and the ACTU regarding economic policy, February 1983.
8 National Economic Summit Conference, 11 April 1983, pp3–5
9 ibid, p33
10 Bill Kelty, personal interview, August 1991
11 The *Sydney Morning Herald*, 2 July 1983
12 The *Australian Financial Review*, 24 June 1983
13 Budget Statements 1983–84, Budget Paper No 1, p55
14 Paul Keating, Speech to the Metal Trades Industries Association (MTIA), 22 October 1984
15 The previous four paragraphs draw upon: Paul Keating, Statement on Economic Issues in the 1984 Election Campaign, 19 November 1984.
16 OECD Economic Surveys *Australia* Paris: OECD, 1984–85, p8

Chapter 4   The Hawke–Keating model: the float

1   Greg McCarthy and Dave Taylor *Float of the Dollar* unpublished manuscript, 1991
2   Bob Johnston, former Reserve Bank Governor, personal interview, March 1991
3   Patrick Weller *Malcolm Fraser PM* Melbourne : Penguin, 1989, pp380–2
4   Philip Ayres *Malcolm Fraser, A Biography* Melbourne: William Heinemann, 1987, pp409–13
5   Ian Harper, 'Why Financial Deregulation?', *Australian Economic Review*, First Quarter, 1986
6   John Phillips, speech, 'Australia's Floating Dollar' March 1984
7   Bob Johnston, personal interview, March 1991
8   Tony Cole, personal interview, June 1991
9   Barbara Ward, personal interview, September 1991
10   Bob Johnston, personal interview, March 1991
11   Paul Keating, personal interview, June 1991; Greg Hywood, the *Australian Financial Review*, 18 December 1989
12   This meant that the Reserve Bank withdrew from its role as underwriter of the official forward market and allowed banks to hold limited foreign currency positions so that they could assume the underwriting role themselves.
13   Edna Carew *Keating* Sydney: Allen and Unwin, 1988, p100
14   John Phillips, speech 'Australia's Floating Dollar', March 1984
15   Johnston, personal interview, March 1991
16   Bob Hawke, personal interview, April 1991
17   Paul Keating, personal interview, May 1991; Carew *Keating* op cit, p103–4
18   ibid, p103
19   Bob Johnston, personal interview, March 1991
20   Bob Johnston, personal interview, March 1991
21   McCarthy and Taylor 'The Float of the Dollar', unpublished manuscript, 1991, op cit
22   John Hewson, 'Australia—Financial Reforms', draft paper, 29 May 1985
23   Ian Harper 'Why Financial Deregulation?' op cit
24   Bob Johnston, personal interview, March 1991
25   Tony Cole, personal interview, July 1991
26   Paul Keating, speech of 14 November 1984
27   Bob Hawke, John Curtin Memorial Lecture, 28 September 1983

Chapter 5   The Liberal revolution

1   Report of the Liberal Party Committee of Review, 1983, p11
2   For John Carroll's depiction, refer Chapter 2, p36
3   Gerard Henderson 'Fraserism: Myths and Realities' *Quadrant*, June 1983
4   Chris Puplick, personal interview, 1990
5   Refer Paul Kelly *The Hawke Ascendancy* Sydney: Angus and Robertson, 1984, pp157–70.
6   This summary of Howard's life draws extensively on Milton Cockburn 'What Makes Johnny Run?' the *Sydney Morning Herald*, 7 January 1989.
7   A. Rattigan *Industry Assistance, The Inside Story* Melbourne: Melbourne University Press, 1986, pp262–71
8   Blanche d'Alpuget *Robert J. Hawke, A Biography* Melbourne: Schwartz, 1982, p150

Endnotes

9 Report of the Liberal Party Committee of Review, 1983
10 ibid
11 Jim Carlton, personal interview, January 1989
12 Peacock speech to the Federal Council of the Liberal Party, 2 October 1983
13 Chris Puplick, personal interview, May 1990
14 *The Australian*, 13 April 1984
15 The *Sydney Morning Herald*, 18 April 1984
16 *The Age*, 17 April 1984

Chapter 6   The attack on Justice Higgins

1 Gerard Henderson 'The Industrial Relations Club' *Quadrant*, September 1983
2 *The Australian*, 31 August 1983
3 Ian Macphee, personal interview, January 1989
4 John Howard, personal interview, January 1989
5 Personal letter, John Howard to Gerard Henderson, 27 September 1983
6 Gerard Henderson, personal interview, January 1989
7 Gerard Henderson, personal interview, January 1989
8 Ian Macphee, personal interview, January 1989
9 See Ian Macphee speeches, 7 October 1983, 'Towards A National Incomes Policy' and 16 April 1984 'The Prices and Incomes Accord—Will It Last?'.
10 Draft Opposition paper on wages and industrial relations (undated), early 1984
11 A comment on the 'Opposition Policy' paper, Henderson to Howard, 17 February 1984
12 Ian Macphee, paper on 'Opting Out', 1984. Macphee quoted Professor Richard Blandy: 'If the Commission does follow the market, at least to the degree that might be expected of, say, a decentralised collective bargaining system, then the gain to society from deregulating the labour market will be much less than hoped for or supposed . . . It is my view that, although the Commission sometimes does not follow the market, mostly it does follow the market, for otherwise it would not have survived.' He also quoted Professor John Niland: 'Even if collective bargaining became pervasive in Australia, actual labour market outcomes probably would not be all that different from those in the present system.' He referred to Dr R.G. Gregory: 'It is also not clear that such a system [decentralised collective bargaining] is possible given our history . . . The Metal Trades Agreement of December 1981 was the outcome of that collective bargaining system. The agreement resulted in a nominal wage increase of between 20 and 30 per cent for a twelve month period at a time when the most commonly accepted forecast of price inflation was about 12 per cent.'
13 Office of the Leader of the Opposition, Discussion paper on Proposals by Mr Macphee and Mr Howard on Opposition Policy on Wages, 24 February 1984
14 Gerard Henderson, A Note on Opting Out, early 1984
15 ibid, Henderson Note on Opting Out, early 1984
16 John Howard, A Note for Shadow Cabinet, 28 March 1984
17 Gerard Henderson, personal interview, January 1989
18 Gerard Henderson, personal interview, January 1989
19 Ian Macphee, personal interview, January 1989
20 Shaun Carney *Australia in Accord* South Melbourne: Sun Books, The Macmillan Company of Australia Pty Ltd, 1988, chapter 6
21 Gerard Henderson, personal interview, January 1989
22 Liberal/National Industrial Relations Policy, 16 April 1984

691

23 Ian Macphee, personal interview, January 1989
24 The *Sydney Morning Herald*, 17 April 1984
25 *The Age*, 21 April 1984
26 Ian Macphee, personal interview, January 1989
27 See Ray Evans' article in John Hyde and John Nurick (eds) *Wages Wasteland* Sydney: Hale and Iremonger, 1985.
28 J.O. Stone, The Shann Memorial Lecture 1984, 27 August 1984

Chapter 7   Beyond White Australia—a new identity

1 *The Age*, 20 March 1984
2 Refer ABC *Nationwide*, 20 March 1984; *The Age*, 3 April 1984.
3 See Geoffrey Blainey *All for Australia* Sydney: Methuen Haynes, 1984, pp158–61.
4 Peter Bowers, the *Sydney Morning Herald*, 12 May 1984
5 Under the classification of the Australian Bureau of Statistics, the official figures for Asia included immigrants from the Middle East.
6 Geoffrey Blainey *All For Australia 1984*, op cit, pp153–163
7 The *Sydney Morning Herald*, 21 March 1984
8 Peter Bowers, the *Sydney Morning Herald*, 12 May 1984
9 Hansard, House of Representatives 8 May 1984, p2010
10 Hansard, House of Representatives 2 May 1984, p1667
11 Hansard, House of Representatives 8 May 1984, p2023
12 Hansard, House of Representatives 8 May 1984, p2025
13 Hansard, House of Representatives 8 May 1984, p2026
14 Hansard, House of Representatives 8 May 1984, p2028
15 Hansard, House of Representatives 8 May 1984, p2029
16 The *Sydney Morning Herald*, 10 May 1984
17 The *Australian Financial Review*, 14 May 1984
18 *The Age*, 12 May 1984
19 Hansard, House of Representatives 10 May 1984, p2226
20 Hansard, House of Representatives 7 September 1984, pp826–29
21 *The Age*, 18 July 1984
22 Gerard Henderson, personal interview, January 1989
23 The *Sydney Morning Herald*, 20 June 1984
24 Australian Broadcasting Commission (ABC), *Pressure Point*, 10 May 1984
25 *The National Times*, 18 May 1984

Chapter 8   Hawke—from messiah to mortal

1 Malcolm Fraser had even sponsored such a referendum but it was undermined from within conservative ranks.
2 ALP Campaign Director's Report—1984 Federal Election
3 The *Sydney Morning Herald*, 18 August 1984
4 Liberal Party Campaign Report, 1984 Federal Election
5 As a result of stronger than expected economic growth in 1984–85, the final outcome showed spending falling as a proportion of GDP, as budget papers the following year revealed.
6 *The Age*, 25 October 1984
7 R.J. Hawke, 1984 Policy Speech, 13 November 1984
8 The *National Times*, 4–10 October 1985

Chapter 9   The Tax Summit

1 *The Age*, 29 April 1985
2 Peter Walsh, personal interview, July 1991
3 *The Australian*, 8 June 1985
4 ibid, 8 June 1985
5 Bob Hawke, National Taxation Summit Proceedings, p4
6 Bob White, National Taxation Summit Proceedings, p5
7 National Taxation Summit Proceedings, p21
8 ibid, p227
9 ibid, p239
10 ibid, p240
11 Hawke–Keating Press Conference, 4 July 1985
12 Bill Kelty, personal interview, August 1991
13 Paul Kelly, *The Sunday Telegraph*, 22 September 1985

Chapter 10   The Peacock surrender

1 Geoff Kitney, the *National Times*, 13 September 1985
2 John Howard, personal interview, January 1989
3 *The Mercury*, 8 December 1984
4 The *Sunday Telegraph*, 12 May 1985
5 John Howard 'Taxation and Australia', 11 April 1985
6 The *Sydney Morning Herald*, 10 May 1985
7 The *Sydney Morning Herald*, 17 July 1985; and the *Canberra Times*, 17 July 1985
8 The *Australian Financial Review*, 2 August 1985
9 *The Age*, 2 August 1985
10 John Valder, personal interview, July 1990
11 *The Australian*, 30 August 1985
12 Peter Bowers, the *Sydney Morning Herald*, 3 September 1985
13 Paul Kelly, *The Australian*, 3 September 1985
14 Paul Kelly, *The Australian*, 4 September 1985
15 The *Sydney Morning Herald*, 4 September 1985
16 The *Sydney Morning Herald*, 5 September 1985
17 ibid
18 Gerard Henderson, personal interview, January 1989
19 The *Sydney Morning Herald*, 5 September 1985
20 John Howard, personal interview, January 1989
21 ibid
22 The *Canberra Times*, 6 September 1985

Chapter 11   The banana republic

1 For an exposition of the Australian Settlement, see the Introduction to this book.
2 Peter Walsh, The Shann Memorial Lecture, 22 October 1991
3 David D. Hale, Chief Economist, Kemper Financial Services, Chicago, 'Structural Change in the Australian Balance of Payments, or Economic Implications of the America's Cup Race, 1986'

4 Peter Drucker 'The Changed World Economy' in *The Frontiers of Management* New York: Truman Talley Books, 1986, pp23–35
5 ibid, pp23–5
6 F. H. Gruen, 1986 Presidential Address to the Economic Society of Australia, August 1986, p4
7 Des Moore 'What Should Be Done' *Institute of Public Affairs* October 1989, p52
8 J. O. Stone, The Shann Memorial Lecture, 27 August 1984
9 ibid
10 Economic Planning and Advisory Committee (EPAC), External Balance and Economic Growth, 20 October 1986, pp7–9
11 Paul Keating, Treasurer, 1985–86 Budget Speech, 20 August 1985
12 Statement No 2, 1985–86 Budget Papers, p13
13 ibid, p67
14 *The Australian*, 26 August 1985
15 *The Australian*, 25 October 1985
16 *The Australian*, 22 November 1985
17 The *Sydney Morning Herald*, 26 February 1986
18 Paul Keating, The Merry Lecture, 21 March 1986
19 Paul Keating, personal interview, July 1991
20 The *Sydney Morning Herald*, 4 April 1986
21 The *Sydney Morning Herald*, 15 March 1986
22 *The Age*, 19 May 1986
23 *The Australian*, 19 May 1986
24 The planned economic meeting was subsequently abandoned on the grounds that it would serve no purpose during a national wage case hearing.
25 *The Age*, 30 May 1986
26 *The Age*, 6 June 1986
27 *The Age*, 31 May 1986
28 David D. Hale, op cit.
29 Edna Carew *Keating, A Biography* Sydney: Allen & Unwin, 1988, p161
30 Peter Walsh, personal interview, July 1991
31 *The Age*, 18 September 1986
32 Statement by the Treasurer, 11 September 1986
33 The *Canberra Times*, 18 August 1986
34 *The Australian*, 24 October 1986

Chapter 12   The Howard leadership

1 David Kemp, Sir Robert Menzies Lecture, 20 February 1986
2 Jim Carlton's speech at the University of Sydney, 11 September 1986
3 Neil Brown, personal interview, January 1989
4 *The Weekend Australian*, 7–8 September 1985
5 John Howard Press Conference, 29 September 1985
6 The *Sunday Telegraph*, 22 September 1985
7 The *Sydney Morning Herald*, 31 July 1986
8 *The Age*, 29 March 1986
9 Gerard Henderson, personal interview, January 1989. There is no suggestion that any of the above-mentioned figures were involved in any of the leaks.
10 Neil Brown, personal interview, January 1989
11 The *Australian Financial Review*, 16 and 20 June 1986, and 4 December 1986
12 Malcolm Fraser, speech at the Southern Cross Hotel, Melbourne, 17 June 1986

13 Chris Puplick, personal interview, May 1990
14 Neil Brown, personal interview, January 1989
15 Patrick O'Brien *The Liberals* Melbourne: Viking, 1985, p28
16 Nick Greiner, address to Liberal State Convention, 10 August 1985
17 B.A. Santamaria, personal interview, May 1991; and B.A. Santamaria *Australia At The Crossroads* Melbourne: Melbourne University Press, 1987, p68
18 ABC *The World Today*, 21 February 1986
19 The *Australian Financial Review*, 7 July 1986
20 ibid
21 John Howard, Address to the Nation, 16 June 1986
22 *The Age*, 15 December 1986

Chapter 13   The New Right

1 David Trebeck, personal interview, January 1989
2 H.R. Nicholls Society *Arbitration in Contempt, the Proceedings of the Inaugural Seminar of the H R Nicholls Society* Melbourne: H.R. Nicholls Society, 1986, p99
3 Peter Costello 'A New Province For Law And Order' 21 March 1991; and personal interview, July 1991
4 *The Age*, 28 July 1986
5 *Carlton/Walsh Report*, ABC Television, 5 September 1985
6 Ray Evans, personal interview, January 1989
7 *Arbitration in Contempt*, op. cit, p314
8 ibid, p17
9 *PM* program, ABC Radio, 21 March 1986
10 Shaun Carney *Australia In Accord* Melbourne: Sun Books, 1988, p96
11 *The Australian*, 16 August 1986
12 Shaun Carney, op.cit, p92
13 The *Bulletin*, 8 October 1985
14 ibid
15 The *Bulletin*, 22 August 1986
16 The *Australian Financial Review*, 5 February 1986; *The Australian*, 6 February 1986
17 Neil Brown, personal interview, January 1989
18 Newspoll, *The Australian*, 10 September 1986
19 Neil Brown, personal interview, January 1989
20 *Business Review Weekly (BRW)*, 5 December 1986
21 ibid
22 The *Bulletin*, 23 December 1986
23 *The Australian*, 8 September 1988
24 *The Weekend Australian*, 2–3 May 1987
25 Chris Puplick, personal interview, July 1990

Chapter 14   Consensus, business and unions

1 The evaluation of Bernie Fraser draws upon my two articles in *The Australian* of 29 and 31 April 1989.
2 ibid
3 P.A. McLaughlin 'How Business Relates to the Hawke Government'
4 National Taxation Summit proceedings, p229

5   The *Bulletin*, 22 October 1985
6   Alan Wood, Australian Financial Review/Syntec Seminar, 17 October 1985
7   Dr Don Russell 'Economic Policy In The Keating Years', 15 October 1991
8   The *Australian Financial Review*, 30 September 1985
9   P.A. McLaughlin, op cit
10 Paul Barry *The Rise and Fall of Alan Bond* Sydney: Bantam Books, 1990, p401
11 P.A. McLaughlin, op cit
12 Bill Kelty, personal interview, August 1991
13 ibid
14 ibid
15 The *Australian Financial Review*, 30 September 1985
16 Dr Don Russell, op cit
17 ibid
18 The *Australian Financial Review*, 30 September 1985
19 ibid
20 ibid
21 Shaun Carney *Australia In Accord* Melbourne: Sun Books, 1988, p186
22 The *Sydney Morning Herald*, 3 October 1985

Chapter 15   Joh for Canberra: the false prophet

1   Brian Ray, personal interview, 1990
2   Mike Gore, personal interview, July 1990
3   *The Australian*, 12 March 1987
4   Joh Bjelke-Petersen, personal interview, July 1992
5   Mike Gore, personal interview, July 1990
6   Alan Gregg, personal interview, February 1992
7   ibid
8   Mike Gore, personal interview, July 1990
9   Sir Robert Sparkes, personal interview, July 1990
10 Mike Ahern, personal interview, July 1990
11 The *National Times*, 25 July 1986
12 For a detailed argument that the Bjelke-Petersen government was then already in decline, see the *Report Arising from A Review of the National Party of Australia*, Queensland, June 1990, by Margaret Bridson Cribb, commissioned by the National Party.
13 Mike Gore, personal interview, July 1990
14 The *Bulletin*, 7 November 1989
15 See the *Canberra Times*, 8 October 1986
16 Joh Bjelke-Petersen, personal interview, July 1992
17 *The Australian*, 3 November 1986
18 Mike Gore, personal interview, July 1990
19 ibid
20 The *Bulletin*, 7 November 1989 and Joh Bjelke-Petersen, personal interview, July 1992
21 *The Australian*, 2 November 1989; House of Representatives, 1 November 1989, p2262
22 Mike Gore, personal interview, July 1990
23 *The Australian*, 3 January 1987
24 *The Australian*, 3, 6 and 13 January 1987
25 Ian Sinclair, personal interview, February 1992

26 National Party of Australia, *The Future, A Report by the Committee of Review*, May 1988, Chapter 4
27 Ian Sinclair, personal interview, February 1992
28 Joh Bjelke-Petersen, personal interview, July 1992
29 ibid
30 *The Australian*, 4 March 1987

Chapter 16 The conservative crisis

1 The *Canberra Times*, 5 March 1987
2 *The Age*, 4 March 1987
3 Section 18 read: 'Unless the Federal Council has decided to the contrary, portfolios in a composite government may be accepted by the National Party.'
4 The *Australian Financial Review*, 5 March 1987
5 *The Age*, 9 March 1987
6 The *National Times*, 22 March 1987
7 The *Courier Mail*, 23 March 1987
8 AAP story print-out, 23 March 1987
9 *The Weekend Australian*, 17 and 24 January 1987; the *Sydney Morning Herald*, 29 January 1987
10 *The Age*, 13 January 1987
11 ABC, *Four Corners*, 30 March 1987
12 The *Australian Financial Review*, 4 March 1987
13 *The Age*, 26 March 1987
14 The *Courier Mail*, 26 March 1987
15 *The Australian*, 30 March 1987
16 Malcolm Fraser, press release, 29 April 1987
17 Alan Ramsey, the *Sydney Morning Herald*, 30 May 1987
18 *The Australian*, 12 February 1987
19 Jim Carlton, personal interview, January 1989
20 David Trebeck, personal interview, January 1989
21 Jim Carlton, personal interview, January 1989

Chapter 17 Hawke strikes

1 Paul Keating, Economic Statement, May 1987
2 The *Australian Financial Review*, 20 December 1991
3 Bob Hawke, media statement, 1 April 1987
4 Bob Hawke, Maurice Blackburn Memorial Lecture, 28 March 1987
5 *The Australian*, 14 May 1987
6 The *Sydney Morning Herald*, 18 May 1987
7 The *Australian Financial Review*, 14 May 1987
8 The *Sydney Morning Herald*, 16 and 18 May 1987
9 *The Australian*, 14 May 1987
10 *The Australian*, 19 May 1987
11 The *Sydney Morning Herald*, 15 May 1987
12 Bob Hawke, 3DB interview, 14 May 1987; Ray Martin *Midday Show*, Channel 9, 13 February 1987
13 *The Australian*, 1 May 1987
14 *The Australian*, 16 May 1987
15 Alan Ramsey, the *Sydney Morning Herald*, 8 August 1987

16 *The Australian*, 6 June 1987
17 *IPA Review*, May–July 1987
18 *The Australian*, 7 March 1987
19 *The Australian*, 6 June 1987
20 Joh Bjelke-Petersen, personal interview, July 1992
21 For a detailed account of this meeting, written at the time, see *The Australian*, 6 June 1987.
22 Personal interview with Sir Robert Sparkes, 14 August 1990
23 *The Australian*, 6 June 1987
24 ibid
25 This version of the meeting in Howard's home draws heavily on my account at the time in *The Australian*, 6 June 1987.
26 *The Australian*, 6 June 1987

Chapter 18 Hawke—Labor's greatest winner

1 *The Weekend Australian*, 30–31 May 1987
2 The *Sydney Morning Herald*, 10 July 1987
3 Bob McMullan, Campaign Director's Report, 1987 election
4 Paul Kelly, Address to CEDA, July 1987
5 *The Australian*, 15 June 1987
6 The *Sydney Morning Herald*, 9 June 1987; the *Sun-Herald*, 14 June 1987
7 Australian Institute for Public Policy, 6 May 1987 Bulletin
8 *The Australian*, 18 June 1987
9 Rod Cameron, personal interview, July 1987
10 *The Weekend Australian*, 27–28 June 1987
11 The *Bulletin*, 14 July 1987
12 Paul Kelly, *The Australian*, 24 June 1987
13 *See* Chapter 20, A Competitive Economy
14 *The Age*, 8 July 1987
15 The *Sydney Morning Herald*, 3 July 1987
16 Paul Kelly, *The Australian*, 11 July 1987
17 *The Weekend Australian*, 1–2 August 1987
18 Clive Bean and Jonathan Kelley, *Politics*, November 1988, p80–94
19 Tony Eggleton, Federal Director's 1987 election report
20 The *Sydney Morning Herald*, 25 July 1987
21 The *Sydney Morning Herald*, 4 November 1987
22 *The Australian*, 13 July 1987
23 Ian Sinclair, personal interview, January 1992
24 National Party Committee of Review, May 1988, p17–19
25 The *Bulletin*, 8 September 1987

Chapter 19 The 1980s boom

1 Peter Walsh, The 1991 Shann Memorial Lecture, 22 October 1991
2 *The Australian*, 22 October 1988
3 Speech by Peter Walsh, 7 August 1987
4 The *Australian Financial Review*, 21 September 1987; and the *Sydney Morning Herald*, 22 September 1987
5 Peter Walsh, personal interview, August 1991
6 The *Sydney Morning Herald*, 16 September 1987

7 Peter McLaughlin, Speech to Institute of Directors, Sydney, 16 September 1987
8 Peter McLaughlin, personal interview, July 1991
9 Ed Shann, speech to the Canberra Economics Society, 16 September 1987
10 David Morgan, personal interview, July 1991
11 Bernie Fraser, personal interview, July 1992
12 Peter Walsh, personal interview, August 1991
13 Don Russell 'Economic Policy in the Keating Years', ANU address, 15 October 1991
14 David Morgan 'The Financial Environment in the 1980s', July 1991, p10
15 Ian R. Harper 'The Australian Macro-Economy in the 1980s', Reserve Bank, p279
16 David Morgan 'Evolution of Monetary Policy Since Financial Deregulation' Sydney, 3 October 1990
17 John Phillips, personal interview, April 1992
18 Bob Johnston, personal interview, July 1991
19 Don Russell 'Economic Policy in the Keating Years' ANU address, 15 October 1991
20 *The Walsh Report* ABC Television, 15 September 1987
21 Bob Johnston, speech, 16 September 1987
22 Bob Johnston, personal interview, July 1991
23 John Phillips, personal interview, April 1992
24 ibid
25 Ed Shann 'Lags and Monetary Policy' paper delivered on 12 August 1987
26 Budget Statements, 1988–89, p12
27 Bob Johnston, personal interview, July 1991
28 The Reserve Bank, Annual Report, 30 June 1988, p14
29 John Phillips, personal interview, April 1992
30 David Morgan, personal interview, July 1991
31 Bob Johnston, personal interview, July 1991
32 Bernie Fraser, personal interview, July 1991
33 John Phillips, personal interview, April 1992
34 Ross Garnaut, H. C. Coombs Lecture, 1 May 1991
35 James Capel Australia, Australian Banking Sector Review, 'From the 80s To the 90s'
36 R. A. Ferguson 'Deregulation and Change' *Current Affairs Bulletin* September 1990
37 V. J. Carroll *The Man Who Couldn't Wait* Melbourne: William Heinemann Australia, 1991, pp 124–5
38 BT Australia, Annual Review, 1990, Directors' Comment, p7
39 The Reserve Bank of Australia, Annual Report, 30 June 1990, p33
40 Bob Johnston, personal interview, July 1991
41 Bernie Fraser, Speech to Housing Finance Institutions, 19 February 1991
42 Refer Alan Kohler, *The Sunday Age*, 17 June 1990
43 The *Sydney Morning Herald*, 13 August 1991
44 John Phillips, personal interview, April 1992
45 Bob Johnston, personal interview, July 1991

Chapter 20   A competitive economy

1 Frederick G. Hilmer *When The Luck Runs Out* Sydney: Harper and Row, 1985, pp5–9

2 John Button, personal interview, July 1991
3 David D. Hale 'The Australian Economy in the 1990s' October 1991
4 Statement No. 2, Budget Papers 1988–89, p49
5 *The Australian*, 25–26 July 1987
6 *The Weekend Australian*, 15–16 September 1990
7 Peter McLaughlin, Speech to the Institute of Directors, 26 May 1988
8 See Dr Peter Barnard, Address to the Industrial Relations Conference, 22 March 1991.
9 John Button, personal interview, July 1990

Chapter 21   The Elliott emergence

1 Geoff Kitney, the *National Times*, 19 July 1987
2 This draws heavily on Peter Denton *Elliott, a Biography* Sydney: Little Hills Press Pty Ltd, 1986.
3 ibid, p178
4 ibid, p172
5 Ben Hills and Kate Legge, the *Herald*, 5 May 1987
6 *The Age*, 8 April 1987
7 *The Australian*, 10 February 1992
8 *The Age*, 18 August 1987
9 Tony Stephens, the *Sydney Morning Herald*, 23 October 1987
10 The *Sydney Morning Herald*, 29 October 1987
11 The *Australian Financial Review*, 20 November 1987
12 *The Australian*, 8 February 1988; also see the *Sydney Morning Herald* editorial, 12 February 1988
13 *The Australian*, 6 February 1988
14 *The Australian*, 8 February 1988
15 *Sunday* program, Channel 9, 27 March 1988
16 Paul Kelly, *The Australian*, 11 April 1988; Alan Ramsey, the *Sydney Morning Herald*, 7 April 1988
17 The *Sydney Morning Herald*, 7 April 1988
18 Paul Kelly, *The Australian*, 11 April 1988

Chapter 22   Howard—the social agenda

1 John Howard, Press Statement, 15 May 1988
2 Dr S. Fitzgerald *Immigration, A Commitment To Australia* Canberra: AGPS, May 1988
3 The *Gold Coast Bulletin*, 22 April 1988; the *Sydney Morning Herald*, 18 April 1988
4 John Howard, Interview on *AM* program, ABC radio, 16 May 1988
5 John Howard, Interview on *Face To Face*, Channel 10, 31 July 1988
6 John Howard, *John Laws Show*, Radio 2UE, 2 August 1988
7 John Howard, Transcript of Press Conference, 4 August 1988; *12.30 Report*, 2GB, 2 August 1988; interview with John Tingle, 2GB, 17 August 1988
8 *The Midday Show*, Channel 9, 15 August 1988; *AM* program, ABC radio, 2 August 1988; *AM* program, ABC radio, 15 August 1988
9 *TV AM*, 12 August 1988; *The World Today*, ABC radio, 15 August 1988
10 *AM* program, ABC radio, 15 August 1988
11 *The Australian*, 17 August 1988

12 The *Melbourne Herald*, 9 August 1988
13 *AM* program, ABC radio, 12 August 1988
14 John Howard, Press Statement, 12 August 1988
15 John Tingle interview, 2GB, 17 August 1988
16 *The Australian*, 20 August 1988
17 *The Australian*, 20 August 1988
18 In the following analysis I have drawn upon some of the ideas of Judy Brett, 'Future Directions' in *Current Affairs Bulletin*, June 1989.

Chapter 23   The Kirribilli pact

 1 The *Sydney Morning Herald*, 29 June 1987
 2 Paul Keating, Address to the Victorian Fabian Society, 11 November 1987
 3 Laurie Oakes, the *Bulletin*, 24 November 1987
 4 The *Australian Financial Review*, 24 November 1987; the *Sydney Morning Herald*, 16 March 1987
 5 The *Australian*, 10 February 1988
 6 The *Sydney Morning Herald*, 16 March 1988
 7 The *Australian Financial Review*, 26 May 1988; the *Sydney Morning Herald*, 29 August 1988
 8 The *Australian Financial Review*, 21 March 1988
 9 *The Australian*, 12 March 1988
10 *The Age*, 17 August 1988
11 The *Sydney Morning Herald*, 20 August 1988
12 The *National Times*, 4–10 October 1985
13 David Morgan, personal interview, July 1991
14 The *Australian Financial Review*, *The Age*, *The Australian*, 25 August 1988
15 The *Sydney Morning Herald*, 27 August 1988
16 *The Weekend Australian*, 27–28 August 1988
17 *The Australian*, 21 December 1991
18 *The Australian*, 12 October 1988
19 *The Australian*, 1 September 1988
20 *The Age*, 5 September 1988
21 Des Moore, former Treasury deputy, was a hardliner and Keating critic who had gone to work for the IPA.
22 *The Australian*, 3 May 1989
23 Bernie Fraser, personal interview, July 1992
24 Paul Keating, transcript of press conference, 3 June 1991
25 Bob Hawke, *Hansard*, Commonwealth Parliamentary Debates, House of Representatives, 3 June 1991, pp4507–4509
26 Bob Hawke, transcript of press conference, 3 June 1991. Hawke declined to discuss the Kirribilli pact when the author was conducting interviews.
27 *The Age*, 24 October 1988

Chapter 24   Elliott denied

 1 On Channel 10's *Face to Face* program on 14 May 1989, Elliott said that he had been 'fairly close' to entering politics the year before.
 2 Andrew Peacock, personal interview, August 1992
 3 Stuart Simson, interviewed on 23 September 1988, ABC Radio 2CN
 4 Michael Kroger, Joe and Enid Lyons Annual Lecture, 25 October 1988

5 Roger Shipton has refused to confirm or deny that he was made such an offer. Hugh Morgan declined to be interviewed.
6 The *Sydney Morning Herald*, 27 October 1988; the *Bulletin*, 1 November and 8 November 1988
7 *The Australian*, 28 October 1988
8 Roger Shipton has refused to confirm or deny that Andrew Peacock discussed the issue of job offers with him.
9 Hugh Morgan, Address to the Liberal Party, Hyatt Hotel, Melbourne, 8 November 1988
10 Kroger had wanted a 50/50 reform of the preselection system between the local branches and head office but settled for the 60/40 split as the best compromise he could secure.
11 Refer Channel 10's *Face to Face* program, 14 May 1989

Chapter 25   The Peacock coup

1 This chapter is based almost entirely upon confidential interviews with a number of the main participants.
2 Peter Shack, ABC Radio interview, 18 May 1989
3 The *Sydney Morning Herald*, 6 February 1989
4 *The Australian*, 7 March 1989
5 The *Sydney Morning Herald*, 8 May 1989

Chapter 26   Towards the recession

1 Compared with the budget forecast of 5.5 per cent
2 Part of this CPI figure was attributable to a statistically exaggerated measure of mortgage interest charges, later modified.
3 The *Sydney Morning Herald*, 1 February 1989
4 *The Australian*, 22 May 1992
5 Channel 10, *Face to Face*, 9 April 1989
6 R. A. Johnston 'Some Reflections of a Retiring Governor' 14 July 1989
7 *The Australian*, 22 May 1992
8 Bob Johnston, personal interview, July 1991
9 John Phillips, personal interview, March 1992
10 Peter Walsh, The 1991 Shann Memorial Lecture, 22 October 1991
11 Kelty says: 'Award restructuring wasn't really my concept. I think it had its origins with people like Laurie Carmichael. I said that if you are going to have award restructuring, you've either got to reform all awards or not bother.'
12 John Phillips, personal interview, April 1992
13 Peter Walsh, personal interview, August 1991
14 Bill Kelty, personal interview, August 1991
15 John Stone, Australian Economic Congress, 2 September 1988
16 Peter Walsh, personal interview, August 1991
17 *The Age*, 8 October 1988; Peter Walsh, personal interview, August 1991
18 Peter Walsh, personal interview, August 1991
19 Bernie Fraser, personal interview, August 1992
20 Geoff Kitney, the *Australian Financial Review*, 22 June 1989
21 Paul Keating, personal interview, July 1991
22 Paul Keating, *Euromoney* magazine, April 1989
23 Peter Walsh, personal interview, August 1991

Endnotes

24 Bill Kelty, personal interview, August 1991
25 I. F. Macfarlane 'Money, Credit and the Demand for Debt' in *Reserve Bank of Australia Bulletin* May 1989
26 ibid
27 I.F. Macfarlane 'Credit and Debt, Part Two' *Reserve Bank of Australia Bulletin* May 1990
28 David D. Hale, William F. Butler Lecture, New York, 13 September 1990
29 —— 'The Australian Economy in the 1990s' October 1991
30 —— William F. Butler Lecture, New York, 13 September 1990
31 *Access Economics Monitor*, January 1992
32 Bernie Fraser, personal interview, July 1992
33 *The Weekend Australian*, 22–23 December 1990
34 ibid
35 Peter Walsh, personal interview, August 1991

Chapter 27 The Liberals falter

1 Tony Eggleton, personal interview, June 1989
2 *The Age*, 24 May 1989
3 Bob Hawke, personal interview, April 1991
4 The *Bulletin*, 13 June and 18 July 1989; *The Australian*, 2 June 1989; the *Sydney Morning Herald*, 9 June 1989
5 Brian Sweeney and Associates, extract from research report, May 1989
6 ANOP, mid-1989 Report
7 Morgan Gallup Poll, 1988 and 1989
8 ANOP, A 1989 Winter Assessment
9 The *Bulletin*, 15 August 1989

Chapter 28 Green power

1 Richard Eckersley *Regreening Australia* Canberra: CSIRO, June 1989
2 Philip Toyne, speech to the Northern Australia Development Conference, October 1988
3 Graham Richardson, personal interview, May 1989
4 ibid
5 ibid
6 The *Bulletin*, 6 June 1989
7 The *Australian Financial Review*, 17 March 1989; the *Sydney Morning Herald*, 18 March 1989; *The Australian*, 16 March 1989
8 The *Australian Financial Review*, 17 March 1989
9 The *Sydney Morning Herald*, 16 May 1989
10 The *Bulletin*, 6 June 1989
11 Graham Richardson, personal interview, May 1989
12 *The Australian*, 30 September 1989; I have substituted the term 'exploration zone' for the original 'conservation zone' to convey a more literal meaning to the reader.
13 *The Australian*, 30 September 1989
14 ibid
15 *The Australian*, 7 October 1989
16 ibid
17 The *Sydney Morning Herald*, 17 October 1989

18 John Kerin speech, 1 November 1989; the *Australian Financial Review*, 2 November 1989
19 John Kerin speech, 1 November 1989
20 Graham Richardson, personal interview, May 1989
21 Philip Toyne, World Wildlife Speech, 8 November 1989
22 Hugh Morgan, Speech to the Australian Mining Industry Council, Canberra, 4 May 1989
23 Chris Puplick, personal interview, August 1990
24 Chris Puplick, speech, 30 November 1989
25 ibid
26 *The Australian*, 7 February 1992

Chapter 29   The Labor revival

1 Geoffrey Cousins, personal interview, August 1992
2 Margaret Bridson Cribb, 'A Review of the National Party of Australia— Queensland', 25 June 1990
3 Wayne Swan, Campaign Director's Report, 10–11 February 1990
4 The *Australian Financial Review*, 8 December 1989
5 Transcript of interview with Andrew Peacock for *The Australian*, 16 January 1990
6 John Phillips, personal interview, April 1990
7 See R. Hogg, Campaign Director's Report, 1990 Campaign

Chapter 30   The 1990 campaign

1 See Tony Eggleton, Campaign Report, 1990, pp4–6
2 ibid
3 *The Weekend Australian*, 24–25 February 1990
4 Richard Farmer, personal interview, May 1990
5 Rod Cameron, ANOP strategy note for the 1990 federal election
6 ibid
7 To get his $50 a week, Keating relied on four components: pay rises flowing from the last wages system, not the new system he was unveiling ($16.10); two pay rises from the new system, the first in October 1990 ($8.30) and the second in autumn 1991 ($12.00); and the announced tax cut expressed not as extra money in the pocket but instead as a pre-tax wage equivalent ($12.50). This meant that the full $50 was operative only by mid-1991 which was sixteen months away.
8 *The Weekend Australian*, 20–21 January 1990
9 Andrew Peacock, personal interview, August 1992
10 Margaret Gibbs, personal interview, June 1990
11 *The Australian*, 7 March 1990
12 Andrew Peacock, personal interview, August 1992
13 Geoffrey Cousins, personal interview, July 1992
14 Paul Kelly, *The Australian*, 19 March 1990
15 Andrew Peacock, transcript of questions and answers at the National Press Club, 20 March 1990
16 Tony Eggleton, 1990 Campaign Report
17 *The Age*, 14 March 1990
18 Paul Keating, ABC *PM* program, 21 March 1990

Chapter 31　Why Labor won

1　Bob Hogg, ALP Campaign Director's Report, 1990 election
2　Bob Hogg, National Press Club Speech, 11 April 1990
3　These estimates are drawn from the analysis by Malcolm Mackerras in 'The Greening of Australian Politics' in *The 1990 Federal Election* Melbourne: Longman Cheshire, 1990
4　ibid
5　These details are drawn from the ALP 1990 election report 'The Environment' prepared by Simon Balderstone
6　Geoffrey Cousins, personal interview, July 1992
7　ibid
8　Margaret Gibbs, personal interview, July 1990
9　John Singleton 'The Conning of Australia' *The Independent Monthly*, 4 April 1990
10　Richard Farmer, personal interview, June 1990

Chapter 32　Hewson—the free market purist

1　John Hewson, personal interview, July 1991
2　*The Weekend Australian*, 20–21 October 1990
3　Ian Sinclair, personal interview, January 1992
4　Speech to Federal Council, 23 October 1990
5　*The Weekend Australian*, 27–28 October 1990
6　John Hewson, personal interview, July 1991
7　*The Weekend Australian*, 20–21 October 1990
8　The *Sydney Morning Herald*, 3 August 1991
9　*The Weekend Australian*, 20–21 October 1990
10　The *Sydney Morning Herald*, 27 July 1991
11　John Hewson, personal interview, July 1991
12　*The Australian*, 22 November 1991
13　The *Australian Financial Review*, 19 September 1991

Chapter 33　The Keating coup

1　Bob Hogg, personal interview, January 1992
2　The *Bulletin*, 3 December 1990
3　*The Age*, 26 November 1990; the *Sydney Morning Herald*, 16 June 1990
4　*The Sunday Age*, 2 June 1991; *The Weekend Australian*, 1–2 June 1991
5　Bob Hogg, personal interview, January 1992
6　The *Australian Financial Review*, 14 December 1990
7　*The Weekend Australian*, 15–16 December 1990
8　The *Sydney Morning Herald*, 14 May 1991
9　Bob Hogg, personal interview, January 1992
10　*The Age*, 25 May 1991
11　*The Australian*, 3 June 1991
12　The *Sydney Morning Herald*, 3 June 1991
13　Hansard, House of Representatives, 3 June 1991, p4510
14　*The Sunday Age*, 30 June 1991
15　*The Australian*, 19 July 1991
16　Paul Keating, 'A Retirement Incomes Policy', 25 July 1991
17　Paul Keating, address at the Collingwood Football Club, 2 November 1991
18　The *Australian Financial Review*, 28 August 1991

19 *The Australian*, 17 September 1991
20 *The Australian*, 20 September 1991
21 *The Age*, 30 September 1991 and 3 October 1991
22 The *Sydney Morning Herald*, 13 August 1991
23 *The Australian*, 4 November 1991
24 *The Age*, 28 September 1991
25 The *Sydney Morning Herald*, 6 December 1991
26 ibid
27 *The Weekend Australian*, 7–8 December 1991
28 *The Age*, 9 December 1991
29 *The Australian*, 11 December 1991
30 *The Sunday Age*, 15 December 1991
31 *The Age*, 12 December 1991
32 *The Age*, 13 December 1991
33 *The Australian*, 13 December 1991
34 The *Australian Financial Review*, 20 December 1991
35 The *Australian Financial Review*, 7 January 1992

Chapter 34   The end of certainty

1 The *Sun-Herald*, 15 December 1991
2 *The Sunday Age*, 25 August 1991
3 Ross Garnaut 'The End of Protection and the Beginnings of a Modern Industrial Economy', 18 March 1991
4 ibid
5 Bob Johnston, personal interview, July 1991
6 David D. Hale 'The Australian Economy in the 1990s', Kemper Financial Services, October 1991
7 Bob Hawke, speech, 'National Wages Policy', Melbourne, 28 May 1992
8 ibid
9 *The Weekend Australian*, 22–23 December 1990
10 Bill Kelty, personal interview, August 1991
11 See Richard Blandy 'Policies and Workplace Wage Determination', Melbourne, May 1992.
12 *Quadrant*, Melbourne, May 1991
13 Industries Assistance Commission, Annual Report, 1988–89
14 *The Australian*, 12 March 1991
15 *Policy*, Autumn 1990, The Centre for Independent Studies, Sydney
16 *The Australian*, 22 May 1992
17 ibid
18 John Phillips, CEDA speech, 13 June 1991
19 —— CEDA speech, 1 March 1990
20 *Policy*, Autumn 1990, The Centre for Independent Studies, Sydney
21 John Phillips 'When The Music Stops', speech, 19 June 1990
22 Bernie Fraser 'Some Aspects of Australia's Foreign Debt', 26 February 1990
23 ibid
24 EPAC, Council Paper No 50, May 1992
25 Ed Visbord, personal interview, October 1991
26 David D. Hale, *op. cit.*
27 ibid
28 Lindsay Tanner 'Labourism In Retreat' in Burchell & Mathews (eds) *Labor's Troubled Times*, Sydney: Pluto Press, 1991

Index

Index

Index

Index

Index

electricity industry, 257–8
Ellicott, Bob, 425
Elliott, John, 42, 265, 561, 602, 605
assessment of, 403–5; assets test, 407, 408; background, 399, 404; BHP takeover bid, 1986, 404–5; business support for, 440; Carlton United Breweries, 404; Carlton, Jim, and, 510; Chaney, Fred, and, 579–81; Drysdale, Alistair, and, 458, 460; Elders IXL, 404, 459, 460, 570; entrepreneur, as, 404–5; Fitzgerald Report (Immigration), and, 421–2; Fosters, and, 570; Harlin Holdings, 406; Hawke, RJ, and, 399, 404, 405, 417, 447
Howard, John, and, 400, 406, 407, 408–17, 420, 467
destabilisation, 1988, 412–17; Adelaide by-election, 410; indirect tax, 411
Elliott support for Peacock challenge, 1989, 467–9, 471, 476, 479, 480; immigration policy, 422, 425; Liberal Party Presidency, 406, 407; rivalry, 403, 408, 412–16
indirect tax, 407, 408, 411, 416; leadership pretensions, 1988, 457–66
Liberal Party, and, 402, 403, 405, 406, 447
interim President, 406–7, 408; membership, 404; President, 400, 406–7, 415, 417
McKinsey's and, 404; Morgan, Hugh, and, 460, 463; Murdoch, Rupert, and, 476; National Crime Authority, and, 570; National Liberal amalgamation possibility, 603; opinion polls, 464
Peacock, Andrew, and, 400, 402, 409, 476
1989 Peacock challenges, 468–9; Elliott support for, 468–9, 471, 476; Peacock assessment, 462; rapprochement, 461, 467–8; rivalry, 403, 461; possible entry into Parliament, 404, 405, 406, 460, 463, 466; Shack, Peter, and, 457, 458, 461, 462; Shipton, Roger, and, 405, 457, 459, 460, 463, 464, 465, 466; tax practices, 460, 465; wets, and, 401

Emerson, Craig, 528
Empire, 11
employment, 54, 60–1, 202, 206, 223, 670, 677
enterprise agreements, 118, 280–1
enterprise bargaining, 9, 120, 201, 255, 275, 284–5, 390, 491, 545, 669–70, 671
entrepreneurs, 9–10, 33, 56, 91, 94, 202, 224, 276, 278, 379–80, 382, 397
environment policy, 524; green power; 1987, 353–4; 1990 election, 578, 589; ALP, and, 525, 533; Antarctic Treaty, 530, 533; Australian Conservation Foundation, 525, 527, 530; Beazley, Kim, 538, 539; Blunt, Charles, 542, 573; Brown, Bob, Dr, 552; Button, John, 539; coalition, 354, 529, 530, 535; Cohen, Barry, 526, 527; Collins, Bob, 538; Constitution, and, 354, 528; Cook, Peter, 529, 539; Coronation Hill mine, 536–8, 632; Dawkins, John, 539; economic policy, and, 525, 530, 531, 535, 537, 540; Environment Ambassador, 534; federalism, and, 528; foreign debt, 540; Franklin Dam case, 528; Fraser government, 542; Fraser Island, 542–3, 631; Gray, Robin, 529; Great Barrier Reef, 538; Green Power, 532; greenhouse effect, 524, 534, 535, 536; Hawke government, 526; Hawke, RJ, 527, 528, 529, 530, 532, 533, 534, 539, 672; Helsham Inquiry, 353, 529; Howard, John, 528; Hyde, John, 536–8, 539–40; Kakadu National park, 353–4, 526, 536–8, 540; Keating, Paul, 530, 531, 532, 534, 535–6, 539; Kelly, Ros, 534; Kerin, John, 539, 540; Liberal Party, 525, 528, 529, 530, 535, 540, 542–3; logging in national estate areas, 353, 526; mining, and, 536–7; National Farmers' Federation, 533; National Party, 529, 542, 573; North Queensland rainforests, 353, 529, 543; ozone layer, 524, 534; preferences, 525–6; Puplick, Chris, 528, 530, 535; Richardson, Graham, 525, 526–8, 529, 530, 531, 532–3, 534, 535, 536–8, 539, 540, 541; soil degradation, 524, 533; sustainable

719

Index

Kelly Ros, 534, 632, 655
Kelman, Brian, 65
Kelty, Bill, 61, 64, 65, 66, 67, 72, 168,
177, 204, 206, 224, 259, 269, 276,
280–1, 282–3, 284, 465, 575, 669
Accord I, and, 66; Accord III, 217,
284, 491; Accord V, 491; Accord
VI, 500; Accord, and the, 61, 281,
490, 500, 670; ACTU, and, 66,
670; BHP takeover bid, 1986, 278;
early 1980s unemployment, 63;
enterprise bargaining, and, 669;
financial deregulation, 89; Hawke,
RJ's view of, 68; indirect tax, 161,
167–8, 173; Industrial Relations
Commission, and, 669; Keating,
Paul, and, 68, 70, 73, 172, 281–2,
284, 435–6, 439, 451, 453–4,
492–3; Keating–Kelty alliance,
640–1; Kerin, John, and, 641,
642–3; Kirribilli pact, 453–5, 618;
Mudginberri, 259; National
Economic Summit, 66; productivity
deal, 282; Reserve Bank governor,
282; superannuation, 282–3; Tax
Summit, 170–1, 173; two-tier
wages system, 285; wages
explosion prevention, 1989, 493;
waterfront, 396; Willis, Ralph, and,
68
Kemp, Charles, 47, 473
Kemp, David, 38, 42, 47, 49, 52, 104,
105, 261, 403, 472–5, 604, 663
Kemp, Rod, 42, 47–8, 52, 261
Kennard, Neville, 42, 47, 261
Kennett, Jeff, 319, 415, 425, 432, 462,
602
Kent, Lewis, 129
Kerin, John, 58, 86, 349, 363, 544, 616,
628, 639, 641–2
1991–92 budget, 643; assessment of,
642–3, 650; environment policy,
529, 531–2, 535, 539–40;
Fightback strategy, 1991, and, 649;
foreign investment, Fairfax, and,
650; Green Power, and, 541; GST,
and, 651; Hawke, RJ, and, 535,
635, 638, 646, 650–1; inflation,
645; interest rates, 642, 644;
Keating, Paul, and, 636, 642;
Keating–Hawke challenge, 635–7;
Kelty, Bill, and, 643; monetary

policy, 645; rural policy, 643;
sacking as Treasurer, 650–1;
superannuation, 640–1; sustainable
development, 540; Treasurer, 635,
639, 642–3, 649–50; Treasury, and
the, 642, 650; wool reserve price
scheme, 642
Kerr, Sir John, 261
Kessell, Keith, 480
Keynes, John Maynard, 624
Keynesian economics, 35, 40, 51, 57,
60, 96
Khemlani, Tirath, 258
Kidman, Peter, 561
Killen, Sir James, 97, 475
Kingston, Charles, 7
Kirner Joan, 646, 672
Kirribilli House, 282–3, 454, 551
Kirribilli meeting,
superannuation/productivity, 1985, 282
Kirribilli pact on Labor leadership, 28,
434, 566, 615, 618, 629–30
Abeles, Sir Peter, and, 453, 454, 619;
breach of, 625–7; Hawke, RJ,
453–5, 618–9, 624, 626–7, 629–32,
636–7; Keating, Paul, 453–5,
618–9, 635; Kelty, Bill, and, 454,
619; Oakes, Laurie, 630, 632;
origins, 453; revelation of, 632, see
also Chapter 23 passim
Klein, Ron, 478, 515, 579, 580, 592,
593
Klemperer, Otto, 233
Knowles, Susan, 485
Kortlang, Ian, 460, 471, 479, 482, 484,
510, 516
Kramer, Dame Leonie, 48, 541
Kristol, Irving, 663
Kroger, Michael, 258, 403, 406, 410,
462–4, 465–6, 472–4, 475, 510, 561
Kuwait, 625

Labor leadership, 23, 216, 657, see also
Hayden, W, Hawke, RJ, Keating, P,
leadership
Labor Party
see Australian Labor Party
labour costs, 61
labour market deregulation, 183, 236,
240, 251, 263, 265, 387, 397–8, 663,
665, 668, 671
BA Statement, 1987, 280; business

Lowy, Frank, 279, 471
Ludwig, Bill, 628, 631
lump sum superannuation, 70, 141
Lynch, Phillip, 39, 49, 50, 51, 69, 97,
  100, 102, 258, 599
Lyneham, Paul, 563
Lyons, Joe, 357
Lyons, Sir Edward, 294

MacBean, John, 161, 168, 278
Macfarlane, Ian, 488, 489, 501, 676
Mack, Ted, 564
MacKay Research, 618
MacKellar, Michael, 133, 425, 427
Mackerras, Malcolm, 355, 577, 588
Mackinnon, Barry, 471
Macmillan, Harold, 238
Macphee, Ian, 51, 103, 104, 108, 114,
  115, 179, 180, 232, 241, 242, 243,
  246, 264, 265, 266, 267, 315, 320
  Accord, and the, 116; affirmative
  action, 320; arbitration, 111;
  assessment migration policy, 130;
  assessment of, 103; Australian
  Settlement, and, 129; background,
  103; ballots, 99, 192; BCA
  meeting, 1986, 264, 265;
  consensus, and, 114, 116, 121;
  crossing the floor, 427; Deakin
  pre-selection, 482, 515; demotion
  to backbench, 321; Fraser,
  Malcolm, and, 103, 321, 475; free
  market policies, and, 103;
  Goldstein pre-selection, 472, 472,
  475, 476, 480; Hawke, RJ, and,
  103; *Herald and Weekly Times*
  takeover, 320; Howard, John, and,
  103, 104, 114, 115, 116, 120, 264,
  265, 320, 321, 401, 472, 473, 474,
  475, 482; immigration policy, 103,
  126, 129, 130, 133, 425; industrial
  relations policy, 111, 114, 115,
  116–18, 119, 120, 263, 264, 265,
  266; Kroger, Michael, and, 472,
  473, 510; Labor Party, and, 103;
  leadership, 103; media, and the,
  474; multiculturalism, 103; New
  Right, and, 103, 267; Peacock,
  Andrew, and, 119, 401, 479, 482,
  483, 510; pre-selection, 1989, 472;
  radical liberals, and, 103; Trade

Practices Act, 116; trade unions,
  103; wets, and, 103, 321, 401
Mahathir, His excellency, Dr, 136
Manchu Court, 173, 216
Mansfield, Bill, 161
marginal seats campaign, 107
Marsh, Jan, 61, 161
Martin Committee, 81, 87
Martin, Ray, 363, 445, 465, 640
Martin, Vic, 81
Maxwell, Robert, 474
May Statements, 69
  1983, 69, 70; 1985, 205; 1987, 324,
  329, 330, 331, 332, 333, 371;
  1988, 384, 392, 393, 439, 616, 667
Maybury, Fred, 294, 312, 336, 337,
  340, 341
Mayne Nickless, 280
McCarrey, Les, 48
McClelland, Jim, 439
McCrann, Terry, 218
McDonald, Bruce, 561
McDonald, Tom, 63, 283
McEwen, John, 6, 26, 35, 43, 98, 102,
  297, 305, 308, 326, 357, 603
McEwen/Westerman Bank (AIDC), 102
McEwenism, 6, 43, 45, 268
McGinty, Jim, 560
McGregor, Craig, 166, 436, 439
McGuinness, PP, 47, 48, 373, 439, 680
McKay, Bernie, 520
McKenzie, Bruce, 169
McKerrow, Shirley, 305
McKinnon, Bill, 102
McKinsey's, 42, 404
McLachlan, Ian, 46, 52, 112, 123, 230,
  247, 252, 253, 256, 257, 261, 268,
  402, 604, 605, 660, 670, 680
  assessment of, 253, 254, 336;
  background, 253, 254; banana
  republic, 257; Bjelke-Petersen, Joh,
  and, 300, 335, 336, 337–9; Hawke,
  RJ, comparison with, 253;
  Hawke–Keating meeting, 257;
  Howard, John, and, 268, 300, 338,
  339; Joh for Canberra campaign,
  300, 335, 336, 337–9, 340;
  leadership, 607; Liberal Party, and,
  268, 300, 301, 339; Liberal Senate
  vacancy offer, 301; live sheep
  export dispute, 112, 255; media,
  and the, 257; Mudginberri, 256;

Index

National Farmers' Federation, 253, 254; National Party, and, 254; new conservative party, 337; New Right, and, 253, 602; Peacock, Andrew, and, 317; protection, and, 606; Sinclair, Ian, and, 337; Sparkes, Sir Robert, and, 301, 335, 336, 337; wets, and, 320; wide combs dispute, 255

McLaughlin, Peter, 276, 365, 366, 394
McLeay, Leo, 444, 449, 647
McLennan, Sir Ian, 404
McLeod, John, 42, 47
McMahon government, 37
McMahon, William, 21, 30, 37, 44, 101, 413, 609
McMullan, Bob, 137, 138, 151, 322, 324, 333, 351, 354, 356
McVeigh, Tom, 308, 317
meat industry, 256
media policy, 56, 278, 320, 650
media, the, 56, 214, 231, 243, 253, 257, 261, 262, 265, 267
1990 press gallery dinner, 621, 622; Blainey, Geoffrey, and, 127; concentration of ownership, 243, 320; effect on politics, 423; elections, and, 586; financial deregulation, 89; Goldstein crisis, 476; Hawke Beijing briefing, 1986, 215, 216; Hawke government, and, 54; Hawke, RJ, and, 449, 636, 651, 665; Hewson, John, and, 608; Howard, John, and, 133, 231, 241, 348, 349, 423, 425, 472, 474, 475, 478, 512, 513; HR Nicholls Society, and, 260, 262; Keating, Paul, and, 26, 224, 384, 435, 449, 496, 621, 622, 636; Labor leadership, 1986, 214, 216; Labor Party, and, 253, 261; Liberal Party, and, 107, 130, 265, 556; Macphee, Ian, and, 474; McLachlan, Ian, and, 257; New Right, and, 253, 267; Peacock, Andrew, and, 515, 522; television, 149, 511, 570, 571, 572
Medibank, 37
Medibank Private, 109, 346
Medicare, 70, 72, 109, 148, 281, 331, 345, 436, 519, 549, 554, 576, 643, 664
Mein, Joy, 412

Melbourne Herald, The, 142
Melbourne Sun, The, 178
Menzies government, 37
Menzies, RG, 3, 20, 21, 29, 35, 37, 96, 99, 100, 103, 121, 200, 228, 229, 230, 231, 244, 245, 246, 271, 297, 357, 430, 431, 485, 603, 604
1949 election, 101, 565; coalition, 304; conservatism, 465; drys, and, 246; family values, 430; federal spending, 37; forgotten people broadcasts, 101, 229, 245; ideology, 230; immigration policy, 128; leadership, 110, 229; Liberal Party, on, 246; liberalism, 245; retirement, 100; state aid, 230; state intervention, 430; state power, 246; voting habit, 246; wets, and, 246; White Australia, 3
Messner, Tony, 235, 327, 459, 485, 512
metal trades industry, 51, 63
Metal Trades Industry Association, (MTIA), 263
micro-economic reform, 48, 201, 498, 668, 669, 671
1980s, 387; 1987, 387; 1988 May Statement, 392, 393; 1989, 395; 1990, 616, 617; Accord, and the, 390, 499; ALP, and, 389; Australian Settlement, and, 386, 398; aviation industry, 671; Business Council of Australia, 394; Button, John, 388; coalition, 1991, 606; coastal shipping, 390, 395, 397; consensus, and, 390, 672; current account deficit, and, 499; Douglas, Roger, 672; farm lobby, 256; financial deregulation, and, 390, 397, 502; foreign debt, and, 397; Garnaut Report, 673, Hale, David, 388; Hawke government, 499, 671; Hawke, RJ, 390, Hewson, John, 671; Howard, John, 249, 663, 672; Keating, Paul, 389, 390; Liberal Party, 250, 517; Peacock, Andrew, 574; privatisation, 391, 392, 393; protection, and, 389, 671; rate of progress, 389; recession, and, 498; Structural Adjustment Committee, 388; tariff, and the, 671; telecommunications, 390, 617, 671, 672; third runway for Sydney

Index

Liberal Party, and, 432; Macphee, Ian, 103; Valder Report, 106
Murdoch, Rupert, 225, 243, 265, 278, 320, 476
Murphy, Lionel, 127, 140
Murray, Wal, 312
Mussolini, Bennito, 276
Mutual Life and Citizens Assurance Company, 81
MX missile crisis, 159, 180, 204

National Association of Forest Industries, 532
National Australia Bank, 617
National Crime Authority (NCA), 140, 141, 570
national debt, 91
National Economic Summit, 59, 65, 197, 276
  Abeles, Sir Peter, 67; Accord I, 66, 67; Bjelke-Petersen, Joh, 67; business support for, 65, 67, 68; business, and, 276; Campbell, Sir Keith, 66; centralised wage fixation, 67; communique, 67; consensus, 65, 66; fiscal policy expansion, 67; Hawke, RJ, 67; inflation, 65, 67; Keating, Paul, 66; Kelty, Bill, 66; participants, 65; Polities, George, 66; scenarios, 66; unemployment, 65; wages policy, 65
National Farmers' Federation (NFF), 42, 43, 45, 46, 117, 253, 254, 255, 256, 261
  Anthony, Doug, and, 45; Country Party, and, 43, 45; economic policy, 257; environment policy, 533; Farm Focus, the 80s, 46; farm lobby, and, 254; fighting fund, 254, 256, 257, 336; formation, 112; free market policies, 45, 680; Houlihan, Paul, 255; industrial reform, 255, 257; Industries Assistance Commission, 44; Joh for Canberra campaign, 295, 336; live sheep export dispute, 112, 225; McLachlan, Ian, 46, 254, 255, 256, 257; Mudginberri, 113, 255, 256; national headquarters, 257; National Party, and, 45; New Right, and, 253; protection, and, 43, 255; radical liberalism, and, 45; radical

liberals, and, 46; small business, 256; tax policy, 167, 235; Trade Practices Act, 112, 277; trade unions, and, 112; Trebeck, David, 254; wide combs dispute, 113, 255
national identification card, 164, 175, 235
  see also Australia Card
national identity, 4, 11, 13, 125, 673
  see also Australian identity; ALP, and, 433; Australian citizenship, 421; Blainey, Geoffrey, 125; flag, 131; free market policies, and, 432; Garnaut Report, 673; Howard, John, 432; immigration policy, and, 125, 421, 422; Joh for Canberra campaign, and, 295, 314; Keating, Paul, 679; Liberal Party, and, 134, 432; republic, 12; Whitlam government, and, 11
National Party, 34, 37, 43, 44, 45, 46, 232, 238, 254, 268
  1987 election, 357; 1989 Queensland election, 552; 1990 election, 573; affirmative action, 320; agrarian socialism, and, 46; assessment of, (Cribb), 552; Bjelke-Petersen, Joh, and, 326, 552; Blunt, Charles, and, 477, 485; coalition, 304, 305, 310, 313, 316, 324, 325, 326, 357, 402, 602, 603; elections, 29; environment policy, 528, 542, 574; Federal Council Meeting October 1985, 254; Federal Council, 1987, 322, 323; Fischer, Tim, and, 602; Fitzgerald Report (Queensland), 522; flat rate tax, 49; float of dollar, 78; free market policies, 517, 602; führer principle, 308; GST, and, 603; Hewson, John, and, 603; indirect tax, 49, 411; Industries Assistance Commission, 44; Joh for Canberra campaign, 305, 307, 309, 313, 357, 588; leadership, 305, 486, 602; Liberal Party, and, 553, 603; National Farmers' Federation, and, 43, 45; New Right, and, 268; NSW National Party, 305, 311, 312; Parliamentary Party meeting, 1987, 306, 307; privatisation, 239; protection, 43, 44, 666; Queensland

Index

Index

White, Brian, 439
White, David, 646
White, Peter, 512
Whitelaw, Bob, 82
Whitlam government, 21, 28, 101, 104
1975, 22; 25 per cent tariff cut, 22;
ACTU, and, 61; assessment of, 61,
436; Bjelke-Petersen, Joh, and, 292;
comparison with Hawke
government, 54; dismissal, 28, 36;
economic management, 22;
economic policy, 19; failures of,
61; federal spending, 38; inflation,
38; Keating, Paul, 26, 436; loans
affair, 258; national identity, and,
11; protection, 667; racial
discrimination, 4; refugees, and,
128; tariff cut, 86; Treasury, and
the, 274; wages explosion, 51, 64
Whitlam, Gough, 19, 21–9, 32, 36, 44,
51, 100, 272, 565, 658, 664, 675,
Keating, Paul, and, 658; 1972
election, 565; ALP leader, 21;
Australian economy, 19; Australian
Labor Party, and, 20, 528;
background, 20; dismissal, 21, 36;
economic policy, 22; ethnic vote,
and, 128; Hawke government,
criticism of, 436; Hawke, RJ, and,
61, 64, 664; Hayden challenge, 27;
Industries Assistance Commission,
and, 44; leadership, 21, 22;
modernisation of ALP, 20;
philosophy, 20; protection, and, 44;
refugees, and, 128, 133; state
power and, 21; unions, and, 23, 24;
unions, views of, 61; wages
explosion 1974, 51, 64; White
Australia, and, 127, 675
Whitlamism, 61, 436
wide combs dispute, 113, 255
Wiesener, Richard, 404
Wilderness Society, 354, 527, 543, 573

Wilkinson, Marian, 510–11
Williams, Pamela, 267
Willis, Ralph, 22–3, 27, 58–9, 60, 86,
214, 224, 265, 636, 643
Accord III, 284; Accord, and the, 61,
68; ERC, 70; executive
remuneration, 277; float of dollar,
84; Hawke, RJ, and, 27, 55, 70,
638; indirect tax, 161–2; Keating,
Paul, and, 636; Keating–Hawke
challenge, 636, 656;
micro-economic reform 397; tax
policy, 175; third runway, 395;
Treasurer, 638, 650
Wills, Dean, 471
Wilson, Geoff, 296
Wilson, Ian, 425, 427
Wilson, Keith, 560
Windsor Hotel, 95, 337, 338, 339
Withers, Reg, 104, 140, 181, 183,
189–91, 317
withholding tax exemption, 220
women, 96, 230, 320
women's liberation movement, 21, 32
women's movement, 32, 431
see also Women's Liberation
Movement
Wood, Alan, 44, 207, 505, 612, 669
Woods, Bob, 604
wool, 642, 667
World Bank, 13
Wran government, 89
Wran, Neville, 19, 22, 29, 57, 136, 170,
278, 526, 552, 591

Year 2000, The—A Radical Liberal
Alternative, 52
Young, Beryl, 294, 338
Young, Mick, 58, 126, 238–9, 324, 326,
333, 438, 551
youth, 96, 123, 230, 272

zero real growth in spending, 221

755